Challenge

Klassen 11–13

Englisch für Berufliche Gymnasien
Niedersachsen

von
Annely Humphreys
Jason Humphreys
Arnd Nadolny

Ernst Klett Verlag
Stuttgart · Leipzig

Challenge Klassen 11 – 13

Englisch für Berufliche Gymnasien
Niedersachsen

Autorinnen und Autoren: Annely Humphreys, Jason Humphreys, Arnd Nadolny
Beratung: Arnd Nadolny, Niedersachsen

Werkübersicht:

Schülerbuch, Klassen 11–13, 978-3-12-809217-1
Workbook und EXAM TRAINING mit Audio-CD, Klassen 11–13, 978-3-12-809219-5
Vocabulary Notebook, Klassen 11–13, 978-3-12-809214-0
Arbeitsmaterial-Paket: Workbook/EXAM TRAINING + Vocabulary Notebook, Klassen 11–13, 978-3-12-809222-5
Lehrerhandbuch inkl. Digitalem Lehrer-Service, Klassen 11–13, 978-3-12-809212-6

1. Auflage 1 5 4 3 2 1 | 17 16 15 14 13

Alle Drucke dieser Auflage sind unverändert und können im Unterricht nebeneinander verwendet werden.
Die letzte Zahl bezeichnet das Jahr des Druckes.

Im Lehrwerk befinden sich ausschließlich fiktive Internet-Adressen, die deshalb auch mit ww#. beginnen anstatt wie üblich mit www.
Die im Buch abgedruckten Mediencodes führen zu interaktiven Zusatzübungen und Hörverständnistexten auf www.klett.de. Die Mediencodes leiten ausschließlich zu optionalen Unterrichtsmaterialien, sie unterliegen nicht dem staatlichen Zulassungsverfahren.

Projektleitung: Matthias Rupp
Redaktion: Astrid Keller
Herstellung: Angelika Lindner

Satz und Gestaltung: Ulrike Promies, Metzingen
Umschlaggestaltung: Projektteam des Verlages
Reproduktion: Meyle + Müller Medien-Management, Pforzheim
Druck: Druckhaus Götz GmbH, Ludwigsburg

Printed in Germany
ISBN 978-3-12-809217-1

ISBN 978-3-12-**809217**-1
9 783128 092171

Das Lehrwerk **Challenge Niedersachsen** entspricht den Lehrplänen für die Jahrgangsstufen 11 bis 13 des Beruflichen Gymnasiums. Alle zu erreichenden Kompetenzen und Prüfungsformate werden intensiv trainiert.

1. **Mit jedem Topic Schritt für Schritt sicher zum Abitur**

   Die ersten fünf Topics (Topic 1.1 bis 1.5) bieten einen leichten Einstieg zur Homogenisierung der unterschiedlichen Niveaus. Die folgenden zehn Topics (Topic 2.1 bis 2.10) dienen der Abiturvorbereitung.
   - Einstiegsdoppelseite Topic: Vorbereitung auf das jeweilige Thema
   - 5 Doppelseiten mit **aktuellen, authentischen Texten** – begleitet von **englisch-deutschen Wortangaben** für einen schnelleren Zugang zum Text und **differenzierten Aufgaben**, die ausgewogen alle Kompetenzbereiche trainieren und auf die in der Abiturprüfung vorgesehenen Prüfungsformate vorbereiten
   - Fokusseite Spot on grammar / language: Wortschatzübungen und Vertiefung der wichtigsten **Grammatikkenntnisse**
   - Fokusseite Hotspot: Handlungsorientierte Themenbearbeitung **mit vielen Projekt- und Internetaufgaben**
   - Doppelseite **Exam practice: Testaufgabe im Abiturformat**
   - **Video lounge**: Authentische BBC-Videos zum Training des Hör- / Sehverstehens
   - Berufsbezug durch **Reading for your exam:** mit je drei Texten zu den Bereichen Technik, Wirtschaft & Verwaltung sowie Soziales & Gesundheit plus Aufgaben

2. **„Your challenge" bietet umfangreiches Material zur individuellen Förderung**
   - **Self-assessment:** Kategorien zur Selbsteinschätzung
   - **Assessment tests:** Thematisch verknüpfte Aufgaben zur Selbsteinschätzung und zur Lernwegdokumentation
   - **Helping hand:** Differenzierungsangebot zu komplexen Aufgabenstellungen
   - **Grading grid:** Bewertungsbogen für Englisch
   - **Skills files:** Alle Kompetenzen prägnant und mit vielen *Phrases* (Redewendungen)
   - **Grammar files:** Kompaktgrammatik zum Wiederholen und Nachschlagen
   - **Dictionary:** Alphabetisches Vokabelverzeichnis

3. **Training und Prüfungsvorbereitung**
   - **Challenge-Code:** Über den Challenge-Code können Sie sich das *Talking vocabulary* (vertonte Wortlisten) als MP3-Dateien zum Anhören der korrekten Aussprache kostenlos unter www.klett.de herunterladen.
   - **3-in-1-Workbook:** Für die Jahrgangsstufen 11 bis 13 bieten wir Ihnen ein Workbook zzgl. Prüfungsvorbereitung und Audio-CD:
     - Grammatikintensivtraining im Arbeitsheft zum Hineinschreiben
     - Hörverstehensübungen mit beiliegender Audio-CD
     - intensive Prüfungsvorbereitung mit Hinweisen zum Abitur und Wiederholung der wichtigsten *Skills* mit Prüfungsaufgaben auf Abiturniveau im *EXAM TRAINING*
   - **Vocabulary Notebook:** Das Vokabellernheft für die Jahrgangsstufen 11 bis 13 ist der thematische Aufbauwortschatz, der gebündelt nur die wichtigen Vokabeln aus den Texten sowie zusätzlichen Wortschatz mit vielen Aufgaben zum Hineinschreiben trainiert.

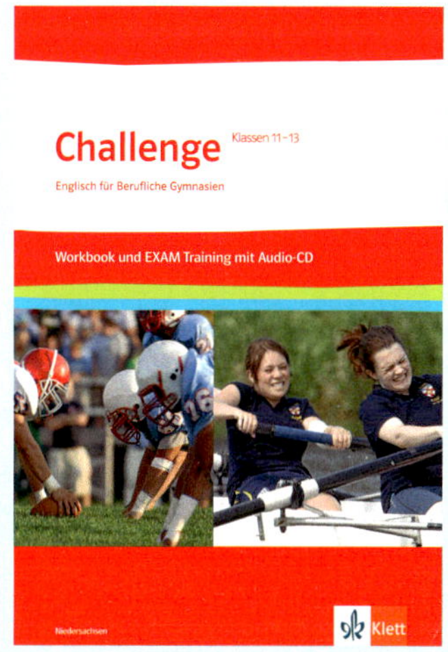

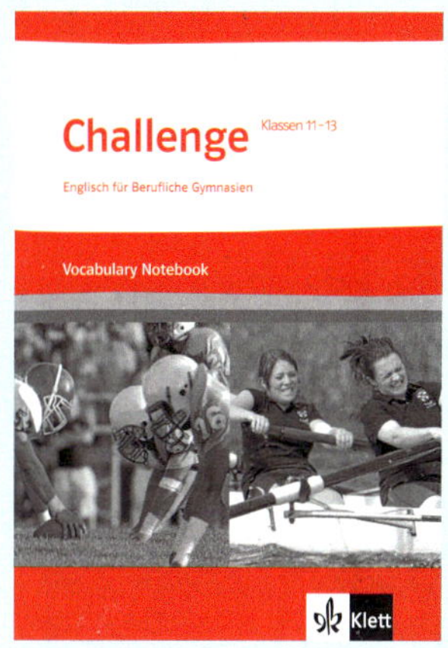

Inhalt

Topic 2.4 World of work 138

Topic 2.5 Science, technology and society 154

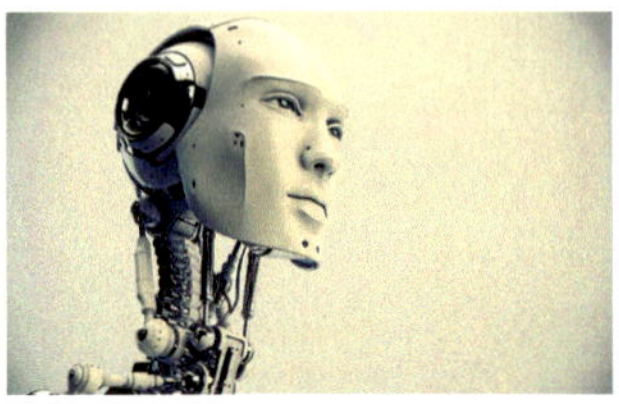

Topic 2.6 The impact of change 170

Topic 2.7 Dreams and visions 186

Symbole und Abkürzungen

p9v2et – Challenge-Code mit *Talking vocabulary*: vertonte Wortlisten als MP3-Download

A1.1 – Audio: Für den Lehrer auf den Audio-CDs im Lehrerhandbuch. Für die Schüler teilweise auf der Audio-CD im Workbook.

[1] **to improve** – (sich) verbessern – Lernvokabular ist in den Topics schwarz hervorgehoben

Partneraufgabe

Gruppenaufgabe

→ Verweise auf die *Skills* und *Grammar files* im Anhang

Aufgaben zur selbstständigen Recherche im Internet

p. 84 Aufgaben mit Differenzierungsangeboten im Anhang (*Helping hand*)

Topic 1.1
Being young today

688ga3

A

B

C

D

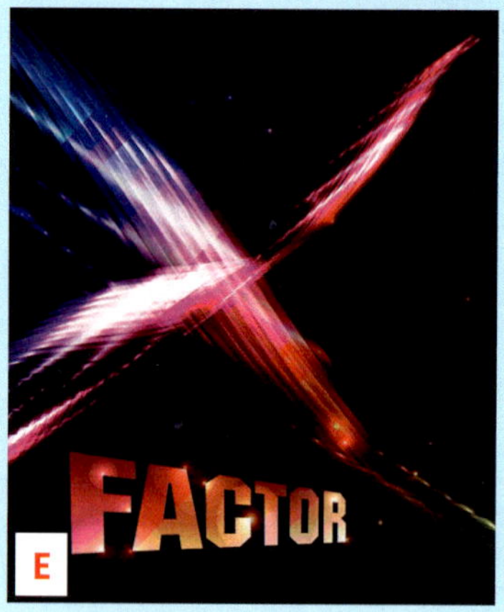

E

F

Getting started

1 **Work on your own. Look at the photos and collect words that both describe and summarise what each photo shows.** → Describing pictures, p. 339

2 **Now get together with your neighbour and compare your results. Then agree on another photo that should be added. Give reasons for your choice.**

3 **Exchange your ideas and your "new photos" in groups. Make a word cluster containing key terms you need to describe young people's lives.**

4 **Vocabulary** → Working with a dictionary, p. 353

a) Collect adjectives that describe what you like/dislike about people your age.

b) In groups, use your list of positive and negative adjectives and make sentences which describe what you like/dislike about people your age, e.g. "I like people who are reliable because it is important that you can trust someone who is your friend."

A survey about growing up in England

In an online survey respondents were asked to name the best thing about being a child or young person living in England. This was an open-ended question, so that the respondents could reply exactly as they wanted to. Their answers were grouped together in the broad themes shown here.

"Don't call me a teenager. From now on, I want to be referred to as a pre-adult."

What is the best thing about being a child or young person living in England?

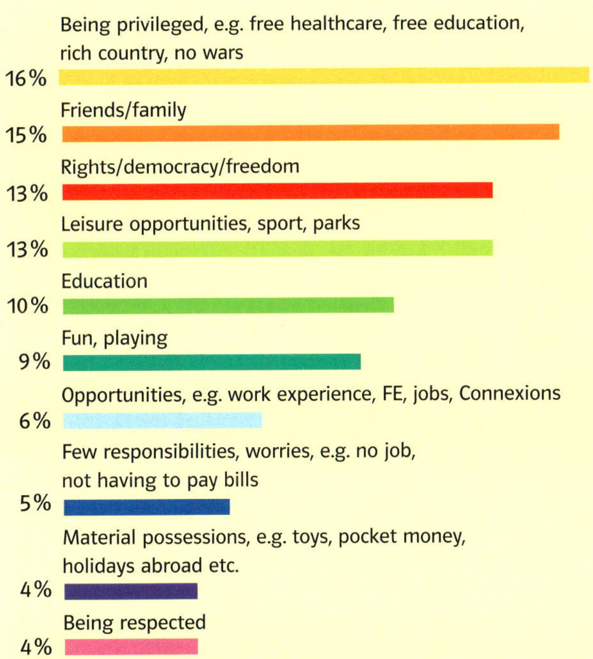

FE further education • **Connexions** a public service for young people aged 13–19, providing advice, information and practical help with things that might be affecting them at school, college, work or in their personal lives • **chav** [tʃæv] *(pej)* working-class young person who is seen to have bad taste in clothes and lifestyle

What is the worst thing about being a child or young person living in England?

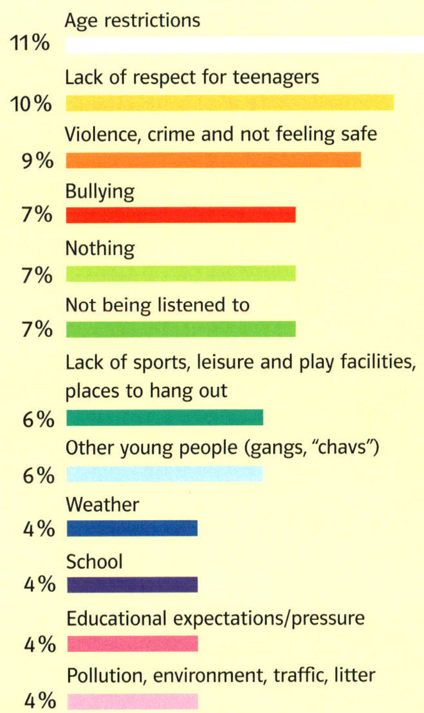

5 **Summarise and comment on the survey results above. Compare them to what you and your classmates would have expected.**

6 **In groups, draw up a survey to find out the best things and the worst things about being a young person in Germany. Ask your classmates to do the survey, then discuss the results.** → Questionnaires and surveys, p. 360

7 **Projects** → Hotspots 1 and 2, p. 23

Word bank

- The survey results show/indicate/prove/suggest that …
- A (high) percentage of …
- A majority/minority of …
- A significant number of …
- Compared with/to …
- A surprising number of …

A Growing up

1 Before you read → Brainstorming, p. 351
Have a look at the following headlines and facts about a Facebook party in Germany. Have you ever been to a flash mob party? What do you think happened? Why do you think all the people came?

A Hamburg girl used Facebook to organise her 16th birthday party but unknowingly broadcast the invitation for all Facebook users to see, leading to more than 1,500 guests turning up for the event.

A spontaneous party in the city of Wuppertal attracted some 800 people.

A flash mob of 5,000 invaded the small North Sea island of Sylt and the community was left to clean up the mess.

The costs of the party (cleaning up, damages, etc.) are estimated to be around €20,000.

2 Comprehension → Understanding non-fictional texts, p. 320
Collect the information mentioned in the text which speaks against Facebook parties.

p. 292

3 Role play → Discussions, p. 344
Prepare a panel discussion with the following roles. Collect arguments and examples that can help you to support your position.

a) A teenager who attends Facebook parties. ("Simply celebrating is not a crime.")

b) The mayor of a town who tries to prevent Facebook parties. ("We cannot guarantee the safety of the teenagers and our citizens.")

1 **interior minister** – Innenminister
2 **recent** – kürzlich, letzte(r/s)
2 **social networking site** – Internetseite eines sozialen Netzwerks
4 **phenomenon** – Phänomen
5 **monitoring** – Beobachtung
7 **inadvertently** – irrtümlich
8 **public order** – öffentliche Ordnung
8 **to ban** – verbieten
8 **in advance** – im Vorfeld
12 **evidence** – Beweis
13 **duty** – Pflicht
14 **municipal** – städtisch
15 **to fuel** – anheizen
16 **appropriate** – angemessen
17 **to intervene** – intervenieren, einschreiten

DW-WORLD.DE
DEUTSCHE WELLE
Search GO

Home | Your link to Germany | DW-World | DW Radio live | DW TV Europe live |

Interior ministers speak out against 'dangerous' Facebook parties

Recent months have seen parties organized over social networking site Facebook overrun by thousands of party crashers who were accidentally sent invitations. Now, German state interior ministers want an end to the phenomenon.

German interior ministers have called for increased monitoring of house parties organized on the social networking site Facebook after several small events organized on the site inadvertently attracted thousands of guests.

"If public order and safety are put at risk then Facebook parties must be banned in advance," Lower Saxony Interior Minister Uwe Schünemann told the weekly *Welt am Sonntag* newspaper.

North Rhine-Westphalia Interior Minister Ralf Jäger echoed these thoughts, telling the newspaper that "if there is concrete evidence of potential danger to participants or innocent third parties ahead of a planned Facebook party, then it is the duty of the municipal police to prohibit the event."

However, Malte Spitz from the Greens said the interior ministers were fueling a "sham debate" with their comments, adding that "police already have appropriate powers to intervene in cases of danger arising from Facebook parties."

c) A representative of a parent organisation. ("As long as they all celebrate together and are monitored by the police, we know what they are doing.")

d) A social worker of a town with fewer than 150,000 inhabitants. ("There's often not much to do for teenagers who aren't 18 yet; Facebook parties that are controlled by local authorities are a good way for them to get to know teenagers from other towns.")

e) Another representative of a parent organisation. ("Parties organised by social networking sites attract all kinds of people; we need to protect those who are underage and so we should forbid such parties.")

f) Any other role you believe is missing in this discussion.

p. 292 △ **4 Text production: Writing an email** → Writing an email, p. 329
On a social networking site you read an invitation to a flash mob pool party in which teenagers in California are called upon to come to an address of a property with a large swimming pool. The person who wrote this invitation used google maps to locate this house. Write an email to this person in which you tell him what you think of the invitation.

p. 292 △ **5 Mediation** → Mediation, p. 343
Summarise the following information in German. Do not translate it.

The amount of time that people from all over the world spend on social networking sites is increasing. According to recent reports, Russians spend an average of over 6 hours per month on these sites compared to Germans (over 4 hours). Facebook alone is said to have about one billion active users. Twitter, MySpace, etc. are popular, too. Spending on online advertising on such sites is predicted to rise to $2.6 billion by 2012 for the USA alone.

Party to remember

In early June, a Hamburg girl used Facebook to organize her 16th birthday party but unknowingly broadcast the invitation for all Facebook users to see, leading to more than 1,500 guests turning up for the event and forcing some 100 police officers to intervene to keep the crowd under control.
Eleven people were detained during the party and one police officer was injured, as well as dozens of people wearing flip-flops who had stepped on shards of glass from broken bottles. Two small fires had to be extinguished and the birthday girl, identified only as Thessa, was forced to flee as the party got out of control.
Shortly after, a spontaneous party in the western city of Wuppertal attracted some 800 people, 41 of whom were taken into police custody and 16 injured.
Hamburg authorities are currently also bracing themselves ahead of a Facebook party planned for September 30 and an expected influx of up to 19,000 partygoers on the city's transport grid.
Schünemann said that in order to prevent such events from occurring, young people using Facebook needed an "Internet drivers license" to educate them about the potential dangers of using the website.
"Young people often don't know what they're getting themselves into," he told *Welt am Sonntag*. "They have to pay for any damages and necessary rubbish collection, and this can cost thousands of euros." (413 words)

20 **to broadcast** – senden, übertragen
22 **crowd** – Menschenmenge
23 **to detain** – in Gewahrsam nehmen
24 **shard** – Scherbe
25 **to extinguish** – löschen, auslöschen
28 **police custody** – Polizeigewahrsam
29 **to brace oneself** – sich rüsten
30 **influx** – Zustrom, Einfall
36 **rubbish** – Müll

B Teenagers and technology

1 Before you read → Brainstorming, p. 351

a) Have a look at the picture. Imagine you had to describe it to someone who doesn't know what mobile phones are.

b) "I'd rather give up my kidney than my phone." What do you think the text is about? What is your first reaction to this quote?

theguardian

News | Sport | Comment | Culture | Business | Money | Life&Style | Travel | Environment

Comment is free > Society   Search [ ] GO

Teenagers and technology: 'I'd rather give up my kidney than my phone'

Text, text, text, that's all they think about: but are all those hours on the phone and Facebook turning teenagers into screen-enslaved social inadequates? Jon Henley finds out.

"I'd rather," deadpans Philippa Grogan, 16, "give up, like, a kidney than my phone. How did you manage before? Carrier pigeons? Letters? Going round each others' houses on BIKES?" Cameron Kirk, 14, reckons he spends "an hour, hour-and-a-half on school days" hanging out with his 450-odd Facebook friends; maybe twice that at weekends. "It's actually very practical if you forget what that day's homework is. Unfortunately, one of my best friends doesn't have Facebook. But it's OK; we talk on our PlayStations."

Emily Hooley, 16, recalls a Very Dark Moment: "We went to Wales for a week at half term to revise. There was no mobile, no TV, no broadband. We had to drive into town just to get a signal. It was really hard, knowing people were texting you, writing on your Wall, and you couldn't respond. Loads of my friends said they'd just never do that." [...]

75% of all teenagers (and 58% of 12-year-olds) now have a mobile phone. Almost 90% of phone-owning teens send and receive texts, most of them daily. Half send 50 or more texts a day; one in three send 100. In fact, in barely four years, texting has established itself comfortably as "the preferred channel of basic communication between teens and their friends".

But phones do more than simply text, of course. More than 80% of phone-owning teens also use them to take pictures (and 64% to share those pictures with others). Sixty per cent listen to music on them, 46% play games, 32% swap videos and 23% access social networking sites. The mobile phone, in short, is now "the favoured communication hub for the majority of teens".

As if texting, swapping, hanging out and generally spending their waking hours welded to their phones wasn't enough, 73% use social networking sites, mostly Facebook – 50% more than three years ago. Digital communication is not just prevalent in teenagers' lives. It IS teenagers' lives.

There's a very straightforward reason, says Amanda Lenhart, a Pew senior research specialist. "Simply, these technologies meet teens' developmental needs," she says. "Mobile phones and social networking sites make the things teens have always done

2 **kidney** – Niere
7 **enslaved** – versklavt
7 **social inadequates** – sozial Benachteiligte
9 **to deadpan** – witzeln
11 **carrier pigeon** – Brieftaube
28 **to swap** – tauschen
29 **communication hub** – Kommunikationszentrum
31 **to weld** – schweißen
33 **prevalent** – vorherrschend
35 **senior research specialist** – leitende(r) Forscher(in)
36 **developmental needs** – Entwicklungsbedürfnisse

– defining their own identity, establishing themselves as independent of their parents, looking cool, impressing members of the opposite sex – a whole lot easier."

Flirting, boasting, gossiping, teasing, hanging out, confessing: all that classic teen stuff has always happened, Lenhart says. It's just that it used to happen behind the bike sheds, or via tightly folded notes pressed urgently into sweating hands in the corridor between lessons. Social networking sites and mobile phones have simply facilitated the whole business, a gadzillion times over.

For Professor Patti Valkenburg, of the University of Amsterdam's internationally respected Centre for Research on Children, Adolescents and the Media, "contemporary communications tools" help resolve one of the fundamental conflicts that rage within every adolescent. Adolescence, she says, is characterised by "an enhanced need for self-presentation, or communicating your identity to others, and also self-disclosure – discussing intimate topics. Both are essential in developing teenagers' identities, allowing them to validate their opinions and determine the appropriateness of their attitudes and behaviours."

But, as we all recall, adolescence is also a period of excruciating shyness and aching self-consciousness – which can make all that self-presentation and self-disclosure something of a perilous, not to say agonising, business. So the big plus of texting, instant messaging and social networking is that it allows the crucial identity-establishing behaviour, without the accompanying embarrassment. "These technologies give their users a sense of increased controllability," Valkenburg says. "That, in turn, allows them to feel secure about their communication, and thus freer in their interpersonal relations."

"Controllability", she explains, is about three things: being able to say what you want without fear of the message not getting through because of that humungous spot on your chin or your tendency to blush; having the power to reflect on and change what you write before you send it (in contrast to face-to-face communication); and being able to stay in touch with untold hordes of friends at times, and in places, where your predecessors were essentially incommunicado. [...] (726 words)

40 **to boast** – angeben
41 **bike shed** – Fahrradschuppen
44 **gadzillion** – Unmenge
49 **self-disclosure** – Selbstoffenbarung
51 **to validate** – bestätigen
53 **to excruciate** – quälen
55 **perilous** – gefährlich
55 **agonising** – quälend
62 **humungous** – riesig
62 **spot** – *hier:* Pickel
63 **to blush** – erröten
65 **untold** – unermesslich
66 **predecessor** – Vorgänger(in)
66 **incommunicado** – isoliert

2 Comprehension → Understanding non-fictional texts, p. 320

a) Summarise each paragraph in a single, simple sentence.

b) Outline why – according to Professor Valkenburg – these communication tools are so popular with teenagers.

c) "[...] being able to say what you want without fear of the message not getting through because of that humungous spot on your chin or your tendency to blush." (ll. 61–63) Explain this sentence in your own words.

A1.1 p. 293 **3 Listening comprehension: Teens, cell phones and texting** → Listening, p. 319
Listen to the text about US teenagers and text messages.

a) When you listen for the first time, write down the central ideas / topics which are mentioned in the text.

b) When you listen for the second time, arrange these central ideas into a cluster and add as much information as possible.

p. 293 **4 Comment** → Writing a comment, p. 327
"Digital communication [...] IS teenagers' lives." (ll. 33–34) Comment on this statement.

C Young people and families

1 Before you read: Do you agree with the following statements? Why (not)?

a) Parents should be role models for their children and should always behave accordingly.

b) Parents should immediately drop their hobbies when their children need their time and attention.

c) Growing up with two parents is always better than living in a one-parent family.

d) The family will always be at the core of western societies.

e) Fathers should always appear strong and confident.

f) Parents should never criticise each other or even argue in the presence of their children.

g) Mothers often have to be tougher than fathers.

h) Families in which the parents do not serve as role models are very likely to be the homes disadvantaged children come from.

Willy Russell
(English writer, born in 1947)

Raymond Marks ("a normal boy from a normal town") is the protagonist of the novel "The Wrong Boy". He grows up living with his mother who split up with her husband when Raymond was still a baby. The following scene tells us why.

5 **to hum** – summen
6 **to acquire** – erwerben
7 **dedicated** – engagiert
7 **determined** – entschlossen
7 **nowt** (northern English dialect) – nichts
8 **to bleed dry** – ausbluten
9 **pram** – Kinderwagen
10 **hire-purchase bills** – Rechnungen über Ratenkäufe

The wrong boy

Apparently my Dad was always coming home with musical instruments that he could never ever play. And at first, my Mam said, she didn't mind.
'That was the reason I fell in love with him,' she said, 'because he was a man who had so much melody in his heart.'
But for all the melody that apparently hummed within the heart of my father and regardless of how fine the instruments he acquired, no matter how dedicated and determined his efforts, he could never wring a tune out of nowt.
'And it was bleeding us dry,' my Mam said. 'You were just a little baby then, still in your pram; and with me just doin' part time at the Kwiky we'd hardly a pair of pennies to knock together. We'd gas bills and electricity bills, hire-purchase bills and the rent to pay. But it never made any difference. We'd all the debts in the world but they were as nowt to your father. I'm not saying it was his fault. It was like a sickness that he had. Johnny just couldn't help himself. With whatever money we did manage to scrape together, he'd set off with the best of intentions in the world, telling me how he was off to the gas showroom or the electricity board to pay off the bills. And me,' my Mam said, 'I always believed Johnny, always believed your father because your father believed himself. But he'd never get to the showroom or the electricity board. He'd turn up back here with a big bass fiddle or a saxophone or flute. And he'd have that dreamy look in his eye again.'

2 Comprehension → Understanding fictional texts, p. 322
In your own words, summarise the role musical instruments play in the family's life.

3 Analysis → Text analysis, p. 326

a) Explain the phrase "it's an addiction and it's bleeding us dry" (ll. 32 – 33) in your own words.

b) Analyse the language the author uses to contrast the worlds the parents live in. Collect relevant words and passages from the text in a table. Indicate the lines as well.

Dad	Mam

c) Taking into account the changing meaning of "a man with melody in his heart" in this extract, outline the relationship the parents have to each other.

4 Partner interview
Interview your partner about the role a family will play in his or her future. The phrases in the box should give you some ideas, but you can and should include your own questions as well.

regularly seeing your brothers and sisters • looking after your parents • getting married • having children • your parents' house • blood is thicker than water

And that's what started the rows between my Mam and my Dad. My Mam said that at first, after the shouting was over, she always found it in herself to forgive him for spending all the money on a Hammond Organ or a xylophone or a trumpet or a bass trombone. […]

And then my Mam came home from the KwikSave one day and saw him with the Rickenbacker guitar that he'd said was an absolute steal at four hundred and thirty-four pounds; my Mam watched him as he stood there, in the middle of the parlour, the guitar strapped around his shoulders as he pretended to play, as he mimed along to an Eric Clapton record, his fingers skittering up and down the fretboard in a wildly haphazard but passionate frustrated frenzy. And my Mam said there were tears dropping down from my father's eyes. And she told him, 'You've got to give this up, Johnny; it's an obsession, it's an addiction and it's bleeding us dry.'

And my Dad did give up the guitar. But when he took it back to the shop he saw a button-key chromatic accordion. He said he got a fantastic part-exchange deal on it.

And that's when my Mam started seeing the holes in the carpet and the flaking paint on the window frames; and with each new instrument my Dad brought home, the flaky paint got flakier, the holes in the carpet grew and my Mam had to work harder and harder at the KwikSave just to keep us all standing still. And that's when my Mam first started to think; that a man with melody in his heart could also be a millstone around a person's neck. (567 words)

24 **trombone** – Posaune
26 **absolute steal** – Schnäppchen
29 **to skitter** – rutschen
30 **fretboard** – Griffbrett
30 **haphazard** – planlos
30 **frenzy** – Rausch
37 **flaking** – abblättern
42 **to be a millstone around sb.'s neck** – jmdm ein Klotz am Bein sein

D Binge drinking

1 Before you read

a) Work with a partner and ask them the following questions:
- How often do you drink alcohol?
- What kinds of alcoholic drinks do you like?
- How much do you usually drink?
- How do you decide when you've had enough?

b) What is 'binge drinking'? With the same partner, come up with a definition and report back to the class.

1 **binge drinking** – bewusstes Rauschtrinken
2 **to throw up** – sich übergeben
3 **humiliating** – demütigend
4 **sociable** – gesellig
4 **undisputed** – unumstritten
4 **appeal** – Anziehung(skraft)
5 **target** – *hier:* Zielgruppe
6 **to tackle** – etw. angehen
16 **to restrict** – begrenzen
19 **shot** – Kurzer
19 **to encourage** – jdn ermutigen
26 **telesales** – Verkauf über das Telefon
26 **pint** – Britische Maßeinheit; 1 Pint = 568ml
27 **to be conscious of sth.** – sich etw. bewusst sein
27 **to affect** – beeinflussen, sich auswirken auf
28 **long-term** – Langzeit-
28 **to discourage** – abschrecken, abhalten

theguardian

News | Sport | Comment | Culture | Business | Money | Life&Style | Travel | Environment

Comment is free > Society   Search [ ] GO

What teenagers think about binge drinking

Units of alcohol are a complicated matter, cheap drinks are welcomed and throwing up is a humiliating but accepted part of growing up. But while teenagers believe they could be better informed about the dangers of alcohol, the sociable side of drinking still holds undisputed appeal. Young people in the UK, among the heaviest drinkers in Europe, are the target of both government and industry campaigns to tackle binge and under age drinking – so the Guardian went out onto the streets of Britain to speak to them about their experiences with alcohol.

Outside a bar called Cuba Libre in Islington's Upper Street in north London, where the bars are wall to wall and happy hour – lasting three conventional hours – is just finishing, Zoe Spittle, 18, says there was "no downside" to cheap drinks offers. "If there wasn't happy hour, we could go to Tesco to get drinks. But it's better to be in a bar where it's more sociable," she says.

Happy hour

Her friend Charlotte Peel, 18, agreed that restricting happy hours "just drives people into their homes to drink." But, she says: "Club nights [in Tottenham Court Road] where it's £1.50 for a shot, encourage binge drinking. I think the answer is more police and more security." [...]

Warnings not taken seriously

In Nottingham, Grace Ennis, 18, who drinks once a week at most, agrees binge drinking needed tackling. She says: "Warnings about binge drinking help, but they're not taken seriously by people because it's a lifestyle – and when people see the news they don't think it's about them."

But telesales worker Alex Wilby, 19, from Beeston, who drinks six or seven pints on a Friday night, is conscious of how much he drinks. "I think it will affect my health more because I'm young," he says. "I think people should be shown the long-term consequences more to discourage them from drinking."

Krishna Owen, 18, also from Nottingham, drinks about five pints when he goes out with friends. "If I went out more I may be concerned about my health, but as it is I'm not worried, though technically, I could be described as a binge drinker," he says. "But I think beer should be labelled with units alongside alcohol percentage: I don't know how many units are in a pint". […] In Leeds, Holly Makin, 20, is a banker who drinks vodka and coke, was recovering from a house party. "There's a big drinking culture here," she says. "There's a club night every night, and house parties all the time. If I wake up with a hangover, I wonder why I drank so much but then go out and do the same again." She says there is pressure to drink: "It's considered the norm. I have a teetotal friend who is constantly being offered alcohol by friends."

Mikey Harrington, 21, from Leeds and a barman, says peer pressure decreases with age. "When I was young I wanted to drink at dinner like my dad. There's pressure to drink at a young age: it's seen as a sign of maturity and adulthood. Now, I just drink because I want to."

He thinks alcohol education in schools needs improving. "Kids should be taught responsibility and how to deal with alcohol properly," he says. Alex Ford, 19, from Leeds, a singer in a post-punk band, agrees. "People should be taught the importance of knowing their limits: it's reckless to get drunk to the point of being paralytic," he says.

Under-age drinkers

Among under-18s, who mainly drink in parties at each other's houses, there was a consensus that "almost everyone drinks." Henry Willmore, 16, lives in north London and drinks beer occasionally with friends – or vodka or Malibu if he's trying to get drunk. "There's no peer pressure to drink, but there's definitely a drinking culture. At parties, everyone's doing it, so some people probably feel left out if they don't drink." Alcohol can help with confidence. "I think it's more if you feel shy or nervous around girls. But I don't feel nervous."

Buying alcohol is no problem, says James Burton, 16. "It's easy to get fake ID that works in off licenses, though not in big pubs or clubs." Lilit Batikyan, 16, from Camden, agreed it's easy to get alcohol. "Older friends supply it, or there are some off licenses in Camden that sell to underage people." […]

In contrast, Lana Rowlett, from Hackney, is enthusiastic about the joys of drinking. The 19-year-old Stella and cocktail drinker, who works with children with learning difficulties, says: "During the holidays I drink more than 50 drinks a week. I know I can stop drinking so it doesn't worry me; it's socialising for me. But if I was still doing this in a few years, I'd have a problem." […]

(800 words)

33 **to label** – beschriften
33 **unit** – *hier:* Alkoholeinheit
33 **alongside** – neben
34 **to recover** – sich erholen
36 **hangover** – Kater
37 **pressure** – Druck
37 **to consider** – ansehen als
38 **teetotal** – abstinent
39 **peer pressure** – Gruppenzwang
39 **to decrease** – zurückgehen, sinken
41 **maturity** – Reife
41 **adulthood** – Erwachsenenalter
42 **to improve** – (sich) verbessern
44 **reckless** – leichtsinnig
45 **paralytic** – betrunken
47 **consensus** – Übereinstimmung
51 **confidence** – Selbstvertrauen, Sicherheit
51 **shy** – scheu
53 **fake ID** – gefälschter Ausweis
53 **off license** – Wein- und Spirituosengeschäft

2 Comprehension
In the text above, a number of young people give their thoughts on binge drinking. Choose at least 6 people from the text and summarise their attitudes towards drinking. Use a table like this one.

Name	Age	Attitude towards drinking
Zoe	18	- likes 'happy hour' because of the cheap drinks - would buy alcohol from the supermarket if bars were more expensive
Charlotte	…	…

3 Text production
A British magazine for teenagers wants to write an article about young people and alcohol in Europe. Write a letter to the magazine in which you give your opinion on drinking among people your age in Germany.

4 Comment
"There's pressure to drink at a young age: it's seen as a sign of maturity and adulthood." (ll. 40–41) Do you agree with this statement?

5 Presentation → Presentation, p. 362
"Kids should be taught responsibility and how to deal with alcohol properly." (ll. 42–43) Work in small groups and come up with a set of rules for responsible drinking. Create a poster and present it to the class. Include pictures and a slogan.

E Young people and the future

1 Think – pair – share

a) Work on your own. Collect the dreams and fears young people have. What are your strategies to achieve what you want in life?

b) Exchange your list with a partner. Which dreams and fears have you both listed? Also compare the strategies you believe can help to achieve what you want in life.

c) Exchange your lists in class and make a cluster on the board. What are the dreams and fears most young people have? How do you believe you can make these dreams come true?

5 **shameless** – schamlos
8 **to be on the right track** – auf dem richtigen Weg sein
13 **to be taken over by fear** – von Angst übermannt werden
15 **to cuss** – beschimpfen
18 **weapon** – Waffe
18 **consumption** – Konsum

The Fear
by Lily Allen

I want to be rich and I want lots of money
I don't care about clever I don't care about funny
I want loads of clothes and fuck loads of diamonds
I heard people die while they are trying to find them

And I'll take my clothes off and it will be shameless
Cause everyone knows that's how you get famous
I'll look at the sun and I'll look in the mirror
I'm on the right track yeah I'm on to a winner

[Chorus]
I don't know what's right and what's real anymore
I don't know how I'm meant to feel anymore
When do you think it will all become clear?
'Cause I'm being taken over by the fear

Life's about film stars and less about mothers
It's all about fast cars and cussing each other
But it doesn't matter cause I'm packing plastic
and that's what makes my life so fucking fantastic

And I am a weapon of massive consumption
And its not my fault it's how I'm programmed to function
I'll look at the sun and I'll look in the mirror
I'm on the right track yeah we're on to a winner

[Chorus]
I don't know what's right and what's real anymore
I don't know how I'm meant to feel anymore
When do you think it will all become clear?
Cause I'm being taken over by the fear

[Bridge]
Forget about guns and forget ammunition
Cause I'm killing them all on my own little mission
Now I'm not a saint but I'm not a sinner
Now everything's cool as long as I'm gettin thinner

[Chorus]
I don't know what's right and what's real anymore
I don't know how I'm meant to feel anymore
When do you think it will all become clear?
'Cause I'm being taken over by the fear

(307 words)

28 **ammunition** – Munition
30 **saint** – Heilige(r)

2 Comprehension → Dealing with songs, p. 325

a) In your own words, summarise what the girl in the song wants to achieve in life. Which strategies does she want to employ?

b) Explain the following sentences in your own words:
- 'Cause I'm being taken over by the fear (l. 13)
- Life's about film stars and less about mothers (l. 14)
- Now everything's cool as long as I'm gettin thinner (l. 31)

.293 **3 Analysis** → Text analysis, p. 326
Analysing the sentence structure and the choice of words, compare the chorus and the five verses. In which way are they different? What is the effect of this?

4 Classroom discussion → Discussions, p. 344
What do you think is the message of Lily Allen's song? Compare it with your list of dreams and strategies (see task 1c).

.294 **5 Comment** → Writing a comment, p. 327
"Lily Allen's song 'The Fear' is typical of the way teenagers think about their future." Comment on this statement.

6 Mediation → Mediation, p. 343
Summarise the following information in English. Do not translate it.

In einer globalen Studie (14 Länder, 5 600 Befragte, Alter zwischen 8 und 34) waren zentrale Ergebnisse: Die Befragten glauben, dass Eltern, Intelligenz und Freunde im Leben weiterhelfen, die Regierung, Arbeitgeber und Religion dagegen einschränken. Dennoch glaubten sie mehrheitlich, dass sie selbst verantwortlich für ihr Leben seien. Weniger als jeder Zweite ist aber der Meinung, dass er/sie einmal mehr als die eigenen Eltern verdienen wird. Zentrale Sorgen der Befragten waren: Bekomme ich einmal einen guten Job? Wie finde ich heraus, was ich wirklich will? Wer bin ich überhaupt? Bin ich attraktiv?

7 Project → Hotspot 3, p. 23

Revision of tenses

→ Grammar, p. 365

a) What is the tense used in the following sentences? Try to explain the correct rule and the appropriate usage. If you need help, look up the grammar section.

1. Today, almost every teenager is familiar with the Internet and communicates by email and text messages. Some even believe they cannot survive without Facebook and online games.
2. In the future, there probably won't be any picture post cards written by teenagers during their holidays anymore.
3. Over the past few decades, teenagers have had more and more freetime.
4. Some even say that teenagers have never had so little responsibility.
5. When the Internet was invented, very large portable phones had already been on the market for quite some time. However, they weren't used for sending SMS.
6. At this very moment, mobile phone users all over the world are sending and receiving more than 200,000 text messages. It might be interesting to know how many of these are being sent by teenagers …

b) Which tenses have not been mentioned? Make sure that you know these rules as well. Come up with more sentences about teenagers and the way they live.

c) Copy the email and fill in the correct words in the correct verb forms.

Hi,

I **1** (write) to you because of a problem I **2** (like) some help with. **3** (you • remember) that I **4** (meet) this good-looking boy at Sophie's party last week? Now he **5** (send) me a text message asking me out on Saturday. He **6** (suggest) we could go to the cinema. I **7** (not be) to the cinema for ages, but that's not the real problem.

He's nearly 18, and at the moment he **8** (prepare) for his driving licence. He already **9** (have) a car of his own which is kind of cool as this **10** (make) him very independent from his parents.

But the thing that I **11** (find) difficult really is that he already **12** (have) a son! He and his ex-girlfriend **13** (have) a child last summer, shortly after which they **14** (split) up. They **15** (seem) to get along OK, but **16** (stop) going out with each other half a year ago. I **17** (know) from a friend of mine that he regularly **18** (see) his son and **19** (spend) a lot of time with him over the weekends.

Now I **20** (be) really confused and **21** (not know) what to do. I think I **22** (like) him but I **23** (not know) if I **24** (should) go out with someone who already **25** (have) a child. Perhaps I **26** (fall) in love with him. What **27** (say) my parents?

28 (like) his son me? What **29** (say) his ex? I **30** (not know) yet if I **31** (want) children at all, I **32** really (not think) about that … **33** (you • think) I should **34** (forget) him before I even get to know him?

Confused, Ann

1 Project: Time to think of your lifestyle → Projects and group work, p. 359

Think of the following questions and develop a personal fact sheet:
- How would you describe yourself? Include positive and negative characteristics of yourself.
- Who are your idols and how do they influence your lifestyle?
- What is your idea of a "best friend"?
- What do you hope to achieve in your life and how do you want to reach your aim?
- What is your motto in life?

Take your time answering the questions and be honest to yourself. Afterwards choose two classmates you'd like to share your personal facts with and present your results to them.

2 Project: What to expect from life → Presentation, p. 362

Work in groups and prepare a presentation for your classmates on one of the following topics:
- a school / university or a company you want to attend after school
- your dream profession: job profile, requirements and companies you could apply to
- a year off: different possibilities (travelling, voluntary work, advantages and disadvantages)

Collect information and prepare a computer presentation telling your classmates all your main points. Don't forget to illustrate your findings with pictures, diagrams and charts.

Finding information
- Ask for information at schools and universities in your area.
- Contact companies in your area (by email, etc.).
- Look for information on the Internet. Use a search engine and try the following search words: study abroad • internship • apprenticeship • gap year • voluntary work

3 Project: Youth studies (Mediation) → Internet research, p. 358

a) Go online and search for youth studies that deal with the following topics: the future, relationships, communication/the media. Prepare a German summary of the main findings of your study and present it to the class.

b) Go online and search for results of the German youth study *Shell Studie Jugend 2010*. Choose one aspect you find interesting (e.g. diagrams, questions asked, interviews with experts, etc.) and summarise it in English.

A1.4

The Observer

What's wrong with today's youth?

In Boston, Lincolnshire, 70 teenagers trashed a 380-acre farm. They crashed 10-ton lorries through a gate on David Benton's farm to deliver alcohol, sound equipment and generators for an all-night rave. Halfway round the world in Australia, firemen in Sydney blamed bored children for the bushfires threatening the city. Fourteen of the 21 arrested were juveniles. Add to these so-called revelries the countless news stories about schoolkids killing each other [...] and you can't help but echo the age-old refrain: what's wrong with today's youth? [...]

To explain their thrill at causing mayhem on a farmer's property or at setting fire to Sydney's national parks, we need to look [...] at the social network they inhabit. And what a threadbare set-up this is; once upon a time, teenagers at a loose end after school could join the Scouts or go to the youth club down the road, where they came face to face with peers and authority figures, and were expected to get on with them all. Here they sampled the give and take of compromise, politeness and demands that colours every encounter within a community. It's an emotional bartering that comes naturally to only a few, and must be learned by the rest of us.

But where can today's youngsters learn to say 'please' and wait patiently in the queue rather than growl and elbow their way to the front? Taking their cues from their disaffected parents, who opt out of politics, clubs and churches, teenagers of all classes have turned away from organised and collective leisure that would have once taught them social skills, and taken up the solo pleasures of the internet.

In virtual chatrooms and through video games, today's generation engages in a new kind of interaction. Yes, you make connections with others – but wholly on your own terms. Should the invisible interlocutor fail to amuse you or to confirm your prejudices or heap sufficient praise upon you, you can simply click your mouse and they're off your screen, to be replaced with someone more amiable or more malleable. [...]

Free of parental interference, and unrestrained by traditional social relationships, young people are turning into socially autistic beings who can only log on and tune out. (375 words)

1 **to trash** – verwüsten

3 **gate** – Tor

6 **to blame sb.** – jmdm die Schuld geben für

8 **juvenile** – Jugendliche(r)

9 **revelry** – ausgelassene Feier

13 **mayhem** – Chaos

16 **threadbare** – schäbig

18 **to be at a loose end** – nicht wissen, was man mit sich anfangen soll

22 **to sample** – ausprobieren

24 **encounter** – Begegnung

25 **bartering** – Austausch

29 **to growl** – sich mürrisch geben

30 **to take one's cue from sb.** – jmds Beispiel folgen

31 **to opt out** – aussteigen

37 **to engage in sth.** – sich mit etw. befassen

40 **interlocutor** – Gesprächspartner

41 **to heap sufficient praise (up)on sb.** – jmdn überschwänglich loben

44 **amiable** – liebenswürdig, freundlich

44 **malleable** – gefügig

45 **unrestrained** – uneingeschränkt

1 Comprehension
Read the text and complete the statements (a–e) by choosing the right answer (1, 2, or 3).

a) Fourteen juveniles were arrested for …
1. making too much noise at a local event.
2. trashing a 380-acre farm.
3. causing a bushfire threatening the city of Sydney in Australia.

b) The social network young people inhabit …
1. can be made responsible for the youngsters' outrageous behaviour.
2. cannot be blamed for their outrageous behaviour.
3. helps them to behave properly.

c) In the past …
1. young people behaved even worse than they do nowadays.
2. young people knew how to get on well with peers and authority figures within a community.
3. young people avoided any useful contact with community members.

d) The current behaviour of young people is the result of …
1. their intensive usage of the Internet.
2. their increasing visits to clubs and churches.
3. the skills they learn at school.

e) Being in virtual chatrooms today's youngsters …
1. want to make conversations on their own terms only.
2. want to communicate mainly with people who have got different visions of life.
3. do not want to amuse themselves but hold talks about serious topics.

2 Analysis → Describing cartoons, p. 340
Analyse the cartoon and state as to whether it is a suitable illustration of the text.

3 Comment: Choose one of the following tasks

a) "[…], young people are turning into socially autistic beings who can only log on and tune out." (ll. 46–48) Discuss.

b) Today's teenagers are said to be faced with many problems former generations did not have. In your opinion, what are the most urgent problems to be dealt with in order to make young people's lives worth living? Discuss, including possible solutions.

Topic 1.2

i7kk55

Personal identities and social relationships

A

B

C

Robert Herrick

Dreams

Here we are all, by day;
by night we're hurled
By dreams, each one,
into a several world.

Getting started

1 Look at the photos and collect as many words as possible that express social relationships, e.g. mother, daughter, mother-in-law, neighbour, friend etc.
→ Brainstorming, p. 351

2 Choose one person in any of the photos. Make up a complex sociogram (see photo F) which represents the social relationships this person might have. Use your imagination, but be as realistic as possible. Label the relationships using the words from task 1.

Ezra Pound

And the days are not full enough

And the days are not full enough
And the nights are not full enough
And life slips by like a field mouse
Not shaking the grass.

3 Work in pairs and interview each other to complete a sociogram for both of you.

4 Find words and expressions that describe the quality and closeness of relationships, e.g. an acquaintance, a friend, someone you know from school, etc. Order them from close to distant.

5 What idea of social relationships is created in the two poems?

6 Bring along a photo or a painting that expresses a special social relationship. Present your illustration in class.

Word bank

relatives • in-laws • colleagues • neighbourhood • leisure activities • to see sb. occasionally / from time to time • best friend • someone you know • partner • grandchildren • grandparents • to be related • to be popular with sb. • to be an outsider

1.2 Personal identities and social relationships

A Friends

1 Before you read

a) In a small group, agree on a short definition of the word "friend".

b) In class, share your results and make a cluster with criteria of friendship.

A 1.8

YoungLife Australia

Search GO

About us | Our Services | Get Involved | Events & News | Contact Us

Friends ain't friends ...

How social media has changed the way young people form friendships

A friend is no longer necessarily a friend. The ongoing influence of social media has derailed the nature of the word's meaning, turned it into a verb, and is altering the nature and the depth of our relationships with others.

In days long gone, the word friend was used to describe someone that you knew, liked and trusted. One joined to another in intimacy and affection. A person with whom you were allied to, a well-wisher who genuinely cared, a patron, a supporter, or a mate you could count on.

That was pre-facebook. Today, friends are more like attractive or quirky collectibles, and merely commodities to be accumulated and traded with the object of many young people being to 'friend' as many people as possible. Indeed, Wikipedia lists another meaning for friends, and that is people who are added to a list of contacts associated with a social networking website.

For the most part, the quality of friendships in the alternate reality that is the internet has been on the slide ever since 2004 when facebook hit the net. And the unfortunate reality is that far too many young people in particular have abandoned the traditional notion of what constitutes a friend and now immerse themselves in the currency of sheer numbers, to find an audience, boost their self-esteem, and prove to others their appeal and importance.

Because many online friendships are distant affairs between people who in a lot of cases have never actually met face to face, it's easy to treat 'friends' in a much more abrupt way than you would in the offline world ... and unfriend, block and banish them at the click of a mouse.

In today's hyper-connected world, we know what our 'friends' are doing ... and often the exact place and time they're doing it ... if their updates and their location posts are to be fully believed.

Dr Damien Maher, a University of Technology Sydney lecturer specialising in social media, is one of many experts tracking the changing face of friendship.

"People have more friends and fewer deep friends. Some have more than a thousand friends and it's changed what it means to be a friend," he told Vanessa

3 **ongoing** – anhaltend
4 **to derail** – entgleisen lassen
8 **well-wisher** – jmd, der einem Gutes wünscht
8 **patron** – Gönner, Schirmherr
10 **quirky** – sonderbar
10 **collectible** – Sammlerstück
11 **commodity** – Ware
11 **to trade** – handeln mit
15 **alternate** – abwechselnd
16 **to be on the slide** – im Rutschen sein
17 **to abandon** – verlassen
18 **notion** – Idee
18 **to immerse oneself** – sich in etw. vertiefen
19 **sheer** – rein, lediglich
23 **to banish** – verbannen

Stubbs of MX in May 2011. "It has a different meaning than it used to. Before the internet, a friend was a person you knew."

"What you put up, in photos, status updates and wall posts, can manipulate the way you represent yourself to people in the real world. So people can reveal what they choose to reveal and online is more accepting of face value," he observes. "But the connection to what is really going on in their lives can suffer."

The overwhelming trend among teenagers is that bigger is better. "Friend numbers confer status," says Dr Maher. "Having more friends is a good thing and somehow means that you're a nicer person, and better to be with."

Leading social researcher Hugh Mackay made an exhaustive study on what makes us tick, investigated the 10 desires that drive us, and published the findings in a book of the same name in late 2010. He sees the key drivers in young people as the need for self-worth, self-respect, and belonging, and spoke on the topic at the Young Life Australia annual Sydney banquet on 20 May 2011.

At the charity event Mr Mackay told the audience that the desire to be taken seriously was one of the big ones for young people. "Not to be seen as serious people ... that would often be frowned upon," he explained. "No, the desire to be taken seriously revolves around the desire to be noticed, to be appreciated, to be acknowledged as the unique individual that we know ourselves to be."

"Generally speaking, this desire is at its most intense in teenagers," said Mr Mackay, "although it does stay with us to a diminished degree as we get older."

"But what happens if we are not taken seriously?" Mackay pondered. "What happens in young people is that if they are belittled, they are mocked, humiliated or marginalised, then they can carry this as a burden, sometimes for life. So many over-compensate in other ways, to try and build themselves up."

This powerful yearning for acceptance, the quest to gain an appealing reputation, and a tribalistic sense of belonging in young people, certainly explains the ever-rising popularity of social media, where collecting as many like's as you can is the modern measure of peer group status. […] (745 words)

35 **to reveal** – enthüllen
36 **face value** – Nennwert
39 **to confer** – gewähren
41 **what makes us tick** – was uns bewegt
48 **to be frowned upon** – Missbilligung erfahren
54 **to belittle** – herabsetzen, verniedlichen
54 **to mock sb.** – jmdn verspotten
54 **to humiliate sb.** – jmdn demütigen
55 **to marginalise sb.** – jmdn an den Rand drängen
57 **yearning** – Verlangen
58 **tribalistic** – Stammes-

2 Comprehension

a) In your own words, show how – according to the text – the understanding of friendship has changed since the arrival of social media.

b) Outline how the researchers Damien Maher and Hugh Mackay explain this change.

p. 294 **3 Analysis** → Describing cartoons, p. 340
Describe and analyse the cartoon.

4 Project → Hotspot 1, p. 39

"If you have any complaints, can you come to me before posting them on Myspace?"

B Family issues

1 Before you read

a) Work with a partner and agree on a list of ten characteristics of good parents.

b) Share your lists in class and agree on a ranking.

2 Comprehension

Summarise the passage in your own words.

Nick Hornby (English writer, born in 1957)

10 **dressing gown** – Bademantel
13 **guess** – Vermutung
17 **to be ashamed of sth.** – sich für etw. schämen
18 **kettle** – Wasserkocher
21 **to babble** – schwafeln
21 **to put sth. off** – etw. hinausschieben
27 **to screw sth. up** – *hier:* zusammenknüllen
27 **fold** – Falte
28 **crease** – Knitterfalte
30 **to smooth sth. out** – glätten

The following text is a passage from "Slam", a novel by Nick Hornby. The story is about Sam, a sixteen-year-old with a passion for skateboarding. When he meets Alicia everything seems great until one moment changes their lives forever. Suddenly Sam is faced with new responsibilities he cannot escape from even though he tries to.

Slam

I'd told Mum I was going out after school, so I had no idea whether she was going to be in or not. I'd told her I was going round to a friend's for tea, and I'd be back around eight. If she knew I wasn't coming back straight after school, she sometimes went out for a drink with someone from work, or went round someone's house for a cup of tea. I'd warned them, but Alicia's mum and dad said that seeing as it was a serious situation, they'd just come in and wait for her if she wasn't there.

Something made me ring on the doorbell, rather than just get out my key and let everybody in. I suppose I didn't think it was right to let Alicia's mum and dad in without warning Mum first. Anyway, there was no answer at first, but just as I'd got my keys out, Mum came to the door in her dressing gown.

She knew something had happened straight away. I think she probably knew what that something was, as well. Alicia, her mum, her dad, four unhappy faces … Put it this way, she probably wouldn't have needed three guesses. It had to be sex or drugs, didn't it?

'Oh. Hi. I was just in the middle of …'

But she couldn't think what she was in the middle of, which I took to be a bad sign. I suddenly got worried about the dressing gown. Why couldn't she tell us she was having a bath? If that was what she was doing? Having a bath is nothing to be ashamed of, is it?

'Anyway. Come in. Sit down. I'll just go and put something on. Put the kettle on, Sam. Unless you'd like something stronger? We've got some wine open, I think. We don't usually, but … And there might be some beer. Have we got beer, Sam?'

She was babbling. She wanted to put it off too.

'I think we're fine, thanks, Annie,' said Alicia's mum. 'Please, can we say something before you get dressed?'

'I'd rather …'

'Alicia's pregnant. It's Sam's, of course. And she wants to keep it.'

My mum didn't say anything. She just looked at me for a long time, and then it was like her face was a piece of paper that someone was screwing up. There were these folds and lines and creases everywhere, in places where there was never usually anything. You know how you can always tell when a piece of paper has been screwed up, no matter how hard you try to smooth it out? Well, even as she was making that face, you could

3 Analysis

a) Characterise Sam and his mother as they appear in this passage.

b) Analyse the relationship between Sam and his mother.

c) Analyse the language the author uses to show the emotions Sam's mother goes through.

4 Text production → Writing an email, p. 329

p.294 a) Write an email to Sam's mother in which you comment on her behaviour in this scene.

b) Starting from line 25 ("Alicia's pregnant. It's Sam's, of course. And she wants to keep it.") write an alternative version of Sam's mother's reaction to the news of Alicia's pregnancy.

5 Projects → Hotspots 2 and 3, p. 39

tell those creases would never go away, however happy she got. And then this terrible noise. I'd never see her if she ever found out I was dead, but I can't imagine the noise would be any different.

She stood there crying for a little while, and then Mark, her new boyfriend, came into the living room to see what was going on. So Mark explained the dressing gown. You didn't have to have any special powers to read the minds of Alicia's mum and dad. Their minds were easy to read, because they were written all over their faces and eyes. You people, I could hear her dad saying to me, even though he wasn't saying anything now, just looking. You people. Do you ever do anything else?

Apart from have sex? And I wanted to kill Mum, which was a coincidence, because she wanted to kill me.

'Of all the things, Sam,' Mum said after what seemed like ages and ages. 'Of all the things you could do. All the ways you could hurt me.'

'I wasn't trying to hurt you,' I said. 'Really. I didn't want to get Alicia pregnant. It was the last thing I wanted to do.'

'Here's a good way of not getting someone pregnant,' said Mum. 'Don't have sex with them.'

I didn't say anything. I mean, you couldn't argue with that, could you? But her argument did mean that I could only have sex two or three times in my life, and not even that many times if I decided I didn't want kids. That decision wasn't mine to make any more, though. I was having kids whether I liked it or not. One kid, anyway, unless Alicia was having twins.

'I'm going to be a grandmother,' said Mum. 'I'm four years younger than Jennifer Aniston and I'm going to be a grandmother. I'm the same age as Cameron Diaz and I'm going to be a grandmother.'

Cameron Diaz was a new one. I hadn't heard her mention Cameron Diaz before.

'Yes,' said Alicia's father. 'Well. There is a great deal about this whole thing that is unfortunate. But at the moment we're more worried about Alicia's future.'

'Not Sam's?' said my mum. 'Because he had a future too.'

I looked at her. Had? I had a future? Where was it now? I wanted her to tell me that everything was going to be all right. I wanted her to say that she'd survived, so I could too. But she wasn't telling me that. She was telling me that I didn't have a future any more. (880 words)

40 **coincidence** – Zufall

58 **unfortunate** – bedauernswert

C Gender stereotypes

1 Stereotypes

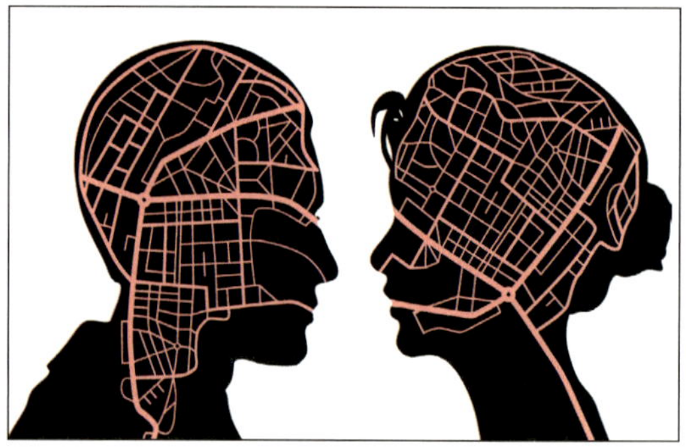

a) Work in groups and collect ten characteristics each for men and women. Try and leave out stereotypes and prejudices.

b) Share your lists with another group. Try to agree on ten characteristics each for men and women.

c) What then – if anything – is typical of a woman, and typical of a man? Discuss in class.

2 Before you read → Brainstorming, p. 351

a) The following text is entitled "Mütter im Berufsleben". Brainstorm ideas that you associate with this.

b) Share your ideas in class and cluster them.

p. 295 **3 Mediation** → Mediation, p. 343
Summarise the German article "Mütter im Berufsleben" in an English text.

DER TAGESSPIEGEL
RERUM COGNOSCERE CAUSAS

Search GO

Home | Berlin | Politik | Sport | Kultur | Welt | Meinung

Mütter im Berufsleben

Das bisherige Rollenmodell bleibt etabliert

Heute sind zwar mehr Mütter als früher berufstätig, dafür arbeiten aber deutlich weniger in Vollzeit. Das hat der jüngste Mikrozensus des Statistischen Bundesamts ergeben. Was bedeutet das?

Die Antwort lautet: Kommt ganz darauf an, was man erwartet. Wenn es etwa darum geht, eine ausgewogene Teilhabe von Frauen und Männern am Berufs- und Familienleben zu erreichen, sind die Zahlen nicht sehr ermutigend.
Zwar ist der Anteil der insgesamt erwerbstätigen Frauen von 1991 bis 2009 gestiegen, bei der Teilzeit in den vergangenen zwölf Jahren sogar um 20 Prozent. Trotzdem kann man die Analysten des Statistischen Bundesamtes so verstehen, dass in Deutschland das bisherige Rollenmodell etabliert bleibt: Vater arbeitet, Mutter ist zu Hause oder arbeitet in Teilzeit.

Diese Aufteilung ist noch immer das mit Abstand häufigste Modell in diesem Land. Im Vergleich zu 1996 sind heute bei Ehepartnern und in Lebensgemeinschaften Frauen viel seltener, minus 20 Prozent, in Vollzeit tätig.
Die Politik und manche Familienforscher konzentrieren sich deshalb gerne auf die Zahl der erwerbstätigen Mütter in Teilzeit, die 2009 auf ein Rekordniveau gestiegen ist. In den neuen Bundesländern hat sich die Zahl der in Teilzeit arbeitenden Mütter sogar verdoppelt. […]
Die größte Gruppe dieser Frauen, die in Teilzeit – oder Vollzeit – arbeitet, ist die der alleinerziehenden Mütter, danach folgen Mütter ab dem 55. Lebensjahr. Innerhalb der Teilzeitbeschäftigung steigen zudem atypische Beschäftigungsverhältnisse an: geringfügig Beschäftigte, Zeitarbeitsverhältnisse. Immer öfter wird die Frau aufgrund der ökonomischen Lage zum Arbeiten gezwungen, beispielsweise weil der Mann arbeitslos wird. Arbeitsmarktforscher kommen in Studien zu dem Schluss: „In Bezug auf die Modernisierung der Geschlechterverhältnisse sind die Arbeitszeiten von Müttern und Vätern ernüchternd. Eine Umverteilung von bezahlter und unbezahlter Arbeit zwischen den Geschlechtern deutet sich bisher nicht an.“ (281 Wörter)

1.11 **4 Listening comprehension: Miss World and women's rights go hand in hand**
.295 → Listening, p. 319
Listen to the recording about Clara Belle, who as a student was strictly against beauty contests and then successfully took part in them. Draw up a table and complete it with information from the recording.

Why Clara Belle was against beauty contests in the past	Reasons that made her change her view	Beauty contests and feminism	Clara Belle's views on contests and pageants in general

5 Analysis → Describing cartoons, p. 340
Describe and analyse the cartoon.

6 Giving a talk → Presentation, p. 362
Prepare a three-minute talk on gender stereotypes in which you include the following aspects:
- male and female characteristics
- stereotypes and prejudices
- gender equality
- any other aspects you consider important

"No, this is not Mel's secretary, this is Mel."

2 **annually** – jährlich
3 **20 billion** – 20 Milliarden
4 **to estimate** – schätzen
7 **single-handedly** – im Alleingang
7 **to cure** – heilen, lindern
8 **disparity** – Ungleichheit
9 **to make sth. worth** – *hier:* etw. belohnen
11 **to make sth. worth one's while** – jmdn für etw. belohnen
12 **for a cause** – für eine Sache
13 **to expend in** – aufwenden für
13 **inconvenience** – Unannehmlichkeit
14 **benefit** – Vorteil
24 **compassion** – Mitgefühl
27 **a shut-in** – jmd, der ans Haus gefesselt ist

D Volunteering

1 Before you read → Brainstorming, p. 351
"Ask not what your country can do for you – ask what you can do for your country."
What message was President John F. Kennedy (1917–1963; 35th President of the US) trying to get across when he spoke these famous words?

Network for Good™ VOLUNTEER

HOME | DONATE | VOLUNTEER | CRISIS RELIEF | MY PROFILE

Participate in the Tradition of Volunteering

- Approximately 109 million American adults volunteer annually – that's 56 % of all adults.
- Volunteers contribute an average of 3.5 hours per week – totalling 20 billion hours with an estimated dollar value of $225 billion.
- 59 % of teenagers volunteer an average of 3.5 hours per week – that's 13.3 million volunteers totalling 2.4 billion hours at a total value of $7.7 billion.

The nonprofit sector cannot take the place of government programs, nor can it single-handedly cure the ills and disparities of society. But each of us can make a difference in a small way, in our own sphere, and can find ways to help that will make our efforts worth the time and trouble we invest in them.

Some of the Best Reasons to Volunteer

Some of the best reasons to give are the ones you may not have considered – the ones that make it worth your while to go that extra step. People who have spent time volunteering for a cause report that they get back in satisfaction and joy more than they ever expend in inconvenience or effort – what you get back is immeasurable. You'll also receive these benefits:

- Volunteering makes you feel needed.
- Volunteering can lead to learning new skills.
- Volunteering can help you deal with some of your personal problems.
- Volunteering helps you meet new people and breaks down barriers of misunderstanding, mistrust and fear.
- Volunteering can create new contacts which may help your business or career.

It's What in the World You Can Do!

You might be thinking, "The little bit that I can do will never help much!" or "What in the world can I do?" If you've ever spent ten minutes reading a book to a lonely child, you know that even that small amount of compassion and attention can make a world of difference. No one person can solve the world's problems, but what little you do can make your little corner of the world – or one far away from yours – a happier, healthier, safer place to live for those who need your help. Each of us can right a wrong, fill a plate, visit a shut-in or clean up a park – and that does make a difference for us all!

(375 words)

2 Mediation → Presentation, p. 362
Use the information of the Network for Good website to prepare a 3-minute talk in German to convince young Germans to go to the US and spend time doing voluntary work. Note down some keywords to structure your talk. Focus on what the Network for Good can / cannot achieve and what personal advantages volunteering offers.

Helping the elderly or disabled

Organising a game for inner-city kids

A1.14

A poem

Compassion's heart

Compassion's ear is not too far
From us in darkest night;
It closely listens to the beat
Of hearts afraid with fright.
Compassion's mouth is not shut tight
When trouble hurts the soul;
Compassion speaks to souls that groan
Its purpose to console.
Compassion's head is never slow
To turn to meet our need;
It meets the foe that hurts us so
With urgency and speed.
Compassion's eye is never closed
To tears that stain the cheek;
Compassion sees the cause of tears
And gives the help we seek.
Compassion's heart is never cold
Or distant in our strife;
It beats from God's own pulse with might
To lift from death to life!

Taking part in political life

Clearing up after a natural disaster

5 **shut tight** – fest verschlossen
7 **to groan** – stöhnen
8 **to console** – trösten
11 **foe** – Feind
12 **urgency** – Dringlichkeit
14 **to stain** – Flecken machen
18 **strife** – Streit
19 **might** – Macht

3 What is the message of the poem? Write it down using your own words.

4 The poet uses lyrical devices such as "personification", "metaphor" and "contrasts". Try to identify them in the poem. → Dealing with poetry, p. 324

5 Together with a partner, think of ways besides volunteering in which individuals can contribute to the society in which they live. You can use the photos on this page as a starting point. Make a diagram showing how the individual and society interact in terms of rights and responsibilities.

E Generation Me?

1 Before you read

a) Look at the picture. Describe and analyse what you see.

b) With the help of the picture, try to predict what the text is about.

A 1.15

1 **self-absorbed** – sehr mit sich selbst beschäftigt

5 **to release** – *hier:* veröffentlichen

6 **empathy** – Empathie, Mitgefühl

9 **counterpart** – Gegenstück

22 **narcissism epidemic** – *etwa:* Epidemie von Selbstverliebtheit

24 **entitlement** – Anspruch

Psychology Today

Search GO

Home | Find a Therapist | Topic Streams | Get Help | Magazine | Tests | Psych Basics

Are today's youth even more self-absorbed (and less caring) than generations before?

Have kids today stopped caring about others?

Earlier this week, Sara Konrath, a researcher at the University of Michigan Institute for Social Research, released her results of a study analyzing and comparing empathy among college students over the last 30 years. The results? The "biggest drop in empathy" in recent history. She writes, "College kids today are about 40 percent lower in empathy than their counterparts of 20 or 30 years ago."

In related survey research, psychologist Jean Twenge has labeled the current generation of young people the "iGeneration," or "Generation Me". In her books she describes how young people today "take it for granted that the self comes first," and has labeled this time a "narcissism epidemic", stating that we are "living in the age of entitlement". Konrath and O'Brien link the self-absorption and lack of empathy together, calling the current generation "one of the most self-centered, narcissistic, competitive, confident and individualistic in recent history ... It's not surprising that this growing emphasis on the self is accompanied by a corresponding devaluing of others."

There are some who argue that this description fits most teens and young adults and is appropriate to some degree for everyone in this developmental phase of life. However, both researchers compare similarly aged kids from other generations and the difference is striking.

This difference raises the question of why? Researchers Konrath and O'Brien hazard a few guesses, most related to the increase in exposure to and use of media. For example, many in this current generation have had repeated lifetime exposure to violent video games and films, and there is a growing body of research suggesting that violent video games (and perhaps films) are a cause of increased aggressive behavior, thoughts, and feelings, and a decrease in empathy and prosocial behavior across both gender and culture. Additionally, the researchers surmise that the ease of having (and ignoring or dumping) online "friends" may make it easy to tune out when they don't feel like responding to the distress of others, and may carry over offline as well. They also add that the inflated expectations of success fueled by "reality shows" create a social environment that encourages self-focus and works against slowing down and listening to someone who needs a bit of sympathy.

Obviously, any statements about an entire generation are not true of every person in that generation. Clearly there are young people today who are deeply emphatic and caring. But the general trends and statistics are alarming, and it would behoove those of us in a position to influence today's youth to pay attention and be proactive about it while we can. Paying attention to the forces that influence children and young people so that they can grow up to be empathic is not only better for them, but ultimately better for us all.

(482 words)

34 **to devalue** – abwerten
36 **appropriate** – angemessen
41 **exposure to** – Ausgesetzt-sein
47 **gender** – Geschlecht
48 **to surmise** – mutmaßen
48 **ease** – Bequemlichkeit, Leichtigkeit
57 **emphatic** – einfühlsam
58 **to behoove** *(old)* – erforderlich sein

2 Comprehension

a) In your own words, summarise what the studies mentioned in the article reveal about today's youth.

b) Outline the influence of the media on teenagers today as mentioned in the text.

3 Analysis → Text analysis, p. 326
Analyse the article in detail and point out where the author includes her personal opinion about today's youth as well.

4 Comment → Writing a comment, p. 327
Write a letter to the author commenting on the article and its findings. Add personal experience to support your ideas.

Reported speech

→ Grammar, p. 380

a) Your group publishes a school magazine and wants to print an interview with Peggy Olsen, an American family counsellor. Here are the questions you ask:

1. How did you become a family counsellor?
2. What do you like about your job?
3. What kind of people do you work with?
4. Do you mostly work from the office, or do you have to travel a lot?
5. What are the most common problems you deal with?
6. Have you ever visited a counsellor yourself?
7. Why do so many families need to see a counsellor these days?
8. Will you always work in this job?
9. Can you give us some tips on how to lead a happy family life?
10. What one piece of advice would you give to all families?

Later Ms Olsen tells her trainee about the interview for your magazine. Write down her exact words. Use different introductory verbs and start like this:
"Today some students from a German school magazine questioned me about being a family counsellor. They wanted to know how I became a family counsellor and asked me …"

b) The following statements are already in reported speech. Put them back into direct speech. Pay attention to whether it is a statement or a question.

1. The woman's friend asked her where she had met her husband.
2. The woman's friend wanted to know if they had liked each other straight away.
3. The woman said that they had hit it off right away.
4. My friend asked me whether or not he should open a Facebook account.
5. I said that I was surprised he did not already have one.
6. He answered that he had been anti-Facebook for a long time but now he realised that it was the only way to keep in touch with his friends in other parts of the country.
7. My mother mentioned that she had been having problems with her neighbours.
8. She told me that they had been playing loud music.
9. I suggested that she try and talk to them before she called the police.
10. My mother said she would discuss it with my father before she made a decision.

1 Project: Parents and children → Presentation, p. 362
Bring along photos or paintings that deal with the relationship of parents and children. Avoid choosing only photos / paintings from today; older ones can be telling, too. Write a short text for each photo / painting which describes what can be seen and why you have chosen this photo / painting. Arrange your photos / paintings
- either in a gallery walk and ask other students from your school to take this walk
- or in a slide show which you accompany with suitable music.

2 Research project: Family types → Internet research, p. 358

a) Search the web for information about family types and household organisations in an English-speaking country of your choice. Compare this information with facts about Germany. Prepare a presentation in which you outline similarities and differences between these two countries.

b) Search the web for information about family types in history in either of the following English-speaking countries: USA, England, Australia. Compare this information with facts about these countries today. Present the developments you have identified in diagrams to your class.

c) Analyse the diagram about household sizes in Germany in 2030. Draw up similar diagrams for either of the following English-speaking countries: USA, England, Australia.

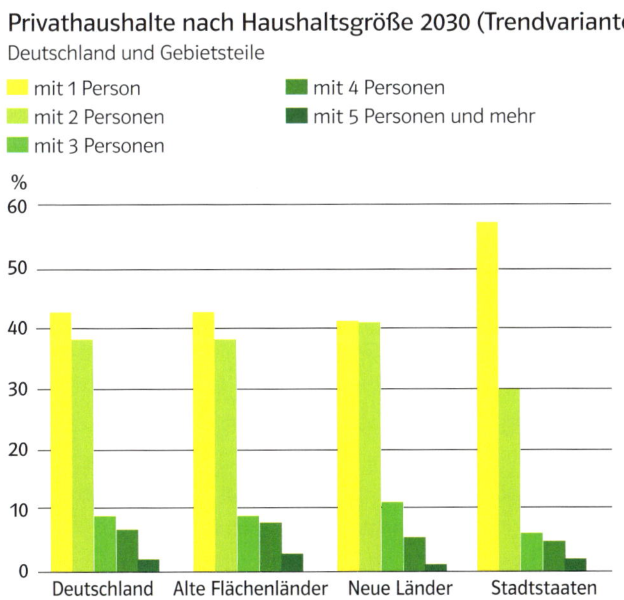

Source: Statistisches Bundesamt, 2011

3 Project: Families in literature → Projects and group work, p. 359
Make a list of a) father figures and b) mother figures in any of the novels or short stories you have read. In class, agree on a set of criteria which can be used to analyse the characters (i.e. loving, egoistic, cold, warm-hearted, tired, ambitious, etc.). Carry out an analysis of these characters. Do you find any gender specific results? Are there any clichés to be found? Do the results you have found out surprise you? Why (not)?

A1.18

1 **homophobia** – Homophobie
2 **to stigmatise** – brandmarken
3 **peers** – Gleichaltrige
4 **stigma** – Makel
4 **to melt away** – *(fig)* wegschmelzen
8 **to redefine** – neu definieren, neu festlegen
8 **masculinity** – Männlichkeit
8 **heterosexuality** – Heterosexualität
9 **to hold sth. in high esteem** – von etw. eine hohe Meinung haben
11 **prejudice** – Vorurteil
16 **to dispel** – verbannen
22 **LGBT (lesbian, gay, bisexual and transgender)** – Lesben, Schwule, Bisexuelle und Transsexuelle
23 **straight** – *hier:* heterosexuell
24 **peculiar** – eigenartig
28 **to ring true** – glaubhaft klingen
29 **to bully** – mobben
33 **to eradicate** – beseitigen
33 **to be embedded** – tief verwurzelt sein
34 **bogus** – falsch
34 **hideous** – abscheulich
36 **to urge** – zur Vorsicht mahnen
37 **shift** – Veränderung
40 **abuse** – Missbrauch
40 **to be dismissive** – *hier:* desinteressiert sein

theguardian

News | Sport | Comment | Culture | Business | Money | Life&Style | Travel | Environment

Comment is free > Society   Search [ ] GO

Homophobia is declining in schools, study claims

Teenagers no longer stigmatise being gay, argues Brunel University sociologist Mark McCormack. Teenagers face far less homophobia among their peers than ever before because the stigma of being gay is melting away in secondary schools, according to a new book.

1 McCormack spent six months in three schools in the same UK town to study attitudes of 16- to 18-year-olds. In his book, *The Declining Significance of Homophobia: How Teenage Boys are Redefining Masculinity and Heterosexuality*, he says that, for this age group, pro-gay attitudes are held in high esteem and homophobia is as unacceptable as racism. **2**

"A lot of prejudice is based on stigma," he added, "and actually the stigma around being gay has dropped off. **3** " The internet had helped to dispel the isolation young gay people have felt in the past, he said. […]

McCormack found teenagers to be open about their sexuality. "It's had a huge impact on the LGBT kids: they are happy, out and proud at school. That's better for gay kids and better for straight kids, too."But he says the change in attitude may well be peculiar to this age group: **4**

"These young people see homophobia as wrong. Guys used to prove they were straight by being homophobic. Now, when young guys want to show they're straight, they do it in a more positive way by joking about being gay."

McCormack's findings do not ring true with everyone. **5** Its 2010 survey of Brighton schools found that 16% of bullied children in primary and 23% in secondary schools reported that the bullying was homophobic in nature. Half of lesbian, bisexual, gay or transgender teens reported homophobic bullying at school or college.

"It remains the second-highest reason children give for bullying," said Allsorts' director, Jess Wood. "I do think to try and eradicate the word 'gay' is a waste of time; it's embedded in the language, but it's a bogus argument to suggest it's anything other than hideous for gay people to hear the negative associations of the word."

Ruth Hunt of Stonewall UK also urged caution. " **6** But plenty are not. Although we are seeing shifts in the way schools think about how boys should be seen to behave, we still see many schools with significant problems. We still have schools who tell us they have no gay pupils."

"As for the abuse of the word 'gay', it's dangerous to be dismissive by using the argument, 'Oh the kids think it's fine and so it's fine'. That doesn't stand up. If the word is being used to mean stupid, then how does it make a young gay person feel? It makes them feel stupid. It's an inevitable connection in their minds."

ONE BOY'S STORY

Lee, 16, says that his life at school has improved since he came out as gay aged 14, but he still suffers homophobic bullying. "Sometimes it feels a bit weird because gay really means rubbish. I don't really like being called gay, I say 'That's so gay' myself. **7** Well, that's not true. I've cried about it a lot. I don't really like walking by myself anywhere. I've been kicked a few times and punched. I try to be myself at school and I've got friends who'll stick up for me, but I wish I could turn it off. I dropped out of one GCSE class because I couldn't take the abuse from one boy. The teacher couldn't see it, and I didn't see why I had to spell it out to him. They don't take homophobia seriously. There's a poster up in our school, one of those 'Some people are gay, get over it' ones. It feels like it's me that's expected to get over it." (744 words)

43 **inevitable** – unvermeidlich
46 **weird** – eigenartig, sonderbar
49 **to punch** – schlagen
50 **to stick up for sb.** – für jemanden eintreten
50 **to drop out of sth.** – aus etw. aussteigen
52 **to spell sth. out** – etw. klarmachen

1 Comprehension

Read the text and choose from sentences A-H the one which fits each gap (1–7). There is one extra sentence that you do not need to use.

A The coming-out narrative is changing too, with parents being OK.
B I can unconditionally agree to it.
C The anti-gay prejudices of the 80s and early 90s are disappearing, claims Mark McCormack, a sociologist at Brunel University.
D "I'm not saying the battle is over against homophobia, but it's getting better."
E He also suggests that the phrase "so gay", used to rubbish things, is unrecognisable to teens as homophobic.
F "It's definitely not our experience, I'm afraid," said Jess Wood of youth support charity Allsorts.
G Yes, I get bullied. It's getting better. But I get called names every single day and I have done since I was at primary school. I don't care anymore.
H I think it matches what we know in that some schools which are good on this are very, very good.

to come out – sich outen
to rubbish sth. – runtermachen
unrecognisable – unerkennbar
charity – Wohlfahrtseinrichtung
to bully – mobben
to match – übereinstimmen

2 Analysis → Describing diagrams, p. 341

a) Examine Lee's feelings about being a young homosexual male.

b) Analyse the statistic from the US and relate it to the text.

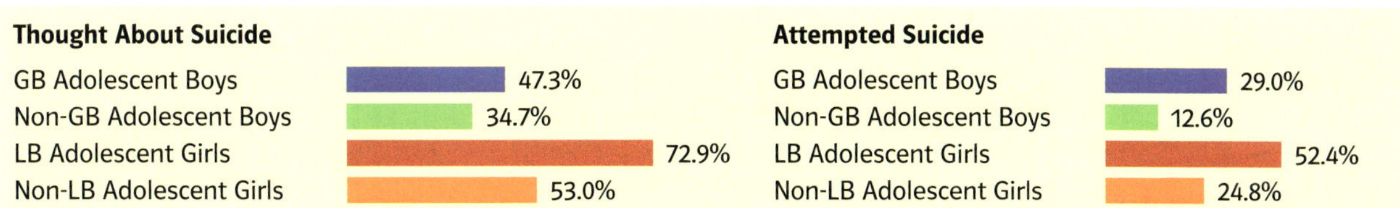

(GB = gay, bisexual; LB = lesbian, bisexual), *Source: Journal of Adolescent Health, 2006*

3 Comment

"I'm not saying the battle is over against homophobia, but it's getting better." Thinking about your own school, do you agree with the statement?

Topic 1.3
Progress and sustainability

8d5i5k

A

B

C

Getting started

1 **Look at the pictures and write down questions for each picture that relate to the concepts progress, sustainability and responsibility, e.g. "Which sources of alternative energy are there?" for picture C. Collect your questions on the board and try to answer as many as you can in class. Are there any questions which nobody can answer?** → Describing pictures, p. 339

D

E

F

G

H

2 Magazine photos

a) Work with a partner and choose one picture you find most impressive. Imagine the picture has been chosen for the front page of a magazine. What type of magazine would it be?

b) Create a title for the picture and write a short caption. Present your results in class.

3 Research project → Hotspot 1, p. 55

Word bank

wind energy • solar panel • renewable energies • nuclear power • nuclear waste • hazardous • recycling • GM food • data protection • hacking • privacy • free-range food • battery farm

A Climate change

1 Before you read → Brainstorming, p. 351
What do you know about climate change? Make a list of changes and their possible consequences. Present your list in class and discuss it.

2 Collect information from the text in note form under the following headings.

Climate change • Geographical changes • Changes in temperature • Changes in atmosphere • Other predictions for the future

8 **carbon dioxide** – Kohlendioxyd
8 **methane** – Methan
8 **nitrous oxide** – Stickoxid, Lachgas
9 **vapour** – Dampf
9 **to trap sth.** – etw. auffangen
9 **to emit** – ausstoßen
14 **fossil fuel** – fossiler Brennstoff
20 **issue** – Thema
32 **human-induced** – von Menschen erzeugt
51 **estimate** – Schätzung
51 **to tie for second place** – zusammen den 2. Platz belegen
54 **glacier** – Gletscher
54 **to retreat** – zurückgehen
55 **extent** – Ausmaß
60 **IPCC (International Panel on Climate Change)** – Internationaler Klimarat
65 **pre-industrial** – vorindustriell

Certainties and uncertainties of climate change

The Earth's climate has varied in the past over many different timescales. Right now we are in an interglacial, a relatively mild period between ice ages. But humans are changing the climate system.

The natural greenhouse effect

Some gases in our atmosphere, for example carbon dioxide, methane, nitrous oxide, and especially water vapour, trap heat emitted from the Earth's surface, keeping the planet about 30 °C warmer than it would otherwise be. This is the 'natural greenhouse effect' and is well understood scientifically.

Human activities, especially burning fossil fuels like coal and oil, have increased the level of these greenhouse gases in our atmosphere. This is throwing the climate system out of balance.

Climate change is the most important environmental issue we face this century. Every one of the hottest 15 years on record has occurred since 1980 – the five hottest since 1997. [...]

Widely accepted facts

- Carbon dioxide and nitrous oxide levels are rising, primarily because of human activities connected with burning fossil fuels.
- Methane levels in the atmosphere more than doubled in the last century. Levels are still rising, though the rise has slowed down.
- Carbon dioxide is responsible for 60 % of human-induced greenhouse warming, methane 20 %, and nitrous oxide and other gases 20 %.
- Carbon dioxide levels in the atmosphere have increased from about 280 parts per million (ppm) in the mid 18th century – the start of the industrial revolution – to around 379 ppm today. You would need to go back millions of years to find another time when carbon dioxide was at such high levels in the atmosphere.
- Nitrous oxide levels are rising by about 0.25 % each year.
- Over the last century, the average global surface temperature rose by around 0.7 °C. Continents in the northern hemisphere have warmed the most.
- 1998 was the warmest year since 1860, the earliest year for which a precise global estimate is possible. 2002 and 2003 tie for second place.
- The majority of the world's mountain glaciers are retreating and Arctic sea-ice appears to be reducing in both extent and thickness.
- Global sea levels have risen 10–20 cm over the past 100 years. [...]

Global consequences

The IPCC has developed a number of scenarios for future greenhouse gas emissions, and has explored these with a range of climate models. They show that:

- Carbon dioxide levels are likely to at least double from pre-industrial levels by the end of this century. When other factors are added, such as increased water vapour, the estimated average global temperature

3 Paraphrasing → Guessing new words, p. 353

With a partner, take turns to paraphrase one of the German terms below in English. See if your partner can guess the English term. (The English terms can be found in the text.)

> fossile Brennstoffe • Durchschnittstemperatur der Erdoberfläche • Treibhausgase • beispiellos, noch nie dagewesen • Eisschicht • Überschwemmungsgefahr • Klimawandel

4 Research project → Hotspot 2, p. 55

rise by 2100 is between 1.5 – 5.8 °C. Though new evidence from climateprediction.net suggests the increase could be as high as 11 °C.

- This rate of warming will be much higher than experienced during the 20th century and is probably unprecedented in the last 10,000 years.
- Global sea level is likely to rise by 10 – 90 cm over this century. Low-lying coasts will flood, affecting many human settlements, including some major cities. Some habitats will be lost.
- If temperatures over Greenland increase by more than about 3 °C – which appears likely based on current model predictions – the ice sheet there will eventually disappear altogether, raising global sea level by several metres over a period of 1,000 years or more.
- Some regions and seasons will become wetter, others drier. Summer droughts are likely to intensify in the interiors of continents. Tropical cyclones may become more severe. Intense cold weather will become less frequent.
- Many areas will experience more extremely hot weather, like the unprecedented heat in Europe in 2003, and heavier rain, with an increased risk of flooding.
- Food production in mid-latitudes could benefit if climate change is not too severe. However, in tropical and sub-tropical regions, the risk of famine is likely to increase.
- Water availability will become even more of a problem for people in regions where it is already scarce, particularly in the sub-tropics.
- The world's vegetation zones will undergo major changes. In particular, the boundaries between grasslands, forests and scrublands may shift.
- The temperature, flow and level in freshwater systems will change, affecting biodiversity, water supplies and water quality.
- Human and animal diseases, such as malaria, will probably spread to new areas, and deaths related to heat stress are predicted to increase.
- 'Environmental migration' is predicted as many people move from high flood risk areas or arid regions. This could drive conflicts and increase health problems. (763 words)

75 **unprecedented** – beispiellos
80 **habitat** – natürlicher Lebensraum
88 **drought** – Dürre
97 **in mid-latitudes** – in mittleren Breitengraden gelegen
103 **scarce** – knapp
105 **boundary** – Grenze
106 **scrubland** – Buschland
107 **to shift** – sich verschieben
110 **biodiversity** – Artenvielfalt
117 **arid** – ausgedörrt

B Alternative energy

1 Before you read
→ Describing diagrams, p. 341
Describe and interpret the chart.

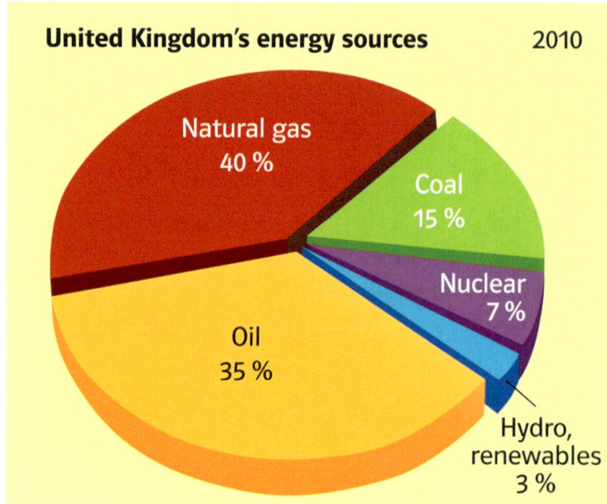

Source: Federal Coordinator, Alaska Natural Gas Transportation Projects

1 **ambitious** – ehrgeizig
1 **doable** – machbar
9 **binding** – bindend
11 **baseline figure** – Ausgangswert
12 **scale** – Ausmaß, Umfang
15 **to exceed** – übertreffen
35 **abundant** – reichlich
39 **Aladdin's cave** – Fundgrube
45 **grid** – Stromnetz
46 **R&D (Research and Development)** – Forschung und Entwicklung
48 **to meet demand** – die Nachfrage decken

theguardian

Britain could be running on 100% renewable energy by 2050

It's ambitious but doable and we will need significant change to our energy systems, says Good Energy CEO

Last week the Committee on Climate Change announced an ambitious target for the UK to reduce emissions by 60% by 2030 – which would require the complete transformation of the UK electricity market. This, it said, would ensure we meet our binding 2050 target of reducing carbon emissions by 80% from a 1990 baseline figure.

Good Energy welcomes the scale of the CCC's ambition – we believe that by turning the energy market upside down the country can exceed these targets, and become 100% renewable by 2050.

We'll need a new approach to how we heat our homes; how we travel; and how we fuel industry. Moving away from oil and gas to increased electrification is the answer. This will push electricity demands to at least double current levels, and meeting this larger demand from renewable sources will be a necessity.

For many generations most of our energy has come from large, centralised fossil-fuelled power stations – not just bad for climate change but for our energy security as we have to import increasingly more fuel. With more than one-third of our current generation capacity set for retirement over the next two decades the UK energy of tomorrow needs to be drastically different from the energy of today – and we need to start making those changes now.

The answer is on our doorstep: renewable energy. With our abundant natural resources the UK has the potential to lead a renewable energy revolution. As the windiest country in Europe, and with over 11,000 miles of coastline, we have instant access to an Aladdin's cave of renewable resources. Renewable resources which are not only abundant, but free.

Good Energy has mapped out a pathway to a 100% renewable future which involves changes to UK energy at every stage of the process, from grid management to investment, and from R&D to transport.

One of the fundamental changes required is managing output; supply must meet demand at all times. Because renewable electricity comes from nature's abundant resources – wind, water and the sun – its generation isn't always predictable. The current systems require massive improvements in how to forecast, store and manage renewable power, and how to back it up. To secure this we will need a highly dynamic and interconnected European electricity grid.

In our model, wind will provide more than half of our electricity – with offshore turbines generating most of our power from an army of over 20,000 turbines. This will require a total overhaul of our planning system so that Nimby's can no longer stand in the way of progress.

Despite the UK having one of the best tidal, wind and wave resources on Earth, a lack of investment has stunted the growth of an emerging technology which has the capability of becoming a world-leading one. Fixing it either requires the government to underwrite the R&D risks or introducing such good incentives that the private sector will take them on board. […]

Transport will need to move away from combustion; petrol and diesel-fuelled cars will be a thing of the past. Electric vehicles, charged by renewables, will need to act as local capacitors through distributed energy systems; providing energy storage for the electricity network – with the potential to sell their excess stored energy back to the grid when demand outstrips local generation.

We will also require a much more intelligent approach to how we use electricity; through encouraging a shift in demand to meet generation. A smarter grid will be needed – for example microchips controlling our fridges and washing machines so they switch on when the local wind farm is generating excess energy.

We also need to change how energy is used in the UK – and individuals need to participate. For too long we have taken for granted that power is available at a low price whenever we want it – at the flick of a switch! Changing our approach to how we use and when we use energy can not only reduce our overall energy consumption but also its carbon content. […]

It won't be easy, but a 100 % renewable future by 2050 is within our reach. (723 words)

62 **overhaul** – Überarbeitung

63 **Nimby** (not in my backyard) – Person, die sich gegen umstrittene Bauvorhaben in der eigenen Nachbarschaft stellt, aber nichts dagegen hat, wenn diese woanders realisiert werden

67 **to stunt** – hemmen

72 **incentive** – Anreiz

75 **combustion** – (Treibstoff) Verbrennung

78 **capacitor** – Kondensator

81 **excess** – überschüssig

82 **to outstrip** – übersteigen

93 **to take for granted** – als selbstverständlich hinnehmen

2 Comprehension

a) What information can you find in the text about the following numbers:

60% • 80% • 100% • 1990 • 2030 • 2050 • 11,000 • 20,000

b) Summarise the new approaches and changes which are required by Britain to be able to run on renewable energy.

21

3 Listening comprehension: Ten tips to prevent climate change → Listening, p. 319

The earth's climate is changing and the effects are worrying. What can we do to stop this?

a) Before you listen, which 5 tips would you give to your friends and family to help prevent climate change?

b) Here are ten tips on small things that help to prevent climate change – every day! Listen to the tips and take notes.

c) Compare your tips with the ones you have just heard and discuss the similarities/differences. Which of them do you find the most/least sensible and practical? Give reasons.

295

4 Comment → Writing a comment, p. 327

"We'll need a new approach to how we […] travel." (ll. 17–18) Write a newspaper article in which you outline arguments for and against mass tourism, which has become an important branch of industry in western consumer societies.

5 Project → Hotspot 3, p. 55

C Saving the planet

1 Before you read
Read the title of the novel extract. What could the novel be about? In your opinion, what makes someone a "friend of the earth"? Discuss with a partner.

2 Comprehension → Understanding fictional texts, p. 322

a) In your own words outline Ty's environmental sins.

b) Describe how Ty's attitude and behaviour change.

T.C. Boyle (American writer, born in 1948)

The story in the novel "A Friend of the Earth" by T. C. Boyle takes place in the 1990s and in 2025. The following extract is set in the future and told from the protagonist Ty's perspective.

A Friend of the Earth

Mexico City, São Paolo, Shanghai, Buenos Aires, Seoul, Tokyo, Dhaka, Cairo, Calcutta, Reykjavik, Caracas, Lagos, Guadalajara, Greater Nome, Sakhalinsky, Nanking, Helsinki – all bigger than New York now. Forty-six million in Mexico City. Forty in São Paolo. New York doesn't even rank in the top twenty. And how does that make me feel? Old. As if I've outlived my time – and everybody else's. Because the correction is under way – has been under way for some time now. Let's eat each other, that's what I propose – my arm tonight and yours tomorrow – because there's precious little of anything else left. Ecology. What a joke.

I'm not preaching. I'm not going to preach. It's too late for that, and besides which, preaching never did anybody any good anyway. Let me say this, though, for the record – for the better part of my life I was a criminal. Just like you. I lived in the suburbs in a three-thousand-square-foot house with redwood siding and oak floors and an oil burner the size of Texas, drove a classic 1966 Mustang for sport and a Jeep Laredo (red, black leather interior) to take me up to the Adirondacks so I could heft my three-hundred-twenty-dollar Eddie Bauer backpack and commune with the squirrels, muskrats and fishers. I went to the gym. Drank in fern bars. Bought shoes, jackets, sweaters and hair-care products. I guess I was dimly aware – way out there on the periphery of my consciousness – of what I was doing to the poor abused corpus of old mother earth, and I did recycle (when I got around to it, which was maybe twice a year), and I thought a lot about packaging. I wore a sweater in the house in winter to conserve energy and turn the flame down on global warming, and still burned fuel and more fuel, and the trash I generated plugged its own hole in the landfill like a permanent filling in a rotten tooth.

Worse, I accumulated things. They seemed to stick to me, like filings to a magnet, a whole polarized fur of objects radiating from my fingertips in slavish attraction. Paper clips, pins, plastic bags, ancient amplifiers, rusted-out cooking grills. Clothes, books, records, CDs. Cookware, Ginzu knives, food processors, popcorn poppers, coffeemakers, my dead father's overcoats and my dead mother's shoes. I kept a

7 **to propose** – vorschlagen
8 **precious little** – reichlich wenig
9 **to preach** – predigen
15 **to commune** – kommunizieren
16 **squirrel** – Eichhörnchen
16 **muskrat** – Bisamratte
16 **fern bar** – schicke Bar
17 **dimly** – trübe
18 **periphery** – Randbereich
18 **consciousness** – Bewusstsein
18 **abused** – missbraucht
25 **fur** – Pelz
25 **to radiate** – ausstrahlen
25 **slavish** – sklavisch
26 **ancient** – antik

296 **3 Analysis** → Text analysis, p. 326

a) Give examples of the author's use of direct address in the text and explain what effect it has on the reader.

b) Analyse the tone of the text. Point out examples of sarcasm, simile and word choice, and say how they influence the tone.

4 Comment → Writing a comment, p. 327
"Because to be a friend of the earth, you have to be an enemy of the people." (ll. 57 – 58) Do you agree or disagree with this statement? Write a comment.

5 Research project → Hotspot 4, p. 55

second Mustang, graffitied with rust, out behind the garage, on blocks. There were chairs in the attic that hadn't been warmed by a pair of buttocks in fifty years, trunks of neatly folded shorts and polo shirts I hadn't worn since I was five.

I drove fast, always in a hurry, and stuffed the glove box so full of tickets it looked like a napkin dispenser in a restaurant. I dated (women, whole thundering herds of them, looking – in vain – for another Jane). I parented. Cooked. Cleaned. Managed my dead father's crumbling empire – you've heard of him, Sy Tierwater, developer of tract homes in Westchester and Dutchess Counties? – and paid bills and collected rents and squeezed down the window of my car to add my share of Kleenex, ice-cream sticks and cigarette wrappers to the debris along the streaming sides of the blacktop roads.

Want more? I drank wine, spent money, spoiled my daughter and watched her accumulate things in her turn. And just like you – if you live in the Western world, and I have to assume you do, or how else would you be reading this? – I caused approximately two hundred fifty times the damage to the environment of this tattered, bleeding planet as a Bangladeshi or Balinese, and they do their share, believe me. Or did. But I don't want to get into that.

Let's just say I saw the light – with the help of a good nudge from Andrea, Teo (may he rot in hell or interplanetary space or wherever) and all the other hard chargers down at Earth Forever! Forces were put in motion, gears began to grind. I sold the house, the cars, the decrepit shopping center my father left me, my wind surfer and Adirondack chair and my complete set of bootleg Dylan tapes, all the detritus left behind by the slow-rolling glacier of my old life, my criminal life, the life I led before I became a friend of the earth. Friendship. That's what got me into movement and that's what pushed me way out there on the naked edge of nothing, beyond sense or reason, or even hope. Friendship for the earth. For the trees and shrubs and the native grasses and the antelope on the plain and the kangaroo rats in the desert and everything else that lives and breathes under the sun.

Except people, that is. Because to be a friend of the earth, you have to be an enemy of the people. (800 words)

29 **rust** – Rost
32 **glove box** – Handschuhfach
33 **napkin dispenser** – Serviettenhalter
34 **in vain** – umsonst
34 **to parent** – erziehen
36 **tract home** – Reihenhaus
38 **debris** – Trümmer
40 **to spoil** – verwöhnen
43 **approximately** – ungefähr
44 **tattered** – zerfetzt
46 **nudge** – Stoß, Stups
48 **gear** – Zahnrad
49 **decrepit** – baufällig
50 **bootleg** – Raub-
51 **detritus** – Müll
51 **glacier** – Gletscher
55 **shrub** – Busch
58 **enemy** – Feind

D GM and designer food

1 Before you read

a) Do you read food labels that inform about a product's ingredients? Why (not)? Which information are you most interested in?

b) Do you think food containing GM ingredients should be labeled? Why (not)?

2 **genetically modified (GM)** – gentechnisch verändert
3 **to insert** – einsetzen
6 **to breed** – vermehren
8 **desired** – gewünscht
8 **traits** – Eigenschaften
9 **breeding** – Züchtung
10 **fickle** – unbeständig
14 **attempt** – Versuch
16 **pronounced** – ausgeprägt
21 **vice versa** – andersherum
28 **purpose** – Zweck, Absicht

Facts on GM food

Genetically engineered or **genetically modified (GM)** foods have had foreign genes inserted into their genetic codes. For thousands of years, farmers have bred plants as well as animals in order to select and pass on desired traits. Selective breeding, however, depends on fickle nature to produce the desired gene. Only then could humans breed animals or produce plants containing that gene in an attempt to make the related characteristics more common or more pronounced. Genetic engineering speeds up this process by moving desired genes from one plant into another – or even from an animal to a plant or vice versa. A more general term is **genetically modified organism (GMO)**, which is applied to all genetically engineered plants, animals or microbes. For example, bacteria were modified to produce insulin for medical purposes as soon as 1978. (136 words)

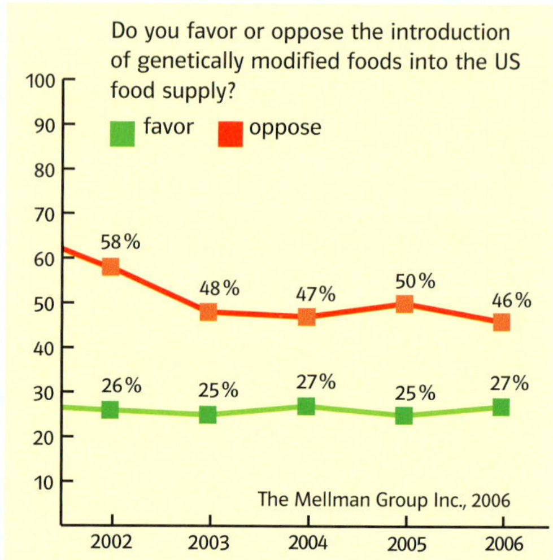

Support for GM food across EU

%	1996	1999	2002	2005
Spain	80	70	74	74
United Kingdom	67	47	63	48
Germany	56	49	48	30
Greece	49	19	24	12

Eurobarometer survey on biotechnology, 2005

p. 296 **2 Analysis** → Describing diagrams, p. 341
Look at the statistics above. Write a short text examining the attitudes towards GM food in Europe and comparing them to the attitudes of the US population.

Facts on Nanotechnology

Nanotechnology is a diverse branch of research and engineering working on the scale of atoms and molecules between 1 and 1000 nano-metres. (1 nano-metre (nm) is one billionth (10^{-9}) of a metre). Nanotechnology is employed to make ultra-small tools and then build powerful mini-machines smaller than a pinhead. A fly could carry a camera on its back!

Nanoparticles are so small that they can pass boundaries within the body, which poses potential safety risks.

Programmable drinks

How could such a beverage be made?

Step 1 Select a colourless, flavourless drink from the refrigerator. Press buttons to select chosen drink and any required additives.

Step 2 Microwaves activate the preprogrammed nanocapsules (milk, vitamin C, caffeine). See the drink change visibly to whisky. Capsules containing unwanted flavour and additives remain inert.

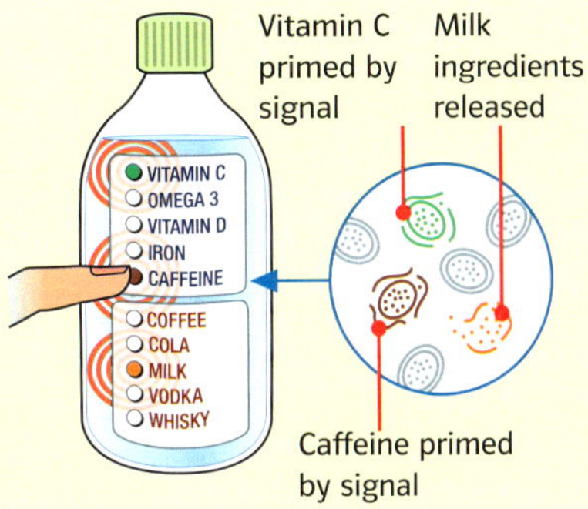

Step 3 As the drink enters the mouth, the particles containing caffeine dissolve at the back of the throat for an instant hit.

Step 4 Capsules containing vitamin C pass unharmed through the stomach and dissolve in the large intestine, passing straight into the bloodstream.

Step 5 All remaining unused capsules pass harmlessly through the body and are excreted.

(191 words)

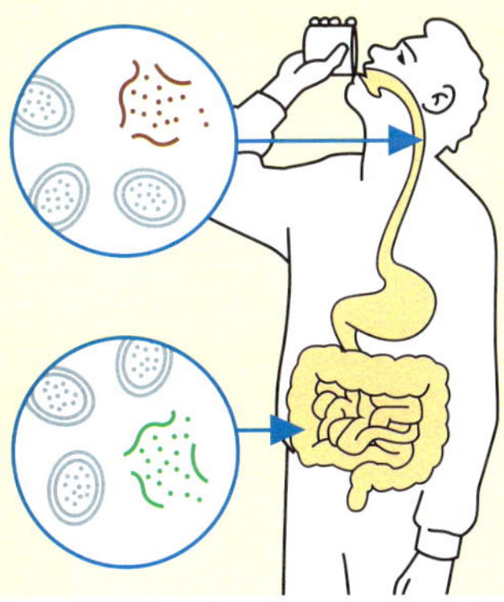

1 **diverse** – breitgefächert
1 **branch** – Sektor
5 **pinhead** – Nadelkopf
7 **to pose a risk** – ein Risiko darstellen
ingredient – Zutat
to release – entlassen
9 **beverage** – Getränk
12 **additive** – Zusatzstoff
17 **inert** – träge, inaktiv
19 **to dissolve** – auflösen
20 **throat** – Hals
20 **instant** – sofort
22 **unharmed** – unbeschädigt
23 **large intestine** – Dickdarm
26 **to excrete** – absondern, ausscheiden

3 Comprehension
Explain in your own words how programmable drinks might be produced, using the information and the pictures above.

4 Panel discussion → Discussions, p. 344

a) Prepare a panel discussion about the pros and cons of GM and designer food. Before you start, decide on roles which should be included in your discussion.

b) Collect arguments to prepare for the roles.

c) Make notes of the best arguments for both sides that come up in your discussion.

5 Project → Hotspot 5, p. 55

E Eco-tourism

1 Before you read

a) Look at the title of the text. What do you think it means to "travel green"? Make some notes.

b) Compare your ideas with a partner. What do you agree on?

c) Share your results with another pair and report back to the class.

d) In the same group, find an opposite for the term "green travel".

1 **to bandy sth. about** – mit etw. um sich werfen
3 **to compile** – zusammenstellen
3 **outstanding** – herausragend
12 **tad** – kleine Menge
23 **bracket** – *hier:* Klasse
23 **unimaginably** – unvorstellbar
26 **to demand** – verlangen
26 **to eschew** – unterlassen
28 **to assess** – beurteilen, bewerten

theguardian

News | Sport | Comment | Culture | Business | Money | Life&Style | Travel | Environment

Comment is free > Society Search GO

What it means to travel green

The word "eco" is bandied about so much, it's difficult to tell what's authentic and what's not. So we've done the hard work for you, compiling a list of 75 outstanding green travel companies.

Nearly 40 years ago I took a three-day train ride from London to Istanbul, a bus from there to Bodrum, and ended up walking to the village of Gumusluk because there was no road. I spent the summer picking and eating peaches and fishing with the locals. Net result: minimum ecological damage, maximum cultural exchange, and a tad fewer octopuses in the Mediterranean. In today's terms, this was as green as travel gets. Now you can get to Gumusluk in a few hours and spend a month there without hearing a word of Turkish. The fish may come from Singapore, the hotels are owned by the British, the villas by the Dutch, and the yachts that call in are in the million-dollar bracket. The place has changed unimaginably in a generation […]. Had I known then what I know now, should I have gone?

Model village … Yachana Lodge in the Ecuadorian Amazon

Yes. Green travel is not just what happens at the destination, or indeed how you get there. It does not demand that you eschew air travel altogether or hotels or comfort, or that your holiday is within 10 miles of your home. Rather, it asks you to pack your brain as well as your swimsuit, and to assess and then act on the impact of your visit. At its best, it's kind to both place and people, and rewards the host as much as the tourist. It is mostly small-scale, unique and personal. It certainly appeals to the intellectually curious, the ecologically and socially responsible, and to the politically aware. It seeks to add to the sum of knowledge and improve, or at least not harm, the natural world. It can be on the other side of the world or down your road, in a forest or in the city. Even flying can be justifiable, if you take a plane only occasionally and are sensible about it. The golden rule must be that if our actions hurt in one way, then we should compensate in another.

Dave Martin, who helps run community-owned Bulungula Lodge in South Africa, argues that rather than cutting out flying, we should be selective about where we visit. Africa is the least polluting continent on Earth but most needs the income, jobs and good development that inspired tourism brings. "Cancel your holidays to the rich world and save up for a worthwhile holiday to the developing world," he says. At its worst, green travel is a cynical lie, told by travel agents, tour operators, airlines and cruise lines claiming to be green but actually peddling mass, crass tourism. It has been used to cover any encounter with indigenous peoples, any foray into a forest or trip by bicycle. Happily that is changing. Hotels used to call themselves green if they offered not to change the towels every day; these days, people demand evidence of real commitment to community, place and the environment.

That is exactly what the 75 companies in Guardian Green Travel List do. Some cater for the adventurous, others for those who like their creature comforts. But they are phenomenally diverse; some are community-run, others are owned by international hotel chains. They range from the English Midlands to the deepest jungle of Ecuador. […] (572 words)

30 **to reward** – belohnen
31 **to appeal** – ansprechen
32 **aware** – bewusst
33 **to harm** – schädigen, schaden
35 **justifiable** – gerechtfertigt
36 **sensible** – vernünftig
37 **to compensate** – entschädigen
39 **to cut out** – weglassen
39 **selective** – wählerisch
43 **worthwhile** – lohnend
44 **cruise line** – Kreuzfahrtgesellschaft
45 **to peddle** – feilbieten
46 **encounter** – Begegnung
46 **indigenous** – einheimisch
46 **foray** – Ausflug
48 **towel** – Handtuch
49 **commitment** – Bindung, Engagement
52 **to cater for** – sorgen für
52 **adventurous** – abenteuerlich
52 **creature comforts** – Annehmlichkeiten

2 Comprehension

a) Describe in your own words how the village Gumusluk has changed since the author of the article first visited.

b) Explain, in your own words, the author's idea of what green travel is and why it can be very attractive.

c) Interpret Dave Martin's statement: "Cancel your holidays to the rich world and save up for a worthwhile holiday to the developing world." (ll. 42–43)

3 Analysis → Describing cartoons, p. 340

Describe the cartoon and relate it to the text.

4 Comment

"The golden rule must be that if our actions hurt in one way, then we should compensate in another." (ll. 36–37) Give examples of how individuals can observe this rule when going on holiday.

5 Project → Hotspot 6, p. 55

The passive

→ Grammar, p. 375

a) Rewrite the sentences below, adding one of the following nouns as a by-agent.

Hurricane Andrew • European leaders • the Weather Office • researchers • the government • scientists

1. A record high temperature was recorded in London today.
2. Hundreds of homes were destroyed last night.
3. A nuclear power plant was closed down.
4. New alternative energy methods are being tested.
5. Further research on GM foods is being carried out.
6. New pollution laws will be voted on next month.

Example:
A record high temperature was recorded in London today *by the Weather Office*.

b) Now transform the following active sentences into the passive. Add the by-agent only where you think it's necessary.

1. European politicians have told large companies to lower their carbon emissions.
2. People consume more energy today than 10 years ago.
3. Experts warn travelers about their carbon footprints.
4. A team of researchers has created a new 'super food'.
5. A group of environmentalists stopped a cargo train carrying harmful waste into the country.
6. The government passed a new law on the sale of GM foods.

c) Transform the following statements and questions into the passive voice.

1. Should schools teach pupils how to recycle their waste properly?
2. Do you think travel agencies should do more to promote eco-tourism?
3. The government should impose large fines on companies that pollute the environment.
4. What can normal people do to help stop climate change?
5. Meteorologists have predicted that extreme weather conditions will become more common in Europe.
6. Should restaurants inform customers when they serve GM foods on the menu?

d) Translate the following sentences into English.

1. Jedes Jahr wird in Deutschland mehr erneuerbare Energie produziert.
2. Wieviel Natur ist bereits durch Massentourismus zerstört worden?
3. Viele Kleintiere werden ausschließlich für die Wissenschaft gezüchtet.
4. Verbraucher sollten über genmanipulierte Lebensmittel informiert werden.
5. Eine Fabrik wurde kürzlich wegen giftiger Gase geschlossen.
6. Werden Umweltverschmutzer in Zukunft härter bestraft werden?

1 Research project: Energy sources → Presentation, p. 362
Work in groups. Choose one of the following energy sources:

fossil fuels • nuclear energy • wind energy • solar energy • hydroelectric energy • biomass • tidal energy • geothermal energy

Research how it is produced, its advantages and disadvantages, where in the world it is mostly produced/used, and its prospects for the future. Present your results on a poster or transparency and give a short presentation to the class. Include charts or diagrams.

2 Research project: Comparison between the US, the UK and Germany
→ Internet research, p. 358
Write an article for a scientific youth magazine on the problem of global warming. Compare how this problem is handled in the US, the UK and Germany and include similarities and differences. Present your article in class.

3 Project: Climate change → Projects and group work, p. 359
Using the information from text A and the notes from the listening activity on page 47 (Ten tips to prevent climate change), design a leaflet for an environmental organisation on the causes and effects of climate change. Include tips on how to prevent it. Display the leaflets in your classroom.

4 Research project: Friends of the Earth → Internet research, p. 358
Get together in groups and search the Internet to find information about the organisation "Friends of the Earth". Watch several of the entries from the "Friends of the Earth" short film competition. Then report on the ones you found most effective. Say what you liked about them.

5 Project: A survey on GM food → Questionnaires and surveys, p. 360
Do a survey on genetically modified food. Develop a questionnaire with at least ten questions concerning GM food and find out what students, your family and friends know about the topic and what they think about it. When writing your questionnaire, consider risks and advantages. Sum up your results in a graph and present it to the class.

6 Project: Working with words → Working with a dictionary, p. 353
This topic deals with different aspects of the environment:

nuclear power • alternative energy sources • climate change • GMF • eco-tourism

Write down important words on each aspect and arrange them in lists, word nets, word families, etc. You can use a dictionary to look up more words and add them to your collection.

Finding information

Look for information on the Internet. Use a search engine and try the following search words:
global warming • GM food • food labelling • Department of Energy and Climate Change • Bundesministerium für Umwelt, Naturschutz und Reaktorsicherheit

A1.24

The Telegraph

Search GO

Home | News | Sport | Finance | Comment | Culture | Travel | Lifestyle | Fashion

New film exposes unsavoury side of US food industry

For millions of Americans, a trip to the cinema involves loading up on popcorn and supersized drinks before the show.

But when the much-anticipated documentary Food, Inc. opens this week, many may find themselves unable to finish their snacks as the film exposes some unsavoury realities about how food reaches the dinner table.

"There are no seasons in the American supermarket," a voice intones in the opening scene as a camera swept past supermarket shelves groaning with plump-breasted chickens, perfect cuts of meat and bountiful fruit, vegetables and grains.

Major food producers would not agree to be interviewed for the movie and they tried to ban the filmmakers from their stock yards, pig farms and chicken barns.

But the producers fought off law suits, grabbing headlines and impressive reviews as they aim to do for the food industry what former Vice President Al Gore's controversial documentary *An Inconvenient Truth* did for debate about climate change.

The documentary was produced by the same company that made *An Inconvenient Truth*, which was widely criticised by global warming sceptics for its apocalyptic approach. Indeed, Food, Inc. has already been dismissed as one-sided propaganda by the food industry.

The documentary claims cows are fattened up on heavily subsidised corn, even though they cannot digest the grain properly and their guts become breeding grounds for deadly E. coli strains as a result.

It also says chickens with oversized breasts are grown to maturity and are ready to be slaughtered twice as quickly as they would be naturally, thanks to chemicals in their feed.

There is also stomach-churning footage of conveyer belts packed with little yellow chicks being pushed around like mechanical parts; a cow, barely alive,

0 **to expose sth.** – etw. enthüllen
0 **unsavoury** – unappetitlich
4 **anticipated** – erwartet
11 **to intone** – anstimmen
13 **plump** – mollig
15 **bountiful** – reichlich
15 **grain** – Getreide
18 **to ban** – verbieten
19 **stock yard** – Hühnerhof
20 **to fight off** – abwehren
20 **law suit** – Rechtsstreit
25 **inconvenient** – ungünstig
30 **sceptic** – Skeptiker(in)
30 **apocalyptic** – apokalyptisch
32 **to dismiss sth.** – etw. abtun
35 **to fatten up** – mästen
35 **subsidised** – subventioniert
36 **to digest** – verdauen
37 **guts** – Gedärme
37 **breeding ground** – Brutstätte
38 **E.coli strain** – Kolibakterium
41 **maturity** – Reife
42 **to slaughter** – schlachten
44 **feed** – Futter
45 **stomach-churning** – widerlich
46 **conveyor belt** – Fließband
48 **barely** – kaum

being dragged around by a forklift; and herds of squealing pigs being forced onto a factory "kill floor".

Knowing they would be cast as the villains of the documentary, food corporations refused to co-operate with the producers. To counter what it says is "a one-sided, biased film" that "demonises" American farmers and a system that feeds more than 300 million people, the agrigiant *Monsanto* is fighting back with its own Web page.

The movie's director Robert Kenner compares the state of American food production to the current financial crisis. "Stupid high risk decisions brought the financial system low," he told *The Daily Telegraph*. "Our food system is unrecognisable from 40 years ago and it could fall off a cliff for the same reasons – unregulated greed and excessive risk-taking."

Eric Schlosser, the author of *Fast Food Nation* and one of the driving forces behind the movie, said: "There is this deliberate veil, this curtain that's drawn between us and where our food is coming from."

"The industry doesn't want you to know the truth about what you're eating because if you knew, you might not want to eat it. We've never had food companies this big and this powerful in our history."

(492 words)

49 **to drag** – ziehen
49 **forklift** – Gabelstapler
50 **herd** – Herde
50 **to squeal** – quieken
53 **villain** – Schurke
55 **to counter** – erwidern, dagegen sprechen
56 **biased** – voreingenommen
56 **to demonise** – verteufeln
67 **cliff** – Klippe
69 **excessive** – übermäßig
71 **driving force** – Antriebskraft
73 **deliberate** – absichtlich
73 **veil** – Verschleierung

1 Comprehension

Read the text and the statements below. Decide whether the statements are true or false. Quote or paraphrase words from the text that confirm or disprove the ideas in the statements. You must give evidence for your decision.

a) The documentary Food, Inc. shows that food is produced under cruel conditions.

b) Food producers were interviewed to comment on the content of the documentary.

c) Food producers accuse the filmmakers of having made an unbalanced documentary.

d) Cows are fattened up in the right way before they get slaughtered.

e) Food producers co-operated with the producers to show the public that they produce in an animal-friendly way.

f) The current food system can be compared with the one people had 40 years ago.

g) There is a certain similarity between the current financial crisis and the state of American food production.

h) The industry wants to report consumer-friendly about how food is produced.

2 Analysis → Text analysis, p. 326

a) Analyse the film review. What is the author's attitude towards "Food, Inc."? Quote from the text to support your answer.

b) Analyse the stylistic devices the author uses and their effect on the reader.

3 Comment → Writing a comment, p. 327

"It is important to know where my food comes from and how it was produced." Do you agree with this statement? Comment on it.

Topic 1.4
Britain and the United States

86p4ig

Getting started

1 Which regions of Britain or the United States do you know best and how did you learn about them (travel, movies, geography lessons, Internet, etc.)?

2 Look at the photos. Which parts of Britain or the United States do they show?

3 Look at the maps of the British Isles and of the United States of America. Match the pictures to the numbers on the maps.

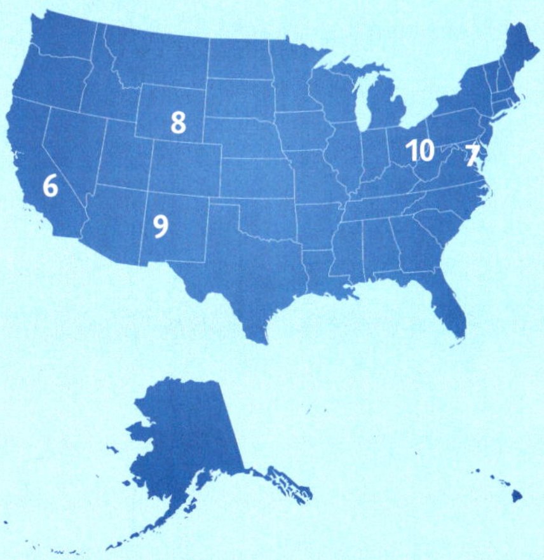

4 Use the phrases in the word bank to describe the locations of the places in the photos. If you need more information, consult the more detailed maps at the front and back of your book.

5 The British Isles consist of five separate countries: England, Scotland, Wales, Northern Ireland and the Republic of Ireland. Which of these countries belong to Great Britain, and which to the United Kingdom?

Word bank

it's located near the … river / ocean / mountains • on the east / west coast • north / south / east / west of • in the north / south / midwest • to the north / south / east / west of • mountainous • flat • northern • eastern • southern • western • northerly • southerly • easterly • westerly

A Britain and the US: A special relationship

1 Each of the boxes describes an important event in the relationship between Britain and the United States. Read the texts and match the events to the timeline. If you are correct, you will get the name of a US state.

2 **Project** → Hotspot 1, p. 71

reluctantly – zögerlich
to found – gründen
persecution – Verfolgung
declaration – Erklärung
independence – Unabhängigkeit
to cut ties – Verbindungen lösen
United Nations Security Council – UN Sicherheitsrat
famine – Hungersnot
fungus – Pilz
harvest – Ernte
to emigrate – auswandern
immigration – Einwanderung

- 2003
- 1973
- 1949
- 1945
- 1941
- 1917
- 1845–1849
- 1776
- 1775–1783
- 1773
- 1620
- 1607
- 1492

A Unlike other European countries, England supports the USA in their war against Iraq.

N Britain reluctantly joins the European Community (now European Union), but still keeps up a "special relationship" with the US.

H Revolutionary War between the thirteen original American colonies and England.

O An English settlement is founded in Jamestown, Virginia, where the settlers begin to grow tobacco.

U The Mayflower – a ship of English Puritans fleeing from religious persecution in England – lands at Plymouth Bay on the coast of Massachusetts.

T The Boston Tea Party: the English settlers in America protest against the high taxes they have to pay to the English king by throwing a load of tea into the harbour of Boston.

O The USA enters World War II, fighting alongside England, France and the Soviet Union against Germany.

C The Declaration of Independence: the American colonies cut their political ties to England.

R The USA joins England and other countries in the war against Germany (World War I).

L The UK and the US become founding members of the United Nations and two of the five permanent members of the United Nations Security Council.

S Searching for a shorter sea route to India, Christopher Columbus discovers the New World.

I Britain and the US become members in the newly-founded North Atlantic Treaty Organization (NATO), a union of western states against the Soviet Union and its allies.

A The Irish potato famine: a fungus destroys the potato harvest in Ireland for a number of years in a row and causes millions of Irish citizens to emigrate to the US. This is one example of many waves of mass immigration from the British Isles to the USA.

B Welcome to America

1 Look at these facts about the US. Write 1–16 onto a sheet of paper and match the numbers with the words and figures in the boxes. Compare your results with those of a partner.

Geography quiz

Location

North America is located between the North Atlantic Ocean and the North Pacific Ocean, with 1 to the north and 2 to the south.

Geographic coordinates

total area: 9,631,420 sq km
land: 9,161,923 sq km
water: 469,497 sq km

Area – comparative

approximately 3 of Russia; about half the size of 4 ; about three-tenths the size of 5 ; a little 6 than China; about 7 as big as the EU

Climate

mainly temperate, 8 in Florida and Hawaii, semiarid in the plains west of the 9 , and arid in the southwest; warm chinook winds in January and February from the eastern slopes of the 10 sometimes increase low winter temperatures in the northwest; 11 in Alaska

Environment – current issues

air pollution causes 12 in the US; the US is the largest single emitter of carbon dioxide from the burning of fossil fuels; water pollution from runoff of pesticides and fertilizers; natural fresh water resources are limited in the 13 part of the country; desertification

Population

314,809,000 (2012 estimate)

Ethnic groups

14 79.6%, black 12.9%, Asian 4.6%, Amerindian and Alaska native 1%, Hawaiian and other Pacific islander 0.2% (2010 estimate)

Languages

English 80.4%, Spanish 15 , other Indo-European 3.7%, Asian and Pacific island 16 , other 0.8% (2010 estimate)

12.2%
2.9%
acid rain
Africa
arctic
bigger
Canada
half the size
Mexico
Mississippi River
Rocky Mountains
South America
tropical
two and a half times
white
western

acid rain – saurer Regen
approximately – ungefähr
temperate – gemäßigt
semiarid – Klima mit sehr wenig Niederschlag
arid – trocken, dürr
chinook wind – Fönwind
slope – Hang
emitter – Erzeuger
fossil fuel – fossiler Brennstoff
runoff – Sickerwasser
pesticide – Pestizid, Schädlingsbekämpfungsmittel
fertilizer – Dünger
resource – Vorrat
desertification – Versteppung
estimate – Schätzung
Amerindian – *kurz für:* American Indian

C City or suburb?

1 Translate the definition of "urban sprawl" with the help of a dictionary.
→ Working with a dictionary, p. 353

> **Urban sprawl** (*also:* suburban sprawl), a term which refers to the rapid and expansive growth of a greater metropolitan area, traditionally suburbs over a large area.
> (*From Wikipedia*)

2 a) List reasons why people often move – either from the city or the country – to the suburbs.

b) What problems might be caused if large numbers of people moved to the suburbs at one time?

3 Vocabulary → Guessing new words, p. 353
Find the three different uses of the verb "to rank" in the last paragraph of the text below. Translate the phrases in which the verb occurs.

2 **tax bill** – Steuerabrechnung
8 **subdivision** – *hier:* Wohngebiet
8 **strip mall** – Einkaufszentrum
10 **habitat** – Lebensraum
13 **relentless** – unablässig
14 **rural** – ländlich
20 **to preserve** – bewahren
21 **condo (AE; short for condominium)** – Eigentumswohnung
21 **town house** – Stadthaus; *meist:* Reihenhaus
25 **mass transit** – öffentliche Verkehrsmittel
30 **development** – Entwicklung
34 **to shell out** *(infml)* – bezahlen, „blechen"
36 **water and sewer lines** – Wasser- und Abwasserleitungen
39 **impact** – Auswirkung
40 **unchecked** – ungehindert, unkontrolliert
41 **foremost** – führend
42 **to predict** – vorhersagen

What urban sprawl costs you

You pay for it. Every time you get stuck in a traffic jam. Every time you get a tax bill. Every time you jump into the car just to go to a store for a loaf of bread. Urban sprawl costs you time and money.

Sprawl defines life in Central Florida – one of the most spread-out regions in the country. Sprawl means one subdivision and strip mall after the next, spread across former farmlands and natural habitat. It's marked by miles of pavement and annoying traffic jams. Sprawl separates homes from businesses. It serves cars rather than people. It is the relentless march of the city outward toward rural areas. And little stands in its way.

"Your yard is starting to mess with my livingroom."

There are some people, however, who think growth can be smarter and more compact with a stronger separation among urban, suburban and rural terrain. Smart growth means better planning and more land preserved. It looks like condos and town houses mixed with single-family homes. Those homes are closer together, linked by walking paths that lead to stores, movie theaters and offices. There may be mass transit. Smart growth in Central Florida is Baldwin Park in Orlando and Celebration by Disney. Across the nation, it's Boston and New York City.

It is hard to quantify, but according to many experts, compact development costs less – in many ways.

TAXES

If Central Florida grows as it always has, Orlando-area taxpayers will shell out $44,955 each in taxes during the next 20 years to pay for roads, water and sewer lines and other services that governments provide as development stretches farther outward, according to a new book, *Sprawl Costs: Economic Impacts of Unchecked Development*.

The authors – some of the nation's foremost experts on urban planning – predict the cost

4 Getting information from the text → Word webs, p. 349
Complete the word web on the right using information given in the text.

5 Preparing a short presentation → Presentation, p. 362, Describing cartoons, p. 340
Look at the cartoon and describe what you see. Prepare a 5-minute presentation based on the cartoon in which you describe the cartoon, name the problem, and talk about the consequences and alternatives. You may use your word web but not the text itself.

p. 296 △ **6 Composition**
Make notes on how you live in Germany (big city, small town, village or rural community, far away or close to shops, cinemas and other commodities, noisy or quiet, etc.).
Write a 200-word composition comparing life in an American suburb as it is described in the text with your own life in Germany.

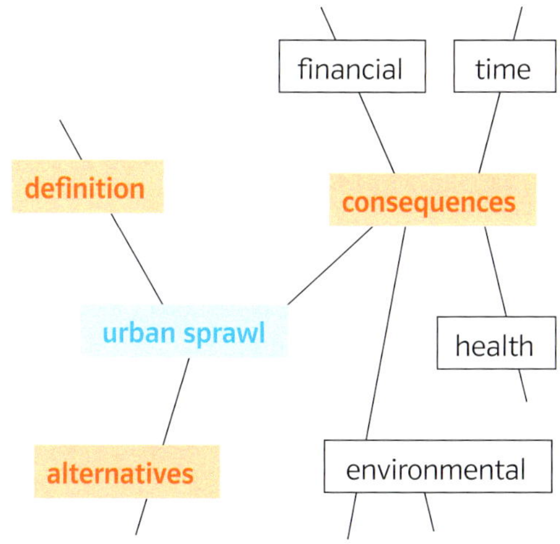

could be reduced by about $2,708 per person if 25 percent of new development doesn't sprawl.
Such compact growth means more condos and town homes, filling vacant lots and rebuilding in already developed areas. The savings could be greater if more new development doesn't sprawl.

HEALTH

You could weigh up to 6 pounds more if you live in a sprawling area, and you may have a higher risk of obesity or high-blood pressure, according to research paid for by the Robert Wood Johnson Foundation.
That's because sprawl makes people spend more time in their car and less time walking to the movie theater, corner store or tavern – locations that are within easy reach in more compact communities that mix homes with businesses.

COMMUTING

Sprawl can get pricey when it comes to roads – from auto expenses to time spent in traffic. In a more compact community, such as Boston, the costs are less.

FARMLAND

Sprawl eats up land. As property gets more scarce, farmers find it more profitable to sell their land to developers. Many of Central Florida's old citrus groves are now residential neighborhoods.
Sprawl also destroys crucial habitat for wildlife, including endangered animals, and interferes with their ability to travel from one natural area to another. Sprawling development also has destroyed many Florida wetlands that serve as breeding and feeding grounds.

HOW OTHER CITIES STACK UP

On the scorecard of sprawl, Central Florida continually ranks among the worst regions in America. A 2005 national study by urban planners, *Sprawl Costs: Economic Impacts of Unchecked Development*, ranked Orlando among the worst sprawling communities nationwide. It ranked 13th while two other Florida cities also joined the top 20: Miami at No. 8 and Jacksonville at No. 20. (583 words)

47 **vacant** – leer stehend, frei
47 **lot** – Grundstück
54 **obesity** – Fettleibigkeit
59 **tavern** – Wirtshaus, Kneipe
60 **within easy reach** – leicht zu erreichen
69 **property** – Grundbesitz
70 **scarce** – knapp
72 **citrus grove** (AE) – Zitronen- oder Orangenhain
72 **residential neighborhood** – Wohngebiet
74 **crucial** – äußerst wichtig
75 **endangered** – gefährdet; *hier:* vom Aussterben bedroht
76 **to interfere with** – *hier:* verhindern
81 **to stack up** – sich mit jmdn/etw. messen lassen
82 **scorecard** *(figurative)* – *hier:* Rangliste

D 9/11

1 Before you read → Brainstorming, p. 351

Do you remember 11 September 2001? In small groups, put together everything you know about 9/11, from your own memory, from what other people have told you, and from the media.

4 **to strike, struck, struck** – treffen
6 **initial** – erste(r/s)
7 **stunned** – betäubt
8 **to chronicle** – aufzeichnen
12 **downing** – willentlich herbeigeführter Absturz
12 **to compound** – verschlimmern
13 **stark** – hart, *hier:* schockierend
14 **to hijack** – entführen
14 **magnitude** – Ausmaß, Größe
15 **overwhelming** – überwältigend
15 **to witness** – mitansehen
17 **to respond to** – *hier:* reagieren auf
18 **janitor** – Hausmeister
18 **executive** – Führungskraft
19 **to file in** – hineingehen (einer nach dem anderen)
19 **heap** – Haufen
20 **rubble** – Schutt
21 **to injure** – verletzen
21 **ultimately** – schließlich
21 **to determine** – *hier:* feststellen
22 **strike** – Schlag
22 **emblem** – Symbol
26 **to hail from** – kommen aus
26 **to gather** – zusammenkommen
27 **donation** – Spende
27 **to avalanche** – niederprasseln
28 **the bereft** – die Hinterbliebenen
28 **onsite** – vor Ort
29 **to boost** – stärken, erhöhen
29 **to vow** – schwören

New York Historical Society | Making History Matter

Search GO

What's new | Visitor information | Exhibitions and collections | Library | Public programs |

Sadness and solidarity

Most citizens of the United States remember exactly what they were doing on the morning of September 11, 2001, when they heard the news – a plane had struck the north tower of the World Trade Center (WTC) complex in New York City. Initial reports were that it was an accident until many of those same people watched, stunned and horrified, as live television chronicled the second plane crashing into the south tower. Thirty-five minutes later, word came that a third plane had hit the Pentagon in Washington, D.C., followed by the downing of a fourth plane in a Pennsylvania field. Compounding the tragedy was the stark realization that the weapons used against the World Trade Center buildings and the Pentagon were hijacked U.S. commercial airliners, full of travelers. The magnitude of lost lives was overwhelming, nowhere more than in the streets of New York where citizens witnessed the crashes with their own eyes. Within minutes, emergency personnel from across the massive city were mobilized to respond to the WTC crash sites.

At 9:59 a.m., as office workers, janitors, and executives fled the World Trade Center – while rescue workers filed in to help them to safety – the south tower suddenly collapsed into a heap of rubble. The north tower followed a half-hour later. Hundreds of rescue workers and thousands of WTC workers and visitors were killed or injured. The U.S. Government ultimately determined that the four attacks on 9/11 were a symbolic strike at the financial and military emblems of the country and were coordinated through a Muslim terrorist group, al-Qaeda, under the leadership of a man named Osama bin Ladin.

In the days after 9/11, New Yorkers pulled together with a new appreciation for each other and their city. Thousands of volunteers hailing from the city and far beyond gathered to offer aid for rescue, recovery, and clean-up efforts, while donations avalanched in from across the country to support the injured and bereft. Mayor Giuliani was onsite at Ground Zero soon after the attacks, and he stayed onsite to boost the morale of workers and volunteers. The city as a whole vowed that it couldn't be brought to its knees by fear-based tactics, and plans were almost immediately put into effect to prove just that.

While the smoke was still rising, New York Governor George Pataki and Mayor Giuliani created the Lower Manhattan Development Corporation to oversee the design and construction of a lasting memorial to the victims of 9/11, while also generating a plan to rebuild and revitalize the area most profoundly affected by the horrific events.

After the smoke cleared, New York City remained the financial powerhouse of the world. The city won't forget the sacrifices made by its citizens on September 11th and on many previous occasions, and it's a city that realizes that the best memorial is to live on. The tourist trade rebounded with surprising speed, and New York City's gritty determination has pulled it through tough economic times not necessarily related to the events of 9/11. The biggest city in the country was built on the diversity of its citizenry – Irish, Jewish, Palestinian, Russian, Italian, Muslim, African, Portuguese, and so many more – and it will continue to be the cultural, financial, and educational heart of the nation. (546 words)

34 **memorial** – Denkmal
34 **to revitalize** – mit neuem Leben erfüllen
35 **profoundly** – stark
35 **to affect** – betreffen, beeinflussen
37 **sacrifice** – Opfer
37 **previous** – vorherig
39 **to rebound** – sich erholen
39 **gritty** – mutig, zäh
40 **tough** – *hier:* hart, schwer

2 Comprehension: True or false?

Read the statements below and decide whether they are true or false. Quote or paraphrase words from the text that confirm or disprove the ideas in the statements.

a) When people first heard about the attacks on the World Trade Center, they thought a plane had lost its way and crashed into the North Tower accidentally.

b) The US government came to the conclusion that what the terrorists really wanted to hurt in the attacks of 9/11 was the economic and military power of the country.

c) The citizens of New York lost all hope and courage after the attacks.

d) Shortly after the attacks the Governor of New York and the Mayor of New York City decided to rebuild the World Trade Center.

e) After 9/11, people soon started to visit the city again.

26 3 Listening: This is too big to comprehend right now → Listening, p. 319

a) As you listen, note down. → Taking notes, p. 352

1. The number of subway stops from Brendan's home to Cortlandt Street.
2. The distance from the subway station to the base of Tower 1.
3. The time Brendan was sitting in his chair.
4. The number of people on Brendan's side of the floor.
5. The amount of time it took people to go down the stairs (sec. / floor).
6. The floor where they met the firefighters.
7. The number of firefighters walking up the stairs.
8. The floor Brendan was at when he realized just how bad the situation was.
9. The time Brendan was on the bridge and heard the sound of Tower 2 collapsing.

b) Complete the following sentences in German.

1. Brendan hatte sehr großes Glück, denn …
2. Eine überwältigende Erinnerung, die Brendan nie vergessen wird, ist, …

4 Research project → Hotspot 2, p. 71

E Talking about Britain

1 Before you read

a) When you think of Britain and the British, what do you think of? Consider people, products, places, food, sports, music, etc.

b) Write down at least three clichés about Britain and the British. Compare your ideas with those of others in your class.

c) Is your own view of Britain and the British based on clichés or on first-hand knowledge? Explain your answer.

2 Your opinion → Brainstorming, p. 351

"Sorry, where did you say you were from again?"

a) If you were asked to make a "German collage", what pictures would you choose? Brainstorm ideas with a partner. Try to come up with a list of ten things that you both agree on as being typically German.

b) Find out what other people in your class think and agree on ten ideas together.

c) Look up on the Internet what the British think about the Germans. Compare your list with this information and give possible reasons for any differences you find.

3 Finding information → Internet research, p. 358

a) Find information about England, Scotland, Wales and Northern Ireland (capital city, main industries, languages spoken, natural resources) and make a table showing it.

Facts and figures

•••

Britain is made up of England, Scotland, Wales and Northern Ireland. Each country has its own capital although the government of all four countries is in London. Britain is a member state of the EU. Its full name is the United Kingdom of Great Britain and Northern Ireland.

Urban and rural population

Half of all Britain's people live in just seven super cities such as Manchester, Birmingham and London, which were formed from smaller towns that grew together. Many of the cities grew up as a result of industries which began to develop in the 19th century. At the beginning of the 19th century 8 out of 10 people lived in the countryside – then Britain had a rural population. Nowadays about 8 out of 10 people in Britain live in a city or town – so Britain has a mainly urban population.

Scene in the centre of Manchester

Population

Britain covers a small area compared with many other countries, but it has a large number of people living in it. The approximate population (mid-2004) is 59,834,300 (England 50,093,100, Wales 2,952,500, Scotland 5,078,400, N. Ireland 1,710,300). The population is spread unevenly across Britain and the way it is spread depends on things like climate, resources, landscape and past history. Population density in England is higher than the rest of Britain, with 375 people per square km. The whole population is now growing, but only very slowly.

b) Work with others in your class to compare your results. Make corrections and additions where necessary. Add two further categories to your table, e.g. famous people, sports, national dishes, etc. Fill in the relevant information in your table.

4 Working with facts → Understanding non-fictional texts, p. 320

a) Divide the class into six groups. Each group is allocated one of the short texts. Read your text carefully, and take notes of the most important information. If your text does not have a heading, find a suitable one. Now close your books.

b) Form new groups. Each group should have at least one student for each of the texts. Now exchange the most important information from the texts with the other group members. Do not open your books again. Use only your notes. Those listening may take notes while you speak.

c) Remaining in the new groups, discuss the following question: What are the most important factors which affect population distribution in Britain according to the information in the boxes? Find as many details as possible.

d) Return to your original groups, exchange and discuss your results.

capital – Hauptstadt
urban – städtisch
rural – ländlich
population – Bevölkerung
approximate – ungefähr
population density – Bevölkerungsdichte
square km – Quadratkilometer
mountain range – Bergkette
densely – dicht
temperate – gemäßigt
depression – *hier:* Tiefdruckgebiet

5 Vocabulary: Find the words in the text which mean ...

a country which belongs to a larger group of countries • a weather condition that causes rain • natural materials like oil, wood, minerals • regions with high hills • the land beside the sea

6 Research project → Hotspot 3, p. 71

• • •

Britain is made up of different landscapes from beautiful mountain ranges and flat open spaces, where few people live, to towns and cities which are densely populated. Not only are the areas of Britain different, they are always changing, for example, when factories close down and workers become unemployed, or when a new industry moves into an area and creates new jobs.

View from Mount Snowdon, Wales

Climate

Britain's climate is generally mild and temperate. There are frequent weather changes but few extremes of temperature. In general the daily weather is influenced by depressions moving eastward from the Atlantic. Winds are mostly south-westerly. There is more rainfall in the mountainous areas in the west and north than in central and eastern parts.

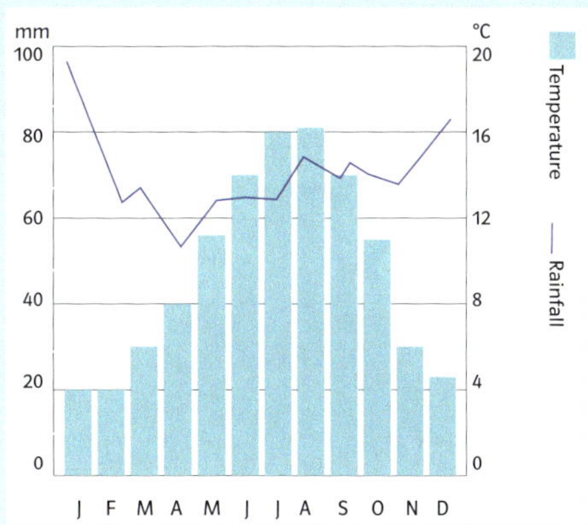

• • •

With an area of about 242,000 square km, Britain is just under 1,000 km from the south coast to the extreme north of Scotland and just under 500 km across at the widest point. The coastline of Britain is 14,549 km long including islands. The most northerly point on the mainland is Dunnet Head, north-east Scotland and the most southerly point is Lizard Point, Cornwall.

(413 words)

F A journey around Great Britain

1 Before you read

The text you are about to read is an extract from the book *The Kingdom by the Sea*, an American writer's experience of travelling around Britain. If you were planning a month-long trip around Britain, what would your itinerary look like? Discuss with a partner and report back to the class.

p. 296 **2 Comprehension**

a) Sum up what Theroux says about the British and British travel writing.

b) Outline why Theroux has "a problem of itinerary" (l. 35).

c) Describe which route Theroux eventually decides to take when travelling in Britain and the reasons for his choice.

Paul Theroux (American travel writer and novelist, born in 1941)

1 **blank** – leer
2 **fastidiously** – akribisch
16 **to simplify** – vereinfachen
16 **muffled** – gedämpft
16 **obliqueness** – Schrägheit
23 **discomfort** – Unannehmlichkeit

The Kingdom by the Sea

There were no blank spaces on the map of Great Britain, the best-known, most fastidiously mapped, and most widely trampled piece of geography on earth. No country was easier to travel in – the British invented public transport. And yet I had seen practically nothing of it. I felt ashamed and ignorant, but when I began to think about traveling around Britain, I became excited – because I knew so little. I wanted to write about it.

Writing about a country in its own language was a great advantage, because in other places one was always interpreting and simplifying. Translation created a muffled obliqueness – one was always seeing the country sideways. But language grew out of the landscape – English out of England – and it seemed logical that the country could be accurately portrayed only in its own language. So what was I waiting for?

The problem was one of perspective: How and where to go to get the best view of the place? It was also a problem in tone; after all, I was an alien.

The British had invented their own solution to travel-writing. They went to places like Gabon and Paraguay and joked about the discomforts, the natives, the weather, the food, the entertainments. It was necessary to be an outsider, which was why

.297 **3 Analysis**

Analyse how Theroux felt about:

a) his upcoming journey around Britain.

b) writing about his travel experiences.

1.32 **4 Listening comprehension: A lonely island** → Listening, p. 319

Listen to the extract from *Notes from a Small Island*, another travel book set in Britain, and decide whether the following statements are true or false.

a) The English Football team is better than the Norwegian one.

b) What is considered a short distance by many Americans can seem like a very long journey to the British.

c) In Britain, there is a sense that America is a lot closer, and that France and Germany and other countries are a lot further away than they really are.

d) After looking at the map, the author's colleagues still don't believe that Bournemouth is actually closer to Cherbourg than to London.

they had never written about Britain in this way. But it was a mystery to me why no one had ever come to Britain and written about its discomforts and natives and entertainments and unintelligible dialects. The British, who had devised a kind of envious mockery of other cultures, and who had virtually invented the concept of funny foreigners, had never regarded themselves as fair game for the travel-writer. They did not encourage aliens to observe them closely. They were like a tribe that plundered abroad and were secretive and inhospitable at home. The British did not make me think of Shakespeare but rather of head-hunters – their travel-writing a literary version of headshrinking that had never been used on them. I was eager to try.

But it was also a problem of itinerary. In a place that was crisscrossed with ant trails, a kingdom of bottlenecks and private property and high fences, my route was a problem, because there were too many routes. To take all the trains would be no more than a mediocre stunt. The buses did not go to enough places. A bicycle was out – too dangerous, too difficult; another stunt. A car was too simple, and anyway I had lived in London long enough to know that driving on English roads was no fun. My route was crucial. It was the most important aspect of travel. In choosing a route, one was choosing a subject. But every mile of Britain had a road through it; there was a track across every field, a footpath in every acre of woods. Perhaps this was why I had never traveled in Britain: I had been unable to decide on the route.

And then I had my way: narrowly, around the entire coast.

It answered every need. There was only one coast, it was one undeviating route, and this way I would see the whole of Britain. (536 words)

27 **unintelligible** – unverständlich
27 **to devise** – erfinden
28 **envious** – neidisch
28 **mockery** – Verhöhnung, Spott
28 **virtually** – praktisch
29 **to regard oneself as sth.** – sich für … halten
29 **fair game** – Freiwild
31 **tribe** – Volk
31 **to plunder** – plündern
31 **inhospitable** – ungastlich
35 **itinerary** – Reiseroute, Reiseplan
36 **bottleneck** – Nadelöhr
38 **mediocre** – mittelmäßig
41 **crucial** – entscheidend, ausschlaggebend
47 **undeviating** – unbeirrbar

Adjectives & Adverbs

→ Grammar, p. 376

a) Write down the missing forms on a separate piece of paper.

	adjective	comparative	superlative	adverb
1.	–	–	–	well
2.	–	more regular	–	–
3.	effective	–	–	–
4.	–	–	easiest	–
5.	recent	–	–	–
6.	–	–	–	efficiently
7.	–	slower	–	–
8.	–	–	fastest	–
9.	–	–	–	carefully
10.	bad	–	–	–

b) Comparisons
Make sentences comparing New York and London using the comparative and superlative form of the adjectives in the box below.

big • expensive • dangerous • interesting • cheap • multicultural • loud • dirty • famous • popular • warm • crowded • exciting • far away • clean • friendly

Example: New York is not as dirty as London. / New York is cleaner than London.

c) Adjective or adverb?
Complete the sentences below by choosing either the adjective or adverb.
1. In Manchester it often rains heavy / heavily.
2. Many people cannot afford to live in Manhattan because the rent is so expensive / expensively.
3. A lot of people in Miami come from Latin America, but they speak English good / well.
4. London is a large city but you can travel around easy / easily on the underground.
5. The weather in California varies greatly / great from the weather in the Rocky Mountains.
6. Despite its reputation, New York is a very safe / safely place to visit.

1 Project: Timeline → Projects and group work, p. 359
Form groups of 2–3 students each. Each group is allocated one of the events on the timeline. Collect information on your event and formulate a short text explaining it. Find pictures relating to your event. Draw the timeline on a long piece of packing paper and mark the given year. Glue your texts and pictures near the correct year and hang the poster on the wall in your classroom.

2 Research project: The boroughs of New York City → Internet research, p. 358
The events of 9/11 will always be remembered and talked about in connection with New York City. Also, the borough of Manhattan is often the place one has in mind when thinking of NYC. However, besides Manhattan, the city has four more boroughs and many more facets that should be known and talked about. The names of the other four boroughs are Queens, Brooklyn, The Bronx and Staten Island. In your class, form five groups and choose one of the five boroughs of New York City each. Go to the library and on the Internet and look for information on your borough. Make a poster on which you collect the most important information and some pictures, including a street map of NYC on which you indicate where your borough is located. Then prepare a short group presentation on your borough.

3 Research project: Facets of Britain → Presentation, p. 362

Work in groups and choose one of the following projects to present in class. Make sure that each member of your group is involved. To check that everybody has listened to your presentation carefully, prepare a short quiz for your listeners to answer and hand in after you have finished your talk.

- **A town or region in Britain**
Your aim is to create a brochure a) for foreign tourists or b) for British tourists in Britain. First decide which city, town or region in Britain you would like to talk about. You may include geographical and socio-economic information, tourist attractions and famous sights, historical and cultural attractions. Don't forget to add pictures and maps, and use an attractive layout.

- **A famous British person**
Decide which person you would like to introduce to your class. You could talk about a famous artist, e.g. a writer, playwright, musician, composer or actor, or you could choose a scientist, sportsman or a member of the royal family. It doesn't matter if the person is still alive or not. Create a poster with pictures as well as biographical information, and say what (has) made them famous.

- **National dishes from Britain**
First brainstorm what you know about British food and decide which dishes you would like to present (no more than four!). Your aim is to create a little cookery book in which you include the ingredients, how the dishes are cooked and where and when they are eaten. Don't forget to add pictures!

- **Typical sports in Britain**
Your aim is to create a poster about a sport that is popular in Britain. Your presentation should include information about the equipment, the rules, and either the national team or a successful club, or some famous players. Pictures or drawings will make your poster more appealing!

- **British customs and traditions**
First brainstorm what you know about British customs and traditions. Think about occasions such as Christmas, Bonfire Night, April Fool's Day, Shrove Tuesday, birthdays, etc. Then select about three or four customs and create a leaflet in which you explain the traditions and their origins.

A1.33

CityBlog

London – love it and leave it

Search GO

There are so many reasons to live in London … and at least as many to leave! That's the conclusion I came to a couple of months ago, talking to a friend who had just returned from a full year of city-hopping, as it were, around the globe. Tony, like me, had spent almost all his life in London. That evening he had declared that he was genuinely glad to be back, which – to my own great surprise – surprised me. Since then I haven't stopped thinking about why, and have begun to open my eyes and look around me.

Well, take the daily journey to and from work on the Tube. I bet that's an aspect of London the bloke had swiftly wiped out of his memory. I would too if I could. There's litter everywhere and overcrowded isn't the word for it: You're more like "sardined" into sweat-drenched carriages, though unlike the tinned fish, you're not quite dead to the world. And why is it that just when you're hurrying to get to an airport or an important interview, trains aren't operating on the line you need? Most Londoners I know also complain that the Tube stops too early, making it difficult to have a good night out.

Overground it's not much better, I notice. The crowds, the grime, the high prices – they all do their bit to grind you down. So you go for a drink with your friends, but before you know it, the pub is closing and you'll be rudely reminded to "drink up". Yes, the law dictating that all pubs must close at eleven was relaxed back in 2005. Yet I find that the pubs around where I live haven't bothered to extend their licensing hours. Of course there are places elsewhere that do business till twelve or one o'clock, not to mention bars and clubs up in town which often stay open till the wee hours – but these establishments are pricier, may require pre-booking, often turn away male-only groups (three blokes make up a group, I'm not kidding), and there's still the problem of how to get home.

2 **conclusion** – Schlussfolgerung
5 **genuinely** – echt, aufrichtig
10 **bloke** *(BE, coll.)* – Kerl
10 **swiftly** – schnell
12 **sardined** – eingequetscht (wie eine Ölsardine)
12 **drenched** – durchnässt
12 **carriage** – Wagen (eines Zuges usw.)
18 **grime** – Schmutz
19 **to grind sb. down** – jmdn zermürben
21 **rudely** – unhöflich
23 **to bother** – *hier:* sich die Mühe machen
23 **to extend** – verlängern, ausdehnen
23 **licensing hours** – Öffnungszeiten (einer Bar mit Alkohollizenz)
26 **wee hours** – frühe Morgenstunden
26 **establishment** – Einrichtung
26 **pricy** – teuer
27 **pre-booking** – Vormerkung
28 **to kid** – Spaß machen

Then, walking towards Regent's Park one evening, I suddenly catch the rosy light of sunset on the creamy facades of the stylish buildings on one side of the street. The park, I notice, is vast and green and tranquil and I am struck by the beauty of the moment. That's when it comes back to me: London is, of course, full of parks, heaths and commons, my favourite being the more unruly Hampstead Heath, the park of my childhood. It's a fact I'd simply taken for granted. I wonder if there's any other city of this size elsewhere as green …

I realise that the best way to find out is to leave London for a while in order to explore cities abroad. And who knows how I'll feel about this place when (or if) I return. (498 words)

31 **facade** – Fassade
32 **tranquil** – ruhig, friedlich
33 **to be struck by sth.** – von etw. beeindruckt sein
34 **heath** – Heide
34 **common** – öffentliche Grünfläche
35 **unruly** – wild, ungebändigt
36 **to take sth. for granted** – etw. als gegeben hinnehmen

1 Mediation
Your younger brother's friend has just seen the city blog about London on your computer screen.
As he is taking a class trip to London next week, he is interested in getting to know what the text says about the city. He has got only limited knowledge of English and asks you to briefly summarise for him the main aspects of the text in German.

2 Analysis
Look at the picture of London. Describe what you can see and analyse the picture as to whether it adds to the images of London presented in the text.

3 Production: Text-based composition
Discuss the pros and cons of using public transport by taking the information from the text into account.

4 Writing
Comment on the following statement: "Big city life is said to make a big contribution to environmental pollution."

Topic 1.5

e2q6wh

Private and professional communication

I don't believe in email. I'm an old-fashioned girl. I prefer calling and hanging up.
Sarah Jessica Parker, American actress

1

A

The more elaborate our means of communication, the less we communicate.
Joseph Priestley, English clergyman (1734–1804)

2

What a lot we lost when we stopped writing letters. You can't reread a phone call.
Liz Carpenter, American writer and feminist (1920–2010)

3

B

Suddenly, it seems as though all the world's a-twitter.
Newsweek, weekly American news magazine

4

C

Getting started

1 **Look at the pictures A–F. Explain what they show.** → Describing pictures, p. 339

2 **Read the quotes. Choose one for each picture.**

D

Electric communication will never be a substitute for the face of someone who with their soul encourages another person to be brave and true.
Charles Dickens, English novelist (1812–1817)

5

elaborate – kompliziert
means of communication – Kommunikationsmittel
clergyman – Geistlicher
substitute – Ersatz
to encourage – ermutigen, ermuntern
philanthropist – Wohltäter(in)
accessible – zugänglich
to found – gründen
to foster – fördern

Communication – the human connection – is the key to personal and career success.
Paul J. Meyer, American businessman and philanthropist (1928–2009)

6

E

F

Talk is by far the most accessible of pleasures. It costs nothing in money, it is all profit, it completes our education, founds and fosters our friendships, and can be enjoyed at any age and in almost any state of health.
Robert Louis Stevenson, Scottish novelist (1850–1894)

7

3 **Share your ideas with your partner and give reasons for your choice.**

4 **In pairs, come up with your own quotation about communication and report back to the class.**

5 **Research project** → Hotspot 1, p. 87

Word bank

Giving opinions
I think that … • In my opinion … • I believe that … • It seems to me … • I agree / disagree because … • What do you think? • What is your opinion on this?

A Communicating online

1 Before you read → Brainstorming, p. 351

a) How much time do you spend online every day? What do you do? What do you think is a "healthy" amount of time to spend online per day?

b) Interview your partner on the same questions. Does he / she spend more or less time online than you? What does he / she do online? Share your findings with the class.

FAMILY MATTERS *is a weekly column which appears on the US online news site mywesttexas.com. In the column, qualified marriage and family therapist Dr. Jim May offers advice and support on personal issues.*

mywesttexas.com

Search GO

Home | News | Sports | Business | Pulse | Life | Multimedia | Data

FAMILY MATTERS:

Time spent chatting online is time lost with family

DEAR FAMILY: My husband somehow started "chatting" with some people on the Internet and has wound up talking to them more now than he does to me. He's not secretive or anything about it; he's just obsessed about having to be on the computer at 9 p.m. so they can all talk. I can come and see what he's doing and it's all very innocent mostly about politics and hunting. I think that is all pretty strange to spend that much time (usually from 9 to 11 p.m.) on the computer talking to people he's never met. When I tell him those people aren't real and that he's ignoring his real family for them, he gets mad at me and clams up.

At any rate, the problem is that we have no time for us anymore. He's a really good father and is involved with our kids, helps them with homework, baths and bedtime stories. But then he's off to the computer until bedtime. I usually am already in bed and sometimes asleep when he comes to bed, so we usually don't talk then. We had had a good sex life but now I'm not willing for him to come to bed and just have

4 **to wind up doing sth.** – schließlich etw. tun
6 **secretive** – geheimnisvoll
7 **obsessed** – besessen
11 **innocent** – harmlos
16 **to clam up** – still werden

sex without any connecting time at all. So he's mad at me about that and I'm mad at him because he's choosing his "friends" over me. Am I just being selfish? We never did a lot together or talk a lot before, but this is ridiculous. Does he have some kind of Internet addiction problem? – LEFT OUT WIFE

DEAR LEFT OUT: You and your husband need to address this problem directly and calmly. I would not characterize your husband as having any kind of addiction problem but he would want to consider re-balancing his life with you and his online activities. Given all of the demands and pressures that are placed on marriage and the family these days, it is even more important that time is set aside exactly for what your husband is doing on the Internet – talking and sharing. This getting-to-know effort is critical in establishing and maintaining healthy family and marital relations.
The main problem with your husband spending so much time on the Internet is that it replaces direct face-to-face interactions and takes away from them. The parts of one's life that should be shared with family and spouse are being shared with others. Strangely enough, those chat-room relationships are real to those involved. They are not real in the face-to-face sense but they are real in terms of real communications. Such communicating does in fact build relationships. The time and energy that should be going to the marriage and family are going to another relationship.
I think at this point you could set aside time to share this column with your husband and reach an agreement on how long he can chat that works for him, you and the family. It is a real compliment to him that you do want to spend time with him. (599 words)

23 **selfish** – egoistisch
24 **ridiculous** – lächerlich
29 **demand** – *hier:* Anforderung
29 **pressure** – *hier:* Zwang, Druck
30 **to set aside** – reservieren
32 **to establish** – aufbauen
32 **to maintain** – aufrechterhalten
32 **marital relations** – eheliche Beziehungen
35 **spouse** – Ehegatte / -gattin

297 **2 Comprehension**
Summarise "LEFT OUT WIFE's" problem and "FAMILY's" answer in your own words.

297 **3 Text production: Writing an email** → Writing an email, p. 329
"[...] chat-room relationships are real to those involved. They are not real in the face-to-face sense but they are real in terms of real communications. Such communicating does in fact build relationships." (ll. 36 – 38)
Do you agree? Can people form relationships without ever meeting face-to-face? Write an email to Dr. May in which you give your opinion on the statement above.

4 Analysis → Describing cartoons, p. 340
Describe and analyse the cartoon and relate it to the text.

Technology continues to improve communication.

B Letter writing – a lost art?

1 Before you read

a) Think about the following questions:
- When was the last time you sent or received a letter?
- What kind of letter was it – handwritten or typed?
- What was the letter about?
- Do people nowadays write more or fewer letters than ten years ago? Why?

b) Discuss these questions with a partner and report back to the class.

theguardian

News | Sport | Comment | Culture | Business | Money | Life&Style | Travel | Environment

Comment is free > Society   Search [ ] GO

A fifth of children have never received a letter

Young people who rely on email and text are missing out on the pleasures and benefits of letter writing, say experts

One in five children in the UK has never received a handwritten letter, according to a survey published today. With young people increasingly relying on email and social networking sites to communicate, a tenth had never written a letter themselves, the research found. Teachers and experts said they feared young people were missing out on the pleasures and developmental benefits of letter writing.

The survey of 1,200 seven- to 14-year-olds, commissioned for children's charity World Vision, found that more than a quarter had not written a letter in the last year and 43% had not been sent one. But in the previous week alone, almost half had either sent or received an email, or a message on a social networking site. Boys were twice as likely as girls never to have written a letter.

Child education expert Sue Palmer, the author of *Toxic Childhood,* said: "If children do not write or receive letters, they miss out on key developmental benefits. Handwritten letters are much more personal than electronic communication. By going to the trouble of physically committing words to paper, the writer shows their investment of time and effort in a relationship. That's why we tend to hang on to personal letters as keepsakes.The effort of writing is a very real one for a child. Painstakingly manoeuvring the pencil across the page, thinking of the best words to convey a message, struggling with spelling and punctuation. It is, however, an effort worth making, because it's only through practice that we become truly literate – and literacy is the hallmark of human civilisation. If we care about real relationships, we should invest in real communication, not just the quick fix of a greetings card, text or email. What's more, if we care about civilised human thought, we should encourage our children to invest time and energy in sitting down to write."

13 **to miss out on sth.** – etw. verpassen
13 **developmental** – Entwicklungs-
15 **to commission** – in Auftrag geben
21 **to commit** – *hier:* niederschreiben
22 **to hang on to sth.** – etw. behalten
23 **keepsake** – Andenken, Erinnerung
23 **painstakingly** – gewissenhaft, sorgfältig
24 **to manoeuvre** – manövrieren
24 **to convey** – vermitteln
25 **punctuation** – Interpunktion
26 **literate** – lese- und schreibkundig
26 **literacy** – Lese- und Schreibfähigkeit
26 **hallmark** – Kennzeichen

Half of 11-year olds were not sure how to lay out a letter and a third of 14-year olds weren't either. The traditional thank you letter was the most common reason for putting pen to paper, making up 70% of children's efforts. Only one in five wrote letters to friends. World Vision carried out the survey for today's National Letter Writing Day. Writing letters to children in developing countries is a key part of its child sponsorship programme. Helen Smith, the headteacher at Lum Head primary school in Manchester, said: "Schools play a central role in child development, and we should always be thinking of new ways to get children writing. This is a great way to help enhance their literacy development."

(575 words)

34 **sponsorship** – Förderung
36 **to enhance** – verbessern

2 Comprehension: True or false? → Comprehension questions, p. 326
Read the statements below and decide whether they are true or false. Quote or paraphrase words from the text that confirm or disprove the ideas in the statements.

a) 25% of children in Great Britain have never been sent a letter.

b) Teachers argue that writing letters is not only fun, but also teaches valuable skills.

c) The survey found out that girls tend to write significantly more letters than boys.

d) For a child, writing a handwritten letter is as easy as writing an email.

e) According to the author, texting, emailing or sending greeting cards to somebody show that this person is important to you.

f) Seven in ten children write a letter after they have received a gift.

g) Helen Smith thinks that teachers are responsible for encouraging children to write.

297

3 Classroom discussion → Discussions, p. 344
Currently, only primary school children are required to practice handwriting in class. However, as the standard of handwriting of older students has deteriorated, some experts argue that secondary schools should introduce special handwriting lessons. This subject would be tested and would contribute to the students' final grades. Would you be in favour of handwriting lessons at your school? What would be the advantages and disadvantages? Think about it from the students' and teachers' points of view.

4 Analysis → Describing cartoons, p. 340
Describe and analyse the cartoon and relate it to the text.

5 Project → Hotspot 2, p. 87

"See kids? This is a LETTER. A LETTER. Back when I was a kid, people would send these all the time. There was no such thing as e-mail."

C Communicating at work

8 **majority** – Mehrzahl, Mehrheit
15 **privacy** – Privatsphäre
24 **to remain** – bleiben
35 **progress** – Fortschritt
38 **destination** – Ziel
41 **intended** – *hier:* bestimmt
46 **enquiry** – Anfrage
46 **offer** – Angebot
46 **order** – Bestellung, Auftrag
48 **brochure** – Prospekt, Broschüre
48 **delivery times** – Lieferzeiten
50 **quotation** – *hier:* Angebot, Kostenvoranschlag
54 **wherein** – worin
59 **to proceed** – fortfahren

Business communication

Communication plays an essential role in any company, and over the years the business world has seen many developments in this area. From the early days of the hand-written letter, to the telephone, computers and the internet, the speed and possibilities of professional communication have increased greatly.

In the majority of professional situations, emails have replaced traditional letters. The advantages are clear: they are fast, can be stored easily, and sent to anywhere in the world, and – thanks to smart phones – at anytime. However, there are also disadvantages. For instance, around 95% of all emails sent worldwide are spam. Then there are the more serious issues of security and privacy – both of which are very important to any business. Emails and attachments may be used to transfer viruses or spyware. And, in terms of privacy, how can you be sure that nobody else is reading your emails?

One thing that has stood the test of time is the telephone. Although it has seen many developments in technology and design over the years, the telephone still has a place on most office desks in the world. It has remained popular for a number of reasons: it is fast, allows you to be spontaneous and make quick decisions, it is relatively inexpensive and simple to use. The major downsides, however, are that it is dependent on the other person being available. For example, if you suddenly have a great idea to put to your partner in Tokyo, you may have to wait six hours for them to wake up before you can tell them. Phone conversations can also lead to misunderstandings, whether due to language difficulties, bad connections, or other factors.

Despite constant technological progress and innovations, the simple written letter (rather cruelly named 'snail mail' as it can take days to reach its destination) still has a key role to play. It offers a level of security missing in emails, i.e. the letter is (ideally) only opened and read by the person it was intended for. Furthermore, a written document with a signature is more formal and may still be required in legal situations.

In the majority of companies, local or international, three types of business letters keep the wheels turning: enquiry, offer and order. An enquiry letter may be general – such as requests for price lists, brochures, or delivery times – or more specific. Such enquiries are often requests for more thorough information, such as detailed quotations.

Once an enquiry has been received the next step is often for the buyer and the seller to agree on a contract. This is generally initiated by an offer letter wherein the seller quotes a price for their goods or services and outlines terms of payments, delivery times and other conditions. After a buyer has received an offer letter from a potential business partner they must decide whether or not to proceed. If the buyer finds the offer satisfactory they will place an order.

The fact that these written documents, and a number of others, still form the backbone of business relations shows that companies still place a great deal of value on having things on paper – not just in the inbox or the answering machine.

(654 words)

1 Comprehension

a) Work with a partner. Make a grid for yourself like the one below. Then read the text again and complete the grid.

	Advantages	Disadvantages
Email		
Telephone		
Letter		

b) Enquiry, offer or order? Match the following phrases with the corresponding type of business letter.

1. "Please supply the following items on the terms stated below."
2. "Please state your earliest delivery date."
3. "We saw your advertisements for laser printers in the October edition of *What PC?* magazine."
4. "We look forward to welcoming you as our customer."
5. "As agreed, payment will be made 30 days from date of invoice."
6. "We can offer a 10% discount on orders over €5,000."
7. "Please send us a quotation for 24 black leather office chairs, article number OCB22."
8. "Please make sure that any glass articles are packed with great care."
9. "We were pleased to hear that you are interested in our products."

2 Listening comprehension: Taking phone calls → Listening, p. 319

38 In her first week at Herkules AG, the new apprentice Sandra Kohl finds herself alone in the office and the telephone rings.

a) Listen to the telephone conversation twice and list as many telephoning phrases as possible.

b) Compare your list with a partner and complete it.

39 **3 Listening comprehension: Taking messages** → Taking notes, p. 352

Listen to the telephone conversation and take the message in German. Use the following message form:

4 Role play: Taking messages → Making phone calls, p. 347

Work in pairs and sit back to back. Partner A "rings" partner B and leaves a short message, e.g. when and where to meet a customer, a response to an enquiry, a telephone order, etc. Partner B takes down the message. Then change roles. Use the phrases from task 2.

Telefonnotiz

Nachricht für: ____________________

Aufgenommen von: ____________________

Anrufer: ____________________

Betreff: ____________________

____

____

5 Project → Hotspot 3, p. 87

D Office life

The new job

From the novel
Martin Lukes: Who moved my BlackBerry?
by Lucy Kellaway

9 **pager** – Funkrufempfänger
9 **BlackBerry** – Smartphone
17 **to make amends** – etw. wiedergutmachen
40 **FTSE 100** – die 100 umsatzstärksten Firmen der Londoner Börse
41 **hush hush** – geheimnisvoll
60 **Sainsbury's** – britische Supermarktkette
61 **yours truly** – mit freundlichen Grüßen

December 2
From: Martin Lukes
To: Sylvia Woods

Hi Sylvia
What's this message to call Sebastian Fforbes Hever? Did he say what it was about? I'm going out now for a spot of lunch. If he calls back, I've got my mobile, pager and BlackBerry with me.
Martin

From: Martin Lukes
To: Jenny Lukes

Darling –
Sorry about last night … had a few too many. Will try to get back early tonite to make amends.
btw one of the top headhunters at Heidrick Ferry has been trying to get hold of me (!) … dunno what it's about
Love you, M xx

From: Martin Lukes
To: SebastianFforbesHever@HeidrickFerry

Hi Sebastian
Thanks for your intriguing email. Yes, indeed, I could find a window to meet up with you tomorrow. I'll have to juggle a couple of meetings, but should be do-able – could see you at your offices in Buckingham Palace Road at around 3ish.
Bestest
Martin Lukes
Marketing Director, A&B (UK)

From: Martin Lukes
To: Jenny Lukes

Darling –
Guess what?? I've been approached to be director of marketing and strategy at a major FTSE 100 company!! All very hush hush … the headhunter wouldn't say which one over the phone, but I'm going to meet him tomorrow.
I know you're really up against it this pm but wld be v grateful if you'd pick up my grey Hugo Boss suit from the cleaners.
Love you M xx

December 3
From: Martin Lukes
To: Sylvia Woods

Hi Sylvia, I'm popping out now. If anyone wants to know where I am, say I'm at a forward planning meeting with Tim at BGF. Will be back 5ish.
Martin

From: Martin Lukes
To: Jenny Lukes

Darling – FANTASTIC meeting with Sebastian just now. The job is marketing director of Sainsbury's!! The role's heaven made for yours truly – I'd be in charge of 350 people globally, $1bn annual budget. Very high profile.

Sebastian didn't mention the package at this stage, but said it wouldn't be an obstacle to finding the right person. I assume at least twice what I'm on now … It's got my name all over it – what they want are unrivalled communications skills, results-driven mentality and an outstanding track record in driving performance … I've got ticks in all the boxes. Coming straight home now.
Love you M xx
Sent from my BlackBerry Wireless Handheld

December 4
From: Martin Lukes
To: Sebastian FforbesHever@HeidrickFerry

Hi Sebastian
Great to meet with you yesterday – I felt we were very much singing from the same hymn sheet. I just wanted to reiterate how positive I am about this position, and how much I have to bring to the party.

Just to re-cap: I'm very can-do, very get-up-and-go – I operate very well within a large company – but have a pronounced entrepreneurial streak that keeps me thinking outside the box.
Look forward to hearing from you.
All my very bestest
Martin

From: Martin Lukes
To: Jenny Lukes

Darling –
I'm on the shortlist!!! I'm going to meet all the top bods at Sainsbury's on Monday. I've got to prepare a presentation on how I would transition the marketing strategy onto a higher plane. As a shopper, have you got any pointers on supermarkets – from the consumer's perspective? Debrief tonite?
Love you, M xx

PS I'll be working flat out all weekend … so don't think I'll be able to make it to your parents on Sunday.

From: Martin Lukes
To: Jenny Lukes

Darling – don't think you understand this is the biggest point in my career to date. I'm sure your parents won't mind – they don't like me anyway …

December 9
From: Martin Lukes
To: Jenny Lukes

Darling – total triumph!! The chief executive of Sainsbury's has the IDENTICAL take on the future of marketing to yours truly. The interview was meant to last an hour, but I got the feeling they had made up their mind after 15 minutes.

My presentation on their marketing strategy was 110 per cent on the button. I was pretty critical – though obviously in a positive sort of way. Basically I said that in the past they've relied too heavily on Jamie Oliver – they need a more flexible approach to winning hearts and minds of today's shoppers.
See you later.
M xx

From: Martin Lukes
To: Jenny Lukes

Darling – Just had a brief chat with Sebastian – and he says they are 'very interested' in me. Re package, we're talking of something in the region of 350k, plus bonuses which could be same again. Obviously share options, pension, health insurance, gym club membership. Car allowance would be

65 **package** – *hier:* Gehalt plus Bonuszahlungen
71 **track record** – Erfolgsgeschichte
89 **to re-cap** – die wesentlichen Punkte wiederholen
92 **streak** – Charakterzug
101 **bods** *(infml)* – Leute
107 **to debrief** – einen Einsatzbericht abgeben
133 **Jamie Oliver** – britischer Starkoch
142 **Re(ferring to)** – Betr(eff)
144 **350k** – 350 Tausend
145 **share options** – Aktienbezugsrecht

154 **count my chickens** – Bezug zur Redewendung: *Don't count your chickens before they're hatched.*

168 **juncture** – Punkt

174 **cheers** *(infml)* – danke

180 **in order** – *hier:* berechtigt

216 **sod** *(coll.)* – Schwein, Sau, Arsch

double so that we could trade in the Mitsubishi Shogun and get a Porsche Cayenne V8 Turbo S.
Love you M xx

From: Martin Lukes
To: Jenny Lukes

Darling – Yes, I know I shouldn't count my chickens. And I'm not. I'm simply repeating what I've been told.
M

December 10
From: Martin Lukes
To: Graham Wallace

Hi Graham
Did you notice that I wasn't firing on all cylinders in the board meeting just now? Between you and me and the gatepost, that could be the last one I'm ever going to attend. I'm up for a big job. It's as good as in the bag, though can't tell you what at this juncture. But put it this way. Think supermarket. Think Jamie Oliver. Think Chief Marketing Officer …
Mart

From: Martin Lukes
To: Graham Wallace

Cheers, Graham. Yes obviously I am totally over the moon. At the end of the day, being marketing director has been a load of fun, but I've outgrown it.
Mart

PS Keep this under your hat till it's greenlighted. Then monster drinks in order.

From: Martin Lukes
To: Sylvia Woods

Hi Sylvia
I think I should let you into a little secret. I'm afraid our ways are about to part. I've been headhunted for a very senior job, so looks like this might be my last week here. If anyone from Sainsbury's or Heidrick Ferry calls in the next hour when I'm in the budget meeting come and get me out.
M

From: Martin Lukes
To: Sylvia Woods

Anyone called?

December 11
From: Martin Lukes
To: Sebastian FforbesHever@HeidrickFerry

Hi Sebastian
I don't want to hassle you, but I just wondered if there was any news?
Bestest, Martin

From: Martin Lukes
To: Sebastian FforbesHever@HeidrickFerry

I don't understand. That wasn't what you implied earlier. I thought the Sainsbury's board loved me.
Is this a joke, or what?

From: Martin Lukes
To: Jenny Lukes

I don't fucking believe it. They've gone and fucking given it to someone fucking else. Sebastian is a fucking lying sod. He said they LOVED my presentation – practically said the job was in the bag. And now he's saying I didn't have the right skillsets, fit not quite right blah, better qualified candidates … blah blah.
I still just can't fucking believe it.
It's so unfair. My dream job.
M

From: Martin Lukes
To: Sylvia Woods

Sylvia I'm feeling very unwell. I think I'm coming down with the flu. I'm going home now.

December 15
From: Martin Lukes
To: Graham Wallace

Just to check – you haven't told anyone about that job, have you? As it happens I've decided against. Basically, I've always believed that work is all about the people. And although it was very flattering to be offered such a mega job at Sainsbury's, at the end of the day, I didn't want to work with them. Feeling a bit rough this am. Hair of the dog later?
M

(1249 words)

241 **hair of the dog** *(infml)* – einen Kater mit Alkohol bekämpfen

1 Comprehension
Summarise what happens in this extract.

2 Vocabulary → Guessing new words, p. 353
Check these expressions in their context and explain what they mean in your own words.

• find a window (l. 27)	• thinking outside the box (l. 93)
• up against it (l. 44)	• the identical take (l. 123)
• I'm popping out (l. 51)	• on the button (l. 129)
• what I'm on now (l. 68)	• firing on all cylinders (l. 162)
• It's got my name all over it (l. 68)	• in the bag (l. 167)
• singing from the same hymn sheet (l. 84)	• Keep this under your hat (l. 179)

3 Analysis → Understanding fictional texts, p. 322

a) Characterise Martin Lukes by showing what his communications with the other characters reveal about him.

b) Compare the content and style of the last three emails.

4 Text production: Writing an email → Writing an email, p. 329
Imagine you are Martin's long-serving secretary Sylvia Woods. You have access to all of the emails above and have decided to write to Martin, who is currently on sick leave. Explain to him why – in your opinion – he probably didn't get the job, and how he can improve his behaviour in the future.

5 Research project → Hotspot 4, p. 87

If-clauses

→ Grammar, p. 373

a) Complete the sentences by using the correct if-clause. Write your answers on a separate piece of paper.

1. If Laura had to, she … (move) to another city for a job; but she would rather stay where she is.
2. Achim will take a job if the company … (offer) him one.
3. If Irene gets the chance to attend the job fair next week in Munich, she … (meet) a lot of prospective employers.
4. If Michael had paid more attention in school, he … (get) better grades.
5. Volunteering … (be) an option for Lena if she doesn't find an internship over the summer.
6. I would drive to work if I … (have) my own car.
7. If you write your application letter too quickly it … (not be) very good.
8. If I had known that you were interested in graphic design, I … (send) you the link to the job advertisement.
9. Lena would have written the application letter by hand if Tim … (not repair) her printer at the last minute.
10. If I … (be) you, I would write more about my hobbies in my CV.

b) Decide which means of communication (telephone, email, letter) is best in the following situations and why. Use the text on page 80 to help you.

1. What will you do if …
   a) … it is 10 am local time and you need some figures from a sales representative in the US?
   b) … you want to meet up with a colleague on the second floor for lunch later?
2. What would you do if …
   a) … you were school headmaster and wanted to inform the parents about a school event?
   b) … you were a fashion designer and had to order some fabric from a supplier in India?
3. What would you have done if …
   … you had injured yourself while working on a machine, and needed medical assistance?

c) Rewrite the following sentences using the appropriate if-clause.

Example:
Michael has a lot of experience doing presentations. He doesn't get nervous.
If Michael didn't have a lot experience doing presentations, he would get nervous.

1. Sally's letter was well written. She has a good chance of getting an interview.
2. Matthew speaks three languages. He was chosen to represent his company at international events.
3. Ruben didn't ask somebody to read through his application letter. His letter was full of mistakes.
4. Teenagers 20 years ago didn't have mobile phones. They had to use payphones.
5. My boyfriend spends a lot of time chatting online. We don't have time to talk to each other.

1 Research project: A timeline → Internet research, p. 358
Search for information on the "history of communication". Create a timeline that shows how communication between people has developed over time. Include predictions for the future in your timeline.

2 Project: Letter writing → Writing a personal letter, p. 331
Draw the name of a classmate at random and keep the name secret. At home, write a short handwritten personal letter to this person. Pay attention to your handwriting, the layout of the letter, spelling and punctuation. Make sure you also include some questions. Here are some things you can write about:

school • family • hobbies • hopes and ambitions for the future • your last / next holiday • ...

Find an envelope and address your letter to this person, and give it to your teacher, who will hand the letters out to the recipients. When you receive your letter, write a reply at home and "send" it the same way.

3 Project: Telephone etiquette → Mediation, p. 343, Presentation, p. 362
Work in groups. Go online and search for English video clips about how to behave correctly on the telephone. In German, create a list of the ten most important tips and copy them onto a transparency. In German, present your results to the class.

4 Research project: German job advertisements
→ Mediation, p. 343, Writing a formal letter, p. 332

a) Work in groups. Go online to find a German job advertisement (*Stellenangebot / Stellenanzeige*) for a job that interests you. You can find ads on the website of every major newspaper. Create a poster that shows the most important information of the job ad in English. Present your poster to the class.

b) In pairs, choose one of your classmates' posters and write a letter of application.

A1.40

3 **creator** – Schöpfer(in), Erfinder(in)

9 **to hinder** – behindern

11 **to take pride in sth.** – stolz auf etw. sein

35 **Pew Internet and American Life Project** – Projekt des amerikanischen Meinungsforschungsinstituts *Pew Research Center*

39 **breezy** – flott, leicht

THE UNIVERSITY OF ALABAMA

Search GO

About UA | Academics | Admissions | Athletics | Giving | Libraries | Life of UA

Text messaging and its effects on teens' grammar

"IYO TXTng = Gd 4 or NME of GMR?" If you cannot understand the previous statement, then you most likely have not been exposed to the language of text messaging. Who are the creators of this language? The answer is today's teenagers. The translation for the opening sentence is, "In your opinion, is texting good for or the enemy of grammar?" Text messaging has surely given our society a quick means through which to communicate, taking out the need for capitalization, punctuation, the use and knowledge of sentence structure and the detail that make good statements great. Some educators suggest that this new age form of messaging may be hindering today's teens' abilities to apply grammar correctly in their writing and social skills. Others, however, take pride in the notion that teenagers are essentially creating their own language of the twenty-first century and see no effect on their students' writing skills. Edutopia, an educational website, conducted an online poll regarding this issue of text messaging vs. grammar. Out of 293 votes, 137 votes (47%) chose "Yes, I believe students are carrying over the writing habits they pick up through text messaging into school assignments." 98 votes (33%) chose "No. I believe students can write one way to their friends and another way in class. They can keep the two methods separate." 55 votes (19%) chose "Maybe. Although text messaging may have some impact on how students write, I don't think it's a significant problem." [...]

Wat do u tnk? (What do you think?) The Sacramento News published an article in April of 2008 about a study conducted by the Pew Internet and American Life Project and the National Commission on Writing regarding text messaging and its effect on teens' schoolwork. The study concludes, "A national telephone poll of 700 youths ages 12 to 17 and their parents found that 64 percent of teens admit that the breezy shortcuts and symbols commonly used in text messaging have appeared in their school assignments." One teacher in the article states, "'When informal language does pop up in papers, I definitely am going to correct it,' she said. 'But it's part of our job as teachers to help students move in and out of formal and informal language.'" This teacher is very correct; in Alabama as well as other states across the United States, one of the standards for teachers of English Language

Arts is to educate students on the difference of and appropriate use of formal and informal language. [...]

Overall, it really is no surprise that text messaging is leaking into students' schoolwork because teenagers are generally known in our society as constant texters. In fact, teens in the United States (ages 13 to 17) statistically, according to phone bills, have the highest levels of text messaging, sending and receiving an average of about 1800 text messages per month. [...]

Many teens, though, go above and beyond the average of text messaging among our youth today. One online article featured a thirteen-year-old girl who text messaged 14,528 text messages in a single month. Her father noted that the online AT&T statement ran 440 pages long. [...] When calculating the amount of hours in a single month, just think about the astronomical amount that this girl is texting per minute. Imagine what this California girl's teachers are probably seeing in her schoolwork. (567 words)

48 **to leak into** – *hier:* sich einschleichen

1 Comprehension

Read the text and answer the following questions in 1–18 words.

a) Who are the creators of text messaging?

b) What are the characteristics of text messaging?

c) What do some educators fear?

d) What is Edutopia?

e) What did Edutopia do?

f) How many voters claimed that writing habits typical of text messaging can be found again in school assignments?

g) How many teens admitted in a study conducted by the Pew Internet and American Life Project and the National Commission on Writing that shortcuts and symbols reappeared in their schoolwork?

h) What do American teens statistically have according to phone bills?

i) How old was the girl who text messaged 14,528 text messages in a single month and where does she come from?

2 Analysis → Understanding non-fictional texts, p. 320

a) Analyse the structure of the article and explain its effect on the reader.

b) Analyse the cartoon and relate it to the text.

3 Comment

"[…] this new age form of messaging may be hindering today's teens' abilities to apply grammar correctly in their writing and social skills." (ll. 9–10)

Do you agree with this statement? Comment on it.

"Possessive pronouns? Um, iPod, yourPod, theirPod?"

Topic 2.1
The English language in use

x8w9uk

163 nations use English to communicate with other UN member states

medium for 80% of the information stored in the world's computers

more than half of the world's technical and scientific periodicals are in English

most widely learned second language in the world

official language in 52 countries

some 380 million native speakers

dominant language in electronic communication

Globish
skills modernity future
global hybrid **language**
lingua tomorrow
immigrants change globalisation worldwide
Mandarin technology international Hinglish Pidgin
negotiations second Shakespeare working
non-native vehicular music
business politics barrier
Internet franca
Asian

influence on cinema, music, broadcasting, science, and the Internet

language with the greatest number of native speakers: Mandarin Chinese

people who count English as their mother tongue make up less than 10% of the world's population, but possess over 30% of the world's economic power

working knowledge is a basic skill in many fields and occupations

of all the world's languages (over 2,700) English is the richest in vocabulary

more than 700 million people speak English as a foreign language

most widely spoken and written language worldwide

Getting started

1 **a)** What aspects of the English language are included in the cluster? What do you know about these aspects? Re-arrange them in a word web adding further details. → Word webs, p. 349

b) Present your word web to your partner.

2 **Study the information on the yellow slips of paper and complete your word web about the English language. Then give a three-minute talk to the class about English as a global language.** → Presentation, p. 362

3 **A class survey about languages** → Questionnaires and surveys, p. 360
Draw up a class survey about the languages which
- you speak,
- you would like to be able to speak (stating your reasons, too),
- are spoken in your homes.

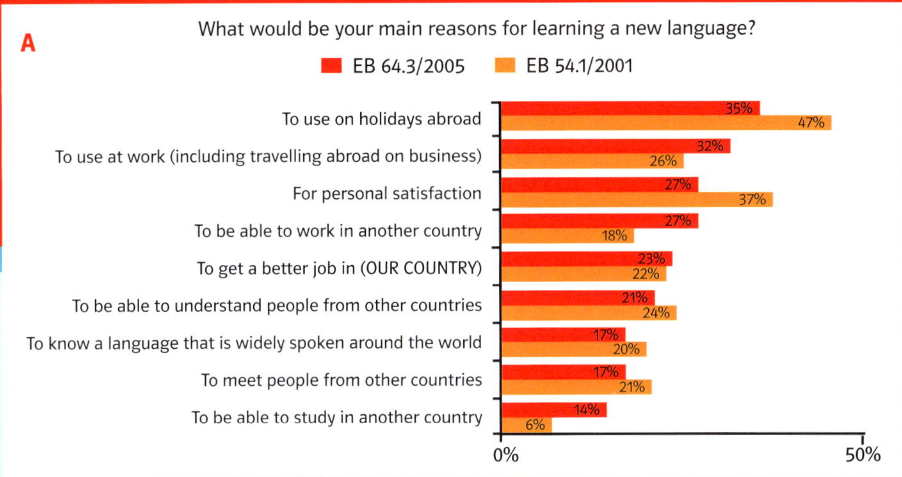

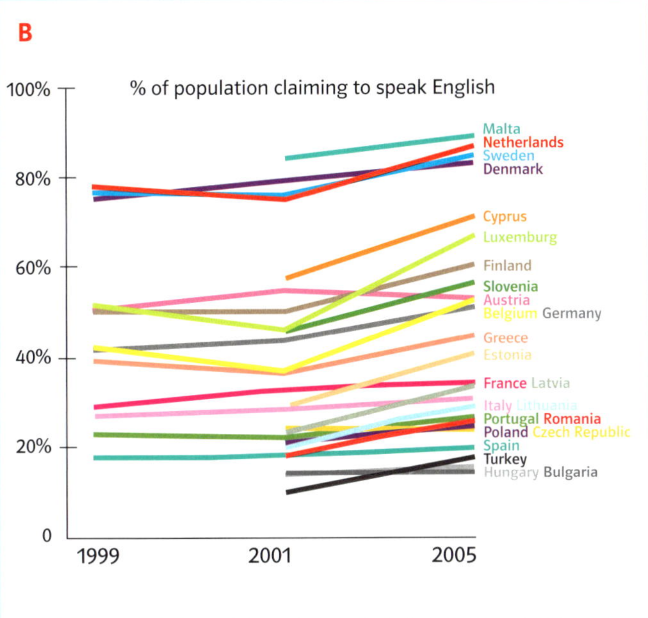

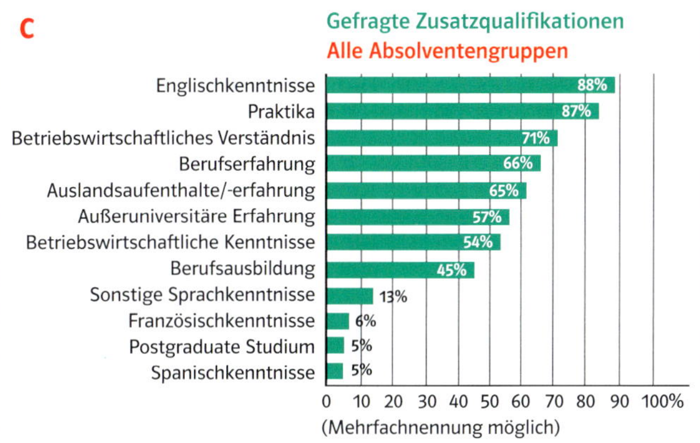

Wer keine Englischkenntnisse und Praktika vorweisen kann, wird es schwer haben, einen attraktiven Arbeitgeber zu finden. Die internationale Geschäftssprache zu beherrschen und praktische Erfahrungen mitzubringen, gehört mittlerweile zum Pflichtprogramm: Jeweils an die 90 Prozent der Unternehmen erwarten dies von ihren Bewerbern. Nur Unternehmen mit Bedarf an Juristen nennen betriebswirtschaftliches Verständnis als zweitwichtigste Kompetenz nach Englischkenntnissen. Auslandsaufenthalte und außeruniversitäre Erfahrungen sind weitere wichtige Pluspunkte beim Berufseinstieg.

Source (A and B): European Union, Eurobarometer

Source (C): Job Trends Deutschland 2011, Staufenbiel Institut

4 The Eurobarometer (EB) is a series of surveys by the European Commission which are carried out in all European member states. → Describing diagrams, p. 341

a) Study and summarise diagrams A and B. What do the two Eurobarometer surveys say about the importance of the English language?

b) Choose one diagram and analyse it in detail.

5 Additional qualifications and skills → Mediation, p. 343
German companies were asked to name the additional qualifications and skills university graduates need to get a job on the German labour market. Summarise the findings in diagram C in English.

6 Research project → Hotspot 1, p. 103

Word bank

highest number of speakers • % of those who took part in the survey say … • international language of business • … % of the population claim to speak English • a good knowledge of English • to be fluent in English • to have work experience • to spend a year abroad • work placement • key qualifications

A English as a lingua franca

1 Before you read → Brainstorming, p. 351

a) Why do people all over the world learn English? Make a list of reasons.

b) This advert by the British council in Hungary tries to motivate people to learn English. Analyse the ad and say if it works. Give reasons.

A 2.1

European Commission

LANGUAGES

Search GO

English as a lingua franca

Throughout history, whenever and wherever different groups have come into contact, there has been a constant need for a common language enabling communities with different mother tongues to communicate. What is new is the scale of international communication today. The past few decades have witnessed unparalleled increases, emphasising the need for one or more vehicular languages that can overcome language barriers. That this role is mainly played by English at the moment can scarcely be disputed. It is against this backdrop that labels such as "World English", "International English", "English as a Lingua Franca", "Global English", or "Globish" have been coined.

Learn English. The most popular language in the universe.

English is the working language or one of the working languages of all international organisations. Besides the United Kingdom, Ireland, the United States, Canada, Australia, and New Zealand, most countries belonging to the former British Empire have adopted it as their – at times sole – official language and new countries are promoting its use (e.g. Rwanda designated English as the official language of education in 2008 and English is gaining ground on French as the chief foreign language even in former French colonies like Algeria, Tunisia and Morocco). It is also the main language of international business and is chosen ever more frequently as the corporate language in multinational corporations and in academic, technological and scientific contexts or in sports events. Its prestige is unchallenged in the media and the entertainment industry worldwide: the number of music bands singing in English instead of their mother tongue clearly shows the appeal of English, as does the number of people drawn to it as the language of their idols.

Thus English has become a symbol of modernity and speaking it means sharing and being part of a global culture through which local barriers can be overcome. Starting mainly from the 1960s and 1970s, through popular music, English has become in many countries a symbol of freedom and rebellion and in serious crises it still proves a powerful weapon against censorship. As the

3 **scale** – Ausmaß

4 **vehicular language** – Verkehrssprache

6 **scarcely** – kaum

23 **corporate language** – offizielle Sprache in einem Unternehmen

25 **prestige** – Prestige, Ansehen

main language of new communication channels, such as blogs and social networks, it has often allowed the opponents of totalitarian regimes to make their voices heard worldwide in spite of the harsh censorship put in place by such governments to crush and silence them. The events which followed the Iranian presidential elections in 2009 very clearly showed the importance of a vehicular language to break isolation and circulate information. The official media did not cover the protests and manifestations which spontaneously broke out in the days immediately after the official results were announced, but news of the riots and casualties could reach the outside world thanks to these new tools, and universal use of English meant that the news spread rapidly and afar.

Even those who fight its supremacy recognise it as a powerful medium to make themselves heard. A few years ago during a march in support of Hindi against English organised in India, demonstrators carried banners in English to reach a wider public. Another interesting example is the protest of fundamentalist Muslims after satirical cartoons making fun of Muhammad were published in Denmark: they protested against the Western world, but did so using slogans in English, even though it is the language of "the Great Satan" and is perceived as the very symbol of Western predominance.

However, whilst the phenomenon is widely acknowledged, it is far from being unanimously welcomed given the perceived risk of serious dangers not only for the survival of other languages, and as a consequence of other cultures, but also for English itself. On the one hand, the more English develops, the more fears are voiced that it propagates a new form of imperialism. According to this view, together with their language, English speaking countries (notably the US) impose their cultures and values, as well as their economic and political supremacy, the final outcome being global uniformity and homogenisation. Therefore, positive and clear action is called for to counter this trend and promote cultural diversity by protecting smaller languages and cultures endangered by the advance of English. On the other hand, the global reach of English is claimed to have a negative impact on English itself, as standards fall and mistakes and local idiosyncrasies increase, leaving native speakers feeling dispossessed of their own language. (711 words)

34 **harsh censorship** – strenge Zensur

40 **supremacy** – Vormachtstellung

46 **predominance** – Dominanz, Vorherrschaft

47 **unanimously** – einhellig

56 **idiosyncracy** – Eigenart

57 **dispossessed** – enteignet, enterbt

2 Comprehension

a) In your own words summarise the reasons for English as a lingua franca that are mentioned in the text.

b) Outline the criticism against English as a lingua franca according to the text.

3 Working with words

a) Read the text again and collect all the technical terms that have to do with English as a lingua franca.

b) Cluster or categorise your technical terms in a logical way (e.g. word web).

4 Having a discussion → Discussions, p. 344

a) Prepare a panel discussion about the pros and cons of English as a lingua franca. Before you start, decide on roles that should be included in your discussion.

b) Collect arguments to prepare for the roles.

c) Make notes of the best arguments for both sides that come up in your discussion.

5 Research projects → Hotspots 2 and 3, p. 103

B The language of tomorrow?

1 Before you read → Brainstorming, p. 351

a) Look at the photo and the headline of the article. What do you think the text is about?

b) Work with a partner and agree on five questions that you expect the text to answer.

THE INDEPENDENT

British schools import China's teachers for lessons in "language of tomorrow"

All the country's 250 specialist language schools have been told by a government adviser that they should put Mandarin on the curriculum as "the language of tomorrow". Sir Cyril Taylor, chairman of the Specialist Schools and Academies Trust, said it should be seen as the key language for future generations to learn – replacing European languages. The trust, which represents 90 per cent of England's 2,950 state secondary schools, has clinched a deal with the Chinese government, which will send 200 teachers a year over to the UK to teach Mandarin in schools. Pupil exchanges are also being arranged, Sir Cyril revealed at a meeting of the Commons Select Committee on Education yesterday. He told MPs: "I want all language colleges to be teaching Mandarin. It is a strategic world language. The difficulty in the past has been getting Chinese teachers. However, exchanges between our schools and Chinese schools will help to change that. We learn from them and they learn from us."

Around 4,000 pupils in the UK are studying GCSE Chinese. However, most of them are of Chinese origin and Sir Cyril wants to extend its take-up. Richard Cairns, headmaster of Brighton College – the independent school which became the first school in the country to make the language compulsory for all pupils and introduced it to youngsters from the age of three – said he believed it would replace German in the "pecking order" of languages. Sir Cyril added: "The state of modern language teaching in this country means we need to do a lot more to promote it. I'd like to see all language colleges having Mandarin on the curriculum as soon as possible and I'd like to extend it to a number of other schools as well." In his government inquiry into language teaching, Lord Dearing successfully argued that ministers should drop the requirement for all schools to teach a European language from the ages of 11 and 14. Instead,

2 **government adviser** – Regierungsberater(in)
4 **curriculum** – Lehrplan
11 **to clinch a deal** – eine Vereinbarung treffen
21 **to make the language compulsory** – eine Sprache verpflichtend machen
23 **pecking order** – Hackordnung

they should be allowed to include Mandarin, Arabic and Urdu on the list of languages that could be taught.
Answering questions from MPs, Sir Cyril also called for schools to use a lottery to determine admissions if they were oversubscribed. He said he would like to see all specialist schools and academies introduce "fair banding" – taking an equal number of pupils from each of several different ability bands. "If a school is oversubscribed, random allocation could be used," he added. Brighton became the first authority in the country to plan the introduction of ballots earlier this year – but the proposal prompted an outcry from parents who believed their children could be denied a place even if they lived near the school.
Sir Cyril argued, though, that it was fair and was already being practised successfully by the Haberdashers' Aske's Academy in Lewisham, south London. He also said that many of the country's brightest pupils were being denied the chance to succeed at A-level – because they had to switch school at 16. "Half of our secondary schools are for 11 to 16-year-olds," he said. "Only 20 per cent of the very able children get three A grades at A-level if they move school at 16." He said schools should work in partnership in their neighbourhoods to ensure post-16 courses for all pupils locally. (561 words)

32 **admission** – Aufnahme (an einer Schule)
33 **fair banding** – Zuordnungsprinzip von Schülern zu Schulen durch ein Testsystem in verschiedenen Kompetenzbereichen
35 **over-subscribed** – *hier:* mehr Anmeldungen als freie Plätze
35 **random allocation** – Zuweisung nach dem Zufallsprinzip
36 **ballot** – Abstimmung
42 **to switch school** – die Schule wechseln

2 Comprehension

a) Which of your five questions from task 1 b) can be answered now?

b) Ask your partner questions about specific information in the text. Your partner has to answer the question and also indicate the line where the correct answer can be found. Example:
How many GCSE students are studying Chinese at the moment?
4,000 GCSE students in the UK are studying Chinese at the moment.
This can be found in line 18 of the text.

.298

3 Mediation → Mediation, p. 343

Prepare a German summary of the text for your school magazine in which you focus on the decision to introduce the Chinese language Mandarin.

.298

4 Analysis → Text analysis, p. 326

Analyse the use of quotes and reported speech in the text and explain its effect on the reader.

5 Text production: A letter to the headmaster → Writing a personal letter, p. 331

As a German living in the UK, you are a parent of a 12-year-old boy attending a specialist language school in an English town. As a result of the *Specialist Schools and Academies Trust* strategy, the school has decided to replace German with Mandarin. Write a letter to the headmaster in which you either criticise or welcome this decision.

6 Making a poster → Presentation, p. 362

Design a poster for an advertising campaign for the *Specialist Schools and Academies Trust* strategy to put Mandarin on the curriculum of the country's specialist language schools. Present your posters to the class and decide which one you like best.

C Language and immigration

1 Before you read
What difficulties might immigrants face if they cannot speak the language of the country they move to? Make a list with a partner and report back to the class.

- 0 **to raise the bar** – *(idiom)* die Messlatte höher legen
- 2 **prospect** – Aussicht, Perspektive
- 2 **policy** – Strategie, Richtlinie
- 3 **to target sb.** – sich jdn zur Zielgruppe nehmen
- 3 **favoured** – bevorzugt
- 4 **fluency** – Flüssigkeit
- 4 **requirement** – Anforderung
- 5 **prospective** – zukünftig
- 5 **to tilt** – neigen
- 6 **pattern** – Muster
- 9 **to gain entry** – eingelassen werden
- 9 **proposed** – geplant
- 10 **to apply to sb.** – für jdn gelten
- 13 **to account for** – ausmachen
- 14 **roughly** – ungefähr
- 17 **to aim at** – zielen auf
- 18 **outcome** – Ergebnis
- 21 **to decline** – abnehmen
- 23 **decade** – Jahrzehnt
- 23 **meanwhile** – mittlerweile
- 24 **predictor (for)** – Anzeichen (für)
- 28 **striking** – auffallend
- 28 **shift** – Verschiebung, Verlagerung
- 29 **to anticipate** – erwarten
- 32 **intake** – Aufnahme

theguardian

News | Sport | Comment | Culture | Business | Money | Life&Style | Travel | Environment

Comment is free > Canada   Search [ ] GO

Canada to raise language bar

Requiring new immigrants to speak English or French to a higher level will improve their economic prospects say ministers but others fear the policy will target favoured nationalities.

The Canadian government's plan to raise language fluency requirements for prospective skilled immigrants has some experts concerned that it may tilt migration patterns toward the English-speaking world.

Canada's immigration minister Jason Kenney said earlier this year that some immigration applicants will soon have to demonstrate high levels of English or French fluency to gain entry to Canada. The proposed new requirements would apply to the largest class of immigrants, the federal skilled worker category, which accounts for nearly 100,000 of the roughly 250,000 immigrants who come to Canada every year. The decision is aimed at improving economic outcomes for immigrants in the country, which have been steadily declining over the last 30 years. Today a new immigrant earns only about 60% of the wages of a similarly educated Canadian-born citizen, compared with nearly 90% three decades ago. Meanwhile a flood of research has shown that language ability is one of the best predictors of rapid integration and economic success.

But Naomi Alboim, a public policy professor at Ontario's Queen's University and a former provincial deputy minister of citizenship, expects the policy will also have other consequences. The most striking will be a significant shift in source countries, she said. Alboim anticipates a decline in the number of migrants from China, for example, and a rise in the number from English-speaking countries.

Such a shift would make Canada's immigrant intake more similar to Australia's. The Australian government raised immigrant language requirements over the last decade and its immigrants have fared better economically than those in Canada. But Australia also receives proportionally larger numbers from English-speaking countries such as the UK, Ireland and New Zealand, who tend to integrate more quickly.

"A focus on language does make eminent sense. But I think we have to be careful about how high we are setting the bar and whether that is going to exclude a whole group of people who can contribute to a very significant degree with a little bit of assistance," Alboim said.

"We don't need to restrict our entire federal skilled worker intake to only those who have a high level of language, because that can develop over time." […]

While anyone can, in theory, learn a language, English or French fluency is more common in some parts of the world and Canada may be taking a step, intentional or not, towards targeting source countries.

Debbie Douglas, executive director of the Ontario Council of Agencies Serving Immigrants, fears that the new policy will screen out people from the global south. "We can't discriminate against folks who don't sound like us. That might mean more propping up of language teaching [for new immigrants] but that's a very small price to pay for helping people contribute to building our country," Douglas said. […]

Kenney has said it is hard to predict what impact the new language requirements might have on source countries, as they tend to ebb and flow for a variety of reasons, including global economic conditions as well as selection criteria. His goal is to create a more flexible language grid that will contribute to improving the economic fortunes of those who are selected. […]

While an emphasis on language might produce better economic outcomes for immigrants in the short term, it could also have other effects. Canada may struggle to find enough people with sufficient levels of fluency to maintain its very high immigration levels, for example. A sudden shift in the attainability of immigration may have an impact on Canada's ties to a country such as China and studies have shown that trade ties increase through immigration. […]

(628 words)

34 **to fare well** – *(ugs.)* gut fahren
38 **eminent** – hervorragend
40 **to contribute** – beitragen
42 **entire** – ganz
48 **to screen out** – aussortieren
49 **to discriminate against sb.** – jdn diskriminieren
50 **to prop up** – (finanziell) stützen
53 **impact** – Auswirkung
56 **grid** – Netz
57 **fortune** – Schicksal
58 **emphasis** – Betonung, Schwerpunkt
60 **to struggle** – sich schwer tun
60 **sufficient** – ausreichend
60 **to maintain** – aufrechterhalten
61 **attainability** – Erreichbarkeit
62 **tie** – Bindung

2 Comprehension: Table completion
Read the text. In a table, collect all the pieces of information the text gives you on the following:

a) reasons why the Canadian government plans to raise the 'language bar",

b) positive effects of this plan,

c) negative effects of this plan.

3 Analysis → Describing cartoons, p. 340
Describe and analyse the cartoon and relate it to the text.

D Whose English is it anyway?

1 Before you listen

"I find children's manipulation of language very exciting. They mix two words up in the bat of an eyelid," she said. "It's incorrect to mix it up but who says it's incorrect? English is a mongrel language anyway."

a) Looking at this quote and the headline *Schoolchildren now speak "The Queen's Hinglish"*, guess what the listening text is about.

b) What is your opinion about the statement: "It's incorrect to mix it up but who says it's incorrect?"

A 2.4 p. 298 **2 Listening comprehension: Schoolchildren now speak "The Queen's Hinglish"**

→ Listening, p. 319

Copy and complete the following table.

Definition of Queen's Hinglish	Development of Queen's Hinglish	Future of Hinglish

A 2.6 **3 Listening comprehension: Whose English is it anyway?**

→ Listening, p. 319, Mediation, p. 343

Listen to the recording. Make notes and summarise them in a German text concentrating on what David Crystal and Bill Bryson say about the aspect of power.

p. 299 **4 Analysis** → Describing cartoons, p. 340

Describe and analyse the cartoon.

E Shakespearian English

1 Shakespeare: Famous quotes and themes

a) The following quotes by Shakespeare are world famous. Match them with the sentences in the right column to express what they mean.

1.	Give every man thy ear, but few thy voice.	A	There is something wrong here.
2.	To be, or not to be: that is the question.	B	Making a fuss about something which is not important.
3.	All the world's a stage, And all the men and women merely players.	C	This is the plain truth.
4.	This is the short and the long of it.	D	Some things look more valuable than they really are.
5.	All that glitters is not gold.	E	Life is just a play.
6.	All's well that ends well.	F	Anything is OK as long as it turns out well in the end.
7.	Much ado about nothing.	G	Listening is often wiser than talking.
8.	Something is rotten in the state of Denmark.	H	Is an unhappy life better than death?

to make a fuss about sth. – viel Aufhebens um etw. machen
to glitter – glitzern
plain truth – reine Wahrheit
ado – Getue, Aufwand

b) In his plays, Shakespeare repeatedly focussed on the following themes. What do they mean in your own words?

The corrupting power of too much ambition • The impossibility of certainty • Fate versus free will, the inevitability of fate • The possibility of justice in the world • Self-interest versus love • The nature of evil • Love as a cause for suffering, love as a cause of death

c) Which of these themes do you consider important today?

Apart from his dramas, William Shakespeare also wrote many sonnets. Sonnet 116 is one of his most famous.

Sonnet 116

Let me not to the marriage of true minds
Admit impediments. Love is not love
Which alters when it alteration finds,
Or bends with the remover to remove:
O no! it is an ever-fixed mark
That looks on tempests and is never shaken;
It is the star to every wandering bark,
Whose worth's unknown, although his height be taken.
Love's not Time's fool, though rosy lips and cheeks
Within his bending sickle's compass come:
Love alters not with his brief hours and weeks,
But bears it out even to the edge of doom.
If this be error and upon me proved,
I never writ, nor no man ever loved.

2 Vocabulary → Working with a dictionary, p. 353
Look up the following words appearing in the sonnet in an English-English dictionary and explain their meaning to a partner.

impediment (l. 2) • to alter (l. 3) • mark (l. 5) • tempest (l. 6) • to wander (l. 7) • bark (l. 7) • sickle (l. 10) • compass (l. 10)

3 Comprehension
A sonnet can be divided into four parts. Find the parts in the sonnet on page 99 and write down what each one is about.

4 Analysis

a) Instead of directly stating what love is, the speaker uses a number of metaphors to define love. List and explain them.

b) Analyse the structure of the sonnet and explain how this supports its main theme.

5 Shakespeare goes interactive
In *Macbeth*, Shakespeare tells a story of prophecy, ambition, murder and fate. Macbeth is prophesied to one day become King of Scotland. In order to speed things up, he and his wife kill King Duncan, but in the end they have to pay for their crime.

theguardian

News | Sport | Comment | Culture | Business | Money | Life&Style | Travel | Environment

Comment is free > Literature   Search [ ] GO

Schools test 'interactive graphic novel' version of Macbeth

Classical Comics is set to launch a multimedia version of the play for children and teenagers, featuring the voices of Juliet Stevenson and Derek Jacobi

Classical Comics' Interactive Macbeth

The latest attempt to get an audience of multimedia-savvy schoolchildren and teens engaged with Shakespeare is an interactive graphic novel version of the play, complete with voiceovers by Derek Jacobi and Juliet Stevenson.

Classical Comics has done well with a series of graphic novels of famous titles (including Jane Eyre, A Christmas Carol and Frankenstein) which it launched two years ago, but the publisher decided that the next step in its quest to make classic stories accessible would be to bring the text alive. Its new version of Macbeth, which it will preview to schools this week before launching in June, takes the artwork of comicbook artist Jon Haward from its original graphic novel and animates it, adding audio from Jacobi and Stevenson.

"That which hath made them drunk hath made me bold: what hath quenched them hath given me fire," proclaims Stevenson as Lady Macbeth, descending a stone staircase framed by gargoyles as two dogs growl over a piece of meat. And later, "I have

4 **multimedia-savvy** – bewandert in Multi-Media
6 **voiceovers** – Synchronstimmen
9 **quest** – Plan, Unterfangen
14 **bold** – mutig, entschlossen
14 **to quench** – Durst löschen
16 **gargoyles** – Wasserspeier

Generations of students have found it difficult to access the original text of what is considered to be one of the world's greatest works of literature. However, there have been modern versions that try to get Shakespeare across to today's audience.

a) If you were asked to make a 400 year old drama more interesting for students, how would you do it? Think about the media you would use, the language, costumes, etc.

b) Go online and watch a demo version of the interactive graphic novel of Macbeth, which was created by *Classical Comics*, a UK publisher. What do you think about it?

6 Comprehension

a) Read the text and outline the reasons for deciding to publish the interactive graphic novel version of Macbeth.

b) In your own words, briefly describe the features of the interactive graphic novel version of Macbeth.

7 Comment

"Publishing Shakespeare dramas as interactive graphic novels helps to get younger readers interested in the work of Shakespeare." Comment.

8 Project → Hotspot 4, p. 103

done the deed," gasps Jacobi as the Thane of Cawdor, gripping two bloody daggers. "Didst thou not hear a noise?"

"It's been in the planning for a while," said Classical Comics managing director Clive Bryant of the Macbeth project. "We thought of it at the beginning of last year and it's taken this long to get it together. Having Derek Jacobi and Juliet Stevenson involved was incredible – we were recording it in a small studio in north London, which had a large contact list, which was how we managed to secure them. It just adds that extra dimension to it: hearing Macbeth with Derek Jacobi in the classroom – you can't get much better than that."

He visualises teachers using the interactive graphic novel (which comes in three versions: the original Shakespearean text, a contemporary rendering, and a quick, reduced version for younger viewers) on the whiteboard for a whole class. Alternatively groups of students might discuss the novel around a computer. Readers can choose to view one panel at a time or sit back and watch in "movie mode", with context notes provided explaining the Shakespearean language.

Jacobi called the concept "truly inspirational, creating, as it does so magnificently, an accessible and fascinating mix of visual and audible drama ... The stage and the page brought vividly to life". "The artwork of Jon Haward is both dramatically compelling and beautifully illustrative," he added. "His pictures illuminate the words to perfection and bring these great works leaping to mind and eye. This format is immediate, vital, energetic and engaging."

If the venture proves popular with schools, Classical Comics is planning a whole range of other interactive graphic novels, including Romeo and Juliet, Julius Caesar and A Midsummer Night's Dream, Bryant said. (497 words)

27 **rendering** – *hier:* Ausgabe, Version
30 **panel** – Blende
35 **compelling** – fesselnd
36 **to leap** – springen

Working with words

These strategies work for all topics. The more words you know for one aspect / idea, the more flexible you become. Looking up words in a thesaurus will certainly help.

a) Synonyms and short definitions

For the following words that have to do with the English language in use, find at least two words or a short definition with the same or a similar meaning, e.g. global: wordwide, all over the world, all-encompassing.

immigrant • lingua franca • negotiations • globalisation • hybrid language • international • skills • technology • texting • abbreviations • multicultural

b) Language functions

For the following verbs, collect as many words with the same language function as possible, e.g. outline: to show, to illustrate, to sketch, to draft.

say • refer to • show • explain • agree • argue • believe • convince • detail • report

c) Odd one out

Find the word which does not belong in the list. Give reasons for your choice.

1. Pidgin • Globish • Hinglish
2. texter • sender • writer
3. communicate • chat • socialise
4. abbreviation • text message • email
5. global • international • multinational
6. language barrier • misunderstanding • unknown words
7. working language • mother tongue • native language
8. communication channel • blog • post

d) Find the words to fill the gaps. Pay attention to the correct forms of the verbs.

misunderstand • combine • discourage • well • abstract • decrease • advantage • polite • difficult • temporary

Some speakers find it very difficult to express **1** ideas in a foreign language.

Misunderstandings **2** learners of a foreign language.

Even when speaking a lingua franca it is very important to remain **3** .

If you learn an international language **4** , you can easily communicate with a variety of people.

In international meetings it is essential not to be **5** .

Therefore, speaking more than one foreign language can be an **6** .

The influence of the English language on other languages is not just **7** .

Many students of English find Shakespeare's dramas **8** to understand.

Children often **9** words from two languages and unknowingly create hybrid expressions.

The percentage of websites in English has **10** .

1 Research project: The influence of English → Presentation, p. 362
Do some research and prepare a talk about the influence of English on German computer/technology language. Make sure to give examples to illustrate what you want to say. Include your own opinion about this trend.

2 Research project: Anglicisms → Internet research, p. 358
Do some research about anglicisms (a word that is borrowed from English to be used in another language, i.e. *Wir müssen das Wording überdenken.*) or the blending of two languages for special effects in advertising, like in the example. Prepare a talk in which you outline how these adverts work. Give further examples and also state your opinion about them.

3 Research project: Lingua francas → Internet research, p. 358

a) Go online and do some research about the following lingua francas and pidgins: Volapük, Esperanto and Interlingua. Present your findings to the class.

b) Go online and do some research on the history of Pidgin English. Include video examples (e.g. Pidgin English spoken on the Solomon Islands, Hawaian Pidgin, Nigerian Pidgin, etc.) in your presentation for the class.

4 Project: Shakespeare's plays → Projects and group work, p. 359
Work in groups. Each group chooses one of Shakespeare's plays, collects all relevant information and then prepares a poster about it. Present your poster to the class.

A 2.9

8 **rise** – increase

10 **to coin** – to invent

11 **paralyzed** – unable to move

12 **to plunge ahead** – to carry on without worries

13 **heedless** – without concern for

15 **latter** – *here:* last

18 **maven** – expert

19 **to riff on sth.** – to say sth. which is based on sth. else

31 **drill** – exercise

35 **parlez** *(French)* – speak

36 **codification** – *here:* list

37 **fraction** – very small part

THE CHRISTIAN SCIENCE MONITOR

Search GO

World | USA | Commentary | Business | Environment | Innovation | Science |

'Globish' and the open-sourcing of English

This form of 'English lite' is out from under the control of native speakers; does that matter?

Do you speak Globish – "global English"? Can you stand it when others do? Globish is a much simplified form of English used, especially in business, where neither party is a native speaker of English. Globish is how a Venezuelan talks to a Chinese, or a Turk to an Algerian. Unlike "Spanglish," for instance, it's not a meld of English and something else. And unlike Basic English or Esperanto, Globish arose naturally.

Its rise would seem to illustrate the saying that Britain and the United States are two countries separated by a common language. Jean-Paul Nerrière, the former IBM executive credited with coining the term "Globish," noticed that at his company's international conferences, Americans and Britons would tend to be paralyzed by the endless minor differences between their two brands of English. Meanwhile, people from other parts of the world would plunge ahead into conversation with one another, heedless of their bad grammar and limited vocabulary.

I'm not sure I buy this. Somehow the idea of an American at a conference hesitating to chat up a British contact for fear the latter would say something like "different to" seems unlikely. On the other hand, anyone who has ever traveled outside his or her linguistic comfort zone has probably found how helpful just a few words in a common language can be.

British language maven Robert McCrum has called Globish "the worldwide dialect of the third millennium." A blogger riffing on Mr. McCrum compared Globish to "open source" software – available for anyone to adapt to his own uses. He added, "I think that if Globish were to be defined by the International community as a whole, this would greatly help to abstract the language from the western, English-speaking culture." But language and culture are so closely linked that culture-free language would be like tasteless food or colorless paint. That idea of ownership, however, is important.

"*Anglophones* no longer own English," the Toronto Star quoted Mr. Nerrière as saying last year. "It's now owned by people in Singapore, Ulan Bator, Montevideo, Beijing, and elsewhere." *Anglophone* isn't used very much in American English, but it's common in French and in officially bilingual Canada. Dictionaries tend to define *Anglophone* as simply one who speaks English – never mind whether as native tongue or something else.

I first learned *Anglophone* at summer school at the University of Aix-Marseille in France. For phonetics drills, we were segregated by mother tongue. The idea was that native English speakers face different issues in learning to make the sounds of French than do, say, native speakers of German. So I tend to think of *Anglophone* as meaning specifically one who makes the sounds of English.

This, I suspect, is how Nerrière understands it, too. His book, "Don't Speak English, Parlez Globish," was a bestseller in France. His codification of Globish has a vocabulary of just 1,500 words – only a fraction of the 615,000 or so of the Oxford English Dictionary.

Globish, Iman Kurdi wrote in the Arab News, "is based on short sentences, simple grammar, repetition and the avoidance of complex syntax. It is rather ugly, clumsy and certainly painful to the ears of native English speakers. But," he continued, "it is also democratic and accessible ... It is something to get you by."

Globish isn't pretty. But it works.

(575 words)

1 Comprehension

Read the text and complete the statements (a–e) by choosing the right answer (1, 2, or 3).

a) Globish …
1. is a simplified form of English spoken by people whose mother tongue isn't English.
2. is limited to speakers from Asian countries only.
3. is the language which is used by native speakers of English and native speakers of other languages.

b) Globish has become popular because …
1. it is too hard for non-native speakers of English to learn the language.
2. English in different varieties has often led to misunderstandings in business negotiations.
3. it is a mix of English and something else.

c) Globish is called …
1. the nationwide dialect of the third millennium.
2. the worldwide dialect of the third millennium.
3. the worldwide language of the third millennium.

d) Globish is compared to open source software because …
1. it is defined by the international community as a whole.
2. it can be used by everyone and be adapted to each person's uses.
3. it helps to abstract the language from the English-speaking culture.

e) Using global English is easy because …
1. grammar knowledge is not essential.
2. long sentences are simplified.
3. simple grammar and short sentences are used.

2 Analysis

→ Describing diagrams, p. 341

Describe and analyse the diagram "Which two languages, apart from your mother tongue, do you think children should learn?"

3 Comment

Taking into consideration the text and the diagram, comment on whether children should learn one or two foreign languages or rather Globish.

Which two languages, apart from your mother tongue, do you think children should learn?

	English	French	German	Spanish
EU25	**77%**	**33%**	**28%**	**19%**
BE	88%	50%	7%	9%
CZ	89%	9%	66%	4%
DK	94%	13%	62%	13%
DE	89%	45%	3%	16%
EL	96%	34%	50%	3%
ES	85%	44%	14%	4%
FR	91%	2%	24%	45%
IE	3%	64%	42%	35%
IT	84%	34%	17%	17%
CY	98%	49%	19%	2%
LU	59%	83%	43%	2%
HU	85%	4%	73%	3%
NL	90%	22%	40%	21%
AT	84%	29%	2%	10%
PL	90%	7%	69%	1%
PT	90%	60%	8%	7%
SI	96%	6%	69%	3%
SK	87%	7%	75%	3%
SE	99%	17%	35%	31%
UK	5%	71%	34%	39%
BG	87%	13%	49%	5%
HR	82%	5%	69%	2%
RO	64%	34%	17%	7%
TR	72%	12%	52%	1%

= **First language**

= **Second language**

Source: European Union, Eurobarometer

Topic 2.2
The United States – then and now

c63e6w

A

"The American Dream is ownership … a house, a car, a vacation home and, even better, your own business."
Mario Batali, famous chef

B

"The American Dream is something that every immigrant brought to this country, as my parents did, and that is the ability to go as far as you can in life, limited only by your own dreams and willingness to work hard. And above all, the American Dream for these folks meant that your children will have the opportunity to do better than you will."
General Colin Powell, former Secretary of State

C

Getting started

1 Think – pair – share

a) Look at the pictures and compile a list of five aspects you consider typically American.

b) Compare your list with that of a partner and agree on five aspects between you.

c) Share your results with another pair and agree on five aspects again. Was it easy to agree? Which of the ideas do you consider stereotypes rather than fact?

"The American Dream is equal protection under the law and equal opportunity. The American Dream does not promise equal results, but it does promise equal opportunity."
The Rev. Jesse Jackson, civil rights activist and political leader

folks *(coll.)* – Leute
attainable – erreichbar
to impel – antreiben
to achieve sth. – etw. erreichen

"The American Dream, whether attainable or not, is to have freedom, freedom in all things. To go as far as ambition impels us, in work, in play, and religion and even in love."
Maya Angelou, author and civil rights activist

"The American Dream is about fulfilling your potential to the max. It's not a chase for material goods; it's about learning what inspires you in life and creating a plan to turn it into your life's work. The way to achieve the dream is to follow the plan and pay attention to the details, because it's those details that make or break you."
Tyra Banks, supermodel and host of 'America's Next Top Model'

2 **From the quotations, filter out the basic idea of the American Dream. Where do these famous Americans agree and where do they disagree? Arrange your answers in a word web.**

3 **In the Declaration of Independence, America's founding fathers declared that God had given us all the right to "Life, Liberty and the Pursuit of Happiness". Discuss in class what these rights mean to you.** → Discussions, p. 344

Word bank

proud • Stars and Stripes • front lawn • rodeo • conservative • religious • extreme views • preacher • protest • demonstration • funeral • coffin • casualty of war • vanity • plastic surgery • appearance • superficial

A The history of the United States

12,000 BC The people we now call Native Americans came from Siberia to Alaska. Recent discoveries suggest, however, that the first humans to arrive in America came from Southeast Asia by boat long before that.

1492 AD Christopher Columbus wanted to sail to India by a new route around the globe. He reached some islands in the Caribbean instead and thought he was in India. That is why he called the natives "Indians". Soon after 1492, the European powers, especially Spain, started to explore and colonize America.

1607 The first permanent English settlement in America was founded: Jamestown in Virginia.

1620 The ship "The Mayflower" brought 102 people (many of them Puritans – the Pilgrims) from England to America. They came for religious reasons. To this day, Americans celebrate the Pilgrims' first harvest as "Thanksgiving" every November.

1675 – 1676 There had always been conflicts between European settlers and Indians, but most of the time there was peace during the early years. King Philip's War in 1675 – 76 (Philip was an Indian chief) was the first serious war and started two centuries of bloody warfare between whites and Native Americans.

1775 – 1783 On July 4, 1776, the American Colonies declared independence from Britain because they were unhappy about the way the mother country treated them. With the help of the French, the American revolutionary army, led by George Washington, won the War of Independence against Britain. Then delegates from the former 13 colonies signed the Constitution of the United States. Washington later became the first president of the US.

1791 The Bill of Rights was added to the Constitution because references to human and civil rights were missing.

1803 After having bought large parts of North America from the French (the Louisiana Purchase), President Jefferson sent the famous explorers Lewis and Clark out West to see what he had bought. As more and more settlers came, the Native Americans were pushed further and further West.

1861 – 1865 The North and the South of the US drifted apart: the South was a slave-holding, agricultural society, the North was more industrialized. Because of these differences, the southern states wanted to be separate, and a terrible Civil War followed (1861 – 65). The victory of the North saved the unity of the United States and freed the slaves in the South.

1869 After the Civil War, the Industrial Revolution spread across the US. The railroad, which was extremely important for linking the different regions of the huge country, was part of it. In 1869 it was finally possible to travel non-stop from East to West by train.

1914–1918 The US Army entered World War I in 1917 and helped to end the war. By that time the US had become one of the leading industrial countries in the world.

1929–1938 The US, together with the rest of the world, entered a period of economic depression. A radical shift in economic policy (President Franklin D. Roosevelt's so-called "New Deal") helped to overcome the crisis.

1939–1945 When Japan attacked the US at Pearl Harbor (Hawaii) in 1941, the US entered World War II to fight against Japan, Germany and Italy. After the war, the US decided to help reconstruct Europe again (with the Marshall Plan) because it needed the western allies against the Soviet Union.

1946–1993 The US and the Soviet Union were rival superpowers until the Soviet Union collapsed in 1993. Several times their "Cold War" almost turned into a nuclear war.

1950s and 60s Rosa Parks and Martin Luther King Jr., among others, protested against the unjust treatment of African Americans. Eventually, protests grew so strong that the policy of segregation came to an end. This, however, didn't mean the end of race problems in the US.

1964–1973 The US fought on the side of South Vietnam against Communist North Vietnam, which was supported by the Soviet Union. In 1975, two years after the US had withdrawn from a war it could not win, North Vietnam invaded South Vietnam and the war was over.

2001 With the terrorist attacks on the World Trade Center in NYC and on the Pentagon in Washington on September 11, Americans realized how vulnerable they were. Fighting terrorism with military means turned out to be very problematic, especially the American invasion of Iraq in 2003. Many of America's allies were against this war.

2009 Barack Obama was elected the first black president of the US.

(756 words)

1 Look at the pictures. Which events in the timeline do they represent?

2 Presentation: A market place → Presentation, p. 362
The class chooses at least six topics from the timeline that are worth considering in more detail (e.g. Native Americans, Bill of Rights, Civil War, 9/11, etc.) and then splits up into groups. Each group works on one of the topics and prepares an informative poster. Display the posters in a market place.

B The American Dream

1 Before you read
What do you associate with the American Dream? Discuss your ideas with your partner.

7 **reliable** – zuverlässig
12 **requisite** – unerlässlich
13 **mobster** – Mitglied der Mafia
13 **to dishonor** – entehren
29 **self-evident** – selbstverständlich
29 **to endow** *(formal)* – ausstatten
30 **inalienable** – unveräußerlich
36 **betrayal** – Verrat, Treuebruch
36 **to hit home** – ankommen (Botschaft)

The American Dream

The Founding Fathers sign the Declaration of Independence, 1776

I'm going to start out today by going back just over a month ago. It's Sunday night, April 16 – the sixth episode of the sixth season of "The Sopranos" is on. Vito Spatafore – the most reliable and loyal captain in the New Jersey crime family run by Tony Soprano – is on the run. The story is out – Vito has a wife, two kids, the requisite mistress, but he's been seen in a gay bar, dressed like the biker in the Village People. The other mobsters want him dead; he's dishonored them all.

Heading north, Vito's been on the road for hours. His cellphone rings; he throws it out the window. He has no idea where he is. His car breaks down. He makes it into the next town, finds an inn, puts his gun under his pillow.

The next day he wakes up in a little New Hampshire village, where gay people walk the streets without fear. In a diner, looks pass between Vito and the counterman. A male couple comes in, sits down, and begins speaking a language Vito has never before heard in the light of day, only in the dark. He's confused: What does it mean to be in a place where, for the first time in your life, you might feel at home in your own skin? Could that even be right?

He goes into an antique shop. He picks up a vase, and the gay owner compliments him on his taste: "That's the most expensive item in the store." But then Vito sees something else, probably the cheapest thing in the store: an old New Hampshire license plate. "Live Free or Die" reads the slogan across the top. […]

Vito stares. "Live Free or Die" – it's as if the metal can talk. It's just a license plate; for him it might as well be the Declaration of Independence, ringing its bell. "We hold these truths to be self-evident, that all men are created equal, that they are endowed by their Creator with certain inalienable Rights, that among these are Life, Liberty, and the pursuit of Happiness," Jefferson wrote – and suddenly, as it has for so many for so long, through that license plate the Declaration is speaking to Vito as if it were addressed to him. "Live free or die" – what if all this, the shock in his face says, was meant for him as much as anyone?

It's one of those signal moments when the whole weight of the national story, its promises and its betrayals, hits home – leaving the citizen at once part of a community and completely alone. It doesn't matter that, well, yes, of course, on the fourth of July,

1776, when the Declaration of Independence was presented, everyone understood that all men meant men, not women; whites, not blacks; Christians, not Jews or Hindi or heathen; decent people, not Sodomites. The idea that "all men are created equal" was not a "self-evident truth", Sen. John Pettit said on the floor of the Senate in 1853: it was "a self-evident lie". It was in the midst of the debates over the Kansas-Nebraska Act; Pettit was arguing for voiding the Missouri Compromise of 1820 and opening the territories to slavery. It was a debate: "The great declaration cost our forefathers too dear," Sen. Benjamin Franklin Wade of Ohio replied to Pettit, "to be so lightly thrown away by their children." [...] "Life, liberty, and the pursuit of happiness" – it's what the rest of the world understands by America when America isn't forcing the rest of the world to understand America as something else. "We are caught in a world of limits where there's no such thing as the self-made man," said a graduate student in France last week; Claire de la Vigne was speaking to a New York Times reporter about the French university system, where doors are made to be closed, not opened. "We are never taught the idea of the American Dream, where everything is possible," she said. It's what Americans understand by America, when the facts of everyday American life somehow recede, and an idea of America takes their place. [...]

There's a way in which you can see every American story as a version of the Declaration of Independence: every story an attempt to make it true, or prove it a lie. In 1941, Henry Luce called the 20th century "the American century"; he meant this was the century when America became a colossus from which the rest of the world would have to step back, trembling with awe. But if that American century was truly American, you can almost see Lincoln reminding us – or, if not Lincoln, the doorkeeper at Independence Hall – that the story of the American century is the story of all sorts of previously excluded, marginalized, scorned, despised, ignored or enslaved people – laborers, women, African-Americans, Asian Americans, Jews, Latinos, gay men and women – entering into full citizenship and full participation in national life. If not full citizenship, a more complete citizenship than even Lincoln or the doorkeeper could in fact have imagined – as, again and again, decade after decade, those echoing words of the Declaration of Independence sounded as if for the first time. (888 words)

by Greil Marcus, delivered as a commencement address at the University of California at Berkeley, 2006

43 **to void** – ungültig machen, auflösen
53 **to recede** – sich entfernen
57 **colossus** – Koloss
58 **to tremble with awe** – vor Ehrfurcht erschauern
60 **marginalized** – an den Rand gedrängt
61 **scorned** – verachtet
61 **despised** – verschmäht

2 Comprehension
What are the main ideas of the Declaration of Independence? How does Vito Spatafore's story compare to the promises made in the Declaration of Independence?

3 Mediation
What meaning does the fulfillment of the Declaration's promise have for those who have previously suffered injustice? Answer in complete German sentences.

4 Vocabulary → Taking notes, p. 352
Make a list of words in this text that you can use to define the American Dream and use them to write a short definition.

5 Comment
"We are caught in a world of limits where there's no such thing as the self-made man." (l. 48). Do you agree with the French student?

6 Research project → Hotspot 1, p. 119

C The American political system

The voters

direct vote

indirect vote (via state electors)

Legislative
- Senate
- House of Representatives

The legislative branch (also known as Congress)
Congress has two chambers, the Senate and the House of Representatives.

- Senate:
  100 Senators, elected for a 6-year term, one third are elected every two years.
- House of Representatives:
  435 members, elected every two years. States with a high population have more representatives than states with a low population.

The House and Senate can reject each other's bills. Congress decides on the federal budget (how federal money is spent).

The Capitol, Washington D.C., the seat of Congress

The President suggests legislation and can veto laws passed by Congress.

Congress can pass laws over the President's veto by a two-thirds majority. Congress ratifies treaties and declares war.

The Court can declare laws unconstitutional.

The President appoints federal judges.

The Senate must confirm the President's judicial appointments.

The Court can declare presidential acts unconstitutional.

Executive
- President
- Cabinet

The executive branch
The President is elected every four years and can hold office for two full terms only. The President is Head of State and Commander-in-Chief of the armed forces. The President appoints a Cabinet and the Cabinet is approved by the Senate. Cabinet members need not be members of Congress.

The US President's office, the Oval Office

Judicial
- Supreme Court
- Federal Courts

The judicial branch
The Supreme Court has nine judges. They are appointed for life. The Supreme Court is responsible for seeing that the Constitution is upheld and that laws that are made are allowed under the Constitution.
There are eleven US Courts of Appeals and 90 US District Courts.

The seal of the US Supreme Court

The electoral process

US citizens over the age of 18 who are registered to vote can do so, but voters must register themselves as there is no automatic registration. At a general election all registered voters vote for the candidate of their choice and the candidate who gets the most votes is the winner (winner-takes-all system).

How the President is elected

The presidential elections are the most important elections of the US. They are held every four years and there are six basic stages.

Stage 1: Who can run for president?

US-born citizens over the age of 35 who had lived in the US for at least 14 years can decide to run for the post of president. Usually there are a number of applicants from the main parties as well as independent candidates.

Stage 2: Primaries

These are state-wide (not nation-wide) elections held between January and June of the election year in which voters choose delegates who will go to the party's national convention to finally select the party's presidential candidate. At the primaries the ordinary party members indicate by selecting their delegates who they would prefer as their party's presidential candidate.

Stage 3: National conventions

Republican and Democratic conventions are held in July or August and at the end of these 4-day meetings with speeches, political declarations and colourful shows, the party's official candidate for presidency is chosen by the delegates and officially announced. Then the candidates start an intensified campaigning tour through all US states.

Stage 4: General election

Election day is the Tuesday following the first Monday in November. Voters cast their vote for their favourite presidential candidate. In fact, the voters are selecting the members of the electoral college, who will finally vote for a certain candidate.

Stage 5: The Electoral College

The number of electors a state has depends on the number of members it has in Congress (e.g. 47 for a big and densely populated state like California, three for the District of Columbia). On the Monday following the second Wednesday in December each elector casts one vote for a presidential candidate. The candidate who wins the majority of electoral votes becomes president (at least 270 out of 538).

Stage 6: Inauguration

The results of the Electoral College vote is declared on January 6 and the newly elected president and vice president are sworn in on January 20 following the November election.

National convention of the Republican Party

12 **applicant** – Bewerber(in)
13 **primary** – *hier:* Vorwahl
16 **convention** – *hier:* Parteitag
18 **delegate** – Vertreter(in), Repräsentant(in)
30 **Electoral College** – Wahlmännergremium
33 **District of Columbia** – Regierungssitz (Washington)
37 **inauguration** – Amtseinsetzung, (feierliche) Ernennung

1 **If you are a party member in the US and want to become president, you have to carry out two successful campaigns. Explain and illustrate the differences in these campaigns.**

2 **Research project** → Hotspot 2, p. 119

D Racial (in)equality

1 Before you read
Make assumptions about the content of the article based on the headline. Share your ideas with a partner.

5 **to ring out** – schallen
10 **eerie** – gespenstisch
13 **irreversibly** – unumkehrbar
19 **uncanny** – unheimlich
19 **premonition** – Vorahnung
21 **to reverberate** – nachhallen
25 **to ascend** – aufsteigen
32 **to detoxify** – entgiften
36 **to expel** – ausschließen

theguardian

40 years after King's death, Jackson hails first steps into promised land

Jesse Jackson has no difficulty remembering his last conversation with Martin Luther King. The leader of the civil rights movement and his young apprentice were preparing to go to dinner with a local pastor. The shot rang out a second later. "Next thing I heard," says Jackson, "someone was saying 'Get low! Get low!' The police were coming towards us with guns drawn. I remember crawling to the steps. There was blood everywhere, and a photographer scooped up a cup of it. It was eerie."

Those few moments, 40 years ago tomorrow, are carved not only into Jackson's memory but into the collective narrative of America. They certainly changed his life, driving an already keen activist, then 26, deeply and irreversibly into the pursuit of racial justice. "It put on us a burden not to stop, to say we must not allow one bullet to kill a whole movement," he says now. But in a wider sense they changed everyone else's reality too. They were what he calls "a defining moment in American history".

Jackson was on stage with King in the Mason Temple in Memphis the night before he was assassinated, when King made his famous "mountaintop" speech. King talked with almost uncanny premonition about the "threats out there" and what might happen to him at the hands of "some of our sick white brothers".

"It doesn't matter with me now," King concluded in words that will forever reverberate, "because I've been to the mountaintop … And I've looked over. And I've seen the promised land."

Forty years on, Jesse Jackson is still weighing up how far up the mountain African Americans have ascended. As someone who has stood at the front of that march for four decades, Jackson believes that there remains some way to go. Politically, he says, African Americans have come a long way. In 1965 there were about 300 black elected politicians in America; now there are some 10,000.

He sees a substantial step forward too in other areas of public life, notably entertainment and athletics. "Take the Super Bowl between the [New York] Giants and the [New England] Patriots. Millions of people watched the game and race never came up. It was the red team versus the blue team. That has detoxified racial relations."

But there are several headline figures that tell a very different story. A quarter of African Americans live in poverty, compared with 8% of whites; seven out of 10 black boys drop out before finishing high school; in several states such as New Jersey black children are 60 times more likely to be expelled from school than whites; there are more black men in jail than in college; and the most shocking statistic: on average black men die more than six years earlier than their white equivalents.

"People of colour have higher infant mortality rates, shorter life expectancy, greater unemployment, less education. We pay more for less. That is our characteristic 40 years later." Jackson has an explanation for this piercing disparity between the advancement of black people in many areas of public life coupled with stagnation or even deterioration in their overall standards of living. He points out that the legal underpinning of Jim Crow segregation in the South was negated in a series of landmark legal actions starting in 1954. Then the civil rights movement led by King began the process that would remove cultural impediments to black progress. But the issue with which he had only begun to grapple at the time of his death – economic inequalities experienced by black as well as white working-class communities – remains a festering sore. "Yes, blacks have been elected to political office, but the economic problems that King had started to turn to are still there. The result is you get black mayors presiding over the worst inner-cities in America, where jobs are leaving, investment is leaving, guns and drugs are coming; where there are first-class jails and second-class schools." (675 words)

39 **infant mortality** – Säuglingssterblichkeit
41 **piercing** – stechend
41 **disparity** – Ungleichheit
42 **deterioration** – Verschlechterung
43 **to underpin** – untermauern
44 **to negate** – zunichtemachen
46 **impediment** – Hindernis
46 **to grapple with sth.** – sich auseinandersetzen mit
48 **to fester** – eitern
48 **sore** – Wunde

2 Comprehension: True or false?

Read the statements below and decide whether they are true or false. Quote or paraphrase words from the text which confirm or disprove the ideas in the statements.

a) Martin Luther King was assassinated while giving a speech.

b) Jesse Jackson was inspired to devote himself to the fight for racial equality after Martin Luther King was killed.

c) Shortly before his death, King predicted that his life was in danger.

d) In Jackson's opinion, sport in America is still heavily affected by debates about race.

e) According to Jackson, the increasing number of black people in American politics shows that economic inequality between black and white Americans is decreasing.

3 Mediation

What evidence does the text give to suggest that black people suffer from a lower quality of life than white people in America? Find six reasons. Answer in complete German sentences.

4 Listening comprehension: Comparing two speeches → Listening, p. 319

Go online and find the texts and the audio files for King's "I have a dream" speech and Malcolm X's "Message to the grass roots" speech. Compare the styles, the references and the aims of the two speeches and how they were delivered.

Word bank

Talking about civil rights
to stage a sit-in • to boycott • to strike • act of non-violence / civil disobedience • to demand / claim / gain your rights • to give / grant / deny sb. his / her rights • to violate sb.'s right

5 Text production

"Forty years on, Jesse Jackson is still weighing up how far up the mountain African Americans have ascended." (ll. 24 – 25)
Describe the development of African Americans' status in US society.

6 Presentation → Presentation, p. 362

Find out in which areas of public life African Americans were segregated before the civil rights movement. Write down the most important cue-words on a transparency and use this to present your findings in class.

7 Research project → Hotspot 3, p. 119

E America's responsibility

Manhattan and the Statue of Liberty on September 11, 2001

1 Before you read

a) Describe the photo taken on September 11, 2001.

b) In your opinion, is this photo historic/memorable/impressive/thought-provoking/symbolic? Why (not)?

c) Work in pairs. Discuss what happened on September 11, 2001 and how the international public and US government responded to this event.

d) From today's perspective, what long-term effects has 9/11 had in political, economic or psychological terms? Consider the different viewpoints, e. g. that of the Americans, of the Europeans, of Muslim fundamentalists, etc.

e) Suggest suitable captions for the photo from each subjective viewpoint.

4 **authoritarian** – autoritär
5 **regime change** – Regimewechsel
10 **to intervene** – einschreiten
14 **to spark** – entzünden
17 **deep-seated** – tiefsitzend

US soldiers cover a statue of Saddam Hussein before tearing it down

America's role in the world: four options

Option 1:
Lead the world to democracy

American values of democracy and freedom are the standard by which all other nations should be measured. Therefore, authoritarian states must become democratic ones through regime change. Relationships with tyrannical regimes should be avoided and the military may be used to keep international troublemakers in check.

- Supporting arguments:
  - Aggressive tyrants and oppressive regimes will be stopped only when the United States intervenes.
  - Democracies are much less likely to start wars. Thus, the world will be more peaceful by spreading democratic values.
- Concerns:
  - Pressuring other governments will spark criticism that the United States is trying to control the world.
  - Many societies reject the US definition of democracy and human rights.
  - Deep-seated forces of history and culture need to be accepted.

Option 2:
Protect US global interests

We must focus on our main interests, i.e. our own security, our trade relationships, our access to crucial raw materials, and stopping the spread of nuclear weapons. We must be prepared to intervene around the globe if our vital interests are at stake.

- Supporting arguments: …
- Concerns: …

Option 3:
Build a more cooperative world

Today's world is interdependent and we cannot stand alone. We must take the initiative to bring the nations of the world together. We have no choice but to play a leadership role in strengthening the UN's role. We must be willing to give up a part of our sovereignty to the UN and to support its initiatives.

- Supporting arguments: …
- Concerns: …

Option 4:
Protect the US homeland

The US has spent billions of dollars on its allies and the developing countries but its recent military involvements overseas have only made it new enemies. It is time for the US to bring its troops overseas home and to face the challenges at home, e.g. a sagging economy, decaying schools, a shaky health care system and the protection against terrorism.

- Supporting arguments: …
- Concerns: …

(343 words)

An American soldier checks a young Iraqi boy during a patrol

Fighter jets fly over Mount Rushmore

2 Comprehension

Read the four policy options and describe the pictures. Discuss to what extent they illustrate the four policy options.

.299 **3 Having a discussion** → Discussions, p. 344

a) Prepare a panel discussion about America's four policy options. Before you start, decide on roles which should be included in your discussion.

b) Collect supporting arguments and concerns about these four options to prepare for the roles.

c) Make notes of the best arguments for each role that come up in your discussion.

.300 **4 Comment** → Writing a comment, p. 327

"After years of waging war against terrorism unsuccessfully, how should the western world respond to the danger of further terrorist acts?" Write a newspaper article in which you give your own opinion on the above question.

Phrasal verbs

a) Read the texts and replace the words in bold type with an appropriate phrasal verb from the box.

break out • call off • draw in • give up • go off • go on • rule against • send in • set off • sign up • step in

The struggle for equality

1954	The Supreme Court **overturns (1)** the law of segregation in public schools. It is now unconstitutional to have separate facilities, as they are inherently unequal.
1955	NAACP member Rosa Parks refuses to **surrender (2)** her seat to a white passenger at the front of a bus. Her arrest **starts (3)** a bus boycott in Montgomery, Alabama, that **lasts (4)** for over a year. The young Baptist minister, Martin Luther King, Jr., leads the boycott and receives national attention for his efforts.
1956	Busses are desegregated in Montgomery, and the boycott is **canceled (5)**.
1957	King's principles of non-violent resistance and civil disobedience **attract (6)** many followers. State and federal troops **intervene (7)** on behalf of the nine African American students who are denied entry to their new high school in Little Rock, Arkansas.
1962	James Meredith is the first black student to go to the University of Mississippi. The violence and riots following his enrollment cause president Kennedy to **dispatch (8)** 5,000 federal troops.
1963	About 200,000 people join the March on Washington. King delivers his famous "I have a dream" speech. Four teenage girls are killed when a bomb **explodes (9)** at the 6th Street Baptist Church in Birmingham, Alabama, a popular location for civil rights meetings. Riots **erupt (10)**.
1965	Black nationalist Malcolm X is shot to death. Activists begin a March to Montgomery in support of voting rights. On this "Bloody Sunday", 50 marchers are hospitalized after police use tear gas, whips, and clubs against them. The Voting Rights Act is passed five months later, making it easier for blacks to **register (11)** to vote.
1968	Martin Luther King is assassinated in Memphis, Tennessee.

b) Translate the phrasal verbs into German.

c) Choose four of the phrasal verbs above and make a sentence with each one.

d) Work with a partner. Choose a text in your book and list all the phrasal verbs you can find. Then try and find synonyms for them and translate them into German. Use a monolingual dictionary to help you. → Working with a dictionary, p. 353

1 Research project: The American Dream → Internet research, p. 358
Research people who have realised the American Dream – e.g. people with a relatively poor background who went from "rags to riches". Then prepare a presentation in class.

2 Research project: 2012 election in the US → Internet research, p. 358
With the help of the map and the Internet, find the names of the 15 most important states for the Electoral College and say which party won them. Comment on the geographical distribution of Republican and Democratic states.

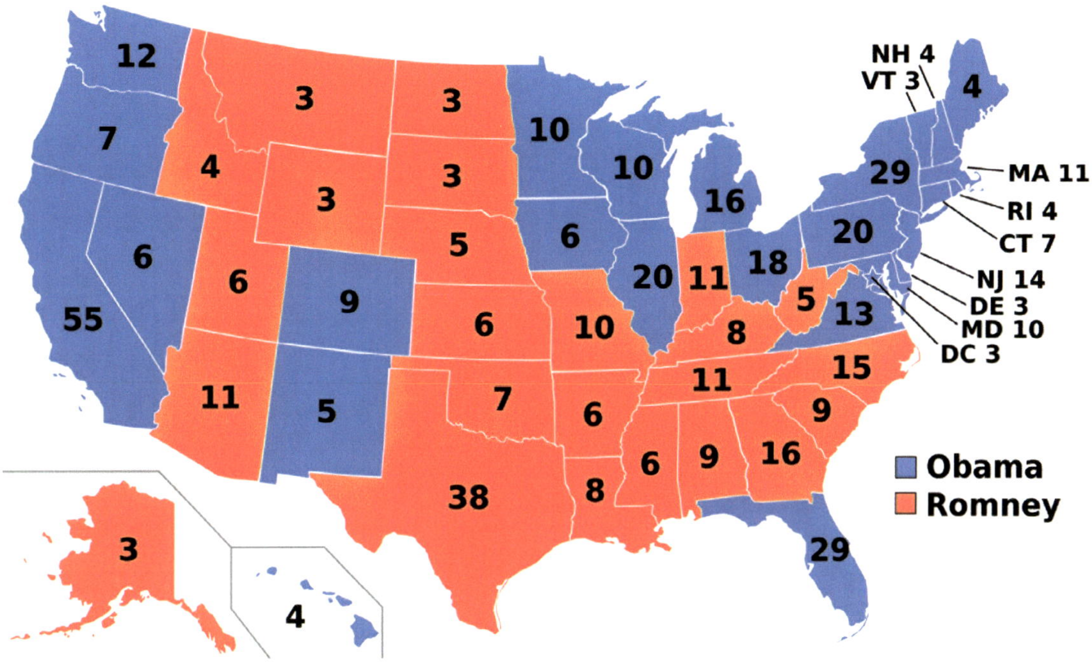

3 Research project: Writing a biography → Internet research, p. 358
Go online and find out about the life of one of the following people:

Malcolm X • Rosa Parks • Jesse Jackson • Martin Luther King

Produce a short biography, creating your own summary of the major events in their life and their contributions to the fight for racial equality. You can choose between the following ways to present your information: a poster, a handwritten text, or a timeline.

A 2.12

4 **to gentrify** – to modernize
8 **subprime mortgage crisis** – US real estate crisis
10 **to foreclose** – to confiscate
12 **to leave sth. in one's wake** – to leave sth. behind oneself
14 **unkempt** – not taken care of
16 **desolate** – abandoned
20 **to deter sb. from doing sth.** – to keep sb. from doing sth.
23 **gloomy** – depressing
24 **foreclosure** – ceditor reclaims property when borrower fails to make payments
26 **to emerge** – to appear
34 **rundown** – in bad condition
36 **commute** – journey to and from work
38 **mass transit** – public transport
42 **to gain momentum** – to increase influence

CNN

Search GO

Is America's suburban dream collapsing into a nightmare?

When Shaun Yandell proposed to his longtime girlfriend Gina Marasco on the doorstep of their new home in the sunny suburb of Elk Grove, California, four years ago, he never imagined things would get this bad. But they did, and it happened almost overnight.

Suburban neighborhoods are becoming refuges for those outpriced in gentrifying innercities. "It is going to be heartbreak," Yandell told CNN. "But we are hanging on."

Yandell's marriage isn't falling apart: his neighborhood is.

Devastated by the subprime mortgage crisis, hundreds of homes have been foreclosed and thousands of residents have been forced to move, leaving in their wake a not-so-pleasant path of empty houses, unkempt lawns, vacant strip malls, graffiti-sprayed desolate sidewalks and even increased crime.

In Elk Grove, some homeowners not only cut their own grass but also trim the yards of vacant homes on their streets, hoping to deter gangs and criminals from moving in. […]

For Yandell, his wife and many other residents trying to stick it out, the white picket fence of an American dream has faded into a seemingly hopeless suburban nightmare. "The forecast is gloomy," he told CNN.

While the foreclosure epidemic has left communities across the United States overrun with unoccupied houses and overgrown grass, underneath the chaos another trend is quietly emerging that, over the next several decades, could change the face of suburban American life as we know it.

This trend, according to Christopher Leinberger, an urban planning professor at the University of Michigan and visiting fellow at the Brookings Institution, stems not only from changing demographics but also from a major shift in the way an increasing number of Americans – especially younger generations – want to live and work.

"The American dream is absolutely changing," he told CNN.

This change can be witnessed in places like Atlanta, Georgia, Detroit, Michigan, and Dallas, Texas, said Leinberger, where once rundown downtowns are being revitalized by well-educated, young professionals who have no desire to live in a detached single family home typical of a suburbia where life is often centered around long commutes and cars. Instead, they are looking for what Leinberger calls "walkable urbanism" – both small communities and big cities characterized by efficient mass transit systems and high density developments enabling residents to walk virtually everywhere for everything – from home to work to restaurants to movie theaters.

The so-called New Urbanism movement emerged in the mid-90s and has been steadily gaining momentum, especially with rising energy costs, environmental concerns and health problems associated with what Leinberger calls "drivable suburbanism" – a low-density built environment plan that emerged around the end of World War II and has been the dominant design in the US ever since.

But now, Leinberger told CNN, it appears the pendulum is beginning to swing back in favor of the type of walkable community that existed long before the advent of the once fashionable suburbs in the 1940s. He says it is being driven by generations molded by television shows like "Seinfeld" and "Friends," where city life is shown as being cool again – a thing to flock to, rather than flee. [...]

Recent market research indicates that up to 40 percent of households surveyed in selected metropolitan areas want to live in walkable urban areas, said Leinberger. The desire is also substantiated by real estate prices for urban residential space, which are 40 to 200 percent higher than in traditional suburban neighborhoods – this price variation can be found both in cities and small communities equipped with walkable infrastructure, he said. The result is an oversupply of depreciating suburban housing and a pent-up demand for walkable urban space, which is unlikely to be met for a number of years.

It is estimated that as a result of the coming structural transformation in 2025 there will be a surplus of 22 million large-lot homes that will not be left vacant in a suburban wasteland but instead occupied by lower classes who have been driven out of their once affordable inner-city apartments and houses. [...]

In Shaun Yandell's neighborhood, this has already started to happen. Houses once filled with single families are now rented out by low-income tenants. Yandell speculates that they're coming from nearby Sacramento, where the downtown is undergoing substantial gentrification, or perhaps from some other area where prices have gotten too high. He isn't really sure. But one thing Yandell is sure about is that he isn't going to leave his sunny suburban neighborhood unless he has to, and if that happens, he says he would only want to move to another one just like it.

"It's the American dream, you know," he said. "The American dream." (786 words)

48 **to mold** – to have a great influence on

50 **to flock to sth.** – to come in great numbers to sth.

53 **to substantiate sth.** – to confirm sth.

56 **to depreciate** – to lessen in value

56 **pent-up demand** – accumulated demand

65 **gentrification** – modernization

1 Comprehension

Read the text. In a table, collect all the pieces of information the text gives you on how the Americans' attitude towards living in either an urban or a rural area has changed.

Living in a rural area	Living in an urban area
– Suburban neighborhoods have become refuges as inner-city apartments have become unaffordable for people with low income. – ...	– Especially young, well-educated Americans tend to work and live in inner cities. – ...

2 Analysis

a) Describe the consequences of the demographic shift from suburban areas to city centres.

b) "Devastated by the subprime mortgage crisis, hundreds of homes have been foreclosed and thousands of residents have been forced to move, [...]" (ll. 8–12) The global financial crisis has changed millions of lives around the world. Illustrate how people in America and beyond have been affected.

3 Comment: Choose one of the following tasks

a) For many people the city is the place to be. In your opinion, is it better to live in an urban area or a rural area? Discuss this, giving arguments for both.

b) People either love or hate the USA. Why does this country arouse such a range of mixed feelings – from admiration to rejection? Comment on it.

Topic 2.3

8qv4b9

The United Kingdom – then and now

"No motto please, we're British."
David, London

"Mind your own business!"
Brian Clacey

"Smile, you're on CCTV."
Les

"Britain – the birthplace of freedom."
Kat

"Dipso, fatso, bingo, asbo, Tesco." JCL

"We apologise for the inconvenience."
Matthew Bailey

In 2007, the Times asked its readers to come up with a national motto for Britain. Over 2,000 ideas were submitted – ranging from tongue-in-cheek suggestions to more serious ones. The newspaper then chose the best 10 and asked readers to vote for their favourite.

> Once mighty empire, slightly used.
>
> J Harris

> Try writing history without us!
>
> Simon Ludkin

D

E

tongue-in-cheek – ironisch
dipso *(coll.)* – jmd, der oft betrunken ist
fatso *(coll.)* – übergewichtige Person
asbo (Anti-Social Behaviour Order) – einstweilige Verfügung wegen antisozialen Verhaltens
Tesco – britische Supermarktkette
CCTV (closed circuit television) – Videoüberwachung

> Free, tolerant, fair-minded & true.
>
> Benj

> Mathematically, we could still qualify.
>
> Wobbly

Getting started

1 Look at the photos A–E. Explain what they show. → Describing pictures, p. 339

2 Read the mottos. Choose one for each picture.

3 Share your ideas with a partner and give reasons for your choice.

4 In pairs, come up with your own motto for Britain and report back to the class.

5 With the same partner, find a similar motto for Germany. What are the differences and similarities between Germany and the UK?

Word bank

Giving opinions
I think that … • In my opinion … • I believe that … • It seems to me … • I agree/disagree because … • What do you think? • What is your opinion on this?

A The British Empire and the Commonwealth

1 Before you read → Brainstorming, p. 351
What comes to your mind when you hear the word "empire"? Brainstorm your ideas with a partner and report back to the class.

3 **hence** – daher, deshalb
4 **foremost** – führend
7 **to encompass sth.** – etw. umfassen
10 **indigenous people** – Einheimische
11 **to aid** – helfen
17 **monopoly** – Monopol
19 **despotism** – Willkür
20 **urge** – Drang, Trieb
21 **to scramble for sth.** – um etw. kämpfen
22 **British Raj** [rɑːdʒ] – British-Indien
25 **longing** – Sehnsucht
39 **suttee** – Witwenverbrennung (in Indien)

How big was the British Empire?

At its height in the nineteenth century the British Empire was the largest in world history, covering about a quarter of the world's land surface, hence the expression "The sun never sets on the British Empire". It was also the world's foremost global power. Ever since the first British colony was established in Jamestown (America) in 1607, the Empire kept changing as Britain gained and sometimes even lost new territories. At different times it encompassed large areas of North America, Australia, Africa and Asia.

How did such a small country come to rule so much territory?

Britain was a powerful and wealthy nation which defeated other European countries and conquered indigenous peoples thanks to its army and navy. In addition, rapid technological advances in the 19th century aided expansion. Inventions such as the telegraph, railroads and steamships meant that Britain had an advantage over local peoples who did not have access to such things.

What were the motives behind Britain's expansion?

The motives behind Britain's expansion were diverse. They included:

- **trade** – the desire to benefit British companies and secure trade routes, e.g. the British-owned East India Company had a monopoly on trade with Asia,
- **economics** – the desire to increase Britain's wealth; George Orwell once wrote that the Empire was "a despotism with theft as its final object",
- **politics** – the urge to prevent other European countries from becoming too powerful, as can be seen with the so-called 'scramble for Africa' at the end of the 19th century,
- **ambition** – Sir James Fitzjames Stephen (1829–1894) wrote that the Raj was "founded not on consent but on conquest",
- **religion** – the desire to spread Christianity,
- **adventure and curiosity** – the longing to explore and learn about new countries and peoples.

What legacy did the British Empire leave?

The British Empire has had a huge impact on the world. The formation of the Commonwealth has meant that most of the former colonies still have links with Britain. Many of them are parliamentary democracies with a legal system based on British law, a military, police and civil service system based on British models, and English is still the main or secondary language.

What changes did the Empire bring about?

The British Empire is often said to have been liberal. It was guided by the principle that colonial government was to be exercised for the good of the subject peoples, who would eventually be given the right to self-rule. Many empire builders thus tried to improve the welfare of the indigenous peoples, giving them better medical care, better legal, education and transport systems, and tried to eliminate practices that they considered barbaric, e.g. suttee, cannibalism and slavery (having, however, first profited from it a century before!). On the other hand, the British often arrogantly considered the indigenous peoples to be 'children' who needed to be 'educated'. Whilst those like the author Rudyard Kipling, who spent years in India, understood that "East is East, and West is West, and never the twain shall meet", others tried to turn the locals into Englishmen. So they not only endured the loss of their lands, but also their culture and met with discrimination and prejudice.

Why did the Empire decline?

The First and Second World Wars not only led to a decline in Britain's wealth and prestige but also lessened the political impact of the Empire. After the wars, the British were more interested in rebuilding their own country than in concentrating on far-away places. They were also beginning to realise that it was no longer feasible to run such a large empire. The dominions (Australia, New Zealand, Canada, the Irish Free State and South Africa) had already officially been given the power to rule themselves by the Statute of Westminster in 1931, even though in practice they had been doing so for some time. This set an example to which many other colonies now began to aspire. The British lost a prized colony, the 'Jewel in the Crown', in 1947, when India was partitioned. After this, colonies were either given self-governing dominion status or became independent. By the late 1960s most of British territories had become independent, although this did not always happen peacefully, especially in the case of Ireland. (718 words)

42 **twain** *(old)* – die Zwei
43 **to endure** – ertragen, aushalten
49 **feasible** – machbar
50 **dominion** *(old)* – Herrschaft, Machtgebiet
53 **to aspire** – anstreben
54 **to partition** – aufteilen

2 Comprehension
In your own words, answer the questions posed in each of the six subheadings in the text. Write between 2–3 sentences for each question.

301 **3 Analysis** → Describing cartoons, p. 340
On July 1, 1997 the UK handed Hong Kong – its last significant colony – back over to China. Describe the cartoon that was drawn at the time and explain the symbols used. What points is the cartoonist making about the British Empire?

15 **4 Listening comprehension** → Listening, p. 319
Listen to the opening of a lecture given in November 2007 by Don McKinnon, the former Secretary-General of the Commonwealth, entitled *The Modern Commonwealth: challenges in the 21st century*. Give short answers in English.

a) Which event led to the downfall of the "British Commonwealth" and when did it happen?

b) How many countries and people make up the Commonwealth?

c) Which two expressions did McKinnon use to describe the values and goals of the Commonwealth?

d) Name two countries in which Commonwealth representatives are active.

e) What positive outcome did an idea of the Commonwealth have for 30 of the world's poorest countries?

f) According to McKinnon, which two characteristics must the Commonwealth have?

5 Research project → Hotspot 1, p. 135

B Britishness

1 Before you read
What do you associate with being British? Together with a partner, make a list, then share your ideas with another pair.

0 **disunited** – entsolidarisiert, uneinig
1 **notion** – Idee
3 **decreasingly** – immer weniger
3 **to rally to sth.** – sich um etw. scharen
4 **division** – Trennung
5 **Marmite** – Hefe-Brot-aufstrich
6 **Coronation Street** – britische Soap
7 **strain** – Belastung, Anspannung
8 **referendum** – Bürger-entscheid
9 **to prompt** – veranlassen
9 **to shatter** – zerschlagen
10 **regardless of** – unabhängig von
15 **grip** – Griff
17 **nationhood** – nationale Identität
19 **arguably** – wohl
21 **to unfold** – sich entfalten
27 **crucial** – entscheidend, aus-schlaggebend
28 **undoubtedly** – zweifellos
28 **extent** – Ausmaß
33 **intriguingly** – verblüffen-derweise
33 **evidence** – *hier:* Befunde
33 **devolution** – Übertragung von parlamentarischer Gewalt

theguardian

News | Sport | Comment | Culture | Business | Money | Life&Style | Travel | Environment

Comment is free > UK > Search GO

Identity crisis: are we becoming a disunited kingdom?

Surveys suggest notions of Britishness are changing

So what makes us? We share the same islands, but we aren't all British. We call ourselves Scots, Irish, Welsh, English and often, but decreasingly, British. Every four years, we rally to the union flag for the Olympics, but when it comes to rugby and football, the divisions open up. There is much shared culture, whether in pop music, clothing, fish and chips, curries and Marmite, comedians and Coronation Street. […]

But now, for the first time in several centuries, that notion of Britishness is under intense strain. Alex Salmond, the first minister of Scotland, will soon lead the country into a referendum that could prompt Scotland to declare independence, a move that would shatter a 304-year-old political union. Regardless of the Scottish referendum, the UK has four separate governments and now the three devolved administrations, in Scotland, Wales and Northern Ireland, are winning greater economic and legal powers, cutting London's grip on the country. And in each part of the UK, notions of nationhood and Britishness are changing and, arguably, the links are weakening.

Because of this unfolding political situation, the Guardian invites readers to enter the debate about national identity and air your attitudes on Britishness. […] We will be asking if it is more and more becoming a "disunited kingdom"?

There is much to suggest this is the case. John Curtice, from the Scottish Centre for Social Research, […] said: "The crucial thing to realise is that in Scotland, British is now very definitely a secondary identity; that's undoubtedly true to a far greater extent than it is in Wales." In England there are plenty of people who, if asked whether they're British or English, will say 'what's the difference?'. Comparing all the latest social attitudes surveys gives us this contrast: if voters are forced to choose, 52% of English voters choose British first compared to 19% of Scots, and 30% of Welsh. […]

Intriguingly, the latest evidence from Wales suggests that devolution may be making the Welsh feel more British. That is one reading of a new study of 3,029 voters by the Economic and Social

Research Council, carried out in the runup to the 2011 referendum, which found overwhelming support for giving the Welsh Assembly greater powers.

Its results […] find that 16% of Welsh voters now feel "British not Welsh", compared to 9% in 2007 and in 2003. Meanwhile, only 19% felt "Welsh not British", a fall from 24% in 2007, with 30% feeling equally Welsh and British.

Roger Scully, from Aberystwyth University and the study's co-author, is cautious about reading too much into the Welsh figures since different survey methods were used in 2011.

"The bigger picture is that basic identity in Wales has not changed much under devolution, or even if you go back and look at the evidence from 1979, since the first devolution referendums," he said. "People have very different views now about how Wales should be governed. But not because they have become, in some crude sense, more Welsh."

In Northern Ireland, identity can be far more complex; loyalty to a larger nation splits between those feeling British and Irish, mostly down religious or ethnic lines. The 2010 Northern Ireland Life and Times surveys […] have shown that 37% see themselves as British, 26% Irish and 29% Northern Irish, with 3% choosing Ulster.

But asked the multiple-choice question, 58% of voters in Northern Ireland in 2007 saw themselves, to varying degrees, as both British and Irish. In 1998, 51% of those given a straight choice said they were British. It is 37% now.

In England last year, 52% described themselves as British and just 34% as English in a straight choice between the two. That is the widest margin since 1997.

Behind such figures emotions run deep. Yet, is national identity in the UK purely a personal badge to be worn with pride at sporting events – or could it fundamentally change the nature of the British (and Northern Irish) state? (670 words)

35 **runup** – Vorlauf
35 **overwhelming** – überwältigend
36 **assembly** – Versammlung
40 **cautious** – vorsichtig
45 **crude** – derb, grob
51 **varying** – wechselnd
54 **margin** – Spanne
55 **badge** – Ansteckschildchen

2 Comprehension

.301

a) What information can you find in the text about the following numbers?

304 • 9% • 16% • 37% • 51% • 52%

b) Describe in your own words why the "notion of Britishness is under intense strain." (l. 7)

c) Outline where in the UK, according to the text, the number of people who feel British might be on the rise. Give reasons.

3 Vocabulary → Working with a dictionary, p. 353

a) Define the following terms. Compare your definitions with the ones in the dictionary.

1. independence • 2. political union • 3. government • 4. national identity • 5. attitude • 6. loyalty • 7. ethnic • 8. emotion • 9. pride

b) Find the corresponding adjectives for numbers 1., 3., 6., 8., and 9.
c) Find the corresponding verb for number 3.
d) Find the corresponding noun for number 7.

4 Presentation → Presentation, p. 362

Think of ideas that characterise Germany. How would you explain "Germanness" to a foreigner? Write down your main points on a transparency and use this to present your ideas to the class.

C The British political system

The House of Commons

The House of Lords

Number 10 Downing Street

16 **approximately** – ungefähr
17 **constituency** – Wahlkreis
19 **advisory** – beratend
20 **to delay** – verzögern
24 **to appoint** – ernennen
36 **assembly** – Versammlung; *hier:* Parlament
40 **predominantly** – vorwiegend

The constitution

The British constitution is not set down in a single document, it is made up of a whole range of laws and conventions instead.

The monarchy

The monarch is the official **Head of State**, the head of the executive and of the judiciary, the Commander-in-Chief of the armed forces and the 'supreme governor' of the **Church of England**. The monarch formally appoints the **Prime Minister** (PM). However, the monarch's duties are largely ceremonial.

Parliament

Parliament is made up of the **House of Commons**, and the **House of Lords**. The Prime Minister decides exactly when a **general election** is to be held within a five year term.

The House of Commons

The House of Commons is where new laws are passed and the main business of government is done. The House of Commons is elected in general elections and consists of approximately 650 **Members of Parliament** (MPs), one from each of the constituencies.

The House of Lords

The House of Lords acts in a mainly controlling and advisory capacity but it can delay bills for up to a year. The number of members is not fixed.

Government and opposition

The party which wins the most seats (though not necessarily the most votes) at a general election forms the Government. The leader of the party is appointed Prime Minister by the Sovereign. The Prime Minister's official residence is **Number 10 Downing Street**. The Prime Minister forms a cabinet by appointing ministers who are usually in charge of a government department. Most ministers are known as "Secretary of State" or "Minister" unless they have a special title, such as the **Chancellor of the Exchequer**, who is responsible for financial and monetary issues. Other important ministers are the **Home Secretary**, responsible for internal affairs and the **Foreign Secretary**, responsible for foreign affairs. The largest minority party in the House of Commons becomes the official opposition with its own leader and "shadow cabinet".
Traditionally Britain has been governed centrally from **Westminster** (London) with Scotland and Wales being represented there by Secretaries of State. Since June 1998 Northern Ireland has had its own assembly (the **New Northern Ireland Assembly**), and since 1999 Wales and Scotland have had their own assemblies with some limited powers.

The political parties

For the past 150 years a predominantly two party system has existed in Britain. After 1945 power was held either by the **Conservative Party** (Tories), a right of centre party, or by the **Labour Party**, a left of centre party. In 2010 the Tories formed a coalition with the **Liberal Democrats** (LibDems), who make up the third biggest party in Britain. There is a Green Party in Britain but it is not represented in parliament, partly because the electoral system gives small parties almost no chance of winning any seats. There are two nationalist parties: **Plaid Cymru** (Welsh Nationals) and the **Scottish National Party** (SNP), which play an important role in Wales and Scotland respectively. In Northern Ireland the most important parties are the Ulster Unionist Party and Sinn Féin, the political wing of the IRA.

The electoral system

For electoral purposes Britain is divided into about 650 **constituencies**. Each constituency is represented by one MP in the House of Commons. The current system that is used at general elections in the UK is the **simple majority** or "first-past-the-post" (FPTP) system. Each **elector** has one vote. Electors vote for the candidate of their choice. The candidate who gets the most votes in a constituency wins the seat. The main advantages of FPTP is that it is simple to understand and produces strong single party governments rather than coalitions, and that it provides a close link between MPs and their constituencies. (613 words)

49 **respectively** – beziehungsweise

59 **to provide** – sorgen für

1 Comprehension: True or false?
Read the statements below and decide whether they are true or false. Quote or paraphrase words from the text which confirm or disprove the ideas in the statements.

a) The British constitution was written in one sitting.

b) The members of the House of Commons are elected in their constituencies.

c) The law-making body is the House of Lords.

d) The electorate decides who will become Prime Minister.

e) The Prime Minister and his ministers form the shadow cabinet.

f) The building of homes lies in the responsibility of the Home Secretary.

g) Coalitions have always been a common phenomenon in Britain.

h) The PM chooses a date for the next general election.

2 Analysis → Describing diagrams, p. 341
Describe and analyse the pie charts.

3 Project → Hotspot 2, p. 135

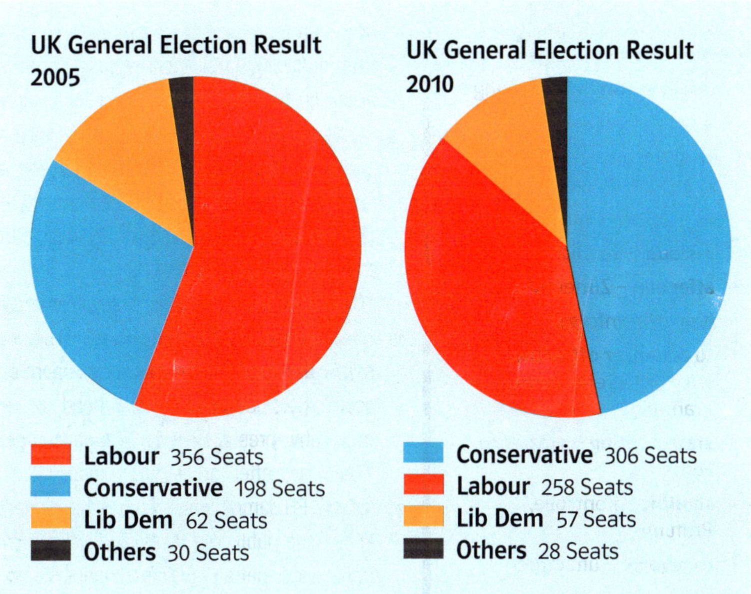

Source: The Huddersfield Daily Examiner

D The Royal Family

1 Before you read
Which members of the royal family can you name? What do you know about them? Discuss with a partner and report back to the class.

2 Comprehension

a) Outline why, according to the text, the royals need an "intense PR campaign" (l. 20) and describe what this campaign includes.

b) Summarise, in your own words, Jennie Bond's and Walter Bagehot's opinions on the new royals.

theguardian

News | Sport | Comment | Culture | Business | Money | Life&Style | Travel | Environment

Comment is free > Society   Search [ ] GO

How the royals became cool

Princes William and Harry are seen as being down-to-earth regular guys. The Duchess of Cambridge is supposedly one of us. How did our stuffy and out-of-touch monarchy suddenly get its mojo back? The other day, Cheryl Cole had a lovely dream. "I married Prince Harry and was a real-life princess," she said. "It's true. And Charles was my father-in-law." The last bit sounds like every girl's nightmare, but that's not important now.

More important are the ramifications of this dream for the British constitution. Until very recently, pop stars didn't dream of marrying members of the royal family, still less blab about it. The royals were too tweedy and facially equine for such dreams to do anything but damage a pop chanteuse's fanbase. But all that has changed. How? […]

"Of course there's a policy," says former BBC royal correspondent Jennie Bond. "The young royals are making the monarchy enormously cool." […] Graham Smith, head of anti-monarchy pressure group Republic, agrees. "There is, after all, a good reason for the intense PR campaign being run by the palace: it knows the public are fast losing interest in the royals, and that as the Queen nears the end of her life any residual affection for her is unlikely

1 **down-to-earth** – bodenständig
2 **supposedly** – angeblich
2 **stuffy** – spießig *(ugs.)*
2 **out-of-touch** – abgehoben, lebensfremd
2 **mojo** – Glücksbringer
6 **ramification** – Auswirkung
10 **tweedy** – konservativ
11 **facially equine** – *hier:* pferdeähnlich aussehend
12 **chanteuse** – Barsängerin
23 **residual** – restlich
23 **affection** – Zuneigung
24 **heir** – Thronfolger
24 **to be better off without sth.** – ohne etw. besser dran sein
25 **state funding** – staatliche Förderung
26 **scrutiny** – Kontrolle, Prüfung
26 **to reverse** – umkehren
27 **alleged** – angeblich
27 **decline** – Rückgang

3 Analysis → Text analysis, p. 326

a) Explain the following terms from the text in your own words:
1. to blab about sth. (l. 9)
2. to trade groovy moves (l. 30)
3. to be off your head (l. 33)
4. pop (l. 34)
5. to be plastered (l. 49)

b) Analyse what effect the use of informal language in the text has on the reader.

c) Explain the following phrase: "I think the biggest enemy is apathy among young people." (l. 52)

.301

4 Comment

"The British Monarchy has no place in modern society." Discuss.

5 Research project → Hotspot 3, p. 135

to transfer to her son and heir,". Smith argues that at least a quarter of Britons believe we'd be better off without the monarchy, more than half want an end to its state funding and two-thirds want the royal household opened up to more scrutiny. Maybe, just maybe, making the royals cool could reverse that alleged decline in interest.

It seems only five minutes ago that Prince Harry was a swastika-sporting throwback who called his Asian friend "paki". Three stories show how his image has changed. During his tour of the Caribbean, Harry traded groovy moves with Jamaican sprinter Usain Bolt, yielding the kind of picture spreads of which no previous British prince, with the possible exception of Henry, Prince of Wales, circa 1505, would have been capable. Then Harry emerged from a 4am lock-in at a bar called Bunga Bunga, dancing to his waiting car like any other twentysomething English yeoman off his head on too much pop. […]

Harry's rehabilitation looks like part of a bigger campaign to make the royals seem normal, while paradoxically – and this would be a brilliant campaign if it could be pulled off – glamourising them and reinforcing their regal status. "It's a marvel to behold," says PR expert Mark Borkowski, "and it seems to be working. What you have now is an amazing PR turnaround in an infinitesimally small amount of time."

The branding of Kate, Duchess of Cambridge, is key to this turnaround. She is simultaneously our future queen, the world's hottest magazine cover girl and a woman feted as a cut-price royal who, while William was bravely defending the Falklands from wicked Sean Penn, modestly made her debut as a public speaker wearing her mother's hand-me-down dress in, there's no easy way to say this, Ipswich. […]

But isn't there a tension for the monarchy in all this? Victorian thinker Walter Bagehot distinguished the dignified from the efficient parts of the constitution. By the former he meant the monarchy, which has a symbolic function; by the latter he meant parliament and government. If the royals seem ordinary, the dignified part of the constitution could be doomed. Where, after all, is the dignity in Harry spilling out of a lock-in evidently plastered?

Bond thinks otherwise. She argues that if the monarchy has a future, then members of the royal family must be like us but cooler. "Not long ago they seemed to be the most dysfunctional family on the planet. Now they're cool. It's brilliant. I think the biggest enemy is apathy among young people." […]

(631 words)

28 **swastika** – Hakenkreuz
30 **to yield** – hervorbringen
32 **capable** – fähig
32 **to emerge** – heraus-kommen
32 **lock-in** – Privat-Party in einer Bar/einem Pub
33 **yeoman** – Freibauer
36 **to pull sth. off** – etw. zustande bringen *(ugs.)*
37 **to reinforce** – verstärken
37 **regal** – königlich
37 **marvel** – Wunderwerk
37 **to behold** – anschauen
38 **infinitesimally** – winzig
41 **to fete** – feiern
41 **cut-price** – Billig-
42 **wicked** – böse
43 **hand-me-down** – gebraucht
45 **tension** – Spannung
45 **to distinguish** – unter-scheiden
46 **dignified** – würdevoll
48 **doomed** – verdammt
48 **to spill out of sth.** – *hier:* aus etw. herauskommen *(ugs.)*
49 **evidently** – offensichtlich
50 **otherwise** – anders
51 **dysfunctional** – gestört, zerrüttet
52 **apathy** – Gleichgültigkeit, Teilnahmslosigkeit

E Britain and Europe

1 Before you read
What advantages and disadvantages might EU membership have for a country? Share your ideas with a partner.

1 **eurosceptic** – Europagegner(in)
1 **entirely** – gänzlich
2 **to be opposed to sth.** – gegen etw. sein
5 **to purchase** – erwerben
8 **recession** – Konjunkturabschwung
9 **free-trade agreement** – Freihandelsabkommen
12 **to govern** – leiten, lenken
12 **European single market** – europäischer Binnenmarkt
13 **to implement** – umsetzen
16 **to deploy** – einsetzen
25 **trade deficit** – Handelsdefizit
25 **leverage** – Einfluss, Druckmittel
25 **opt-out** – Ausstiegsmöglichkeit
26 **rebate** – Nachlass, Ermäßigung
29 **to impose** – auferlegen
30 **tariff** – Zoll
30 **likelihood** – Wahrscheinlichkeit
34 **bloc** – Staatenblock
35 **overseas** – ausländisch

THE INDEPENDENT

What if Britain left the EU?

Eurosceptics want a vote on the ultimate question – and the PM does not seem entirely opposed. Ben Chu examines the consequences of saying bye bye to Brussels

Exports

The European Union is easily Britain's biggest single export market, with 53 per cent of our goods purchased by our fellow European nations in 2011. This sector of our economy, directly and indirectly, supports three million jobs, according to Sir Iain Begg, a professorial research fellow at the European Institute of the London School of Economics. Without export growth last year, we would have fallen back into recession much earlier. If we were to leave the EU, we would almost certainly still be allowed to sell goods into the single market. Norway, Iceland and Switzerland already do so through a free-trade agreement. The difference would be that the UK would not be able to set the rules that govern the European single market. It would, of course, have to implement those rules to keep selling into those markets though. The argument sometimes deployed by those who want out of the EU is that leaving would, somehow, encourage British manufacturers to concentrate on exporting to the likes of China, Brazil and India.

Imports

Britain also imports a great deal from other nations in the EU – more than it exports, in fact. In 2011, we exported £159bn of goods to the EU and imported goods worth £202bn – an annual trade deficit of £42bn. Some argue that this deficit gives us leverage to demand more opt-outs and budget rebates from our European partners. The argument is: "They need us more than we need them." The problem is that we import a lot of European goods, not because we are doing the Europeans a favour, but because our people want to buy things that cannot be produced at home – think of all those German cars and French luxury goods. If Britain were to leave the EU, the Government might decide to impose large tariffs on European imports, but this probably wouldn't prove very popular. The likelihood is we would still run a trade deficit with the EU, but, as with imports, we would have no say over the rules governing the single market. […]

Growth

Would foreign capital still want to invest in the UK if it were not part of the EU bloc? Some economists say overseas investors would be put off. The National Institute of Economic and Social Research, for example, estimates that foreign direct investment would fall. And, mainly for this reason, it argues that our GDP would permanently be 2.25 per cent lower if we left the EU. However, Capital Economics argued last month that, because of the eurozone crisis, levels of foreign investment in the UK could actually go up if we left the EU, because we would seem like a safe haven.

Immigration

If Britain left the EU, the Government would not be required to permit the free movement of all citizens of the 27 nations of the union into Britain, nor their right to work here. About 165,000 EU citizens migrated to the UK in the year to September 2011, after 182,000 arrived in the 12 months to September 2010. Proponents of withdrawal argue that stopping such flows would improve quality of life because there would be less strain on public services and infrastructure. Opponents argue that immigrants are an economic benefit for Britain, filling holes in our labour market and boosting overall productivity. But the free movement of people is two-way. An estimated 748,010 Britons live or work in the European Union. Many have holiday homes in France and Spain. If we decided to restrict inflows of EU citizens to Britain, the European Union would be likely to respond in kind. […]

Politics

Europe is more social democratic than the UK. Even countries with centre-right governments tend to tax more, spend more on welfare and are less laissez-faire when it comes to markets. Those on the left in Britain tend to be in favour of the UK's continued membership because they feel it will help to move the country in this direction. Those on the right tend to be opposed for similar reasons; they feel Europe is helping to undermine Britain's social and economic freedoms. Yet there are global politics to consider, too. The right wants to rely on Britain's "special relationship" with the US, but Washington prefers Britain to work in closer partnership with the EU. Rising Asian giants such as India and China also seem to regard Britain's membership of the EU as a good reason to build economic and diplomatic ties with us.

(772 words)

36 **GDP (Gross Domestic Product)** – Bruttoinlandsprodukt
39 **safe haven** – sicherer Ort
41 **to permit** – erlauben
44 **proponent** – Befürworter(in), Anhänger(in)
44 **withdrawal** – Ausstieg
45 **strain** – Belastung
45 **opponent** – Gegner(in)
46 **labour market** – Arbeitsmarkt
46 **to boost** – in die Höhe treiben
51 **to tax** – besteuern
52 **welfare** – Sozialwesen
52 **laissez-faire** – lax
55 **to undermine sth.** – etw. untergraben
56 **to rely on** – setzen auf, bauen auf
58 **to regard** – betrachten
58 **tie** – Beziehung, Bindung

2 Mediation → Mediation, p. 343
You are doing an internship at a local German newspaper. The editor would like to print an article based on the text above in the newspaper's international section. Summarise the text in German using the subheadings to help you.

46 **3 Listening comprehension: A British vision for Europe** → Listening, p. 319
Listen to the article and find out whether Angela Merkel's or David Cameron's points of views are reflected in the following statements:

a) We want to be less involved with Europe.

b) We are, for the most part, Eurosceptics.

c) Us European countries should work more closely together.

d) We did not choose to be in charge, but it is our responsibility.

e) If you expect us to support you financially, you have to listen to what we have to say.

f) We are in a dilemma: if we step back, you say we are not interested, and if we take the lead, you accuse us of pushing you around.

g) What we need is a "networked Europe".

h) 49% of our citizens want to leave the EU, anyway.

4 Project → Hotspot 4, p. 135

Transitions

The purpose of transitions is to connect. They lead into the next paragraph and the next point or make a connection back to the previous paragraph before introducing a new point. Transitional phrases or sentences come at the end of one paragraph or at the beginning of the next.

This may be a reason for … Another reason for this is … That's not the only reason for … Furthermore, … In addition, … In fact, …	Another example is … Let's take a look at another example. For example/instance … To demonstrate … To illustrate … In particular, …	On the other hand, … More importantly, … Even before … In order to … With this in mind … In comparison/contrast to …

a) Read the first part of the comment below and improve the flow of the text by adding transitions.

The pros and cons of moving to the United Kingdom
There are many reasons why people choose to move to the UK: **1** there might be more employment opportunities. While a person's native country may have a weak economy and a high unemployment rate, it is possible that the UK offers a great deal of job possibilities. **2** some countries may be politically unstable, making them unsafe for people to live. **3** the person or people may have fled the country to escape a civil war. **4** a large number of immigrants leave their home country and move to the UK for this reason.
5 not all people move countries for these reasons. **6** some people may simply move because of the lifestyle, or for personal reasons. For many people, moving to the UK offers them a fresh start. **7** these people can also face many problems. **8** they may not speak English or be able to adapt to British culture. Or, **9** they could find that their new home does not offer the opportunities they had hoped for or had been promised.
10 migrants may find themselves under pressure not only to support themselves in a new country, but also the friends and relatives they have left behind in their country, especially those from poorer parts of the world. […]

b) Find more arguments and continue writing the comment using transitions.

c) Look at a comment you have recently written and improve its style by adding transitions where possible.

1 Research project: The British Empire and the Commonwealth
→ Internet research, p. 358

a) In groups, create an illustrated timeline on the British Empire and/or the Commonwealth, including dates, pictures, short texts, and if possible quotations.

b) Go online and find out more about the Commonwealth Games. Look at the history of the Games, the most recent Games, and how they differ from the Olympics.

2 Project: 2010 elections in the UK → Projects and group work, p. 359
The general elections in the UK in 2010 caused a completely new situation in the political landscape in the UK. Find out about the results of this election and explain the new situation.

3 Research project: Monarchies in Europe → Internet research, p. 358
Use the Internet to find out which countries in Europe still have a monarch as head of state. Find out what role they play, how much political influence they still have, and what relationship they have with their people.

4 Project: Britain and Europe → Discussions, p. 344
Work in small groups. Read the fact file and then look at the cartoon. What point is the cartoonist making? Do you agree with him? Give reasons and report back to the class.

Britain and Europe
After twice being denied membership, Britain finally joined the Common Market in 1973. This was mainly for economic reasons such as to promote trade. During the Thatcher era (1980s), opposition to a "United States of Europe" was strong. Nevertheless, Britain did sign the Single European Act in 1987 and join the Exchange Rate Mechanism in October 1990. In 1994 the opening of the Eurotunnel lessened Britain's geographical isolation. When the Labour government came to power in 1997, Britain signed the Social Charter (guaranteeing social and economic human rights), which the Conservatives had refused to do, thus giving the country a more pro-European image. However, one of the biggest issues is the euro. Britain has stayed with its decision to keep its own currency unless the people choose to accept the euro in a referendum. Whatever the British feel about Europe, they cannot really leave. As Gordon Brown said, "The European Union is essential to the success of Britain and a Britain fully engaged in Europe is essential to the success of the European Union."
(177 words)

A 2.20

0 **aid** – (financial) help
0 **row** – fight
1 **to underlie** – to be the cause or basis of
2 **myth** – common belief
6 **to take off** – to start
12 **to remain** – to stay
13 **malnourished** – starved
15 **childbearing age** – age from which women can have children
15 **anaemic** – not having enough blood
20 **to unleash** – to release
23 **disparity** – inequality
23 **obscenely** – *here:* greatly
27 **to fuel** – to inflame
30 **to prompt** – to start
30 **accusation** – a charge or claim that someone has done sth. illegal or wrong
31 **ingratitude** – ungratefulness
34 **violation** – breach
35 **rationale** – philosophy
36 **to promote** – to support
41 **to reveal** – to make known
47 **ballooning** – increasing
47 **expenditure** – money spent
49 **blast** – explosion
53 **GDP (Gross Domestic Product)** – the total value of goods and services that is produced by a nation, measure of a nation's economic activity
54 **sanitation** – the provision of clean drinking water and adequate sewage disposal
54 **affordable** – not too expensive
57 **to reshape** – to reform
62 **benefit** – advantage
66 **to terminate** – to stop

theguardian

News | Sport | Comment | Culture | Business | Money | Life&Style | Travel | Environment

Comment is free > Society   Search [ ] GO

Why India needs aid

Most of its population are still poor. The row over British aid shows how many people confuse rapid growth with wealth.

Underlying the debate raging over British aid to India is the myth that the subcontinent's strong, market-driven growth of the past two decades has pulled hundreds of millions out of poverty. The economy is taking off; its people no longer need much aid, it is said.

In reality, since 1991, during which time India has experienced the highest growth in recent history, there has been no significant reduction in poverty or hunger. Two in every five children remain malnourished. A third of adults have an abnormally low body-mass index. Half of women of childbearing age are anaemic, a proportion far higher than in sub-Saharan Africa. More than 500 million Indians have no electricity, and less than a third have toilets.

The neoliberal policies unleashed by the prime minister, Manmohan Singh, when he was finance minister in the early 90s, have widened class disparities obscenely. Numbers such as 8% growth, and the fact there are 153,000 dollar millionaires, mean little to most Indians.

The debate in the UK was fuelled by anger at India's decision to buy French Rafale jets rather than the Eurofighter Typhoon, prompting shrill accusations of "ingratitude". International development secretary Andrew Mitchell even admitted that the focus of aid to India included "seeking to sell the Typhoon" – in violation of the stated rationale of British overseas aid, to fight poverty and promote health and education.

So if India can spend billions on nuclear weapons, aircraft carriers and nuclear submarines, and on a moon mission, does it deserve aid? As was revealed this weekend, India has itself told Britain it doesn't want aid.

But this confuses the nature of aid – which is about poor people, not poor countries. Many Indians question the government's

ballooning military expenditure, which has more than tripled since the 1998 nuclear blasts. Instead they want substantially improved public services, including food security, drinking water, healthcare (India's public health spending proportionate to GDP is among the world's lowest), sanitation, and education at affordable prices. Great struggles are under way on these issues, which have the potential to reshape Indian politics.

Besides, aid is much less wasteful than commonly thought. A small part of the international development department's budget might go towards GPS devices on buses in Bhopal, with dubious benefits. But more than 60% has gone in recent years into education and healthcare. […]

Britain would be morally and politically wrong to terminate aid to India, home to the largest number of the world's poor. Giving aid not only acknowledges the injustice of colonial exploitation, it also arises from an obligation to redress the gross structural imbalances that continue to mark the world despite recent power shifts between states. Good aid programmes can make humane existence possible for millions who have been denied it. Rather than Mitchell's aim to "invest more in the private sector" and public-private partnerships – which charge user fees the poor cannot afford – Britain should target schemes with a social transformation potential. Programmes that resemble a sovereign wealth fund and seek financial returns are less beneficial than building up people's human potential.

(533 words)

68 **to acknowledge** – to recognize
68 **injustice** – unfairness
69 **exploitation** – misuse
70 **to redress** – to set right
70 **gross** – large
72 **shift** – change
81 **to resemble** – to be similar to
82 **beneficial** – useful

1 Comprehension

Read the text and complete the statements (a–e) by choosing the right answer (1, 2, or 3).

a) The consequence of rapid growth in India is that …
1. hundreds of millions of people do no longer need aid.
2. there has been a significant reduction in poverty and hunger since 1991.
3. nonetheless, poverty and hunger have not been reduced significantly.

b) In the UK people are furious as …
1. India spends billions on different projects but not enough on health and education.
2. India wants to buy the Eurofighter Typhoon.
3. class disparities could be reduced in India.

c) Many Indians want …
1. the government to increase their military expenditure.
2. public services to be provided at reasonable prices.
3. more rich Indians to help the poor.

d) For Britain it would be wrong …
1. to give money to India in the future.
2. to stop giving money to India as the largest number of the world's poor living there must be helped.
3. to remember the injustice of colonial exploitation.

e) A good aid programme …
1. should invest more money in the private sector.
2. should support public-private partnerships.
3. should build up people's human potential.

2 Analysis

Analyse whether the author of the text supports or opposes British aid to India. Quote examples from the text to support your answer.

3 Comment → Writing a comment, p. 327

Write a letter to the author of the text in which you discuss the pros and cons of foreign aid to poor places such as India or Africa, taking into account the aspects mentioned in the text.

Topic 2.4
World of work

r8tj62

A

B

C

D

Word bank

to have an interview • to be nervous / creative • CV • to design • to work overtime / outdoors • dangerous • to install • solar panel • green company • to be responsible for • to work in education / with children

Getting started

1 Work on your own. Look at the photos and brainstorm words that describe what is shown in each of them. → Describing pictures, p. 339

2 Compare your list of words with a partner and agree on a final list of five words for each photo.

3 With the same partner, think of three questions you would like to ask each of the four young people shown in the photos.

You're logical and enjoy learning.
Your ideal job: one where you need to solve problems and that has a high salary, e.g. an IT specialist or a marketing manager.

You're active and practical.
Your ideal job: one that needs a lot of energy, e.g. a police officer, an electrician, an athlete.

You're friendly and helpful.
Your ideal job: something where you can assist people, e.g. a flight attendant, a nurse, a sales assistant.

You're communicative and creative.
Your ideal job: something that involves interaction or artistic talent, e.g. a makeup artist, a journalist, an actor/actress.

You're smart and independent.
Your ideal job: something with language and words, e.g. a writer, a language teacher.

You're creative and practical.
Your ideal job: something that needs organisational skills or creative talent, e.g. a tourist guide, a secretary, a graphic designer.

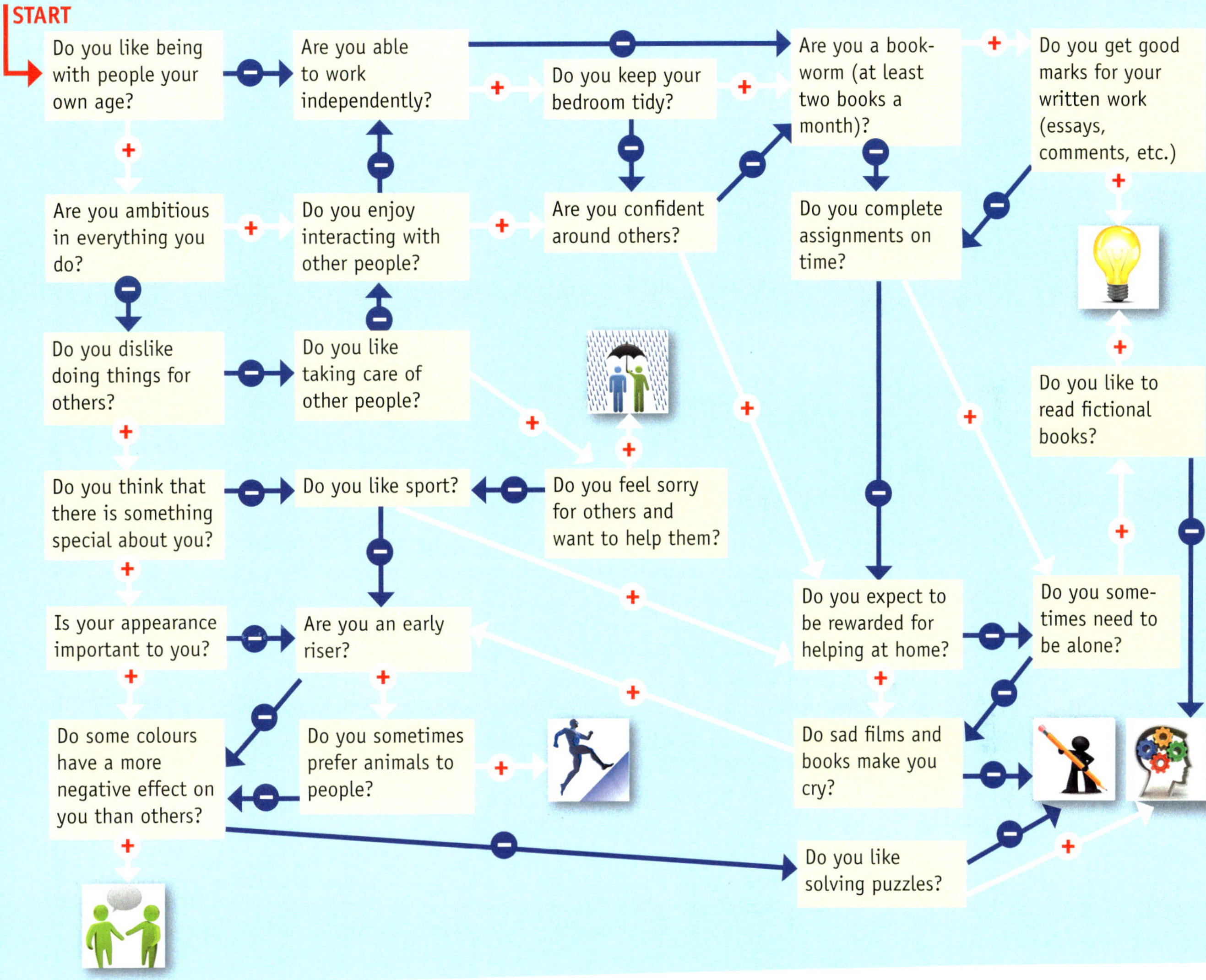

4 **Do you already know what you're going to do when you leave school? If not, don't worry. Check out the chart, find out what kind of person you are and which direction you should take.**

a) Work with a partner. Partner A asks the questions in the chart, partner B closes his/her book and answers the questions truthfully with "yes" or "no". When you get to one of the symbols, look at the list for a suitable job. Then swap roles.

b) What do you think about your results? Does this reflect your interest? Would you consider one of the jobs? Why (not)?

A Applying for a job

1 Before you read

a) Do you know which documents are generally included in a job application? Look at the box below and find the correct documents.

copy of driving license • curriculum vitae (CV)/résumé • pictures of your family • bank details • letter of application • school certificates • references • birth certificate • medical records

b) Compare your answers with a partner, then report back to the class.

2 **to crowd** – überfüllen
3 **killer** *(coll.)* – *hier:* sehr gut
5 **to expand on** – aufbauen auf
5 **hard-copy** – in Papierform
6 **recommendation** – Empfehlung
6 **sample** – Beispiel
7 **to compile** – zusammenstellen
10 **binder** – Ordner
11 **zippered** – Reißverschluss-
13 **table of contents** – Inhaltsverzeichnis
13 **divider** – Trennblatt
14 **customization** – Anpassung
15 **to gather** – sammeln
15 **to assemble** – zusammenstellen
16 **objective** – Absicht
17 **expertise** – Fachkenntnis
17 **trait** – Charakterzug
17 **transcript** – Zeugnis
18 **to verify** – belegen
21 **applicant** – Bewerber(in)
21 **to track** – verfolgen
21 **to reject** – ablehnen
22 **to comply with** – übereinstimmen mit
23 **work sample** – Arbeitsprobe
23 **spreadsheet** – Tabelle
23 **P&L (profit & loss) statement** – Gewinn- und Verlustrechnung
24 **annual report** – Jahresbericht
24 **to showcase** – demonstrieren
24 **training manual** – Schulungshandbuch
25 **survey** – Umfrage
28 **confidential** – vertraulich
28 **proprietary** – geschützt

eHOW Search [ ] GO

family | food | health | home | money | style | more

How to make a job skills portfolio

A CBS News report stated there are 4.5 job seekers for every open position. With so many qualified individuals crowding the job market, the successful candidate needs more than a killer résumé. An old idea, generally reserved for artists, designers and architects, is making a comeback for anyone looking for a job. The job portfolio expands on the traditional résumé with hard-copy examples of past work, projects, recommendations, writing samples and other documented items. It is worth the time to write and compile this powerful tool to give life to résumés through concrete examples of past work.

Instructions: Things you'll need

Three-ring portfolio binder   Copies of sample work documents

1. Compile your documents in a three-ring portfolio. A zippered style looks professional and will keep everything neat and clean. Organize the portfolio into sections with a table of contents and dividers. You should be able to easily remove and replace the sections for job customization.

2. Write, gather and assemble the documents. Begin the portfolio with a clear objective statement and summary of your work experience. Include your past experience, areas of expertise and personal traits. Request copies of transcripts, certifications or other documents verifying education or certification training and include them in a separate section.

3. Prepare regular and scannable versions of your résumé. Many companies scan résumés into their applicant tracking systems. Your résumé may be rejected if it does not comply with their system.

4. Include work samples relevant to the position. Sample spreadsheets, P&L statements or annual reports showcase your work as an accountant. Training manuals or employee satisfaction surveys are relevant to a human resources position. Reports, projects, PowerPoint presentations, technical drawings, graphic design projects showcase your particular skills that set you apart from the others. Be sure work samples do not include confidential or proprietary information.

5. Share awards and recognitions. Include copies of award certificates, letters of recognition, reference letters, customer appreciation letters and emails. Remove any personal information such as email addresses, street addresses, and phone or fax numbers from outside correspondence. This can be provided in a second interview.

6. Select relevant material. While jobs require a variety of skills and experience, do not overload the portfolio. Help prospective employers focus on significant information. Too much can be confusing and appear disorganized.

7. Create an electronic version of the portfolio. Scan the documents and copy to a flash drive or CD to include in the portfolio. Plastic dividers for electronic media will give your portfolio an updated look. (517 words)

29 **recognition** – Anerkennung
29 **letter of recognition** – Empfehlungsschreiben
30 **appreciation** – Wertschätzung
37 **flash drive** – USB-Stick

2 Comprehension: Multiple choice

Read the text and choose the answer (1., 2., or 3.) which you think fits best according to the text.

a) According to the text, there are currently
1. more qualified applicants than available jobs.
2. more available jobs than qualified applicants.
3. as many qualified applicants as available jobs.

b) At the start of your portfolio, you should have
1. school certificates.
2. a reference from a former employer.
3. information about your previous jobs.

c) Your portfolio should not contain
1. personal details.
2. samples of your work.
3. examples of positive feedback from customers.

d) Having a hard-copy of your job skills portfolio is
1. unnecessary.
2. recommended.
3. obligatory.

302 ## 3 Mediation → Mediation, p. 343

A friend of yours would like to apply for a job at a company in the USA, and for her application she needs to make a *job skills portfolio*. Use the text above and create a list of tips. Write your answers in complete German sentences.

23 ## 4 Listening comprehension: A job interview → Listening, p. 319, Taking notes, p. 352

Barbara Meyer has applied for a summer job in a coffee shop.

a) Listen to the interview twice and find out the following information:

1. name of manager • 2. opening hours (weekdays) • 3. opening hours (Sundays) • 4. working hours • 5. possibility of working overtime • 6. duties (three items) • 7. necessary qualifications

b) What does the manager learn about Barbara Meyer? Write down the notes she might have made about: 1. Barbara's age; 2. nationality; 3. family; 4. her English skills; 5. experience; 6. place of residence. Then listen again and check your answers.

5 Projects → Hotspots 1 and 2, p. 151

B Work placements

1 Before you read → Brainstorming, p. 351

a) Have you ever done a work placement? If you could do a three-month work placement with any company, which one would you choose? Give reasons for your choice. Share your ideas with the class.

b) Would you be prepared to pay €2,000 for the work placement you have just chosen? Explain why or why not.

theguardian

News | Sport | Comment | Culture | Business | Money | Life&Style | Travel | Environment

Comment is free > Career   Search [ ] GO

Career-boosting internships for sale

The pressure to get experience on their CV leads students not only to work for free in internships, but to pay for the privilege … if they can afford it.

About a decade ago the word internships was barely used in a British context. Today, internships are both ubiquitous and highly contentious. There are campaigns denouncing the ethics of requiring young people already saddled with thousands of pounds of debt from their degree studies to do unpaid work, and debate over the morality of a system that allows those from well-to-do families to exploit their connections and secure opportunities that give them even greater advantage over those from humbler backgrounds.

Growing numbers of recent graduates are paying thousands of pounds to companies that specialise in securing placements overseas. And auctions held in aid of charity continue to offer internships to the highest bidder.

Work experience placements donated to four charities by the auction house Christie's over the last year have each raised up to £3,000, while, in November, the charity Pilotlight, which sends volunteers from the world of business into small charities to help them work more efficiently, attracted a top bid of £3,000 in an online auction for a week at GQ magazine.

Meanwhile firms offering to arrange internships abroad for a fee, usually in China or Australia, are growing in size and number. One, CRCC Asia, has increased the number of placements it offers in Beijing and Shanghai fivefold in three years.

This year, 3,600 students applied for its one or two month internships, easily filling the 1,300 places. Students, who are assessed for suitability, pay £1,495 for a month in Beijing and £100 more for Shanghai. As well as a fee for arranging the placement, the figure includes accommodation, a visa and other extras. But students must cover their flights and living costs while in China, separately.

The one-year-old company Standout Internships offers placements in Sydney, in everything from finance, banking and law to fashion and event planning. Jonathan Manning quit his City job to co-found the firm with a friend after seeing graduate friends struggle to get jobs because of a lack of work experience. Manning says, "The fact that students are doing an internship helps them in their applications for a paid job. You need the experience to get the job and if you have to pay for it then it is worth it."

3 **privilege** – Privileg
4 **to afford sth.** – sich etw. leisten können
7 **ubiquitous** – allgegenwärtig
8 **contentious** – umstritten
8 **to denounce** – verurteilen
10 **debt** – Schuld, Schulden
13 **well-to-do** – wohlhabend
13 **to exploit** – ausbeuten
14 **humble** – bescheiden
16 **overseas** – im Ausland
16 **in aid of** – zur Unterstützung von
16 **charity** – Wohltätigkeit, Wohltätigkeitsverein
17 **bidder** – Bietende(r)
18 **to donate** – spenden
19 **volunteer** – Freiwillige(r), Ehrenamtliche(r)
22 **fee** – Gebühr
26 **to assess** – beurteilen
26 **suitability** – Eignung
27 **accommodation** – Unterbringung
30 **to co-found** – mitgründen

Critics disagree. Already concerned that unpaid internships put poor students at a disadvantage, they say asking students to spend large sums for such opportunities harms social mobility even more.
Sophie Corcut applied for an internship through CRCC Asia after studying history and French at Bristol and finding herself unsure what career she wanted to pursue. While at university she had already done several unpaid placements, mostly arranged through personal contacts.
Using a combination of savings, paid work and a loan of £1,500 from her parents, she got together the £3,500 she needed to cover the trip, including flights, and spent two months in Beijing doing a marketing internship at a fair trade company. On her return she was quickly accepted on a graduate scheme at management consultants Accenture.
Corcut says she is sure the internship played a big role in her getting the job. "Coming back from China, you've got this one thing on your CV that makes you stand out," she says.
Martin Birchall, managing director of High Fliers Research (HRF), says it's no surprise graduates are so keen to find placements. "Employers have been looking for more than just the basic degree for some time, and the recession accelerated that process," he says. "In the past work experience was a 'nice to have'. Now it has, in effect, becoming a pre-requisite." (852 words)

39 **to pursue** – verfolgen
41 **loan** – Darlehen, Kredit
43 **graduate scheme** – Traineeprogramm für Hochschulabsolventen
49 **to accelerate** – beschleunigen
50 **pre-requisite** – Voraussetzung

302 **2 Comprehension: Table completion**

a) What are the pros and cons of the kind of internships described in the text? Make a table and list as many pros and cons as you can find.

Pros	Cons

b) Explain the following sentence in your own words: "[…] asking students to spend large sums [of money] for such opportunities harms social mobility […]" (l. 36).

3 Role play → Discussions, p. 344
Prepare a panel discussion with the title "Internships for sale: a fair trade?" with the following roles. You can use the pros and cons you have collected in task 2 to prepare your arguments.

a) A recent graduate who is looking for work experience to increase his career prospects. ("I'd rather not have to pay, but if it gets me the job …")

b) A parent of a recently graduated student who is not able to support their child financially. ("We simply can't afford it.")

c) A human resources manager from a major company. ("Nowadays, work experience is a pre-requisite.")

d) The manager of a company selling overseas work placements. ("You need the experience. If you have to pay for it, then it's worth it.")

e) Another role you believe is missing in this discussion.

24 **4 Listening comprehension: Work experience** → Listening, p. 319, Taking notes, p. 352
Listen to a British teenager talking about her work experience in a London store. Take notes about her work experience and make a grid. Use the following keywords:

employer / type and location of company • length of stay • feelings before starting work • first impressions • normal duties • additional duties • positive aspects of the job • negative aspects of the job • achievements

5 Projects → Hotspots 3 and 4, p. 151

C Teenage unemployment

1 Before you read → Brainstorming, p. 351
The following text is about Neets, i.e. teenagers who are *not in education, employment or training*. It provides us with facts and figures, reasons for the present situation and also names measures to fight this problem. Before you read, discuss the following questions in class:

a) What might be reasons for young people to become Neets?

b) Which measures might be taken to fight this problem?

BBC NEWS EDUCATION & FAMILY
Search GO
Home | UK | Africa | Asia-Pac | Europe | Latin America | Mid-East | South Asia

Rise in youths out of work and education in England

The proportion of 16-24-year-olds not in employment, education or training in England at the end of 2010 was up on previous years, official figures show.
A total of 938,000 – 15.6% of 16-24-year-olds – were in this category (Neet) in December 2010, the highest final-quarter figure since 2005. The government said the number was "still too high". Last week the youth unemployment rate hit a new peak. Critics called for more investment in education rather than cuts. (...) The increase comes amid concerns that young people have been hit particularly hard by the recession, as rising numbers of graduates battle for jobs and fill vacancies traditionally taken by school and college leavers.

'Back of the queue'

The proportion of 16-18-year-olds not in education, employment and training, however, has reached its lowest level, 162,000 (8.5%) since 2005. This follows a push in recent years to encourage more 16-year-olds to stay on in education. A government spokesperson said: "The number of young people who are Neet is still too high. It is young people who bear the brunt in any recession or downturn, which is why we are so focused on tackling the deficit and promoting growth." The Conservative-Liberal Democrat coalition says it plans to fund 75,000 extra adult apprenticeship places, as well as offering a new Work Programme to provide "personalised support and training to help unemployed young people into work".
A spokesman from youth charity The Prince's Trust said: "As thousands of unemployed graduates flood the jobs market, Britain's most disadvantaged young people are being pushed to the back of the queue. These young people may have come from households where no-one works, with no positive role models, or struggled at school, leaving with few qualifications. It is these vulnerable young people who need our support to help them into jobs," the spokesman said.
Last week, the youth unemployment rate reached 20.5%, its highest since comparable records began in 1992.
The government has axed the Education Maintenance Allowance study support grant for low-income students in England, and the Future Jobs Fund, which has been used to fund temporary employment for 18-24-year-olds in England, Scotland and Wales who have been out of work for more than six months.

6 **to hit a peak** – den höchsten Stand erreichen
9 **to battle** – kämpfen
9 **to fill vacancies** – freie Stellen besetzen
14 **to encourage** – ermutigen
16 **to bear the brunt** – die volle Last tragen
16 **to tackle** – angreifen
21 **youth charity** – Jugendhilfsorganisation
22 **disadvantaged** – benachteiligt
25 **vulnerable** – verletzlich
29 **to axe** – *hier:* abschaffen

Sally Hunt, general secretary of the University and College Union, said these moves, at a time when youth unemployment was at its highest in years, "could come back and haunt this country".
"Instead of erecting barriers to study, such as tripling the cost of tuition fees, the government should be following the example of other countries and be investing in education, not cutting the very services young people need," she said. Figures for Neet young people are published separately in Wales, Scotland and Northern Ireland.

(466 words)

34 **to haunt** – *hier:* später zu schaffen machen
36 **to erect barriers** – Barrieren errichten
36 **to triple** – verdreifachen
36 **tuition fees** – Studiengebühren

2 Comprehension: True or false?
Read the statements below and decide whether they are true or false. Quote or paraphrase words from the text which confirm or disprove the ideas in the statements.

a) The proportion of 16-18-year-olds not in education, employment and training, however, has reached its highest level in many years.

b) Only a fifth of all 16-24-year-olds in England were in education, employment and training at the end of 2010.

c) One reason for this increased youth unemployment is the recession of 2010.

d) Many disadvantaged young people in Britain simply do not want to be trained or work.

e) Critics of the government demanded that more money should be invested in education and training.

f) A high number of Neets come from households where no-one works, with no positive role models.

g) The Future Jobs Fund is a government programme to help young people in England, Scotland and Wales who have been unemployed for over half a year.

h) The government has already been criticised for increasing tuition fees making education more expensive.

3 Analysis → Understanding non-fictional texts, p. 320
Analyse the function of the quotations in the text. In order to get a better overview, first copy and fill in the table below:

quotation by	summary of quotation in your own words	function of this quotation

302 **4 Analysis** → Describing cartoons, p. 340
Describe and analyse the cartoon.

5 Research project → Hotspot 5, p. 151

"Yes, I've been looking for a job but I haven't seen any yet."

D Corporate culture

1 Before you read

a) Look at the photo. What can you see?

b) Find words that best describe the kind of working environment you think it represents.

c) Would you like working in a large office? Why (not)?

2 Comprehension → Understanding fictional texts, p. 322
In your own words, describe a day at the office for the employees in the text.

Joshua Ferris (American writer, born in 1974)

Then We Came to the End *is set during the downturn of the Internet boom at the end of the 1990s. The story takes place in an advertising company in Chicago and is a satire of American office environment.*

Then We Came to the End

WE WERE FRACTIOUS AND overpaid. Our mornings lacked promise. At least those of us who smoked had something to look forward to at ten-fifteen. Most of us liked most everyone, a few of us hated specific individuals, one or two people loved everyone and everything. Those who loved everyone were unanimously reviled. We loved free bagels in the morning. They happened all too infrequently. Our benefits were astonishing in comprehensiveness and quality of care. Sometimes we questioned whether they were worth it. We thought moving to India might be better, or going back to nursing school. Doing something with the handicapped or working with our hands. No one ever acted on these impulses, despite their daily, sometimes hourly contractions. Instead we met in conference rooms to discuss the issues of the day.

Ordinarily jobs came in and we completed them in a timely and professional manner. Sometimes fuckups did occur. Printing errors, transposed numbers. Our business was advertising and details were important. If the third number after the second hyphen in a client's toll-free number was a six instead of an eight, and if it went to print like that, and showed up in Time magazine, no one reading the ad could call now and order today. No matter they could go to the website, we still had to eat the price of the ad. Is this boring you yet? It bored us every day. Our boredom was ongoing, a collective boredom, and it would never die because we would never die.

1 **fractious** – mürrisch
3 **to lack sth.** – etw. vermissen lassen
11 **unanimously** – einstimmig
11 **to revile sb.** – jmdn schmähen
12 **infrequently** – selten, unregelmäßig
13 **astonishing** – erstaunlich
13 **comprehensiveness** – Umfang
15 **handicapped** – Behinderte(r)
16 **to act on** – auf etw. reagieren
16 **despite** – trotz
17 **contraction** – Zusammenziehen
19 **ordinarily** – für gewöhnlich, normalerweise
20 **transposed** – vertauscht
22 **hyphen** – Bindestrich
22 **toll-free** – kostenlos

303 △ **3 Analysis** → Text analysis, p. 326

a) Analyse the language the author uses to show how the employees in this company feel. First, collect positive and negative examples showing the employees' attitudes towards their job and workplace in a table. Then use this information to explain their feelings. Include the corresponding lines.

b) Explain the phrase "No matter they could go to the website, we still had to eat the price of the ad." (ll. 24–25)

c) Analyse the perspective from which the text is written and its effect on the reader. Give some examples from the text to support your answer.

303 △ **4 Comment** → Writing a comment, p. 327
Imagine you have been offered a job at the company in the text. Would you like to work there? Give reasons for and against.

We didn't know who was stealing things from other people's workstations. Always small items – postcards, framed photographs. We had our suspicions but no proof. We believed it was probably not for the loot so much as the excitement – the shoplifter's addictive kick, or maybe it was a pathological cry for help. Hank Neary, one of the agency's only black writers, asked, "Come on, now – who would want my travel toothbrush?"

In those days it wasn't rare for someone to push someone else down the hall really fast in a swivel chair. Games aside, we spent most of our time inside long silent pauses as we bent over our individual desks, working on some task at hand, lost to it – until Benny, bored, came and stood in the doorway. "What are you up to?" he'd ask. […]

It could have been any of us. "Working" was the usual reply. Then Benny would tap his topaz class ring on the doorway and drift away.

How we hated our coffee mugs! Our mouse pads, our desk clocks, our daily calendars, the contents of our desk drawers. Even the photos of our loved ones taped to our computer monitors for uplift and support turned into cloying reminders of time served. But when we got a new office, a bigger office, and we brought everything with us into the new office, how we loved everything all over again, and thought hard about where to place things, and looked with satisfaction at the end of the day at how well our old things looked in this new, improved, important space. There was no doubt in our minds just then that we had made all the right decisions, whereas most days we were men and women of two minds. Everywhere you looked, in the hallways and bathrooms, the coffee bar and cafeteria, the lobbies and the print stations, there we were with our two minds. There seemed to be only the one electric pencil sharpener in the whole damn place.

We had visceral, rich memories of dull, interminable hours. Then a day would pass in perfect harmony with our projects, our family members, and our co-workers, and we couldn't believe we were getting paid for this. (762 words)

29 **suspicion** – Verdacht
30 **loot** *(AE, coll.)* – Geld
31 **addictive** – süchtig machend
31 **pathological** – krankhaft
35 **swivel chair** – Drehstuhl
41 **mug** – Becher
43 **uplift** – Auftrieb
43 **cloying** – anwidernd
47 **satisfaction** – Zufriedenheit
48 **doubt** – Zweifel
49 **whereas** – während, wohingegen
54 **visceral** – tief sitzend
54 **dull** – langweilig
54 **interminable** – unendlich

E Job satisfaction

1 Before you read → Brainstorming, p. 351

a) Work on your own. Write a list of at least five things which you would need to be happy in your future job.

b) Write a short definition of "job satisfaction" and share it with the class.

1 **tangible** – materiell
2 **reward** – Belohnung
2 **generous** – großzügig
2 **benefit** – Leistung, Vorteil
3 **increasingly** – zunehmend
4 **intangible** – immateriell
7 **gorgeous** – sehr schön
9 **praise** – Lob
9 **supervisor** – Leiter(in), Kontrolleur(in)
9 **to go out of one's way** – keine Mühen scheuen
10 **to bother** – sich die Mühe machen
16 **sincere** – aufrichtig
17 **accomplishment** – Leistung
18 **to escalate** – sich zuspitzen
19 **to appreciate sth.** – etw. schätzen
23 **survey** – Umfrage
24 **honesty** – Aufrichtigkeit, Ehrlichkeit
28 **to nurture** – etw. fördern
32 **executive** – leitende(r)
33 **merely** – nur
35 **to determine** – bestimmen
37 **sympathetic** – mitfühlend
37 **crucial** – entscheidend, äußerst wichtig

THE CHRISTIAN SCIENCE MONITOR

Search [ ] GO

World | USA | Commentary | Business | Environment | Innovation | Science |

Seven things employees want most to be happy at work

Ask bosses what makes employees happy at work, and many are likely to think in terms of tangible rewards: a good salary, a pleasant office, generous benefits.

Those play a role in job satisfaction, of course. But increasingly, workplace specialists are discovering that for many workers, the "happiness factor" depends heavily on intangibles, such as respect, trust, and fairness. Here are seven intangibles workers want most, according to experts:

1

"If the office is gorgeous, the pay is good, and the work is interesting, of course that helps," says Michal Ann Strahilevitz, a marketing professor at Golden Gate University in San Francisco. "However, there is one huge factor that does not cost an employer money: praise. So many supervisors go out of their way to let employees know what they have done wrong, but don't bother to congratulate and praise them for success. Praise does not cost anything to give, but its benefits on employee morale are priceless."

2

"The most important factor in keeping employees happy is treating them with fairness and respect," says Pamela Skillings, a career coach in Jackson Heights, N.Y. "People want to be paid what they're worth, treated like adults, and rewarded for their good work." Those rewards can be simple and spontaneous. "A sincere thank you or short note often means a great deal when it is recognizing an accomplishment or specific effort," says Mrs Sarikas, Career Specialist, Northeastern University, Boston. She finds that job dissatisfaction escalates when employees are not treated with respect or feel that their work is not appreciated.

3

Going hand in hand with respect is trust. "You have to trust the people you work for, and enjoy the people you work with," says Julie Clarkson, assistant professor of business at Wartburg College in Waverly, Iowa. In a nationwide survey of 500 employees about what matters most in their relationship with a manager, 90 percent of workers rank honesty, fairness, and trust as their top three needs, says Terry Bacon, author of "What People Want."

4

What people also want is an opportunity to grow and learn on the job. "No matter how we make a living, each of us is nurtured by our own professional and personal growth," says Michael Neece, cofounder of Pongo.com, which provides résumé-writing services. "Employees want to understand how their efforts contribute to the business and want to feel that they are making a difference to their team, their department, and the company." "The presence of money is a condition of work, and its absence is a demotivator," says Alan Weiss, an executive coach in East Greenwich, R.I. "But if you give more money to an unhappy employee, you merely have a wealthier, unhappy employee."

5

Bosses also play key roles in determining a worker's happiness factor. More than half of employees responding to an annual job-satisfaction survey by Yahoo! HotJobs admit that they don't leave companies, they leave bosses. "Having a fair, sympathetic manager who makes employees feel valued is a crucial element to an employee's job satisfaction," says Tom Musbach, managing editor of Yahoo! HotJobs. By contrast, if bosses aren't honest with workers, don't listen to them, and don't care about them, employees either leave or become disengaged in their work, says Terri Levine, president of Comprehensive Coaching U in North Wales, Pennsylvania.

6

"You need to feel good about the people you work with and the people you work for," Sarikas says. "You don't have to be best friends and probably shouldn't be, but you need to be able to respect them for their knowledge and experience as well as for their ethics." Similarly, employees need to find an organization where the corporate culture fits their personality and work style. For some, that includes work-life balance.

7

"Most people find happiness at work when they feel connected to the core purpose of the organization," Clarkson says. "When we are able to find work that uses our capabilities and allows us to address important values in our life's purpose, it is the best way to find happiness at work."
Whatever an individual's personal recipe for happiness on the job, Jeff Garten, author of the forthcoming book "Career Contentment," urges people to take the long view. "Career contentment is different from job satisfaction," he says. "It is a deeper state of mind about one's direction, fulfillment, calling, engagement. Job satisfaction comes and goes with each job, but career contentment is a lifelong quest and mind-set." (944 words)

40 **disengaged** – gelöst
45 **ethics** – Werte
49 **core** – Kern
50 **capability** – Fähigkeit
52 **recipe** – Rezept
53 **to urge** – drängen
54 **calling** – Berufung
55 **quest** – Suche
56 **mind-set** – Einstellung

2 Comprehension: Multiple matching → Scanning, p. 319

a) Look at the headlines below and match them with the appropriate sections (1–7) of the text. There are three headlines that don't fit.

Compatible co-workers • Financial rewards • Appreciation • A good boss • Trust • Individual growth • Generous holidays • Respect • Social events • A sense of purpose

b) Summarise each of the 7 sections in one or two sentences. Use your own words.

c) Compare the definition of job satisfaction given in the text with your definition. What are the similarities and differences?

303 **3 Comment** → Writing a comment, p. 327
"A high salary is the most important factor for job satisfaction." Comment on this statement.

4 Partner interview: School satisfaction → Discussions, p. 344
Interview your partner about the things that are necessary for him or her to be satisfied at school. Ask them how satisfied they are in these areas. The words in the box should give you some ideas, but you should also include your own.

marks • teachers • classmates • timetable • tests • catering • location of school • facilities • …

27 **5 Listening comprehension: Job satisfaction** → Listening, p. 319
Listen to an interview with the director of Oxfam in Britain, Barbara Stocking, and find out the following:

- What did Barbara want to be as a child? Why?
- How did she get the job at Oxfam?
- What are Barbara's top interview tips?
- How does she describe her work-life balance?

Oxfam
Deutschland

Oxfam International is a confederation of 13 organisations which work together with more than 3,000 partners in over 100 countries to find long-term solutions to poverty and Injustice.

Formal and informal language

a) Choosing the right register
Decide for the following words and expressions if they are formal, informal or part of a professional register (a variety of a language that is used in a particular professional context). Find a formal term for informal expressions.

what makes us tick • incentives • rewards • household pattern • bestie • friend • mate • parents • pal • sista • bro • dad • old man • fam • relatives • mommy • big daddy • peer support • social networks • peer pressure • motivation chart • marriage patterns • family structures • sibling • guardians • push factors • to save sth. for a rainy day

b) Rewriting a text
You have been asked to write a short text for your school's partner college in England. They would like you to write about German teenagers, friendships and finding the right job. Put the notes into a formal English text. You can use a thesaurus (= a book of synonyms, often including related and contrasting words and antonyms) to help you. Online thesauruses are a fast way of finding the words and expressions you need.

Notes:

- the German teenagers I know are open and don't have any stereotypes, they just get along well with everybody no matter if boy or girl, German or foreigner
- they just ask one question: do I like this person, are they cool?
- when it comes to finding the right job after school: no typically male / female job; only concern: What am I good at? What will my mates do? Will I lose touch when I go somewhere else?
- many of them have a hard time finding the perfect job for themselves
- but then they help each other because they're going through the same things
- when choosing a job, money doesn't seem that important as long as the people are cool and the work is fun
- they don't like others nagging all the time and telling them what to do, they want to be independent and also share responsibility
- if someone is getting on their nerves, they might freak out and risk getting into trouble
- all in all the teenagers I know are open and honest …

Start like this:
I was asked to write a short text about German teenagers, friendships and finding the right job. Of course I cannot speak for all German teenagers; I can only speak from my own experience. Generally speaking, German teenagers are open-minded and do not have any particular prejudices. …

1 Project: A job skills portfolio → Presentation, p. 362
Prepare a job skills portfolio for yourself. You do not need to write out full sentences. However, be prepared to tell your classmates what you would like to include in your job profile when applying for a job.

2 Project: Interview do's and don'ts → Projects and group work, p. 359

a) Work in groups of four. Go online and find a video with expert advice about job interviews. While you are watching, make a list of the do's and don'ts mentioned in the clip. Type "job interview, do's and don'ts, video clip" into a search engine.

b) Discuss your results in your group and add your own ideas.

c) Split the group into two smaller groups. Group 1 should write a script for a good interview, and Group 2 for a bad interview.

d) Act out your interviews in front of the class and ask them to point out the do's and don'ts.

3 Project: "Duales Ausbildungssystem" (Mediation) → Presentation, p. 362
Imagine you work in a German company with business partners abroad. In the near future, your boss is going to be visited by some Chinese business partners. He asks you to prepare a short presentation on the *duales Ausbildungssystem* in Germany. You can use a search engine and these two German key words to find information. Sum up the most important ideas about the German dual vocational education system in English. Prepare a transparency with key words to use in your presentation.

4 Project: "Juniorenfirma" (Mediation) → Projects and group work, p. 359

a) Some schools in Germany have a so-called "Juniorenfirma". Find out which class at your school is in charge of it. Then prepare a list of questions in English to ask the students involved. Collect information that you can use to create a leaflet about the "company" in English. You can present your findings at the end of this short project.

b) If there is no such "Juniorenfirma" in your school, imagine you are asked to set one up. Which services and products could you offer in your school? List your services and products, invent a marketing slogan to go with each item and think up a name for your company.

5 Research project: Job descriptions and necessary skills → Internet research, p. 358

a) Go online and find the job description for a job that interests you. Make notes on the most important tasks and necessary skills and qualifications for this job.

b) Now go online again and find a report from an intern/trainee about their experiences in the job you have chosen. What positive and negative experiences did they have and how useful was it for their future careers?

c) Copy your results from a) and b) onto a transparency and present them to the class.

A 2.29

1 **to ditch** – to give up
4 **to be set** – to be about to
11 **to reckon** – to estimate
12 **partially** – partly
14 **high-flying** – successful
17 **to commission sth.** – to order sth.
24 **to account for** – to constitute
29 **to skip sth.** – to leave out
32 **in demand** – desired
38 **remote working** – working from home
40 **gain** – benefit
45 **to fund** – to finance
51 **disability** – handicap
54 **solicitor** – lawyer
62 **valued** – appreciated
63 **you're more likely to …** – there's a higher chance that you …
66 **supervision** – *here:* guidance

THE INDEPENDENT

Working at home grows in popularity

Billions of people have ditched the commute to the office in favour of working from home – and the number of home-based workers is set to rise dramatically.

According to research […] by consumer think tank the Future Foundation, 8.6 per cent of the work force – 2.5 million people – work from home for one or more days a week.

It expects that number to rise by 200,000 a year for the next four years. By 2020, it reckons that 16 per cent of the working population will be at least partially based at home.

Employers increasingly allow well-paid, high-flying professionals, as well as traditional teleworkers, to work away from the office. The report, commissioned by Brother, the electronics and manufacturing company, also identifies a new type of worker, who is based at the office but e-mails clients from their BlackBerry on the train or makes work-related phone calls from home.

Describing them as "free workers", it says this group accounts for 46 per cent of the work force but will rise to 80 per cent by 2020.

"The question by then will be not who sometimes works at home but who doesn't," says report author William Nelson. "There are positive benefits to skipping the daily commute and increasing productivity by working at home. Highly-skilled workers who are in demand may find their company would rather allow them to work flexibly, rather than lose them."

In a separate report, published recently by the Management Consultancies Association, a third of the 1,200 respondents claimed that remote working is now common in their organisation. However, despite the potential gains for the employer, 93 per cent said it was the employees who were choosing to work away from the office, rather than their employer encouraging them to do so.

It also found that the majority of companies were unwilling to fund the arrangements. Only 40 per cent said that their employer covered the costs of remote working.

The Flexible Working Regulations, which came into force in 2003, provide parents with children under six – or 18 if the child has a disability – with the right to request flexible working arrangements, which may include working from home.

The employment solicitor James Upton, from Hill Dickinson Solicitors, says: "This means an employer has to follow certain procedures to consider their request for flexible working. It doesn't mean they are automatically able to work from home. Neither does it mean that employees without children can't ask their boss to let them work from home."

If you're a valued employee with bags of experience, you're more likely to convince your employer that you can work from home effectively, than if you're fairly junior, only started last month and need constant supervision. […]

(461 words)

1 Comprehension
Read the following statements (a-l) and put them into the correct order for a complete summary of the text. There is one extra statement that you do not need to use.

a) Commuting to and from work does not take place anymore and productivity might increase as well.

b) In most cases employees ask their employers to enable them to work from home.

c) Reports say that one third of the companies which have been asked recently confirm that working from home has become common for them.

d) The Flexible Working Regulations limit the number of people who should be allowed to work away from the office.

e) The number of people working from home has risen enormously and has already reached about 9% of the work force.

f) Those workers will get in contact with clients from their office as well as from their home or by using their smartphones.

g) The costs of working from home have mostly to be covered by the employees themselves.

h) A new type of worker, called "free worker", will make up to about 80% of the work force by 2020.

i) Especially well-qualified employees and teleworkers are allowed by their employers to work from home.

j) Last but not least there is no obligation for the employers to allow their employees to work flexibly.

k) The Flexible Working Regulations agreed on in 2003 make it easier for certain groups of people to apply for a job from home.

l) Working flexibly has got lots of advantages for employers and employees.

2 Analysis → Text analysis, p. 326
Analyse the language and structure used in the text and show whether the authors' opinions about teleworking become perceptible to the reader. Quote from the text to support your findings.

3 Comment
Comment on the benefits and inconveniences of teleworking for both employers and employees.

Topic 2.5

gq988z

Science, technology and society

A

> “Men have become the tools of their tools.” Henry David Thoreau

> “Civilization advances by extending the number of important operations which we can perform without thinking of them.” Alfred North Whitehead

> “Everybody gets so much information all day long that they lose their common sense.” Gertrude Stein

> “Any sufficiently advanced technology is indistinguishable from magic.” Arthur C. Clarke

B

Getting started

1 **Look at the photos and think of different ways in which technology is part of our lives. What are the positive effects, what are the negative developments?**

2 **a)** Choose one of the technologies in the pictures and imagine life without it. What would your life look like? Discuss with a partner.

b) Choose one of the technologies in the pictures and discuss some positive and negative effects of this technology with a different partner.

“Our technological powers increase, but the side effects and potential hazards also escalate.” Alvin Toffler

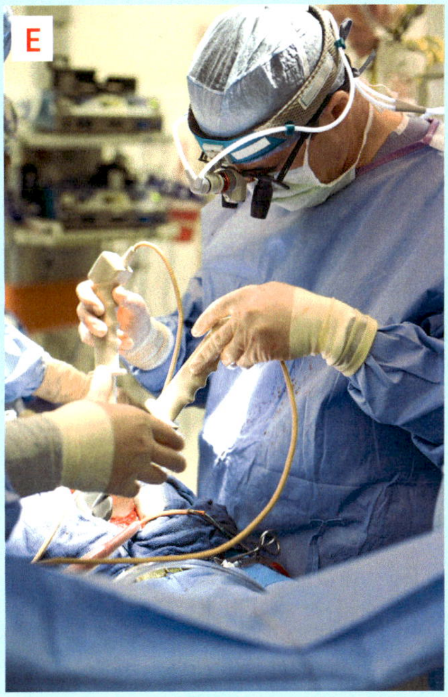

“Technology is the knack of so arranging the world that we don't have to experience it.” Max Frisch

“The real problem is not whether machines think but whether men do.” B.F. Skinner

“It is only when they go wrong that machines remind you how powerful they are.” Clive James

3 Work in groups. In your group, agree on the most important machine in history. Collect arguments and convince your classmates of your choice.

4 Famous quotes

Choose two quotes that in your opinion best describe the role technology plays in our lives. Give reasons for your decision and share your arguments with your classmates.

5 Research project → Hotspot 1, p. 167

Word bank

minimally invasive surgery • robotic arm • wind power station • nuclear power plant • solar panels • to advance • to progress • to live without sth. • it's hard to imagine • not all that is possible is acceptable • to meet the demands • to develop solutions • to make life easier • a double-edged sword

A Genetics

1 Before you read

Do you agree with the following statements? Why (not)?

- Couples should be allowed to use genetic engineering to make sure that they have a healthy baby.
- Insurance companies should be allowed to use genetic testing before giving someone health or life insurance.
- Sports officials should be allowed to use genetic testing of young athletes before supporting and sponsoring careers.
- Scientists should be allowed to clone human embryos to grow organs for transplant operations.

0 **stem cell** – Stammzelle
0 **to dawn** – beginnen
5 **a spring in his step** – federnder Schritt, er strahlt Zuversicht aus
5 **to conduct** – durchführen
7 **approval** – Zustimmung
7 **regulatory agency** – Prüfbehörde
8 **macular degeneration** – Makuladegeneration, Verlust von Sehkraft am „Gelben Fleck"
10 **to give the go-ahead** – grünes Licht geben
12 **spinal cord** – Rückenmark
13 **tissue** – Gewebe
14 **trial** – Versuch
15 **to gauge** – beurteilen, messen
15 **US Food and Drug Administration (FDA)** – amerikanische Regierungsinstitution, die für die Sicherheit von Nahrungsmitteln, Medizin etc. verantwortlich ist
16 **testimony** – *hier:* Beweis
16 **advance** – Fortschritt
19 **fertility treatment** – Fruchtbarkeitsbehandlung
20 **oligodendrocyte** – eine Form von Gehirnzellen
20 **precursor** – Vorläufer(in)

The Telegraph Search GO

Home | News | Sport | Finance | Comment | Culture | Travel | Lifestyle | Fashion

Stem cell research: a new age dawns in healthcare

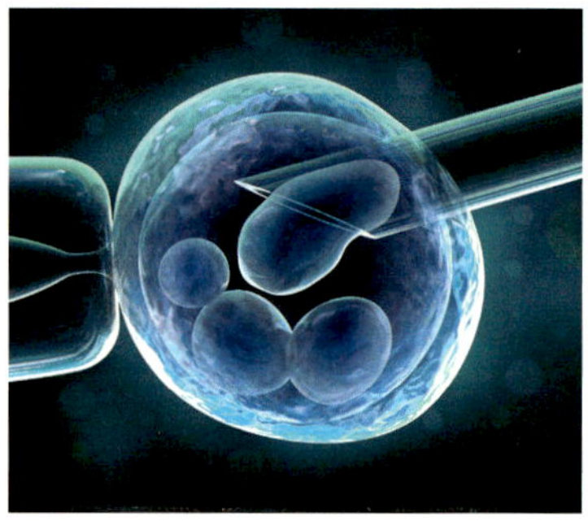

Scientists working in stem cell research believe that they are about to change medicine forever, writes Michael Day.

Professor Pete Coffey, of University College London, like many other stem cell scientists, has a spring in his step these days. His team is set to conduct the first test of an embryonic stem cell-based treatment on patients in the UK.

Approval from the Medicines and Healthcare products Regulatory Agency (MHRA) to test a therapy that he hopes will cure macular degeneration, the most common form of blindness among older people in the western world, is unlikely before 2012. However, Prof Coffey is confident that the regulator will give the go-ahead.

This is due in no small part to events in the US, where it was announced last week that doctors had begun the first trial in which patients with spinal cord injuries will receive tissue grown from human embryonic stem cells. The study by the Geron Corporation is primarily designed to test the safety of the procedure; larger trials will be needed to gauge its effectiveness. But the fact that the US Food and Drug Administration approved the trial is testimony to important advances in stem cell research. [...] The other important change is political. With George W. Bush out of the White House, the US, the world's powerhouse for biomedical research, is once more publicly funding medical research with embryonic stem cells left over from fertility treatments. The Geron scientists have grown oligodendrocyte precursor cells from their stem cells.

They hope that, once injected at the site of recent spinal injury, these will populate the area and help regenerate damaged tissue.

Prof Coffey's group is using stem cells to develop cells that support the retina, the photosensitive area at the back of the eye. In patients with macular degeneration, these cells start to disappear. He hopes that a patch containing the reared cells delivered behind the retina will restore patients' vision. "If we start testing, we should know quite quickly whether it works. The question is simple: can the patients see again?"

He believes treatments for conditions like macular degeneration, which are well-understood and don't require complex interactions between curative cells and host tissue, will be the first to appear. "Liver disease, heart conditions, perhaps diabetes, where the concept of getting insulin-producing cells into the body is quite simple, might be the first to be treated."

He predicts stem cell treatments for more complex and less well-characterised conditions, including brain diseases like Alzheimer's or Parkinson's, will take longer to appear. But ultimately he is in no doubt that stem cells "will change medicine for ever". This is a view shared by his UCL colleague Chris Mason, professor of regenerative medicine bioprocessing. "There are still many years of rigorous testing ahead and there will be setbacks and failures before we have safe and effective cell-based therapies," he says. "But this first in man [Geron] study marks the dawn of the 'Stem Cell Age'."

(502 words)

22 **to regenerate** – neu beleben
23 **retina** – Netzhaut
25 **patch** – Flicken, Pflaster
25 **reared** – herangezüchtet
26 **to restore** – wiederherstellen
30 **curative** – heilend

2 Comprehension: True or false? → Comprehension questions, p. 326

Read the statements below and decide whether they are true or false. Quote or paraphrase words from the text which confirm or disprove the ideas in the statements.

a) The tests for a stem cell-based cure for macular degeneration have been approved by the regulatory agency.

b) In the USA, a study has been started that will find out how well stem cell therapy works in healing spinal cord injuries.

c) Former US president George W. Bush was opposed to funding medical stem cell research.

d) Researchers hope to make blind patients see again by introducing photosensitive cells grown from stem cells into the patients' eyes.

e) Parkinson's and Alzheimer's will soon be curable as well.

304 **3 Mediation** → Mediation, p. 343

Summarise the current developments and possibilities of stem cell research and stem cell treatment as mentioned in the article in a German text.

304 **4 Analysis** → Text analysis, p. 326

Analyse the structure of the text and state if the author includes his personal opinion about stem cell research in this article. Quote examples from the text to support your answer.

5 Research project → Hotspot 2, p. 167

B Human spare parts

1 Before you read → Brainstorming, p. 351
Why do people have babies? Discuss reasons with a partner. To what extent can these reasons influence a person's relationship with his / her parents, and what effect might this have on their self-image and self-esteem?

2 Comprehension → Understanding fictional texts, p. 322

a) Make a list of the reasons the narrator gives for why people have babies.

b) Briefly outline the circumstances surrounding the narrator's own birth.

3 Analysis
Explain the sentence: "[…] we practically set a place for Death at the dinner table." (ll. 41 – 42)

Jodi Picoult (American writer, born in 1967)

The following text is a passage from "My Sister's Keeper", a novel by Jodi Picoult.

Anna

When I was little, the great mystery to me wasn't how babies were made, but why. The mechanics I understood – my older brother Jesse had filled me in – although at the time I was sure he'd heard half of it wrong. Other kids my age were busy looking up the words penis and vagina in the classroom dictionary when the teacher had her back turned, but I paid attention to different details. Like why some mothers only had one child, while other families seemed to multiply before your eyes. Or how the new girl in school, Sedona, told anyone who'd listen that she was named for the place where her parents were vacationing when they made her ("Good thing they weren't staying in Jersey City," my father used to say).
Now that I am thirteen, these distinctions are only more complicated: the eighth grader who dropped out of school because she got into trouble; a neighbor who got herself pregnant in the hopes it would keep her husband from filing for divorce. I'm telling you, if aliens landed on earth today and took a good hard look at why babies get born, they'd conclude that most people have children by accident, or because they drink too much on a certain night, or because birth control isn't one hundred percent, or for a thousand other reasons that really aren't very flattering.
On the other hand, I was born for a very specific purpose. I wasn't the result of a cheap bottle of wine or a full moon or the heat of the moment. I was born because a scientist managed to hook up my mother's eggs and my father's sperm to create a specific combination of precious genetic material. In fact, when Jesse told me how babies get made and I, the great disbeliever, decided to ask my parents the truth, I got more than I bargained for. They sat me down and told me all the usual stuff, of course – but they also explained that they chose little embryonic me, specifically, because I could save my sister Kate. "We loved you

1 **mystery** – Rätsel
2 **mechanics** *(pl)* – Ablauf
12 **to file for divorce** – die Scheidung einreichen
17 **flattering** – schmeichelhaft
20 **to hook up** – *hier:* zusammenfügen
21 **precious** – wertvoll
23 **more than I bargained for** – mehr als ich erwartet hatte

4 Role play → Discussions, p. 344

a) Write down two or three sentences in which you describe the relationship between the characters in the text. Since the text isn't explicit about this, you have to use your imagination. Write about how:
- the narrator feels about her parents / her sister / herself,
- the parents feel about their daughter Kate / the narrator.

b) Now prepare a role play in which the family come together to discuss their feelings. Work in groups of four and assign a role to each person. Then, on your own, collect arguments to support your position. You can use your ideas from exercise a) to help you.

5 Comment
Is it ethically acceptable to artificially create a child in order to save another life? Discuss this question using the results from the previous task.

6 Project → Hotspot 3, p. 167

even more," my mother made sure to say, "because we knew what exactly we were getting."

It made me wonder, though, what would have happened if Kate had been healthy. Chances are, I'd still be floating up in Heaven or wherever, waiting to be attached to a body to spend some time on Earth. Certainly I would not be part of this family. See, unlike the rest of the free world, I didn't get here by accident. And if your parents have you for a reason, then that reason better exist. Because once it's gone, so are you. […]

My parents tried to make things normal, but that's a relative term. The truth is, I was never really a kid. To be honest, neither were Kate and Jesse. I guess maybe my brother had his moment in the sun for the four years he was alive before Kate got diagnosed, but ever since then, we've been too busy looking over our shoulders to run headlong into growing up. You know how most little kids think they're like cartoon characters – if an anvil drops on their heads they can peel themselves off the sidewalk and keep going?

Well, I never once believed that. How could I, when we practically set a place for Death at the dinner table?

Kate has acute promyelocytic leukemia. Actually, that's not quite true – right now she doesn't have it, but it's hibernating under her skin like a bear, until it decides to roar again. She was diagnosed when she was two; she's sixteen now. Molecular relapse and granulocyte and portacath – these words are part of my vocabulary, even though I'll never find them on any SAT. I'm an allogeneic donor – a perfect sibling match. When Kate needs leukocytes or stem cells or bone marrow to fool her body into thinking it's healthy, I'm the one who provides them. Nearly every time Kate's hospitalized, I wind up there too. (680 words)

38 **to run headlong into sth.** – überstürzt in etw. hineinrennen

39 **anvil** – Amboss

43 **promyelocytic leukemia** – Promyelozytenleukämie

44 **to hibernate** – überwintern, *hier:* vorübergehend inaktiv sein

46 **relapse** – Rückfall

46 **granulocyte** – eine Form weißer Blutkörper

46 **portacath** – transportabler Katheder, durch den ständig Medizin in den Körper geleitet werden kann

47 **SAT (scholastic aptitude test)** – Test vor der Zulassung zu einem College

47 **allogenic donor** – Spender, dessen Gene ähnlich, aber nicht identisch mit denen des Empfängers sind

48 **bone marrow** – Knochenmark

C Green clubbing

1 Before you read

a) Many people think that nightclubs are loud, create lots of rubbish and use large amounts of energy. But how can nightclubs be 'green'? Work with a partner and make a list of ideas.

b) Share your list with the class. Which ideas do you think would be easy/difficult to introduce? Discuss.

SPIEGEL ONLINE

Search [ ] GO

Home | Berlin | Politik | Sport | Kultur | Welt | Meinung

Erste Öko-Disco der Welt: Schwoofen für Strom

Hüpfen, schwingen, springen – jede Tanzbewegung im „Club Watt" erzeugt Strom. Das aktuell produzierte Energie-Level der Tänzer lässt sich von Leuchttafeln ablesen. Die erste Öko-Disco der Welt hat jetzt in Rotterdam eröffnet.

Rotterdam – Diesen Werbeslogan kann man wörtlich nehmen: „We want your energy" heißt es in der ersten Öko-Disco der Welt. Wer in dem Beton- und Glasbau an der West-Kruiskade im einst als Drogenquartier berüchtigten Chinesenviertel von Rotterdam tanzt, erzeugt Strom und hilft damit der Umwelt. In der Nacht zum Freitag wurde der Club von energiegeladenen Tänzern eröffnet. „Man fühlt sich dabei wie ein Kraftwerk", schwärmte eine Besucherin aus Deutschland. „Der erste nachhaltige Dance Club der Welt setzt einen Trend", hofft der Architekt Herman Kossmann. „Er beweist, dass Umweltschutz und Spaß bestens zusammenpassen." Früher war der Laden als „Nighttown" für aufregende Shows von Iggy Pop, Nirvana oder Amy Winehouse berühmt. Stars werden auch künftig kommen. Doch jetzt heißt die mit Millionengeldern niederländischer Privatinvestoren völlig neu gestaltete Disco „Club Watt" – und wer hier auftritt, legt damit auch ein grünes Bekenntnis ab.

Das Kernstück der Öko-Disco ist die flexible elektromechanische Tanzfläche. Der Boden unter den Füßen gibt um einige Millimeter nach. Die durch Schwingungen erzeugte Bewegungsenergie wird nach dem Dynamo-Prinzip in Elektrizität umgewandelt und in Akkus gespeichert. Fast ein Drittel des Stroms, den die DJ-Bühne verbraucht, sollen die Tänzer als „menschliche Energieerzeuger" liefern.

Tanzt, auf dass die Birnen erglühen

Leuchtdioden im Boden sowie Lampen an der Bühne zeigen an, wie stark die Stromerzeugung jeweils ist. Wer sich austobt, sorgt für eine individuelle Lichtshow. „Leute, tanzt auf dass die Birnen erglühen!", feuert DJ Ted Langenbach die Gäste an. Der 48-jährige Party-Guru der

Rotterdamer Szene gehört zu den Initiatoren des „Club Watt". „Dieses Projekt hat mich gefesselt. Es gibt eben doch noch etwas Neues auf dem alten Tanzboden."

Allerdings ist die Eigenstromerzeugung gemessen am Gesamtbedarf des Clubs, der 2000 Gäste aufnehmen kann, mit bis zu zehn Watt pro Tanzendem noch gering. Doch dabei soll es nicht bleiben. „Dies ist Club Watt in der Version 1.0", sagt Martin Jordans vom Rotterdamer Architektenbüro Döll. „Wir arbeiten bereits an verbesserten Konzepten mit weit höherer Ausbeute."

Dafür werden auch die künftigen Erfahrungen des Italieners Lucien Gambarota berücksichtigt, der als einer der „Väter" der Nutzung „menschlicher Energie" gilt. Gambarota richtete in Hongkong den „California Fitness"-Club ein, wo Sporttreibende immerhin so viel Strom erzeugen, dass damit die Beleuchtung, die Musik und Elektronik der Trainingsgeräte betrieben werden können.

Anfragen aus aller Welt

Im „Club Watt" geht es nicht allein ums Stromsparen. Im „Club Watt" ist alles verpönt, was Abfall erzeugt oder unnötig Ressourcen verbraucht. So werden die Toiletten mit Regenwasser gespült. Die eingesparte Wassermenge soll dem Jahresbedarf von 13.000 Menschen entsprechen. Und an den beiden Zero-Waste-Bars (etwa: Null-Müll-Theken) werden Getränke ausschließlich in wiederverwertbare Hartplastikgläser eingeschenkt. Wegwerfprodukte sind verpönt, darunter auch Flyer.

„Den meisten Leuten ist noch gar nicht bewusst, dass normale Discos mit allem drum und dran enorme Stromfresser und Umweltverschmutzer sind", sagt der Miterfinder des „Club Watt"-Konzepts, Michel Smit. Mit seiner Firma SDC – die Abkürzung steht für Sustainable (nachhaltiger) Dance Club – hofft er auf Aufträge aus aller Welt. Wohl nicht zu unrecht.

Vor Anfragen - darunter auch aus Berlin und anderen deutschen Städten - können sich die „Watt Club"-Macher inzwischen kaum retten. (538 Wörter)

2 Vocabulary → Working with a dictionary, p. 353

Find the German equivalents of the following words in the above text.

illuminated panel • sustainable • environment protection • private investors • electromechanical • vibrations • kinetic energy • to transform • storage battery • bulbs • lighting • taboo • waste • annual consumption • exclusively • recyclable • disposable products • enquiries

3 Mediation → Mediation, p. 343

You are doing an internship at an international event management company in Dublin. Your boss has heard about *Club Watt* and asks you to find out more about it. Use the information in the text and summarise the main points for her in English.

4 Presentation → Presentation, p. 362

It is not only nightclubs which produce a lot of waste and use masses of energy, but any place where many people gather and spend time - for example, your school. How could you make your school greener? Work in small groups and think of some ideas to make your school more environmentally friendly. Present your ideas to the class, using a poster to display your main points.

D Smart homes

1 Before you read
Look at the picture and the headline of the article. What do you think the text is about? Which features would your own smart house have? Why?

BBC

Search [ ] GO

News | Sports | Travel | Weather | TV

Building smart homes of the future

1

You come home after a long, hard day at work. Having grabbed a frozen meal on the way home, you set it down on the coffee table and turn the kettle on. Seems normal, right? Only that your frozen meal has smart packaging and the coffee table has induction coils built in. So that as soon as you set the meal down – anywhere on the table – it starts to defrost the meal and keep it at that temperature. And because the kettle is also powered wirelessly, you can leave it anywhere in the house. The surface senses a kettle has been set down and starts to power it up. The surface is using magnetic fields to heat directly into the metal inside the product, and only the coil, meaning that you will not burn your hand if you put it next to your thawing meal or boiling kettle.

2

That may seem far-fetched, but according to Dave Barman of the US firm Fulton Innovations – which makes this cordless induction-heating technology – we could be only three years away from this being a reality if manufacturers want it to happen. "It's more efficient than gas and electric," he says. "When installed properly, there shouldn't be any cost difference between the traditional method and an induction zone."

3

The smart home of the future, featured in science fiction movies and cartoons like the Jetsons, is almost upon us. While we are not quite at the state of transporters and instant food makers a la Star Trek, our homes are getting smarter and more sophisticated. Real-time monitoring of every aspect of your house is here already, from plumbing to electrics, while companies like Google are trying to get the internet into your TV. But it takes a lot of power to make this happen, and a much more sophisticated approach to home construction, presenting opportunities for a whole slew of companies out there.

4

In the UK, for example, low-energy "green" buildings are extremely uncommon, according to John Alker, head of policy at the UK Green Building Council, an industry body

1 **to grab** – sich etw. schnappen
2 **kettle** – Wasserkocher
3 **induction coil** – Induktionsspule
5 **to defrost** – auftauen
6 **surface** – Oberfläche
6 **to sense** – *hier:* registrieren
15 **thawing** – tauend
17 **far-fetched** – weit hergeholt
26 **sophisticated** – *hier:* hochentwickelt
27 **real-time** – Echtzeit
27 **monitoring** – Kontrolle, Überwachung
30 **slew** – Menge

formed by the biggest homebuilders in the country. But this is set to change. The new government has stuck to targets mandating that all new residential homes must be carbon neutral by 2016, with commercial and public buildings to follow three years later.

5

A UK firm, Green Structures, is developing a passive heat recovery system using heat pipes and a thermal accumulator that stores the night's cool or hot air for daytime release, saving both the cost of air-conditioning and winter heating. This technology can also provide savings to the public sector – albeit in macabre ways. Mr Alker says that one council recently announced it was going to warm its swimming pool using wasted heat – from the local crematorium.

6

Fulton Innovations is also trying to reuse wasted energy, by for example having the sensor on urinals powered by the energy of the flush, or a shower radio derive its charge from the shower itself. But this only goes so far. The shower cannot power the washing machine or the heating system, as it would take too much power out of the system. "If you try to push too much power from the plumbing, it goes back to the source," Mr Barman says. "We're not trying to get free energy." That, at least, is a long way off yet. (579 words)

34 **to mandate** – anordnen
34 **residential** – Wohn-
35 **carbon neutral** – CO2-neutral
37 **recovery** – Rückgewinnung
38 **pipe** – Rohr
38 **accumulator** – *hier:* Speicher
39 **release** – Freisetzung
40 **albeit** – obgleich, wenn auch
40 **macabre** – makaber, grausig
44 **urinal** – Pissoir, Urinal
44 **flush** – Spülung
44 **to derive sth. from** – etw. beziehen aus

2 Comprehension: Multiple matching → Scanning, p. 319

a) Read the text and choose from the headings A – H the one which fits each gap. There are two extra headings that you do not need to use.

A Green buildings • **B** Smart but limited • **C** Intelligence at a price • **D** Convenient cooking • **E** Recycling heat • **F** Fiction becoming reality • **G** Hidden dangers • **H** More efficiency, same costs

305 **b)** In your own words, summarise the features that smart homes of the future might have, and the opportunities they could offer.

3 Vocabulary → Working with a dictionary, p. 353
Find one synonym and one antonym for the words below. Use an English-English dictionary if necessary.

smart (l. 3) • properly (l. 22) • traditional (l. 23) • sophisticated (l. 26) • uncommon (l. 31)

4 Analysis → Describing cartoons, p. 340
Describe the cartoon, analyse it and relate it to the text.

5 Project → Hotspot 4, p. 167

"Sorry I'm late. My smart house overslept."

E The next fifty years

1 Before you read

a) Look at the picture and brainstorm adjectives that express how you feel when looking at the cyborg. Agree on five words in your group.

b) Based on the discussion in your group, come up with ten sentences that all begin with "In fifty years' time there will be (won't be) …".

c) Share your adjectives and your sentences with your classmates. Which predictions do you find promising or useful, which ones do you rather find threatening? Explain why?

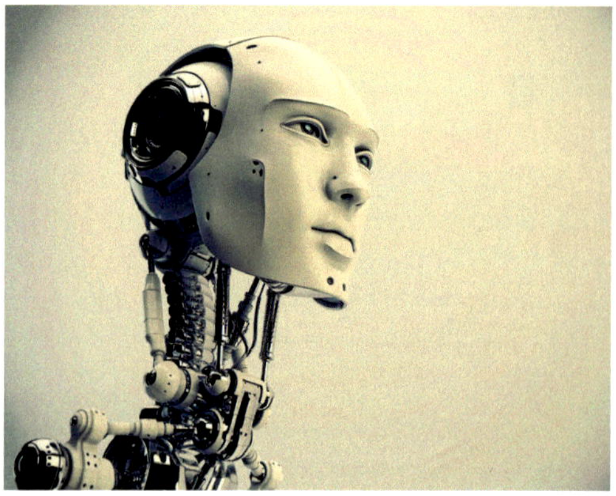

Promising predictions	Threatening predictions

2 **nanotech (nanotechnology)** – Nanotechnologie
2 **hyped** – angesagt, hochgejubelt
3 **disruptive** – bahnbrechend
8 **clone** – Klon
12 **traits** – Charaktermerkmale
14 **hereditary** – Erb-
17 **enhancement** – Verbesserung
22 **foreseeable** – vorhersehbar

Five trends that will transform science and technology

Nanotechnology

Nanotech is the hyped technology of the new millennium. It's unlikely to disappoint either, because it's disruptive. Nanotech will affect every industry from aerospace and construction to energy and medicine and will create products that we cannot possibly imagine now. However, public debate about it will be almost invisible until there is a major high-profile nanotechnology accident.

Biotechnology

We had Dolly the cloned sheep in 1996 and since then we've had cloned mice, cows, rabbits, horses and dogs. A human clone can't be far away, although it's unlikely that it will come from a US or Western laboratory. A clone will certainly grab the headlines, but a more threatening concept is perhaps the idea of genetically enhancing humans to strengthen or remove certain traits. There is also the alarming prospect of tests to judge personality or future actions based on genetic makeup and hereditary factors. In the future, everything from careers to relationships will involve genetic issues. Anyone for genetically engineered mosquitoes? How about one that glows in the dark so that you can see it coming? Or what about genetic enhancements and tests for unborn children?

Emotionally aware machines

Much has been written about artificial intelligence, but personally I think that AI in any meaningful sense is a long way off. Having said that, can you imagine the implications if an internet of the future did actually become aware of its own existence? Ohmygawd. As for the foreseeable future, a more immediate driver of change will be emotional intelligence – or emotionally aware machines. In the future we will see cars that link the emotional state of the driver with various safety controls and mood-sensitive features, computers that can tell whether we are in a good mood and voice-recognition systems that can judge if we are king. How about therapeutic robots or radios and televisions that tune into happy programs when we're feeling sad? Or what about online retailers tailoring their home pages, product offerings and even product descriptions to the emotional state of individual customers?

Ethics

Science and, to a lesser extent, technology have always operated within a political context, but until recently they were more or less left alone. Not any more. Both will come under the microscope as society debates not whether something is possible but whether its consequences are desirable. Top of the list of gatekeepers will be government, with its own national and international agenda based on political philosophy, the economy and defense. Privacy will also become a key issue once people realize that computers are everywhere and almost no place on Earth is free from surveillance. No form of communication will be safe. Other people will know who you are, where you are, what you are doing and perhaps even what you are thinking. Privacy in a digital and connected age is dead. Gen Y knows this and doesn't care. Gen X and the Boomer Generation either don't realize or are horrified. In the future we will even debate questions such as whether it is wrong for an adult to love a machine or whether people should marry robots or have sex with them.

Robotics

Robotic soldiers anyone? They're coming, but should such machines feel pain or regret? And if (when) there's an accident, who should be held responsible? Would you trust a robot to administer a general anaesthetic and perform surgery on you? Or what about when someone makes a robot that your child loves more than you? The convergence of a handful of trends is about to transform the field of robotics. First, the cost of computing power (processing and storage) is dropping fast. Second, distributed computing, voice and visual-recognition technologies and wireless broadband connectivity are similarly becoming cheaper and more available. Personal robots will be cleaning floors, dispensing medicine and keeping an eye open for intruders, while industrial robots will operate dangerous machinery and handle hazardous materials. On a smaller scale, robots could carry our bags from the supermarket, work as guide dogs for the visually impaired, or replace care workers in hospitals or nursing homes. Whether a machine will ever fully replace human or animal contact is a big question, to which most people currently answer no. However, attitudes may shift over time. (719 words)

from: Richard Watson, Future files: A brief history of the next 50 years

28 **to tailor** – maßschneidern
35 **gatekeeper** – Türsteher, Kontrolleur
39 **surveillance** – Überwachung
48 **anaesthetic** – Narkosemittel
48 **to perform surgery** – operieren
50 **convergence** – Annäherung, allmähliche Übereinstimmung
52 **visual-recognition** – visuelle Erkennung, biometrische Erkennung
56 **hazardous** – gefährlich
56 **scale** – Ausmaß
57 **impaired** – eingeschränkt, behindert

2 Comprehension: Table completion
Complete your table "Promising predictions – Threatening predictions" with information from the text.

3 Analysis → Text analysis, p. 326
Analysing the language used in this extract, show how the author includes his personal opinion in his predictions about the future and what effect it has on the reader.

4 Listening comprehension: The next fifty years → Listening, p. 319
Listen to the recording and complete your table "Promising predictions – Threatening predictions".

5 Project → Hotspot 5, p. 167

Connectives

Connectives are conjunctions, adverbs or phrases that make the logical link between two clauses or two sentences explicit. Their functions are to indicate, for example, addition, contrast, reinforcement, explanation, the cause or result of something, etc.

a) Complete the statements.

1. Rationalisation and automation meant the introduction of many new machines, so …
2. The Industrial Revolution saw the invention of many machines. Above all, …
3. In the near future nanotechnology will become more important. Presumably …
4. Technology is becoming more complex. Consequently, …
5. Life without sophisticated technology would be less comfortable, but …

b) Odd one out

Find the odd one out, i.e. the word that does not have the same function as the others.

1. moreover – besides – otherwise – furthermore
2. to start with – then – next – so
3. above all – instead of – especially – indeed
4. all in all – moreover – finally – in summary
5. meanwhile – therefore – thus – consequently
6. but – however – still – likewise
7. for instance – for example – such as – except
8. yet – but – above all – however

c) Synonyms

Think of a connective with the same function as the word or phrase given in the left column. Then use the new connective to develop the idea of the prompt given in the right column. Be careful: some connectives are used to link two clauses in the same sentence (a), some connectives are used to begin a new sentence (b).

1. therefore	Hard and dirty work has become unpopular …

Examples:

a. Hard and dirty work has become unpopular, so we have invented a lot of machines.

b. Hard and dirty work has become unpopular. Consequently, we have invented a lot of machines.

2. but	Technology means more comfort …
3. furthermore	More machines meant fewer jobs …
4. as a result	Today's global problems demand intelligent solutions …
5. however	With the help of technology, possibilities seem to be endless …
6. because	Today's technology is extremely complex …

1 Research project: Rationalisation and mechanisation → Internet research, p. 358
Do some research on rationalisation and mechanisation in the past. Here are some aspects you might want to consider:
- Which technology was introduced?
- What was the effect on the labour market?
- How did people react at that time?
- How is this development seen today?

2 Research project: Stem cell research → Internet research, p. 358
Find out more about stem cell research. Make sure that you include the following aspects in your presentation: pros and cons of stem cell research, arguments of supporters and opponents, government positions, current projects. Feel free to add any aspects you have strong opinions about.

3 Project: Organ donation → Projects and group work, p. 359

a) In groups of about four, do one of the following tasks:
- Design a brochure or poster informing people about organ transplants and trying to persuade them to give their consent to being a potential donor.
- Design a brochure or poster against organ donations, pointing out dangers and ethical concerns, and trying to get people to withhold their consent to being a potential donor.

b) Present your results in class and discuss your own attitudes towards organ donation.

4 Project: The home of tomorrow → Projects and group work, p. 359
You have been asked to design the "home of tomorrow" as part of an international architecture competition. Think about the features the house would have and what it might look like. Prepare a poster or an information flyer and present your ideas to the class.

5 Project: Panel discussion → Projects and group work, p. 359
Prepare a panel discussion of the question: "Have we become dependent on technology in our lives?" Before you start, decide on roles that should be included in your discussion. Then collect arguments to prepare for the roles.

Finding information

Check the websites of the following organizations and institutions:
Deutsche Stiftung Organtransplantation • Organspende (Bundeszentrale für gesundheitliche Aufklärung) • UK Transplant • The BBC (Health section) • The US Government of Organ & Tissue Donation and Transplantation

DIE ZEIT

Immer überall erreichbar

Die Revolution der deutschen Medienlandschaft begann am 1. April 1963. Das Zweite Deutsche Fernsehen ging auf Sendung. Nun hatte der Zuschauer die Wahl, später auch eine Fernbedienung. Aber konnte damals, vor 43 Jahren, jemand voraussehen, dass uns heute mehr als 500 Fernsehkanäle zur Verfügung stehen, dass wir uns mit E-Mails, Handys, DVD-Playern durch ein Meer elektronisch verfügbarer Information pflügen?

Absolut nicht. [...] Erstens, weil sich ausgerechnet die Zukunft der Digitaltechnik, auf der alle Kommunikationstechnik heute beruht, nur schwer vorhersagen lässt, und zweitens, weil die Kommunikation von der Kultur bestimmt wird – und deren Entwicklung hat sich bislang jeder Langzeitprognose entzogen. Ein paar Überlegungen lassen sich indes anstellen. Beginnen wir mit der Technik; jede Prognose über Kommunikation hängt von den Annahmen über die Technik ab.

Ausgangspunkt ist eine Vermutung von Gordon Moore, dem Mitbegründer der Chipfirma Intel. Vor gut 40 Jahren sagte er voraus, dass sich die Dichte elektronischer Schaltungen etwa alle 12 Monate verdoppeln werde. Dieses Mooresche Gesetz wurde in den folgenden Jahren immer wieder revidiert und neu formuliert. Es handelt sich natürlich um kein Gesetz, sondern um die Entwicklungspläne der Halbleiterindustrie. Sollten sich diese fortsetzen wie bisher, dann, so schreibt das amerikanische Unternehmen Montgomery Research, könnte im Jahre 2050 die Computerleistung sämtlicher heutiger Rechner der Firma Google in einem Kasten von der Größe eines Handys untergebracht werden. [...]

Bis zum Jahr 2030 könnte nach Ansicht der britischen Medienwissenschaftlerin Sue Thomas das „Internet der Dinge“ Wirklichkeit sein. Anknüpfend an eine Idee, die der Zukunftsforscher Alex Pang im Januar 2006 in seinem Weblog *The End of Cyberspace* publik machte, postuliert sie eine Welt, in der nicht bloß die Computer als Guckkästen in die Cyberwelt miteinander vernetzt sind, sondern so ziemlich alle Dinge unseres Alltags. Die Teekanne weiß dann, wo die Tassen stehen, das Buch ist erst ein Nietzsche und dann ein Marx, kennt aber auch die Links der beiden zu Hegel; die Bahnfahrkarte informiert über Verspätungen und Zuganschlüsse, und die Wäscheladung einigt sich ohne Zutun des Menschen mit der Waschmaschine auf dasjenige Waschmittel, das sich am besten eignet, ordert es und stellt die Maschine an. Oder so ähnlich. Jedenfalls umgäbe alle Dinge eine digitale Aura, die sich mit geeigneten Brillen oder anderen Instrumenten sichtbar machen ließe; das Schlagwort heißt *ambient intelligence*. Diese umgebende Intelligenz verzaubert dann nicht nur die Dinge. Jeder Mensch könnte eine solche unsichtbare, nur mit Zugangscode sich enthüllende „digitale Blase" (wie der für die British Telecom arbeitende Zukunftsforscher Ian Pearson sie nennt) um sich errichten, die beispielsweise alle seine jemals verfassten Briefe oder Anträge, Steuererklärungen oder Bestellzettel enthielte – es sei denn natürlich, er möchte sie löschen. Science-Fiction? Gewiss. Nur so gelangen wir in die Kommunikationswelt des Jahres 2050.

(440 Wörter)

1 Mediation

Gemeinsam haben Sie sich in Ihrem letzten Englischkurs mit den unterschiedlichsten Medien als Mittel der Informationsbeschaffung und -verwendung beschäftigt und diese auch auf Ihre Zukunftsfähigkeit hin analysiert. Zurzeit machen Sie bei einer englischen Lokalzeitung in Birmingham ein Praktikum und erhalten vom zuständigen Redakteur den Auftrag einen kurzen Artikel über die Zukunft von Informationstechnologien zu verfassen. Bei Ihrer Recherche im Internet finden Sie diesen deutschsprachigen Zeitungsartikel.
Stellen Sie die historische und zukünftige Entwicklung von Kommunikationstechnologien dar und gehen Sie dabei auch kurz auf die im Artikel verwendeten Begriffe „Mooresches Gesetz", „Internet der Dinge" und „ambient intelligence" ein. Ihr Text soll etwa 200 Wörter umfassen.

2 Analysis

Describe and analyse the picture.

3 Comment

"The rapid development of communication technologies is bad for elderly people as they will lag behind those developments and have problems to adapt to it."

Do you think that this applies to elderly people in general? Discuss.

Topic 2.6

The impact of change

ep5225

Getting started

1 Study the words in the word bank and check their meanings.

2 Describe the pictures. What do they stand for? Relate the words in the word bank to the pictures. What have they got to do with the impact of change?

→ Describing pictures, p. 339

3 Work in small groups. Agree on five terms which you consider very important when talking about change. For each term, start and complete a word web.

→ Word webs, p. 349

4 The table on p. 171 shows some groundbreaking inventions and innovations.

a) For each of them, say why it stands for change. Use words from your word web to help you.

b) Which inventions or innovations should be added to the list, and which should be removed? Give reasons.

Word bank

automation • shiftwork • mass production • progress • working conditions • rationalisation • work-life balance • demographic change • virtual reality • 24-hour society • machines • impact • online

Invention / Innovation	Year	Invention / Innovation	Year
wheelchair	1595	non-figurative art	1910
art auction	late 17th century	assemby line	1913
ball bearing	1794	stainless steel	1914
battery, electricity storage	1800	television	1923 / 1927
food canning	1809	frozen food	1924
kindergarten	1837	blood bank	late 1930s
refrigerator	1842	credit card	1950
jeans	1873	cardiac pacemaker	1952
shift work	large scale after the invention of the light bulb in 1879	botox	1967
airconditioning	1902	Internet	1969
decaffeinated coffee	1905	mobile phone	1973
convenience food	1905	virtual reality	1989
electric washing machine	1907	eBay	1995

5 a) List five things that you believe really made the world a better place. Explain your choice.

b) List five things which have at least as many negative as positive effects. Give reasons.

306 **6 Describe and analyse the cartoon.**
→ Describing cartoons, p. 340

7 Project → Hotspot 1, p. 183

A Convenience food

1 Before you read → Questionnaires and surveys, p. 360
What type of convenience food (i.e. food that has been industrially prepared so that it requires very little preparation time) do you consume and how often? Interview at least three students about their eating habits and report back to the class.

theguardian

News | Sport | Comment | Culture | Business | Money | Life&Style | Travel | Environment

Comment is free > Society > Search GO

The rise and rise of convenience food

The news that Heinz is developing ready-made beans on toast has sent Britain reeling. But is it with horror – or delight? What is it about ready meals, dinner in a can and tea granules that keeps us coming back for more? Tim Dowling reports

This was the gist of the news: baked beans on toast, Britain's most popular convenience food, was about to get even more convenient. "Instant" baked beans on toast, a frozen, fused sandwich that goes in the toaster, is to be tested by Heinz in New Zealand and if successful, launched in the UK. It's the subject that everyone is talking about, but you have to ask: why are they doing it? [...]

A classic TV Dinner of fried chicken, mashed potatoes and corn.

Once upon a time convenience foods consisted largely of ready-made or at least easy-to-make versions of foodstuffs which had a reputation for being difficult to produce from scratch. Instant gravy and custard powder were nothing like their real-life counterparts, but they came out roughly the right colour. Baked beans were introduced to the UK in 1905; the first frozen foods appeared in 1937. The US company Swanson paved the way for the modern-day ready meal when it introduced the TV dinner in 1954, selling 10 million the first year the product went national. The next year saw the introduction of the fish finger to Britain. Certain popular dishes from the heyday of convenience food, such as faggots in gravy, blancmange and chicken kiev, are now best known in their frozen, tinned or reconstituted form.

Britain was meant to have turned a corner in terms of its attitude to food. Farmers' markets are springing up everywhere. A chastened Jamie Oliver has brought the woeful state of the nation's school dinners to public attention. Manufacturers have been pressured into reducing the salt content of processed foods, and everybody is meant to understand the importance of fresh, healthy, simply prepared meals. And yet Britain now spends £900m in a year on ready meals, with 31,000 more of them bought every month than a year ago.

0 **convenience food** – Fertiggerichte
1 **to send sb. reeling** – *hier:* jmdn in Aufruhr bringen
8 **fused** – schmelzflüssig
11 **to launch** – *hier:* auf den Markt bringen
18 **from scratch** – grundlegend
18 **instant gravy** – Fertigsoße
18 **custard powder** – Pulver für Vanillesoße
20 **to pave the way** – den Weg bereiten
22 **fish finger** – Fischstäbchen
23 **heyday** – Blütezeit, Hochzeit
23 **faggot** – Frikadelle
24 **blancmange** [blə'mɒnʒ] – Pudding, Flammeri
24 **to reconstitute** – wiederherstellen
25 **to turn a corner** – über den Berg kommen / sein
26 **to chasten** – züchtigen
26 **woeful** – traurig, elend
28 **processed foods** – industriell verarbeitetes Lebensmittel

Sales of baked beans, meanwhile, have risen by 13% since 2001 and are expected to increase by another 30% in the next five years. Spam is enjoying an unlikely resurgence in sales, as is canned pasta and tinned corned beef. Roast beef and yorkshire pudding, steak and kidney pie, even omelette and chips - there's almost nothing you can't get in a can. Sales of tinned food have risen 10% in the past year, to reach £660m. Perhaps it's a mark of patriotism: it was a British merchant, Peter Durand, who patented the tin can in 1810, and two Britons, John Hall and Bryan Dorkin, who opened the first commercial canning factory three years later. [...]

But does the convenience outweigh the cost? How busy do you have to be to need precooked rice? What are you going to do with the extra nine minutes? Let's bear in mind that rice simmering on the stove does not require the sort of concentration that's going to spoil the last bit of EastEnders. The value added here, from the consumer's point of view, is virtually nil. The cost, however, is considerable. Ordinary, unadulterated, precooked rice sells at about £5 per kilo, as opposed to 84p for the normal, just-add-water-and-cook sort. [...]

Inevitably a lot of this stuff is targeted at children, and the lessons it presents are dreadful. For a start, it teaches them that cooking is a loathsome chore, and that time spent cooking is time wasted. It teaches them that unpackaged, perishable, non-value-added food is inherently undesirable, that cheese string is cheese and that a Pot Noodle with a bit less salt in it is some kind of healthy option. At a point when we are meant to be revamping our thinking about food, we are actually coming up with bizarre convenience versions of convenience foods. On my last trip to the supermarket I saw ready-made six packs of jelly which don't seem to require any form of refrigeration to stop them going gloopy. Few of us have the time or resources to produce gourmet meals from the finest, freshest ingredients every day of the week, but if you can't be bothered to make your own jelly you haven't got any business having a kitchen.

(726 words)

32 **spam** – Frühstücksfleisch
32 **resurgence** – Wiederauferstehung
37 **canning factory** – Konservenfabrik
40 **to simmer** – köcheln
40 **to spoil** – verderben
41 **EastEnders** – populäre britische Fernsehserie
42 **unadulterated** – unverfälscht
44 **to target at sb.** – auf jmdn gerichtet sein
45 **a loathsome chore** – eine mühselige Aufgabe
46 **perishable** – verderblich
46 **inherently** – an sich, von Natur aus
48 **to revamp** – aufpolieren
50 **jelly** – Götterspeise
51 **gloopy** – matschig

2 Comprehension

a) Summarise the history of convenience food as mentioned in the article.

b) Outline the basic facts the text provides about convenience food today.

c) In your own words, summarise the arguments against convenience food mentioned by the author.

3 Analysis → Text analysis, p. 326

Analyse the way the text is written (structure, choice of words) and show how Tim Dowling tries to influence the readers of his opinion about convenience food.

306

4 Text production: Writing a letter/an email → Writing an email, p. 329

"Few of us have the time or resources to produce gourmet meals from the finest, freshest ingredients every day of the week, but if you can't be bothered to make your own jelly you haven't got any business having a kitchen." (ll. 51–53)
Write a letter / an email to the editor in which you comment on the final sentence of the newspaper article.

5 Research project → Hotspot 2, p. 183

B Lifelong learning

1 Before you read → Brainstorming, p. 351

a) Brainstorm reasons why elderly people decide to attend a computer class. Which other classes do older people you know take?

b) Explain the title of the article "Lifelong learning is the secret to happiness in old age" in your own words.

c) In how far does learning in old and young age differ?

theguardian

News | Sport | Comment | Culture | Business | Money | Life&Style | Travel | Environment

Comment is free > Society   Search [ ] GO

Lifelong learning is the secret to happiness in old age

Not only can learning during the later stages of life bring happiness, wellbeing and a connection to the wider community for those studying, it can also reduce dependency on welfare. […]

McNair, a semi-retired National Institute of Adult Continuing Education research fellow, says that in all the guidance about wellbeing, education is central. "[It is] particularly important for those in the latter stages of life when one is less mobile and having to cope with the death of partners and friends: getting out of bed and feeling one has a purpose can be particularly challenging."

This is clearly not an issue for 84-year-old Jim Kelly, winner of an Adult Learners' Week award in 2010, who has in recent years dedicated himself to a wide range of study – everything from gardening to the 1688 "glorious revolution". After school days blighted by poverty and bullying teachers, the impetus to study came from his granddaughter Becky who, as a two-year-old, grew frustrated with his inability to answer her questions. "Don't you know anything granddad?" she would ask. Now, 14 years later, he tells the teenager he's pleased she asked that question.

Evidence of the benefits of learning during the latter stages of life is overwhelming, from research by the Alzheimer's Society showing delayed onset of the disease, to reduced dependency on welfare support.

Melissa March is executive director of Learning for the Fourth Age, a charity dedicated to bringing trained volunteers into care settings where they work with residents. "Our volunteers help people with everything from recovering piano-playing after strokes to wanting to tackle Welsh for the first time," she explains. "There is lots of interest too in IT and the connections that email can bring. Our work helps break down older people's fears about young people and opens our volunteers' eyes to the lives of older people with very different experiences from their own." […]

John Salinas, at 91, is also embracing IT. Each week he drives to his computing class and has progressed rapidly from not even knowing how to plug in his laptop, to using digital photography. "John is an inspiration in the learning group of over-60s participants by being an example of

5 **dependency** – Abhängigkeit
6 **semi-retired** – in Altersteilzeit
7 **research fellow** – Forschungsbeauftragte(r)
8 **guidance** – Anleitung, Beratung
10 **latter** – letztere(r/s)
15 **to dedicate oneself to sth.** – sich einer Sache widmen
16 **blighted** – vereitelt
17 **impetus** – Schwung, Elan
21 **onset** – *hier:* Ausbruch
25 **stroke** – Schlaganfall
25 **to tackle** – in Angriff nehmen
29 **to embrace** – belegen, einbeziehen

someone committed to learn, and not letting age or knowledge be a barrier to 'getting digital'," says Iona Gibbons, a community learning development worker with Bath and North East Somerset county council.

Sharing with friends

For John, the benefits of lifelong learning are clear – the weekly classes have given him a new zest for life. "I want to remain active in myself for my own health but also access all the information that is on computers, to benefit from community opportunities and to meet other people who are in the same boat as me," he says. "I see my computer learning as now firmly part of my life and can share what I learn with my family and show them what I can do."

For 84-year-old Len Street, a committed contributor to the University of the Third Age (U3A) since its creation 19 years ago, it is the companionship while learning that leads to a healthier life. He currently runs opera and art-history study groups. "When people leave work it is often the company of others they miss most – education in older age can be a lifesaver."

The value of learning is no exaggeration, says Fiona Aldridge, Niace programme director and author of a recent report into lifelong learning in care settings. "The benefits of ensuring that ongoing learning is a part of a care package is hard to deny when one learns of some of the best practice in this area. It has significant benefits in terms of improving people's mental health and reducing their reliance on medication." (629 words)

32 **committed** – entschlossen
36 **zest** – Eifer
43 **opera** – Oper
45 **exaggeration** – Übertreibung
46 **care** – Pflege
47 **best practice** – Positivbeispiel
48 **mental health** – geistige Gesundheit
49 **reliance** – Verlass
49 **medication** – Medikation, medizinische Behandlung

2 Comprehension

In your own words, summarise the benefits of lifelong learning according to the text.

3 Analysis → Text analysis, p. 326

Analyse the function of quotes in the text "Lifelong learning is the secret to happiness in old age."

4 Mediation → Mediation, p. 343

Summarise the following German text in about 130 words in English.

Lebenslanges Lernen: Studie bescheinigt Deutschland nur Mittelmaß

In Deutschland sind die Voraussetzungen für das lebenslange Lernen im Vergleich zu anderen europäischen Ländern nur mittelmäßig. Zu diesem Ergebnis kommt eine Studie der Bertelsmann Stiftung, die dem SPIEGEL exklusiv vorliegt. Der Grund: Investitionen in Schulen und Hochschulen seien zu gering.

Bei einer europäischen Bildungsstudie der Bertelsmann Stiftung hat Deutschland ein mittelmäßiges Ergebnis erreicht: Die Bundesrepublik bleibt bei einem Vergleich des „Lernklimas" deutlich hinter Dänemark, Schweden, den Niederlanden und Finnland zurück. Diese Länder hätten „in Europa bislang am besten die Idee vom lebenslangen Lernen in die Tat umgesetzt". […]

Aus den vielen Zahlen errechneten die Forscher mehrere Rankings. Deutschland erreicht dabei insgesamt einen Platz nur knapp über dem Durchschnitt. Das mäßige Abschneiden ergibt sich laut den Fachleuten vor allem daraus, dass die Bundesrepublik vergleichsweise wenig Geld in Schulen und Hochschulen investiere. […]

Die Forscher entdeckten zahlreiche Zusammenhänge zwischen einem guten Lernklima in einem Staat und dem Wohlstand oder dem Wohlergehen dort. Staaten mit einem hohen Wert auf der Bildungsskala zeichneten sich unter anderem dadurch aus, dass dort Korruption weniger verbreitet ist, mehr Vertrauen in politische Institutionen herrscht und die Gefahr der Armut niedriger liegt.

Ein Fazit der Studie: „Lernen macht reich, produktiv und wettbewerbsfähig". Außerdem würden der „gesellschaftliche Zusammenhalt" und das „gesellschaftliche Grundvertrauen" gefördert. […]

Weil sich Investitionen in Bildung nur langfristig auszahlten, würden ihre positiven Effekte allerdings häufig unterschätzt, beklagte die OECD. (228 Wörter)

5 Project → Hotspot 3, p. 183

C Health education

1 Before you read → Brainstorming, p. 351

a) Brainstorm important aspects that contribute to a healthy lifestyle. Agree on a definition of a "healthy lifestyle".

b) Collect ideas about how these aspects can be taught to children.

c) Do you live a healthy life? Explain why (not).

A 2.39

Life123
Answer at the speed of life

Search [ ] GO

Arts | Beauty | Career | Vehicles | Hobbies | Food | Health | Entertaining | Home

Teaching children about living a healthy lifestyle

Teaching children about living a healthy lifestyle is not as hard as you may think. As parents, you should model the lifestyles you want your child to follow. Living an active way of life and eating healthy foods will help your child stay fit. People joke about being a couch potato, but the truth is that a sedentary lifestyle leads to unhealthy habits. Jump off the couch and jumpstart your child's way to a healthy life. If you and your child spend a lot of time in front of the TV or computer screen, shut it off. One hour of activity each day is a good starting point. Introducing a variety of activities is important. It cuts down on the number of

2 **model** – *hier:* Vorbild
4 **sedentary** – bewegungsarm
5 **to jumpstart** – auf die Sprünge helfen

times you hear "I'm bored" and it develops a broader scope of skills. Take a walk, play a game, ride a bicycle. Participation in a team sport not only enhances physical development, it also builds self-esteem and teamwork. Being active as a family will also increase your child's activity level. If you find it difficult to keep your child engaged, consider motivation techniques. Reward charts and recognition of achievements provide evidence of your child's growth and development. Plus, your child can take ownership and track his improvements. […] (216 words)

9 **scope** – Spektrum
10 **to enhance** – verbessern
13 **reward** – Belohnung
14 **evidence** – Beweis

2 Comprehension

a) In your own words summarise the advice given by the author on how to live a healthy life.

b) Outline the role of parents according to the text.

.40
3 Listening comprehension: Healthy eating → Listening, p. 319

Listen to the second part of the text and answer the following questions:

a) What does a balanced diet include?

b) How much fruit and vegetables do young children and teenagers need?

c) What are examples of 'healthy snacks'?

d) Which drinks should be avoided and which are recommended?

307
4 Mediation → Describing diagrams, p. 341, Mediation, p. 343

Summarise and explain the two German diagrams below in a short English text.

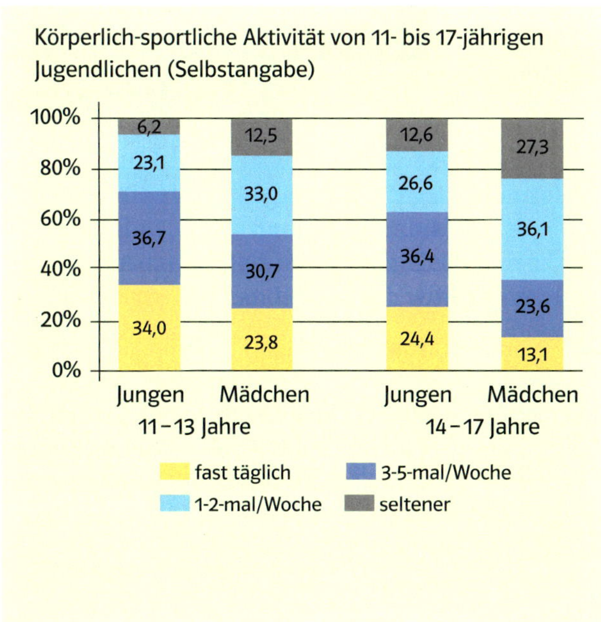

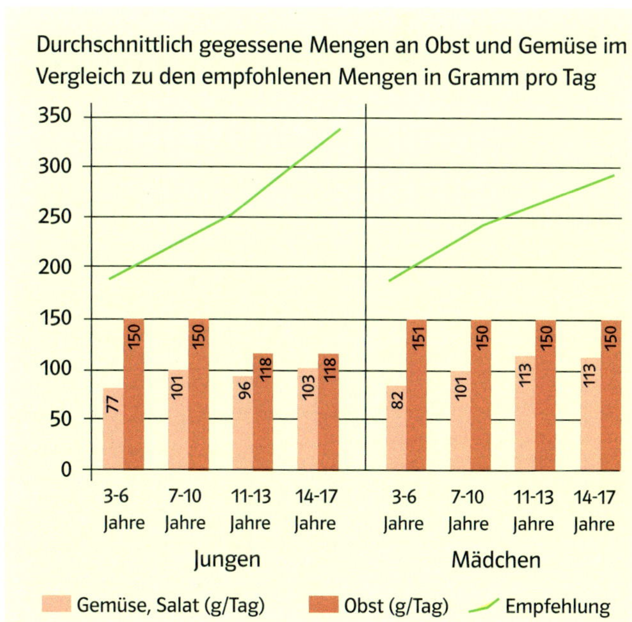

Source: Robert-Koch-Institut

D Digital media

1 Before you read → Brainstorming, p. 351
Compare your own use of media with that of your parents. Note down your ideas and share them with the class.

1 **native** – Ureinwohner(in)
9 **to transform** – umwandeln
18 **essential** – notwendig, wesentlich
23 **immigrant** – Einwanderer
24 **to come to terms with sth.** – mit etw. zurechtkommen
24 **to rule** – herrschen, regieren
36 **to indulge in** – sich etw. hingeben
39 **stimuli** *pl (sg* stimulus) – Anregung, (An-)Reiz
40 **scary** – Angst machend, erschreckend
42 **to chart** – vermessen, skizzieren
47 **attention span** – Aufmerksamkeitsspanne
48 **gnat** – Stechmücke

THE SUNDAY TI

The next step in brain evolution

Emily Feld is a native of a new planet. While the 20-year-old student may appear to live in London, she actually spends much of her time in another galaxy – out there, in the digital universe of websites, e-mails, text messages and mobile phone calls. 1 It may even be the next step in evolution, transforming brains and the way we think.

"The other day, I went to meet a friend in town, when I realised I'd left my mobile phone at home. I travelled the five miles back to collect it. I panicked. I need to have it on me at all times. I sound really sad, but everyone I know is the same. Technology is an essential part of my everyday social and academic life. I don't know where I'd be without it. I've never really been without it."

2 Her mother, Christine, on the other hand, is a 'digital immigrant', still coming to terms with a culture ruled by the ring of a mobile and the zip of e-mails. Though 55-year-old Christine happily shops online and e-mails friends, at heart she's still in the old world. "Children today are multitasking left, right and centre – downloading tracks, uploading photos, sending e-mails. It's nonstop," she

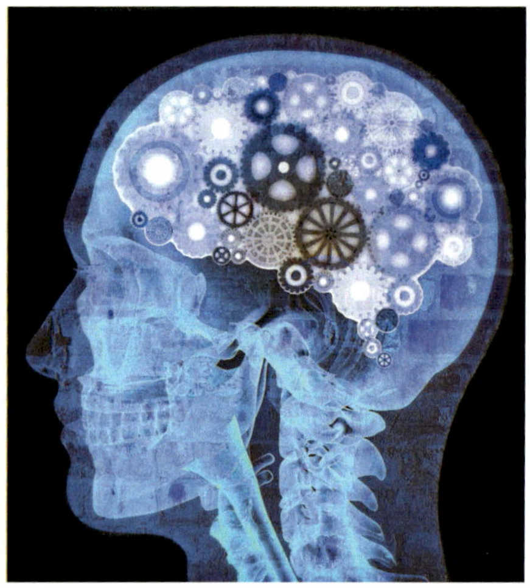

says. "They find sitting down and reading, even watching TV, too slow and boring. I can't imagine many kids indulging in one particular hobby such as birdwatching, like they used to."

3 To some, a world flooded with endless info bits and constant stimuli is scary; to others it is full of possibility and fascinating questions. Are digital natives charting a new course for human intelligence? And if so, is it better, faster, smarter? Many parents still fear that children who spend hours glued to computer screens will end up nerdy zombies with the attention span of a gnat. But it need not be like that, say some experts.

4 "Is this a different way of thinking? Well, a bit. […] People are becoming more visual than verbal." […]

The mass of visual, auditory and verbal information in the modern world is forcing digital natives to make choices that those who grew up with only books and television did not. "Younger people filter more," says Helen Petrie, a professor of human-computer interaction at the University of York. "But I don't think attention spans are diminishing per se. If we find something that is engaging, then our attention span is just as long as it has always been." […]

Where is it all leading? 5 […] Faster broadband speeds, easier interfaces, smaller hardware – innovation is happening at such a pace that what was science fiction a few years ago is looming as fact. (538 words)

54 **auditory** – auditiv, mit dem Gehör wahrnehmbar
57 **to make choices** – Entscheidungen treffen
63 **to diminish** – kleiner werden
64 **per se** – an sich
65 **engaging** – einnehmend, faszinierend
69 **interface** – Schnittstelle
71 **pace** – Geschwindigkeit, Gangart
73 **to loom** – sich abzeichnen

2 Comprehension: Multiple matching

Read the text and choose from the sentences A – F the one which fits each gap (1–5). There is one extra sentence that you do not need to use.

A	This generational divide has been evident for a while, but only now is its impact becoming clear.
B	Only one thing seems clear: changes propelled by the digital world are just beginning.
C	Research shows that children between 7 and 11 spend up to five hours a day playing computer games.
D	"Computer games can improve some aspects of attention, such as the ability to quickly count objects," says Dr Anders Sandberg, who is researching "cognitive enhancement" at Oxford University.
E	The behaviour of Feld and her generation, say experts, is being shaped by digital technology as never before.
F	That's what makes Emily a 'digital native', one who has never known a world without instant communication.

evident – erwiesen, offensichtlich
impact – Auswirkung
cognitive enhancement – Wahrnehmungssteigerung
to shape – formen
instant – sofortig

3 Mediation → Mediation, p. 343

Erstellen Sie auf Deutsch eine Liste aller im Text genannten Auswirkungen, die die digitalen Medien auf die junge Generation haben. Schreiben Sie vollständige Sätze.

4 Comment: Choose one of the following tasks

a) "[…], innovation is happening at such a pace that what was science fiction a few years ago is looming as fact." (ll. 70 – 73)
Comment on this quotation from the text by giving examples of inventions for which this is true, and examples of inventions that still seem impossible today.

b) Explain how digital innovations have changed the world of work in the past decades.

5 Research project → Hotspot 4, p. 183

Ben Elton (English writer and comedian, born in 1959)

0 **contestant** – Teilnehmer(in) an einem Wettbewerb
0 **surveillance** – Überwachung
0 **to evict** – *hier:* ausschließen

1 **to drawl** – gedehnt sprechen
1 **distinguished** – angesehen, bedeutend
4 **baying crowd** – johlende Menge
5 **to vanquish** – bezwingen
6 **poll** – Umfrage
7 **to leech off** – sich wie ein Parasit von etw. ernähren
8 **loftily** – arrogant, von oben herab
11 **shadow minister for home affairs** – Schatteninnenminister
16 **to deny** – verweigern
17 **overwhelming** – überwältigend
19 **crucial** – entscheidend
22 **genuine** – echt, aufrichtig
25 **to grieve** – trauern

E New TV culture

1 Before you read

Many television viewers are obsessed with a new TV culture that focuses on reality and casting shows. Choose any reality or casting show you know and explain why it is popular among viewers. Why do people take part in such shows? Would you want to take part in them?

The following text is a passage from "Dead famous", a novel by Ben Elton. 'House Arrest' is a television show in which ten contestants are forced to live together under constant camera surveillance. In the course of the show, the contestants can nominate each other to be evicted from the show. One day, Kelly, one of the 'inmates', is found murdered on the toilet. The television producers decide to air a ninety-minute special edition including the lead-up to the murder, the murder itself and a live discussion programme "about the morality of their having continued to broadcast the show at all".

Murder on air

"Reality television, as it is called," drawled the distinguished broadcaster, "is a return to the gladiatorial arenas of ancient Rome. What we are watching is conflict, conflict between trapped and desperate antagonists who compete for the approval of the baying crowd. Like the plebeians of old, we raise and lower our thumbs to applaud the victor and condemn the vanquished. The only difference is that today we do it via a telephone poll."

Geraldine shifted in her seat. She hated the way supposed intellectuals leeched off popular culture while loftily condemning it.

"Personally," the distinguished broadcaster continued, "I am astonished that it has taken so long for murder to become a tactic in these entertainments."

"Yes, but does that justify its being broadcast?" the shadow minister for home affairs leapt in, angry that the discussion had been underway for two minutes and that he had yet to speak. "I say most definitely not. We have to ask ourselves what sort of country we wish to live in."

"And I would agree with you," said the distinguished poet, "but will you have the courage to deny the mob? The public must have its bread and circuses."

Geraldine swallowed an overwhelming desire to unleash a four-letter tirade and resolved to be reasonable. That was, after all, why she had come on the show. The last thing she needed at this crucial moment in her career was to be taken off the air.

"Look," she said. "I don't like what has happened here any more than you do."

"Really?" sniffed the poet. [...]

"There is a genuine public interest here in what is, after all is said and done, a major public event. The audience feel, I think legitimately, that they are part of this murder. In many ways they feel some responsibility for it. They have been shocked and traumatized. They are grieving and they need to heal. They need to remain connected to what is happening in order to begin that healing process. We cannot suddenly cut

2 Comprehension: Table completion

How does Geraldine, one of the show's producers, justify showing Kelly's murder on TV? What are her real reasons? Collect the relevant information from the text and complete the following table:

Reasons stated by Geraldine	Geraldine's real reasons
genuine public interest in major public event …	…

3 Analysis

Characterise Geraldine as she appears in this extract.

4 Projects → Hotspots 5 and 6, p. 183

them out of the loop. Kelly was much loved, an enormously popular contestant. She truly was the people's housemate, and in many ways this is the people's murder."

It was a brilliant, jaw-droppingly audacious gambit, and totally unexpected. Everybody knew that the real reason Geraldine and the channel wanted to continue broadcasting was money, pure and simple. The stark truth was that Kelly's murder had turned House Arrest from a moderately successful programme into a television colossus. Episode twenty-six, the last to be shown before the murder, had achieved a 17 per cent audience share. The episode that had just been broadcast, the one that included the murder, had been watched by almost 80 per cent of the viewing public. Almost half of the entire population. Thirty-second advert slots in one of the three commercial breaks had sold at fifteen times their normal price.

"To prevent further broadcasts would be entirely élitist," Geraldine continued. "What we would be saying is that we know what is good for the public. We, the high and mighty, the great and the good, will decide what the proles can be trusted to watch. That is totally unacceptable in a modern democracy. Besides which, let me remind you that this event has already been live on the Internet. It's already part of the culture. It is already out there. Do you condone the social disenfranchisement of people who do not own a computer? Are they to be denied their chance to grieve? To come to terms with Kelly's death just because they are not on-line?"

Even the distinguished poet and broadcaster was caught off balance by such a breathtaking display. […]

"As I believed I implied," he said, "in many ways this event crosses the Rubicon in the democratization of the human experience. Reality television has already shown us that privacy is a myth, an unwanted cloak which people eagerly discard like a heavy garment on a summer's day. Death was the last truly private event, but thanks to House Arrest it is private no longer. In our open, meritocratic age, no human experience need be seen as 'better' or more 'significant' than any other, and that includes the final one. If Kelly had the right to be seen living, then surely we must grant her the right to be seen dying."

(724 words)

27 **to be in the loop** – auf dem Laufenden sein
29 **jaw-droppingly** – umwerfend
29 **audacious** – kühn
29 **gambit** – Schachzug
43 **disenfranchisement** – Entrechtung
46 **to be caught off balance** – überrascht werden
50 **cloak** – Umhang
50 **to discard** – wegwerfen, abwerfen
52 **a meritocratic age** – ein Zeitalter, in dem Leistung belohnt wird

Improving your style

Complex structures are characteristic of written language. You can link different ideas by combining a main clause with subordinate clauses such as conditional clauses or relative clauses. Another way of forming complex sentences is by using gerund or participle constructions.
Gerunds and present participles are easy to confuse because they both look similar (-ing form). The basic difference is that a gerund functions as a noun while a participle describes another word in the sentence. The past participle is formed like the simple past in regular verbs, in irregular verbs it is the third form of the verb.

Examples:
The smart phone's most useful function is **connecting** its user to the Internet, anytime anywhere. → Here *connecting* is a gerund which has the function of a noun.

The smart phone started **uploading** my photos onto Facebook as soon as it connected to my laptop. → In this case, *uploading* is a (present) participle describing what the smart phone was doing.

The pictures **uploaded** by my smart phone are always of good quality. → The past participle *uploaded* is used here as a shortened relative clause (for "The pictures which are uploaded ...").

a) Determine whether the -ing form in the following sentences is a gerund or a present participle construction, and identify the past participles.

1. In computer classes, elderly people learn new skills, allowing them to keep up with technological changes.
2. Designed by innovative developers, the smart phone is not only smart, but also stylish.
3. The *Volkshochschule* is one of the German institutions offering lifelong learning for everyone.
4. In the UK, an even wider range of convenience foods will soon be sold, making life easier for working mothers.
5. Living to the age of 100 will have become the norm by the year 2050.
6. The celebrity world depicted in the media is often based on gossip and rumours.

b) Rephrase the participle constructions (present and past participles) by changing them into subordinate clauses, or make two sentences out of the one sentence.

c) Rewrite the following sentences. Link the two ideas by using a gerund or a participle construction.

1. The new heating system heats your rooms automatically. It does not use much energy.
2. With your automated vacuum cleaner you don't have to clean the floor yourself anymore. You can relax instead.
3. My smart phone wakes me up every morning. I am very grateful.
4. Don't just press the 'start' button. You must always read the instructions first.
5. You can live longer. Just eat healthily.
6. The dinner party went well. My new food processor did everything for me.

1 Project: Songs about change → Projects and group work, p. 359
Work in groups of 4–6. There are many songs that are called "change" or which have got this word in their title.

a) Make a list of songs. Prepare to present these songs (lyrics, music, etc.) to the class.

b) Which topics that have to do with change do they deal with in particular?

c) Bring along pictures that represent the topics and the aspects mentioned in the songs.

d) Prepare posters that show your understanding and interpretation of these songs.

e) Present the posters to the class.

2 Research project: Change → Internet research, p. 358

a) Agree on one topic which in your opinion most strongly represents change (i.e. the Internet, working conditions, family structures, etc.)

b) Make a list of four to five sub-topics which are essential for the overall topic.

c) Go online and collect information about these sub-topics in the past and at present.

d) Compare and analyse your findings.

e) Forecast the importance of this topic for 2050 and explain your reasons.

Finding information

Look for information on the Internet. Use a search engine and try the following search words: guardian.co.uk • mirror.co.uk • independent.co.uk • sundaymirror.co.uk • bigissue.com • sundaysun.co.uk • theherald.co.uk • British newspapers • American newspapers

3 Project: Further education classes → Projects and group work, p. 359
Make a flyer with the aim of attracting senior citizens to take part in further education classes. Include information from the texts in this topic and your own research results. Present your flyers to your classmates.

4 Research project: Mass media → Internet research, p. 358
Research the development of the mass media (books, newspapers, the cinema, radio, television, computer technology, the Internet) and draw up a timeline. Make assumptions about the future of different forms of mass media.

5 Project: Panel discussion → Discussions, p. 344
Think of at least six interest groups that might have strong opinions on the question whether the show should have been stopped after Kelly's murder.
Form groups that represent each of these interest groups. Also nominate two chair-persons to lead the discussion.

6 Project: A new TV show → Projects and group work, p. 359
Create a concept for a new TV show, e.g. game show, reality show, talent show etc. Present it to the class and explain why it is likely to become a huge success.

A 2.41

1 **compulsory** – obligatory
1 **retirement** – time when one no longer works after a certain age
4 **to peg** – *here:* to connect
11 **aberration** – abnormality
25 **incremental** – step-by-step
27 **increment** – level
28 **redistribution** – reallocation
30 **discretionary time** – free time
32 **elusive** – hard to achieve
37 **prevailing** – common
39 **peril** – risk

theguardian

News | Sport | Comment | Culture | Business | Money | Life&Style | Travel | Environment

Comment is free > Society   Search [ ] GO

A shorter working week would benefit society

Ending compulsory retirement is a good idea – but we can do more to create a sensible and sustainable work-life balance

Phasing out compulsory retirement must be a sensible idea. Providing for a right to retire at an age pegged to rising life expectancy may be a sensible next step. No one should feel trapped in paid employment as the years advance beyond 70, but – who knows – it may not be long before 70 is the new 60.

The real problem lies with the whole idea of retirement as something that falls across our path like a tree in a storm. And that is because we have such fixed ideas about a "normal" working life. Why should everyone be expected to work at least eight hours a day, five days a week – and often much more? Why do we look upon the rise in "part-time" employment as some kind of aberration, instead of a step in the right direction?

The New Economics Foundation is calling for a move towards a much shorter working week, over a decade or more, with a goal of 21 hours as the new standard. Instead of settling for high rates of unemployment, why not share the work out, with shorter hours for all allowing more people to join the labour force? No one imagines this will be easy, but an incremental shift would leave time to put compensating measures in place – a higher minimum wage, more training, flexible working conditions and a gradual trade-off between pay increments and working time.

The benefits of a shorter working week could be very substantial. Think of it as a redistribution of paid and unpaid time. People who are currently out of work get a chance to earn a living. Everyone gets more discretionary time – so they have more freedom to play their part as parents, carers, friends, neighbours and active citizens. It begins to make sense of the notion of "work-life balance", which has proved so elusive – especially for parents and carers – in a long-hours culture. It could even help to realise some of the more honourable intentions of the "big society" – how else, after all, are citizens and voluntary organisations to find the time to take more control over what happens to them at a local level?

There is evidence that people who work shorter hours are more productive hour-for-hour, so that's got to be good for business. And at the same time it helps to shift prevailing values away from high-rolling consumerism, where we work to earn, earn to consume and consume at the peril of our planet. We might give more careful thought to how much stuff we really need to buy and, therefore, why we need to work such long hours to earn the money to buy it.

It would help to promote equality, both by lowering unemployment rates and by sharing paid and unpaid labour more equally between women and men. There would be less mental and physical ill-health, since both are associated with long hours as well as with joblessness. And it would transform the way we deal with later life. People who work shorter hours throughout their lives are less likely to burn out by 65. Down-shifting for older workers could be a very gentle affair, with no great contrast between "normal" and pre-retirement patterns of work. Most people could go on working until well into their 70s, if they chose to do so, gradually reducing their time. The point is not to force people to work shorter – or longer – hours, but to change what we think of as the most sensible and sustainable way to lead our lives.

(613 words)

45 **down-shifting** – *here:* working fewer hours
46 **gentle** – smooth
49 **sensible** – reasonable

1 Comprehension

Read the text and the statements below. Quote words or phrases from the text that explicitly express the ideas found in the statements.

a) There should be no fixed date when people should be allowed or even forced to retire.
Example: Phasing out compulsory retirement must be a sensible idea.

b) The author wonders why people should always have a nine-to-five job.

c) Earning less money due to reduced working hours can make us more environmentally conscious.

d) "Work-life balance" would reduce the number of diseases.

e) In the future, there should be individual ways about how to deal with different forms of work.

f) Shorter working hours mean that more people could be offered employment.

g) Working part-time should not be condemned but seen as a good alternative.

h) "Work-life balance" is the right way to have more time to care for things after work.

i) There should be a move towards shorter working hours that only add up to 52.5% of a former 40-hour week.

2 Analysis

Describe and analyse the diagram about total working time worldwide.

3 Comment

"[…] we work to earn, earn to consume and consume at the peril of our planet. We might give more careful thought to how much stuff we really need to buy […]" (ll. 38–40)
Working less and consuming less – would that be an option for you? Comment.

Total working time is lowest in Western Europe and highest outside Europe

Total minutes worked, paid and unpaid, per day

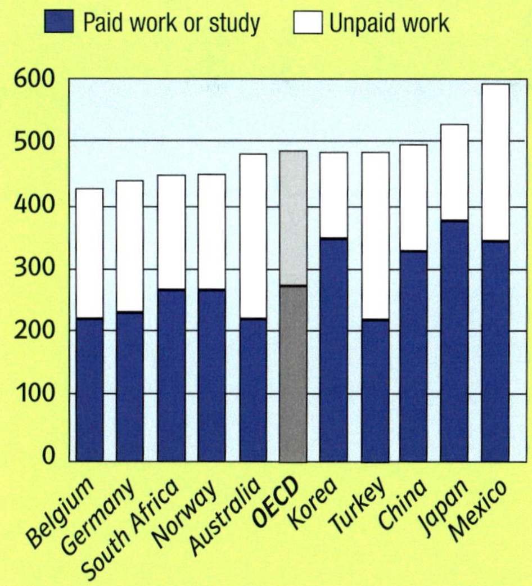

Population aged 15–64. Unpaid work is the production by family members of goods and services that are not sold on the market.

Source: OECD, 2011

Topic 2.7
Dreams and visions

py68st

A

B

C

D

E

Getting started

1 Look at the pictures above. Work with a partner and brainstorm what dreams and visions you think these pictures show. Create a list of at least five key words or expressions for each picture.

2 With the same partner, come up with three more images which show your dreams and visions for the future.

3 Share your ideas with the class and explain your choices.

In the year 2525

In the year 2525
If man is still alive
If woman can survive, they may find

In the year 3535
Ain't gonna need to tell the truth, tell no lies
Everything you think, do and say, is in the pill you took today

In the year 4545
Ain't gonna need your teeth, won't need your eyes
You won't find a thing to chew
Nobody's gonna look at you

In the year 5555
Your arms hanging limp at your sides
Your legs got nothing to do
Some machine doing that for you

In the year 6565
Ain't gonna need no husband, won't need no wife
You'll pick your son, pick your daughter too
From the bottom of a long glass tube

In the year 7510
If God's a-comin, he oughta make it by then
Maybe he'll look around himself and say
"Guess it's time for the judgment day"

In the year 8510
God is gonna shake his mighty head
He'll either say "I'm pleased where man has been"
Or tear it down and start again

In the year 9595
I'm kinda wonderin if man is gonna be alive
He's taken everything this old Earth can give
And he ain't put back nothing

Now it's been ten thousand years
Man has cried a billion tears
For what he never knew
Now man's reign is through

But through eternal night
The twinkling of starlight
So very far away
Maybe it's only yesterday

In the year 2525
If man is still alive
If woman can survive, they may find

In the year 3535

Words and music: Zager and Evans, 1969
In the Year 2525 K/T: Evans, Richard S © OV: Chelsea-Music Publ. / SV: Nordton Edition

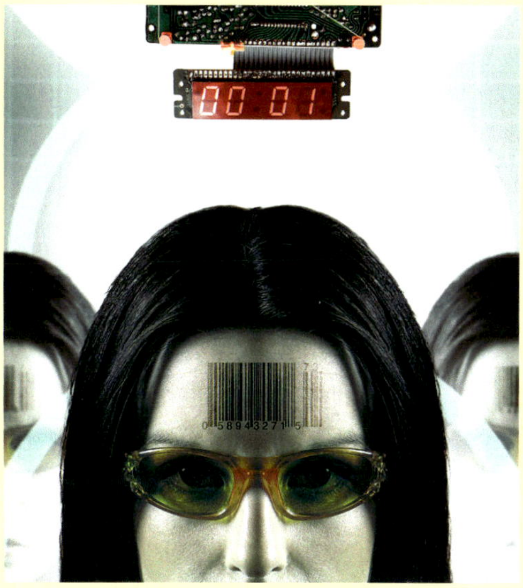

4 **Read the lyrics of the song. What topics does the song deal with?**

5 **Analyse the song in detail. In your opinion, does it paint a more positive or negative vision of the future? Explain.**

Word bank

racism • prejudices • (violation of) human rights • pollution • clean environment • war • peace • old/young generation • mutual respect • helping each other • In my opinion, the song deals with the topic of … • I think the song is about … • rationalisation • genetic engineering • punishment • destruction of the planet • exploitation

A European issues

1 Before you read
The term the 'American Dream' is well-known. But what could be the 'European Dream'? Work with a partner and brainstorm some ideas.

theguardian

News | Sport | Comment | Culture | Business | Money | Life&Style | Travel | Environment

Comment is free > Politics — Search [ ] GO

Why national dream is a foreign concept

Confidence in a better tomorrow is a notion that comes more easily to Americans with a century of economic and, latterly, political dominance behind them than to the British.

Flags in front of the European Parliament in Brussels, Belgium

When Ed Miliband told Labour supporters in Gateshead about his fear that young people today were no longer sure of a better future than their parents had enjoyed he was careful to admit that Britain lacked an upbeat popular catchphrase to match "the American Dream". But when he invoked the idea of a broken "British promise" as over-hasty coalition spending cuts bite deep into the delicate fabric of society that was clearly what Miliband meant to convey: the chance of decent education and jobs for all, a secure environment, free healthcare and confidence in a better tomorrow. It is a notion that comes more easily to Americans with a century of economic and, latterly, political global dominance behind them, though the half century of rising living standards that followed the Great Depression and second world war has given way to far greater uncertainty for millions. Until recently postwar Europeans have made similar assumptions, but they started from a different, darker place. The US had been peopled for 400 years by immigrants – all of them eager volunteers apart from African slaves – determined to make a new and freer life in the New World.

By contrast most Europeans had vivid memories of war, tyranny and rigid class hierarchies. Mostly they admired America while also thinking Americans materialistic, uncouth and noisy. It was admiration which prompted France to donate Bartholdi's Statue of Liberty to New York in 1886, complete with Emma Lazarus's famous lines "Give me your tired, your poor, your huddled masses yearning to be free …" Reality was not always like that in the sweat shops of New York or on the thin soil of Nebraska. But the dream of self-betterment had been powerful since religious dissenters sought to

2 **notion** – Konzept
4 **latterly** – in letzter Zeit
11 **upbeat** – optimistisch
11 **catchphrase** – Schlagwort
13 **to invoke** – anführen
14 **over-hasty** – übereilt
15 **delicate** – empfindlich
17 **to convey** – vermitteln
24 **assumption** – Annahme
25 **eager** – eifrig, willig
27 **vivid** – klar
29 **uncouth** – ungehobelt
29 **admiration** – Bewunderung
29 **to donate** – *hier:* schenken
31 **huddled** – zusammengedrängt
31 **to yearn** – sich sehnen
33 **dissenter** – Systemkritiker(in), Dissident(in)

build their "shining city on a hill" in New England or make a fast buck growing tobacco in Virginia. The idea was embodied in the life, liberty and pursuit of happiness pledge of the constitution of 1776 when Americans overthrew the British rule they thought stood in the way of their goal. Millions crossed the Atlantic to join the pursuit. In the 19th century the fertile inventor Thomas Edison's rise to fame and fortune was said to embody the American Dream. In fact the phrase only attracted capital letters after James Truslow Adams, himself a wealthy writer, wrote about it expressing the idea of limitless success for the hard-working. It was as late as 1931.

Margaret Thatcher tried to foster a "British Dream" tradition, as did Tony Blair. Even the more prosaic Gordon Brown sought to blend European social democratic traditions of fairness with American entrepreneurial zeal. But Miliband gets it because the concept is in his blood. Like Emma Lazarus, a Jewish refugee from Russian pogroms, his own Jewish ancestors fled west to seek a better life. By 1940 they had reached Belgium where grandfather and his then-teenage father, Ralph, escaped to Britain from what would probably have been death in the camps. Britain gave them shelter, education and a chance to start afresh, he said – pure Americanism of the kind you do not hear in France, where patriotism is expressed in terms of republican virtue, though Nicholas Sarkozy, another child of Jewish refugees from Hungary, openly admires America as French leaders rarely do in public. The irony is that Ronald Reagan and Margaret Thatcher's response to emerging globalisation deliberately sought to create more risk-prone unequal societies, theoretically more meritocratic but in reality restoring the advantages of privilege which the mid-century shook off. Twenty-five years on, working- and middle-class skills and salaries are stagnant and declining while the wider world, which also admired the American Dream, decided they would build it at home in Shanghai or Bangalore rather than emigrate as their ancestors did. Dream or promise, both are under pressure in the west, regardless of who sits in No 10 or the Oval Office. (684 words)

34 **to make a fast buck** – schnelles Geld verdienen
35 **to embody** – verkörpern
35 **pursuit** – Streben
41 **limitless** – grenzenlos
42 **to foster** – fördern
43 **prosaic** – nüchtern
43 **to blend** – mischen
44 **zeal** – Eifer, Begeisterung
45 **refugee** – Flüchtling
50 **virtue** – Tugend
54 **risk-prone** – risikoanfällig
54 **meritocratic** – leistungs-orientiert
55 **to restore** – wieder-herstellen
56 **stagnant** – stagnierend

2 Mediation
A friend has to give a presentation on the American Dream and whether there is such thing as a 'European Dream'. He finds the article above in the Internet but has problems understanding it. Therefore, he asks you to sum up the main points for him in German.

3 Analysis → Describing cartoons, p. 340
Describe the cartoon, analyse it and relate it to the text.

08 **4 Comment** → Writing a comment, p. 327
"Ed Miliband told Labour supporters […] about his fear that young people today were no longer sure of a better future than their parents had enjoyed […]" (ll. 6–10)
As a European do you think your generation will have better future prospects than your parents' generation? Discuss.

5 Research project → Hotspot 1, p. 199

"I'M GLAD THE AMERICAN DREAM IS STILL ALIVE AND WELL SOMEWHERE."

B Global protests

1 Before you read

a) Describe the picture below.

b) What do people protest against? In Germany? Europe? Around the world? Work with a partner and make a list.

1 **to redefine** – neu definieren
3 **peak** – Höhepunkt
6 **battle-scarred** – kampf-erprobt
7 **lefty** – Linke(r)
10 **taxation** – Besteuerung
11 **to be held responsible for** – verantwortlich gemacht werden für
11 **due to** – auf Grund von
12 **greed** – Habgier
12 **trestle table** – Klapptisch
25 **uprising** – Aufstand
27 **shabby** – schäbig
28 **subsequent** – anschließend, nachträglich
30 **to be misplaced** – unan-gebracht sein
30 **to chime** – läuten

theguardian

News | Sport | Comment | Culture | Business | Money | Life&Style | Travel | Environment

Comment is free > Politics   Search [ ] GO

Global protests: Is 2011 a year that will change the world?

Will this year go down in history as one of those that redefined global politics? Just what are the parallels – if any – with 1968 and 1989?

Midway through last month, when the Occupy movement was at its peak and the New York police department was keeping its distance from Zuccotti Park, I was in Berkeley, California. Outside a branch of Bank of America, a compact local Occupy camp had sprung up, apparently drawing on a mixture of battle-scarred lefties, students from the University of California, and the sizeable local homeless population. Their line of argument was captured on A4 flyers that were pasted on to every available surface in the surrounding streets, the most direct of which read thus: “Are you pissed [off] yet? You should be! No taxation of the rich. Endless war. Bankers not held responsible. Corrupt politicians. Destruction of the planet due to politicians’ and corporations’ greed. Can it get any worse than this?” On a trestle table lay small piles of a leaflet credited to the “Bureau of Public Secrets”, which quoted 69-year-old Kalle Lasn, the editor of the Canada-based countercultural magazine Adbusters: “We are not just inspired by what happened in the Arab spring recently. We are students of the situationist movement. Those are the people who gave birth to what many people think was the first global revolution back in 1968 when some uprisings in Paris suddenly inspired uprisings all over the world.”

Looking at the shabby camp in front of me, any talk of Paris in 1968 seemed absurd – but then again, subsequent events in nearby Oakland, where thousands of Occupy supporters took to the streets on 3 November maybe suggested that such reference points were not completely misplaced. The 1968 reference also chimed with an article, not from any anarchist leaflet, but from the Financial Times, titled

2011: The Year of Global Indignation, and written by the paper's foreign affairs columnist, Gideon Rachman. "Many of the revolts of 2011 pit an internationally connected elite against ordinary citizens who feel excluded from the benefits of economic growth, and angered by corruption," he wrote. "The creation of a global mood is a mysterious thing. In 1968, before the word 'globalisation' or the internet were even invented, there were student rebellions around the world. The year 1989 saw not just the fall of the Berlin Wall but the Tiananmen Square revolt in China." And then a tentative question: "Perhaps 2011 will come to rank alongside 1968 and 1989 as a year of global revolt?"

This year has so far seen convulsive events in Tunisia, Egypt, Libya, Bahrain, Syria and Yemen. Mass protests against economic breakdown and austerity in Greece, Italy and Spain. Marches and protest camps in Chile and Israel. The arrival of Occupy Wall Street – which was cleared by police yesterday, though it will surely return in some form – and a movement-cum-meme which quickly arrived in London and beyond. And all the time, from Arab dictatorships, through to the world's banks and the Murdoch empire and now the vast edifice of the EU, the sense that interests and institutions, that once seemed invincible are either cracking or being questioned as never before, while mainstream politics is left looking bereft not just of answers, but even ideas. But what connects the crowds who are making all the noise? What could link a student camped outside St Paul's to Mohamed Bouazizi, the Tunisian vegetable seller who, having set himself on fire, died on 4 January, and thereby set in motion the events we now know as the Arab spring?

Sometimes, the answer seems to lie in actual links between the people at the centre of events. On 26 October, for example, Occupy Wall Street was visited by a group of activists drawn together by the Egyptian Facebook-based 6 April movement, who blessed the camp with the spirit of Tahrir Square; a fortnight ago, demonstrators outside St Paul's Cathedral conducted a live video linkup with pro-democracy activists in Syria. Such moments highlight the kind of people who have taken the lead in spreading the message of protest and dissent: a new political breed, unlike their politicised predecessors in some respects; but in others, remarkably similar.

(714 words)

32 **indignation** – Empörung
33 **to pit sth. against sth.** – etw. an etw. messen
34 **excluded** – ausgegrenzt
39 **tentative** – vorsichtig
41 **convulsive** – erschütternd
42 **austerity** – Einschränkung
45 **meme** – Gedankeneinheit, die sich durch Kommunikation weiterverbreitet
47 **edifice** – Gebäude
48 **invincible** – unbesiegbar
49 **bereft** – beraubt
57 **to bless** – segnen
57 **spirit** – Geist
57 **fortnight** – vierzehn Tage
58 **to conduct** – ausführen
59 **to take the lead** – die Führung übernehmen
60 **to spread** – verbreiten
60 **dissent** – Widerspruch
60 **breed** – *hier:* Generation
61 **predecessor** – Vorgänger(in)
61 **remarkably** – bemerkenswert

.308
2 Comprehension

a) Sum up in your own words what, according to this article, people are protesting against.

b) Outline what happened in 1968 and 1989.

3 Presentation → Presentation, p. 362

Divide the class into two groups. The first group should focus on the "Occupy Movement" and the second group should focus on the "Arab Spring". Divide the two topics into sub-topics (i.e. background, locations, impact, timeline, etc.) and prepare a presentation for the class. Use the Internet to help you.

.308
4 Comment → Writing a comment, p. 327

"Global protests: Is 2011 a year that will change the world?"
Do you think that the events of 2011 have changed the world? Discuss.

C Political speeches

1 Before you read
Which emblem represents the United Nations (UN) and what does it show? What are the other two? What do you know about the UN?

Ban Ki-moon, UN Secretary-General since 2007

2 **headquarters** – Hauptquartier
4 **remark** – Äußerung
4 **non-governmental organization (NGO)** – Nichtregierungsorganisation
6 **to appreciate** – (wert) schätzen
7 **commitment** – Engagement
11 **passion** – Leidenschaft
12 **crucial** – entscheidend, sehr wichtig
12 **to forge** – formen, schmieden
12 **sustainable** – nachhaltig
13 **prosperity** – Wohlstand
15 **summit** – Gipfel(treffen)
15 **landmark** – Meilenstein
16 **biodiversity** – Artenvielfalt
16 **awareness** – Bewusstsein
16 **to soar** – hochschnellen
18 **disarmament** – Abrüstung
20 **to dismiss sth. as** – etw. als … abtun
20 **pie-in-the-sky ideal** – Luftschloss
23 **transition** – Übergang
23 **remarkable** – bemerkenswert
25 **to draft** – entwerfen
26 **judiciary** – Gerichtswesen

UN NEWS CENTRE

Search [ ] GO

Home | Press Room | Tools & Services | Resources | News Focus

Secretary-General Ban Ki-moon
UN Headquarters
26 October 2011

Remarks to Non-Governmental Organizations

Good morning, Ladies and Gentlemen,

It is a great pleasure to meet you today. Thank you very much for taking time and I appreciate your strong commitment and leadership and willingness to work together with the United Nations in addressing many important challenges which we are facing these days.

Perhaps the most important thing I wanted to tell you is to say is: thank you. Thank you very much for all you have been doing for humanity. Thank you for everything you do to support the United Nations. We simply could not do without your passion, your ideas – and your criticism, too. […] Your voices and views are crucial. The world needs to forge a common agenda for sustainable peace, prosperity, freedom and justice.

I see three areas where your efforts will be especially important.

First, sustainable development. The first Earth Summit in 1992 was a landmark. It produced Agenda 21 and binding conventions on climate change and biodiversity. Global awareness soared. So did NGO engagement. Next year's Rio + 20 conference is a chance to build on that spirit.

The second area where NGOs can make a big difference is disarmament. We have seen encouraging progress in recent years, advanced in large measure by civil society and organizations such as yourselves. […] Too many people dismiss disarmament as a pie-in-the-sky ideal. Let us work together to bring disarmament down to earth.

Ladies and Gentlemen,

The third major opportunity: helping countries in transition. This year has been a most remarkable year for all of us. Not only those countries in the Middle East and North Africa – Tunisia, Egypt and Libya – face major challenges organizing elections, drafting new constitutions, promoting democratic practices, building independent judiciaries and free media. There can be no success

2 Comprehension

a) Divide the speech into parts and give each part a heading.

b) Outline which goals Ban Ki-moon mentions in his speech and the suggestions he makes on achieving them.

3 Analysis

a) Analyse the language Ban Ki-moon uses to connect with and engage his audience.

b) Explain the following sentence in your own words: "Too many people dismiss disarmament as a pie-in-the-sky ideal." (ll. 20–21)

4 Mediation → Mediation, p. 343
Write a short German newspaper article in which you outline the challenges the world faces, according to Ban Ki-moon.

5 Project → Hotspot 2, p. 199

without a healthy civil society. Please, do your part. Help these women's groups, social media activists, human rights defenders and others to take their rightful place in society … in government, in parliament, in every public institution.
Ladies and Gentlemen,
One of the most important lessons I have learned as Secretary-General is the power of partnerships. Governments cannot do it alone. We need support from business communities, civil societies, philanthropists, and faith leaders, and we need coalitions, we need alliances, multistakeholder platforms. This is our business model, and we know that it works. Thanks to the power of partnership, we are closing in on a day when we can eliminate deaths from malaria. Our target is 2015. By that time, we expect that there will be no malaria-related deaths. […] Together, in close coordination and cooperation, we can achieve outsized results on virtually every aspect of our shared agenda. And we will continue.
Dear Friends,
These are difficult economic times. Tight budgets. Cutbacks. Belt tightening. You are living all of this, too. Everywhere, people are living in fear … fear of losing their jobs, fear of being unable to feed their families, fear that governments and public institutions will fail them yet again. It is up to us – organizations like yours and mine – to help restore that faith. To deliver for people in need; to not forget people in need, especially now when times are so hard. […] During this era of new austerity, I often say that we must learn to "do more with less." In fact, however, we must think and act in a deeper way. The austerity challenge is not merely about quantity; it is about quality. It is not merely about "doing more with less" but about "doing better with less". By that, I mean increasing the impact of our work … making a bigger and measurable difference in the daily lives of real people. I know that we can do that with you by our side – as partners across the full spectrum of our work. That is the power of partnership.
Let me close on a more personal note. Many of you have told me, often more than once, that we do not see one another often enough. That we must do more to cement this partnership and amplify its potential power. […] Let me say that I understand. And I am committed to doing what I can to nurture and deepen this UN-NGO relationship. In our modern world, so complex and fast-changing, no nation or institution can prosper alone. Only by working in concert, in strong partnership, can we advance our common goals.
Thank you very much for your strong support for United Nations goals and your own personal engagement and leadership. Thank you. (760 words)

33 **philanthropist** – Wohltäter, Menschenfreund
33 **multistakeholder** – Interessensvertreter
37 **outsized** – übergroß
40 **tight** – eng, knapp
40 **cutback** – Kürzung
43 **to restore** – wiederherstellen
45 **austerity** – Entbehrung, Einschränkung
46 **merely** – lediglich
48 **measurable** – messbar
52 **to amplify** – verstärken
55 **in concert** – gemeinsam

D Social responsibility

1 Before you read
Here is a definition of the word "entrepreneur":

> **entrepreneur (n)** [ˌɒn.trə.prəˈnɜː]: *a person who sets up a business or businesses, taking on financial risks in the hope of profit*

What do you think is the difference between an entrepreneur and a social entrepreneur? Share your ideas with the class.

2 Comprehension
Summarise each of the projects in your own words.

3 Analysis
Explain the phrase "tackling financial illiteracy" (l. 9) in your own words.

theguardian

News | Sport | Comment | Culture | Business | Money | Life&Style | Travel | Environment

Comment is free > Society   Search GO

The Guardian Social Entrepreneurship Awards

Elisabetta Lapana, London – Young People's Bank
The project will be a bank in secondary schools set up and run by students. Its objectives are to enable young people to become more enterprising and to develop a new approach to tackling financial illiteracy. The students will be able to invest and take out small loans for personal development and will also be empowered to improve the social and economic make-up of their communities. The students will learn valuable finance skills and schools could gain specialised status as financial literacy is high on the government agenda. An UnLtd award will cover the costs of computer equipment and volunteer expenses.

Jonathan Burr, Windsor – The Beam
This programme is targeted at 12 to 15-year-old boys who have a body mass index of over 30. It will cover nutrition, fitness, self-awareness and self-esteem. Jonathan hopes to run the programme for up to 15 teenagers and include their parents in at least one of the modules. He believes that weight issues are a major source of poor self-esteem and unhappiness in young British males and wants to

5 **objective** – Ziel
6 **to enable** – ermöglichen
7 **enterprising** – unternehmenslustig
9 **to tackle** – in Angriff nehmen, bekämpfen
9 **illiteracy** – Analphabetismus
12 **loan** – Darlehen, Kredit
13 **to empower** – befähigen
14 **valuable** – wertvoll
14 **to gain** – bekommen
16 **volunteer** – Freiwillige(r)
16 **expense** – Kosten
19 **nutrition** – Ernährung
19 **self-awareness** – Eigenwahrnehmung
19 **self-esteem** – Selbstwertgefühl
21 **weight** – Gewicht
21 **issue** – Frage, Problem
21 **major** – Haupt-

309 **4 Mediation** → Mediation, p. 343
Choose the two projects that interest you the most and sum up the key information in German.

5 Having a discussion → Discussions, p. 344
Which of the projects deserves to be given an award for social responsibility? Exchange arguments in class and take a vote.

3.1 **6 Listening comprehension: Social entrepreneur of the year** → Listening, p. 319
Listen to the recording and find out what a social entrepreneur is and what his/her main aims are. You do not have to write full sentences.

7 Research project → Hotspot 3, p. 199

provide participants with knowledge of alternative health choices. Project costs include venue hire, professional fees, travel and insurance.

Ben Ward, Bristol – World Jungle
This project aims to provide life-changing opportunities to young people and individuals in Ben's rural community through dance, music and art activities. World Jungle will give the young people a chance to learn about social and environmental issues facing other cultures. Ben already has links with Ghanaian, Indian and Moroccan dancers, drummers, speakers and relevant festival and carnivals organised to take young people to. Ben hopes this project will encourage the young people he is targeting to explore other cultures and challenge prejudices. Project costs include travel, venue hire, dancers, admin and publicity.

Jessica Sherlock, London – The Amoosi Project
This project will engage designers at the beginning of their careers to work with recycled clothing and textiles. Rather than see these materials go to landfills or be sold in developing countries, Jessica wants young fashion designers to develop their skills while using these materials. She strongly believes that these designers can influence the fashion industry as a whole. Project costs include: marketing materials, website hosting, sample production, company registration and advertising.

Helen Thomas, Cornwall – Film Kitchen
This will be a mobile film and food facility designed to enable films to be screened in a variety of locations including village halls, schools and outdoor locations. The aim of the project is to promote healthy food to the local community, introducing themed/multicultural food, while bringing a variety of films to people who would otherwise not be able to travel to their nearest cinema. The project will offer the local community a facility that educates, inspires and encourages them to get together. Project costs include a projector, speakers, sound mixer and further technical equipment. (482 words)

23 **to provide** – geben, bieten
24 **venue** – Veranstaltungsort
24 **fee** – Gebühr
24 **insurance** – Versicherung
27 **rural** – ländlich
32 **to explore** – erkunden
32 **to challenge** – herausfordern
32 **prejudice** – Vorurteil
33 **admin** – Verwaltung
35 **to engage** – involvieren
36 **landfill** – Deponie
39 **website hosting** – Bereitstellen von Speicherplatz für eine Webseite
40 **sample** – Muster
42 **facility** – Einrichtung
42 **to screen** – vorführen
44 **to promote** – fördern
46 **otherwise** – ansonsten
48 **projector** – Beamer

E Future living

1 Before you read

a) How do you think your hometown will change in the next thirty years? Discuss with a partner what you believe will change for the better and what you fear will change for the worse. Report back to the class.

b) Brainstorm ideas which express what your hometown would ideally look like in thirty years' time.

c) Discuss in class what you believe are aspects of an imaginary ideal place to live in.

1 **utopia** – Utopie
1 **dystopia** – Antiutopie, Dystopie
2 **to derive from** – sich ableiten von
3 **imaginary** – erfunden
4 **current** – aktuell
4 **progress** – Fortschritt
6 **transformative** – umgestaltend
7 **anxiety** – Angst
7 **resistance** – Widerstand
8 **decade** – Jahrzehnt
9 **terrifying** – furchterregend
9 **to intensify** – verstärken
10 **inhuman** – unmenschlich
11 **to enslave** – versklaven
11 **citizen** – Bürger
12 **to portray** – abbilden
13 **implicitly** – implizit
14 **to project** – projektieren
14 **contemporary** – gegenwärtig
14 **to get out of hand** – außer Kontrolle geraten
16 **significant** – bedeutend
16 **impact** – Auswirkung
17 **emergence** – Aufkommen
17 **surveillance** – Überwachung
17 **to give rise to** – etw. entstehen lassen
18 **advance** – Vorstoß
19 **caste system** – Kastenordnung

Utopia and dystopia

Utopia is derived from the Greek words for 'good' and 'place', which sums up what utopias are all about: imaginary societies, set in a different place or the future, which are better than our current society. Technological progress was largely viewed with optimism until well into the 19th century, and positive utopian visions of the future were therefore common. Towards the turn of the century and in the early 20th century, however, the speed and transformative power of industrialisation and of scientific progress also created anxiety and resistance. In the following decades, the experience of the two World Wars, of totalitarian states and terrifying weapons, intensified this feeling. Pessimistic visions of the future (so-called 'anti-utopias', or more commonly 'dystopias') were understood as warnings against inhuman totalitarian states that dominate or enslave their citizens.
The main aim of both utopian and dystopian art is to portray alternative societies, implicitly criticising tendencies in contemporary society either by offering a better society or by projecting a dangerous contemporary development into a future where it has gotten out of hand. Technological progress does not have to play a role in this, but it often does because new technologies have such a significant impact on the structure of society. For example, the emergence of mass media and surveillance technology gave rise to dystopian visions of totalitarian regimes that control every aspect of citizens' lives, and advances in biotechnology inspired dystopias of genetic caste systems. (277 words)

2 Comprehension

a) In your own words, outline the difference between utopia and dystopia.

b) Sum up what triggered the vision of the dystopia.

3 Vocabulary → Working with a dictionary, p. 353

Find the German equivalents of the following words in the text on page 197:

renewable energies • researcher • breakthrough • emission-free • inventors • emissions • solar power • sun collector • solar power station • fertiliser • car-free transport system • railway lines • solar-fuelled • cabin • evaporated

p. 309

4 Mediation → Mediation, p. 343

Summarise the main points of the article on the next page in English.

Hightech für die Umwelt: Die Stadt der Zukunft

Magnetschwebekapseln statt Autos, Photovoltaik statt Erdöl: Abu Dhabi plant im Rahmen der Masdar-Initiative eine „Grüne Stadt". An wichtigen Forschungsprojekten sind deutsche Institute federführend beteiligt.

Abu Dhabi nennt sein ehrgeiziges Projekt zur Entwicklung erneuerbarer Energien „Masdar" („Quelle"). Denn das Projekt will Quelle sein für Erfindungen, Innovationen und Unternehmergeist. Es will die besten Forscher zusammenführen und ausstatten, es will diesen Forschern Unternehmer an die Seite stellen, die ihre Erfindungen umsetzen. Masdar wird damit ein nachhaltiger Impuls, um den erneuerbaren Energien zum großen Durchbruch zu verhelfen und um das Zeitalter, in dem das Erdöl versiegen wird, in die weite Zukunft zu verschieben. Im Mai 2007 stellte das Emirat sein Projekt erstmals vor. Sein sichtbarster Teil wird die emissionsfreie „Grüne Stadt" sein, ein sechs Millionen Quadratmeter großer Komplex, der stadtplanerisch von dem britischen Architekturbüro Foster and Partners betreut wird. Abu Dhabi will für das Projekt die besten Forscher bündeln. Wo bei erneuerbaren Energien Exzellenz gefragt ist, sind deutsche Institutionen dabei. Ein wichtiger Baustein von Masdar ist das Research Network. In dieses hat Masdar sechs der führenden Forschungseinrichtungen der Welt eingeladen, zwei von ihnen kommen aus Deutschland: die Rheinisch-Westfälische Technische Universität (RWTH) Aachen und das Deutsche Zentrum für Luft- und Raumfahrt (DLR).

Um den Austausch zwischen Forschung und Industrie zu erleichtern, richtet Abu Dhabi eine Sonderwirtschaftszone ein, die „Grüne Stadt". In ihr werden die Institute und die Unternehmen angesiedelt, in ihr werden die Erfinder und Innovatoren leben und arbeiten. Diese neue Stadt am Rand des heutigen Abu Dhabi ist das für Außenstehende spektakulärste Projekt von Masdar. Die Stadt soll auf sechs Quadratkilometern Pilotprojekt und Modell zugleich sein. Sie soll nichts Geringeres werden als das Silicon Valley für erneuerbare Energien. In ihr wird kein Auto fahren und es wird keine Emissionen von Kohlendioxid geben. Sie wird mit Solarstrom auskommen, der aus Sonnenkollektoren auf den Dächern gewonnen wird und von einem benachbarten Solarkraftwerk. Der Müll wird zu Düngemitteln verarbeitet, und in der autofreien Stadt wird ein Transportsystem die Beförderung der Menschen sicherstellen: Auf Trassen werden solarbetriebene Kabinen verkehren, die jeden Einzelnen mindestens bis zu 200 Meter an jeden Punkt innerhalb der Stadt steuern. Ein „intelligentes" Dach wird Schatten spenden und mit verdunstetem Wasser die Temperatur in den Straßen regeln – trotz der extremen klimatischen Bedingungen in Abu Dhabi mit Außentemperaturen bis zu 50°C. (374 words)

310 **5 Analysis** → Describing pictures, p. 339
Describe the picture on the right in detail and compare its vision of a city of the future with that of the Masdar project.

310 **6 Comment: Choose one of the following tasks**

a) Imagine you have been offered the chance to spend one year living in the "Green City". Discuss whether you would accept the offer or not, outlining arguments for and against.

b) If you had to paint a picture of the future in, say, 2150, would it be more utopian or dystopian? Give reasons.

7 Research project → Hotspot 4, p. 199

Paraphrasing

Paraphrasing means putting information into your own words. When you answer questions on a text, write a summary or otherwise refer to a particular text, you should not copy the exact sentences but use your own words as much as possible.
Use introductory phrases (e.g. *The author says/claims that … / According to the text/ author …*) if the ideas you are writing about are not yours.
If you use synonyms, remember to change the sentence structure, if necessary (e.g. *For politicians, being informed about current events is very much a part of daily life. → For politicians, being informed about current events is very important in daily life.*).

a) Read the following sentences and choose the paraphrase which you consider better. Give reasons for your choice.

Examples:

1. Although people around the world are protesting against a variety of things, these issues are not completely independent from one another.
   - People around the globe have many reasons for protesting but these do not exist independently from each other.
   - Although people all over the world are protesting about different issues, they are not completely independent from one another.

2. Instead, different protests are often connected by feelings of powerlessness and anger.
   - Instead, feelings of anger and powerlessness often connect different protests.
   - Instead, protests are often connected by the anger and powerlessness felt by the people protesting.

b) Now paraphrase the following sentences yourself. You can use an English-English dictionary or a thesaurus for help.

1. The year 1989 saw not just the fall of the Berlin Wall but the Tiananmen Square revolt in China.
2. The Occupy movement is an international protest movement primarily directed against economic and social inequality.
3. The Occupy Wall Street movement was initiated by the Canadian activist group Adbusters.
4. Just after midnight on November 9 in Ontario, police evicted protesters from the city's Victoria Park.
5. Later, on the night of November 14, authorities forcefully closed down camps around the world in cities such as New York, Oakland and Zurich.
6. However, protestors immediately regrouped and vowed to continue protesting.
7. The series of demonstrations and protests across the Middle East and North Africa has been labeled the "Arab Spring".
8. As of February 2012, governments in four countries have been overthrown.

1 Research project: The American Dream → Presentation, p. 362

a) Go online and find a definition of the American Dream.

b) Find Emma Lazarus's poem "The New Colossus", analyse it and relate it to the concept of the American Dream.

c) Come up with a definition for a "European Dream". Present your results to the class.

2 Project: The role of the UN → Presentation, p. 262
In groups do some research and find some United Nations peacekeeping missions. Who is at conflict? Since when? Over what? What are the chances of a peaceful solution? How is the UN involved? Present your findings to the class.

3 Research project: Social entrepreneurship in Germany → Internet research, p. 358
Do you know of any social entrepreneurship in Germany? Use the Internet to gather information about German projects that have innovative business ideas aimed at tackling society's most pressing social problems. Choose a project that interests you and prepare a 3-minute talk to introduce the project to your classmates.

4 Research project: Cities of the future → Internet research, p. 358
Go online and look for information about projects similar to the Masdar project, e.g. green cities, sustainable cities, zero emission cities, etc. Prepare a short talk in which you outline the most important details and the aims of the project.

A 3.3

1 **glittering** – sparkling
1 **to bristle** – to stand upright
2 **to straddle** – to extend across
2 **metropolis** – city
3 **Perspex** – acrylic glass
5 **painstaking** – done with great care
5 **grave** – severe
5 **understatement** – the presentation of sth. as being smaller or less good or important than it really is
7 **to comprise** – to make up
8 **meticulously** – exactly
8 **crafted to scale** – made in proportion
12 **faithfully** – in detail
15 **indulgence** – luxury
17 **planning permission** – allowance to build sth.
18 **to date** – up to now
18 **to cast** – to spread
19 **blueprint** – plan
19 **at a glance** – with one quick look
21 **dwarfed** – made to look very small
27 **casual observer** – normal person
28 **striking** – surprising
35 **barely** – just
35 **inch** – 2.54 cm
39 **blank** – empty
39 **canvas** – strong cloth
40 **proliferation** – increase in number
41 **writ large** – clear, obvious
43 **to reside** – to live
44 **to reveal** – to disclose, to show
46 **to inform** – *here:* to influence

BBC NEWS EDUCATION & FAMILY

Search GO

Home | UK | Africa | Asia-Pac | Europe | Latin America | Mid-East | South Asia

London 2030: Modelling the future

A forest of glittering new skyscrapers bristles from the City of London, the completed Olympic Park transforms the East End and the £17bn Crossrail line straddles the metropolis at last. This is London 2030. But made entirely of Perspex.

To describe the construction of this model as painstaking is a grave understatement. Some 50,000 individual buildings or blocks comprise the urban landscape, each meticulously crafted to scale [...].

Every street and park – not to mention the familiar curve of the Thames – has been faithfully reproduced [...]. And a total of 5,000 hours of labour by model-making firm Pipers has gone into the 12-metre-long (36ft) result. But this is no mere indulgence – there is a definite purpose behind the creation of the model. For alongside the familiar structures – Buckingham Palace, the London Eye and the Houses of Parliament – sits every major development given planning permission to date. Some 500 unborn buildings are cast across the landscape, reproduced from architects' plans and blueprints.Thus, at a glance, the observer can see London in two decades' time.

Canary Wharf dwarfed

Model makers used plans of future buildings such as The Shard, under construction at London Bridge

Nick McKeogh, director of Pipers, explained: "The model was first made in 2005, in the middle of a huge building boom. Not since Victorian times had London seen such development." [...] To the casual observer, the number of new skyscrapers is particularly striking. In London's financial district the Gherkin – designed by Norman Foster – has six new partners among the clouds. And four buildings across the miniature landscape dwarf the UK's current tallest skyscraper, Canary Wharf – despite being barely half an inch high in the model. Observers are left in no doubt: the skyline of 2030 will be a very different sight. But Mr McKeogh said: "It's not Shanghai-on-Thames. There are still a huge amount of low buildings, [...]. A few years ago people thought everything old and low was being knocked down to make way for big towers." [...]

"Blank canvas"

While the proliferation of skyscrapers points firmly towards the future, the mark of history is still writ large, with clues to how developments of the past were carried out. Debbie Whitfield, director of New London Architecture, in whose galleries off Tottenham Court Road the model resides, said: "Although the model is quite simplified it's incredible what it reveals. It shows how the [historically] Roman walled City of London was largely built over the medieval street plan just as it was before the Great Fire of London. The medieval street plan informed the shape of developments that were built later."

Ms Whitfield continued: “Architects building there (the City) had to respond to very different circumstances than elsewhere in London. For instance you have Canary Wharf, which was a blank canvas. When you come out of the Tube there you could be in Tokyo – the complexity of London is its beauty.”
The city’s complexity can be confusing for new inhabitants. Many new Londoners experience the epiphany of turning the corner to recognise a whole other district of London they had no idea was so close. And for those wanting to connect up the mental jigsaw the model provides a strong rival to peering through clouds from an aeroplane window.
“It’s amazing to get a feel for where things are in relation to each other,” Ms Whitfield said. [...] “It highlights that the distance between Stratford and the Square Mile is roughly equidistant to that from the Square Mile to Paddington. Most people tend to think of Stratford as being much further out.” The model, built to a 1:1,500 scale, is constantly updated as new developments are approved. But will the London of 2030 be a better place? Or are developers putting profit over civic improvement? While his pride in the model is evident, Mr McKeogh retains a healthy cynicism. “I would not say all of these things will contribute to a better London,” [...]. (655 words)

52 **epiphany** – eye-opening experience
53 **jigsaw** – puzzle
54 **rival** – competitor
54 **to peer** – to look
57 **equidistant** – of the same distance
58 **scale** – size
59 **to approve** – to give permission
60 **civic** – community
61 **evident** – clear
61 **to retain** – to keep
61 **cynicism** – scepticism

1 Comprehension

Read the text and answer the following questions in 1–25 words.

a) What is entirely made of Perspex?

b) What was the intention to create such a model?

c) When was the model first made?

d) What will be special about the new London that prevents it from becoming “Shanghai-on-Thames”?

e) What does the model reveal about the history of London?

f) Which experiences might new inhabitants of London make that could confuse them at first?

g) What is the model a rival to if people want to piece together the mental puzzle about London?

h) What constantly happens to the model?

i) What is Mr McKeogh’s explanation as to if London will be a better place in 2030?

2 Analysis

a) Explain what the following statement says about London: “Many new Londoners experience the epiphany of turning the corner to recognise a whole other district of London they had no idea was so close.” (ll. 51–53)

b) Interpret McKeogh’s statement: “I would not say all of these things will contribute to a better London.” (ll. 61–62)

3 Comment

‘Your town 2030’. What will your hometown look like in 2030? What changes will have taken place and how will they affect the people living there? Write a text explaining your vision of your hometown in the future.

Topic 2.8
Cross-cultural issues

u25ye8

In my country

Walking by the waters
down where an honest river
shakes hands with the sea,
a woman passed round me
in a slow watchful circle,
as if I were a superstition;

or the worst dregs of her
  imagination,
so when she finally spoke
her words spliced into bars
of an old wheel. A segment of air.
Where do you come from?
'Here,' I said, 'Here. These parts.'

Jackie Kay

Jackie Kay

Pat Mora

Legal alien

Bi-lingual, Bi-cultural,
able to slip from "How's life?"
to "Me están volviendo loca",
able to sit in a paneled office
drafting memos in smooth English,
able to order in fluent Spanish
at a Mexican restaurant,
American but hyphenated,
viewed by Anglos as perhaps exotic,
perhaps inferior; definitely different,
viewed by Mexicans as alien,
(their eyes say, "You may speak
Spanish but you're not like me")
an American to Mexicans
a Mexican to Americans
a handy token
sliding back and forth
between the fringes of both worlds
by smiling
by masking the discomfort
of being pre-judged
Bi-laterally.

Pat Mora

6 **superstition** – Aberglaube
7 **dregs** *(pl)* – Bodensatz
10 **to splice** – *hier:* aufsplittern

3 **me estan volviendo loca** *(Spanish)* – Sie machen mich verrückt
4 **paneled** – getäfelt
5 **to draft** – schreiben
5 **smooth** – *hier:* fließend (Sprache)
8 **hyphenated** – mit einem Bindestrich verbunden
10 **inferior** – minderwertig
16 **token** – *hier:* Spielstein
18 **fringe** – Rand
20 **to mask** – verbergen

Getting started

You are going to read three poems which all deal with living between different cultures. The poets are Jackie Kay, a black Scottish poet, who was adopted at birth by a white couple; Pat Mora, born in Texas to a Mexican family; and John Agard, a Caribbean poet who moved to Britain from Guyana in 1977.

A 3.7 **1 Listen to and read the first poem. Then answer the following questions.**

a) Who is the speaker of the poem and what experience does the poem describe? How does the title relate to the message of the poem?

b) Explain how the metaphor of the river and the sea relates to a society with ethnic minorities.

A 3.8 **2 Listen to and read the second poem. Then answer the following questions.**

a) What do you understand by the term "legal alien", and how does it relate to the situation described in the poem?

b) What does the speaker mean by the phrase "American but hyphenated" (l. 8)?

c) The speaker talks about "sliding back and forth between the fringes of both worlds" (ll. 17–18). How is this idea emphasised by the structure of the poem?

Windrush child

Behind you
Windrush child
palm trees wave goodbye

above you
Windrush child
seabirds asking why

around you
Windrush child
blue water rolling by

beside you
Windrush child
your Windrush mum and dad

think of storytime yard
and mango mornings
and new beginnings
doors closing and opening

will things turn out right?
At least the ship will arrive
in midsummer light

and you Windrush child
think of grandmother
telling you don't forget to write
and with one last hug
walk good walk good
and the sea's wheel carries on
spinning

and from that place England
you tell her in a letter
of your Windrush adventure
stepping in a big ship
not knowing how long the journey
or that you're stepping into history

bringing your Caribbean eye
to another horizon
grandmother's words your shining
beacon

learning how to fly
the kite of your dreams
in an English sky

Windrush child
walking good walking good
in a mind-opening
meeting of snow and sun

John Agard

John Agard

3 **Compare the two poems on page 202** → Dealing with poetry, p. 324

a) To what extent are the experiences described in both poems similar, to what extent are they different?

b) How do the speakers feel about their experience? How is this expressed in the two poems?

3.9 **4** **Listen to and read the third poem. Then answer the following questions.**

a) Who is the "Windrush child" addressed in this poem? What situation is being described here?

b) The poem contains references to the past and what has been left behind, the present and the future of the addressee. Copy this table into your exercise book and add similar references. Summarise each column of the table in one sentence.

Past	Present	Future
palm trees	seabirds	new beginnings
storytime yard	blue water	doors opening
…	…	…

0 **windrush** – *Empire Windrush* ist der Name des Schiffes, auf dem im Jahr 1948 die erste große Gruppe von Einwanderern aus der Karibik nach England kam.

36 **beacon** – Leuchtfeuer

38 **kite** – Drachen

Word bank

The writer wants to express … • The message of the poem is … • The person in the poem feels … • The choice of words suggests that … • In my opinion, … • … is a metaphor for …

2.8 Cross-cultural issues

A Racial stereotypes

1 Before you read → Describing cartoons, p. 340

a) Discuss what stereotypes of ethnic or other groups you know of. To what extent does your personal experience confirm or contradict these stereotypes?

b) Describe the cartoon. Who or what is the target of the cartoon? How is irony used to emphasise the point being made?

to spot – entdecken
split second – der Bruchteil einer Sekunde

Racial stereotypes can be unconscious but reversible

Negative stereotypes about various racial groups bombard us every day in the mass media and deposit their residue deep into our minds, often without our realizing it, says Brian Lowery. Even among the most well intentioned and consciously egalitarian people, says the associate professor of organizational behavior, non-conscious associations about ethnic groups still have a pernicious effect on behavior and attitudes.

The good news, he says, is that we can also be influenced for the better, particularly by social relationships with people who strongly value egalitarian ideals. Lowery's work moves the dialogue on racism beyond simple dichotomies that divide people into categories of "good" and "bad" according to their views on people of a different race or ethnicity. "The situation is much more complex," he says. Even people who consciously disavow prejudice can fall into racist traps.

In one study, for example, Lowery demonstrated how racial stereotypes subtly operate in the penal system. Los Angeles police and probation officers were asked to make judgments about a hypothetical adolescent (whose race was not identified) who had allegedly either shoplifted or assaulted a peer. Certain officers were first subliminally exposed to words commonly associated with African Americans (such as ghetto, homeboy, dreadlocks, etc.) on a rapidly flashing computer screen so that they took in the information subconsciously. In contrast to subjects who did not receive this "priming", officers with the subconscious messaging attributed more negative traits and greater culpability to the hypothetical offenders, and they endorsed harsher punishment – all typical responses to black as opposed to white offenders.

In other words, by simply unconsciously thinking about black people, officers suddenly began seeing a neutral situation in racially stereotypical terms – without even knowing it. The subliminal priming was all it took to activate the entire program of material these officers held about African Americans. The phenomenon held sway even for officers who reported – and truly believed – they were tolerant and non-biased toward non-whites. "What's particularly interesting is that many of the officers were African Americans themselves," Lowery notes. "This shows the degree to which even African Americans can be affected by the negative associations in the environment." When participants who

2 **residue** – Rückstand, Rest
3 **egalitarian** – egalitär, auf politische oder soziale Gleichheit ausgerichtet
4 **pernicious** – schädlich
8 **dichotomy** – Zweiteilung
10 **to disavow** – verleugnen, von etw. abrücken
11 **subtly** – fast unmerklich
11 **penal system** – Strafvollzug
12 **probation officer** – Bewährungshelfer
13 **allegedly** – angeblich
13 **to assault** – angreifen
14 **subliminal** – unterschwellig
17 **priming** – Grundierung; Vorbereitung
17 **trait** – Eigenschaft
18 **culpability** – Strafbarkeit
18 **offender** – Straftäter(in)
18 **to endorse** – billigen, unterstützen
24 **biased** – voreingenommen

had received the subliminal priming were later debriefed and told about the results, Lowery reports, they were extremely uncomfortable. "People are very reluctant to believe their scores reflect anything about their attitudes, and they instead try to invalidate the measures," he says.

In other research, Lowery examined just how readily people associate particular social groups with certain kinds of feelings. In a subliminal word-association exercise, black people's faces were more quickly associated with negative words, while white faces were linked with positive words. Lowery found, however, that such associations would change when subjects were exposed to someone who displayed egalitarian attitudes (as evidenced by wearing a T-shirt with an anti-racism message). The presence of an egalitarian African American person or white person who was friendly and appealing was enough to shift participants' unconscious racial associations to become less negative about blacks. Interestingly, the presence of an unfriendly though egalitarian researcher did not result in such a shift. "When we like or identify with people, we're more likely to emulate their attitudes and behaviors," Lowery explains. His research also confirms that children who identify strongly with parental figures tend to pick up their parents' racial views.

What's hopeful about these latter results, Lowery says, is that a change in viewpoint toward another ethnic group can come from within a social group through positive and appealing role models who exhibit justice-minded attitudes – an important factor given that widespread segregation often makes it difficult for various groups to interact. By exploring such possibilities, Lowery's work is helping to expand the research on ethnic stereotyping in new directions. In addition, by working with participants in live settings such as the juvenile justice system – and not relying exclusively on student subjects as researchers in the laboratory typically do – he is also helping to demonstrate how racism operates in populations where such issues can literally be a matter of life and death.

(685 words)

[27] **to debrief** – eingehend befragen
[28] **reluctant** – widerwillig, widerstrebend
[28] **score** – *hier:* Ergebnis
[29] **to invalidate** – für nichtig erklären, entkräften
[34] **to evidence** – ausdrücken, zeigen
[38] **to emulate** – nachahmen
[46] **juvenile** – Jugend-

2 Comprehension: True or false?

Read the statements below and decide whether they are true or false. Quote or paraphrase words from the text which confirm or disprove the ideas in the statements.

a) There is no clear division between people who are racists and people who aren't.

b) The officers who were shown the words on a flashing computer screen were not aware that they thought the offender was black.

c) Officers who said they weren't racists did not associate negative qualities with the offender, although they had received the "priming".

d) Negative stereotypes are subconscious and cannot be changed.

e) Lowery's research is important because it shows the influence of racial stereotypes on people who make important decisions about the lives of many others.

311 **3 Comment** → Writing a comment, p. 327

Discuss how both individuals and society as a whole can try to challenge and overcome racial stereotyping.

4 Group discussion → Discussions, p. 344

In your multicultural neighbourhood in Germany, some people are not quite happy with how little contact there is between the different ethnic groups. Some say that they don't feel welcome, while others say that some ethnic groups don't really want to mix and integrate. In your community centre, representatives of the different ethnic groups come together and discuss what can be done to improve the situation. Form groups to represent different ethnic groups and prepare arguments for a class discussion. Talk about how you perceive the situation, explain your reasons for behaving as you do, and then discuss plans to change things.

B National identity

1 Before you read

a) Which recent events can you remember that are connected to religious radicalism? Discuss with a partner.

b) In your opinion, what drives people to join extremist organisations?

A 3.10

Reflections of a former British Muslim extremist

The following interview with Ed Husain, a former Muslim extremist and author of the controversial book The Islamist *(2007), was recorded in February 2008.*

Ms Tippett: You were born and raised in Britain. You were not an immigrant. You were perhaps living in a culture that was defined by immigrants but, you know, talk to me a little bit about your British identity and why your link to that was susceptible or vulnerable or tenuous so that you were captured by some of these ideas.

Ed Husain: We have a real problem in Britain. It was the case when I was growing up and it's still the case now in that it's extremely difficult to define Britishness. Whereas in America it's different. You have a very clear sense of national identity. We don't have that here. There's the Welsh issue, the Scottish issue, and the Irish issue that compounds this problem. And then bring into the mix people who arrived in Britain in the 1960s after the winding up of the British Empire in the West Indies and in India. You have a group of people who arrived here, you know, my parents' generation, initially for economic purposes with some hope of, you know, going back as it were one day. That going back never happened. So my generation, born and raised here, we're confused as to where our parents stood. At home we were exposed to one culture; at school we were exposed to another. So Britishness was never clearly defined for my generation growing up. And the fact that we've got communities up and down the country that live totally separate lives – I mean, in the name of multiculturalism we've created these monocultural ghettos in Bradford, Birmingham, Burnley, parts of London where there is no interaction between, you know, native white English communities and the children of immigrants. And so it's very much a live problem here in Britain.

Ms Tippett: And I have a sense that when you first became attracted to a kind of politicized Islam, initially not necessarily extremist, but just that some of the words you used to describe what you found worthy in what you were experiencing was that, you know, it sounds like it almost seemed to bridge some of these different aspects of your identity that weren't bridged in the culture. You said it was English-speaking, educated, rooted in faith.

Ed Husain: You see, when we went to mosques – when I went to mosques – most of the imams came from Pakistan, Bangladesh, India. They spoke about an Islam that was very much village-based, a folkloric Islam. It wasn't something that people like myself, born and raised here in Britain in a different cultural-social-political setup, could easily relate to. We were always given Islam in a second language, the language of our parents – Urdu, Bengali, whatever. But suddenly when I reached my teens, there were these young people who spoke Islam in the language that I easily identified with, i.e., English. So it took me a while to cotton on to the fact that the sort of Islam they were trying to sell to people like myself was an Islam that was at odds with my parents' more Sufistic,traditional orthodox Islam. But the English-speaking radicals were trying to promote a sense … a type of Islam that was, you know, Islamist, politicized.

5 **susceptible** – anfällig, beeinflussbar
5 **vulnerable** – angreifbar, verwundbar
5 **tenuous** – schwach
10 **to compound** – verschlimmern
11 **to wind up** – enden
16 **to be exposed to sth.** – etw. ausgesetzt sein
30 **to relate to sth.** – sich mit etw. identifizieren
33 **to cotton on to sth.** – anfangen, etw. zu verstehen
34 **to be at odds with sth.** – zu etw. im Widerspruch stehen
35 **Sufistic** – sufistisch

But against that, there was something else going on in the early 1990s here in Europe that people often forget. And that was the entire Balkan crisis.

Ms Tippett: Right.

Ed Husain: Between '91 and '94, you had large numbers of Muslims in Bosnia, who were white, blond, blue-eyed, being slaughtered in their thousands. And when people from, you know, Arab countries who had taken political refuge in Britain – Omar Bakri and others – came and said to us that, 'Look, two hours away from London's Heathrow Airport, you've got people who are being slaughtered in their thousands despite being European Muslims for 600 years. What chance do people like you and I, who are brown-skinned, black-haired, got in the long term here in Britain?' So for a 16 year-old who is not entirely comfortable in being in Britain, that message, you know, has a strong resonance. [...] And I think the same thing is going today with Iraq with lots of young people, but most certainly Bosnia politicized me. Yes. [...]

Ms Tippett: Right. And over the years I've spoken with a number of people who – and not just Muslims – who as young people, you know, tends to be the rule became drawn into extremist movements. And, you know, one of the things they've talked about to me is the intoxication and the power that comes with that that meets something in adolescence and young adulthood, where one's identity is fragile, where one is looking for a cause and identity. Was that your experience too, I mean, could you talk about the appeal of this idea to you at that point in your life and in this milieu, you know, you really describe British universities and schools where these kinds of ideas were everywhere. [...] (872 words)

51 **intoxication** – Rausch
53 **fragile** – zerbrechlich, schwach

2 Comprehension

a) Summarise in your own words why, according to Ed Husain, his generation has had problems establishing a British identity.

b) Outline the reasons Husain and Tippett give for young Muslims being drawn into extremist movements.

3 Discussion

Work with a partner. Having read the first part of the interview with Ed Husain, which other things would you like to know about him? Write down at least five questions.

.12

4 Listening comprehension → Listening, p. 319

311

Listen to the second part of the interview and answer the questions.

a) What impressed Husain about his Muslim scholars such as Iman Hamza and Yusuf Hanson?

b) What does Husain say about Muslims in America?

c) In which year did the 7th July terror attack in London take place, and how many people were killed?

d) Why, according to Husain, was this attack a kind of "wake-up call" for the UK?

e) What is, in the political far right's view, responsible for extremist movements in the UK?

5 Research project → Hotspot 1, p. 215

C Cross-cultural attitudes

Chris Cleave
(British writer and journalist, born in 1973)

1 **coin** – Münze
3 **fickle** – flatterhaft
4 **corner shop** – Tante-Emma-Laden
9 **gunfire** – Schüsse
9 **thatch** – Dachstroh
14 **to disguise oneself** – sich verkleiden
15 **property** – Eigentum
16 **to trap sth.** – etw. einfangen
18 **sorcerer** – Zauberer
18 **to pursue** – verfolgen
18 **to shed** – abwerfen
18 **tail** – Schwanz
19 **to seize** – packen
25 **to leap** – springen
25 **turnstile** – Drehkreuz
26 **to dodge** – ausweichen
26 **tackle** – Angriff

1 Before you read

What do you think are the problems that asylum seekers face when they come to a new country? Make a list and report back to the class.

"Little Bee", written by British author Chris Cleave in 2008, is a story about a Nigerian asylum seeker in Britain. It focuses on the treatment of refugees by the asylum system.

Little Bee

MOST DAYS I WISH I was a British pound coin instead of an African girl. Everyone would be pleased to see me coming. Maybe I would visit with you for the weekend and then suddenly, because I am fickle like that, I would visit with the man from the corner shop instead – but you would not be sad because you would be eating a cinnamon bun, or drinking a cold Coca-Cola from the can, and you would never think of me again.

We would be happy, like lovers who met on holiday and forgot each other's names. A pound coin can go wherever it thinks it will be safest. It can cross deserts and oceans and leave the sound of gunfire and the bitter smell of burning thatch behind. When it feels warm and secure it will turn around and smile at you, the way my big sister Nkiruka used to smile at the men in our village in the short summer after she was a girl but before she was really a woman, and certainly before the evening my mother took her to a quiet place for a serious talk.

Of course a pound coin can be serious too. It can disguise itself as power, or property, and there is nothing more serious when you are a girl who has neither. You must try to catch the pound, and trap it in your pocket, so that it cannot reach a safe country unless it takes you with it. But a pound has all the tricks of a sorcerer. When pursued I have seen it shed its tail like a lizard so that you are left holding only pence. And when you finally go to seize it, the British pound can perform the greatest magic of all, and this is to transform itself into not one, but two, identical green American dollar bills. Your fingers will close on empty air, I am telling you.

How I would love to be a British pound. A pound is free to travel to safety, and we are free to watch it go. This is the human triumph. This is called, *globalization*. A girl like me gets stopped at immigration, but a pound can leap the turnstiles, and dodge the tackles of those big men with their uniform caps, and jump straight into a waiting airport taxi. *Where to, sir?* Western Civilization, my good man, and make it snappy.

.311 **2 Comprehension** → Understanding fictional texts, p. 322

a) What do we learn about Little Bee? Summarise the information given in the text.

b) Outline why, according to Little Bee, it is so desirable to be able to speak the Queen's English.

.311 **3 Analysis** → Text analysis, p. 326

a) Analyse how the author illustrates Little Bee's feelings and experiences.

b) Explain the phrase "Learning the Queen's English is like scrubbing off the bright red varnish from your toenails, the morning after a dance." (ll. 51–52)

4 Research project → Hotspot 2, p. 215

See how nicely a British pound coin talks? It speaks with the voice of Queen Elizabeth the Second of England. Her face is stamped upon it, and sometimes when I look very closely I can see her lips moving. I hold her up to my ear. What is she saying? *Put me down this minute, young lady, or I shall call my guards.*

If the Queen spoke to you in such a voice, do you suppose it would be possible to disobey? I have read that the people around her – even kings and prime ministers – they find their bodies responding to her orders before their brains can even think why not. Let me tell you, it is not the crown and the scepter that have this effect. Me, I could pin a tiara on my short fuzzy hair, and I could hold up a scepter in one hand, like this, and police officers would still walk up to me in their big shoes and say, *Love the ensemble, madam, now let's have a quick look at your ID, shall we?* No, it is not the Queen's crown and scepter that rule in your land. It is her grammar and her voice. That is why it is desirable to speak the way she does. That way you can say to police officers, in a voice as clear as the Cullinan diamond, *My goodness, how dare you?*

I am only alive at all because I learned the Queen's English. Maybe you are thinking, that isn't so hard. After all, English is the official language of my country, Nigeria. Yes, but the trouble is that back home we speak it so much better than you. To talk the Queen's English, I had to forget all the best tricks of my mother tongue. For example, the Queen could never say, *There was plenty wahala, that girl done use her bottom power to engage my number one son and anyone could see she would end in the bad bush.* Instead the Queen must say, *My late daughter-in-law used her feminine charms to become engaged to my heir, and one might have foreseen that it wouldn't end well.* It is all a little sad, don't you think?

Learning the Queen's English is like scrubbing off the bright red varnish from your toenails, the morning after a dance. It takes a long time and there is always a little bit left at the end, a stain of red along the growing edges to remind you of the good time you had. So, you can see that learning came slowly to me. On the other hand, I had plenty of time. I learned your language in an immigration detention center, in Essex, in the southeastern part of the United Kingdom. Two years, they locked me in there. Time was all I had. (967 words)

30 **stamped** – geprägt
32 **guard** – Wache
34 **to disobey** – nicht gehorchen
37 **tiara** – Diadem
37 **fuzzy** – kraus
39 **ensemble** – *hier:* Outfit
41 **desirable** – erstrebenswert
46 **mother tongue** – Muttersprache
48 **engaged** – verlobt
49 **heir** – Erbe
51 **varnish** – Lack
53 **stain** – Fleck
55 **immigration detention center** – Auffanglager für Einwanderer

D Immigration

1 Before you read → Brainstorming, p. 351
For what reasons do people leave their home country and start a life somewhere else? Make a list and compare it with your partner.

A 3.13

7 **niece** – Nichte
7 **nephew** – Neffe
14 **raspberry** – Himbeere
17 **to keep track of sth.** – über etw. Aufzeichnungen machen
21 **agricultural** – landwirtschaftlich
25 **papers** – offizielle Unterlagen, z. B. Aufenthaltserlaubnis
27 **resident** – Bewohner(in)
27 **permanent residency** – Daueraufenthalt
29 **green card** – Wohnsitznachweis für Ausländer(innen) in den USA
33 **to mind one's own business** – sich um seinen eigenen Kram kümmern
34 **jealousy** – Eifersucht

An immigrant's long journey

Armando and his family

What aspects of your life in Mexico made you leave your home?

It wasn't me … it was my mom's decision. I was still young. My mom wanted more opportunities for a more successful life for her kids – all seven of us plus some of her nieces and nephews who counted more on her for support than on their own mother.

Was it easy to find jobs? What were they and how much did you earn?

I was only 13 when I arrived in the US, but I did work in the fields with my mom during the summer and after school. I worked in the raspberry fields where my mom worked. She earned about $2 per can (about the size of a large coffee can) of firm raspberries and $1 per can of softer raspberries, used for jams and juices. On good days, we would pick about 40 cans full of raspberries per day, three people (my mom, my sister and I) working for 14 hours on my mom's ticket. Each worker has a ticket that keeps track of how many cans they've collected. That's basically what they use to calculate your pay check for the week. The raspberry season is only about half the year and the good days are only about half of that time. Needless to say, the pay was minimal and sporadic. There was no future planning with agricultural jobs. The only non-agricultural job I was able to get without papers was at a fast food restaurant that paid me $4.50 per hour.

How did you go from being an illegal immigrant to becoming a US citizen? Was your story typical of the other immigrants you know?

Actually, all of my brothers and sisters now have their papers, thanks to the people they married. My route was faster because I married a US citizen, whereas they all married permanent residents. I was able to earn my permanent residency within one year of getting married, whereas they have had to wait at least 5 years for their green card. The only way I know of people getting their green cards is through marriage. What I've noticed about people who come to this country is that the relationship with their families is easily broken. It wasn't that way back home. In Mexico, there's more respect passed on to children. Children are looked after by all the neighbors when they play in the streets. Here everyone is expected to just mind their own business. With more money it seems that more jealousy and many more problems come. People are so busy working all day long, sometimes working two or three jobs. While in Mexico, life is lived day by day. We were poor in Mexico and we still gave to those who had less than we did.

Migrant fruit pickers at work

How did you meet your wife?

Mimi came to Watsonville, California, as a volunteer. She used to pick up the kids at the labor camp where I lived and take them to the Penny Club for after-school activities. At first I thought she was too serious, but I think that was her reaction because she had never seen people living in such poor conditions. After she finished her volunteer year, we began dating and got married civilly about a year later. The only people who were present were two of my sisters and my mom. Mimi didn't tell her parents until after we were married.

I wouldn't say that her family immediately welcomed me, but slowly I grew on them. I think in part it was because they didn't expect such a commitment so soon.

How would you describe your present situation?

I am very thankful to my family and Mimi's family for where I am today. I'm also thankful for our two beautiful and healthy boys, Luis and Rafa. I try to live simply and work hard every day. I make time to play soccer with my two sons. I'm fortunate to be able to help my mom in California and my aunt in Mexico financially. This is due in part to the fact that Mimi's parents "gave" us one of their houses so we don't have a mortgage to pay. As a laboratory technician and a teacher, we do not earn a lot of money, but we make enough to provide for our family and save a little for the future. (738 words)

Interview with Uli Nürnberger

39 **volunteer** – Freiwillige(r)
40 **labor camp** – Arbeitslager
43 **to marry civilly** – standesamtlich heiraten
47 **commitment** – *hier:* Bindung
51 **fortunate** – glücklich
54 **mortgage** – Hypothek
55 **to provide for** – sorgen für, versorgen

312 **2 Comprehension**

Armando is representative of many immigrants from Latin America. Make a list of these typical aspects.

3 Analysis

Explain what elements of his story are not very typical of an immigrant's story.

14 312 **4 Listening comprehension** → Listening, p. 319

Listen to the second part of the interview and complete the sentences.

a) For Armando Perez, the *American Dream* is …

b) The first attempt to cross the border failed because …

c) They were eventually able to cross the border because …

d) In the USA they were helped by …

e) Illegal immigrants often work as …

f) The two things taken away from immigrants' paychecks are …

g) The government doesn't want to legalise undocumented workers because …

h) Many American citizens wouldn't do the jobs that illegal immigrants do because …

312 **5 Text production: A letter** → Writing a personal letter, p. 331

Write a letter to Armando in which you comment on his story. Include information about the situation of migrant workers in Germany.

6 Research projects → Hotspots 3 and 4, p. 215

E Patriotism

1 Before you read – Think-pair-share

a) What does patriotism mean to you? Write down five key words or expressions that you associate with this term.

b) Compare your list with that of a partner and agree on five words/expressions between you.

c) Share your results with another pair and agree on five words/expressions. Which of your words have negative or positive connotations? Discuss with the class.

2 **to spoil** – verderben
4 **to reinforce** – verstärken
4 **notion** – Idee
5 **to avoid** – vermeiden
7 **Aussie** – *(ugs.)* Australier(in)
7 **despite** – trotz
8 **to commemorate** – gedenken, feiern
8 **to found** – gründen
8 **penal colony** – Strafkolonie
8 **downtrodden** – unterdrückt
9 **to sentence** – verurteilen
9 **punishment** – Bestrafung
10 **loaf of bread** – Brotlaib
11 **over the top** – übertrieben
11 **reverence** – Verehrung
12 **sheepish** – kleinlaut
14 **to gather** – zusammenkommen
15 **sacred** – heilig
16 **to stage** – veranstalten
16 **fundraiser** – Benefizveranstaltung
20 **to highlight** – hervorheben
21 **invidious** – gehässig
23 **to witness** – beobachten
24 **spectator** – Zuschauer(in)
25 **peninsular** – Halbinsel
25 **coachload** – Busladung

theguardian

News | Sport | Comment | Culture | Business | Money | Life&Style | Travel | Environment

Comment is free > Australia Search [ ] GO

It's Australia Day. Don't let the 'we grew here, you flew here' crew spoil it

Australians do patriotism much better than Brits – but some are using our national day to reinforce notions of us and them.

One of the many things Australia does particularly well – apart from sport and avoiding the global financial crisis – is patriotism. And never more so than today, Australia Day.

There have never been any flies on us Aussies as we celebrate our national day, despite the fact that it commemorates the founding 223 years ago of a penal colony for downtrodden Brits, who could find themselves sentenced to seven years' transportation as punishment for as little as stealing a loaf of bread.

Not for us, the over-the-top religious reverence of the United States (Australians never ask God to bless their country) nor the slightly sheepish British patriotism (because you always have to feel guilty about the empire). Instead, Australians today enjoy a day off work and gather for their most sacred ritual – the backyard BBQ (this year staged as fundraisers for the Queensland flood victims).

At least, that's what I thought. But a shadow is falling over the sunburnt country and its patriotic celebrations, highlighted by the growing use of an invidious new phrase: "We grew here, you flew here."

I have always thought Australian patriotism left British patriotism for dead. I once witnessed two Australian spectators at a tennis tournament show more support for the Aussie player than the rest of the British arena. When Australians visit the Gallipoli peninsular in Turkey in their coach-

2 Comprehension

a) Describe in your own words why, according to the author, Australia does patriotism "particularly well" as opposed to the USA and the UK. Give examples from the text.

b) Outline the recent developments in Australian patriotism the author has noticed, and how he feels about them.

3 Analysis

Explain the statement "We grew here, you flew here." (ll. 1–2)

4 Comment

Football players are often criticized for not singing the national anthem before international matches as this is seen to be unpatriotic. Do you agree with this criticism? Discuss.

loads, they alight at the little cove that marked the landing site of that disastrous first world war military action and cry.

I think the moment it hit home that Britain had a lot to learn from its former colony about national pride was when London won the 2012 Olympics. The contrast 12 years earlier when Sydney won the 2000 Olympics was total. Then thousands of Aussies stayed up until 3am, walked over the Harbour Bridge to Circular Quay to watch Sydney announced the winner on giant TV screens. Everyone expected Beijing to win so the place went wild. Twelve years later, Guardian colleagues gathered around the office TV for the 2012 announcement. Everyone thought Paris would win. When London was announced only one person leapt out of their chair in excitement – me.

One of the best aspects of Australianess, for me at least, is its elasticity. This is not to deny problems of racism but you can become Australian, by and large, because you want to. Thus over the years Australians have claimed as their own people as diverse as the late heart surgeon Victor Chang (born in China), Tony Grieg (born in South Africa, England cricket captain), Russell Crowe (born in New Zealand), Mel Gibson (born in New York) and Nicole Kidman (born in Hawaii).

It is a tradition pleasingly maintained by the man the nation awarded the honour of delivering this year's Australia Day address – Michael Parkinson.

But in recent years Australia Day is being used by some to reinforce notions of us and them. I first heard about this two years ago from friends who visited Australia's nicest and dullest city, Adelaide, and were shocked by how blonde and blue-eyed Australians gave their patriotic celebrations an aggressive, anti-ethnic edge.

Now David Koch, the avuncular breakfast presenter, has zeroed in on this problem with a provocative column for national opinion website The Punch, entitled "What I hate about Australia Day". His answer:

"I hate blonde-haired, blue-eyed yobbos prancing about in the Australian flag who intimidate people who don't look like them."

He recounted how he was haunted by not confronting racist sentiments when he came across them and urged readers to "let's not politely ignore derogatory race-related comments from friends and relatives".

In a way, it is because Australia has done so much to tackle racism that the growing divisiveness of Australia Day is so depressing.

Like Koch, I am proud of Australia and don't believe it a racist country. But yes, some of its residents are. (680 words)

26 **to alight** – aussteigen
26 **cove** – Bucht
28 **to hit home** – *hier:* klar werden
34 **to leap** – springen
35 **elasticity** – Anpassungsfähigkeit
35 **to deny** – abstreiten
37 **heart surgeon** – Herzchirurg(in)
40 **to maintain** – aufrechterhalten
43 **dull** – langweilig
45 **edge** – *hier:* Ton
46 **avuncular** – onkelhaft
46 **to zero in on sth.** – auf etw. fokussieren
49 **yobbo** – Rowdy
49 **to prance about** – herumtanzen
49 **to intimidate** – einschüchtern
51 **to recount** – erzählen
51 **to haunt** – verfolgen
51 **sentiment** – Ansicht
52 **to urge** – ermahnen
52 **derogatory** – abschätzig, abwertend
54 **to tackle** – bekämpfen
54 **divisiveness** – Gespaltenheit
57 **resident** – Einwohner(in)

Avoiding mistakes: German-English interference

In the following exercises, you are asked to identify some of the mistakes often made by German learners of English.

a) Read the sentences and then decide which answer is correct. Give a reason for your choice.

Pablo Jamirez **1** in San Diego for three years now.	lives	has lived
He **2** from Ecuador three years ago.	came	has come
In Ecuador, Pablo Jamirez studied to be **3**.	dentist	a dentist
In San Diego, however, he works as **4**.	fruit picker	a fruit picker
He **5** his family in Ecuador because the trip is too expensive, …	visits never	never visits
… but he writes letters and explains **6** why he can't come.	them	to them
Some days ago, his cousin called him and asked him about life in the USA. He gladly gave her the **7** she had asked for.	information	informations
He told her that in the USA **8** a lot of jobs for people who are willing to work hard.	are	there are
There are **9** Americans who are willing to pick raspberries all day long in the summer heat.	few	a few
Once they have a work permit, **10** people find better-paid jobs and don't pick fruit any more.	most	the most

b) Error-spotting: Read the following sentences and correct the mistakes.

The Notting Hill Carnival

1. The society has changed a great deal over the last decades, becoming much more multicultural.
2. In England live people from many different countries such as India, Pakistan and the Caribbean.
3. In the 1950s there have been fights between white youth gangs and the Caribbean immigrants.
4. As a response, a Caribbean street festival was celebrated during which people enjoyed to dance in the streets and to eat Caribbean food.
5. The Notting Hill Carnival is celebrated every summer in August since 1966.
6. Some people complain themselves about the noise and all the rubbish that is left in the streets.
7. However, the most people think it is a great symbol of the new multicultural Britain.
8. Seeing the costumes and hearing the steel drums is a good thing because many British people do not have enough informations about other cultures.

1 Research project: Writers and their roots → Internet research, p. 358
Work in small groups. Choose one of the following writers:

Pat Mora • John Agard • Ed Husain • Jackie Kay

Collect information on their ethnic background, their work, and how cross-cultural issues such as ethnic diversity, immigration, prejudice, and racism influence their writing.

2 Research project: Ethnic minorities → Internet research, p. 358
Divide the class into three groups, one for the United States, one for Britain and one for Germany. Within your group, research the main ethnic minorities living in that country and form small subgroups. Prepare a short presentation about the minority group you have researched, including information about their history within the new country:

- When and why did members of that ethnic group immigrate?
- Is immigration still going on?
- What is the situation of that ethnic group in the country (legal, social, etc.)?

3 Research project: Traces of German immigrants in the USA → Presentation, p. 362
The influence of German immigrants was very strong in the United States especially during the 19th century, and many traces can be observed to this day. Form different groups and find out about:

- **German place names in the US:** Select three or four cities which have German names and read up on their histories. Why were they given their names?
- **German words in the English language:** Use the Internet to find German words that have been adopted into the English language (you call this "borrowing"). Explain why these specific words were borrowed.
- **German food in the US:** Look for German restaurants in US cities on the Internet. Where are many of them located? Find out what specialties they offer.
- **German culture:** Find out about the Goethe-Schiller monument in Weimar. There are copies of this monument in four US cities. This is only one example of the influence of German culture in the US. Explain this and/or find further examples. One way to go about this is to type the name of a famous German person (Goethe, Schiller, Heine, etc.) plus "USA" into the search engine and see what results you get.
- **Famous German immigrants or descendants of German immigrants:** These are easy to find on the Internet. Choose a few prominent examples and present their stories.
- **In 2010, a German-American museum opened in Washington, D.C.:** Introduce this museum to the class.

Present your findings to the class in the form of a poster, a short presentation, an interactive mini-lesson, etc. It is possible to divide some of the topics between two groups.

4 Project: Immigration to Germany
Which ethnic groups are represented in your class? Interview your classmates with ethnic backgrounds and find out the reasons why their families immigrated to Germany. Present your results to the class.

A 3.16

Julian Baggini (British author, born in 1968)

1 **to point the finger** – to accuse

2 **Mail (Daily Mail)** – a British newspaper

2 **editorial** – a newspaper article that expresses the editor's opinion

3 **impact** – a strong effect

4 **to eschew** – to avoid

5 **to walk on eggshells** – to be very careful

13 **perception** – awareness of how sth. is

17 **to dilute** – *here:* to make weaker

It's no use pointing the finger at ethnic minorities

The Mail expressed the dominant view of multiculturalism in an editorial on 17 July: "[The] malign impact of multiculturalism and political correctness has for years seen Britain segregated into inward-looking communities that eschew British values while the forces of law and order walk on eggshells, desperate not to offend." **1** Interestingly, although we're not a particularly religious country, most people do think our values are in some important way Christian ones. A BBC poll reported that 61 % believe that "our laws should respect and be influenced by UK religious values", with even 49 % of those with no religion agreeing.

Antipathy towards British Asians in particular is thus based largely on the perception that they do not wish to adopt the 'British way of life' or that their numbers are getting so large that the English way is being diluted too much by their mere presence. [...] **2** Again it should not be presumed that this is racism in disguise. The mainstream wants to expel

1 Comprehension

Read the text and choose from sentences A-G the one which fits each gap (1–6). There is one extra sentence that you do not need to use.

A The first is that it is true that many minorities do not fully integrate into mainstream English culture. This is plain fact.

B The generally accepted solution is simple: live like the English or get out.

C As long as staying apart isn't threatening, it is not only accepted, it is actually what people want.

D Put more positively, and in pub terms, it's that people "don't mind who lives here, whether they're black, white or green, as long as they follow our way of life."

E We all like to feel that we're open-minded people who can be friends with anyone, and we also can probably come up with a few examples of friends who do not match our demographic profile to prove our lack of insularity.

F Many minorities have already been successfully integrated into mainstream English culture.

G For the most part, people mix and marry with people mainly of their own cultural background, as determined by a combination of country, family origin or religion.

insularity – interested only in your own country or group from society, through enforced emigration or incarceration, all sorts of people who refuse to conform, and the fact that the majority of those they currently want out have different coloured skins is a historical accident.

The argument may be flawed but it is based on several truths that we would be foolish to ignore. **3** Ethnic minority populations do concentrate in particular areas. [...] Although mixed race marriages are on the rise, they still comprise only 2% of all marriages. Only 6% of British Indians, 4% of Pakistanis and 3% of Bangladeshis have married a non-Asian. In contrast 29% of black Caribbean men and 48% of other black men have married non-black women. **4** This is the same the world over. For instance, while in Spain I saw a newspaper report on a study which showed that 75% of immigrants there did not have a Spanish friend.

The key point, however, is that every sector of society does this. It's no use pointing the finger at ethnic minorities. England is a patchwork of almost hermetically sealed sub-worlds, in which class as much as race is a crucial factor. [...] **5** [...] But if we are honest, the vast majority live, work and socialize overwhelmingly with people of a similar social type. [...]

The point about multiculturalism is therefore a red herring. All sorts of social groups don't mix very much, yet we don't chastise them for it. The trouble is not caused by not mixing, but refusing to do so in ways which seem to threaten other groups. **6** (588 words)

From: Julian Baggini, Welcome to Everytown

23 **incarceration** – to put or keep sb. in prison
26 **flawed** – having mistakes
36 **patchwork** – sth. that is made up of different things
37 **crucial** – very important
40 **red herring** – a wrong track
41 **to chastise** – to punish

2 Analysis → Describing cartoons, p. 340

a) Explain the author's view on the lack of mixing between the minority groups mentioned in the text.

b) Decribe the cartoon, analyse it and relate it to the text.

3 Comment
→ Writing a comment, p. 327
"As long as staying apart isn't threatening, it is not only accepted, it is actually what people want."
Discuss to what extent you agree with this statement. Choose examples from what you have learned about minorities in the US or Britain, or from your own experience.

Topic 2.9
The global challenge

7mz39c

A

B

C

D

E

F

Getting started

1 **a)** Identify seven different personal objects in the classroom (clothes, watches, etc.) that originated from seven different countries by checking the labels. Find the countries on a world map. Make a grid.

Object	Produced in	What you know about the country
mobile	…	…
trainers	…	…

b) Which of these findings surprised you most? Why?

c) How did the objects that were not made in Germany get into the classroom?

d) Why were none of these objects produced in Germany?

e) Were they ever made here? When? Where? How?

Globalization Blues

You can't hide in your bed;
You can't hide in your head.
They'll run over you; you'll be worse
off than dead.
I'm talkin' globalization, globalization.
Drug-dealing, money-stealing
globalization blues.

They say forget your suspicions;
Work in sweatshop conditions.
Sew some more sneakers and guard
these munitions.
It's globalization, globalization.
People-bashing, job-smashing
globalization blues.

They say your country's in debt
And you've got to pay.
If you want to eat, then do what we say.
That's globalization, globalization.
Slave-made, world-trade globalization
blues.

Since you can't get away,
Better fight them today.
From Seattle to Prague, Manila Bay to LA,
It's globalization, globalization.
On the street, we're gonna beat the
globalization blues.

Words and music: Ray Korona

3 **to be worse off than sb./sth.** – schlechter dran sein als jmd/etw.
8 **suspicion** – Misstrauen
9 **sweatshop** – Ausbeuterbetrieb
10 **to sew** – nähen
10 **sneakers** – Turnschuhe, Sportschuhe
11 **munitions** – Munition
13 **to bash** – schlagen, schlechtmachen
15 **debt** – Schuld
19 **slave** – Sklave, Sklavin

2 With a partner, make a word web and then write a definition for globalisation as you understand it now. → Word webs, p. 349

19 **3 Listening comprehension** → Dealing with songs, p. 325

a) Make a list of the aspects of globalisation that the song "Globalization Blues" focuses on.

b) Write a headline for each of the four verses.

c) Analyse the choice of words used in this song. What is their effect on the listener?

d) Which of the pictures (A – F) can be linked to the song, and why?

e) Which aspects of globalisation are illustrated by the other pictures?

4 Projects → Hotspots 1 and 2, p. 231

Word bank

developing / developed country • global player • with a highly developed / deficient infrastructure • a free market economy • an exporter / importer of … • raw materials • manufactured goods • state-of-the-art technology

A Discovering globalisation

1 Before you read

a) When do you think globalisation really started? Collect your ideas in class.

b) Look at the photos. The heading of the text states three eras of globalisation. From what is shown on the photos, try to guess what these three eras could be.

2 Comprehension: Table completion → Taking notes, p. 352
Make a three-column table and fill in the main features describing each of the three great eras of globalisation. Use your own words as far as possible.

The three eras of globalization

There have been three great eras of globalization. The first lasted from 1492 – when Columbus set sail, opening trade between the Old World and the New World – until around 1800. I would call this era **Globalization 1.0**. It shrank the world from a size large to a size medium. [...] In this era, countries and governments (often inspired by religion or imperialism or a combination of both) led the way in breaking down walls and knitting the world together, driving global integration.

The second great era, Globalization 2.0, lasted roughly from 1800 to 2000, interrupted by the Great Depression and World Wars I and II. This era shrank the world from a size medium to a size small. In **Globalization 2.0**, the key agent of change, the dynamic force driving global integration, was multinational companies. These multinationals went global for markets and labor, spearheaded first by the expansion of the Dutch and English joint-stock companies and the Industrial Revolution. In the first half of this era, global integration was powered by falling transportation costs, thanks to the steam engine and the railroad, and in the second half by falling telecommunication costs – thanks to the diffusion of the telegraph, telephones, the PC, satellites, fiber-optic cable, and the early version of the World Wide Web. It was during this era that we really saw the birth and maturation of a global economy, in the sense that there was enough movement of goods and information from

4 **to shrink** – schrumpfen
6 **to knit sth. together** – etw. verknüpfen
8 **roughly** – ungefähr
13 **to spearhead** – anführen
13 **joint-stock company** – Aktiengesellschaft
17 **diffusion** – Verbreitung
18 **fiber-optic cable** – Glasfaserkabel
19 **maturation** – Reifung

3 Presentation → Presentation, p. 362

Read the quotation by Byron Dorgan and prepare a 3-minute talk to explain to your class what he might have meant when he said it.
"I am not someone who believes we should build fences around our country but I do believe there ought to be some fairness with respect to the rules of this globalization."
Byron Dorgan (former United States Senator from North Dakota)

4 Analysis → Describing cartoons, p. 340

p.313

a) "Globalization 3.0 is shrinking the world from a size small to a size tiny [...]." (l. 24). Explain this quote in your own words.

b) Explain the term "[...] to plug in and play." (l. 38).

c) Examine the author's attitude towards globalisation.

d) Describe the cartoon, analyse it and relate it to the text.

5 Comment

"Where do I as an individual fit into the global competition and opportunities of the day [...]" (ll. 32–33)
Discuss to what extent you feel fit for the global market.

continent to continent for there to be a global market, with global arbitrage in products and labor. [...]

Right around the year 2000 we entered a whole new era: **Globalization 3.0.** Globalization 3.0 is shrinking the world from a size small to a size tiny [...]. The dynamic force in Globalization 3.0 – the force that gives it its unique character – is the newfound power for individuals to collaborate and compete globally. [...] People all over the world started waking up and realizing that they had more power than ever to go global as individuals, they needed more than ever to think of themselves as individuals competing against other individuals all over the planet, and they had more opportunities to work with those other individuals, not just compete with them. As a result, every person now must, and can, ask: Where do I as an individual fit into the global competition and opportunities of the day, and how can I, on my own, collaborate with others globally? [...] Globalization 1.0 and 2.0 were driven primarily by European and American individuals and businesses. [...] Globalization 3.0 is going to be more and more driven not only by individuals but also by much more diverse – non-Western, non-white – groups of individuals. [...] Globalization 3.0 makes it possible for so many people to plug in and play, and you are going to see every color of the human rainbow take part. (490 words)

from: "The World is flat" by Thomas L. Friedman

Thomas L. Friedman (American journalist, born in 1953)

21 **arbitrage** – Arbitrage, Nutzung der Kursunterschiede an verschiedenen Börsen
25 **unique** – einzigartig
26 **to collaborate** – zusammenarbeiten
26 **to compete** – konkurrieren
34 **primarily** – hauptsächlich, vornehmlich

B A fair world?

1 Before you read

a) Go online and find the official English *Fairtrade* homepage. Use the online information to come up with a definition of Fairtrade.

b) Do you know any Fairtrade shops or supermarkets that sell Fairtrade products in your area? Have you ever been there? What did you buy? If you do not know anything about Fairtrade shops in your area, find out if there are any and give a short presentation to introduce them to your class.

2 Comprehension → Understanding non-fictional texts, p. 320
Work with a partner. One of you reads the leaflet on the left, the other reads the one on the right. Summarise the texts for each other.

Fairtrade International

FAIRTRADE INTERNATIONAL

HOME | ABOUT US | ABOUT FAIRTRADE | STANDARDS | PRODUCTS

TRADING UP

THE FAIRTRADE MARK GIVES SMALL FARMERS A STRONGER POSITION IN WORLD MARKETS

In the Windward Islands, in the Caribbean, thousands of families make their living growing bananas on small, hilly farms. During the 1990s, many of them were forced out of business by large-scale Latin American banana plantations where labour is cheaper and costs are lower.

"When prices dropped, the economy went down to zero because bananas are the heartbeat of the country," explains Amos Wiltshire, National Fairtrade Coordinator for Dominica, one of the Windward Islands.

Amos joined forces with other farmers who saw Fairtrade as the only way to survive in a cut-throat market. Through Fairtrade, producers learn how best to sell their products and what the international market and consumers want. Today, nearly 100% of Dominica's banana farmers are members of Fairtrade groups.

"FAIRTRADE HAS BEEN THE SAVIOUR OF THE FARMERS IN DOMINICA – OF AGRICULTURE AND THE WHOLE ECONOMY. WITH FAIRTRADE, SMALL FARMERS HAVE BEEN TRANSFORMED FROM MARGINALISED FARMERS INTO BUSINESSMEN.
AMOS WILTSHIRE, BANANA FARMER, DOMINICA"

0 **to trade sth. up** – mit etwas Hochwertigerem ersetzen
0 **mark** – *hier:* Zeichen
2 **to make a living** – seinen Lebensunterhalt verdienen
2 **to grow** – anbauen
4 **to be forced out of business** – gezwungen werden, den Betrieb einzustellen
5 **large-scale** – *hier:* riesig
6 **labour** – Arbeitskräfte
12 **to join forces** – zusammenarbeiten, sich zusammenschließen
13 **to survive** – überleben
13 **cut-throat** – Verdrängungs-
saviour – Retter(in)
to marginalise – ins Abseits drängen

.20 .313 **3 Listening comprehension: Making globalisation work** → Listening, p. 319

Listen to the thoughts of American economist and university professor Joseph Stiglitz on globalisation. Take notes in English and answer the following questions:

- Which problems and anomalies of globalisation does Stiglitz mention at the beginning of the text?
- How have French workers been affected by globalisation?
- Contrast the USA's and Scandinavia's approach to remaining competitive and efficient in a globalised world. What have been the results?
- Which solutions to the current issues of globalisation does he suggest?

4 Project → Hotspot 3, p. 231

TACKLING POVERTY AND EMPOWERING PRODUCERS THROUGH TRADE

PRODUCERS | RESOURCES | NEWS   Search [ ] GO

A BETTER DEAL

THE FAIRTRADE MARK MEANS A CLOSER LINK BETWEEN SHOPPERS AND PRODUCERS

FAIRTRADE INTERNATIONAL

More and more of us want to know where our shopping comes from and that the people who produce it have received a fair deal. Fairtrade encourages more direct trading relationships so that producers get a bigger share of the export price.

Sweet rewards

In Ghana, liberalisation of the internal cocoa market created big challenges for small farmers; they responded by forming Kuapa Kokoo, a farmer-owned business. Their decision proved wise: Kuapa Kokoo now owns a one-third share in a UK-based company selling Fairtrade chocolate. As well as supplying the cocoa, they have a direct share in the company's success.

"I WANT TO BE SURE THAT FARMERS GET A FAIR PRICE AND BENEFIT DIRECTLY FROM MY PURCHASE. AS THE DAUGHTER OF A GHANAIAN FATHER, I KNOW HOW IMPORTANT FAIRTRADE IS TO SMALL PRODUCERS. WITH MORE SHOPS STOCKING MORE GREAT QUALITY PRODUCTS CARRYING THE FAIRTRADE MARK, IT'S A WIN-WIN SITUATION. WE CAN EAT AND DRINK IN GOOD HEALTH AND GOOD CONSCIENCE." **ADJOA ANDOH, ACTRESS (PICTURED TOP RIGHT)**

(351 words)

21 **to encourage** – ermutigen
22 **share** – Anteil
24 **reward** – Belohnung
25 **liberalisation** – Liberalisierung
26 **challenge** – Herausforderung
26 **to respond** – reagieren
28 **to prove wise** – sich als klug erweisen
30 **to supply** – liefern
33 **to stock** – führen
35 **conscience** – Gewissen

C Global players

1 Before you read
If corporations were persons, which characteristics would you give the following ones?

BÖRSE ▸ ONLINE

Search GO

GLOBAL PLAYER: Auf der ganzen Welt zu Hause

Wenn Unternehmen die Vorzüge der internationalen Expansion anpreisen, dann fällt oft der Begriff Abhängigkeit von bestimmten Märkten. Global agierende Konzerne machen Einbußen auf dem Heimatmarkt im internationalen Geschäft wett.

Irgendwo ist immer Wachstum – auch wenn Südeuropa mit einer Schuldenkrise kämpft oder die US-Konjunktur auf der Kippe steht. Für Anleger sollte es sich daher lohnen, nach Aktien weltweit präsenter Unternehmen zu fahnden.

„Wo Firmen ihr Geld verdienen, wird für Investoren immer relevanter", erklärt HSBC-Stratege Garry Evans. So kommt den global agierenden Konzernen derzeit entgegen, dass die Konjunktur in Fernost brummt. „Für den Export sieht es weiter gut aus. Wir profitieren vom Boom in Asien", sagt WestLB-Volkswirt Jörg Lüschow. Der Ländermix hilft den Unternehmen, günstige Währungseffekte auszunutzen und Ertragsrisiken zu streuen.

Ein klassisches Beispiel für eine Weltaktie ist Coca-Cola. Mit einem Markenwert von 58 Mrd. Dollar zählt der Name zu den top drei weltweit. Beinahe überall wird die Brause getrunken – in New York und Peking, auf Grönland und in Kapstadt. Allein in Europa setzte der Softdrinkhersteller aus Atlanta 2009 ein Drittel um.

Boeing 787 Dreamliner

Auch der Flugzeughersteller Boeing gibt wieder eine gute Figur ab. Die peinliche Serie von Entwicklungspannen beim neuen Langstreckenflieger Dreamliner ist passé. Der Supervogel soll in den kommenden Tagen auf der Flugschau in Farnborough vorgestellt werden. Der dickste Auftragsbrocken wartet aber zu Hause: Die US-Luftwaffe will insgesamt 534 Tankflugzeuge ordern. Der Auftrag ist 100 Mrd. Dollar schwer. Um den Zuschlag für die fliegenden Zapfsäulen buhlt auch der Rivale EADS. Doch Brancheninsider rechnen dem US-Unternehmen bessere Chancen aus.

Eine deutsche Weltaktie kommt aus Ludwigshafen. Dort hat BASF die Idee des Verbundstandorts entwickelt: Die Produktionsanlagen sind so miteinander verknüpft, dass sich effiziente Wertschöpfungsketten ergeben. Die Nebenprodukte einer Fabrik dienen an anderer Stelle als Einsatzstoff. Das führt zu Synergien und senkt die Herstellungskosten. BASF hat das Konzept in die Welt exportiert: in die USA nach Freeport und Geismar, in Asien nach Nanjing (China) und Kuantan (Malaysia). Diese Globalisierung der Produktion machte BASF zum führenden Chemiekonzern. Immerhin 16 Prozent der Erlöse erwirtschaftet der Konzern in der Region Asien/Pazifik, in Nordamerika sind es 18 Prozent. Bis 2020 will der Chemieriese den Gesamtumsatz auf mehr als 90 Mrd. Euro fast verdoppeln. Dabei soll das Branchenwachstum jährlich um zwei Prozentpunkte übertroffen werden. (373 words)

2 Vocabulary → Working with a dictionary, p. 353
Find the German equivalents of the following words in the text:

advantages • to praise • dependency • losses • domestic market • growth • debt crisis • economic cycle • shares • Far East • to boom • currency • effects • yield risk • to spread • brand value • to turn over • long-distance aircraft • contract • production facilities • value-added chain • byproducts • production material • production costs • total turnover • to exceed

313 **3 Mediation** → Mediation, p. 343
Sum up the main points of the text for an English youth magazine.

4 Analysis → Describing diagrams, p. 341
Describe the table and analyse it.

5 Research projects
→ Hotspots 4 and 5, p. 231

Rank	Previous Rank	Brand	Region/Land	Sector	Brand Value ($m)	Change in Brand Value
1	1	Coca-Cola	United States	Beverages	77,839	8%
2	8		United States	Electronics	76,568	129%
3	2	IBM	United States	Business Services	75,532	8%
4	4	Google	United States	Internet Services	69,726	26%
5	3	Microsoft	United States	Computer Software	57,853	-2%
6	5	GE	United States	Diversified	43,682	2%
7	6	M	United States	Restaurants	40,062	13%
8	7	intel	United States	Electronics	39,385	12%
9	–	SAMSUNG	South Korea	Electronics	32,893	40%
10	11		Japan	Automotive	30,280	9%
11	12		Germany	Automotive	30,097	10%
12	–	BMW	Germany	Automotive	29,052	18%

Source: Interbrand 2012

D Corporate power

Max Barry (Australian writer, born in 1973)

1 Before you read → Brainstorming, p. 351
Look at the following quote from the novel *Jennifer Government*:
"But now America has all the best companies and all the money because everyone works and the Government can't spend money on stupid things like advertising and elections and making new laws. They just stop people stealing or hurting each other and everything else is taken care of by the private sector, which everyone knows is more efficient." Brainstorm pros and cons of this vision of the future.

2 Comprehension
In your own words, outline the world that Hayley lives in.

The following text is an extract from Jennifer Government, *a novel written by Max Barry. The story is set in a dystopian alternate reality, in which most countries (now controlled by the USA) are dominated by large profit-seeking corporations.*

3 **to hotfoot (it)** – hasten
9 **to suck** – ätzend sein
11 **to jot** – schnell notieren
13 **arch** – Bogen
14 **to abolish** – abschaffen
18 **crack-up** – etw. zum Totlachen
26 **a smattering of sth.** – ein bisschen
26 **to guess** – glauben, schätzen
27 **to work up enthusiasm for** – Begeisterung aufbringen für
27 **to head for sth.** – etw. ansteuern

McDonald's

Until she stood in front of them, Hayley didn't realize how many of her classmates were blond. It was like a beach out there. She'd missed the trend. Hayley would have to hotfoot it to a hairdresser after school.

"When you're ready," the teacher said.

She looked at her note cards and took a breath. "Why I Love America, by Hayley McDonald's. America is the greatest group of countries in the world because we have freedom. In countries like France, where the Government isn't privatized, they still have to pay tax and do whatever the Government says, which would really suck. In USA countries, we respect individual rights and let people do whatever they want."

The teacher jotted something in his folder. McDonald's-sponsored schools were cheap like that: at Pepsi schools, everyone had notebook computers. Also their uniforms were much better. It was so hard to be cool with the Golden Arches on your back. "Before USA countries abolished tax, if you didn't have a job, the Government took money from working people and gave it to you. So, like, the more useless you were, the more money you got." No response from her classmates. Even the teacher didn't smile. Hayley was surprised: she'd thought that one was a crack-up.

"But now America has all the best companies and all the money because everyone works and the Government can't spend money on stupid things like advertising and elections and making new laws. They just stop people stealing or hurting each other and everything else is taken care of by the private sector, which everyone knows is more efficient." She looked at her notes: yep, that was it. "Finally I would like to say that America is the greatest group of countries in the world and I am proud to live in the Australian Territories of the USA!"

A smattering of applause. It was the eighth talk this period: she guessed it was getting harder to work up enthusiasm for capitalism. Hayley headed for her seat.

3 Analysis → Text analysis, p. 326

a) Analyse Hayley's attitude towards the world she lives in. Include quotes from the text to support your answer.

314 △ **b)** Illustrate Hayley's character. Once again, use quotes from the text to support your answer.

c) Examine the emotions that Hayley goes through during her presentation, and show how the writer puts these across to the reader.

d) Analyse the teacher's attitude towards Hayley's presentation.

314 △ **4 Comment** → Writing a comment, p. 327
"McDonald's-sponsored schools were cheap like that: at Pepsi schools, everyone had notebook computers. Also their uniforms were much better. It was so hard to be cool with the Golden Arches on your back." (ll. 11–14) Some people claim that major companies and their brands have too much influence on modern society. Do you agree? Discuss.

"Hold it," the teacher said. "I have questions."

"Oh," Hayley said.

"Are there any positive aspects to tax?"

She relaxed: a gimme question. "Some people say tax is good because it gives money to people who don't have any. But those people must be lazy or stupid, so why should they get other people's money? Obviously the answer is no."

The teacher blinked. He made a note. That must have been an impressive answer, Hayley thought. "What about social justice?"

"What?"

"Is it fair that some people should be rich while others have nothing?"

She shifted from one foot to the other. She was just remembering: this teacher had a thing about poor people. He was always bringing them up. "Um, yeah, it's fair. Because if I study really hard for a test and get an A and Emily doesn't and fails" – renewed interest from the class; Emily raised blond eyebrows – "then it's not fair to take some of my marks and give them to her, is it?"

The teacher frowned. Hayley felt a flash of panic. "Another thing, in non-USA countries they want everyone to be the same, so if your sister is born blind, then they blind you, too, to make it even. But how unfair is that? I would much rather be an American than a European Union … person." She gave the class a big smile. They clapped, much more enthusiastically than before. She added hopefully, "Is that all?"

"Yes. Thank you."

Relief! She started walking. A cute boy in the third row winked at her.

The teacher said, "Although, Hayley, they don't really blind people in non-USA countries."

Hayley stopped. "Well, that's kind of hypocritical, isn't it?"

The class cheered. The teacher opened his mouth, then shut it. Hayley took her seat. Kick ass, she thought. She had aced this test. (628 words)

31 **gimme** *(coll.)* – gib mir
33 **obviously** – offensichtlich
34 **to blink** – blinzeln
34 **impressive** – beeindruckend
35 **justice** – Gerechtigkeit
38 **to shift** – wechseln
41 **renewed** – erneut
43 **to frown** – die Stirn runzeln
43 **flash** – *hier:* Anflug
50 **relief** – Erleichterung
50 **cute** – süß
50 **to wink at sb.** – jmdm zuzwinkern
53 **hypocritical** – scheinheilig, heuchlerisch
54 **to cheer** – jubeln
55 **to ace** – *hier:* die Note 1 bekommen

E Water poverty

1 Before you read

a) Describe the picture and relate it to the title of the article.

b) How do you think limited access to clean drinking water would affect your everyday life? Discuss with a partner and report back to the class.

2 Comprehension: Short answer questions
Read the text and answer the following questions in 5–20 words.

a) What did the United Nations say about the consequences of a lack of access to clean water?

b) What effects does a lack of access to clean water have on women and girls?

c) What is GWC?

GWC **GLOBAL WATER CHALLENGE** Search GO

1 IN 8 PEOPLE LACK ACCESS TO SAFE WATER

Around the globe, nearly 800 million people lack access to water and over 2.5 billion lack access to sanitation. The scope and impact of this crisis are staggering. The United Nations has reported that more people die from water- and sanitation-related disease than from all forms of violence, including war. According to the United Nations Development Program, every US$1 spent on water and sanitation generates a return of US$9 in saved time, increased productivity and reduced health costs in Africa.
Beyond loss of life, water poverty and inadequate sanitation cripple all development efforts. A lack of adequate water and sanitation facilities keeps children, especially girls, from attending school. Women spend an average of 3-5 hours each day fetching water, missing out on opportunities to perform other tasks or engage in economically productive activity. Parents miss work due to water-related illness or caring for sick family members. Existing medical conditions, such as HIV/AIDS, are exacerbated because of unsafe water and inadequate sanitation. Climate change, population growth, industrialization and urbanization all threaten to make the global WASH [Water Sanitation and Hygiene] crisis much worse.
Fortunately, there is room for hope. Waterborne illness is preventable and lasting water supply and sanitation solutions exist. Through concerted efforts by governments, corporations, foundations and nongovernmental organizations, roughly 200 million people have gained access to clean water during the past decade. However, even with these efforts, many countries are unlikely to meet the Millennium Development Goal (MDG) for water and even fewer will reach the MDG for sanitation. Unprecedented collaboration between all sectors of society is needed in order to achieve sustainable solutions to this challenge. [...]
Founded in 2006, Global Water Challenge (GWC) is a nonprofit [...] coalition of leading organizations committed to addressing water and sanitation issues. Drawing upon the experience, expertise and assets of its members, GWC is able to create partnerships that achieve far greater results

0 **access** – Zugriff
2 **sanitation** – sanitäre Einrichtungen
2 **scope** – Ausmaß
3 **staggering** – überwältigend
12 **facility** – Einrichtung
18 **to exacerbate** – verschlimmern
19 **urbanization** – Verstädterung
21 **waterborne** – durch Wasser übertragen
21 **preventable** – vermeidbar
22 **concerted** – gemeinsam
26 **unprecedented** – beispiellos
26 **sustainable** – nachhaltig
30 **asset** – Vermögen

d) In which countries has GWC invested in school programs?

e) How have the students in these schools benefitted?

f) How successful are the GWC's water and sanitation projects?

g) What makes a water and sanitation project 'sustainable'?

3 Analysis
Describe and analyse the cartoon.

4 Presentation → Presentation, p. 362
Access to safe water is not something to take for granted and those in the developed world must learn to use water more responsibly – but how? Work in a small group and create a poster that gives 5–10 tips on how people can save water every day. Present your posters to the class.

5 Research project → Hotspot 6, p. 231

than any one organization could by itself. Since its inception, GWC is a powerful catalyst for fostering collective action in the water sector. GWC serves three core functions:

CONNECTING.
GWC is a platform for collaboration that unites corporations, implementing nonprofits, research institutes, and governmental agencies in partnerships that leverage their unique resources and expertise. In addition, GWC connects citizens with policymakers to increase the priority placed on water and sanitation globally.

INVESTING.
GWC has invested in and collaborated with members on innovative programs and campaigns globally. Some examples include:
Schools Programs: GWC's investment in schools programs has benefited nearly 500,000 students in Kenya, El Salvador, Guatemala, Honduras, Nicaragua, Tanzania, and Mexico. These programs have enhanced children's health and education, paving the way for more opportunities for the students, their families and their countries. [...]

LEARNING.
GWC is committed to improving the long-term impact of investments in the sector by working with its members and other partners to identify and share important lessons and best practices. [...]
To achieve our goal of universal access to clean water and safe sanitation, all GWC projects are sustainable, replicable and scalable by local communities and national governments. GWC is committed to learning from past projects, connecting those who can help each other, and investing and leveraging financial or policy support for innovative projects.

Sustainable
All projects must have long-term plans. It is estimated that half of all water and sanitation projects fail after 5 years. Sustainable projects maintain the local water source and build local capacity in order to maintain and operate a water system. This requires the involvement of the local community, local government, and local businesses. For each system that doesn't have to be replaced, more resources will be available in the future for new projects.

Replicable
GWC measures impacts and benefits consistently, communicating these clearly throughout the project. Monitoring programs and sharing information helps communities, governments, local entrepreneurs, and non-profits working in this sector. Having access to results allows leaders in the field to replicate the program on their own.

Scalable
GWC invests in successful models with the potential to expand beyond a particular area. These models should be flexible enough to meet the demands of individual localities. (676 words)

31 **inception** – Gründung
31 **catalyst** – Beschleuniger
31 **to foster** – fördern
32 **core** – Kern-, Haupt-
34 **to implement** – einführen
35 **to leverage** – etw. wirksam einsetzen
43 **to enhance** – steigern
43 **to pave the way for sth.** – den Weg ebnen für etw. *(fig.)*
47 **best practice** – beste Vorgehensweise
49 **replicable** – replizierbar
49 **scalable** – anpassbar
54 **to maintain** – aufrecht-erhalten
60 **to monitor** – überwachen
64 **to expand** – ausdehnen

Mastering assignments

How to write a comment about positive or negative aspects/effects, pros and cons, advantages and disadvantages:

Topic: Many large fashion retailers have their goods produced in Asian countries like India or Bangladesh, where production is cheap. Discuss the pros and cons of this trend.

a) Write an introduction to the topic. There are several ways of writing a good introduction:
- You can start with a rhetorical question, or one that people might ask in relation to the topic.
- You can use a quote that is related to your topic.
- You can begin with an interesting fact that is related to the topic.
- You can use an analogy or a paradox, but make sure that it is easy to understand.
- You can use examples from your own experience.

Example: Have you ever looked at the labels in your clothes? Do you know where your new jacket was made? Do you care? Many high street fashion chains have their clothing produced in Asian countries like India or Bangladesh, where production is cheap. This trend has advantages and disadvantages and there are winners and losers.

Which of the above listed methods were used to write this introduction?

b) Brainstorm pros and cons in relation to the topic. Here is a list of pros and cons of producing clothes in Asian countries. Make a table and sort them into the correct column.

pros	cons

many jobs in industrialised countries are lost • companies can save money because labour is cheap • companies are exploiting workers in developing countries • local shops and small family-owned businesses can't compete with global players • low cost = clothing companies can update clothing range more often • brings jobs to poorer countries • harms the environment because of global transport • poor quality • keeps prices low for consumers • poor working conditions • possible use of child labour • wide range of products due to low production costs • avoiding strict European environmental regulations (e.g. waste disposal)

c) Now you need to choose the pros and cons which you think are the most important. But make sure that you have something to say about each of them. Look at the table and choose the three or four most important arguments on each side.

d) The next step is to write the main part of your comment. Use connectives (see the list at the back of your book) to connect your thoughts. Don't make the mistake of just listing your arguments in one sentence. Elaborate by giving details and examples. If you are more inclined to support production of clothing in Asian countries, start with the cons, and vice versa. Write the main part of the comment.

e) The last part is the conclusion. Sum up the arguments above and draw conclusions from them. Finally, state your point of view. Don't forget to use connectives. Write a conclusion to the comment.

1 Project: Songs about globalisation → Presentation, p. 362
Go online and find the song "My Global Mind" by Queensrÿche. Listen to the song and complete the following activities:

a) In your own words outline the singer's state of mind.

b) Compare the music and the message of this song to those of "Globalization Blues" at the beginning of this topic.

c) Find the metaphors in the song and explain their effect on the listener.

d) Now find another song about globalisation and collect additional information such as facts about the artist or video clips and prepare a short presentation. Is it a protest song or is it in favour of globalisation? Give your presentation to the class.

2 Research project: How products are made → Internet research, p. 358
Work in small groups. Choose one of the objects from exercise 1a) on page 218. Go online and find out how your chosen object is made, explaining the production process from the raw materials to the finished product. Create a collage that illustrates this process and present it to the class.

3 Project: A talk show on globalisation → Discussions, p. 344
Organise a serious TV discussion on the topic "Globalisation – blessing or curse?" First decide who will be the talk show host / guests. Give your guests different roles e.g. local food producer, African coffee farmer, restaurant owner, representative of large discount supermarket chain, etc. Discuss the following topics:
- food miles
- prices
- competition
- exploitation
- etc.

4 Research project: A case study → Internet research, p. 358
Go online and find an example of a German company that has outsourced parts of its business (services or the manufacturing of products) to another country. Collect information on the reasons behind the decision. If possible, also outline the effects it has had on the company itself, the customers, and the country it has outsourced to.

5 Research project: German global players → Internet research, p. 358

a) With the help of the Internet, create a ranking of Germany's biggest companies by turnover/revenues or profit. Compare your group's ranking to another group's. Did you get the same results?

b) Chose one of the companies in your ranking that interests you and collect background information on it, e.g. the company history, its key products or services, the number of employees, its future prospects, etc. Present your findings to the class.

6 Research project: Virtual/embedded water → Internet research, p. 358
Work in small groups and research the concept of 'virtual/embedded water' on the Internet. Find out what this concept is, give some examples, outline the impact it has on water supplies around the globe, and explain who the winners and losers are.

A 3.25

1 **gloomy** – dark, depressing
1 **prospect** – outlook
2 **bleak** – poor
3 **downturn** – decline
5 **beyond** – over and above
6 **to reshape** – to change
7 **root** – origin
7 **abject** – pitiful
7 **failure** – mistake
7 **governance** – ruling
8 **neglect** – ignorance
9 **to reveal** – to show
11 **lack of sth.** – sth. missing
13 **prosperous** – wealthy
14 **to ensure** – to make sure
14 **to gain** – to profit
15 **to expose** – to uncover
16 **unprecedented** – never seen before
19 **to prevent** – to keep from happening
20 **legitimate** – rightful
22 **to affect** – to influence
23 **urgent** – pressing
23 **multilateral** – varied
26 **welfare** – well-being
27 **equity** – justice
27 **afterthought** – second thought

No country, no matter how powerful … can control the forces of globalisation on its own

[…] The world looks a gloomy and uncertain place. Every day the prospects for the global economy look bleaker. We don't know how deep or long-lasting the downturn will be. But we do know there is plenty of pain to come.

In every crisis, however, there is opportunity. If we have the courage to learn the lessons of the past […] and put them into practice beyond the economic sphere, we can put in place new foundations to reshape our world for the better.

For the roots of this crisis go beyond an abject failure of financial governance and neglect of warnings of the risks being run. Connections between economies have been revealed which were clearly not fully understood, let alone regulated. There may have been endless talk of globalisation. But it is very clear there has been a lack of recognition of what this means for us all.

We have now learnt decisively that no country, no matter how powerful or prosperous, can control the forces of globalisation on its own. The lack of inclusive processes and institutions needed to manage the risks and ensure all gain from the benefits has also been exposed.

The present crisis has already led to unprecedented international co-operation. There has been co-ordinated action to protect the financial system from collapse, to try to stimulate the global economy and find new rules and structures to prevent this disaster being repeated. But while the G20, combining rich nations with emerging market countries, is a better and more legitimate forum than the G8, it does not go far enough to give the poor and excluded a voice. After all, they are the ones most affected by the decisions made. The real lesson of the past year is the urgent need to build on and extend this multilateral approach. It means accepting that the rich and powerful alone can no longer rule the world.

It means, too, recognising that the only lasting and effective solutions to the challenges we face will be those which have the security, opportunity and welfare of all at their heart. Fairness and equity can no longer be an afterthought. No

1 Comprehension

Read the text and the statements below. Decide whether the statements are true or false. Quote or paraphrase words from the text that confirm or disprove the ideas in the statements. You must give evidence for your decision.

a) In Annan's view, the current situation of the global economy might become worse.

b) Things that went wrong in the past could be done better in the future.

c) The reason behind the crisis only lies in the failure of financial governance.

d) The G8 is the best forum to give the poor and excluded a voice.

e) Market forces can solve the problems of fairness and equality in the world.

one's stability, security and prosperity can be guaranteed unless we strive to tackle the gross inequality of wealth, opportunity and influence in our world.

What is needed is a fundamental change of mindset. Solutions to the financial crisis must look beyond the impact on the market, financial institutions and developed countries. They must also focus on jobs, family incomes and the effect of the slowdown on the poorest countries. Market forces are the engine for economic growth. But they need to be well regulated to ensure fairness and equal opportunity for all.

The present crisis has underlined the importance of government in effective regulation of the market. But governments must also look beyond their borders and at the long-term picture. Richer countries cannot use the excuse of tighter finances to renege on their aid promises to the poorest on the planet. As global trade contracts and protectionist instincts are emboldened, the danger is that those least responsible for the present crisis will be hardest hit. [...]

We can waste no time. Only by working together can we hand over a healthy and sustainable planet to future generations. [...] There must be a radical, effective and universal agreement at Copenhagen this year based on climate justice and the principle that the polluter pays.

The developed economies must accept their responsibilities to our planet and future generations. They must take the lead in cutting their emissions. They must also fund the transfer of knowledge needed to help the rest of the world to grow their economies sustainably and to adapt to the inevitable change in our climate already underway. No other approach will work.

The consequences for our children if we fail to rise to this challenge are immense. Breaking our addiction to fossil fuels and investing in green technologies will also help us to deliver energy security, jobs, prosperity and sustainable economic growth.

This will, however, require robust and inclusive global economic, financial and political institutions. We need fundamental reform to involve a far wider range of countries and voices meaningfully in decision-making. (720 words)

Kofi A. Annan (Secretary-General of the United Nations from 1997 to 2006)

28 **to strive to do sth.** – to try hard to achieve sth.
28 **to tackle** – to fight
30 **mindset** – opinion
31 **impact** – effect
33 **engine** – driving force
39 **to renege** – to withdraw
40 **to embolden** – to encourage
47 **to take the lead** – to be in control
49 **inevitable** – unavoidable

f) Mr Annan emphasises the importance of climate justice.

g) Money has to be invested in green technologies to make our planet a healthy one.

2 Analysis → Text analysis, p. 326
Point out the rhetorical devices that Annan uses to get his message across, and the effects they have. Give examples from the text.

3 Comment → Writing a comment, p. 327
"We can waste no time. Only by working together can we hand over a healthy and sustainable planet to future generations." (ll. 43 – 44) How can you as an individual contribute to solving the global problems mentioned in Annan's speech?

Topic 2.10
Marketing and media

3fc22h

A

> Advertising is the greatest art form of the twentieth century.
>
> Marshall McLuhan, Canadian social scientist (1911–1980)

> You can tell the ideals of a nation by its advertisements.
>
> Norman Douglas, Scottish author (1868–1952)

> What is the difference between unethical and ethical advertising? Unethical advertising uses falsehoods to deceive the public; ethical advertising uses truth to deceive the public.
>
> Vilhjalmur Stefansson, Canadian explorer & ethnologist (1879–1962)

B

Getting started

1 Describe the different forms of advertising shown above and say what you think of them.

2 Which forms of advertising do you regularly encounter? How do you react to them?

3 Which other forms of advertising are part of our daily lives? Think of some examples.

C

> Many a small thing has been made large by the right kind of advertising.

Mark Twain, US humorist and novelist (1835–1910)

> Advertising is legalised lying.

H.G. Wells, British author (1866–1946)

D

> Advertising is the modern substitute for argument; its function is to make the worse appear the better.

George Santayana, US (Spanish-born) philosopher (1863–1952)

> Advertising may be described as the science of arresting the human intelligence long enough to get money from it.

Steven Leacock, Canadian economist & humorist (1869–1944)

4 **Explain what you understand by each of the quotations above and then give your opinion on how true you think each statement is.**

5 **What is advertising in your opinion? Collect statements of your classmates which begin with "Advertising is . . .".** → Brainstorming, p. 351

Word bank

sponsorship • billboard • neon signs • merchandising • to receive spam • text message • to target • to bombard • to convey a message • campaign • to deceive • to persuade • to place an ad • brand

A The influence of advertising

1 Before you read → Brainstorming, p. 351

a) When you think about TV ads, what is the first ad that comes to your mind? Write down what the ad is for, what happens in it, and what made you remember it.

b) Has this ad affected the way you think about the product or service advertised? How? Why?

c) Share your ideas with a partner and report back to the class.

0 **sustainable** – nachhaltig
0 **behaviour** – Verhalten
0 **desirable** – wünschenswert, erstrebenswert
1 **armpit** – Achsel
8 **obvious** – offensichtlich
10 **habit** – Gewohnheit, Angewohnheit
12 **brand** – Marke
15 **to enlist** – *hier:* in Anspruch nehmen
19 **to draw on sth.** – an etw. anknüpfen
19 **obsession** – Besessenheit
20 **embarrassment** – Beschämung, Peinlichkeit
22 **to dash for** – losstürzen, rasen
25 **anxiety** – Angst
25 **desire** – Wunsch, Verlangen
26 **unique** – einzigartig
27 **decade** – Jahrzehnt

theguardian

News | Sport | Comment | Culture | Business | Money | Life&Style | Travel | Environment

Comment is free > Society — Search GO

Can brands make consumers see sustainable behaviour as desirable?

Well, with one campaign (and a pig in an armpit) they managed to change the routines of Russian women

In Russia, in 2007, most women used deodorant only on special occasions. They would spritz their armpits with the sweet-smelling stuff to party, but not every day. As a result, Russians got through less than one pack of deodorant each per year, compared with five in the UK. For obvious reasons, this was not a habit that pleased Russian deodorant brand Rexona or its makers Unilever, so they set about changing it.

To do this they enlisted the help of cultural analyst Greg Rowland, who identified some key cultural themes in Russia to draw on, including "an obsession with glamour and beauty" and "a culture of embarrassment". In the resultant advert, a seemingly glamorous woman raises her arm in a lift only to find – to her horror – that the smell makes the guy next to her dash for the exit. In case the viewer doesn't get it, there's also a drawing of a pig on her underarm. The advert helped significantly increase deodorant use in Russia.

By playing on cultural anxieties and desires, Rexona managed to change Russians' morning routines. This is not unique; brands and businesses have influenced the way we live for decades, in a bid to sell us more stuff. But as the burgeoning corporate sustainability movement has matured some firms have started using these well-honed tools to a different end. Companies such as Unilever have realised that for some products the biggest environmental impact comes from their customers' behaviour – people using soaps and shampoos in a hot shower, for example – and have begun trying to promote more sustainable choices and habits. [...]

One of the most obvious tools at their disposal for this is marketing. "Brands have the ability to make sustainable behaviours aspirational," says Madden. This can take the form of a campaign like Sainsbury's Love your Leftovers, which tries to change the way people see food waste, or Ariel's Turn to 30, which plays on the idea that the detergent is so powerful that washing at high temperatures is unnecessary, and is credited with increasing the number of people washing at 30°C.

More subtle marketing can also help combat the fact that sustainable behaviours are often perceived as "not attractive and not normal" says Lucy Shea, CEO of sustainable communications agency Futerra. A green version of product placement – adverts featuring recycling bins or people cycling instead of driving, for instance – could be an interesting way of making those behaviours more normal and desirable, says Shea. [...]

Some firms' business models already coincide with environmental aims – bus companies trying to get people out of cars and on to buses, for example. The car-sharing companies Streetcar and Zipcar, for example, offer their customers mobility when they need it (in the form of a car on a street near them to hire when they want) without the need for everyone to own their own car. [...] (726 words)

28 **burgeoning** – aufkeimend
28 **corporate** – Unternehmens-
28 **sustainability** – Nachhaltigkeit
28 **to mature** – reifen
29 **well-honed** – gut geschliffen
29 **to use sth. to an end** – etw. für einen Zweck einsetzen
31 **impact** – Auswirkung
34 **at one's disposal** – *hier:* zur Verfügung
35 **aspirational** – erstrebenswert
36 **leftovers** – Reste
38 **detergent** – Waschmittel
39 **to credit sb. with sth.** – jmdm etw. zuschreiben
41 **subtle** – dezent
41 **to combat** – bekämpfen
42 **to perceive** – wahrnehmen
44 **to feature** – *hier:* zeigen
47 **to coincide** – übereinstimmen

2 Comprehension

315
a) Summarise in your own words the problem faced by deodorant companies in Russia, what Unilever did to combat this, and what the result was.

b) Aside from selling products, outline what aim businesses have become more interested in recently and what the key to achieving this is.

c) Table completion: Collect all the pieces of information the text gives you about the following companies regarding sustainable consumer behaviour:

Sainsbury's	Ariel	Streetcar/Zipcar

3 Analysis → Analysing advertisements, p. 342

a) Explain how product placement can be used to make sustainable behaviour more attractive.

b) Find an advertisement that appeals to you. Analyse it in detail and present the results to the class.

4 Projects → Hotspots 1 and 2, p. 247

B New media and infotainment

1 Before you read: News media → Questionnaires and surveys, p. 360
→ Describing diagrams, p. 341

a) Draw up a class survey about where your classmates get their daily news from.

b) Present your results in a suitable graph.

2 Comprehension → Scanning, p. 319

a) What information can you find in the text about the following numbers:

20 • 28 • 49 • 62 • 64 • 72 • 87 • 1000

b) With the help of the information in the text, draw two bar graphs. The first should show the most frequently used news media in Australia. The second graph should display people's trust in different forms of media.

smh.com.au

The Sydney Morning Herald

Search GO

NSW | World | Business | Sport | Environment | National Times

New media fail to click on the reliability scale

Australians trust the ABC more than its commercial rivals, while supposed "old" media such as newspapers, television, and radio fare much better than the internet, a survey of attitudes to media has found. An Essential Research survey of 1000 people showed that despite the recent protestations of web media proprietors, traditional media is still the dominant source for information on news and current affairs, and is also more highly trusted than its internet counterparts.

The survey found commercial TV news and current affairs is the most frequently consumed news media, with 87 per cent of people saying they watched at least once a week. Daily newspapers came second, with 72 per cent reading at least weekly. In contrast, just 28 per cent of people said they accessed blogs at least once a week, but in results that will give some comfort to the mainstream media proprietors behind major news websites, 62 per cent of people said they accessed them at least weekly. The consumption habits also reflected people's trust of different forms of media. Asked the extent to which they trusted commercial TV news and current affairs, 64 per cent said "a lot" or "some", with daily newspapers closely behind on 62 per cent. The affiliation with a major media outlet appeared to bolster the trust in news and opinion websites, which sat at 49 per cent, but internet blogs, which are usually independently run, were trusted by just 20 per cent.

Essential Research's director, Peter Lewis, said the figures showed consumers sought a distinction between news and opinion, which was more prevalent in newspapers than online.

"It gives some encouragement to professional journalists that there is in the public's mind a difference between news and opinion, and as long as that separation remains in the public's eyes, there's always going to be a place for quality journalists," he said. [...] (355 words)

0 **to fail** – scheitern
0 **reliability** – Glaubwürdigkeit, Vertrauenswürdigkeit
1 **ABC (Australian Broadcasting Corperation)** – öffentlich-rechtliche Rundfunkgesellschaft in Australien
1 **rival** – Konkurrent(in)
2 **to fare better** – besser abschneiden
3 **protestations** – Beteuerungen
4 **proprietor** – Besitzer(in), Eigner(in)
5 **current affairs** – aktuelle Nachrichten, Zeitgeschehen
5 **counterpart** – Gegenüber
18 **affiliation** – Verbindung, Zugehörigkeit
19 **to bolster** – stärken
22 **prevalent** – verbreitet
23 **encouragement** – Ermutigung
24 **separation** – Trennung

c) Taking into account the information you collected in tasks a) and b), sum up the most important information of the article in your own words.

315 **3 Mediation** → Mediation, p. 343

Prepare an English summary of the following text for your email pen pal in Australia, who is very interested in cars and technology.

WinFuture

WINDOWS ONLINE MAGAZIN

Search GO

Software | Hardware | Spiele | Internet | Sicherheit | Mobiles

Infotainment-Systeme im Auto immer beliebter

Glaubt man diversen Marktforschern, werden integrierte GPS-Navigationsgeräte sowie Kameras und Sensoren für leichteres Einparken schon bald zur Grundausstattung von Autos gehören. Stattdessen werden neue Technologien die entscheidenden Kaufargumente darstellen. Nachdem die Automobilindustrie 2008 und 2009 einige Probleme zu bewältigen hatte, scheint sie nun das Internet als Wachstumsfaktor für sich entdeckt zu haben. Laut Instant Research werden bereits in diesem Jahr rund 15 Millionen so genannte In-Vehicle Infotainment-Systeme (IVI) verkauft. Bis 2015 soll diese Zahl auf über 35 Millionen anwachsen. Die Analystin Stephanie Ethier erklärt, dass die Automobilindustrie in diesem Jahr mit den Innovationen der Unterhaltungselektronik mithalten muss, um wettbewerbsfähig zu sein.

Gab es 2009 nur etwa eine Million Fahrzeuge, die mit dem Internet verbunden waren, so werden es 2017 bereits mehr als 42 Millionen sein, prophezeien die Marktforscher aus dem Hause iSuppli. Man hat erkannt, dass das Internet für die Menschen inzwischen das wichtigste Medium ist, um verschiedene Inhalte zu konsumieren. Diese Möglichkeiten auch in Autos anzubieten, ist ein logischer Schritt, der erfolgversprechend ist.

„Die Leute wollen Erfahrungen, die sie bereits von zu Hause oder von ihren mobilen Geräten kennen", erklärt Joe Pitarresi, Forscher bei den Intel Labs. „Sie wollen Unterhaltung und Zugriff auf Online-Dienste, die sie bereits von außerhalb des Fahrzeugs kennen." Die Produkte für Autos müssen so entwickelt werden, dass sie ein sicheres Fahren ermöglichen, erklärt Pitarresi, der bei Intel nach Möglichkeiten forscht, das Internet in Autos auf sichere Art und Weise zu integrieren. Der Wunsch nach Infotainment-Systemen kann bei Fahrzeugbastlern bereits seit mehreren Jahren beobachtet werden. (254 words)

315 **4 Analysis**

→ Describing cartoons, p. 340

Describe and analyse the cartoon, and relate it to the above text.

"It's the new iPed. It's a pedometer, a GPS, and it has apps that show you the nearest ice cream parlors and dessert shops."

5 Group discussion → Discussions, p. 344

If you had to invent the ultimate news medium for people your age, what would it look like?

6 Project → Hotspot 3, p. 247

C Consumer protection

1 Before you read → Brainstorming, p. 351

a) What do you think targeted advertising is?

b) How good is your Internet English? Match the terms with their definitions.

1. cookie	a) The program people use to access the World Wide Web.
2. spyware	b) An add-on for a program that adds functionality to it.
3. browser	c) A small amount of data generated by a website and saved by your web browser. Its purpose is to remember information about you.
4. plug-in	d) Software that can capture information like web browsing habits, usernames and passwords, etc.

0 **targeted advertising** – gezielte Werbung
1 **to slam** – scharf kritisieren
1 **to launch** – auf den Markt bringen
1 **behavioral advertising** – verhaltensbezogene Werbung
2 **advocate** – Befürworter(in)
3 **proposal** – Vorschlag
3 **user tracking** – Benutzerverfolgung
5 **to exploit** – ausbeuten, ausnutzen
6 **to maintain** – behaupten
11 **to engage in sth.** – sich an etw. beteiligen
18 **to opt out of sth.** – sich abmelden, aussteigen
19 **to solicit** – erbitten
20 **beta (software)** – Testsoftware
20 **deputy** – Stellvertreter(in)
21 **to rely on sb./sth.** – sich auf jmdn/etw. verlassen
22 **consistent with** – übereinstimmend mit
23 **beyond sth.** – über etw. hinaus
23 **requirement** – Anforderung

NETWORKWORLD

Search GO

Security | Wans & Lans | UC/VoIP | Cloud Computing | Infrastructure Mgmt

Privacy groups rip Google's targeted advertising plan

Two online privacy groups slammed Google for launching a behavioral advertising program, with one advocate calling Google's plan a privacy "disaster."

Google's proposal would bring user tracking to the world's largest ad network, said Marc Rotenberg, executive director of the Electronic Privacy Information Center. "It's a disaster," he said. "It's about whether the most dominant Internet media firm should be able to exploit its access to Internet user data for advertising purposes. Google long maintained it would not do this type of advertising. Indeed, they claimed they didn't need to and they went after others who did." Google privacy officials, as recently as early 2008, said they had no plans to engage in behavioral advertising. Behavioral advertising doesn't work, Google officials said then.

Rotenberg called on the U.S. Federal Trade Commission to halt Google's plans.

The plan, announced Wednesday on Google's official blog and its public policy blog does allow people using Google's AdSense network and YouTube to change their advertising preferences and to opt out of being targeted at all. Google solicited advice from several groups before launching the behavioral advertising beta, wrote Nicole Wong, Google's deputy general counsel. "We talked to many users, privacy advocates and government experts," she said. "By listening to them and by relying on the creativity of our engineers, we built a product that's not only consistent with industry groups' privacy principles, but also goes beyond their requirements."

Google is one of the first Internet companies to allow users to see and to change their advertising profile, according to some privacy advocates. The Google plan got a mixed review from

Ari Schwartz, vice president and chief operating officer of digital rights group the Center for Democracy and Technology. While he praised Google for allowing users to change their advertising profiles, he criticized the difficulty of opting out. Schwartz is also disappointed that the Internet advertising industry has not gotten together to come up with better ways for Web surfers to control their advertising experiences, he said. Google chose a flawed way of honoring opt-out requests – by putting a cookie on users' machines, similar to a frequently criticized model offered by the Network Advertising Initiative.

Many users and spyware software programs frequently delete cookies, Schwartz noted, although Google has offered a browser plug-in that will prevent the Google opt-out cookie from being deleted. "The cookie opt-out doesn't work, it's a bad idea," he said. "People who care about their privacy enough to opt out also are the same people who delete their cookies."

(497 words)

30 **flawed** – fehlerhaft
30 **to honor** – anerkennen
31 **frequently** – häufig
34 **to prevent** – verhindern

2 Comprehension: True or false? → Comprehension questions, p. 326

Read the statements below and decide whether they are true or false. Quote or paraphrase words from the text which confirm or disprove the ideas in the statements.

a) Marc Rotenberg works for Google and supports the use of targeted advertising.

b) In 2008, Google said they wouldn't use advertising based on consumer behaviour.

c) People who use Google's AdSense network and YouTube cannot influence which ads they are exposed to.

d) Google claims that their new tracking software agrees with privacy standards.

e) Ari Schwartz sees no positive aspects to Google's behavioural advertising program.

f) Users can "opt out" of Google's targeted advertising by deleting their cookies.

316 **3 Analysis** → Describing cartoons, p. 340

Describe the cartoon, analyse it and relate it to the text.

28 **4 Listening comprehension: Too much choice**
→ Listening, p. 319

Write down short answers only.

- Where and when does this scene take place?
- What did the narrator want to do?
- What was typical of the coffee stand he went to?
- What did listening to the other customers' orders make the narrator want to do?
- How does he describe the other customers' orders?
- What did he order himself?
- Name three details the salesperson asks the narrator.
- What time is it now and how long has the narrator been in line for the coffee?
- How does he threaten the salesperson?
- How does the narrator characterise himself?

5 Research project → Hotspot 4, p. 247

D Food consumption: We are what we eat

1 Before you read → Brainstorming, p. 351

a) What is your favourite food? Where does it come from and how is it produced?

b) How do you interpret the statement "You are what you eat"? Do you agree with the statement. Discuss with a partner.

THE INDEPENDENT

Search GO

Opinion | Environment | Sport | Life & Style | Arts & Ents | Travel | Money | Indy Best

Organic movement split over air-freighted food

For the conscientious, food shopping poses many ethical dilemmas: are organic bananas better than FairTrade or English tomatoes preferable to imports?

Britain's booming organic movement has been wrestling with one such dilemma for years and the debate has become so heated it can no longer be ignored. From today, the country's organic farmers, suppliers and shoppers are being asked for an answer to an awkward question: is it acceptable to air-freight organic food?

On this one question could hinge the prosperity of thousands of African farmers, fruit and vegetable importers, the integrity of the organic movement and, to some extent, the health of the planet itself.

If the body which certifies three-quarters of organic food (in Great Britain), the Soil Association, rules that the climate change pollution cannot be justified, it may ban all flown-in food.

A ban might split the organic movement: one side with strict environmental standards and another with looser standards that factor in the development of the Third World. The argument arises from the rapid rise of the UK organic movement, which has burgeoned into a £1.6bn-a-year business.

Farmers have struggled to grow enough food and in 2005 supermarkets imported one-third of their organic range, mostly by air.

Nationally "food miles" are at a record high, with air-freighting up 136 per cent between 1992 and 2002. Yet flying food thousands of miles from poor farmers to wealthy Westerners generates substantial amounts of CO_2 just as climate change is being recognised as an emergency. Shoppers find the dissonance uncomfortable: a Soil Association survey found that eight out of 10 would prefer to buy conventional local food rather than an organic import.

0 **to be split over** – geteilter Meinung sein über
0 **air-freighted** – per Luftfracht
1 **conscientious** – die Bewussten
2 **to pose** – darstellen
12 **awkward** – seltsam
14 **to hinge** – abhängen
22 **to rule** – *hier:* entscheiden
28 **to factor in** – berücksichtigen, einbeziehen
31 **to burgeon** – entwickeln
44 **dissonance** – Unstimmigkeit

At Britain's biggest vegetable box supplier, Riverford Farm in Devon, air-freighted food is banned. The self-imposed ban is sometimes difficult but Guy Watson, its founder, believes the environment must take priority. He tells customers: "Most out-of-season vegetables imported to the UK are flown in from Africa and South America causing horrendous emissions, or trucked from southern Europe with less, but still substantial, environmental impact." About 80 per cent of the company's 35,000 customers' food comes from the UK, with the rest arriving by road or ship.

By contrast, the importer Blue Skies in Northamptonshire buys fresh pineapple, mango and coconuts from Ghana, where it employs 1,500 people. "We would see any change to the rules as unfair to us and unfair to Africa," said the founder, Anthony Pile. "The carbon emissions for air-freighted food is something like 1 per cent of the total emissions. Why hit farmers who have a tiny carbon footprint and often live without electricity?" he asked. In its consultation, the Soil Association is setting out the case for five options. Maintaining the status quo would help faraway producers but might damage the organisation's credibility. A gradual or total ban would damage exporters but help tackle climate change and encourage more sustainable agriculture. Warning stickers or offsetting flights would be a compromise.

Anna Bradley, of the Soil Association's Standards Board, explained that the rules had to evolve over time and the time had come for a definitive answer on aviation. "It's quite clear right now that these issues of climate change and CO_2 are much more important than they were 10 years ago and it feels much more pertinent to talk about them," she said. But Britain's organic trailblazer could lose business by raising its standards, just as it did when it tightened its rules on poultry farms. "That cost us licensees but it has … retained the integrity of the standard," she said. (598 words)

51 **self-imposed** – selbst auferlegt
58 **horrendous** – übermäßig, horrend
72 **to hit** – *hier:* benachteiligen
76 **to set out** – *hier:* (im Detail) darlegen
81 **to tackle** – bewältigen
82 **sustainable** – nachhaltig
83 **to offset (offsetting)** – ausgleichen, *hier:* CO_2-Emissionsausgleich tätigen
93 **pertinent** – relevant
94 **trailblazer** – Wegbereiter
96 **poultry** – Geflügel
97 **licensees** – Lizenznehmer
98 **to retain** – behalten

2 Comprehension: Table completion → Taking notes, p. 352

a) Collect all the pieces of information the text gives you about the arguments for and against air-freighted food in the view of the people listed below:

Guy Watson, Riverford Farm	Anthony Pile, Blue Skies	Anna Bradley, Soil Association	Kenyan organic farmer	British conventional farmer	British shopper

b) Choose the three arguments you find most convincing. Give reasons.

3 Comment

"Food miles are at a record high." (ll. 37 – 38) Food miles are part of our carbon footprint. Discuss several ways you can reduce your individual carbon footprint.

4 Presentation → Presentation, p. 362

Some time ago, a "slow food movement" came into existence. Find out where it started and what its advantages and disadvantages are. Write down the most important cue-words on a transparency and use this to present your findings in class.

E The art world

1 Before you read
Which pieces of art do you know? Why do people spend a fortune on buying art for private collections? Discuss with a partner and report back to the class.

Steve Martin (American actor, comedian and writer, born in 1945)

2 Comprehension → Understanding fictional texts, p. 322

a) Outline where Lacey and her companion are, what they are doing, and why.

b) Summarise in your own words how the art world is presented in the text, and how this contrasts with the reality of a young person working in this world.

c) After reading the text, what do you think the title of the book might refer to?

Steve Martin is a renowned comedian and actor who has starred in many Hollywood films. His book, An Object of Beauty, *is a story set in the Manhattan art world.*

3 **offshore** – vor der Küste
4 **exploit** – große Tat
12 **a class act** – *hier:* eine Person, die sehr schick und eindrucksvoll erscheint
12 **to blare** – plärren
12 **to zero in on** – auf etw. abzielen
13 **to wince** – zusammenzucken
14 **to deter** – abschrecken
15 **to zip up** – den Reißverschluss zumachen
15 **to emerge** – herauskommen
17 **cleavage** – Ausschnitt, Dekolleté
18 **to mutter** – murmeln
19 **barrette** – Haarspange
20 **instantly** – sofort
20 **to mature** – reifen
21 **broke** – pleite

An Object of Beauty

LACEY'S LIFE AND MINE have paralleled each other for a long while. When we were twenty-three, our interest in art as a profession landed us both in New York City at a time when the art world was building offshore like a developing hurricane. Our periodic lunches caught me up with her exploits. Sometimes she showed up at a Manhattan cafe with a new boyfriend who was required to tolerate my unexplained presence, and when she excused herself to the restroom, the boyfriend and I would struggle for conversation while he tried to discover if I was an ex-lover, as he soon would be. [...]

"Come with me," she said after coffee. "Where to?" "I'm buying a dress. I'm interviewing at Sotheby's tomorrow and I have to look like a class act." The New York heat baked us till we found the inside of a moderately cooler downtown dress shop that featured recycled class-act clothing. Music blared as Lacey zeroed in on a dark blue tight skirt and matching jacket. She winced at the price, but it did not deter her. She pulled the curtain of the changing room, and I could hear the rustle of clothes. I pictured the skirt being pulled on and zipped up. She emerged wearing the jacket loosely opened, with nothing on underneath – which created a sideways cleavage – and started buttoning it up in front of the mirror, surveying herself. "I've got a blouse at home I can wear with this," she muttered to me. She straightened up and pulled the barrette from her hair, causing the blond mix of yellows and browns to fall to her shoulders, and she instantly matured.

"They're going to love you," I said. "They goddamn better because I'm broke. I'm down to seven thousand." "Last week you said you had three thousand." "Well,

3 Analysis → Text analysis, p. 326

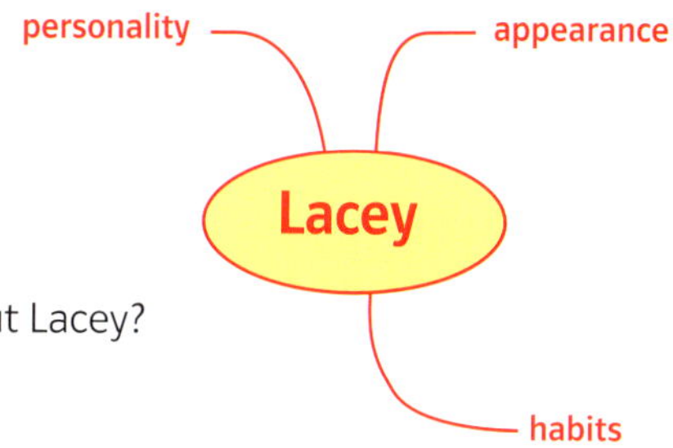

a) What sort of person is Lacey? Use the word web to collect information about her. You should also include extracts from the text to support your answer.

b) What does the extract tell us about the narrator? How does he feel about Lacey?

c) Analyse the language the author uses to show the youthfulness of the characters. Collect relevant words and passages from the text. Indicate the lines as well.

d) Explain the phrase "And so Lacey joined the spice rack of girls at Sotheby's." (l. 27) in your own words.

e) Using your results from a), b), c) and d), characterise Lacey as she appears in this extract.

316 △ **4 Comment** → Writing a comment, p. 327
"To those that have, shall be given." Many people believe that being beautiful makes it easier for you to be successful in life. Do you agree? Comment.

---

if I've got three, I'm fucked. So let's call it seven." Lacey turned from the mirror for the first time and struck a pose in the preowned Donna Karan, "You look great. A lot of people our age don't know how to go in and apply for a job," I said. Lacey stared at me and said, "I don't go in and apply for a job. I go in and get a job." And so Lacey joined the spice rack of girls at Sotheby's. Sotheby's and Christie's, the two premier auction houses in New York, drew young, crisp talent from Harvard and its look-alikes. Majors in art history were welcomed over majors in art making, and pretty was preferred in either sex. The houses wanted the staff to look swell as they crisscrossed the busy galleries on exhibition days, holding in their arms files, faxes, and transparencies.

Because the pay was low, the young staff was generally financed from home. Parents thought well of it because their children were at respectable firms, working in a glamorous business, with money of all nations charging the atmosphere. The auction houses seemed not as dull as their financial counterparts on Wall Street, where parents of daughters imagined glass ceilings and bottom patting. Sotheby's was an institution that implied European accents and grand thoughts about art and aesthetics coexisting with old and new money in sharp suits and silk ties. This was a fresh and clean New York, where you dressed nicely every day and worked in a soaring, smoke-free, drug-less architectural building filled with busts, bronzes, and billionaires. What the parents forgot about were the weekends and evenings when their children left the Cezannes and Matisses and crept underground, traveling back to shared downtown spaces where they did exactly the same things they would have done if they had joined a rock band.

(681 words)

24 **to strike a pose** – eine Pose einnehmen
24 **preowned** – gebraucht
27 **spice rack** – Gewürzregal
28 **crisp** – *hier:* frisch
30 **major** – Studiengang, Hauptfach
31 **staff** – Angestellte(r), Personal
31 **swell** – großartig
31 **to crisscross** – durchkreuzen
31 **exhibition** – Ausstellung
32 **file** – Akte
35 **to charge** – aufladen
36 **dull** – langweilig
37 **glass ceiling** – unsichtbare Decke, an die Frauen auf der Karriereleiter stoßen
37 **bottom patting** – Klaps auf den Hintern
38 **to imply** – implizieren
39 **sharp** – *hier:* schick
40 **silk tie** – Seidenkrawatte
41 **soaring** – hoch aufragend
42 **bust** – Büste
44 **to creep** – kriechen

Word families – word building

a) Read the sentences and fill the gaps with a word belonging to the same word family as the word given on the right.

Teachers call for a ban on **1** of all unhealthy food and drink on all TV channels before the 9 pm watershed.	advertise
Teachers should not be **2** into using commercial materials in the classroom.	pressure
Will most of the seafood stocks really be **3** by the year 2048?	depletion
Unethical advertising uses falsehoods to **4** the public.	deception
Advertising is **5** lying.	legal
Online advertising is constantly **6** and developing itself.	innovation
Television was **7** developed without advertising in mind, whereas online developments were driven by advertising revenues.	initial
The favoured method of advertising online is through paid-for search, which is **8** by Google.	domination

b) You can link two words with a hyphen and so get a new word or part of speech.
Example: hi + tech = hi-tech

Make more new words like this by combining the following words:

ad-	consumer-	paid-	owned	cal	based
cut-	peanut-	medium-	range	sized	week
job-	UK-	farmer-	related	consuming	scale
large-	two-	time-	tech	friendly	for
low-	free-	hi-	related	like	throat

Make a meaningful sentence with each of your word combinations.

c) What preposition normally follows each of these words?

- opinion, ban, based, spending, impact
- amounted, addicted, intended, linked, lead
- account, in return, advertising, inappropriate, substitute

Make a meaningful sentence with each of the words plus their prepositions.

d) Write a text of at least 150 words on the topic of marketing. Include at least five of the following words:

consumerism • advertising • target • sexploitation • ban • addiction • fair • fairtrade • choice • campaign

1 Project: Creating an ad campaign → Analysing advertisements, p. 342
Work in groups. You work for an advertising agency and have been asked to create an ad campaign for one of the following products:

smart phone • energy drink • perfume/aftershave • pain killer • car • product/service of your choice

Design an ad (poster, power point presentation, script for TV/radio ad etc.) for it. Think about the name of the product, its design and packaging, the target group, the image, the price, where it will be sold and the slogan. Use the AIDA formula (see Skills files, p. 342) to help you. Present your ideas to the class.

2 Project: Scandalous advertising → Presentation, p. 362

a) Can you think of any scandalous advertising campaigns? What were they about and why were they considered scandalous?

b) Search the Internet for examples of scandalous advertising. Use a search engine for images, enter "scandalous advertising" and choose three of your findings to present to your class: Describe the ad image, say what makes it scandalous and add your own impression and reaction to the image.

3 Project: Media preference → Describing diagrams, p. 341
The graph on the right shows people's preference of news media around the globe. Work in groups. Analyse the graph and find a new way of presenting the information shown (e.g. pie chart, bar graph, written report, word cloud). Use a transparency or poster to present your results.

Media preference when gathering news and background information

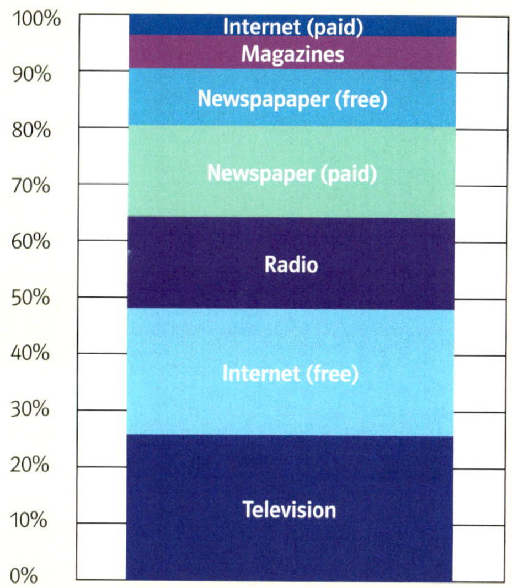

4 Research project: ASA → Internet research, p. 358

a) When carrying out advertising campaigns in the UK, advertisers may come into contact with the ASA. Check the web to find out more about the ASA and to answer the following questions:
- What is ASA short for?
- What does the ASA do?
- What role does the ASA play in ad regulation in Europe?

b) Find out about advertising campaigns that had to be withdrawn. You may use a search engine or the websites of newspapers such as *USA Today* and *The Independent*. You can enter key words such as "ad campaign" and "withdraw". The ASA website also lists controversial ad campaigns. Present your findings to the class after considering the following points:
- a description of the campaign
- reactions to it
- consequences for the advertisers / company.

c) Find out what "greenwash" is. Look for examples to illustrate this advertising technique.

A 3.30

4 **to call for** – to publicly ask for

6 **9 pm watershed** – a time each evening after which certain material may be shown, e.g. sex and violence

8 **union** – association

10 **unashamedly** – without shame

10 **to target** – to aim at

11 **to exploit sb.** – to take unfair advantage of sb.

11 **to pester sb.** – *here:* continually asking sb. for sth. until you get it

16 **treats** – an event or item that is out of the ordinary and gives great pleasure

19 **to cite** – to quote

29 **pole-dancing kit** – equipment needed for pole dancing

30 **lace lingerie** – erotic underwear

32 **to remove** – to take away

34 **padded** – stuffed

34 **bra** – women's underwear

35 **naughty** – indecent

37 **to be pressurised** – to be put under pressure

39 **schemes** – program

39 **voucher scheme** – coupon system

41 **crisps** – potato chips

44 **in this regard** – in this respect

48 **to be extended to** – *here:* to be applied to

49 **to cover** – *here:* to broadcast, to air on TV

57 **celebrity endorsement** – advertising with celebrities

61 **lace knickers** – erotic underpants

66 **inappropriate** – unsuitable

THE INDEPENDENT

Search GO

Opinion | Environment | Sport | Life & Style | Arts & Ents | Travel | Money | Indy Best

Teachers' call for "sexploitation" of children to end

Teachers' leaders have demanded an end to the "sexploitation" of children through commercial marketing. They also called for a ban on the advertising of all "unhealthy" food and drink on all TV channels before the 9 pm watershed.

A report published by Britain's biggest teachers' union, the National Union of Teachers (NUT), warned: "Companies are unashamedly targeting their campaigns to exploit children's 'pester power'."

"Growing up in a Material World"

The report – "Growing up in a Material World" – argued that this included targeting "day to day purchases of food and drink, through treats, such as meals out, to clothes and toys which can include expensive electronic equipment".

The report cited figures from Ofcom, the television regulator, which showed that products with high sugar, salt or fat content accounted for between 82 per cent and 92 per cent of all food and drink advertising before the 9 pm watershed.

It also cited examples of what Steve Sinnott, the union's general secretary, described as the "sexploitation of young children" – such as Tesco marketing a pole-dancing kit on the toys section of its website, Asda selling pink and black lace lingerie to children and Next being forced to remove T-shirts for young girls with the slogan "so many young boys, so little time" and BHS selling padded bras with a "Little Miss Naughty" logo.

It also warned teachers "not to be pressurised into using commercial materials in the classroom or take part in schemes such as voucher schemes".

"Parents are collecting vouchers for chocolates with Cadbury's and for crisps with Walkers in return for books," said Mr Sinnott. "We need to change the culture of this country in this regard."

New regulations introduced this week will mean all children's TV channels have to ban advertising for junk food by January 2009. They will also be extended to other channels covering children's programmes by January 2008.

"We need to change the culture of this country in this regard."

However, the NUT said this did not go far enough and demanded a ban on all junk food advertising before the 9 pm watershed. It also wants the ban extended to cover "sponsorship, celebrity endorsement, mobile phone, internet, e-mail and publications aimed at children".

Asda said it had stopped the sale of its lace knickers, while Tesco said the pole-dancing kit was not sexually orientated and was "clearly aimed at adults who wanted to improve their fitness".

However, Mr Sinnott argued: "All of this sexualisation of childhood is inappropriate for youngsters."

(425 words)

1 Comprehension
For questions a)–e), choose the right answer (1, 2, or 3) which you think fits best according to the text.

a) What do teachers' leaders complain about?
1. They complain about the advertising of unhealthy food and drink by targeting young children before the 9pm watershed.
2. They call for a general ban on advertising on TV.
3. They want young children to stop watching TV before the 9pm watershed.

b) What is said about the products that are advertised on TV before the 9pm watershed?
1. All the products contain a very low percentage of sugar.
2. The products contain high percentages of sugar, salt or fat.
3. The products contain neither sugar nor salt.

c) According to Steve Sinnott, what is the "sexploitation of young children" in commercial spots on TV?
1. Products are sold which are not seen as suitable for young children as they contain sexual allusions.
2. The producers force the children to buy those products.
3. The producers want to tell young children the facts of life with the help of their products.

d) What should teachers do to tackle the problem of commercial marketing aimed at young children?
1. They should use commercial materials in their classrooms to please the children.
2. They should take part in voucher schemes instead.
3. They should not feel pressurised to use commercial materials in their classrooms.

e) What does the "National Union of Teachers" additionally want?
1. It doesn't want the ban extended to other fields of advertising for young children.
2. It wants the ban extended to other fields of advertising for young children.
3. It wants celebrities to support the ban on certain products aimed at young children.

2 Analysis → Describing cartoons, p. 340
Describe the cartoon, analyse it and relate it to the text.

3 Comment → Writing an email, p. 329
Do you think that some companies are taking the saying "sex sells" in advertising too far? Write an email to the NUT, stating your opinion.

"Your vital signs are all healthy..."

1 Binge drinking

Topic 1.1

BBC Motion Gallery

Before watching

a) According to the dictionary, binge drinking is *"the activity of drinking a large amount of alcohol in a short period of time, usually in order to become drunk"*. What is your personal opinion on binge drinking? Have you experienced it in one way or the other?

b) Why do you think people binge drink?

c) Share your ideas with a partner. Decide on three final reasons.

d) Discuss your ideas with the class.

While watching

Watch the video and take notes on the following questions. Short answers will do.

a) The report states "Nearly half of all men and a quarter of all women have become binge drinkers." How does the report define binge drinking?

b) How much does binge drinking cost the UK economy? How is this figure calculated?

c) In what age group has there been the largest increase in binge drinking numbers?

d) What does the report say about the effect of binge drinking on the nation's health? What figures are mentioned to support this assessment?

e) What does the government want to do about the problem?

f) What do charities think needs to be done to stop binge drinking?

After watching

a) Write a German summary of the video using your notes.

b) Why do you think approximately twice as many males than females are binge drinkers? Share your ideas with a partner.

c) Work in groups of 3–4 and design an anti-drinking poster to be put up around high schools to stop young people from binge drinking.

2 Kid's Company

Topic 1.2

BBC Motion Gallery

This video is about *Kid's Company*, a London-based charity that works for neglected and abused children. It is run by Camila Batmanghelidjh.

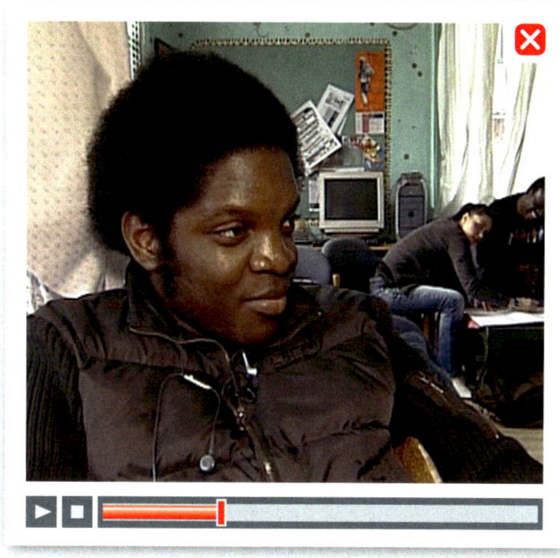

Before watching

a) Discuss in groups what kind of help neglected and abused children need.

b) Here are some quotes from the video. What do you think the film is about?

Every single one of these children is worth every minute of my time.

Here in London, a brave experiment is changing lives.

A boy who might end up in gangs is studying to be a fashion designer.

There are only two places you can end up: dead or in jail.

Trouble is that kind of thing that just naturally folllows me, unfortunately.

It's the everyday one-on-one help which is key to turning troubled lives around.

While watching

a) Watch the video for the first time. What are its main parts?

b) Watch the video again, concentrating on the following aspects. What is Batmanghelidjh's approach to neglected and abused children? What role do former gang members play in *Kid's Company*?

After watching

a) Write a short report about the activities and the success of *Kid's Company*.

b) Go online and search for further information about *Kid's company*. Summarise the main aspects of this charity in a short German text for your school newspaper.

c) Discuss whether the following statement by Camila Batmanghelidjh is true for any kind of care for neglected and abused children: "It's the everyday one-on-one help which is key to turning troubled lives around."

d) You work in the personnel department of a company that is looking for trainees. You receive an application from a young man who offers the qualifications and work experience your company is asking for. All this experience was gained in a project similar to *Kid's Company*. Do you think you should invite him to a job interview? Discuss in groups and agree on one opinion. Present your opinion to the class and exchange your views.

3 Green Fuel from Pond Scum

Topic 1.3 BBC Motion Gallery

The film introduces the idea of hydrogen-fuelled cars and explains different ways of producing the hydrogen needed.

Before watching

a) Make a list of fossil fuels and a list of renewable energy resources.

b) Which of these resources are currently used to power cars? Which ones do you consider green?

c) Copy and complete the word web about green technologies in cars.

green technologies in cars
- disadvantages of using green fuels in cars
- advantages of using green fuels in cars
- types of green fuels available
- anything else you know

d) Agree on one statement which expresses your opinion about green technologies in cars, e.g. "We believe that more has to be done to develop alternative technologies because at the moment green technologies are so expensive that not everyone can afford to drive a green car." Collect these statements in class.

While watching

span the US • is produced from natural gas • clean car laws • hydrogen fuel cells • by a third by 2014 • from renewable sources of energy • harmless water vapour

a) Complete the sentences with suitable information from the box.
1. The real trick would be to get hydrogen …
2. The car prototypes shown are powered by … that make electricity.
3. The only exhaust is …
4. Politicians in California believe the hydrogen revolution will …
5. The only problem about using hydrogen to power cars is that much of the hydrogen …
6. California law says that greenhouse gas emissions from cars must be reduced …
7. California leads the world with its …

b) Apart from the traditional use of natural gas, the film shows two new ways of producing hydrogen. Copy and complete the table with information from the film.

solar foil	pond scum

After watching

a) In groups, agree on one statement which expresses your opinion about green technologies in cars. Compare these statements with the ones you made before you watched the film. Has your attitude changed?

b) Summarise the information shown in the film about hydrogen-fuelled cars in a short German text.

c) Find out about hydrogen-fuelled cars on the German market. Inform your classmates about technical details, prices, etc. Based on the information in the film, make a poster to advertise the idea of buying cars powered by renewable energy sources.

4 The Interview

Topic 1.5

BBC Motion Gallery

Before watching

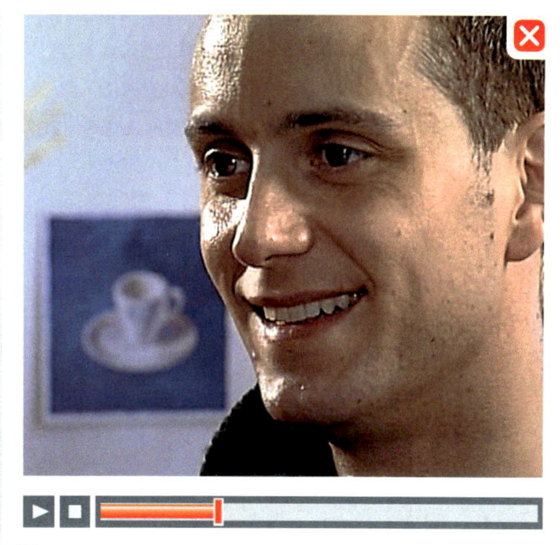

a) What three tips would you give somebody going to a job interview?

b) Discuss your ideas with a partner and decide on a final list of three.

c) Share your tips with the class and be prepared to explain your choices.

While watching

a) Why has working in a café become more attractive?

b) What qualities is the HR & Training Director looking for in the applicants?

c) What criticism does the expert have of the first applicant (two things)?

d) What question does the interviewer ask the second applicant?

e) According to the expert, what is the worst question you can ask as an applicant and why?

f) Watch the film again and find out the following information:
1. What are the applicants' names?
2. What position are they applying for?
3. What countries do the applicants come from?
4. Which applicant is successful?

After watching

a) Imagine you are the interviewer. Work together with a partner and come up with a list of positives and negatives about each applicant based on what you have seen in the video.

b) In groups of 3-4, discuss which applicant you would choose for the job and why.

c) Share your thoughts with the class and see if you have chosen the same person.

5 If ... Cloning Could Cure Us

Topic 2.5

BBC Motion Gallery

Stem cells have the potential to develop into many different cell types in the body. They can also serve as an internal repair system, dividing limitlessly to replenish other cells. When a stem cell divides, each new cell can either remain a stem cell or become another type of cell with a more specialized function, such as a muscle cell, a red blood cell, or even a brain cell.

Scientists all over the world are working on methods to infuse stem cells into a patient where – once they are integrated into the tissue – they ideally divide, growing more and more of the surrounding tissue and thus regenerating damaged cells.

Based on a fictionalised case, this film deals with the controversial subject of cloning and stem-cell research.

Before watching

a) Work with a partner. Agree on five sentences beginning with "If cloning could cure us ...".

b) Collect pros and cons of therapeutic cloning.

c) Find out more about the ethical and social issues of stem cell research and therapeutical cloning.

d) Take a class vote: Who is in favour of therapeutic cloning?

While watching

Watch the film and collect phrases in the word field of "therapeutic cloning". Divide the class into two groups and watch the film again.
Group A: Collect arguments in favour of therapeutic cloning.
Group B: Collect arguments against therapeutic cloning.

After watching

a) Collect information about the legal status of stem cell research in five countries of your choice including GB / the USA.

b) Search the Internet and collect information about the main arguments of those strictly in favour / against stem cell research. Present the results to the class.

c) Form groups, each with at least two people from group A and two from group B. Discuss the pros and cons of therapeutic cloning using the notes you made. Then take a second vote: Who is still in favour of therapeutic cloning? Why have you (not) changed your mind?

6 A Brit in Berlin

Topic 2.6

BBC Motion Gallery

Seema Prabhu is a 26-year-old English journalist who is living in Berlin at the moment. In the video, she talks about her life in the city and her ideas about Europe.

Before watching

Look at the vocabulary in the box and complete the sentences.

- I was supposed to go to New York but I changed **1** and went to Washington DC.
- When you fly, you are allowed to take 20 kg of baggage. Your **2** is 20 kg.
- At the weekend, I often **3** my friends in town.
- The sea is within **4** of the town and in summer everyone **5** to the beach.
- The first thing I did when I arrived in London was to **6** at a language school.
- They had nothing when they arrived in the new country. They had to **7** from **8**.
- However, they worked hard, made friends and slowly they got it **9**.
- There's a Mc Donald's in **10** every city in the world now.
- The **11** from being a student to having a job and working isn't always easy. People often have to do some **12**.
- Have you found an apprenticeship yet? – No, but I'm **13** it!
- Life in modern Europe is really interesting. There's **14** exciting **15**.

A **I was supposed (to do)** *ich sollte (etwas tun)*
B **I changed my mind** *ich habe es mir anders überlegt*
C **be within easy reach** *leicht erreichbar sein*
D **decamp (to)** *aufbrechen (nach)*
E **transition** *Übergang*
F **baggage allowance** *Freigepäck(menge)*
G **start from scratch** *bei Null anfangen*
H **get it together** *sein Leben in den Griff bekommen*
I **enrol** *sich anmelden*
J **work on (doing sth.)** *dabei sein (etw. zu tun)*
K **Soho** *Stadtteil Londons*
L **sign from God** *Zeichen Gottes*
M **serve a purpose** *einen Zweck erfüllen*
N **do some readjusting** *sich neu einstellen*
O **pretty much** *so ziemlich*
P **hang out (with someone)** *(mit jmdm) herumhängen*
Q **there is sth. going on** *es passiert etwas*

While watching

Take notes and answer the following questions. Short answers will do.

1. Why did Seema come to Berlin?
2. What did she do on her first weekend in Berlin?
3. How did she find her first couple of weeks there?
4. What did she find in a street in Soho in London? How did this help her?
5. Why is the language school in Berlin good for Seema?
6. How do Seema's parents feel about her decision to go to Berlin?
7. What does Seema say at the end about Europe and living in Europe?

After watching

Listen one more time and write a short text for your school newspaper's "English page" about Seema Prabhu in Berlin.

7 American Immigration

Topic 2.8

BBC Motion Gallery

This film shows the situation at the US-Mexican border. Every day, many Mexicans try to enter the US illegally. The film portrays both illegal immigrants and those who try to defend the border.

Before watching

a) In many cases, emigration seems to be the only solution for people who want to make a better life for themselves. Due to strict border controls in both the countries of origin and some potential host countries, migrants have to take the risk of crossing borders illegally. Make a list of how people try to do this and also consider the dangers involved.

b) Collect information about the US-Mexican border.

c) Estimates say that there are between 10 and 15 million illegal immigrants living in the US, more than half of them from Mexico. Brainstorm reasons why these people leave their home country to come to the USA illegally.

While watching

Take notes on the following questions.

1. How do most illegal immigrants cross the border? What risks do they take? Why do they do it?
2. What is being done about illegal immigration? How do US residents view illegal immigration?
3. What is said about the scale of illegal immigration?

After watching

a) Using the information above as a starting point, prepare a report on illegal immigration in the US. Find out how many immigrants cross the border from Mexico every year, how many illegal immigrants live in the US, what the chances of being granted permanent residence are, and how the government plans to deal with the situation. Work in groups and, using statistics where necessary, present your results as an oral report to the class.

b) Research arguments for and against a permanent wall along the US-Mexican border.

c) Search the Internet for information about the novel "Tortilla Curtain" by T.C. Boyle (plot, characters, setting, topics, etc.). Present the results to the class.

d) Search the Internet for information about the film "Sugar" (storyline, characters, setting, topics, etc.) It shows the story of a young baseball player from the Dominican Republic who comes to the USA. Present your findings to the class.

e) Compare the fictional stories of Tortilla Curtain and Sugar. Which one do you like better? Why?

8 Cocoa Children

Topic 2.9

BBC Motion Gallery

The Ivory Coast in West Africa supplies half the world's cocoa. This video tells the story of Marc, a young boy who is one of the country's 'Cocoa Children'.

Before watching

Look through the English expressions below and match them with the German translation.

1. stagnation (economics)	a) ausrotten
2. belt	b) Machete (Buschmesser)
3. barely	c) (sich) hacken
4. poverty	d) (Wirtschafts)Flaute
5. to eradicate	e) kaum
6. to set out	f) Armut
7. machete	g) *(hier:)* Region
8. to hack (oneself)	h) sich auf den Weg machen

While watching

a) Why do so many farmers in this region of Africa grow cocoa?

b) Why do so many children work on the farms?

c) What important 'protocol' was signed in 2001?

d) Who did the BBC reporters meet in the bush?

e) What did they find in the village? (WARNING! Shocking images!)

f) The reporters meet Marc again when they leave the village. Summarise what Marc tells them.

g) What question does the video ask at the end? What do you think is the answer?

After watching

Write a summary of the video in English. Begin like this:
In this video called 'Cocoa Children', a reporter from the BBC visits the Ivory Coast, the West African country which supplies half the world's cocoa. He wants to find out about …

1 **ceiling** – the upper interior surface of a room

2 **piece of kit** – equipment

6 **incandescent** – emitting light as a result of being heated

7 **to sap** – to drain

7 **orb** – a round object or shape

11 **humble** – modest

16 **inconvenient** – difficult, causing trouble

21 **array** – a number of

22 **to resemble** – to be similar to

28 **to phase out** – to gradually withdraw

31 **diode** – a semiconductor device with two terminals, typically allowing the flow of current in one direction only

32 **anode** – the positively charged electrode by which the electrons leave an electrical device, the opposite of cathode

32 **cathode** – the negatively charged electrode by which electrons enter an electrical device, the opposite of anode

36 **to deposit** – to place

36 **semiconductor** – a solid substance that has a conductivity between that of an insulator and that of most metals

37 **to impregnate** – to fill

38 **impurity** – substance inside a confined amount of liquid, gas or solid

41 **to emit** – to produce and discharge

42 **property** – specification

49 **predictable** – foreseeable

65 **fortuitous** – lucky

BBC NEWS Technology | Search | GO

Home | UK | Africa | Asia-Pac | Europe | Latin America | Mid-East | South Asia

LED bulbs: The end of the lightbulb as we know it?

Look up at the ceiling above you, and chances are there is a centuries-old piece of kit swinging from a cord. The light bulb has been hanging around for more than 150 years. [...] But now the days of the traditional incandescent bulb look numbered. These electricity-sapping glass orbs have fallen out of favour with environmentally-conscious governments and consumers. And waiting in the wings is a new breed of hi-tech light based on the humble LED (light-emitting diode), the small lights found in everything from TV remote controls to bike lights. [...]

Already, the efficiency and long life of LEDs is making them a popular – if costly – option in places where changing bulbs is inconvenient or expensive, such as in motorway lights, traffic signals, airport runways or on large buildings and bridges. [...]

But the real hope of the LED industry is that arrays of these tiny twinklers packed into something that resembles a bulb will become the light of choice in your bedroom, bathroom or study, allowing them to grab a slice of a global lighting market that was worth an estimated €52bn in 2010. Their cause is helped by the numerous governments around the world which have chosen to phase out the sale of incandescent bulbs. [...]

As their name suggests, LEDs consist of a simple diode. In traditional electronics these are two metal posts – an anode and a cathode – placed very close to one another, through which power can only flow in one direction. In LEDs, the anode and cathode are formed by depositing two areas of semiconductor that have been "doped" – impregnated with impurities – next to one another. As power flows through the junction between these two patches, some of it is unable to make it through and is instead emitted as photons of light. The colour of the light is dictated by the properties and structure of the semiconductor used to make the LED. [...] Although this may sound complicated, the manufacturing process to create LEDs is well understood.

And – like all processes involving semi-conductors – it is coming down in cost all the time, and at predictable rates. In fact, the rates are so predictable that there is even a law – called Haitz's law – that describes the fall. This states that every decade, the cost of producing useful light will fall by a factor of 10, whilst the amount of light generated increases by a factor of 20. This is crucial for LEDs, which are currently around ten times more expensive than incandescent bulbs. Yet decreasing costs are only one part of the excitement.

In traditional incandescent bulbs, only about 5% of the electricity used is converted into light, while the rest is wasted as heat – the bulbs are therefore little more than tiny electric heaters which give out light as a fortuitous side-effect. But LEDs can be up to ten times as efficient. [...]

And LEDs have another environmental trick up their sleeve: they last far longer than most other light sources. Incandescent bulbs last around 1,000 hours before burning out. LEDs do not burn out in the same way but simply get dimmer over time, and when they fall to 70% of their initial brightness their useful life is considered over. A good LED light should have a useful life of between 30,000 and 50,000 hours, and maybe up to 70,000 in the future, meaning less are thrown away and less are made.

But LEDs do not have it all their own way. One of the biggest challenges they face is the quality of the light that they produce. LED bulbs tend to generate a stark, cold light – a world away from the warm, yellowish light we are used to from incandescent bulbs. [...] To get around this, scientists and manufacturers are now working on using a combination of blue LEDs and less efficient red ones to create a warmer glow. [...]

Since white light is made up of a spectrum of different colours, the possibility of manipulating the light spectrum emitted by LED lights offers some of the most intriguing possibilities. For example, it should be possible to tune lights to give out a dose of near-violet light that would have antiseptic-like qualities. These could be used to keep countertops in kitchens clean, or to help maintain sanitary conditions in washrooms. It may be possible to design lamps that emit tailored light for students to use, to help them study more effectively, or ones that counter natural circadian rhythms to help night workers to stay awake. [...]

(757 words)

82 **stark** – severe or bare
92 **intriguing** – interesting
97 **countertop** – work surface
98 **to maintain** – to keep
98 **sanitary conditions** – cleanliness
100 **tailored** – customised
102 **circadian rhythm** – biological clock

1 Comprehension: Short answer questions

Read the text and answer the following questions in 5–20 words.

a) What does the LED industry hope will happen, and why?

b) What determines the colour of the LED light?

c) What is Haitz's Law?

d) How much electricity is wasted as heat in a traditional lightbulb?

e) When is an LED's 'useful life' over?

f) What is currently one of the LED bulb's biggest disadvantages?

g) What could an LED emitting near-violet light be used for in the future?

2 Analysis

Describe and analyse the graph and link it to the text.

3 Comment

"[...] LEDs [...] are currently around ten times more expensive than incandescent bulbs." (ll. 56–57). Many 'environmentally-friendly' products are more expensive than the alternative. Are you as an individual prepared to pay extra for such products? Explain your answer.

Energy Saving vs. Energy Consumption

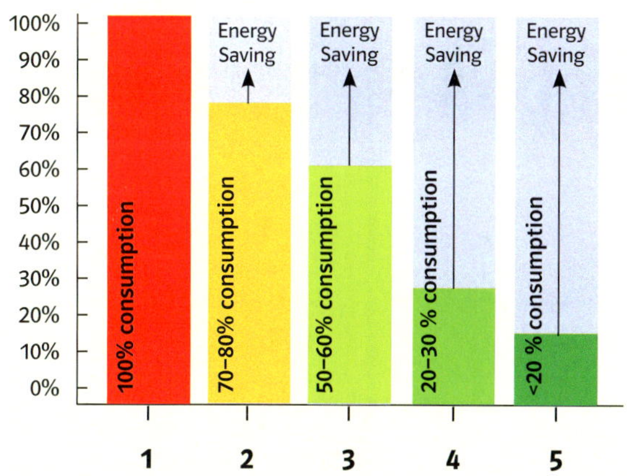

1 – Conventional incandescent bulbs
2 – Improved incandescent bulbs (class C of the energy label, halogen lamp with xenon gas filling)
3 – Improved incandescent bulbs (class B of the energy label, halogen lamp with infrared coating)
4 – Compact fluorescent lamps (CFLs)
5 – Light-emitting diodes (LEDs)

Source: European Commission, 2009

3 **inconsiderate** – selfish
3 **congestion** – traffic jam, heavy traffic
4 **malaise** – problem
4 **range** – distance
4 **anxiety** – fear
5 **to strike** – to hit
20 **poster child** – role model, example
23 **internal combustion engine** – engine which generates motive power by the burning of petrol, oil, or another fuel
32 **coil** – a length of something wound in a joined sequence of rings
32 **embedded** – built-in
35 **coupling** – joining together

BBC NEWS Technology | Search GO

Home | UK | Africa | Asia-Pac | Europe | Latin America | Mid-East | South Asia

Wireless highway charges electric cars as they go

Researchers are close to developing a system that allows electric cars to recharge while they are moving ... via a recharging road.

Road works. Inconsiderate drivers. Congestion. Today's drivers have their fair share of stress already. But now there is a new malaise for the modern motorist: range anxiety.

That is the term given to drivers of electric cars that are struck by the sudden fear that their vehicle does not have enough charge to reach its destination. Most of us have experienced that sinking feeling when the little orange indicator light comes on to tell us we are low on petrol, but there is not a gas station in sight. Imagine that, combined with the feeling that you get when your cellphone starts beeping because the battery is low, and you are nowhere near a plug. That gets you close to the feeling of range anxiety.

It is an interesting phenomenon, particularly when you begin to look at how many of us actually use our cars. According to the US Bureau of Transportation Studies, 78% of drivers do less than 40 miles (65km) a day – a trivial distance for many of today's electric cars. In fact, the poster child of electric cars – the Tesla – has a range of 300 miles (485km) using some batteries.

According to Dr Richard Sassoon, of Stanford University, there are "three main reasons" that many of us choose the internal combustion engine over its cleaner, quieter alternative.

"One is the short range that an electric vehicle can travel between charges, and that's based on the size of the battery," he said. "The second is the lack of a sufficient charging infrastructure, and the third is that even if you can charge, it takes a long time to charge – several hours. That means you're going to have to take a break in your trip in order to charge your vehicle."

Researchers and firms are trying to tackle all of these problems. Firms, such as Better Place, have started building battery "switching stations" that allow drivers to pull in and swap their batteries as easily as filling up with gas, whilst countless researchers are developing more efficient batteries.

But Dr Sasson believes there may be another answer: recharging roads.

Engineers in his lab are developing a way to wirelessly charge electric cars from magnetic coils embedded into the road. The car would pick up the power via another coil, meaning – in theory – that you would never have to make a charging stop again.

The system works using a technique called "magnetic resonance coupling". You can think about resonance as the phenomenon that allows an opera singer to smash a glass using only the power of their voice. In that case, when the singer hits a note that has the same resonant frequency as the glass, they couple and energy begins to build up in the glass, eventually causing it to smash.

Instead of using acoustic resonance, the Stanford team use the resonance of electromagnetic waves. A coil in the road that is connected to a power line is made to vibrate with the same resonance frequency as the coil on the bottom of the car, allowing energy to flow between them. […]

They have come up with designs of coil that allow 97% efficient transmission of power over a distance of about 2m (6ft). Using models, they estimate they can transfer up to 10kW of power.

"That number is about the number we'd probably want to transfer to vehicles" says Dr Sasoon.

And to turn this principle into a practical "recharging road" is not as difficult as it seems, he says.

"Road beds are made of asphalt or concrete, but there is often a lot of steel in the roads – a lot of rebar, a lot of ties between the segments of the road and so on," he said. "What we want to do is use that to our advantage."

He believes they could use much of the metal in the roadbed as part of the transmitter, and then the receiver would use the metal of the car body, again avoiding too many extra structural components.

It may take years, if not decades, until roads are retrofitted in this way. But various firms, including an MIT spin-out called WiTricity, are already taking the first steps by building charging stations for car parks, garages and beyond. […]

Dr Sasoon believes electric cars will become the technology of choice, displacing our current love of gas guzzlers and banishing the concept of range anxiety forever.

"You never need to worry about stopping and filling up," he said. […] (773 words)

46 **concrete** – cement

46 **rebar** – reinforcing steel used as rods in concrete

49 **roadbed** – the material laid down to form a road

51 **to retrofit** – to add a component to something that did not have it when manufactured

52 **spin-out** – subsidiary

54 **to displace** – to replace

54 **gas guzzler** – car that uses a lot of petrol

55 **to banish** – to get rid of permanently

1 Comprehension

a) In your own words, outline why people still prefer petrol cars to electric cars.

b) Outline how researchers have tried to tackle the problems connected to electric cars.

c) Describe how the 'recharging road' (l. 31) works.

2 Analysis

a) Explain the term 'range anxiety' (l. 4).

b) Describe and analyse the bar graph and relate it to the text.

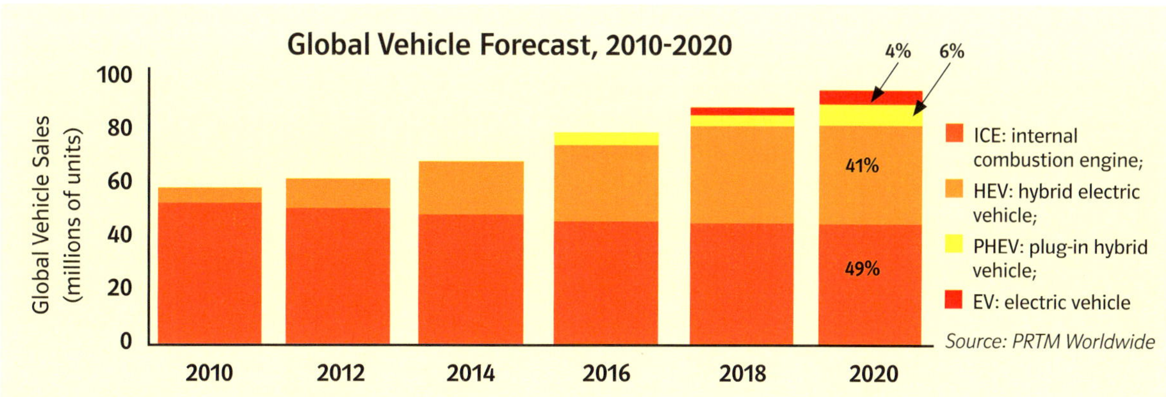

3 Comment

"[…] electric cars will become the technology of choice, displacing our current love of gas guzzlers […] forever." (ll. 54–55) Do you think people will be prepared to give up their petrol cars for electric cars in the near future? Discuss.

0 **dawn** – Morgendämmerung, Beginn

5 **think tank** – Expertenkommission

8 **to prompt** – hervorrufen

8 **to equal** – gleich sein, an etw. herankommen

8 **row** – Streit

17 **to back** – unterstützen

20 **drone** – Drohne (männliche Biene), *hier:* kleiner Flugkörper

21 **to stalk** – sich an jmdn/etw. heranpirschen

22 **to ferry** – befördern

22 **supplies** *(pl)* – Vorräte

theguardian

News | Sport | Comment | Culture | Business | Money | Life&Style | Travel | Environment

Comment is free > Work   Search [ ] GO

Dawn of the age of the robot

The robots are coming. The second decade of the 21st century will see the rise of a mechanised army that will revolutionise private and public life just as radically as the internet and social media have shaken up the past 10 years. Or so says Marina Gorbis, futurologist and head of Californian think tank *The Institute for the Future*. [...]

Gorbis says robots will increasingly dominate everything from the way we fight wars to our work lives and even how we organise our kitchens.

Robots are likely to prompt a political storm to equal the row over immigration as they increasingly replace workers, says Gorbis. But it's not all bad news. "When IBM's Deep Blue became the first computer to beat chess grand master Gary Kasparov, people said, that's it, computers are smarter than people," she says. "But it didn't mean that at all. It means they are processing things faster, not that they are thinking better." Working together, she believes, robots and humans will be able to create a world of new possibilities impossible before our new industrial revolution.

Gorbis says the robots are already here. The US military is backing the development of a four legged, mechanical, pack-carrying robot, called the BigDogs. Guided by its own sensors, BigDog can navigate treacherous terrain carrying 150 kg on its back. In the air, robot drones are stalking targets in Afghanistan, remote controlled helicopters are ferrying supplies.

Military technology from the Roman road to the internet has a habit of hitting the mainstream, and robots are already spreading their influence. Robots may soon do building work. The University of Southern California has developed a system called Contour Crafting that allows machines to construct buildings in layers, guided by computers. The system can reduce construction times and costs by 75%, according to USC.

In South Korea robots assist teachers in language classes, repeating words and phrases over and over and assessing how well they are parroted back. Google is working on cars that drive themselves. "What is that other than a robot," says Gorbis. Amazon and shoe retailer Zappos' huge warehouses are organised by an army of squat orange robots designed by Kiva Systems.

Inevitably the rise of the robots will put people out of work. Gorbis believes that this and other trends will mean unemployment will remain around 10% in many parts of the developed world over the coming years. "We are in transition. It is similar to when we mechanised agriculture. After that we went through a period of high unemployment as people transitioned to new kinds of jobs. People learned to do other things," she says.

There is potential for a huge backlash. "But once a technology is invented, it is very rare that it disappears. You can delay the introduction but it is going to be used. If someone can produce something cheaper and faster, you are competing in that environment." [...]

We too are likely to become more robotic, she believes. "We have been modifying ourselves with technology forever, with eyeglasses, cochlear implants. We are going to see more of that. Sensors are going to be on our bodies, in our bodies, letting us and others know what we are doing, what is going on with our health. All kinds of applications we haven't even thought of yet."

Gorbis says she is often asked if the future is arriving faster than ever. "I'm not sure that it is," she says. "We know more, we have access to more information, but if you lived during the period of electrification or the building of railroads, I'm sure you really felt the pace of change too. It's all relative."

With all this information being bombarded at us it is no wonder that people worry, she said. "I feel schizophrenic myself. Half the time I feel really depressed when I look at, say, climate change or the potential to misuse technology. But then I get really excited about how we are reinventing ourselves through technology." (672 words)

23 **habit** – Gewohnheit
27 **layer** – Schicht
30 **to assess** – beurteilen
31 **to parrot** – nachplappern
33 **squat** – gedrungen
35 **inevitably** – zwangsläufig
38 **transition** – Übergang
38 **agriculture** – Landwirtschaft
40 **to transition to** – wechseln zu
42 **backlash** – Gegenreaktion
43 **to delay** – hinauszögern
47 **cochlear implant** – Innenohrprothese
50 **application** – Anwendung
53 **access** – Zugang
55 **pace** – Geschwindigkeit
61 **to reinvent oneself** – sich neu definieren

Mediation

You are a member of the school newspaper team. The newspaper's editor would like to publish an article about the growing influence of robots, and has found the above text. He asks you to sum up the most important information for him in German.

theguardian

News | Sport | Comment | Culture | Business | Money | Life&Style | Travel | Environment

Comment is free > Work   Search [ ] GO

A working life: The app developer

Many of those familiar with the world of smartphones and other handheld computers will have daydreamed of inventing a killer app, one of the simple and often brilliantly useful little programs that run on touchscreen phones and tablet computers like the iPad. Perhaps we imagine our idea will become part of the zeitgeist, be downloaded millions of times and generate unfathomable profits, spawning lucrative toys, T-shirts and other merchandise.

As I stroll along Oxford Street to the head offices of Grapple Mobile, I think of a couple of my own money-spinning ideas: a football stadium app telling you where in the ground your seat is, local amenities and the ability to message other fans. Or how about an app that could tell you the real-time gender mix in a bar or club? But it doesn't take much time chatting to Justin James, head of development at Grapple, for me to realise I have no chance of turning my app fantasies into reality. […]

Justin James, head of development at Grapple.

James impressed the Grapple bosses enough to become head of development after just four and a half months, having worked on successful launches such as a multi-platform app for wine magazine *Decanter*, as well as client pitches. "We often get asked to build something speculatively for a client and it's great fun to let your imagination run wild, especially if the app ends up being given the green light," he explains. It is the experimentation that James clearly savours. […]

James tells me what his job is all about. "It often involves taking large chunks of data and making it work for the user. It's about coming up with different solutions to the same problems. You're building on stuff all the time, taking what has worked with something else and applying it to a new app."

Most often, a corporate client will approach Grapple with what they want from an app, Grapple will take that idea, cost it out, produce wireframes (walkthroughs of how the app will work) and a design aesthetic (if needed) and build the app for as many different types of mobile platform as the client needs. […]

James's job is to take a brief from the client, create the app and deliver it on time and on budget. It is easier said than done: "It can be straightforward or it can be difficult. With the Decanter wine app, we had a huge database of wines and regions that the user had to be able to access. We had to find a way of displaying that information quickly and we decided to force the app to access the internet to do it. Even then, that's a large chunk of data for a mobile phone to process so we had to find ways to slow the user down and stop them getting angry if it took too long to find what they wanted."

4 **unfathomable** – impossible to understand
5 **to spawn** – to produce a large number of sth.
5 **merchandise** – official goods
8 **amenities** – facilities
11 **gender** – sex
21 **launch** – an occasion where something new is introduced
22 **pitch** – sales talk
24 **to savour** – to enjoy
29 **corporate** – business
30 **wireframe** – an image which displays
33 **brief** – a set of instructions
34 **straightforward** – simple

James calls the solution to these problems "the twist", as in: "The client owns the app, but we bring the twist." And clients pay handsomely for it, too. Apps can cost a corporate client around £30,000, even more for a quick turnaround. […] Grapple has in-house testers to ensure the finished product ticks all the boxes and, most importantly, is exactly what the client wanted.

I leave James with his colleagues as they discuss their work schedules for the week and as I saunter along Oxford Street once again, my head quickly becomes full of more app possibilities. It's not long before I've got another cracking idea – the one that could make me a fortune. All I need is £30,000 and someone like James to build it for me. (609 words)

41 **to pay handsomely** – to pay well

45 **to saunter** – to walk casually

46 **a cracking idea** – an excellent idea

1 Comprehension

a) Summarise the information given in the text about Justin James and his career at Grapple.

b) Describe James' role in developing apps at Grapple.

2 Analysis

Describe and analyse the bar graph below, and give possible reasons for the figures shown.

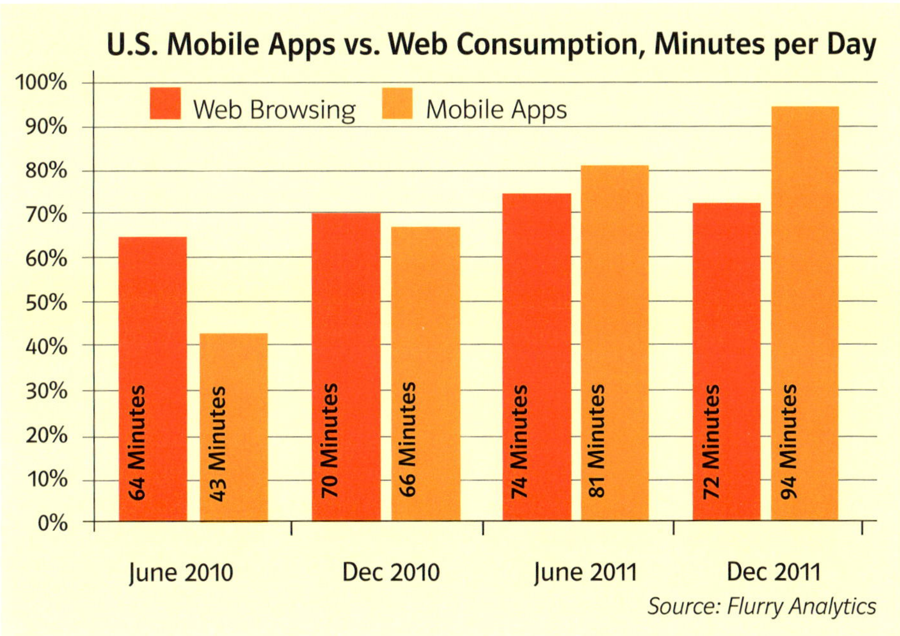

3 Comment

"Many of those familiar with the world of smartphones and other handheld computers will have daydreamed of inventing a killer app […]" (ll. 1–2). If you were asked by Grapple to develop an app, what would it be? Explain your choice, thinking about your own experiences with apps.

3 **bunch** – *hier:* Völkchen
4 **to stride** – große Schritte machen
5 **stiff upper lip** – kontrollierte Emotionen
5 **old school tie** – alte Seilschaft aus der gleichen Schule
10 **reserve** – Scheu, Förmlichkeit
10 **to crumble** – zerfallen, sich auflösen
17 **born-and-bred** – einheimisch
19 **to fumble around** – herumfummeln
22 **chit-chat** – Geplauder
27 **at the outset** – am Anfang

The Economist

World politics | Business & finance | Economics | Science & technology | Culture | Blogs

Doing business in London

London is not a difficult place to do business. Forget the stereotypes you might have heard elsewhere: in general terms, the transport systems work, the weather is okay and the British are a tolerant bunch. These tips below should help you to stride into meetings with that extra bit of confidence. Stiff upper lips and old school ties are much rarer than they used to be, but Londoners are still relatively shy. Buy a round of drinks in the pub later in the day, though, and you'll find the reserve starts to crumble.

Meeting and greeting

London is a multicultural city. It is worth finding out where your contact is from. You are quite as likely to be dealing with an Indian or an Australian as you are with a born-and-bred Londoner. Business cards are typically exchanged at the end of a meeting. But it is not unusual for a Brit to forget about them entirely. If your contact fumbles around for his card, or fails to produce one, don't take it personally.
The British tend to be punctual, and meetings generally follow the Anglo-Saxon norm, with brief chit-chat swiftly followed by a focused, action-oriented discussion.

Working habits

E-mails perfectly suit the famous British reserve. In general, they are promptly responded to and are often the preferred method of communication, at least at the outset. As a relationship strengthens, and certainly if complex negotiations are involved, expect face-to-face meetings and telephone conversations. The strongest relationships are forged after work – be that in a pub or at an informal evening meal. The line between work and private life is not as clearly delineated as in America, and the British tend to socialise with colleagues quite regularly. Drunken behaviour on a Friday evening will

be laughed off the following Monday, and in some cases is quite the norm. The woes of public transport are a sure-fire way of reviving flagging conversation. London's motorists have to pay a congestion charge to drive into the city. Your contacts will be sure to have an opinion on whether the experiment is working.

Eating and drinking

A business lunch can just as easily mean a quick sandwich and coffee as a slap-up meal in a smart restaurant. Breakfast meetings are rare. Most Brits subscribe to Oscar Wilde's claim that "only dull people are interesting at breakfast." Midday drinking has declined, but it is still normal to have a glass of wine or a beer, with food or without.

Likewise, smoking has fallen off dramatically. Smoking was banned in all public spaces (including restaurants and bars) from July 2007 and the smoky haze that used to be a feature of many pubs is but a memory. If you want to smoke, you have to be outside. When in a pub, do not expect table service, unless you are seated in the restaurant area. And don't tip the bar staff unless they bring the drinks and bill over to you.

Table manners are keenly observed as a subtle sign of good breeding. Never talk with your mouth full; never reach across the table; do not wave cutlery around or yell "I'm done" to the waiter. London's top restaurants are expensive (£100 a head is not unheard of). Furthermore, an increasing number insist on taking credit card details before accepting a booking. The British are less politically correct than their American counterparts. Wittiness can still mean an agility with sexual innuendo, with a pint in one hand and a cigarette in the other. (589 words)

35 **delineated** – abgegrenzt
43 **woes** – Leiden, Probleme
43 **sure-fire** – todsicher
43 **to revive a flagging conversation** – ein erschlaffendes Gespräch beleben
44 **congestion charge** – Staugebühr
50 **to subscribe to a claim** – sich einer Behauptung anschließen
50 **dull** – langweilig
55 **smoky haze** – rauchiger Schleier
59 **good breeding** – gute Erziehung
64 **counterpart** – Gegenstück, Pendant
65 **wittiness** – Witzigkeit
65 **agility** – Gewandtheit
65 **innuendo** – Anspielung

Mediation

You are doing a work placement at a German marketing company. The company has just acquired an important English client based in London, and some of your company's representatives are about to travel there for the first round of meetings. The head of your department has found the above information online and has asked you to put together an information sheet on 'Doing Business in London' in German.

theguardian

News | Sport | Comment | Culture | Business | Money | Life&Style | Travel | Environment

Comment is free > Business   Search [ ] GO

Top tips for web startups

Are you curious about starting up online, but concerned about the legalities? Olivia Perrott and Nick Atkins give some key advice for internet startups.

Web-based businesses can in theory be set up overnight with a very limited budget. However, the following legal issues are worth bearing in mind to minimise risk and optimise the value of investment.

Prepare for success

Consider how your business should be structured to provide the flexibility to bring in investment and grow.

1

Compared with operating as a sole trader, a limited company has the key advantage of limiting your personal liability. Your company can then borrow – although most lenders and some suppliers will ask for personal guarantees – and enter into contracts in its own right. UK corporation tax rates are currently low. Ordinarily, the advantages of incorporating will outweigh the administrative burdens of running a company, which include annual accounts and other filings.

As it grows, a company provides you with a platform to issue shares to investors in return for important growth capital. As is particularly common in the IT industry, share schemes can also be put in place to incentivise and help retain talent in your business. [...]

As well as companies limited by shares, there are other types of legal entity, such as limited liability partnerships, but in our experience private limited companies by shares are the most popular for web-based businesses. [...]

Domain names and trade marks

2

Carrying out some basic searches will help you rule out potentially problematic domain names, and more sophisticated clearance searches can be carried out by trade mark agents.

1 **legality** – level of accordance with the law
10 **sole trader** – a business owned and run by one person
10 **limited company** – a private company whose owners are legally responsible for its debts only to the extent of the amount of capital they invested
11 **liabililty** – the state of being legally responsible for sth.
13 **incorporating** – joining together
15 **filing** – bookkeeping
16 **to issue** – to give out
18 **to incentivise** – to make sth. appealing
18 **to retain** – to keep
19 **entity** – a thing with distinct and independent existence
22 **domain** – a distinct part of the Internet
22 **trademark** – brand
24 **to rule out** – to exclude
25 **sophisticated** – *here:* thorough

1 Comprehension: Multiple matching

Read the text and choose from the sentences A–F the one which fits each gap (1–5). There is one extra sentence that you do not need to use.

A	Important details to consider include ensuring that the deadlines which the parties will work towards are set out in writing.
B	Having the benefit of the experience of someone who has gone through the process themselves can be invaluable to a new business.
C	User-generated content can enhance your site, but entails certain risks.
D	In most cases this will mean setting up a limited company in which you, your business partners and investors can hold shares.
E	Advertising your products online can be very lucrative if you choose the right site.
F	When naming your site, you should avoid using a name which is the same, or similar to the trade mark or name of another business.

You may wish to register your business name as a trade mark, which means you can prevent others from using the mark or a similar mark for the same kind of goods or services. Doing this at an early stage is a good idea as your business name will not otherwise be protected until you have established a reputation in the market. It will also provide you with a valuable asset which can be attractive to investors.

Website and software development

If you use independent website developers you should review the terms of their contract carefully.

3

Also, that the developers are required to provide some support to you once the site goes live; and that the obligation to pay for the services does not arise until you have had the opportunity to test and accept the site. [...]

If you are creating your own software, make sure you check that any code which appears to be open-source – so free to download – has no awkward conditions attached to its use.

Third party material

If you plan to use third party copyright material on your site, such as music, video or text, you risk being liable for copyright infringement unless permission has been obtained for its use, or other limited circumstances exist.

4

The content may be infringing because it contains third party copyright material, defamatory or illegal and as website operator you may be liable for it in certain circumstances. It is therefore important to include a prohibition in your site's terms and conditions against the use or uploading of illegal, infringing or defamatory content and reserve the right to remove this content at your discretion. [...]

Information about users

New regulations provide that any website which uses cookies must provide users with clear and comprehensive information about their use on the site and the purpose, and in most circumstances obtain consent from each user to use them.

Many web-based businesses will process users' personal data in some way. Personal data is essentially any information from which an individual can be identified. [...]

Learn from others

Talk to a trusted mentor from an early stage so they can guide you through the startup process.

5

(724 words)

29 **reputation** – beliefs or opinions that are generally held about someone or sth.

29 **asset** – sth. of value

35 **obligation** – responsibility

35 **to arise** – to appear

38 **awkward** – *here:* complex

41 **infringement** – violation

to entail – to include

44 **defamatory** – damaging the good reputation of someone

46 **prohibition** – ban

47 **at one's discretion** – based on one's own decision/ judgement

invaluable – very valuable

2 Analysis

Describe and analyse the cartoon and link it to the text.

3 Comment

Internet shopping has changed the face of retail forever. Discuss the pros and cons of shopping on-line.

"Honey, look how cute ... The kids have started their own little business."

0 **holistic** – comprehensive
0 **approach** – way of doing sth.
3 **to tackle** – to try to stop
6 **to forge a link** – to make a connection
11 **denial** – refusal to admit sth. is true
12 **to ease out** – to help out
17 **sustainable** – can be kept at a constant level
17 **paediatric** – branch of medicine dealing with children
18 **dietician** – nutrition expert
20 **hands on approach** – a practical approach

theguardian

News | Sport | Comment | Culture | Business | Money | Life&Style | Travel | Environment

Comment is free > Health   Search [ ] GO

New holistic approach to treat child obesity

Clinical team joins forces with community services to tackle child obesity

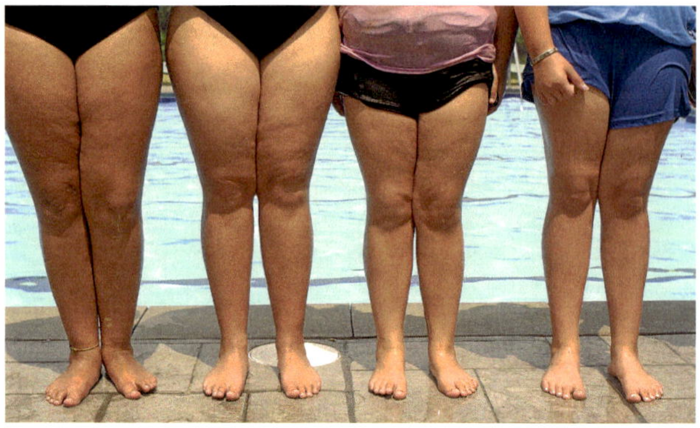

Mary Haddow is a specialist nurse working on a new scheme that forges links between healthcare professionals and community services to tackle obesity. The most enjoyable part of her job is helping children and families, but her task is not an easy one.

"Denial, guilt and low self-esteem are linked to obesity so it can be a real challenge getting children and families to attend appointments," says Mary. "So we try to find ways to ease children out of their comfort zone. A walk along the beach with our exercise instructor can be a crucial first step."

The new scheme brings together a range of healthcare professionals and services to offer personalised care and support for children with obesity problems. It is based on a local, holistic and sustainable approach and brings together a multi-disciplinary 'paediatric healthy weight team' – consisting of doctors, nurses, a dietician, psychologist and physical instructor – providing medical assessment, dietary advice, exercise programmes and nursing support. Children and parents also work with community services offering a hands on approach to empower them to improve diet, physical activity and confidence. Services include cooking classes, exercise programmes and fun activities.

1 Comprehension: Multiple choice

Read the text and choose the answer (1., 2. or 3.) which you think fits best according to the text.

a) Obese children and their families
1. are keen to meet with healthcare professionals.
2. have difficulty getting appointments with healthcare professionals.
3. do not often initiate meetings with healthcare professionals.

b) Parents of obese children
1. have an active part in the scheme to help their children.
2. are not involved in the new scheme.
3. are required to pay a fee for their children to attend the scheme.

c) Since its launch seven months ago, the scheme
1. has been heavily criticized.
2. has cost the government a lot of money.
3. has proven to be successful.

"By getting out into the community, children can make new friends, develop new skills and more confidence," says Mary, adding that it is, ultimately, a lifestyle choice that the scheme is aiming to change. And this is where community services play a crucial role.

Around 110 children have been referred to the scheme from paediatric services, school nurses, health visitors and GPs. There have been positive results since its launch seven months ago and an evaluation will be undertaken by the University of East Anglia.

Mary was responsible for setting up the day-to-day running of the scheme, and has developed a range of managerial and organisational skills with the experience of setting up a whole new scheme, coordinating services and working closely with community services.

"It has been a fascinating role, a good challenge and a huge learning curve," says Mary. "Many people, even health professionals, do not know what is available in the community," she says. There are good services in place but effective co-ordination is needed to bring these together.

While the extra workload has been a struggle, good communication and a supportive team with a "can do" attitude has helped to deliver the comprehensive service, she explains. Every child and family is unique, and with a range of services on offer, it is important to think creatively and outside of the box to deliver personalised care and support and to ensure no child or family slips through the net, she explains.

Hilary Class, president of the paediatric and child health royal society, praised the scheme: "The biggest challenge in overcoming a problem like childhood obesity is that there isn't a single solution; there are multiple factors at play. So any solution must necessarily draw on a range of people if it's to really work."

"This kind of innovative approach rightly sees obesity as a complex problem; but one that with joined-up working and interventions from healthcare professionals and parents alike, can be overcome."

"We need to monitor the success of such services carefully; and where they're seen to work well, look to replicate elsewhere," she added.

But while these community services have been shown to work, with some recommended by NICE as a front line treatment to obesity, less than 5% of overweight and obese children have access to these type of programmes, says Paul Sacher, chief research and development officer at MEND. "Obesity is widely considered as one of the most serious public health threats facing our society, but there is a lack of funding for such treatments and programmes," says Sacher. […]

Meanwhile, Mary is enthusiastic: "This is a new service and as long as everyone pulls together and are keen to try different things, we have an opportunity to make it work." (666 words)

24 **ultimately** – put simply
37 **unique** – one of a kind
48 **to replicate** – to copy
49 **to recommend** – to strongly suggest
49 **NICE** – National Institute for Health and Clinical Excellence
51 **MEND** – healthy-lifestyle program for 7–13 year-olds who are overweight
52 **threat** – danger
53 **lack of** – the state of being without or not having enough of sth.
53 **funding** – financial support

d) Despite obesity being one of the most serious health problems today,
1. there is not enough financial support available to tackle it.
2. there is still a lack of physical activity in schools.
3. parents still do not pay enough attention to what their children are eating.

2 Analysis
Describe and analyse the cartoon and link it to the text.

3 Comment
"Obesity is widely considered as one of the most serious public health threats facing our society […]" (l. 52). Give reasons as to why more and more children are becoming obese and suggest what could be done to tackle this problem. Use the text to help you.

theguardian

News | Sport | Comment | Culture | Business | Money | Life&Style | Travel | Environment

Comment is free > Society   Search [ ] GO

Just another day in court as a social worker

Aggressive cross-examinations, a lack of privacy and tense confrontations with angry parents are all part of the process – one social worker in Ireland shares their experience.

Depending on your cases, court can be a big or a small part of the job of a social worker, but it is always part of the job at some stage; each trip to court filled with waiting, nervous tension and more waiting. Most of it is hidden from the world by the confidentiality rules of family law.

Each day in court begins with everyone crowding into a small hall with no windows, no ventilation and no seating – at least that's my experience – and the day spent standing around in this small hall outside the actual courtroom waiting. First, we wait for the judge to arrive and get proceedings under way, then we wait for lawyers and barristers to negotiate, and finally waiting for your case to be heard.

There is no clear timetable for cases, so you could be done in two minutes, or wait around several hours before being heard. This is just one of the many things that makes a day at court so unpredictable, time-consuming and ultimately frustrating.

It's not just the social workers in this corridor, the families are all here, waiting around endlessly too. They are waiting to have a judge take their child away,

0 **court** – building where legal cases happen

1 **cross-examination** – questioning of a witness called by the other party in court to challenge or extend testimony already given

1 **tense** – strained

7 **confidentiality** – discretion

20 **barrister** – a lawyer who specializes in courtroom advocacy, drafting legal pleadings and giving expert legal opinions

20 **to negotiate** – to agree on terms

24 **unpredictable** – uncertain

1 Comprehension

a) In your own words, describe a day in court for a social worker.

b) Outline what could make a social worker's job easier.

2 Analysis

Describe the picture and relate it to the text.

waiting for access to be refused, waiting for the worst to happen. Standing there in front of them are the social workers, the people who are inflicting this on them, adding tension to the already stuffy atmosphere.

The clients usually end up hating us, undermining any relationship, which has been so carefully built up. Running around among this crowd are lawyers and barristers from both sides – arguing, negotiating, and doing their best to fit social work's shades of grey into the black and white world of law.

And still we wait thinking about all the work you need to do but can't. No matter what is happening in your other cases, everything is dropped while you are in court. Without access to a room of our own with adequate privacy, even simple phone calls prove difficult, and anything more complex, such as case notes or referrals, is never going to happen.

Eventually you wind up in the courtroom itself in front of a judge. The courtrooms are often the complete opposite of the corridor we wait in. Earlier in the day you don't have any idea which judge you will be in front of, but this can really matter. It is worrying how much a judge's personality can actually impact a case, and it's hard to know if you and the child at the centre of the case will win or lose this judicial lottery.

I try and remember it's not personal. When the lawyers verbally assault me during cross-examination, they are just doing their job; when judges shout at me, they are just doing theirs.

At the end of the day there is a child, or sometimes several children, whose future depends on this spectacle. That is the worst part, and the most stressful part. We as social workers try to do our best, but if the court doesn't agree for whatever reason that can have real and serious consequences. These are the cases where you can easily be haunted by the personal doubt of "did I do enough?"

Is there anything that can make this better? Simple things like giving the social workers some office space, maybe even with a computer hooked up to our case database, or just some privacy to allow work to be done would help. This separation can also reduce the tension with parents.

On a deeper level, a complete overhaul of how the courts work would make a significant difference, replacing the combative nature of common law with an inquisitorial system that is not acting as referee between two sides. This, however, is a huge change to our legal system and not without controversy. (676 words)

29 **to inflict sth. on sb.** – to cause sth. to happen to sb.
30 **stuffy** – unfriendly
31 **to undermine** – to ruin
39 **referral** – an act of referring someone or sth. for consultation, review, or further action
45 **judicial** – relating to the administration of justice
46 **to assault** – to attack
53 **to be haunted by sth.** – to be plagued by sth.
58 **overhaul** – major changes
59 **combative** – aggressive
60 **referee** – person who mediates/judges

3 Comment

Your school requires you to complete a four-week internship in the social work field. The local council is offering internships as a social worker. Based on your knowledge of social work and what you have read in the text, would you be interested in this opportunity? Explain your answer.

0 **vocational** – beruflich, Berufs-
3 **to kit out** – ausrüsten
3 **safety goggles** – Schutzbrille
17 **peak** – Höchststand
19 **aborted** – abgebrochen
20 **to be on a par with sth.** – sich mit jdm./etw. messen können
20 **casualty** – Opfer
21 **humanities** – Geisteswissenschaften
22 **to abandon** – *hier:* aufgeben
30 **to investigate** – erforschen, untersuchen

theguardian

News | Sport | Comment | Culture | Business | Money | Life&Style | Travel | Environment

Comment is free > Education   Search [ ] GO

Has England finally found the formula for vocational education?

It's an unusual sight in a British school. Michael Micallef is kitted out in safety goggles and blue overalls, expertly operating machinery that wouldn't look out of place on the workshop floor of one of Europe's top manufacturers.

The 18-year-old says – with considerable pride – that what he does feels more like working for a company than going to school. He is one of a growing number of teenagers to attend a new kind of school in England known as a university technical school or UTC.

Pupils, parents, employers and government ministers have high hopes that these schools will reduce youth unemployment – at a near 20-year peak – by equipping youngsters with the sorts of skills the country's engineering and manufacturing firms have long cried out for.

In the past 30 years, there have been a number of aborted attempts at introducing a vocational education system on a par with Germany's. [...] The latest casualty has been "academic diplomas" in humanities, languages and science, which were to combine work-based training and traditional study. They were abandoned in 2010, a year before they were to be officially introduced.

UTCs, however, herald a promising fresh start.

Micallef's UTC in Rocester, Staffordshire, is named after the world's third-largest construction equipment manufacturer – JCB – whose headquarters are down the road. [...]

The schools have a specialism, which tends to be engineering but for some will be construction, digital media or anything that requires practical skills and specialised equipment. [...]

Pupils at UTCs, who are aged 14 to 19, are set real workplace tasks, such as designing a pump for a jet engine or investigating the materials needed to help trains change direction.

During the year, students at Micallef's school are assigned five eight-week projects. After each task, they present their findings to a panel of employees from companies that work with the school and help design the projects. [...]

The schools are state-funded. Neither the companies nor the university provide extra cash – just their employees' time. [...]

Micallef believes he has improved his job prospects by going to a UTC. "In interviews, I can talk about the practical side of things," he says. "I can show them I know how to use a lathe and I've got a portfolio of work for them to view. In a community school, you learn a subject and then you sit a test."

Jim Wade, the headteacher, says there are more companies interested in becoming involved in the JCB academy than he has space for. Pupils know these firms are under no compulsion to hire them, but, as Charlie Crawshaw, 14, says, "at least we have the sense that we have a foot in the right door".

More than 100 senior engineers come to the school each year to help pupils with their work. Will Wainwright, 18, who hopes to study engineering at university, says these visits are "the greatest way to learn". "You just listen to what they say – they've had 20-plus years of experience in their field."

The first cohort of pupils will leave the JCB academy this summer and, so far, their prospects are looking rosy. Half have offers to study engineering at university and the other half are waiting to hear whether they have been successful in interviews for apprenticeships.

Wade says at most of England's schools, pupils very often move between lessons – and therefore subjects – every 50 minutes and this makes it harder for them to acquire the skills they need for the workplace.

"By spending that much longer with our students because of the project work we do, we can help them develop team-building and communication skills," he says. Pupils are more likely to see the relevance of what they are learning because it is set in the context of the "real world", he argues.

But, while some politicians hope for at least 100 UTCs to be open by 2015, Wade is not getting carried away. UTCs are probably suitable for about 10% of the school population, he says. "If you want to be a dancer, for example, you wouldn't come here."

There is another problem that is likely to prevent UTCs from opening up in great numbers across the country in the near future: British snobbery.

"We're still at the stage where if someone asks a young person what they are studying and they say Latin, we reply 'how fantastic'," Wade says. "If they say they are doing a diploma in engineering, we say 'oh, right'."

"As a country, we still make value judgments about technical education, but at least there's now clearly a recognition that we need to do something about that." (773 words)

32 **panel** – Gremium
37 **lathe** – Drehbank
41 **compulsion** – Zwang
42 **to hire** – einstellen
48 **cohort** – Gruppe
50 **apprenticeship** – Berufsausbildung, Lehre
62 **snobbery** – Snobismus
66 **value judgment** – Werturteil
67 **recognition** – *hier:* Erkenntnis

Mediation

You have recently completed school in Germany and are interested in studying engineering at a UTC in England. As your parents are a little sceptical about the idea, you need to convince them. In German, summarise the key information about UTCs and how students learn there to persuade them that it is a good idea.

Self-assessment – Selbsteinschätzung

Nachdem Sie die Aufgaben (Seite 280 – 291) bearbeitet haben, können Sie die Ergebnisse mit den Lösungen vergleichen. Schätzen Sie dann bitte Ihre Leistung in den folgenden Kategorien selbst ein: Leseverstehen, Hörverstehen, Schreibfertigkeit und Sprechfertigkeit. Bitte beurteilen Sie für jede Kategorie, ob Sie die einzelnen Stufen „überhaupt nicht erreicht", „voll erreicht" oder Ihrer Meinung nach „deutlich überschritten" haben.

In den danach folgenden Kategorien Wortschatz, grammatische Strukturen, Aussprache und Flüssigkeit sowie Aufbau und Gedankenführung wählen Sie die Kategorie, die Ihre Leistung am besten beschreibt.

Leseverstehen

Stufe 1
Wenn ich einen unbekannten englischen Text lese, kann ich oft die wesentlichen Punkte erfassen. Die Texte sollten nicht zu kompliziert und nicht zu lang sein, es ist leichter, wenn sie ein Thema behandeln, bei dem ich mich gut auskenne. Die Informationen, die ich benötige, finde ich dann schnell. Mit dem vorliegenden Text hatte ich nach wiederholtem Lesen keine großen Schwierigkeiten, ich habe alle gesuchten Informationen ohne sehr große Probleme gefunden.

Stufe 2
Ich lese englische Texte insgesamt sehr selbstständig und verstehe auch dann vieles, wenn ich Fachartikel lese. Längere Texte machen mir meistens keine Schwierigkeiten, Zeitungsartikel zu aktuellen Fragen verstehe ich zum größten Teil. Den vorliegenden Text habe ich schnell auch im Detail verstanden, nur wenige Sätze musste ich mehrfach lesen.

Stufe 3
Ich verstehe fast alle englischen Texte. Ich kann lange, komplexe Texte im Detail verstehen, auch wenn sie ein Thema behandeln, mit dem ich mich nicht gut auskenne. Manchmal lese ich komplizierte Passagen mehrmals, aber ich fühle mich im Lesen von englischen Texten insgesamt sehr sicher. Den vorliegenden Text fand ich insgesamt leicht, er hat mir keine Probleme bereitet. Alle Details habe ich sehr schnell gefunden.

Hörverstehen

Stufe 1
Ich verstehe die Hauptaspekte in Redebeiträgen zu alltäglichen oder vertrauten Themen. Das Hörverstehen fällt mir leichter, wenn die Sprecher(innen) deutlich artikulieren. Die Beiträge sollten aber nicht sehr lang sein.

Stufe 2
Ich verstehe die Hauptaussagen in Redebeiträgen auch zu komplexeren Themen. Wenn der Akzent vertraut ist und deutlich gesprochen wird, verstehe ich auch Fachdiskussionen zu weniger vertrauten Themen. Das Hörverstehen fällt mir leicht, wenn die Sprecher(innen) deutlich artikulieren.

Stufe 3
Wenn ich einen längeren englischen Redebeitrag höre, kann ich meist die wesentlichen Punkte erfassen. Die Texte können auch fremde und komplexe Themen behandeln. Ich verstehe auch Unterhaltungen mit zwei oder mehr Sprecher(inne)n ohne Probleme, leichte Probleme habe ich eigentlich nur bei fremdem Akzent.

Texte verfassen

Stufe 1
Ich kann zu bekannten oder alltäglichen Themen zusammenhängende Texte verfassen, in denen eine klare Struktur zu finden ist.

Stufe 2
Ich kann in strukturierten, zusammenhängenden Texten Vor- und Nachteile von bestimmten Standpunkten darlegen und meine Meinung besonders zu vertrauten Themen aus meinem Interessengebiet darlegen. Hier kann ich auch Detailinformationen klar und überzeugend präsentieren.

Stufe 3
Ich kann klar, flüssig und gut strukturiert über komplexe Themen schreiben, es fällt mir nicht schwer, bestimmte Punkte besonders hervorzuheben. Mein gedanklicher Aufbau ist mit Standpunkt(en), Beispielen und klarem Ende gut nachzuvollziehen.

An Gesprächen teilnehmen

Stufe 1
Die meisten vorhersehbaren Situationen kann ich in Gesprächen so lösen, dass mein(e) Gesprächspartner(in) versteht, was ich sagen möchte. Ich kann Informationen austauschen, meine Meinung darlegen und Argumente für vertraute Sachverhalte vorbringen.

Stufe 2
Ich kann mich soweit fließend und spontan verständigen, dass ein normales Gespräch über verschiedene Freizeit-, aber auch berufliche Themen möglich ist, ohne dass mein(e) Gesprächspartner(in) sich anstrengen muss, mich zu verstehen. Ich kann mich auch über einen längeren Zeitraum an Gesprächen beteiligen und habe keine Mühe, ein Gespräch durch meine Initiative aufrechtzuerhalten.

Stufe 3
Ich kann mich fast mühelos spontan und fließend ausdrücken. Mein Wortschatz ist groß genug, um immer auch Umschreibungen für das zu finden, was ich sagen möchte. Schwierigkeiten habe ich nur bei Fachthemen, bei denen mir zum Teil Begriffe unbekannt sind. Ich kann flexibel auf Gesprächspartner(innen) eingehen und eigentlich immer alles ausdrücken, was ich sagen möchte, dies schließt auch z. B. Scherze, Emotionen usw. ein.

Wortschatz

Ich denke, mein Allgemein- und Fachwortschatz ist …

… sehr differenziert, d.h. ich kann fast alles sagen, was ich möchte, bei vielen Wörter kenne ich auch andere Wörter mit gleicher oder ähnlicher Bedeutung oder die jeweiligen Gegenteile; die Wörter kann ich auch alle korrekt schreiben.

… differenziert, ich kann vieles sagen, was ich möchte, manchmal kenne ich Wörter mit gleicher oder ähnlicher Bedeutung; ich mache sehr wenige Rechtschreibfehler.

… weniger differenziert, d.h. manchmal fehlen mir auch alltägliche Wörter; für viele Aspekte kenne ich nur jeweils ein Wort. Insgesamt kann ich aber vieles sagen, was ich sagen möchte, auch wenn ich ab und zu Rechtschreibfehler mache.

… begrenzt, d.h. häufig fehlen mir auch alltägliche Wörter; nicht immer kann ich sagen, was ich sagen möchte; die Zahl der Rechtschreibfehler ist insgesamt hoch.

… deutlich begrenzt, ich weiß viele Wörter nicht, die ich schon vor Jahren gelernt habe; häufig muss ich im Wörterbuch nachsehen, ich mache auch bei einfachen Wörtern sehr viele Rechtschreibfehler.

… stark begrenzt; ich kann sehr vieles (auch Alltägliches) nicht sagen; die Wörter, die ich dann im Wörterbuch finde, habe ich häufig noch nie gehört; die Grundregeln der englischen Rechtschreibung kenne ich nicht.

Grammatische Strukturen

Ich denke, die von mir benutzten grammatischen Strukturen …

… haben einen sehr hohen Grad an Korrektheit, ich weiß, dass ich kaum Grammatikfehler mache; gelegentliche Fehler kann ich als Fehler erkennen und entsprechend schnell korrigieren.

… haben einen hohen Grad an Korrektheit, ich mache nur gelegentlich Grammatikfehler, diese kann ich selbst erkennen und korrigieren, wenn ich in einer Grammatik nachschlage.

… zeigen, dass ich eigentlich die englische Grammatik beherrsche, obwohl ich vermehrt Fehler mache; ich kenne die wichtigsten grammatischen Regeln, sie sind nur im Sprachgebrauch nicht immer selbstverständlich für mich.

… sind bei einer ziemlich hohen Fehlerzahl noch im Rahmen; ich weiß, dass ich einige Regeln im Detail wiederholen müsste, aber ich habe von den wichtigsten Regeln schon gehört und kann sie eigentlich auch anwenden, wenn ich sie wiederholt habe.

… zeigen, dass ich im Bereich Grammatik ziemliche Lücken habe; ich mache sehr viele Fehler und weiß auch oft nicht, was an meinen Sätzen von der Grammatik her falsch ist.

… zeigen, dass ich die englische Grammatik kaum beherrsche; ich kenne auch sehr elementare Regeln nicht und bin auch nicht in der Lage, meine Fehler ohne Hilfe zu korrigieren.

Aussprache und Flüssigkeit

Ich denke, meine Aussprache ist …	… klar, korrekt, flüssig; die Zuhörer(innen) können immer sofort verstehen, was ich sagen möchte, meine Sprechgeschwindigkeit ist recht hoch.
	… weitgehend klar, korrekt, flüssig; manchmal zögere ich kurz, wenn ich ein Wort nicht sofort weiß, aber das bedeutet keine langen Pausen.
	… so, dass die Zuhörer(innen) mich eigentlich schon verstehen, auch wenn ich manchmal recht langsam spreche; die Aussprache bei einigen Wörtern fällt mir manchmal schwer und ich weiß nicht alle Wörter sofort.
	… ist bei einer ziemlich hohen Fehlerzahl noch im Rahmen; ich weiß, dass ich Wörter falsch ausspreche, aber meine Beiträge sind weitgehend zu verstehen, auch wenn ich manchmal Pausen mache.
	… geprägt von einigen Aussprachefehlern, ich zögere vielfach, manchmal sind die Pausen auch länger.
	… geprägt von vermehrten Aussprachefehlern, das Verständnis ist nicht gesichert, für die Zuhörer(innen) ist eine Unterhaltung mit mir insgesamt anstrengend.

Aufbau und Gedankenführung

Meine Gedankenführung halte ich für …	… stringent, komplex und differenziert; ich kann einzelne Aspekte und die gedanklichen Verbindungen zwischen Aspekten sehr gut darstellen.
	… klar, stringent und nachvollziehbar.
	… angemessen, da ich immer eine Gliederung habe und meine Ausführungen nachvollziehbar sind.
	… verbesserungswürdig, da ich oft Schwächen im logischen Aufbau habe; ich schaffe es trotzdem, eine grundsätzliche Gliederung zu erstellen.
	… häufig zusammenhanglos; ich weiß, dass ich mir oft widerspreche und dass man eine Gliederung kaum erkennen kann.
	… sehr unzureichend, da mir eine Strukturierung und Gliederung dessen, was ich sagen möchte, fast nie gelingt.

Assessment test 1.1 – Diagnose

A1.42 **1 Listening comprehension: Teenagers and social networking sites** → Listening, p. 319
Listen to the recording about social networking sites and say whether each statement is true, false or not in the text.

a) More than 500 million teenagers worldwide use Facebook.

b) Facebook is more popular than MySpace.

c) Social networking sites have become integrated into the everyday social lives of teens.

d) These online platforms can only be accessed by personal computers.

e) Teenagers use these sites to stay in touch or make new friends.

f) Flirting with somebody online is not very common.

g) The majority of teenagers do not like posting photographs.

h) A large number of teenagers do not see a risk when posting confidential information such as telephone numbers or postal addresses.

i) These confidential pieces of information may be passed on for advertising reasons or can even be misused for identity theft.

j) Parents warn teenagers not to post photos.

Mail Online

Search GO

Home | News | U. S. | Sport | TV & Showbiz | Femail | Health

How spending too much time online 'can increase the chances of your teenager taking drugs'

Those regularly glued to screens are 'far more likely to engage in risky behaviour'

Spending time online increases the likelihood of a teenager taking drugs or having unprotected sex, it has been claimed. Research revealed those who are regularly glued to their screens are far more likely to engage in risky behaviour than their peers. The researchers from the Queen's University in Canada found that young adults who logged the most hours on their computers were 50 per cent more likely to engage in a cluster of six 'multi-risk behaviours'. These included smoking, drunkenness, cannabis and illegal drug use, having unprotected sex and not using seat belts.

Research author Valerie Carson, said: 'This research is based on social cognitive theory, which suggests that seeing people engaged in a behaviour is a way of learning that behaviour. Since adolescents are exposed to considerable screen time – over 4.5 hours on average each day – they're constantly seeing images of behaviours they can then potentially adopt.'

3 **glued to the screen** – vor dem Fernseher kleben

3 **to engage in sth.** – sich an etw. beteiligen

4 **likelihood** – Wahrscheinlichkeit

5 **to claim** – *hier:* behaupten

5 **to reveal** – *hier:* veröffentlichen, zeigen

6 **peer** – Gleichaltrige(r)

11 **social cognitive theory** – Kognitions- und Lerntheorie, die u.a. besagt, dass man lernt, indem man andere beobachtet

15 **to adopt** – anpassen

One explanation behind the findings is that a considerable amount of advertising that used to be shown on TV is now being shown on the internet. In addition, computer usage by adolescents has increased considerably in recent years. 'TV and video games have more established protocols in terms of censorship, but Internet protocols aren't as established,' Ms Carson said. 'Parents can make use of programs that control access to the Internet, but adolescents in this age group are quite savvy about technology and the Internet. It's possible that these types of controls aren't effective in blocking all undesirable websites.'

The research, recently published in the Journal of Preventative Medicine, suggests that future studies should examine the specific content adolescents are being exposed to in order to help strengthen current screen time guidelines for youth. (314 words)

[19] **protocol** – *hier:* Ordnung, Vorgabe
[20] **access** – Zugang
[24] **preventative** – vorbeugend
[26] **to strengthen** – verstärken

2 Comprehension → Word webs, p. 349
Copy and complete the word web with relevant information from the text.

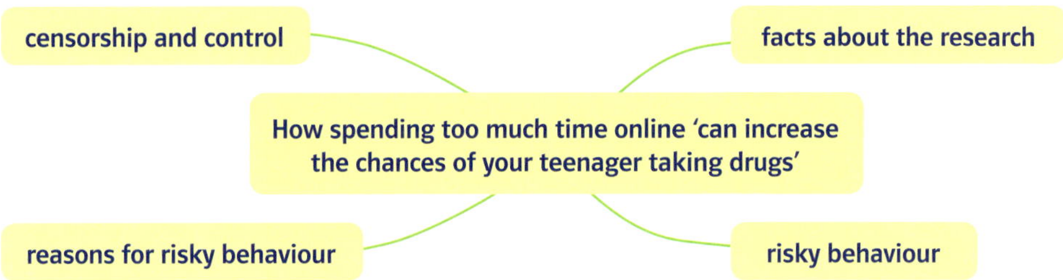

3 Comment → Writing a comment, p. 327
"Teenagers' access to the Internet should be limited to a maximum of 2 hours a day." Comment on this statement, also with reference to the findings presented in the text. Make sure that you include pros and cons!

4 Role play: Teenagers and the Internet → Discussions, p. 344
Now prepare for a role play. There are four roles. Work on your own and collect arguments to prepare for the discussion.

a) You are a teenager and are strictly against limiting Internet access for teenagers.

b) You are a parent and are concerned about your children spending too much time on the Internet. However, you do not know if a limit would really help.

c) You are a parent and are strongly in favour of limiting your teenage child's Internet access to a maximum of two hours a day.

d) You are a teacher. You believe that for many teenagers the Internet has replaced all other communication media, but you are also concerned that the contents children and teenagers are consuming can no longer be controlled.

Assessment test 1.2 – Diagnose

A1.43

1 Listening comprehension: Globetrotters – a radio documentary → Listening, p. 319

Listen to the interview with Max Ranter, a popular musician who travels all over the world with his band. Copy and complete the word web with information from the interview.

2 Comprehension: Teenagers and music

Work through the table of facts about teenagers and music and choose the correct answer. Be careful! Sometimes more than one answer is correct.

3 **destructive** – zerstörerisch
5 **drug abuse** – Drogenmissbrauch
11 **to estimate** – schätzen
14 **to enhance** – verbessern
16 **motor control** – Motorik
21 **guidance** – Führung, Orientierung
26 **to bridge** – überbrücken
33 **average** – durchschnittlich
43 **outlet** – *hier:* Ventil

Parents should ask for professional help if a teenager is often lost in music that has very destructive themes and if they see changes in behaviour (isolation, depression, alcohol or other drug abuse).	Music is so powerful because it is a universal language. It addresses universal human feelings and bridges gaps between cultures. Music brings people much closer together than languages do.
A survey found out that on average teenagers consider £6.58 a fair price for a CD album.	75 per cent of teenagers say that they have watched a music video online.
Music also plays a powerful social role: it brings young people with similar tastes together.	Music is often a key part of a teenager's own personal world. It is quite common for teenagers to keep adults out of this world.
Record companies estimate that illegal peer-to-peer filesharing accounts for 95 per cent of all digital music downloads.	According to record companies, on average 43 per cent of the music owned and enjoyed by teenagers has not been paid for.
Scientists say that music enhances brain functioning. Playing music activates a variety of brain functions simultaneously: motor control, imagination, hearing, sight, memory, etc.	Many people agree that whatever you are doing becomes more intense when it is accompanied by music: a sporting event, a movie scene, a romantic situation, even driving your car.
Nearly 3/4 of 15–24s said they don't feel guilty about illegally downloading music.	60 per cent of 16–24 year olds would rather go without meeting friends for a week.
Especially for teenagers, music can serve as a source of moral or social guidance.	Music is generally believed to be a form of expression and an emotional outlet.
40 billion songs are downloaded illegally worldwide every year.	More than 80% of the teenagers interviewed said that listening to music made them feel good.

a) 1. More than 80% of teenagers do not feel guilty about illegal downloads.
2. Half of the teenagers say illegal downloads are acceptable.
3. Nearly 75% of teenagers do not mind downloading music illegally.

b) 1. Teenagers often do not want to share their music with adults.
2. Teenagers ask parents for advice if their music deals with destructive themes.
3. Adults encourage teenagers to listen to music because it has a positive influence on them.

c) 1. Record companies say that nearly 40 billion songs are downloaded illegally every year.
2. Teenagers share passwords to download songs.
3. More and more adults download music illegally as well.

d) 1. Music makes you feel good whatever you do.
2. Whatever you do becomes more intense when you listen to music.
3. Music is suitable as an emotional outlet.

e) 1. Music makes it easier to get to know other people.
2. Only language is more powerful in bringing people together.
3. With the help of music, differences between cultures can be overcome.

f) 1. Some kind of music can even serve as emotional or moral guidance.
2. Whenever you listen to music, you feel better.
3. Music stimulates various activities in your brain.

g) 1. On average, teenagers spend £6.58 for music online every week.
2. Teenagers are not prepared to pay more than £6.58 for an album.
3. On average, teenagers say that £6.58 is a fair price for an album.

3 Text production: Writing an email → Writing an email, p. 329
A friend of yours called Marleen sends you the following email. Write an email in reply giving Marleen some advice.

Hi,
You know that we've been playing in our band for the last couple of years now; you also know that we have never been that successful. For me it was crystal clear that music would be nothing more than a hobby … But then last year all of a sudden things started to change. We got more gigs than in the years before and now we have even been contacted by a record company. They want to offer us a contract on the condition that I stop school and become a full-time musician. I really don't know what to do … On the one hand, music is my life – but on the other hand, leaving college now means I would end up without any qualifications at all. Can I please have your advice?
Cheers,
Marleen

4 Role play: A work placement in Australia → Discussions, p. 344
After finishing school, you (aged 18) first want to do a work placement and then see what comes next. So you have decided to work in the music industry for six months because music is extremely important in your life. You have sent applications to a German record company and an Australian music label. Now, both have offered you a placement, and they want a decision soon. That's why you now find yourself in a discussion with your family and your boyfriend / girlfriend.

a) You want to go to Australia because you believe this is a once-in-a-lifetime chance.

b) Your father / mother understands that you see this as a real chance but is worried nevertheless.

c) Your boyfriend / girlfriend fears that your relationship will suffer if you go away for so long.

d) Your older brother / sister supports your plans and encourages you to go abroad.

Assessment test 1.3 – Diagnose

A1.45

1 Listening comprehension: Teenagers as consumers → Listening, p. 319
Listen to the text about teenagers as consumers and summarise the most important aspects in German.

2 Comprehension → Understanding non-fictional texts, p. 320
Copy and complete the table with information from the text.

Information about the study	Negative effects of working during school	Positive effects of working during school	Recommendations

5 **to hamper** – erschweren
7 **delinquency** – Kriminalität
14 **sophomore** – amerikanischer Student (2. Jahr)
19 **decade** – Jahrzehnt
22 **attainment** – Leistungen
23 **substance abuse** – Drogenmissbrauch

THE 10 O'CLOCK NEWS

Search GO

HOME | NEWS | WEATHER | HEALTH | MONEY | SPORTS |

Study: Too much part-time work harmful for students

A part-time job may seem like a sweet deal for teens raising money for college or wanting to buy their own things, but a new study warns that too many work hours may be harmful to a teen's development.
The study, led by University of Washington researcher Kathryn Monahan, suggested that working during the school year can hamper school performance and cause behavior problems like drug abuse and delinquency.
"Especially in a recessed economy, many adolescents may feel pressure to work during high school," Monahan told the *University of Washington news service*. "The study suggests that working during the school year is perfectly fine, so long as the work hours for adolescents are restricted to fewer than 20 hours per week."
Monahan, a research scientist with UW's School of Social Work, used data from nearly 1,800 high school sophomores and juniors who were followed for two years in the late 1980s. There was almost an even mix of boys and girls with ethnically and socio-economically diverse backgrounds from nine high schools in Wisconsin and northern California.
While the research was decades old, she said that work and teens have not changed that much. The study, as reported by *USA Today*, showed that students who worked more than 20 hours a week had lower expectations for educational attainment and were less engaged in school. They also showed more problem behavior such as substance abuse.

At the same time, the same students had slightly higher grade point averages than teens without jobs and were more independent in their decision-making. *USA Today* said researchers attributed some of the higher GPA to working students taking easier classes and spending less time on homework. Even after the teens cut down their hours or stopped working, *US News* and *World Report* said, the study showed that the negative behavior still continued.

"Although working during high school is unlikely to turn law-abiding teenagers into felons or cause students to flunk out of school, the extent of the adverse effects we found is not trivial ...," Monahan said. She said parents, educators and employers should be careful about letting teens work too many extra hours during the school year. The study is published in the January/February issue of the journal *Child Development*. (382 words)

24 **grade point average (GPA)** – Notendurchschnitt
36 **issue** – Ausgabe

3 Comment → Writing a comment, p. 327
Write a text commenting on the advert "No money. No problem." which the Standard Bank uses to attract young people as customers. Take into account the slogan and also the text.

4 Role play: TweenPlus account
Standard Bank wants to start a large advertising campaign to promote their children's bank account, tweenPlus.

Here are the facts:

children (aged 11+) can open their own bank account with as little as £1 • earn credit interest – the more you save, the more interest you'll earn • StandardBank Cash Card for withdrawing up to £50 a day from cash machines • pay pocket money straight into your account • no monthly fee

Now prepare for the role play. There are four roles. Work on your own and collect arguments to prepare for the discussion.

a) You are a bank manager and defend your tweenPlus account.

b) You are a concerned parent and are worried that your child will end up in debt if they have an account of their own.

c) You are a member of a consumer watchdog organisation that criticises banks for massively targeting teenagers as potential customers.

d) You are a 16-year-old teenager and are all in favour of this kind of bank account.

Assessment test 2.1 – Diagnose

A 3.33 **1 Listening comprehension: A news report** → Listening, p. 319
Listen to the recording and complete the sentences with information from the listening text.

a) Immigrants represented more than …

b) People entering Britain from outside Europe and the Commonwealth …

c) Immigrant communities make up …

d) The largest groups came from …

e) There were major increases in immigration from countries such as …

f) Nearly 20 per cent of people born in India …

g) Fewer than half of new immigrants from Bangladesh …

h) The expansion of the European Union is resulting in …

2 Comprehension: True or false? → Comprehension questions, p. 326
Read the statements below and decide whether they are true or false. Quote or paraphrase words from the text which confirm or disprove the ideas in the statements.

a) The percentage of ethnic minorities in the British population is expected to grow from 8% to 20% in the course of 50 years.

b) The trend of ethnic groups to concentrate in certain places will continue.

c) Many of the immigrants coming to Britain in the coming years are expected to be white.

theguardian

News | Sport | Comment | Culture | Business | Money | Life&Style | Travel | Environment

Comment is free > Society   Search GO

Ethnic minorities to make up 20% of UK population by 2051

Projection of British population over 40 years shows sharp growth in ethnic groups outside of white British majority

Ethnic minorities will make up a fifth of Britain's population by 2051, compared with 8% in 2001, according to new projections published today by the University of Leeds. The figures, which show Britain's total population growing to 77.7 million, also indicate that the UK will become far less segregated as ethnic groups disperse throughout the country. In October, the Office for National Statistics predicted the population would exceed 70m by 2029. Researchers found striking differences in the respective growth rates of the 16 ethnic groups studied. White British and Irish groups are expected to grow the most slowly, while the so-called other white group is projected to grow the fastest, driven by immigration from Europe, the US and Australasia. Traditional immigrant groups of south Asian origin (Indian, Pakistani and Bangladeshi) will also grow rapidly. The initial findings of the three-year study include population projections for 352 local authorities in England, as well as projections for Wales, Scotland and Northern Ireland, for each year until 2051.

"The ethnic makeup of the UK's population is evolving significantly," said Professor Philip Rees of Leeds University. "Groups outside the white British majority are increasing in size and share, not just in the

6 **to disperse** – to spread out over a larger area

7 **to exceed** – to be more than a specific number or amount

7 **respective** – belonging to each of the different items that are mentioned

14 **to evolve** – to go through a development gradually

d) Asian and African groups will remain in poorer areas.

e) Trends in demographic change can be predicted with great accuracy.

f) The British government considers the regulation of immigration a necessary measure.

3 Text production: Blog entry → Writing a blog entry, p. 330
Write a blog entry in which you comment on the question whether it is OK to restrict migration into Germany, allowing only skilled people with the qualifications needed and shutting out others.

4 Role play: Immigration to Germany → Discussions, p. 344
Now prepare for a role play. There are four roles. Work on your own and collect arguments to prepare for the discussion.

a) You are a politician who is strictly in favour of limiting the numbers of unskilled immigrants. You fear that the state can no longer afford to finance them if they do not find a job.

b) You are a Pakistani who runs a small shop in a large German town. You believe that Germany is no longer as attractive as other European states like, for example, Spain, but also think that Germany needs immigrants.

c) You are a politician who is strictly against immigration restrictions. You think it is time to officially acknowledge that Germany is a multi-cultural country.

d) You are a social worker who sees the danger of ghettos in larger German towns. You fear that many immigrants do not want to assimilate, while at the same time many immigrants feel excluded.

areas of initial migration, but throughout the country, and our projections suggest that this trend is set to continue through to 2051." He added: "At a regional level, ethnic minorities will shift out of deprived inner-city areas to more affluent areas, which echoes the way white groups have migrated in the past. In particular black and Asian populations in the least deprived local authorities will increase significantly." The research team investigated ethnic population trends on a local scale in the UK and built a computer model to project those trends under a variety of scenarios. They used existing data on the 16 ethnic groups recognised in the 2001 census, along with demographic factors such as immigration, emigration, fertility and mortality.
The research shows the white British population shrinking from 87.1% to 67.1% and the white Irish group shrinking from 2.5% to 2.1%. The other white group's share grows from 2.5% to 9.9% – the greatest gain. Asian groups increase their share by three percentage points, black groups by two percentage points and Chinese and other ethnic groups by 2.6 percentage points. The researchers said their data generated five different scenarios for population makeup for each year until 2051, with each of the five projections yielding different absolute figures for ethnic groups and the population size as a whole. This, they cautioned, highlighted the difficulty in predicting trends such as migration.
"It is impossible to predict exactly how people will move into, out of and within the country in the coming decades as all of these trends are influenced by a whole range of socio-economic factors," said Rees. "However, our results suggest that overall we can look forward to being not only a more diverse nation, but one that is far more spatially integrated than at present." The immigration minister, Damian Green, said Britain had always benefited from being outwardlooking and having a population with diverse backgrounds, but added: "Problems arise in periods when the population changes too fast for comfort. That's why the government wants to control the level of immigration so that we can benefit from the arrival of talented people from all over the world without putting pressure on our public services." (582 words)

17 **to shift** – to move from one position to another
17 **deprived** – poor
18 **affluent** – wealthy
27 **to generate** – to cause sth. to exist
34 **spatially** – relating to space
36 **too fast for comfort** *(idiomatic)* – so fast that one doesn't feel good about it

Assessment test 2.2 – Diagnose

A 3.34 **1 Listening comprehension: The situation of women agricultural workers in Chile**
→ Listening, p. 319
Listen to the report about women agricultural workers in Chile. Take notes and answer the questions.

a) Why doesn't it help that there are more temporary jobs now in Chile?

b) Where does the money for exported products end up?

c) In what three senses are the women workers poorer than before?

d) Why can't the agricultural labourers take holidays?

e) How does Rosa Paleres feel about her situation?

f) What does she want from the government?

g) How many free trade agreements has Chile signed?

h) What is the price of a container of grapes?

i) Name three important export products in Chile's agricultural industry.

2 Comprehension → Comprehension questions, p. 326

a) Complete these sentences with information from the text.
1. Diets in China and India have changed as prosperity has grown, creating …
2. With the price of crude oil high, farmers are …
3. There is a war for resources between …

THE TIMES

To eat … or to drive?

Finishing her bag of Karu cheese-flavoured snacks, Shoko Taketani blushes and admits that she still feels oddly peckish. It is not her imagination: Japanese crisp packets contain 10 per cent fewer crisps than they did a month ago. In Munich, beer at this year's Oktoberfest will be the most expensive in the festival's history. […]
In Kuala Lumpur, Rhosdi is mulling a decision he thought would always be beyond him: whether to trade in his motor scooter for his first car. He is one of the 1.2 million Malaysian civil servants who have just received a windfall pay increase – their first in 15 years. Though geographically diverse and apparently unrelated, these developments are in fact connected, symptoms of a new global trend. Stomachs and petrol tanks are for the first time in competition and farmers everywhere are asking themselves a novel question: am I planting food or energy? There is no single source for the revolution sweeping across every continent. But one starting point is Jim Curl's 350-acre farm in Brahman, Oklahoma. This year he planted a third of it with genetically modified corn instead of the area's traditional crop of wheat. This amounts to 100 acres or so, a mere flap of a butterfly's wings in the great scheme of things. But by the time the impact of Mr Curl's decision has made its way to the other side of the world, the results are seismic. The economics of food – what is affordable, what it costs, and what that money buys – are creating unprecedented waves through all continents. From nut plantations in Indonesia to barley fields along the Rhine, farmers are all adjusting to this new world. Part of the result is tortilla riots in Mexico, the astonishing leap in Brazilian chicken leg prices and mayonnaise price spikes in Western Europe. These, say industry insiders, are the first skirmishes of a conflict that could soon dominate geopolitics: the war for resources between the world's 800 million cars and

1 **to blush** – to turn red
2 **peckish** – feeling slightly hungry; having an appetite
5 **to mull a decision** – to think about a decision long and hard
7 **windfall** – *here:* an expected event that brings good fortune
10 **novel** – *here:* new
11 **to sweep** – to move fast
13 **crop** – agricultural produce, such as grain, vegetables, or fruit
13 **wheat** – type of corn *(Weizen)*
13 **flap of a butterfly's wings** – *Flügelschlag eines Schmetterlings* – represents the idea in Chaos Theory that a very small event can have global consequences
15 **seismic** – relating to or caused by earthquakes
16 **unprecedented** – unparalleled
17 **barley** – type of corn *(Gerste)*
18 **leap** – jump
19 **price spike** – sudden and dramatic rise in prices
19 **skirmish** – a short fight

4. The war centres largely on global demand for "green" replacements …
5. Farmers are making a …

b) Put these statements into a logical order.
1. there is not enough of the crop on the market
2. soya oil prices have risen
3. much more corn will be grown in the near future
4. price was 50 per cent higher than the previous year.
5. the US wants to increase the use of ethanol
6. increase in corn production has already led to a cut in soya cultivation

3 Comment → Writing a comment, p. 327

Write a comment in which you outline what you think about the war for resources between the world's 800 million cars and its six billion stomachs. In your opinion, what is more important: fuel or food?

4 Role play: Fair trade or cheap products? → Discussions, p. 344

Now prepare for a role play. There are four roles. Work on your own and collect arguments to prepare for the discussion.

a) You are a teenager and do not have much money for expensive alternatives to cheaper products.

b) You are a parent and are concerned about your children growing up in a world of abundance.

c) You are a retail manager and justify low prices in developing countries.

d) You work for a fair trade organisation which tries to secure higher prices for Kenyan coffee farmers.

its six billion stomachs. In the developed world, the war will come down to price and choice; in the developing world it could come down to survival. The war centres largely on global demand for biofuels – "green" replacements for petrol, such as ethanol, that can be produced from sugar, corn and other agricultural products rather than fossil fuels.
Farmers are making a perfectly rational economic choice. With the price of crude oil high, they are planting crops to meet demand for cheaper biofuels. But converting more crops into energy means there is less to go into foodstuffs. And so the prices of those foodstuffs rise. The price increases for German beer, for instance, arise from replacing barley fields with ethanol feedstocks. […]
The US is a driving force in such change. In January President Bush called for a massive increase in the use of ethanol over the next decade – a move regarded by traders as setting the battle lines of the future conflict. This decision has momentous consequences. Planting more corn for ethanol has meant a 15 per cent cut in the amount of land devoted to soya. So soya oil prices are rising. That in turn has opened the door to cheaper palm oil – 90 per cent of which comes from Malaysia and Indonesia.
That surge in sales of palm oil is, in Malaysia in particular, creating dramatic social change overnight. Government coffers are so full that last month all civil servants were given pay rises of between 7.5 per cent and 42 per cent. […] Diets in China and India have (also) changed as prosperity has grown, creating greater demands for meat and, as a consequence, the crops that feed livestock. […] But it is corn – global inventories are at a record low and the price of the crop is 50 per cent higher than it was last year – and edible oils where the greatest impact is being felt. […] Within a year, say economists, China could reach the hugely significant point of becoming a net importer of corn. Oils give food a sophistication that more and more Chinese and Indians are getting a taste for. Shoko Taketani, with her empty crisp packet in Tokyo, knows this to her cost. (715 words)

25 **crude oil** – unrefined oil
36 **surge** – sudden increase
41 **edible** – which can be eaten
43 **sophistication** – having a good knowledge of others and their culture

Assessment test 2.3 – Diagnose

A 3.35

1 Listening comprehension: Is shopping your drug of choice? → Listening, p. 319
Listen to the recording and complete the table with information from the listening text.

Characteristics of compulsive shopping	Shopping addiction as a vicious circle	Indications that shopping is an addiction

2 Comprehension

a) In your own words, describe what FarmVille is and how Lady Gaga uses it to promote herself.

b) Summarise in your own words why advertising through online games is attractive to bands and musicians.

2 **casual** – *here:* occasional
3 **to reap** – to collect
3 **bumper crop** – large crop
11 **to partner with sb.** – to work together with sb.
14 **unicorn** – mythical horse-like creature with a horn on its forehead
16 **roughly** – approximately
17 **demographic** – relating to the structure of populations
17 **appeal** – attraction
17 **broad** – far-reaching
18 **leek** – a type of vegetable
19 **to harvest** – to collect

theguardian

News | Sport | Comment | Culture | Business | Money | Life&Style | Travel | Environment

Comment is free > Society   Search [ ] GO

Get down on the FarmVille

Aimed at older women and 'casual gamers', FarmVille has reaped a bumper crop of 60 million global users. No wonder Lady Gaga wants in.

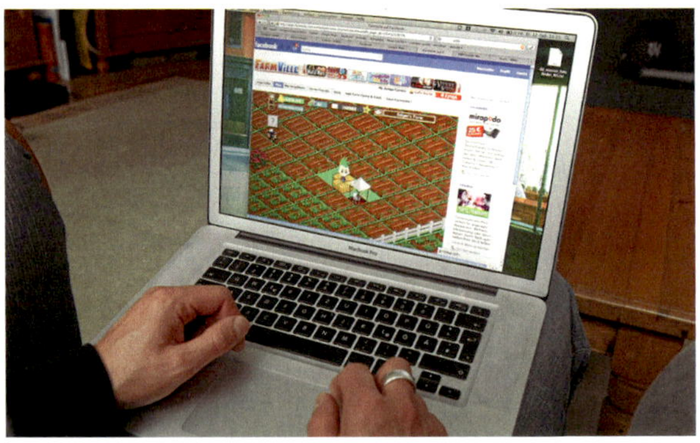

Lady Gaga, pop supremo, wearer of meat dresses, the star who has sold more than 15m albums worldwide, announced on Wednesday that she is partnering with games company Zynga to release exclusive songs through their Facebook game, FarmVille. The singer's fans will be able to visit GagaVille, a specially designed farm inside the virtual farming simulation game, which will contain unicorns and crystals.

Lady Gaga's choice of FarmVille makes sense: it's an enormous market. The game has around 60 million players worldwide – that's roughly the same size as the population of the UK. And FarmVille's demographic appeal is broad.

In FarmVille, players plant virtual crops – strawberries, bell peppers and leeks are just some of the many choices – wait a few hours, and then harvest them to receive coins that allow them to buy more farming supplies. Of course, the best farming goods can't be bought with ingame

3 Comment → Writing a comment, p. 327
Comment on the fact that websites primarily designed for entertainment or games are increasingly used for marketing purposes.

4 Role play: Pressure by advertising → Discussions, p. 344
Now prepare for a role play. There are four roles. Work on your own and collect arguments to prepare for the discussion.

a) You are a social worker and witness an increasing pressure among teenagers to buy. Mobile phones, clothes, shoes – very soon teenagers will fear becoming an outsider if they cannot keep up with the others.

b) You are a parent and are concerned about your children growing up in a material world. The advertising industry is responsible for the enormous pressure teenagers face today. Why is a cool pair of sneakers more important than character traits?

c) You work for an advertising agency and reject the criticism that you are responsible for people becoming shopping addicts or getting into debt.

d) You work for a debt councelling agency. More and more people face bankruptcy because they buy more than they can afford.

coins, but need real money, with items ranging from a few pence to a few pounds. As the New York Times pointed out in a profile of FarmVille's founder Mark Pincus last year, "the sums are small, but add up quickly when multiplied by millions of users".

But the genius of the game is that players advance much more quickly if they rope their friends in too. My Facebook account is littered with requests such as: "I'm trying to nourish my baby lamb! Could you send me a bottle?" Some find these requests hard to turn down and by exerting this social pressure FarmVille has consolidated a solid user-base. Lady Gaga's not the first to spot the business potential of a tie-in with such a popular brand: the last time I entered FarmVille's virtual space I was offered a "free windmill from American Express". They've also partnered with McDonald's in the past, as well as raising money for earthquake victims in Haiti.

The growth of FarmVille is just the latest and most obvious expression of a change in gaming demographics over recent years. The media's image of a "gamer" might still be of a man in his teens or 20s sitting in front of Call of Duty for six-hour stretches, but that stereotype is now more inaccurate than ever.

FarmVille, of course, is unashamed about being a game. It's partly that playful style that makes it a good partner for Lady Gaga, an artist famed for antics and experimentation. Gaga has also used social media to develop a deep connection with her fans – she surpassed Britney Spears last year as the most-followed user on Twitter, and topped a survey of the most popular musical artists in online social media.

But Gaga isn't the only musician tapping into the increasing reach of games. Adrian Hon, CCO of Six to Start, a games company, [...] says: "Games are a good way for bands to connect with their younger fans, to engage with the sort of people who buy music and go to concerts. Labels and publishers have seen the internet primarily as a place to advertise and a source of worrying piracy, but artists tend to be much more interested in the creative possibilities."

The games industry is growing by somewhere between 10% and 20% a year, a figure that the film and the music industry could only dream of. We might not all be wearing meat dresses in 10 years' time, but in hooking up with an online game, Lady Gaga is likely to be a forerunner of things to come. (743 words)

24 **to rope in** – *here:* to involve
25 **littered** – full of
25 **to nourish** – to feed
27 **to exert** – to apply
27 **to consolidate** – to build up
28 **tie-in** – combination
30 **earthquake victim** – sb. who has suffered because of an earthquake
33 **stretch** – *here:* length of time
33 **stereotype** – popular assumption
34 **inaccurate** – false
35 **unashamed** – not embarrassed
36 **to be famed for sth.** – to be well known for sth.
36 **antics** – fooling around
37 **to surpass** – to outdo
40 **to tap into sth.** – to take advantage of sth.
47 **forerunner** – pioneer

Helping hand – Differenzierung

Topic 1.1

A 3 Role play → p. 12

Here are some arguments to start you off:

- The greater the number of young people who gather in one place, the more likely it is that the party will get out of control.
- There will always be some who go against the rules. In most cases, this means alcohol and drugs.
- Police operations on this scale cost the taxpayer a lot of money.
- You can't just go round having fun at someone else's expense.
- The partygoers certainly won't clean up when they leave.
- Especially younger people, who are under a lot of peer pressure, might easily be influenced by those who misbehave.
- Why can't you just have a bit more trust in young people? Always calling in the police beforehand shows what you think of them!
- As long as they celebrate in public places, everything is just fine.
- These parties are a brilliant way of getting to know other people.
- Where's the difference to your Schützenfest? Just because we're young?
- Adults just need to accept that life is changing because of the Internet. Everything is faster, more spontaneous, even freer.

A 4 Text production: Writing an email → p. 13

Here are some sentences you might want to use in your email:

- Dear …, on Facebook I just read that you are inviting people in California to a flash mob party at someone else's house – to the home of someone you do not know.
- Even though I do not know you and we will probably never meet, I would like to tell you what I think about this idea. Using someone else's property – in this case someone else's pool – is …
- Especially the fact that you cannot estimate how many people will eventually turn up …
- Have you thought about …
- You also might want to consider…
- Let me tell you about an incident which took place in Hamburg, Germany…
- So, all in all, I believe that your idea of inviting strangers to a stranger's house for a party is …

A 5 Mediation → p. 13

Follow these basic rules when doing a mediation task:

- Do not translate word for word.
- Just try to get the key message and the central ideas of the text across.
- Your new text can have a different line of argumentation or a different sequence.

For this task, you might want to include the following ideas:

- Menschen verbringen mehr Zeit auf Internetseiten von sozialen Netzwerken (Facebook, Twitter, MySpace usw.), Russen mehr als sechs Stunden im Monat, Deutsche etwa vier Stunden
- Facebook hat ca. 1 Milliarde aktive Mitglieder
- voraussichtliche Werbeausgaben auf diesen Seiten nur für die USA (2012) – 2,6 Miliarden Dollar

B 3 Listening comprehension: Teens, cell phones and texting → p. 15

These are the main topics which are mentioned in the audio text:

- American teenagers are increasingly using mobile phones and text messages to communicate with each other.
- Parents and schools find it difficult to set limits.
- Some teenagers already prefer texting to face-to-face conversations.

B 4 Comment → p. 15

Here are some ideas that might help you in your line of argumentation:

- There are those who admire teenagers for their ability to use digital communication with ease.
- They envy them for being able to stay in touch with the world around them effortlessly.
- There are those who say that teenagers are wasting their lives on social networking sites or on texting dozens of messages a day.
- They point out that teenagers are becoming increasingly technology-enslaved.
- Parents are worried that their children might be losing touch with the outside world as they replace it with a virtual one.
- They fear that today's teenagers might lose their ability to interact with people in the real world.
- Life is much more than digital communication. There is no substitute for authentic experience and real encounters.
- Digital communication offers huge advantages to those who have the knowledge and the skills to use it to fulfil their wishes.
- Digital communication is fast, easy, keeps people in touch and does not exclude people because of the way they look or speak. In this sense, it is fairer and more respectful.

E 3 Analysis → p. 21

Here are some ideas that might help you in your line of argumentation:

Chorus	Verses
words showing insecurity: don't know, fear	words showing determination, power and success: want, don't care, I'll, fucking, weapon, massive, winner
negative sentence: I don't know, question adressed to sb. else (When do you think …)	
repetition (When do you think it will all become clear? Cause I'm being taken over by fear) at the end of every verse	affirmative sentences: I want, I'll, I am

E5 Comment → p. 21

In your comment, the following phrases might help you:

- On the one hand Lily Allen's song portrays …
- The singer manages to show …
- The lyrics clearly emphasise what society …
- To many teenagers, the idea of their future consists of …
- On the other hand the dominant fear plays an important role …
- Hardly any teenager today believes that…
- While Lily Allen's song ends with …, for many teenagers …
- All in all I believe that you cannot say that teenagers today …
- There's no such thing as …

Topic 1.2

A3 Analysis → p. 29

The following sentences will help you with your analysis of the cartoon:

- The black-and-white cartoon shows …
- The father is … He is traditionally dressed and is …
- His son who is … is standing …
- There is a caption under the cartoon saying …
- This means that the public discussion of family matters on social media …
- A normal conversation or even an argument between family members …
- The father seems to be more concerned about his image on MySpace …
- For the son making his complaint public seems to be …
- So the cartoonist is making the point that …
- I think the cartoon is …

B4 a) Text production: Writing an email → p. 31

Your email to Sam's mother could include the following aspects and ideas:

- show an understanding for the shock she is feeling
- show an understanding for the difficulty of raising Sam alone
- say what you think of Sam's behaviour
- show some sympathy for her and acknowledge the fact that she may feel guilty or that she has made a mistake
- comment on how she talks to her son in front of other people
- offer advice on how she could behave in the future

C3 Mediation → p. 32

The following keywords might help you with your mediation:

- census by *Statistisches Bundesamt*, Germany
- traditional role model still valid today
- but: more working mothers, most work part-time
- fathers mostly breadwinners, mothers stay at home or work part-time (still most common role model in Germany)
- numbers of mothers working part-time have increased dramatically, this especially applies to single mothers
- generally speaking: more women than in the past feel that they must work part-time to make ends meet

C4 Listening comprehension: Miss World and women's rights go hand in hand → p. 33

Match the following jumbled clues with the headings in the table. This will help you understand the listening text.

Why Clara Belle was against beauty contests in the past	Reasons that made her change her view	Beauty contests and feminism	Clara Belle's views on contests and pageants in general
Rebecca Mordan's criticism: women are reduced to the "sum of their parts"	pageants and women's rights can go hand in hand; they celebrate the diversity of appearances; underline contestant's individuality contestant gains confidence, friendship and a broadened mind	she believed these contests were degrading and humiliating to the young women	she discovered people who • are motivated, shared a desire to contribute to their community and be a part of something positive • seek recognition • represent views or causes that are important to them

Topic 1.3

B4 Comment → p. 47

Here are some arguments for and against to help you write your newspaper article:

Arguments for	Arguments against
• financial benefits – for tourism industry + people living in tourist destinations • increased tourism = increased investment in infrastructure: good for tourists + local residents • culture, tradition, food, language, art of one local area is promoted around the world • everyone should see the world • new cultures, influences, opportunities	• local cultures are destroyed by influx of tourists • culture changed / watered down to suit visitors • visitors do not see 'real life' • mass tourism damages environment: long-haul flights, waste, etc. • sites of natural beauty ruined by overcrowding

C3 Analysis → p. 49

Here are some points to help you with the text analysis:

Examples from the text	Effect on the reader
• "… I was a criminal. Just like you." (l. 11) • "… Want more? I drank wine, spent money, …" (l. 40) • "And just like you – if you live in the Western world, and I have to assume you do, or how else would you be reading this?" (ll. 41–42)	• provoke the reader – ask the reader questions • awakens the interest of the reader • reader is challenged, involved • reader must make up their mind

D2 Analysis → p. 50

Here are some points to get you started:

Attitudes toward GM food in Europe	Comparison with USA
• support in Spain remained quite constant – high level • support in UK unstable – sharp decline from 1996 – 1999 and sharp increase from 1999 – 2002 • Germany: steady drop in support • Greece: extreme drop in support from 1996 – 2005: 49% – 12% • conclusion: support in Europe varies but decline is noticeable	• opposition to GM food has declined 10% • support for GM food stable • half US population against GM food, one third in favour • percentage of support for GM food higher in Spain, UK & Germany than in USA

Topic 1.4

C6 Composition → p. 63

Here are some ideas that might help you write the composition:

American suburbs	Life in Germany
• cities spread very fast, taking over what used to be inhabited land • very large suburbs • large distances between homes and shops, places of work, facilities, etc. • car is always necessary • lack of or poor public transport	• cities don't spread as fast; there is less uninhabited land in Germany • smaller suburbs • homes generally closer to shops, etc. • life without a car is more possible as you can walk to more places • public transport more widespread

F2 a) Comprehension → p. 68

Use the ideas below to help you answer the comprehension question:

- British people have their own unique way of writing about other countries and people
- tend to mock other cultures
- British writing seems to suggest that other countries are not as advanced/developed as Britain

F3 a) **Analysis** → p. 69

Your analysis should include the following points:

- excited as he had little knowledge of Britain
- full of anticipation – what would it be like?
- eager

Topic 1.5

A 2 Comprehension → p. 77

Here are some points you might want to include:

LEFT OUT WIFE's problem:

- Her husband is chatting to other people on the Internet.
- He is spending a lot of time on the computer and less with her and their children.

FAMILY's answer:

- The wife should confront her husband with how she feels.
- They should have an honest, open discussion.

A 3 Text production: Writing an email → p. 77

You might want to include the following arguments:

For	Against
• Technology allows you to see and hear your partner online. • People may be more honest and open when conversation isn't face-to-face.	• If you only write to one another you cannot see body language, facial expressions nor get a sense of emotions, so it is impossible to really get to know somebody. • It is easier to be untruthful online than it is face-to-face.

B 3 Classroom discussion → p. 79

Here are some ideas to start you off:

Advantages	Disadvantages
• improves standards of handwriting • improves spelling skills • may increase students' vocabulary	• takes away time from "more important" subjects (languages, maths, etc.) • handwriting can be seen as an expression of "one's personality" • setting general standards could detract from uniqueness • boring, monotonous lessons

Topic 2.1

B3 Mediation → p. 95

Here are some aspects which you might want to use in your text:

- Abkommen zwischen dem britischen *Specialist Schools and Academies Trust* als Vertreter von 90% aller britischen staatlichen Sprachschulen und der chinesischen Regierung.
- 200 Lehrer nach England.
- Mandarin als verpflichtende strategische Weltsprache der Zukunft.
- Europäische Sprachen aus dem Lehrplan verdrängen.

B4 Analysis → p. 95

The following aspects might help you with your analysis:

- All the people who are quoted or referred to in indirect speech are experts and support the idea of introducing Mandarin and other Asian languages in language teaching.
- Direct speech gives the impression of closeness and authenticity, the reader gets the impression that Richard Garner, the author of the article, was very close to Sir Cyril Taylor.
- Reported speech gives the impression of knowledge about people in the background, they are not that important but support the same idea.
- No personal opinion of the author is found in the text.

D2 Listening comprehension: Schoolchildren now speak "The Queen's Hinglish" → p. 98

The following facts are mentioned in the listening text:

- Queen's Hinglish is a mixture of English and South Asian languages such as Hindi, Urdu and Punjabi in South Asia.
- Modern blend of standard English, Indian English and South Asian languages.
- Hinglish has already moved into the mainstream and is used on musical channels and in advertising.
- In the UK, Hinglish has appeared in TV programmes.
- Hinglish is used increasingly throughout the United Kingdom, particularly in playgrounds.
- Collision of languages has produced colourful phrases.
- People are becoming more and more comfortable with mixing words from languages such as Hindi, Urdu and Punjabi with English.
- Hinglish could soon become the most widely spoken form of English on earth.

D4 Analysis → p. 98

The following sentences might help you to analyse the cartoon:

- English class for immigrants, students look foreign (turban, headscarf, moustache etc.).
- Teacher in front looking at one angry student holding up a sign saying "I have tried telling you several times my name is Ken and I am from Glasgow".
- Cartoon makes fun of the fact that immigrants have to take English classes where they are taught how to speak English.
- English consists of so many varieties and dialects that not all native speakers of English can communicate with each other.
- The student from Scotland surely has told his English teacher several times that he speaks English, still the teacher has not been able to understand him or has not accepted this as English. That's the reason why he is attending / has been made attend this class.

Topic 2.2

E3 Having a discussion → p. 117

Here are some arguments to help you plan your panel discussion:

Option 1

For	Against
• strengthened patriotism amongst Americans • America doing its duty / helping the world • world becomes a more peaceful place • standing up for human rights • new democracies need military support • tyrants must be stopped	• Americans fear for their safety • America a target for others • many societies reject US's view of democracy / human rights • opens the US up for international criticism • other political systems must be respected • democracy cannot be enforced

Option 2

For	Against
• no room for idealism in world unstable with global terrorism / economic competition • necessary to engage with world pragmatically / selectively to promote US interests • US interests often require friendly relations with undemocratic governments	• acting without regard for other nations' interests leads to resentment, international violence, undermines international cooperation • relationship with dictators may endanger worldwide movement towards democracy • cooperation with undemocratic leaders = possible acceptance of genocide, ethnic cleansing, etc.

Option 3

For	Against
• global problems (environmental pollution, financial crises, refugees, AIDS, nuclear proliferation) require international cooperation • USA has power and influence to bring nations together • US cooperation with EU, UN, NATO cannot be criticised	• handing over power to international institutions: loss of international influence • American values in conflict with those of large parts of the world – therefore cooperation may not work / could be dangerous • USA can no longer respond flexibly / quickly to international changes.

Option 4

For	Against
• 9 / 11 has shown vulnerable USA – security at home is top priority • USA has wasted money on allies and should concentrate on domestic threats • military action / spending should be concentrated on defense • international action only brings criticism / anti-US feeling • US's first priority = protect its residents	• foolish to pretend the rest of the world does not matter • in the US's interest to promote democracy / human rights around the world • best way to protect the US homeland is through a wise foreign policy • many countries need the US's help

E4 Comment → p. 117

Here are some ideas to help you write your newspaper article:

- Western world needs to understand what it is fighting against
- must learn exactly what al-Qaeda / other extremists stand for
- change foreign policy – avoid alienating the majority of Muslims (war of hearts and minds)
- perhaps be less aggressive in conflicts around the world
- Germany: should support the rest of the world in the methods mentioned, should be consistent in its approach, but should not put itself in unnecessary danger.

Topic 2.3

A 3 Analysis → p. 125

The following bullet points might help you to analyse the cartoon:

- the cartoon depicts a tired and injured old lion covered in flies, wearing a battered crown
- the lion is standing against a setting sun whose rays form the stripes of the Union Jack
- the exhausted, dying lion stands for Britain and the end of the British Empire
- the cartoon is making the point that with the loss of Hong Kong, the British Empire is now a thing of the past
- the sun has finally set on it; allusion to the saying "The sun never sets on the British Empire"
- the British lion is now too weak to rule over an empire

B 2 a) Comprehension → p. 127

Here are some points to help you:

- the union between England and Scotland is 304 years old (2011)
- in 2007, 9% of Welsh voters felt "British not Welsh"
- now (2011), 16% feel "British not Welsh"
- in 2010, 37% of Northern Irish people saw themselves as "British"
- in 2007, 51% of Northern Irish people saw themselves as "British"
- last year (2010), 52% of English people described themselves as British

D 4 Comment → p. 131

You might want to include the following points:

For	Against
• British monarchy is famous all over the world, iconic • British monarchy is a tourist attraction • thus it brings money into the country • the Queen has a very high status, can use her international influence and popularity to help Britain • thanks to the monarchy, old traditions are continued • the monarchy is a political institution and stands for political stability • the royals do a lot of charity work • part of British national identity	• British monarchy and its traditions can be regarded as being archaic • the monarchy costs the British tax payer a lot of money (£32 million in 2011) • some members of the royal family don't really behave very "royal", image is crumbling, embarrassment for Britain • fancy lifestyle of the royals; makes them more celebrities than representatives of an old and honored institution

Topic 2.4

A 3 Mediation → p. 141

Here are some points you might want to include:

- Ringordner für Dokumente; Inhaltsverzeichnis; Trennblätter
- Zielformulierung; Zusammenfassung und Dokumentation der Arbeitserfahrung; Dokumente über bestimmte Fachkenntnisse; Charaktereigenschaften; Zeugnisse; Bescheinigungen über besuchte Fortbildungen
- eingescannte Version des Job Skills Portfolios; manche Firmen nehmen Bewerbungen digital in Empfang; Einpflegung in Systeme
- nur relevante Arbeitsproben integrieren; Abhebung durch Berichte, Projekte, PowerPointPräsentationen etc.; keine vertraulichen oder geschützten Informationen und Daten
- besondere Leistungen sollten ersichtlich werden; Auszeichnungen; Empfehlungsschreiben oder positives Kundenfeedback; Entfernung von persönlichen Daten
- Portfolio nicht überladen, Gefahr der Unübersichtlichkeit
- Portfolio auf digitales Medium kopieren und beifügen

B 2 a) Comprehension → p. 143

Here are some arguments to start you off:

Pros	Cons
• The money raised by "selling" internships is often donated to charity. • More students are gaining work experience abroad.	• Young people already have enough debts from their time as students. • Families with more money or "powerful" friends may have an advantage over less wealthy or influential families.

C 4 Analysis → p. 145

Here are some sentences which you might want to include in the description and analysis of the cartoon:

- A boy is lying on his bed looking out of the window with a pair of binoculars.
- The cartoonist uses the double meaning of "looking for sth." in his cartoon. On the one hand this means … On the other hand, however, looking for a job …
- I think the cartoon is funny because the cartoonist makes the point that some teenagers simply …
- I do not really like the cartoon because the cartoonist is clearly exaggerating. In today's world, no teenager…
- In my opinion the cartoon works because it addresses a topic …

D3 a) Analysis → p. 147

Here are some quotes to start you off:

Positive	Negative
• "Most of us liked most everyone […]" (l. 6) • "We loved free bagels in the morning." (ll. 11–12) • "Our benefits were astonishing in comprehensiveness and quality of care." (ll. 12–13)	• "Our mornings lacked promise." (ll. 2–3) • "We thought moving to India might be better, or going back to nursing school. Doing something with handicapped or working with our hands. No one ever acted on these impulses, despite their daily, sometimes hourly contractions. Instead we met in conference rooms […]." (ll. 14–17) • "Our boredom was ongoing, a collective boredom, and it would never die because we would never die." (ll. 26–27)

D4 Comment → p. 147

Here are some arguments to start you off:

Reasons for wanting to work at the company:

- The pay is good.
- Most people liked one another.
- Advertising work may be interesting.

Reasons for not wanting to work at the company:

- The work sounds boring.
- Some of the colleagues are a little strange.
- It seems as if there is often a bad working atmosphere.

E3 Comment → p. 149

Here are some arguments to start you off:

Arguments for the statement:

- A high salary is an indication of the importance of the job.
- You are respected if you earn a lot of money.
- Having a lot of money can make you happy.

Arguments against the statement:

- The amount of money you are paid cannot influence how much you enjoy your daily tasks.
- A job should be rewarding in itself.
- Working just for the money is a short-term outlook.

Topic 2.5

A 3 Mediation → p. 157

The following notes might help you with the German summary of the text:

- Beispiel Professor Pete Coffey vom University College in London
- aktuelle Forschungen und medizinische Entwicklungen im Bereich der Stammzellentechnologie
- Professor Coffey: mit Hilfe von aus Embryonen gewonnenen Stammzellen Behandlungsmöglichkeiten zur Augenkrankheit Makuladegeneration entwickeln
- Positivsignal der britischen Genehmigungsbehörde
- Regierungswechsel in den USA
- Stammzellenforschung hofft auf mehr an Genehmigungen für die Forschung aus Fruchtbarkeits-behandlungen gewonnenen Stammzellen
- Professor Coffey: Stammzellentechnologie wird Medizin in die Lage versetzen Leber- und Herz-erkrankungen und möglicherwiese Diabetes, langfristig auch Alzheimer und Parkinson zu behandeln.

A 4 Analysis → p. 157

The following aspects will only serve as starting point for your analysis, you need to go into more detail and of course support this by quoting from the text:

- positive picture of Pete Coffey
- calls the USA the world's powerhouse of biomedical research
- more detailed account of Coffey's project
- no opponent of stem cell research mentioned
- positive aspects and hopes are dealt with
- author never includes his personal opinion

D2 b) Comprehension → p. 163

Here are some ideas to start you off:

Features	Benefits
• voice recognition for household functions such as doors, windows, lights, …	• no need to have keys for doors • can turn on / off lights when hands are full • children or disabled / elderly / blind people will find it easier to get around the house
• automated cleaning, recognises when something is dirty / dusty, cleans automatically	• no need to do the cleaning yourself • house always looks clean and tidy, even when guests arrive unannounced
• waste disposal system that automatically separates waste and arranges for it to be picked up and taken away	• more efficient waste separation • no need to keep so much waste in the house
• adjustable modes, for example, holiday mode, party mode, etc.	• you will be able to set your house to do certain things automatically • different modes have different benefits
• heated driveway	• no need to shovel the driveway clear
• smart fridge that orders food when things run out	• no need to go to the supermarket

E3 Analysis → p. 165

The following aspects will only serve as starting point for your analysis, you need to go into more detail and, of course, support this with quotations from the text:

- includes himself when talking about the future
- adjectives or exclamations which very clearly express his opinion
- rhetorical questions
- presentation of possible negative developments as something factual and irrevocable

Topic 2.6

6 Describe and analyse the cartoon → p. 171

Below is a list of words and sentences which you might need to describe and explain the cartoon:

- to make a confession
- to confess
- to commit a sin
- to repent
- words of forgiveness
- to contradict the idea of sth.
- value of a face-to-face conversation
- active listening

- The cartoon consists of an illustration of an elderly woman in a confessional.
- In the partition wall of the confession box there is an intercom; in a normal confessional there would be the priest on the other side of the wall listening to the person making the confession.
- The text in the speech bubble next to the intercom says: "Thank you for choosing our automated service, for venial sins, press one …"
- The elderly woman looks startled and surprised by this recorded voice.
- The elderly woman is a stereotype of an elderly churchgoer.

A 4 Text production: Writing a letter / an email → p. 173

This is how you could start your letter / email to the editor:

- In the newspaper article *The rise and rise of convenience food*, which was published in the online edition of the Guardian, the author Tim Dowling …
- He concludes by …
- His final remark in his report …

The following phrases for expressing your opinion might be helpful for your letter:

- I believe that …
- I strongly doubt if …
- I wonder whether …
- I think …
- I feel …
- I don't think …
- In my opinion, …
- If you ask me, …

B 3 Analysis → p. 175

The following ideas might help you to get started with your analysis. Make sure that you give them a logical structure before you start writing your text:

- two active participants: John Salinas, 91, and 84-year-old Len Street
- all just point out the extremely positive aspects of adult learning; no word of criticism
- experts underline positive aspect of lifelong learning; no need for the author to include his opinion
- experts quoted: McNair, a semi-retired National Institute of Adult Continuing Education research fellow; Melissa March is executive director of Learning for the Fourth Age; Iona Gibbons, a community learning development worker and Fiona Aldridge, Niace programme director and author
- other quotes are by two senior learners who at the age of 84 and 91 are active participants
- almost all quotes in the text are by either scientists or those in charge of adult education programmes, all are experts

C 4 Mediation → p. 177

The following results will surely help you with your text about the two diagrams:

- two diagrams showing levels of physical activity and consumption of fruits and vegetables of 11 – 17 year olds
- diagram 1: physical activity; boys and girls, two age groups 11 – 13 and 14 – 17
- more than 1 / 3 of younger boys do sports almost daily, 37% 3 – 5 times a week: nearly 70% in that age group are physically active;
- 1 / 4 of the boys in that age group are physically active 1 – 2 times a week, only 6% say that they rarely do sports;
- girls are not that active, only 1 / 4 report daily physical activity, 30% say that they do sports 3 – 5 times a week; slightly more than 50% are physically very active;
- 30% report occasional physical activity, 12% say that they rarely do sports
- slightly different trend for age group 14 – 17, slight decrease in physical activity for boys (2 – 3% less), major change for girls: only 13% are physically active every day, just above 20% 3 – 5 times a week: more than 60% do sports only 1 – 2 times a week or even less than that
- diagram 2: consumption of vegetables / fruits compared to daily recommendations
- four age groups; youngest age group closest to recommendations; the older the boys get, the less they consume in terms of fruits / vegetables; age group of 14 – 17 year old boys: only one third of recommended amount; girls half of the daily recommendations, consumption remains unchanged but the recommended quantities rise

Topic 2.7

A4 Comment → p. 189

Here are some points to help you write the comment:

Yes	No
• no major war involving Europe • open borders between EU member states = more international job opportunities • higher standard of living • higher mobility through improved transportation • women have more career choices nowadays	• more opportunities = increased competition • younger people under more pressure to succeed • European economy unstable (problems with the Euro currency) • environmental damage / climate change / unpredictable weather

B2 a) Comprehension → p. 191

Here is some information to get you started:

- higher tax for rich
- war
- irresponsible / greedy behaviour by bankers
- corrupt politicians
- climate change / global warming
- globalisation being out of control
- people being exploited
- people feel excluded from decision-making

B4 Comment → p. 191

Here are some arguments to help you write the comment:

Yes	No
• Arab Spring / Occupy Movement have shown that people will stand up for themselves if pushed too far • people will no longer be threatened • people no longer scared of government violence • the events of 2011 brought global struggles to the eyes of the world – more people aware of what goes on and quicker to support those protesting • political world showed support for the people in undemocratic states (Libya) • 2011 demonstrated an increased willingness to go onto the streets and be more active • the use of social media was revolutionary	• it takes more than protests to change the world long term • more important to see how the affected parties / countries react • Arab Spring may have changed the world in terms of the scale of the protests, but how will they change the fate of North Africa and the Middle East? • Occupy Movement only small victories for the man on the street against upper classes • small number of successful protests compared to unsuccessful protests

D4 Mediation → p. 195

Here is some help for your mediation:

Young People's Bank
- Schüler eröffnen und führen eine Bank in der Schule.
- Fähigkeit der Schüler, mit Geld umzugehen und finanzielle Transaktionen durchzuführen soll verbessert werden.
- Motivation zu unternehmerischer Aktivität.
- Schüler können investieren und kleine Kredite erhalten.

The Beam
- Zielgruppe: Jungen im Alter von zwölf bis 15 Jahren mit BMI von 30 und mehr.
- Inhalte des Projekts: Ernährung, Fitness, Selbstwahrnehmung, Selbstvertrauen.
- Eltern sollen integriert werden.
- Wissen um eine gesunde Ernährung soll gesteigert werden.

World Jungle
- Ziel dieses Projekts: jungen Menschen kulturelle Möglichkeiten bieten.
- Aktivitäten: Tanz, Musik und Kunst.
- Fokus auf soziale und wirtschaftliche Probleme anderer Kulturen.
- z. B. indische, marokkanische und ghanaische Tänzer, Trommler und Sprecher, die bei Festivals auftreten.
- Vorurteile sollen abgebaut werden.

The Amoosi Project
- Designer, die am Anfang ihrer Karriere stehen sollen Möglichkeit erhalten, mit recycelten Kleidern und Textilien zu arbeiten.
- Fähigkeiten sollen entwickelt werden.
- Es soll vermieden werden, dass die Materialen auf Müllhalden landen.
- Designer sollen Modeindustrie mit ihren Kreationen beeinflussen.

Film Kitchen
- Mobile Filmvorführ- und Essenszubereitungseinrichtung.
- Filme sollen an verschiedenen Orten wie Gemeindehallen, Schulen und im Freien gezeigt werden.
- Ziele des Projektes: 1. Gemeinden gesundes und multikulturelles Essen vorstellen; 2. Menschen, die ansonsten keine Möglichkeiten haben, ein Kino zu besuchen, Filme anbieten; 3. Gemeindemitglieder inspirieren und zur Zusammenkunft motivieren.

E4 Mediation → p. 196

Here are some points you might want to include in your mediation:

- Abu Dhabi planning "green city"
- two German institutes involved in project
- project named *Masdar*: means "source", "fountain"
- project aim: to promote renewable energy resources
- size of city: approximately six million square meters
- Abu Dhabi to enlist scientists from the world's leading research institutes
- aim: to create ecological equivalent of Silicon Valley in the USA
- the city will rely totally on renewable energy

E5 Analysis → p. 197

The following ideas might help you to describe the picture and link it to the text:

- painting
- very colourful
- scene of a futuristic looking city
- foreground: people standing in front of a tall golden building → people appear to be staring up at building
- people are wearing multi-coloured clothing → do not look human
- golden building = temple of some kind?
- background: other high buildings of different colours → smoke coming from the buildings
- sky: large planet → looks like Saturn
- sky is a dark blue: impression of being in space

Connection to Masdar vision of the future:

- picture can be linked to the text in that it shows how cities of the future could look
- may be a utopian vision of the future
- alternatively: may show a more dystopian image → what can happen when development does not work as planned
- perhaps picture shows what may happen when there are too many people → "green" energy is not sufficient / war breaks out, etc. for instance → lot of pollution in this city
- it is possible that the city in the picture started out with utopian ideals, like Masdar, but things did not progress in the right way

E6 a) Comment → p. 197

You might want to consider the following points in your comment:

Arguments for spending one year in Masdar	Arguments against spending one year in Masdar
• wonderful opportunity to be a part of the experiment • chance to live in another part of the world • opportunity to experience renewable energy first hand • learn a lot about using renewable energy • see if such utopian visions can work • Masdar: safe and healthy place to live – no cars, pollution • life would be more convenient and comfortable – new transport system, controlled climate	• miss your family / friends • if you go alone → lonely • Masdar has no natural beauty – mountains, lakes, forests, etc. • if no sense of community, (then) it will not be a pleasant place to live • feeling of claustrophobia could set in after some time • city surrounded by desert • no guarantee everything will function as planned • due to international interest in project, it may be like living in a fish bowl – i.e. under constant observation

Topic 2.8

A3 Comment → p. 205

You might want to consider the following points:

- important for people to be open-minded and tolerant
- people should try to get to know members of other cultures and races and try and understand their traditions and way of life → visit cultural events
- people could join sports or social clubs → meet new people
- parents should be good role models for their children
- children must understand that people cannot be judged on their colour / race / gender / religion
- children must be taught to speak up against racism / prejudice
- encourage mixed-race pre-school → children learn to mix at an early age
- governments / administrations can hire more ethnic minorities

B4 Listening comprehension → p. 207

The following words and phrases might help you with the listening comprehension:

- intelligent, spoke English, embodied compassion, justice and love – showed him the spiritual side of Islam
- US Muslims are patriotic / proud to be American and Muslim
- 2005, 52 killed
- after the attack, Britain realised: violent extremist movements exist
- far right blames immigration

C2 a) Comprehension → p. 209

Here are some key words to help you answer the question:

- African girl from Nigeria
- has experienced war → talks about "the sound of gunfire and the bitter smell of burning thatch behind"
- has a mother and an older sister called Nkiruka
- experienced problems at immigration at the airport
- speaks English; but not "the Queen's English"
- previous experiences with the police
- two years in an immigration detention centre

C3 a) Analysis → p. 209

The following sentences might help you to analyse the text:

- author uses an analogy with a pound coin
- pound coin represents life Little Bee would like to lead, and the experiences she would like to have → this is contrasted with her actual experiences and feelings

Examples:
- "Most days I wish I was a British pound coin instead of an African girl. Everyone would be pleased to see me coming." (ll. 1–2) → pound coin welcome everywhere, but immigrants are not
- "It can cross deserts and oceans and leave the sound of gunfire and the bitter smell of burning thatch behind." (ll. 8–10) → pound coin can go wherever it wants and can escape danger. She, however, was not always safe in Nigeria – needed to find a way to escape

D2 Comprehension → p. 211

Here are some points to help you:

- economic reasons causing immigration
- immigrants crossing the border illegally on foot
- illegal immigration often needs several attempts to succeed
- working as fruit pickers
- low pay for work
- Armando now has papers; feels integrated into US society

D4 Listening comprehension → p. 211

The following words and phrases might help you with the listening comprehension:

- work, house, comfortable life
- group too large, were discovered
- change of guards
- strangers: gave them money for food; Mexican family: shower in their home, fed them, gave them clothes; Mexican restaurant: food; hotel: stay overnight; Armando's cousin: plane ticket to San Francisco
- fruit pickers, canneries, poultry farms, other agricultural areas
- taxes, social security
- refund the workers tax and social security taken from their wages; also, difficult to find people to do the low-paid work if immigrants had the necessary papers to work in better jobs
- hard work, low pay – slave labour

D5 Text production: A letter → p. 211

The following points will help you write the letter:

- just listened to your interview; wanted to write a letter
- interested in your story
- can imagine that it was tough for you – starting work aged 13, picking fruit for low pay
- also difficult for migrant workers in Germany – many from Turkey, Poland, Italy, etc.
- main problems for migrant workers: splitting up of families, language problems, integration, working conditions, insurance.
- some are successful – start a new life for themselves / their families.
- your story is an inspiration

Topic 2.9

A4 a) Analysis → p. 221

Here are some useful keywords to help you explain the quote:

- trade, telecommunications and internet had already "shrunk" the world
- more global companies = more people connected around the world
- technological innovations: faster information, 24/7 news
- low-cost travel: go anywhere, anytime

B3 Listening comprehension: Making globalisation work → p. 223

Use the following points to answer the listening comprehension:

- Problems and anomalies of globalisation: unfair trade regime (blocking development), unstable financial systems, expensive medication not available to places that need it the most, flow of money from poor to rich.
- Effect on French workers: lower wages, less job protection.
- USA's approach: tax cut for rich, reduce welfare state. Results: USA = rich country with poor people.
- Scandanavia's approach: invest in education, research, strong social security system for poor. Result: more productive/competitive economy + higher living standards for majority.
- Solutions to current issue: understand global problems more, look for causes of problems, implement policies that benefit the most people.

C3 Mediation → p. 225

Here are some points to help you with your mediation:

- One advantage of having presence in foreign markets = "brand dependency".
- Global players: offset losses in domestic markets with lucrative international business operations.
- Always growth somewhere in the world.
- Global companies attractive to investors.
- Acting globally = companies can exploit currency exchange rates/spread risk.
- Coca Cola is prime example of globally-active business: brand worth 72 billion US dollars.
- Boeing recovered from setbacks concerning the 'Dreamliner' to receive huge contracts all over the world.
- BASF business model: production facilities are connected – byproducts from one factory used as production materials in another.
- BASF exports production worldwide (China, Malaysia).
- BASF is leading pharmaceutical company: aims to have total turnover of more than 90 billion euros.

D3 b) Analysis → p. 227

Here are some ideas to get you started:

- she is easily distracted – "Until she stood in front of them, Hayley didn't realize how many of her classmates were blond." (ll. 1–2)
- wants to "fit in" – "She'd missed the trend." (l. 2)
- not well educated? – "Before USA countries abolished tax, if you didn't have a job, the Government took money from working people and gave it to you." (ll. 14–15); "Some people say tax is good because it gives money to people who don't have any. But those people must be lazy or stupid, …" (ll. 31–32)
- does not question the state of the world – "Finally I would like to say that America is the greatest group of countries in the world …" (ll. 23–24)

D4 Comment → p. 227

Here are some arguments to help you write the comment:

Agree	Disagree
• Everyday life invaded by brands. • Sponsorship (major sporting events, football teams and television programs, etc.) brings brand names into the home. • People (mostly younger people) can become addicted to brands. • Children bullied in school if they do not wear the "fashionable"/"cool" brands. • Brand consciousness at young age = peer pressure. • Brand names becoming more important than quality products. • People get into debt spending too much money on clothes, electronic devices, etc. that they do not need. • Wearing brand names = walking advertisements for companies. • Result of brand influence: people associate quality with high prices.	• Nothing wrong with brands influencing consumers' buying decisions. • Brands are powerful because products are highest quality. • People not as easily influenced as quote suggests. • Big brands and big companies = more competition amongst businesses = good news for consumers. • Brand names help people choose – for example, if you want to buy a laptop, you can use Apple as a reference point. You know the Apple costs €X, so you can see how good value Brand Y is when it costs €Z. • Influential brand is result of successful company or product – surely the goal of running a business. • Influential brand helps the consumer make the right choice.

Topic 2.10

A2 a) Comprehension → p. 237

Here are some keywords to help you answer the question:

- Russian women: deodorant for special occasions only
- consequence: low sales for deodorant companies
- solution: funny ad campaign
- idea behind campaign: use cultural attitudes towards beauty, glamour and embarrassment
- result: successful ad; increased deodorant sales in Russia

B3 Mediation → p. 239

The following keywords might help you with your mediation:

- new technologies in cars will become decisive in choosing a car
- automobile industry sees internet as opportunity for growth
- in 2011 around 15 million IVIs sold
- 35 million IVIs by 2015
- car makers need to keep up with the latest consumer electronics to remain competitive
- more than 42 million cars connected to the Internet by 2017 – approximately one million in 2009
- people want the same connectivity and entertainment in their cars as they enjoy at home

B4 Analysis → p. 239

The following sentences might help you to analyse the cartoon:

- cartoon shows two women jogging
- one of the women is carrying a small handheld device
- device is called iPed and is clearly inspired by Apple products
- woman is explaining that it has many different functions
- one function is an application that points out the nearest ice cream parlor and cake shops
- what makes the situation funny is the fact that the two women are obviously trying to be healthy; however, they seem to be using the new iPed to locate places where you can buy unhealthy food
- cartoon relates to the text as it shows people's desire to be connected, entertained and informed anytime, anywhere
- iPed demonstrates our desire for new "gadgets" that we believe make our life more interesting or easier

C3 Analysis → p. 241

The following sentences might help you to analyse the cartoon:

- three people standing at a bus stop, waiting for the bus
- people are standing next to bus shelter, in the rain, and they all look very unhappy
- inside the bus shelter: speaker playing an advertisement, telling the people to buy things
- seems as if people would rather stand in the rain than listen to advertisement in bus shelter
- could suggest that people are tired of hearing / seeing ads everywhere
- relation to text: people being exposed to advertising more and more
- text suggests: people would be unhappy about being monitored and tracked; cartoon shows: people trying to get away from advertising

E4 Comment → p. 245

You might want to consider the following points:

Arguments for	Arguments against
• most Hollywood stars / music stars are good looking • for many (often highly-paid) jobs, attractiveness is a prerequisite • attractive people often use their good looks to get what they want • good-looking people are often more self-confident • attractive people often climb the career ladder more easily • by nature, humans are drawn to physical beauty • not so attractive people have to work harder to be noticed / have to distinguish themselves through their skills	• for the most important / influential jobs in the world looks are not as important • some of the most famous / successful actors and musicians are not good-looking in the classical sense • skills, knowledge and experience are more important in gaining success than good looks • charisma, sense of humour and intellect have no relation to physical appearance • not everybody is impressed or influenced by good looks • some attractive people might even have to work harder to prove that they are "more than just a pretty face"

Aspekt	Gewicht	Note	sehr gut	gut	befriedigend	ausreichend	mangelhaft	ungenügend
		Punkte	15 14 13	12 11 10	9 8 7	6 5 4	3 2 1	0
Wortebene	**Allgemeiner Wortschatz**		sehr differenziert, treffsicher und umfangreich, sehr hoher Grad an Korrektheit	differenziert und meist treffend, hoher Grad an Korrektheit	weniger differenziert bei vermehrter Fehlerzahl	begrenzt, teils ungenau, recht hohe Fehlerzahl	deutlich begrenzt, Verständlichkeit beeinträchtigt, hohe Fehlerzahl	stark begrenzt, Verständlichkeit erheblich beeinträchtigt, sehr hohe Fehlerzahl
	Fachwortschatz, Funktionswortschatz		sehr differenziert, treffsicher und umfangreich, sehr hoher Grad an Korrektheit	differenziert und meist treffend, hoher Grad an Korrektheit	weniger differenziert bei vermehrter Fehlerzahl	begrenzt, teils ungenau, recht hohe Fehlerzahl	deutlich begrenzt, Verständlichkeit beeinträchtigt, hohe Fehlerzahl	stark begrenzt, Verständlichkeit erheblich beeinträchtigt, sehr hohe Fehlerzahl
Satzebene	**Grammatische Strukturen**		sehr hoher Grad an Korrektheit	hoher Grad an Korrektheit	grundlegende Beherrschung trotz vermehrter Fehlerzahl	noch angemessene Beherrschung, recht hohe Fehlerzahl	hohe Fehlerzahl, zum Teil auch bei elementaren Strukturen	durchgängige Verstöße, auch bei elementaren Strukturen
	Satzbau und Satzverknüpfungen, Idiomatik		sehr differenziert und variantenreich, treffsichere Verwendung auch von idiomatischen Konstruktionen	differenziert und variabel, gelegentliche Verwendung von idiomatischen Konstruktionen; meist treffende Verwendung von Konstruktionen	eher einfache Konstruktionen, erkennbare Variabilität	meist einfache Konstruktionen, kaum Variabilität, gelegentliche Stilbrüche	sehr einfacher Satzbau, keine Variabilität, Verständlichkeit beeinträchtigt auch durch unidiomatische Wendungen und zahlreiche Stilbrüche	durchgängig sprachuntypische Syntax, Text wirkt wie übersetzt, Verständlichkeit erheblich beeinträchtigt
Textebene	**Aufbau / Gedankenführung**		sehr stringent, komplex und differenziert, überzeugende Hervorhebung und Verbindung von Gedanken; sinnvoller und funktionaler Einsatz von Zitaten, in hohem Maße eigenständig, flüssig	klar, stringent, nachvollziehbare Schlussfolgerungen; überzeugende Darstellung von Aspekten; eigenständige Leistung, flüssig	Gliederung und gedankliche Zusammenhänge nachvollziehbar; zum Teil Anlehnung an Vorlage	Gliederungselemente und gedankliche Zusammenhänge erkennbar, Schwächen im logischen Aufbau, häufige Anlehnung an Vorlage	mangelnde oder widersprüchliche Gliederungselemente, teils zusammenhanglos, sehr enge Anlehnung an Vorlage	unzureichende Strukturierung, Aufbau und Gedankenführung zusammenhanglos, übernommene Passagen
	aufgabenformattypische Versprachlichung		souveräne Beherrschung des zu erstellenden Textformats; überzeugende Anwendung der entsprechenden sprachlichen Konventionen	sichere Beherrschung des zu erstellenden Textformats, sprachliche Konventionen getroffen	angemessene Beherrschung des zu erstellenden Textformats, sprachliche Konventionen weitgehend getroffen bzw. dem Zieltext angemessen	durch Aufgabenformat vorgegebene Textsorte erkennbar, formattypische Merkmale stellenweise vorhanden	nur Ansätze der Konventionen der zu erstellenden Textsorte erkennbar	Versprachlichung insgesamt nicht der Textsorte entsprechend, erforderliche sprachliche Konventionen nicht beherrscht

Listening

As with all comprehension, watch out for **key words** and try to get the gist.

When you are involved in a **conversation** (e.g. on the telephone) or asked to interpret for someone, you can always request the speaker to **repeat or explain** what you haven't understood. When you not only hear but also see people talk, their **body language** helps you to understand what they say.

Announcements contain important information, usually in clear, simple language. They are often **repeated** several times to make sure everyone understands them.

Following **radio programmes** is more difficult because the only help you can get is from the speakers' **intonation**.

Be aware of the most important differences between **British and American English**, and be prepared for other variations such as **regional pronunciation**.

When you listen to **longer speeches or interviews**, take notes in a systematic way, e.g. in a grid or a checklist.

Useful phrases

Excuse me, can you say that again, please? • Could you repeat that for me, please? • Sorry, I don't understand the word … • What does it mean? • Can you spell that for me, please? • Have I got that right? • Sorry, would you mind explaining that again, please?

Skimming

Skimming means finding the **main ideas in a text** in order to get an impression of its content.

- Read the title, the introduction or the first paragraph, the first sentence of every paragraph and any headings and sub-headings.
- Note any pictures, charts or graphs.
- Pay attention to any words or phrases in italics or bold print.
- Read the last paragraph, which often offers a short summary of the text.

Scanning

Scanning is useful for finding **specific information** quickly, e.g. you have a question in mind and read a passage to find the answer.

- Decide what **specific information** you are looking for. Ignore unrelated information.
- Look out for **relevant key words**. Stop when you find one and read that part of the text carefully. Make notes if necessary.
- How might the information be given in the text? For example, if you need a date, only look at the numbers in the text.
- **Headings** can help you to identify sections which might contain the information.
- **The first sentence** in a paragraph should indicate whether the information you need could be there, or not. Do not read the text in detail.

Understanding non-fictional texts

A **non-fictional text** is a text whose **content is based on facts**. The writer refers to people and places which really exist and incidents which really took place. Typical examples are **newspaper** or **magazine articles**, **essays**, **comments** or **advertisements**.

1 Reading a non-fictional text

- Read the text carefully.
- Look up unknown vocabulary if necessary, but try to concentrate only on key words that block your understanding of the text.
- Ask yourself the following questions and write notes:
  What type of text is it? • What is its central idea / main theme / message? Can you state it in a single sentence?
- Structure the text. Divide it into different units and underline important passages.

2 Understanding a non-fictional text

What kind of text is it?

- What kind of text is it? A newspaper / magazine article, an essay, etc.?
- Who is the author?
- When was it written?
- Where was it published? In a newspaper, on the Internet, etc.?
- Why was it written? What is the target group?

What is the text about?

- What is the central idea / main theme / message?
- What parts can it be divided into?
- What is the purpose of the text?
- What is the author's point of view / intention?
- What arguments or examples does the author use?
- What is special about the text?

Newspaper reports

We are confronted with a wide range of different newspapers from all around the world. On the one hand there are quality newspapers. They present the news in a neutral way and separate information from opinion so that the reader can form his /her own view. On the other hand, there are popular newspapers (tabloids). Their news reports are often sensational with big pictures and headlines. Popular newspapers often mix information and opinion, offering the reader a ready-made opinion.

Example:

quality newspaper **popular newspaper**

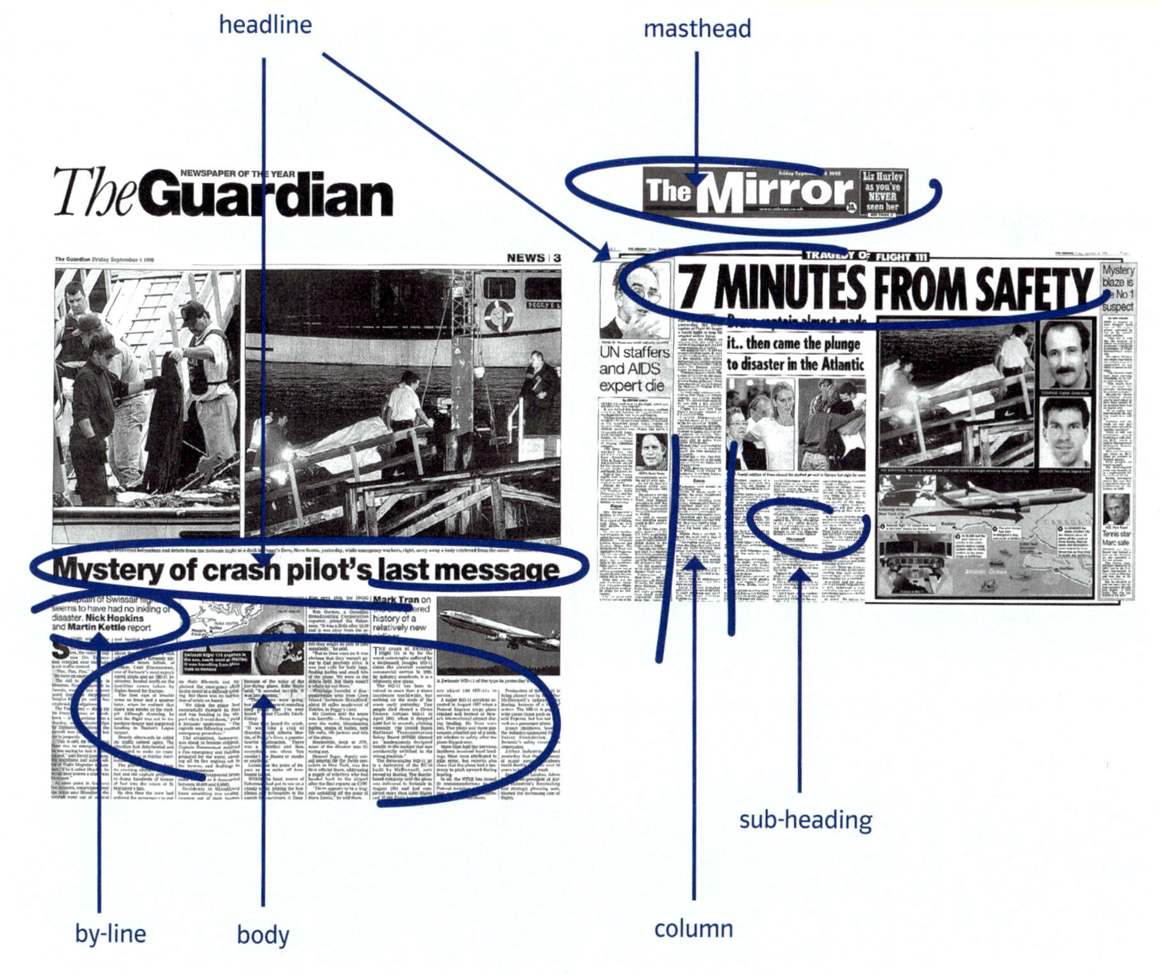

Understanding fictional texts

A **fictional text** is a literary work whose content is based on the **imagination of the author** and not necessarily on facts. There are three **literary genres: poetry** (poems, songs), **drama** (plays) and **fiction** (novels, short stories, fables, fairy tales, etc.).
By reading a fictional text, the reader is transferred into a different world and the author's intention is often a matter of interpretation. Pictures in the reader's mind are produced to create a new reality, and atmosphere and emotions are often more important than hard facts.

1 Reading a fictional text

- Read the text carefully.
- Look up unknown vocabulary if necessary, but try to concentrate only on key words that block your understanding of the text.
- Ask yourself the following questions and write notes:
  What is the story about? • What is its central idea/main theme / message? Can you state it in a single sentence?
- Structure the text. Divide it into different units and underline important passages.

2 Understanding a fictional text

When you analyse a text, you should follow these steps. Answer the questions and write notes.

What kind of text is it?
- What is the literary genre of the text? Poetry, drama or fiction?
- What kind of text is it (poem, song, short story, etc.)?
- Who is the author and when was it written?

What is the text about?
- What is the central idea / main theme / message?
- Who is the narrator?
- What is the setting?
- What is the plot?
- Who are the characters?

How we learn about the characters in a story:
- outward appearance
- language
- actions, behaviour, mood
- main traits
- motives, influences from the past
- roles, social background
- character's function in the constellation of characters

3 Character grid

outward appearance	*athletic, attractive, blond, elegant, fat, tall, young, …*
language	*excited, gentle, polite, rude, …*
actions, behaviour, mood	*angry, embarrassed, emotional, irresponsible, terrified, upset, …*
main traits	*honest, intelligent, jealous, kind, show-off, shy, sympathetic, violent, …*
roles, social background	*boss, daughter, girlfriend, broken home, criminal, lonely, married, rich, …*
function in the constellation of characters	*enemy, friend, rival, …*

4 Special features of the text

- What parts can it be divided into?
- Is there a turning point in the plot?
- What kind of language is used?
- What atmosphere is created and how?
- What else is special about the text?

The features of a short story

A **short story** is a short fictional prose text which is meant to be read in a single sitting. It can be as short as 500 and as long as 15,000 words. A lot of short stories follow different patterns but the following points apply to many of them.

- There may be one main **character** or a group of equally important characters.
- There is often only a single **setting** (i.e. the time and place of the action does not change). Longer short stories might have more than one setting.
- The setting helps to create a certain atmosphere.
- The reader may be led into the story through an **exposition**.
- In modern stories the action often starts in the first sentence.
- The action develops logically through **conflicts or crises**, reaching a climax or **turning-point** near or at the end (emphasis on action and suspense).
- Some stories concentrate on a decisive moment in the main character's life (emphasis on character and psychology).
- There is often a surprise **ending**, a happy / unhappy ending or an open ending.

The features of a play

Plays are very different from short stories or poems because they are not written to be read but to be **performed** and **watched**. Outside school or university, people do not normally sit down to read a play, unless they are planning a trip to the theatre. When a **playwright** or **dramatist** sits down to put pen to paper, he has **directors, stage managers** and **actresses / actors** in mind.

- A dramatic text usually consists of two parts: **dialogue** and **stage directions**. In a play, **dialogue** covers all the spoken language, not only the conversation of two characters.
- The **stage directions** give information about how to perform the play. This might refer to the setting, scenery, the characters' movements, tone of voice, etc.
- When you analyse a play, look at the **setting**, the **action** and the **characters** (→ Understanding fictional texts p. 322).
- Don't forget to describe the **atmosphere** of the play.
- Finally, give an **interpretation** of the play.

Dealing with poetry

Poetry may look shorter than other literary forms, but it can be more demanding. Here are some ideas on how to improve your feeling for and understanding of poetry.

- Read the poem and try to get the gist or message of the poem first. Then sum it up in your own words.
- Read the poem aloud to stress the relationship between certain words and ideas.
- Take a close look at structure and form:

stanza: the way the lines of a poem are grouped together
rhyme pattern: groups of words that rhyme
repetition: when words or sounds are repeated

- Look for comparisons and contrasts (metaphors and similes). Identify images and symbols, and what impressions or ideas they give you.
- Find devices that are used to bring out certain feelings and to create an atmosphere, e.g. colours, sounds.
- Describe any characters who appear in the poem.
- Who is the speaker? What do we learn about the setting?

Example:

Films

Some films are sad – you watch them and cry. A
You know that the hero is going to die. A

Some films have spies – they fight, run and jump. B
When they crash their cars, there's a very big bump! B

Sometimes aliens come down from space. C
That often means trouble for the human race. C

And then there are ghost films – ghosts come out at night D
And give everybody an awful fright. D

But the worst films are love films where all the stars kiss. E
Those are the films that I want to miss! E

William Sears

stanza: five stanzas with two lines each
rhyme pattern: AABBCCDDEE
repetitions: some(times) (lines 1, 3, 5), you (lines 1, 2), films (lines 1, 3, 7, 9, 10)

Useful phrases

The poem consists of / is divided into … stanzas / sections / lines … • It has an unusual layout. • It follows a clear rhyme scheme. • It is an example of unrhymed verse. • The rrangement of the rhymes is … (e. g. aabb). • A number of lines do not rhyme at all. • Lines x and y rhyme. • The poet aims to express a certain message poetically. • The vocabulary is simple / difficult. • The words mainly belong to the word field of … • The repetition of the words '…' creates a … atmosphere. • There is a strong contrast between '…' and '…'. The tone of the poem is serious / calm / sad / ironical / cheerful / … This is heightened by words such as …

Dealing with songs

Songs are **similar to poems**, but they additionally contain a **musical aspect**, which is particularly important. It is always useful to look for background information on the songwriter and / or the artist performing the song, who shouldn't be confused as they aren't necessarily the same person. Look at all the information you have got. If something is missing that could help you to understand the song better, try to find out more. The Internet is probably the best source of information for you. You can follow these steps:

Background information
- What is the title of the song?
- Who is / are the singer(s) / the band?
- Who wrote the lyrics? Who wrote the music?
- When was the song written?
- Was the song a success?

Music
- What kind of music is it?
- What instruments are used?
- What does it sound like?
- Can you describe the rhythm?
- What feelings are created by the music?
- What is the structure of the song (verses, chorus)?

Lyrics
- Examine the song text (verses and chorus). Look at form, structure and the language which is used (→ Dealing with poetry p. 324).
- Do the lyrics tell a story? What happens and what is the setting?
- What feelings are expressed by the words?
- Is there a message?

Comprehension questions

There is no general rule for answering comprehension questions. However, the following guidelines can be helpful:

- If the task refers to the text, **scan** the text for points you want to use, **take notes** and order them.
- For an **introductory sentence** it can be useful to refer to the words used in the task.
- Sometimes it is unavoidable to use the words from the text but you should try to use **your own words** as much as possible.
- Use **linking words** or **connectives** to show the logical development of different points, ideas or arguments of your answer.
- If your text is longer, divide it into **paragraphs**.
- Find a sentence that **concludes** your answer adequately and has the form of a general statement.

Text analysis

For all texts
- text type
- author
- target group
- purpose
- (historical) context
- structure
- language, register, style and tone
- relationship between style and content
- atmosphere
- other remarkable features
- effect on the reader
- your personal impression (if asked for)

For literary texts
- literary genre
- narrator and point of view
- setting
- characters (direct / indirect characterisation)
- main theme
- plot
- exposition, climax, turning point, rising / falling action, dénouement
- narrative techniques (chronology, frame story, suspense, tone, descriptions, comments, etc.)

Tips
- Secure your comprehension of the text by looking for keywords and taking notes.
- Considering background information about the text, its historical context, and its author can be helpful.
- Answer questions on the text precisely and to the point. Watch out for the way questions are asked: Do exactly as you are told when you are asked to *analyse, examine, describe, discuss, compare, summarise, interpret* or *comment* on things.
- Don't forget to relate the individual points to each other, i.e. look for similarities or contrasts in the characters, the atmosphere, the language, and find reasons for the author's choice of genre and style for a particular content.
- Explain everything in your own words, but use quotations from the text to support your statements, marking them clearly as quotations and giving line references.
- Clearly distinguish between facts and your interpretation.
- Avoid repetition.
- Never state your opinion without giving reasons, and only if you are asked.
- When you write about a text, think of using connectives and structuring devices as well as suitable adjectives and adverbs to give precise descriptions of characters, action and circumstances.

Writing a comment

An comment is a **clearly structured** piece of writing in which important arguments on a topic are presented.

Comments are generally written in the **simple present**. When you are asked to write a comment, always read the task carefully.

1 Preparation

- **Define** the topic clearly.
- **Brainstorm ideas**. Write down what you know about the topic in a word web, diagram or table.
- If necessary, **collect facts, arguments and other information**.
- Formulate your **opinion** on the topic.

2 Arranging your material

- Decide on the **most important facts, arguments or pieces of information** that you want to include.
- For each main argument try to think of two **supporting arguments**.
- Put your facts or arguments in a **logical order**. For example, you could:
  - start with general ideas and then go on to talk about details.
  - put things into chronological order.
  - start by giving all the arguments in favour and then give all the counterarguments.
  - follow each argument in favour with a counter-argument.

3 Writing your comment

The introductory paragraph
- The introductory paragraph should **introduce your topic** and catch the reader's interest.
- In your introductory paragraph you should also:
  - say clearly what your comment is going to be about in one or two sentences.
  - ask a question or questions which you will answer in your text.
  - give a **brief outline** of the problem / topic.

The main paragraphs
- Start a **new paragraph for each new idea**.
- Begin each paragraph with a **main idea or argument**.
- Write simple sentences.
- Arrange sentences in a logical order.
- Join sentences using suitable **connectives**.
- Use adverbs to emphasise points.
- Use **examples** where possible.

The conclusion
- Do not introduce new ideas!
- Make a **brief concluding statement** summarising what you have said in your comment.

4 Checking your comment

- Check that all your **sentences are complete** and that they make sense.
- Check your comment for **grammar, spelling and punctuation** mistakes.

5 Writing a model comment

Expressing your opinion To be quite honest, I do not think that/I cannot (fully) agree with …/I am not convinced by …/ I would like to question the view that …/I reject the idea that … • In my opinion/view this argument is wrong/weak/unconvincing because …	I do not think anyone would disagree • In fact/As a matter of fact, I believe it is fully justified to say that … • I am of exactly the same opinion as … • I share the view that … • To my mind, … • this argument is very strong/powerful/convincing/plausible
Making concessions To a certain extent, I can accept … • However, we shouldn't forget that … • Most of the arguments are hard to dismiss. • Yet there are experts who … • I agree in principle, but … • Personally, I would not go so far as to say that … • Although …, we should accept/must admit that … • In spite of all this, … • Admittedly, …, but …	**Giving arguments/reasons** One reason for my criticism/scepticism is that … • Another/A second/A further/An additional argument I would like to present is that … • I would also argue that … • Another point I would like to make is that … • The main reason, however, is that … • The most convincing argument is that … • That brings me neatly to my final and most important point: …
Your conclusion/summary To sum up, … • In short, … • Considering all these arguments, … • I would conclude that … • I have come to the conclusion that … • It is safe to say that … • I would support the view that … • My suggestion is that … • My appeal to … is: … • In conclusion … • Having weighed up all the arguments, I would like to	

Writing a newspaper/magazine article

The following steps can help you to write a newspaper or magazine article:

- Remember the **ABC of news writing**:
  Accuracy (be exact, all the facts have to be correct)
  Brevity (keep it short and to the point)
  Clarity (make sure everyone understands).
- Remember also the five Ws: **Who? What? When? Where? Why?** (sometimes How? and So what?)
- Give **answers** to these questions.
- Attract the **reader's attention** with the headline and the lead, which is usually the first word, sentence or paragraph of the story. The lead contains the most important, most exciting point and makes the reader go on reading.
- The **structure of a newspaper article** is basically an inverted pyramid: The most important thing is at the top, in the lead. More facts and additional details follow, the least important ones at the end, so that you can stop reading any time after the lead should you feel you have enough information. If the story is written well, however, or if you are interested in the details, you can read on till the end.
- Good news **style** is **active, informative, to the point**. Nothing is repeated and nothing is said that is not necessary. Everything must be logical and easy to understand.
- News articles often contain **anecdotes, examples and quotes**. If you use quotes when writing, make sure they express the speaker's intention. Without the right context, they may be misunderstood. Only use them when they make a point clearer.
- A **good ending** rewards the reader for finishing the article by making some kind of reference to the lead.

5 Writing a model comment

Expressing your opinion
To be quite honest, I do not think that/I cannot (fully) agree with …/I am not convinced by …/ I would like to question the view that …/I reject the idea that … • In my opinion/view this argument is wrong/weak/unconvincing because …

I do not think anyone would disagree • In fact/As a matter of fact, I believe it is fully justified to say that … • I am of exactly the same opinion as … • I share the view that … • To my mind, … • this argument is very strong/powerful/convincing/plausible

Making concessions
To a certain extent, I can accept … • However, we shouldn't forget that … • Most of the arguments are hard to dismiss. • Yet there are experts who … • I agree in principle, but … • Personally, I would not go so far as to say that … • Although …, we should accept/must admit that … • In spite of all this, … • Admittedly, …, but …

Giving arguments / reasons
One reason for my criticism/scepticism is that … • Another/A second/A further/An additional argument I would like to present is that … • I would also argue that … • Another point I would like to make is that … • The main reason, however, is that … • The most convincing argument is that … • That brings me neatly to my final and most important point: …

Your conclusion/summary
To sum up, … • In short, … • Considering all these arguments, … • I would conclude that … • I have come to the conclusion that … • It is safe to say that … • I would support the view that … • My suggestion is that … • My appeal to … is: … • In conclusion … • Having weighed up all the arguments, I would like to

Writing an email

From: r.moll@doppelsechssports…de
To: purchasing@citysports.co…uk
Cc: s.bauder@ doppelsechssports…de
Sent: 20…-12-04 13:34
Attachments: Doppel Sechs Winter Specials.pdf
Subject: Order Confirmation_15 May

Dear Mr Warren ← *Salutation*

Thank you for your order of 21 February. I can herein confirm that 22 units of item number WSB554, 18 units of item number QPR414, and 16 units of item number MUX982 have been dispatched to the given delivery address. Please find attached our Winter Specials catalogue, with many special offers for the Christmas and New Year season. If you require any further information or have any queries, please do not hesitate to contact us. ← *Body of email*

Kind regards ← *Complimentary close*

Roman Moll ← *Signature block*
Senior Export Clerk

Roman Moll ← *Signature footer*
Doppel Sechs Sports
Hohe Straße 6
50667 Köln
Germany
Tel: + 49 221 4569…
Email: info@doppelsechssports…de
ww#.doppelsechssports…de

From:	The sender's email address will appear here automatically.
To:	Pay attention when writing the recipient's email address. One small typing mistake and the email will either be sent to the wrong person, or returned.
Cc:	This stands for 'carbon copy'. Here you enter the email address of anybody you would like to also receive the message.
Bcc:	This stands for 'blind carbon copy'. This has the same function as 'carbon copy' but the addresses under Bcc do not appear in the message header of the other recipients.
Sent:	This may also be labeled 'Date'. The correct date and time the message was sent will be added automatically.
Attachments:	Any kind of file, such as MS Word (.doc), MS Excel (.xls), PDF (.pdf) or pictures (.jpg) can be attached to an email.

Subject:	You should always mention the precise subject of your email. This will help all people involved deal with the mail, and will prevent it from being deleted.
Salutation:	Very formal salutations such as 'Dear Sirs' are not used in emails. Instead use 'Dear …' wherever possible. In the English-speaking world emails are personalised as often as possible – Dear Ms Dietrich, Dear Kevin, etc. To avoid 'Dear Sirs' you can use 'Dear East Slope Furnishings'.
Body of the email:	Begin the first word with a capital letter.
Compliment-ary close:	There are a number of expressions to choose from: Best/Kind regards Best wishes Regards Yours sincerely (considered very formal in emails)
Signature block:	Write your job title or department underneath your name.
Signature footer:	Write your company's full name, address and telephone number.

Writing a diary / blog entry

- When you write a diary or blog entry, it is often necessary to **slip into the role of a different character**.
- Try to put yourself into the character's situation (age, background, job, sex, etc.).
- Try to imagine **the character's thoughts, feelings and ideas**.
- Although in a diary entry the main focus is on the past, present emotions and dreams and hopes about the future may also play a role.
- Write your entry from the **first-person point of view**.

Writing a personal letter

A **personal letter** is a letter you write to someone you know well **on a personal basis**, e.g. a friend or relative. There are no special rules which you have to follow when you write to people you know well. The model letter below shows you what an informal letter generally looks like in English. You can use **informal language** in a personal letter, as if you were speaking to the person.

Thomas Reiter
Dinkelstr. 1
70183 Stuttgart
Germany

Your address goes in the top right hand corner.

May 3, 20...

Write the date under the address.

Start the letter: Dear + name

Dear Frank

Use a capital letter for the first word.

Just a few lines to let you know I'm still alive! Sorry for not having written for so long, but I've been very busy at college with exams.

How are things with you? What are you doing for the summer? Unfortunately my applications for jobs in the States have all been turned down so far. Oh well, I'll keep trying...

Group your news, etc. in paragraphs.

Please drop me a line when you have a minute. We really must keep in touch. Give my regards to the family.

Finish the letter with one of these phrases: All the best • Best wishes • Bye for now • Love • Lots of love

All the best

Thomas

P.S. If I do get to the States, I'll let you know my address. Maybe we'll be able to meet up!

Writing a formal letter

A formal letter can be **a letter of application, a reservation, a request for information**, etc. **Commercial correspondence** refers to formal letters written in a business context, i. e. from one company to another. There are different ways of layouting these types of letters. The model letter below is in 'block form', which is probably the best to use because it is accepted everywhere. The parts in **blue** are only necessary in **commercial correspondence**.

Punctuation: In 'block style' you don't use commas in the address, salutation or complimentary close.

Weltweit Services
Thomas Reiter
Dinkelstr. 1
70183 Stuttgart
Germany
Tel: 0711 7682...
Fax: 0711 7682...
Email:
ww#.

Writer's address. In commercial correspondence you should include the company name, telephone, email, Internet address and fax number.

Addressee, including name and position, if known.

Personnel Manager
Import Export
11270 White Blvd.
Los Angeles CA 91430
USA

Your ref:
Our ref: TR

In commercial correspondence include references. 'Our ref:' is usually the initials of the person who wrote the letter. (TR = Thomas Reiter)

11 January 20...

Date: The British write day, month, year (11.1.200...). Americans write month, day, year (1.11.200...). So it is best to write the date in full to avoid confusion.

Dear Mr ... / Ms ...

In commercial correspondence include a subject line beginning 'Re:'.

Re: Your advertisement in the Sun Times of April 28

With reference to your advertisement in the Sun Times of April 28, I would like to apply for the position of bilingual buying assistant.

I am particularly interested in this job as I would very much like to gain work experience abroad. As well as speaking fluent English and Spanish, I have a working knowledge of French. My mother tongue is of course German.

I can supply references from former employers if you wish.

I enclose my curriculum vitae. Please do not hesitate to contact me if you should require further information.

Main part of letter: State your reason for writing in formal, polite language. Group your points in paragraphs.

Complimentary close

Yours sincerely

Signature

Thomas Reiter

Name in full

Thomas Reiter

In commercial correspondence: Writer's position in company.

Trainee buyer

Enc.

Enc. = Enclosures: Indicates that additional material is being sent with the letter.

Salutation	When used	Complimentary close
Dear Sir or Madam	to a company and when you don't know the person's name or sex	Yours faithfully
Dear Madam	to a woman, when you don't know her name	Yours faithfully
Dear Sir	to a man, when you don't know his name	Yours faithfully
Dear Mr Brown	to a man, whose name you know	Yours sincerely
Dear Ms / Mrs Brown	to a woman, whose name you know	Yours sincerely
Note: Nowadays the use of *Yours faithfully* and *Yours sincerely* is not always divided up as strictly as given above.		

Useful phrases

Explaining the purpose of the letter
We are writing / I am writing … • in connection with … • … with reference / regard to … • … to advise you of … • … to confirm … • … to let you know … • … to tell you that … • … to ask / enquire (whether) … • …to inform you of … • … to request you to …

Stating a reference
Thank you for your mail of July 1st. • Many thanks for your letter dated 26th July. • We refer to your order for … • I have received your enquiry regarding … • Further to our telephone conversation today, … • With reference to your mail of June 5th, … • With regard to your enquiry of June 5th about …

Giving good news
I am delighted to tell you that … • You will be pleased to hear that …

Giving bad news
We regret to inform you that … • I am afraid that … • We are sorry to have to tell you that … • Unfortunately we are unable to …

Making a request
Please … • Please could you … ? • Could you possibly…? • We would be grateful if you could/would … • We would be much obliged if you could … • I would appreciate it if you could … • … would be very much appreciated.

Offering help
If you wish, we would be happy to … • Would you like us to …? • At your request we would gladly …

Giving information
We wish to advise you that … • We are pleased to inform you that … • For your information: …

Enclosing documents
I am enclosing … • Please find enclosed … • Please find attached … (= attachment / papers fixed to the letter with a paper clip / …)

Thanking
Thank you for sending me … • Many thanks for … • I am grateful to you for … • I am much obliged to you for sending me … (formal)

Useful phrases

Apologising
I am sorry about the delay in replying. • We were (very / extremely / most) sorry to hear about the problem. • We regret that this problem has occured. • We apologize for any inconvenience caused.

Assuring
Please rest assured that we will do our utmost to help you. • We assure you that we will do our best to put the matter right. • We promise to look into the matter immediately. • You can count on us to ensure smooth delivery in future.

Making concessions
We agree to reduce the price by (percentage / sum of money). • We are happy to grant you a discount of 3% on the goods. • We will let you have the goods at a reduced price of …

Closing remarks
If you have any questions, please do not hesitate to call me / us on (tel. no.). • Should you have any questions, feel free to contact me / us. • If you require further information, please do get in touch / ask. • Should you require further details, please contact us again. • If we can help in any way, we would be happy to be of assistance.

Referring to future contact
We look forward to hearing from you soon / meeting you next week / seeing you on the 29th. • We are looking forward to receiving your proposal / order.

Writing an enquiry

East Slope Furnishings
32 North Street
Brighton
BN1 2RG
Tel: + 44 1273 6307…
Email: purchasing@esfurnishings.co…uk
ww#.esfurnishings.co…uk

Möbelwelt GmbH
Gaußstraße 7
51503 Rösrath
Germany

Your ref:
Our ref: ELG/ag

17 November 20…

Dear Sir or Madam

Re: Product enquiry

Your address was passed on to us by a business partner who recommended your products. Our company, East Slope Furnishings, is a young and rapidly growing home furnishing company with outlets in six cities across the south of England. We supply affordable and stylish furniture and home accessories.

Source of address

Introduce your company

We have visited your website and were very impressed with your product range. Consequently, we are interested in adding a number of your products to our collection.

Reason for enquiry

Could you please send us a copy of your latest brochure and an up-to-date price list? Please also supply us with information regarding your terms of payment, delivery times, possible discounts, as well as the minimum quantity for a trial order.

Ask for further information – sales literature, terms and conditions, delivery times, etc.

Thank you in advance and we look forward to hearing from you.

Polite ending

Yours faithfully

E. Lloréns Gómez
Elisabet Lloréns Gómez
Purchasing manager

Writing an offer

Möbelwelt GmbH
Gaußstraße 7
51503 Rösrath
Germany
Tel: + 49 2205 4569...
Email: info@moebelwelt...de
ww#.moebelwelt...de

East Slope Furnishings
32 North Street
Brighton
BN1 2RG

Your ref: ELG/ag
Our ref: MD/jh

24 November 20...

Dear Ms Lloréns Gómez

Re: Your enquiry of 17 November 20...

Thank you very much for your enquiry of 17 November. We are pleased to hear of your interest in stocking our products in your store.

Reference to enquiry

Please find enclosed, as requested, a copy of our latest brochure as well as an up-to-date price list.

Respond to enquiry / make offer

Our prices are quoted DDP Brighton and Möbelwelt GmbH has a minimum order policy of 100 for deliveries to the United Kingdom. Nevertheless, trial orders can be arranged on an individual basis. Please also refer to our catalogue and website for special offers.

Our usual terms of payment are bank transfer to our account with the European Bank within 30 days from date of invoice. Regular customers are granted open account terms.

State terms of delivery and payment

Standard delivery times to the United Kingdom are 2-3 working days, although express overnight delivery is available on some orders.

Refer to the delivery time

Should you have any further questions or queries, please do not hesitate to contact us.

Polite ending / creating goodwill

Yours sincerely

M. Dietrich
Meike Dietrich
Senior Export Clerk

Enc.

Writing an order

East Slope Furnishings
32 North Street
Brighton
BN1 2RG
Tel: + 44 1273 6307…
Email: purchasing@esfurnishings.co…uk
ww#.esfurnishings.co…uk

Möbelwelt GmbH
Gaußstraße 7
51503 Rösrath
Germany

Your Ref: MD/jh
Our ref: ELG/ag

30 November 20…

Dear Ms Dietrich

Re: Your offer of 24 November 20...

Thank you very much for sending us your brochure and price list. We also appreciate you outlining your delivery terms and conditions. ← *Reference to offer / previous contacts*

We have studied your catalogue and are very impressed with your products. We would like to order 16 units of item number AQW445 and 16 units of item number AQR457. ← *Place an order*

As agreed, we will make payment by bank transfer to the previously named bank within 30 days from date of invoice. Delivery is to be made DDP Brighton. ← *Confirm method of payment / terms of delivery / delivery time*

We look forward receiving the goods in time and to doing further business with you in the future. ← *Polite ending / creating goodwill*

Yours sincerely

E. Lloréns Gómez
Elisabet Lloréns Gómez
Purchasing manager

Writing a CV

CV is short for 'Curriculum Vitae'. There are no rules about how to write a CV in English. Use the following 'Dos and Don'ts' and the model CV below as a guide.

Dos

Do include skills and interests which are relevant to the job, if possible.
Do give the English equivalents of German terms, where possible.

Don'ts

Don't write more than one page.
Don't necessarily include a photo, unless asked to.
Don't use handwriting for your CV.
Don't sign your name at the end.

Curriculum Vitae

Name:	Ute Braun
Address:	Musterstraße 1, 50400 Köln, Germany
Telephone:	0211 / 2345...
Email:	u.braun@e-mail...de
Date of birth:	6.5.1988
Nationality:	German
Schools attended:	2004–2006: Language College, Stuttgart 1997–2004: Pfeiffer Realschule (Comprehensive)
Qualifications:	Diploma course as a bilingual secretary (English, Spanish)
Work experience:	July 2005 – September 2005: kitchen work at McDougall's July 2004 – September 2004: office assistant in the export department of Bosch
Skills, Interests and Experience:	fluent English and Spanish, a working knowledge of French; good computer skills (Word, Excel); clean driving license; tennis and member of the local repertory company (latest role: the Nurse in Romeo and Juliet)

Describing pictures

1 Types of pictures

photo(graph) • print • transparency • slide • painting • drawing • sketch • picture • illustration • image • collage • electronic image • snapshot • skyline • panorama • close-up • action photo • still (from a film) • scene • sequence

2 Describing a picture

First impression
- Where is the image from?
- What type of image is it?
- What does the image (roughly) show?
- Who created it?
- When and why was it drawn / taken?

Description
- Describe in detail what can be seen in the picture.
- Talk about what you can see in the foreground and in the background, from the left to the right and from the top to the bottom.
- Don't forget to look at the details. Describe the setting or situation, the quality of the picture, the characters and their appearance and body language.

Interpretation
- What message is given by the picture?
- Is it aimed at a particular target group?
- Did the person who created the picture intend it to have a certain effect on the viewer? If so, how is this achieved?

Evaluation
- Do you think the picture has the intended effect?
- Which elements are responsible for its success or failure?
- If it is a historical picture, compare the effect it might have had in its original context with the one it has on a viewer now.

Useful phrases

First impression
This is a photo / an illustration of …• This photo was taken in … • The illustration shows …• In this illustration / photo you can see (that) …• My first thought when I saw the picture was … • The photograph is shocking/disgusting / amazing / spectacular / special … • The picture reminds me of … • It shows … • It was probably taken in / at … • The photograph looks as if it was staged to achieve a certain effect. • It is a realistic picture.

Description
on the right-hand / left-hand side of the picture • in the centre • in the foreground • in the background • at the top • at the bottom • in the upper right-hand corner • in the lower left-hand corner • The picture was painted by … • It is a portrait / cartoon / still life / landscape / an oil / watercolour painting. • In the middle /centre of the picture there is … • to the left / right of … • in the top left-hand / bottom right-hand corner • There is a contrast

Useful phrases

between … • … is clearly visible • The focus is on … • The field size is a close-up / medium shot / long shot • The colours are bright / dark. • … is seen from above / below / the front / the back • This creates a … atmosphere.

Interpretation
The person in the picture looks … (*+ adjective, e.g. happy*) • The photo / illustration supports the point made in the text that … • The photo / illustration gives you the impression that … • The illustration makes me feel … (*+ adjective: e.g. worried*) • The colours the artist has chosen make me feel … (*+ adjective: happy / sad / worried / …*) • In my opinion the illustration would be better, if … (*+ simple past: e.g. if it was more life-like*)

Evaluation
The artist aims to present … • The picture is (not) convincing because …

Describing cartoons

A cartoonist aims to be both **funny and critical**. When looking at a cartoon, the most important thing is to try to work out what point the cartoonist is making. Generally **the point is made by a combination of the text and the illustration**, so it is important to analyse and understand both. **Illustrations** generally show caricatures of **well-known people or particular stereotypes.** To understand a cartoon, you need to recognise and define the person or group of people illustrated.

To analyse a cartoon, you can follow the steps in the skill 'Describing pictures' → p. 339.

Useful phrases

Describing the cartoon
The cartoon consists of an illustration of … • The illustration shows … • There is a caption under the cartoon, which says "…". • In the (first) speech bubble it says "…". • The text in the speech bubble is spoken by … • The figure is a stereotype / caricature of … • The drawing is detailed / clear / sketchy / abstract.

Talking about the point
The cartoonist is making fun of … • The cartoonist is satirising … • The cartoon is funny because of the misunderstanding between …

Giving your opinion
I think / I don't think the cartoon is (very) funny because … • I get the joke / point. / I don't get the joke / point. • I think / I don't think the cartoon is easy to understand because … • I agree / I don't agree with the point the cartoonist is making because …

Describing diagrams

As you know, **diagrams sum up a lot of statistics or information in very little space** and can make information easier to understand. The kind of diagram you choose to use (bar chart, pie chart, flow chart, line graph, etc.) depends on what you want to show.

A pie chart shows percentages of 100 %:

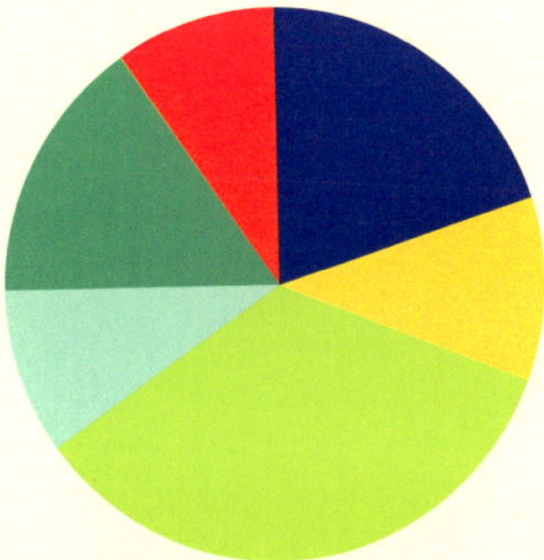

A bar chart is used to compare figures directly:

A line graph shows a development over a certain amount of time:

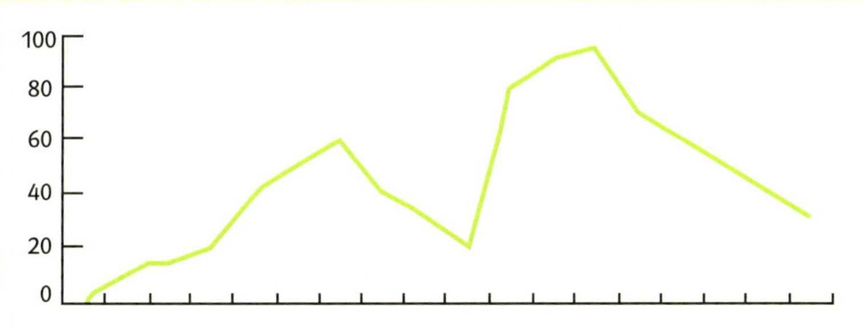

A flow chart shows the links between elements and their influence on each other. It is best used to describe processes that contain decisions at certain points, where alternatives need to be shown:

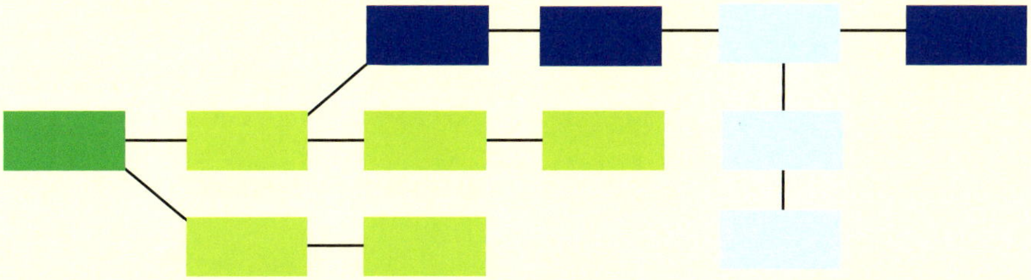

Useful phrases

Describing an increase
to rise • to increase • to have increased by • growth • an increase / a rise (in the number of ...)

Describing a decrease
to decrease • to drop • to decline • a decrease • a decline • a drop (in the number of ...) • a reduction (in the number of ...)

Useful adjectives and adverbs
sharp(ly) • slow(ly) • steady / steadily • continuing / continual(ly) • gradual(ly) • significant(ly) • insignificant(ly) • negligible...negligibly • large • high • small

Expressing numbers & figures
the figures for the last year / the last month / ... • the latest figures • the total number of ... • a (significant/insignificant / ...) number of ... • a (high / ...) percentage of ... • the statistics • a majority / minority of ...

Useful nouns
amount • proportion • sum • level • figure(s)

Useful verbs
to show that ... • to indicate that ... • to suggest that ... • to give information about ... • to make it clear that ... • to illustrate ... • to represent ... • to depict

Qualifiers
a total of • over • under • nearly • more / less than • between • the same number as • the same amount of • from over / under ... to just over / under • half • a third • two thirds • a quarter • (25) per cent • twice as many • three times as many • on average • averagely • roughly • exactly • precisely

Analysing advertisements

When you want to analyse an advertisement, you need to think of the following aspects:

- What is being advertised?
- What is the advertising medium (e.g. a poster, internet pop-up?)
- Who is the ad targeting? What is the product's target group? – men, women, older people, kids, etc.
- What image of the product does the ad try to give? – healthy, hi-tech, value-for-money, ...
- How does it try to do this? What "devices" does it use? Think of pictures, text and layout. Ads can be complicated or simple, serious or funny, etc.
- What do you think of the ad? Do you think it is effective, entertaining, awful, clever, sexist, ...?

Advertisers often use the AIDA formula to plan advertisements. Ads can also be analysed by using this formula:

Attention: How does the ad attract your attention?
Interest: How does the ad create interest in the product?
Desire: How does the ad arouse desire?
Action: How does the ad make you take action (i.e. buy the product)?

Useful phrases

Design
The advertisement is divided into … / consists of … • In the foreground / background … / On the left / right … • It features a … / It shows an image of … • The product is presented / depicted as a …

Impact
The design is colourful / simple / bold / … • It grabs / catches the reader's attention by … • The eye is drawn towards … • The arrangement of text and images has the effect of … • The most striking feature is … • The use of … conveys an impression of … • The choice of font creates a retro / modern look

Product and target market
The product / service being advertised is … • It might appeal to people who … • The advert seems to be directed / aimed at … • It appeals to the desire for status / prestige / security / …

Claim and message
The slogan / strapline promises the customer … • It claims to … • The claim is supported with statistics / endorsements / … • The hidden / underlying message seems to be that … • It makes fun of … / It plays with the idea of … • The language is flowery / plain / straightforward / … • It makes use of alliteration / pun / wordplay / irony … • It prompts / urges the reader to …

Mediation

Mediation means **communicating the main points of a text**, written in one language, **in another language.** For example, the text may be in English and you have to formulate the main points in German, or the text may be in German and the text you produce should be in English. Mediation is not a word-for-word translation. Instead, it is about **getting a message** or **the main points of a text** across in a different language.

Tips

- Read the **task description** carefully to understand what you are supposed to do.
- Read the text and **underline the words** you need to look up in a dictionary.
- Read the text again and **mark the most important points** based on the task description. You can also write **key words** in the margin.
- Pay attention to words such as 'but', 'however', and other signals which indicate a new point.
- You do not normally need to include examples in your mediation text as these usually only illustrate the main points in the original text.
- **Plan the structure** of your mediation text: Think of a good introduction to your text. Which points will you start with? Do you want to include a conclusion?
- Your mediation does not need to have the same structure as the original text.

Discussions

1 Rules for a discussion

- Always be polite!
- Look at the person / the people you are talking to but don't stare at them.
- Don't interrupt unless you feel it is really necessary.
- Listen carefully to what other people are saying.
- Keep to the point.
- Don't talk too much.

2 The role of a discussion leader

A discussion leader makes sure the **discussion is held in an orderly way** and that participants are always polite to each other. He / She always remains neutral (i. e. doesn't give his / her own opinion).

Useful phrases

Introducing the topic and the participants
(As you know,) our discussion today is about… • On my right / left I have … *(name of person or group)*, who is / are in favour of / against …

Choosing whose turn it is to speak
Who'd like to open the discussion? • … , would you like to open the discussion? • The next person to speak is … , followed by … and then …

Making sure everyone has an equal chance to speak, including people who are shy
Is there anything you'd like to say, …?

Making sure no one person monopolises the discussion
I'm sorry to interrupt you, but I'm afraid you'll have to stop there. • Sorry, but I must give the others a chance to put forward their arguments now.

Making sure that only one person speaks at a time
Please wait your turn, you'll have a chance to speak in a minute! • If you'd just let … finish, please.

Noting down the most important points and summarising the discussion at the end
Time is running out, so I'd like to sum up what we've been discussing. • We heard from … that …

Thanking everybody at the end
Thank you for taking part in the discussion! • And finally I'd like to thank all the participants for holding a fair / friendly / … discussion.

Making a suggestion
Let's consider … • I suggest/propose that you / we … • I suggest/propose (+ -ing form) • What do you think about …? • If I were you, I'd …

Responding to a suggestion
That's a good idea! / Fine! • OK / Yes, why not? • OK, if you want, I don't really mind. • I think it would be a better idea to talk about / consider … • Couldn't we look at this / do this another way? • What about …? • I'm not sure. How about …?

Useful phrases

Asking for an opinion
What do you think / feel about …? • What is your view / opinion on / about …? • What would you say? • I'd like to hear what you think about …

Giving an opinion
As far as I'm concerned … • I think / feel / believe / am of the opinion that … • To my mind … • In my opinion … • In my view …

Agreeing
You're (quite / absolutely) right. • That's a very good point! • Absolutely! / Exactly! • I agree (with you / Susie / …). • You have a point there. • You might / could be right. • I think you're right to a certain extent / up to a point.

Disagreeing
I disagree (entirely). • I'm sorry, but I completely disagree. • Stop exaggerating! • I think you're oversimplifying things. • That's an interesting point, but … • That's not the point. • You've missed the point (entirely).

Interrupting someone
Sorry to interrupt, but could you please explain / repeat the point you've just made. • Excuse me for interrupting, but I don't understand what you've just said. • Sorry for interrupting but …

Dealing with being interrupted
Can I just finish what I was saying, please? • Just a second. I haven't quite finished. • Would you let me / allow me to make my point, please. • You could at least let me finish my sentence!

Changing the subject
There is something else that I'd like to say … • Have you ever thought of / considered …? • On the other hand … • Try looking at things another way / from a different angle. • I'd like to bring up another point.

Returning to the original subject
Let's get back to what we were saying / discussing. • Let's get back to the point. • As I was saying before, … • Getting back to what we / you / … said earlier …

Asking for a further explanation
Did I get that right? • Do you really mean that …? • Did I understand correctly that you think …? • Could you explain what you just said / the point you just made / … again, please? • Could you give me / us a concrete example, please?

Saying that a point has been misunderstood
That's not what I meant to say (at all)! • You've got me (completely) wrong. • You've (completely) misunderstood me. • That's not what I was trying to say! • I didn't make myself clear. I'll try and explain again.

Tips for everyday conversation

Always make sure your **language and behaviour is appropriate for the situation** at hand. If it's a formal situation and you know what will be talked about, prepare by looking up useful words and facts.

When you are talking to older or more **experienced people or to your boss**, you should use more **polite phrases** and not be too direct. With **people of the same age or people you know really well**, you probably feel more at ease and can **be a little more direct**. In any case, always show that you are interested in what the person has to say and that you respect him / her.

Give **precise and clear information** and remember to **be tactful** when telling people something that affects them personally.

Always pick up on what your conversation partners have said to show that you **respect and sympathise** with them, that you are listening carefully and judging the content fairly. Use **supportive intonation and body language** as well as the following phrases, where appropriate.

Useful phrases

please • thank you • you're welcome • don't worry • not at all • Could I …? • Would you …? • May I …? • I'd like … • Yes, I will • No, I don't • Yes, that's true, but … • I agree, but … • It's just … • of course • I see • you know • I mean … • Really? • Are you sure? • What a pity. • That's very kind of you. • I appreciate that.

Small talk

Small talk is **light (casual) conversation**. It is a way of showing interest in others, communicating in a friendly way and avoiding conflict at all times! At a **social event**, such as a party, you might spend the whole time in casual conversation. At a **business meeting, on the phone, at an interview, etc.** you can start (and end) with **a little small talk**.

Topics for small talk

- The weather (especially popular in Britain!)
- A journey (to or from the place where you are)
- Where you live / Where your conversation partner lives
- Your family and / or your conversation partner's family (if you know them)
- A recent / well-known TV programme or film
- Tips about what to see and do in a certain town or city (i.e. cultural events, attractions, restaurants, local specialities, etc.)
- Sport (e.g. a current sports event)
- A vacation
- Where you / your conversation partner went to school or university
- What you do for a living / what your conversation partner does for a living
- Hobbies and interests
- An experience / event that you and your conversation partner are both currently involved in or have been involved in
- A non-controversial item in the news

Useful phrases

Starting a conversation
Hi! / Hello! • What are you up to? • Do you mind if I join you? • Nice to see you (again)! • How are you? • How are you doing? • How are things?

Finding a topic
Did you see … on TV last night / at the weekend / …? • Have you seen the new … film yet? • Did you read about … in the newspaper this morning? • Terrible / Beautiful weather, isn't it? • How was your journey? • How did you get here? • What made you decide to come here? • Have you ever been here before? • Who do you think is going to win … this evening?

Making plans
Shall I pick you up? • Let's arrange to meet at … • Sorry, I can't manage Friday. I'm meeting … then. • I've got an appointment with … at … • Thursday would suit me better / best. • That's no good, I'm afraid. What about …? • I've got a date with … on … • I'm seeing … then. • Shall we book seats / tickets / a table? • When does the performance start? • It starts at … • If there's a problem, call me.

Responding & showing surprise
Really? • I don't believe it! • That's incredible! • Well, I've never heard of anything like that before! • That's the funniest / most interesting / strangest thing I've heard in ages! • I've never thought of it like that before. • I couldn't agree more! • That's funny! Exactly the same thing happened to me the other day / two weeks ago / … .

Finishing a conversation
It was nice talking to you! • Goodness / Oh no, is that the time? • Excuse me, / What a shame, I've got to go now. • Hope to see you again soon. • Hope you get home safely. • Take care. • Give my regards to … . • Don't forget to say hello to … for me!

Making phone calls

1 Preparing a phone call

- **Prepare yourself** thoroughly. Make **notes in English** or write out a rough draft of the main things you want to say. This is especially important when making formal or business calls.
- If possible **find out the name and number** of a direct contact person in advance.
- **Think of things** the contact person is likely **to ask or say** and work out responses.
- **Be prepared to spell words**, especially people's names and names of places.

2 During the phone call

- **Speak clearly and slowly**. State your requests clearly and to the point.
- Don't worry about making mistakes.
- **Be polite!** Say *please* when you ask for information and *thank you* when you receive help.
  Remember: *please = bitte • you're welcome / not at all = bitte schön; gern geschehen*
- When making a social call, give your first name only.
- When making a formal / business call, give your first name and surname.

- **Address people** you know well by their first names. In a formal / business situation address people using *Mr, Mrs* or *Ms* [mz] + surname.
- **State telephone numbers** as single digits. When the same number occurs twice consecutively, you can say *double* (e.g. *33 = double 3*). *0 = Oh* (BE & AE) or *zero* (AE)
  Example: *07145 14406: Oh / zero – seven – one – four – five – one – double four – oh / zero – six*
- **Ask the caller to spell names**, etc. for you to avoid confusion.
- **Repeat important information** (times, names, addresses, prices, etc.) to be sure that you have understood everything correctly.
- Don't expect to understand every single word that is said.
- If you are not sure if you have understood something:
  – **Ask the person to repeat** what they have just said: *Could you repeat that, please?*
  – **Ask the person to explain** something in a different way: *So what you're saying is …?*
  – **Ask the person to speak more slowly**: *Could you speak a little more slowly, please?*
- If you can't hear the caller properly, **ask the caller to speak more loudly**.
- If you think you've got the wrong number, check and apologise. Don't just hang up.
- If the caller has got the wrong number, explain politely. **Don't just hang up**.

Useful phrases

The kind of things you may want to say
Hello. Is that Mr Brown speaking? • Could I speak to Mr Brown, please? • This is … I'm calling from Germany. • I'm calling about … • I'd like to enquire about … • I hope I'm not calling at an inconvenient time. • I've got a few questions/ a complaint about … • I'd like to make an appointment to see the doctor/ dentist / … • Shall I ring back later? • Could you take a message/ give him / her a message, please? • What time would be most convenient? • Could you repeat that, please? • I'm afraid the line's very bad/ we've got a bad connection.

What you may hear at the other end of the line
Brown and Wilson Car Rentals. Can I help you? • Speaking! • I'll just fetch him. Hang on a moment, please. • I'm afraid he's not available / he's in a meeting. I'm afraid the line is engaged at the moment. • Could you call back later? • Can I take a message? • I'll give you his extension. • I'll put you through to the … department… • I'll connect you. Please hold the line. • Sorry. I think you've dialled the wrong number. • The person you are calling is not available at the moment. Please leave a message afterthe tone. • If you wish to contact the sales… complaints…customer service department, please press ONE…TWO…

A job interview

If a company finds your letter of application and CV interesting, their human resource department may invite you for an interview. For the interviewee, the interview process starts beforehand with **good preparation**.

1 Preparation

- **Find out about the business or institution** where you will have your interview.
- **Think of questions** that you might be asked, and come up with **suitable answers**.
- Have a friend ask you the questions (plus some surprise ones) and give you a constructive feedback on how you answered them.
- **Think of questions to ask the interviewer** about the business or institution. You want to show that you already know something about them.
- **Dress nicely and arrive early** so that you can collect your thoughts before the interview.

2 During the interview

- **Smile and maintain eye contact** with your interviewer (although it isn't a good idea to stare).
- The interviewer knows that you are nervous, so he or she might try to lighten the atmosphere with **small talk** (→ Small talk p. 346). Be prepared to chat with him or her.
- **Speak clearly and not too quickly!** It is perfectly alright to pause for a moment and think about what you want to say.
- If necessary, ask the interviewer to repeat or explain a question. This also gives you more time to think!
- **Do not answer questions with only *yes, no,* or *I don't know*.** However, keep answers clear and concise. This is your chance to convince the interviewer that you are the right person for the job!
- If possible, **ask the question(s) about the business or institution** that you thought of.
- **Thank** your interviewer at the end.

3 After the interview

- After a short time, **send a short, follow-up mail** thanking your interviewer and expressing interest in the position again. If you haven't been told when the decision will be made, ask politely when you can expect a reply.
- **If you don't get the job, don't worry!** Think of what you can do better next time, and work on these points. As with any other skill, the more interviews you do, the better you will get!

Useful phrases

As you can see from my CV … • I trained in … • I graduated / will be graduating from school in … • I enjoy dealing with clients / working with people. • I have excellent … skills / good knowledge of … • I'm PC literate. • I'm accustomed to working hard. • I'm prepared to work overtime. • During my time at school I did internships at …

Word webs

Word webs are useful for **collecting and organising a large amount of information** about a certain topic. You can make a word web for yourself or as a group. The basic structure of a word web is always the same.

1 How to make a word web

- **Use a pencil** so that you can easily delete things or change their position, if necessary.
- Write your main topic in the middle of a page and draw a circle around the word or phrase. (Fig. 1)
- Think of **important things** directly related to the main topic. Write each idea (subtopic) in a **circle** around the outside of your first circle. **Draw lines** connecting the subtopics to the main topic. (Fig. 2)
- Now add more circles with related ideas around the subtopics. (Fig. 3) Instead of drawing circles you can use lines with 'branches' for subtopics. (Fig. 4)

2 Ways of using word webs

- To **brainstorm for ideas on a given topic:** Write the topic heading in the centre circle and add all new and related aspects.
- To **organise information from a text** (or other source): Start with the most important point in the text, add the main subtopics, then add relevant detailed information or quotations from the text.
- To **develop word fields**: Start with the generic term and add all related words.
- To **organise arguments**: Start with the topic of discussion. Add a branch or circle: 'for' and another one 'against'. Continue by adding further branches / circles with arguments 'for' and 'against'.

Fig. 1

Fig. 2

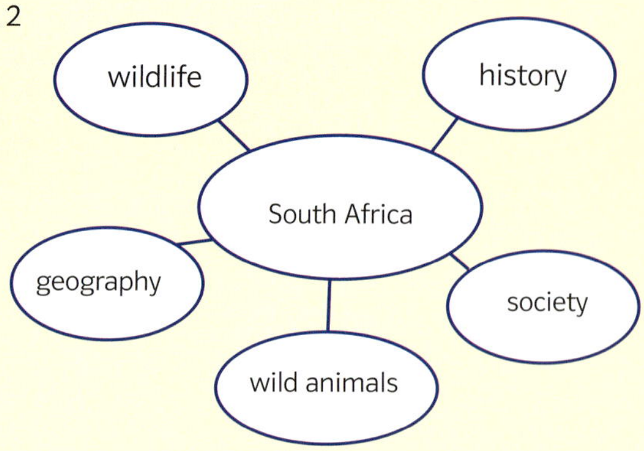

Fig. 3

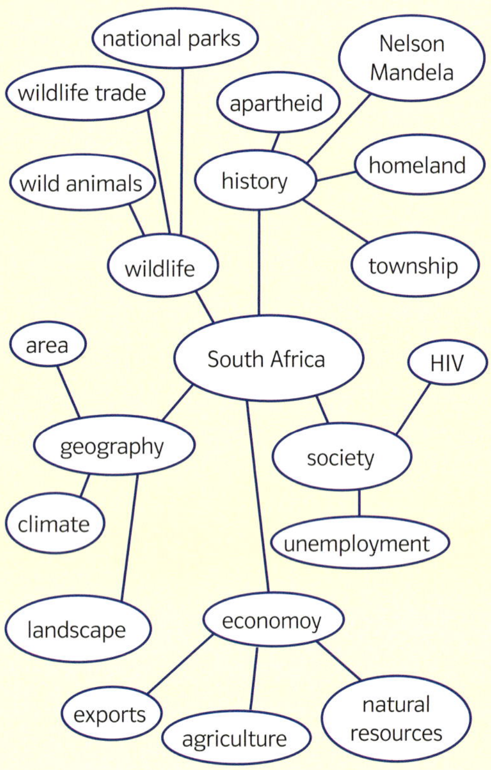

Fig. 4

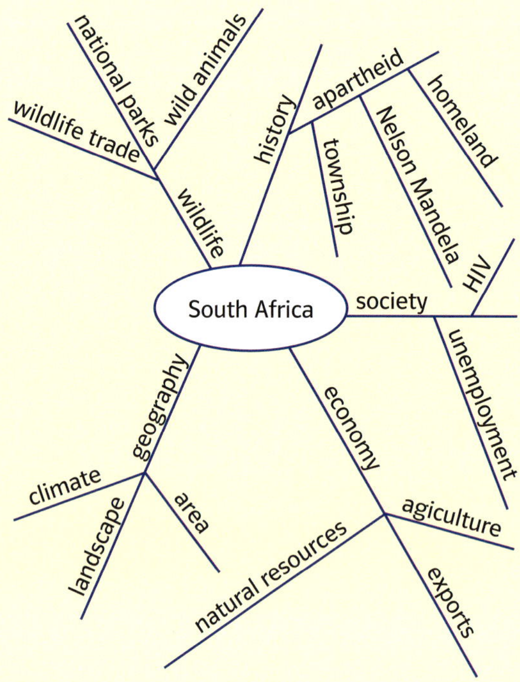

Brainstorming

Brainstorming is the first step when you want to **collect ideas on a specific topic**. You can brainstorm on your own, with a partner or in a group.

1 Individual brainstorming

- First write down **each idea that comes to mind** when you think of the topic.
- In a second step, go through your collection of ideas and choose those which you really want.
- **Structure** your ideas in a grid or a word web.

2 Brainstorming in a group (placemat)

- Form groups of four. Write down the topic in the middle of a big sheet of paper (placemat). Each of you works in one corner.
- Collect your ideas on the topic and write them down in your corner.
- Discuss all ideas and decide on the ones you find best or most important. Write them in the middle of your placemat.

Example:

- landscape (interior plateau, hills, narrow coastal plain
- agriculture (maize, wheat, wine)
- natural resources (gold, diamonds, metals, minerals)

- apartheid (blacks, whites, other ethnic groups)
- townships, homelands
- wildlife (national parks, wild animals, protection of wild animals)

South Africa
- apartheid (blacks, whites, townships, homelands)
-
-
-

- history (settlers, apartheid, democracy)
- HIV
- unemployment
- problems between blacks and whites

- national parks
- wild animals
- wildlife trade
- protection of animals
- safaris
- holiday

Taking notes

Taking notes means writing down information from a spoken source (speech, interview, etc.) in short form.

- Only write down the **most important information**. It is impossible to note down everything.
- Only write down **key words**, never complete sentences. Key words are often names, times, numbers and places.
- Try to order your notes systematically. If possible, use headings, sub-headings or grids.
- Use **symbols** for certain relationships, for example: = ≠ →
- Make sure that you can read your handwriting!

Marking up a text

When you read a text, it can be useful to mark up **information that you will need later** for answering questions, etc. Remember that you can only mark up texts **in photocopies or in books that belong to you**.

- When you read the text, keep in mind **which information** you are looking for.
- Mark relevant information by **underlining, circling or highlighting** the words or phrases.
- If you want to mark different kinds of information, choose **different colours**.
- You can also write down **key words in the margins**.
- When you read the text again later, you can **concentrate on the marked words** and phrases and on your notes in the margins.

Example:

The struggle against apartheid

Apartheid (meaning *separateness* in Afrikaans) was a system of legalised racial segregation in South Africa. Apartheid had its roots in the history of colonisation and settlement of southern Africa. *definition and roots*

The first Europeans who settled in South Africa were the Dutch in 1652. In 1806 the British arrived. The discovery of diamonds in 1867 and gold in 1886 led to increased immigration and brought wealth which, however, native Africans were denied. The Union of South Africa was formed in 1910 and racial segregation was generally accepted although the policy of apartheid didn't become official until 1948, when the National Party came to power. *first settlers*

Apartheid classified inhabitants and visitors into racial groups (black, white, coloured, and Indian or Asian). South African blacks had to move to small and economically unproductive areas of the country known as 'homelands'. Blacks who worked in factories and mines had to live in 'townships', i.e. poor and underdeveloped living areas which were built around the major cities. The government also segregated education, medical care and other public services. The services for black people were greatly inferior to those of whites and the black education system was designed to prepare blacks for life in the labouring class. *apartheid examples*

Guessing new words

Don't be afraid of texts containing new words. You already know many different ways of guessing their meanings. After applying your guessing technique there will still be some words you don't know, but don't worry, you will probably understand the most important points in the text.

Guessable words	**Examples:**
• Words that are used in a German context.	*bestseller, boycott, clown, laptop, track, …*
• Words that are similar to German words → but watch out for false friends!	*individuality, inner, install, parallel, to wander, …*
• Words that are similar to words you know from another foreign language (French, Latin, Spanish, Italian) → but watch out for false friends!	*academic, announcement, artificial, descendant, dignity, disrespect, individuality, junior, minor, pasta, phase, …*
• Compounds of words you already know.	*handwriting, heartfelt, mixed ability, single-sex, washing machine, wholeheartedly, …*
• Words from a word family you already know.	*adventurous, announcement, importation, to mirror, nationalism, relevance, …*
• Words you already know, but with a different meaning, the new meaning being guessable from the context.	*to admit, light, plain, pretty, to report sb…*
• Words whose meaning you can guess from the context.	*(he) dozed off (in his chair); (it's old-fashioned) out of date*

Working with a dictionary

1 English-German, German-English

When using an English-German or German-English dictionary, make sure to check the following information in your dictionary.

- What part of speech is the word?
- What does it go together with?
- What topic or word field does it belong to?
- How is it pronounced?
- Are there irregular forms?
- What translations are given?
- Which of the translations can only be used in a limited context (*AE, formal, slang*, etc.)?
- Which of the translations fits the context?

Example:

fo·cus['fəʊkəs] <*pl* **focuses, foci**> [*pl* 'fəʊsaɪ] *s* ❶ (MATH OPT) Brennpunkt *m* ❷ *(fig)* Brennpunkt, Herd *m,* Zentrum *nt;* ~ *(un)scharf eingestellt;* ~ scharf einstellen *vt* ❶ (OPT PHOT) einstellen *(on* auf) ❷ *(fig)* konzentrieren *(on* auf); **focus group** *s (in marketing)* [ausgewählte] Test-

2 English-English

This type of dictionary is best used for **writing an English text** when you are not quite sure which is the best word in a given context. The more English you read, the more you will improve your language! An English-English (monolingual) dictionary provides you with the following information:

- What part of speech is the word?
- What does it go together with?
- What topic or word field does it belong to?
- How is it pronounced?
- Are there irregular forms?
- What synonyms and / or definitions are given?
- Which of the given meanings fits the context?
- Examples show how the word is typically used.

Tips for using an English-English dictionary

- Before looking up a word identify whether it is a verb, noun, adjective, adverb, etc.
- When you have found the entry for the word, make sure you look at the meaning for the correct class of word.
- Read any additional information which the dictionary gives you about the word.
- Take your time to read the entry carefully.
- Make sure you find the entry which matches the use of the word in the given context.

Example:

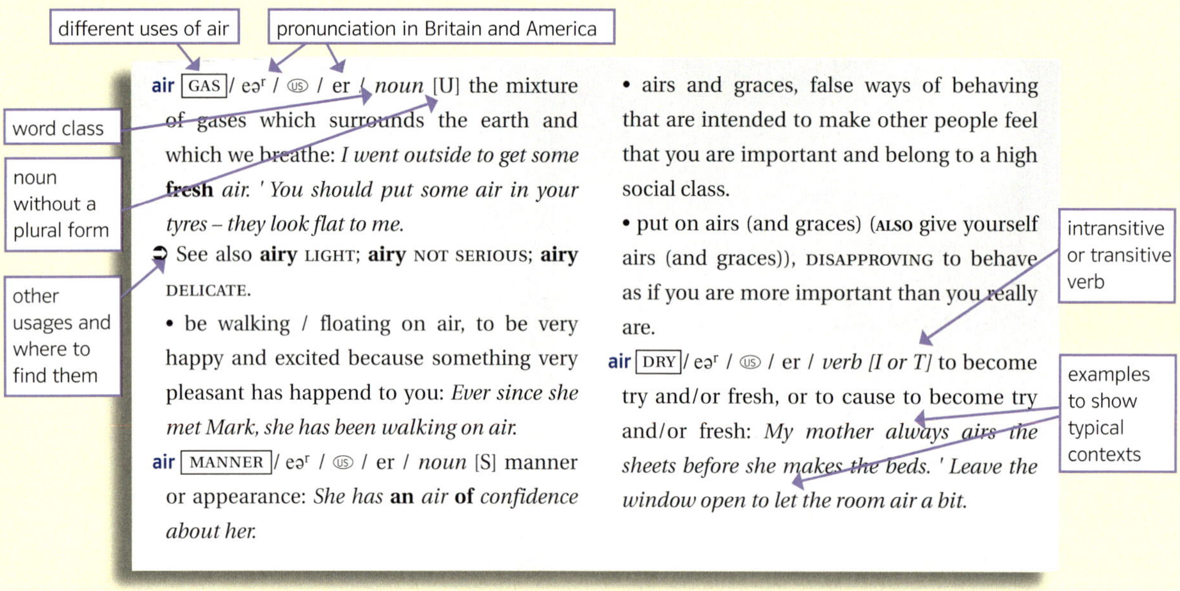
air GAS / eəʳ / (US) / er / *noun* [U] the mixture of gases which surrounds the earth and which we breathe: *I went outside to get some* **fresh** *air. ' You should put some air in your tyres – they look flat to me.*
➲ See also **airy** LIGHT; **airy** NOT SERIOUS; **airy** DELICATE.
• be walking / floating on air, to be very happy and excited because something very pleasant has happend to you: *Ever since she met Mark, she has been walking on air.*

air MANNER / eəʳ / (US) / er / *noun* [S] manner or appearance: *She has* **an** *air* **of** *confidence about her.*
• airs and graces, false ways of behaving that are intended to make other people feel that you are important and belong to a high social class.
• put on airs (and graces) (ALSO give yourself airs (and graces)), DISAPPROVING to behave as if you are more important than you really are.

air DRY / eəʳ / (US) / er / *verb [I or T]* to become try and/or fresh, or to cause to become try and/or fresh: *My mother always airs the sheets before she makes the beds. ' Leave the window open to let the room air a bit.*

Working with films

An interesting way of dealing with a specific topic is by watching and analysing related films. A film usually tells a story, so you **can analyse the plot, setting, characters and narrative techniques** exactly the way you do with a fictional text (→ Understanding fictional texts p. 322). In addition to the content, you can analyse the **audiovisual aspects** of the film.

1 Important film genres

action • adventure • comedy • crime • drama • epic / historical • horror • musical • science fiction • war • western • fantasy • romance • melodrama

2 Choosing a film

- If you are looking for a film that deals with a specific topic, you can search on the Internet. Use a search engine or check the *International Movie Database*.

3 Analysing a film

- **Choose a scene** from the film.
- Make a **list of the types of camera shots.**
- Say what effect each shot creates, e.g. it shows a character's emotions, it includes the viewer in the scene, it shows where the action is going to take place, etc.
- If you have access to **different versions of the film**, compare the same scene in both. What similarities / differences do you notice?
- If the film is **based on a novel, short story or play**: How much of the original plot has been used in the film? Have characters been cut out / added in? Why is this the case, do you think? Compare the message of the film with that of the original text. Which do you prefer – the book or the film? Why?
- Is the **music** memorable? Does it create a particular atmosphere? What effect does the music have on the scenes?
- If you have the film on DVD, also watch the **special features** (director's commentary, interviews, cut-out scenes, trailers, etc.)
- If you have got the **film script**, compare it to the film version, concentrating on one or two scenes. What changes were made in the film?
- Choose two actors / actresses from the film. Find out about other films they acted in. Then say whether you found them suitable in their role in the film you are analysing.
- Describe the **film poster and / or film trailer**. What aspects of the film does it emphasise? Most modern films have homepages which include the poster and trailer.
- Write a **review** of the film in which you **outline the plot and the roles** played by the actors. Say whether you liked the film and would recommend it or not.
  Explain why.
- Check the Internet for online reviews and comments by people who have seen the film. Compare their evaluation with yours.

4 Camera operations

5 Important aspects of one or more film scenes

setting	contemporary / historical? • science fiction? • city / country? • exterior / interior?
characters	how many? • who? • appearance? • costumes? • body language?
story and storyline	dialogue? • interaction? • fight? • narrative structure?
camera	field size? • view? • zooming? • panning? • tracking?
light	colours? • brightness / darkness? • atmosphere?
cut	tempo? • rest? • correspondence with actions?
sound and music	voices? • atmosphere?
special effects	animation? • slow / fastmotion?

6 Presenting a film in class

- **Start by giving your audience more information** than just the title:
  - Who directed it?
  - Who acted in it?
  - Who produced it?
  - When was it made?
  - Who wrote the music?
  - Was it a success?
  - If the film is based on a literary text, say which one.
- Then briefly **introduce the setting and the characters and sum up the plot.**
- Say what is **good or bad** about the film and why you like it or not.
- **Present a scene** that has an important function in the film. The scene should enable you to say something about the characters, their relationship with each other, their role in the plot, their language and body language, the atmosphere of the film and what is typical of the way it tells its story. You should also be able to say at what point in the film it comes and what its function is.

Useful phrases

In the foreground / background there is … • The camera takes a long / medium / close-up / extreme close-up shot. • This brings us close to … / creates a distance between … • The camera position is … • The view of … is frontal / from above / below / behind. • The focus is on a … detail. • The camera zooms in / out of … • The camera pans from … to … • … is introduced in a panning shot. • The movement of … is followed in a tracking shot. • The shots follow each other quickly. / The … shot lasts for a while. This creates a / an … atmosphere. • … is shown in slow / fast motion.

Internet research

1 Subject searches and key word searches

- Browse a **subject guide or directory**, e.g. *Yahoo*, to choose a category, then a subcategory and so on, e.g. *travel > travel guides > United States > Las Vegas*.
- Use a **search engine**, e.g. *Google*, to look for certain key words, e.g. *history apartheid Mandela*.
- Most of the search engines use OR as a default. This means that you will get a list of sites that include any one of any of the key words you entered, e.g. you will get sites for South Wales (in Britain) as well as New South Wales (in Australia) if you enter *new south wales*.
  With most search engines you can **use + or – signs in front of certain key words** to make sure they are included or excluded from your search, e.g. *+martin +luther -king*. If you look for a certain phrase, like the title of a book, put it in **inverted commas**, e.g. *"lord of the rings"*.
- To get better results, it may help to put the **most unusual or relevant word first**.
- If you don't get many hits, check your spelling, try similar key words or use fewer words.
- If you get too many hits, be more specific and add some words.

2 Bookmarks *(Favoriten)*

- To make it easier to return to a site you like, you can add a **bookmark** either by clicking on the bookmarks *(Favoriten)* menu, by pressing Control-D *(Strg-D)* or by clicking on your right mouse button.
- If you forgot to add a bookmark, you can go back to sites you have visited during the last few sessions by using the forward or back buttons or by pressing Control-H *(Strg-H)*.

3 Evaluating your results

- Don't believe everything you read! Remember that anyone can publish anything on the Internet.
  Judge the reliability of a website before using information from it. Is it similar to *www.harvard.edu* or more like *www.aol/users/joedoe*?
- Is it a commercial website? Then it might be interested in selling something rather than giving objective information.
- Does it contain **facts or just opinions**?
- Is the **author** someone who is likely to know something about a subject, e.g. a university teacher or a journalist?
- Also check if the website has been **updated recently**, especially if you are looking for the latest news on a topic.

Projects and group work

1 Finding information

Set up an **'information centre'** in your classroom (or of your own) in which you keep a record of where to find information. Find and keep a record of:

- The name, address, email address, telephone and fax number of:
  - your local library
  - the nearest university or college library
  - your twin-town association (if your area has one)
  - the nearest newsagent or bookshop which stocks English newspapers and magazines. (Tip: Try your nearest main station.)
- The **website addresses** of search engines, schools and colleges, youth organisations, political parties, newspapers, magazines, government agencies in America and the UK.
- The names of classmates who have **contacts** (penfriends, relatives, friends, etc.) **in the English-speaking world**, and who might be willing to help you.
- The names of classmates or people in your neighbourhood who have an **English-speaking parent / parents** and who might help you. Collect **brochures** from travel agencies and tourist information bureaus. Collect material while you are on holiday (leaflets, magazines, postcards, advertisements, menus, timetables, etc.). Add information and addresses to your files when you find new material.

2 Doing a project

- Read the information you are given about the **project task** carefully.
- In your groups, **brainstorm** to find ideas about:
  - what you all already know about the topic.
  - which aspects you want to concentrate on.
  - where you can find information.
- If necessary, **decide which points are more important** (concentrate on these) and which are less important (and can possibly be left out).
- Decide **which tasks each member of the group are going to do**. Make sure the workload is divided equally.
- If not specified in the task, decide how you want to **present your material**.
  You can produce: a talk using visual aids • a video • a CD • a leaflet • a brochure • a file of written information • a written report • a poster or wall chart • a website.
- Remember to **keep a record of your sources**, i.e. where you found material, where quotes or extracts from original material were taken from, etc.

Questionnaires and surveys

1 Before doing a survey

- It is important to have a clear idea of **what kind of information** you hope to get from your survey.
- Write one or two **sentences describing your topic** and explaining why you are doing the survey. (Later you can include these sentences at the start of your questionnaire so that the people you ask (interviewees / participants) have a clear idea of what the survey is about.)
- Briefly **state what you expect the results of your survey to be** – or give alternatives.
- Decide **how many people** you want to interview and **which social groups** they should belong to. For example, is the age of participants important? Should they be male or female? Should they have a certain job or hobby?

2 The questionnaire

- The success of a survey depends largely on **how good your questions** are.
  If possible, ask an independent person to answer your questions before you carry out the survey to make sure your questions are clear.
- Decide what **type of questions** you want to ask. The most common types of questions are described in the box below.
- Your questions need not all be of the same type, but it is best not to include too many different types.
- Always keep the **aim of your survey** in mind when you are formulating questions.
- Word your questions **clearly and concisely**. Use formal language.
- **Don't ask too many questions** (between 10 and 15 is usually enough).
- Put your questions in **logical order**.
- Group questions relating to particular aspects together.
- Start off with simpler, more general questions and then go on to more detailed questions.
- Your last question can be an open-ended question.

3 Types of questions

Multiple choice questions

The interviewee chooses from given answers.

Which of the following do you own?

a) a TV ☐ *b) a DVD player* ☐
c) an MP3 player ☐ *d) a CD player* ☐

Yes / No questions

Questions that can be answered with 'Yes' or 'No'.

Do you exercise more than three times a week?

☐ *YES* ☐ *NO*

Graded questions

The interviewee has to choose to what extent they agree / disagree with, like / don't like / … something.

How often do you eat fruit or vegetables on average per day?

☐ *never*
☐ *less than three times*
☐ *more than three times*

Open-ended questions

Questions to which the interviewees must give their own answer.
The questions usually begin with a question word: who, what, when, where, why or how.

How, in your opinion, could the recycling system in your area be improved?

____

4 Presenting the results

- When you summarise and present your results, always **think of your aims**, for example:
  - proving a certain expectation right or wrong
  - comparing the answers of different groups
  - giving the majority opinion
  - presenting the most surprising results.
- Never forget to say **how many and what kind of people took part** in your survey! Most answers can be turned into statistics straight away, so you can present your statistics as percentages and use diagrams to support the presentation visually.

Example:

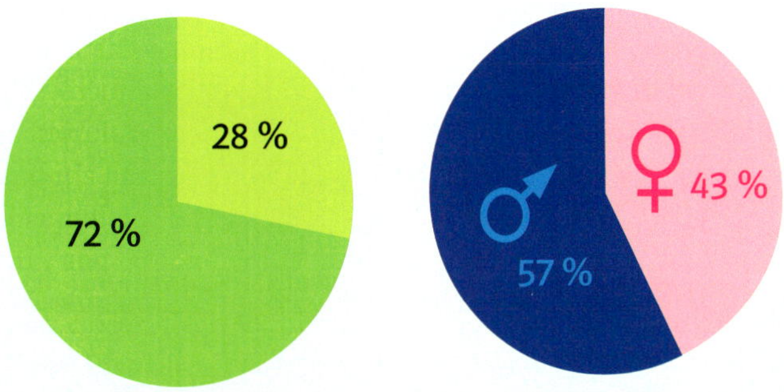

Of all the pupils in the tenth form at our school 72 % have got their own computer, 57% of them are boys.

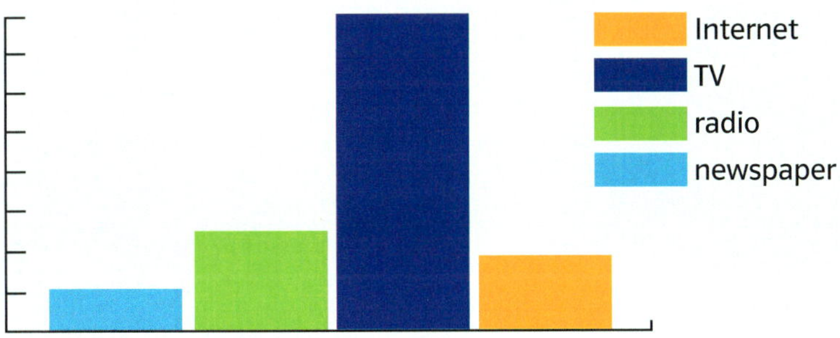

Popular sources of information for tenth graders

- Ratings may require a different **form of presentation**, e.g.:
  When asked about the importance of foreign languages, 26 out of 30 people answered that foreign languages were generally very important to them, 3 out of 30 thought foreign languages were only important in some situations, and only one person said they were not important at all.
- Presenting **answers to open-ended questions**, you may be able to make a top three, five or ten using similar answers or you may quote the most surprising ones, e.g.:
  The top three breakfast favourites in our class are: 1. rolls 2. cereals 3. jam.

Presentation

1 Preparation

Gather material on your topic:
- Brainstorm to find ideas on the topic and make a word web.
- Find information from relevant sources (library, school books, the Internet, newspapers, etc.)

Choose which main points you want to talk about.
Make a set of prompt cards in English, which you can look at during your talk to remind you of what you want to say (→ prompt cards p. 363).
- Write down the key words, phrases and vocabulary which you will need.
- Note down any examples or quotations.
- Note down any visual aids (OHPs, photographs, posters, flip charts, etc.) which you plan to use.

Arrange your prompt cards in logical order. You could present points:
- in terms of importance, from the most to the least important (or vice versa)
- chronologically
- with all those in favour first, followed by all those against.

Make a prompt card for your introduction (→ card 1 p. 363). Catch the listeners' attention with:
- an interesting question or fact
- a quote or joke
- a picture or cartoon on an OHP transparency.

Make a prompt card for your conclusion (→ card 7 p. 363):
- Note the point(s) you want to emphasise.
- Write down key words and phrases.
- Make a note of a final quotation or an example you wish to use.

2 Giving a talk or presentation

- **Practise your talk or presentation** out loud, preferably in front of a mirror, or ask a friend/relative to listen to you!
- **Speak slowly and clearly!**
- Use short, clear sentences.
- **Vary your voice** so that you don't sound boring. For example, emphasise particularly important points by speaking a little more loudly.
- **Look at your audience** as often as possible. Don't look at your prompt cards all the time.
- Try not to make distracting movements such as waving your hands, etc.
- **Smile!** (But don't laugh nervously!)
- **Start by introducing yourself** (if necessary) and your topic. **Finish by thanking** your audience for listening. Ask if anyone has any questions.

3 A market place

- **Form groups** and **prepare** your product.
- Choose a **speaker** for your group.
- **Present** your product in the classroom. Your classmates walk around and look at the different products. The **speaker** presents the product to the people who pass by and answers their questions.
- **Discuss** the products in class.

4 A gallery walk

- **Prepare** your product (on your own or in a group).
- Prepare an **evaluation sheet** in class.
- **Present** your product in the classroom and give the evaluation sheets to your classmates.
- Your **classmates** walk around, look at the different products and **fill in the evaluation sheet**.
- **Discuss** the results of the evaluation sheets in class.

5 Prompt cards

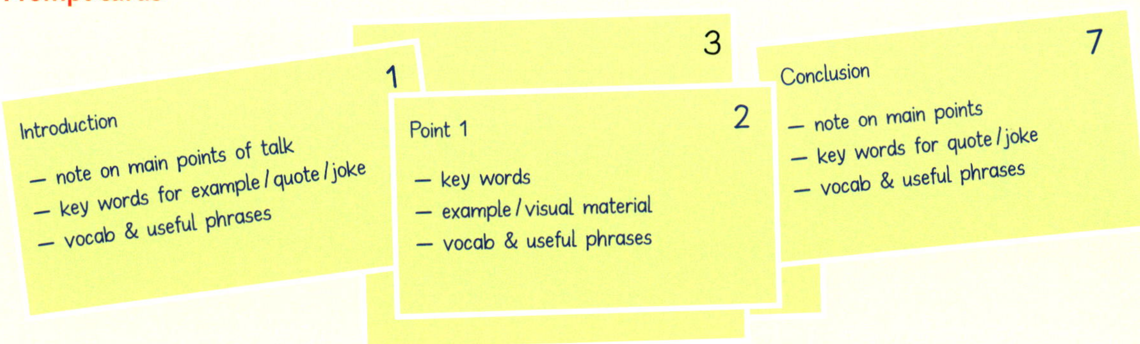

Useful phrases

Good morning / afternoon, my name is … • Today I'm going to talk about … • The subject of my talk today is … • Can everyone hear me alright? • Can everyone see the board / screen / etc.? • I'd like to begin by (+ *-ing form*) … • Let me start by saying a few words about … • Let me give you an example. • As you can see on the chart / graph / cartoon … • I'd like to finish / conclude by (+ *-ing form*) … • Let me finish by (+ *-ing form*) … • Finally … • Thank you very much for your attention. • I hope you all enjoyed my talk. • I'd be happy to answer any questions

Grammar files

Tenses

Simple present

Positive sentences	Negative sentences	Questions
I play football. You play football. He/she/it plays football. We play football. You play football. They play football.	I don't play football. You don't play football. He/she/it doesn't play football. We don't play football. You don't play football. They don't play football.	Do I play football? Do you play football? Does he/she/it play football? Do we play football? Do you play football? Do they play football? Questions with question word: Why do I play football? Why do you play football? Why does he/she/it play football? Why do we play football? Why do you play football? Why do they play football?
! Be careful with these verbs: be, have		

Examples of typical use:

1. Facts and general statements: Cats eat mice.
2. Everyday activities or habits: Our team plays football on Sundays.
   Tense markers: always, often, sometimes, never, usually, every day/week/month/year, on Mondays/…, at 7 o'clock/…
3. A set sequence of events or actions: The two knights fight, the Queen screams, and then the King saves her.
4. For scheduled future events with an adverbial phrase of time: The train leaves at 14:35.

Present progressive

Positive sentences	Negative sentences	Questions
I am singing. You are singing. He/she/it is singing. We are singing. You are singing. They are singing.	I'm not singing. You aren't singing. He/she/it isn't singing. We aren't singing. You aren't singing. They aren't singing.	Am I singing? Are you singing? Is he/she/it singing? Are we singing? Are you singing? Are they singing?

Positive sentences	Negative sentences	Questions
		Questions with question word: What am I singing? What are you singing? What is he/she/it singing? What are we singing? What are you singing? What are they singing?

! Some verbs are never used in the progressive form, especially those which express feelings or belief: believe, love, hate, seem, have (in the sense of own), can, mean, want to, feel, notice, realise

Examples of typical use:

1. An activity that is going on right now and will continue for a certain limited or temporary period of time: Greg is cooking dinner (now).
   Tense markers: now, just now, at the moment
2. Planned future events with an adverbial phrase of time: They are visiting us in three weeks.

Simple past

Positive sentences	Negative sentences	Questions
I played football. You played football. He/she/it played football. We played football. You played football. They played football.	I didn't play football. You didn't play football. He/she/it didn't play football. We didn't play football. You didn't play football. They didn't play football.	Did I play football? Did you play football? Did he/she/it play football? Did we play football? Did you play football? Did they play football? Questions with question word: Why did I play football? Why did you play football? Why did he/she/it play football? Why did we play football? Why did you play football? Why did they play football?

! Be careful with irregular verbs

Examples of typical use:

1. For activities that began and ended at a specific time in the past: They returned from Canada a week ago.
   Tense markers: yesterday, ago, last week/month/year, in 2007/…, on Tuesday/…
2. For a series of events in the past as in a story, often called the 'narrative past':
   As the train left the station, Helen looked around the compartment. There was no one else in sight. She took out the letter and started to read it.

Past progressive

Positive sentences	Negative sentences	Questions
I was singing. You were singing. He/she/it was singing. We were singing. You were singing. They were singing.	I wasn't singing. You weren't singing. He/she/it wasn't singing. We weren't singing. You weren't singing. They weren't singing.	Was I singing? Were you singing? Was he/she/it singing? Were we singing? Were you singing? Were they singing? Questions with question word: What was I singing? What were you singing? What was he/she/it singing? What were we singing? What were you singing? What were they singing?

Examples of typical use:

1. An activity in the past that was already in progress when something else happened:
   They were cleaning the house when the guests arrived.
2. Several activities or events that were happening at the same time in the past:
   While Patty was mowing the lawn, Sid was cleaning the windows.

Present perfect simple

Positive sentences	Negative sentences	Questions
I have finished. You have finished. He/she/it has finished. We have finished. You have finished. They have finished.	I haven't finished. You haven't finished. He/she/it hasn't finished. We haven't finished. You haven't finished. They haven't finished.	Have I finished? Have you finished? Has he/she/it finished? Have we finished? Have you finished? Have they finished? Questions with question word: What have I finished? What have you finished? What has he/she/it finished? What have we finished? What have you finished? What have they finished?

! Be careful with irregular verbs
With the present perfect simple the result of the action is usually more important than the action itself.
Never use the present perfect with adverbs of past time, e.g. yesterday, last week, three years ago, in 2007.

Examples of typical use:

1. Activities that happened recently, and whose effects are still felt in the present:
   They have moved to Stratford and they are still living there.
2. With certain adverbs: just, so far, ever, never, recently, lately, today, this week, already, (not) yet
   The test results have just arrived. – I have had good marks so far this year. – Have you ever been to New York?
3. With for and since, for activities that started in the past and are continuing:
   I haven't eaten chocolate for three weeks! – I haven't seen Melanie since 2008.

Present perfect progressive

Positive sentences	Negative sentences	Questions
I have been waiting. You have been waiting. He/she/it has been waiting. We have been waiting. You have been waiting. They have been waiting.	I haven't been waiting. You haven't been waiting. He/she/it hasn't been waiting. We haven't been waiting. You haven't been waiting. They haven't been waiting.	Have I been waiting? Have you been waiting? Has he/she/it been waiting? Have we been waiting? Have you been waiting? Have they been waiting? Questions with question word: Why have I been waiting? Why have you been waiting? Why has he/she/it been waiting? Why have we been waiting? Why have you been waiting? Why have they been waiting?

Examples of typical use:

1. Activities that have either been going on either continuously or at intervals up to the present, often with adverbials of time such as all day, for a week, etc.: We have been looking for a camping site all day.
2. With no mention of time, the activity has taken place very recently and the result is clearly visible:
   It has been raining.

Past perfect simple

Positive sentences	Negative sentences	Questions
I had finished. You had finished. He/she/it had finished. We had finished. You had finished. They had finished.	I hadn't finished. You hadn't finished. He/she/it hadn't finished. We hadn't finished. You hadn't finished. They hadn't finished.	Had I finished? Had you finished? Had he/she/it finished? Had we finished? Had you finished? Had they finished?

Positive sentences	Negative sentences	Questions
		Questions with question word: What had I finished? What had you finished? What had he/she/it finished? What had we finished? What had you finished? What had they finished?

! Be careful with irregular verbs

Examples of typical use:

1. An activity that happened before another activity in the past, showing the connection between the two activities:
   When we arrived at the station, the train had already left.
   After I had watched the news, I decided to go out.
2. In reported speech, when the original statement is in the past or present perfect:
   Jane said that she had forgotten to do her homework.

Past perfect progressive

Positive sentences	Negative sentences	Questions
I had been waiting. You had been waiting. He/she/it had been waiting. We had been waiting. You had been waiting. They had been waiting.	I hadn't been waiting. You hadn't been waiting. He/she/it hadn't been waiting. We hadn't been waiting. You hadn't been waiting. They hadn't been waiting.	Had I been waiting? Had you been waiting? Had he/she/it been waiting? Had we been waiting? Had you been waiting? Had they been waiting? Questions with question word: Why had I been waiting? Why had you been waiting? Why had he/she/it been waiting? Why had we been waiting? Why had you been waiting? Why had they been waiting?

Examples of typical use:

1. A past activity that occurred before another where there is a direct relation to the activity that followed:
   He was tired because he had been working so hard.
2. In reported speech, when the original statement is in the present perfect progressive:
   He said that he had been working hard.

Going to-future

Positive sentences	Negative sentences	Questions
I am going to leave early. You are going to leave early. He/she/it is going to leave early. We are going to leave early You are going to leave early. They are going to leave early.	I'm not going to leave early. You're not going to leave early. He/she/it's not going to leave early. We're not going to leave early. You're not going to leave early. They're not going to leave early.	Am I going to leave early? Are you going to leave early? Is he/she/it going to leave early? Are we going to leave early? Are you going to leave early? Are they going to leave early?

Examples of typical use:

1. For an action in the future that has already been planned or prepared:
   They're going to buy Tom a new computer for his birthday.
2. For a prediction about the future, when you can see that something is about to happen:
   Look at those clouds. It's going to rain soon.

Future simple (will-future)

Positive sentences	Negative sentences	Questions
I will play football. You will play football. He/she/it will play football. We will play football. You will play football. They will play football.	I won't play football. You won't play football. He/she/it won't play football. We won't play football. You won't play football. They won't play football.	Will I play football? Will you play football? Will he/she/it play football? Will we play football? Will you play football? Will they play football? Questions with question word: Why will I play football? Why will you play football? Why will he/she/it play football? Why will we play football? Why will you play football? Why will they play football?
! English will = German werden English want = German wollen		

Examples of typical use:

1. Things that are likely to happen at a defined or undefined time in the future:
   You'll be a great movie star some day.
2. For forecasts, such as the weather forecast: On Saturday, there will be rain for most of the day.
3. In 'if'-clauses Type 1 – future situations that are probable/possible:
   If the weather is fine, I'll play football.

Future progressive

Positive sentences	Negative sentences	Questions
I will be singing. You will be singing. He/she/it will be singing. We will be singing. You will be singing. They will be singing.	I won't be singing. You won't be singing. He/she/it won't be singing. We won't be singing. You won't be singing. They won't be singing.	Will I be singing? Will you be singing? Will he/she/it be singing? Will we be singing? Will you be singing? Will they be singing? Questions with question word: What will I be singing? What will you be singing? What will he/she/it be singing? What will we be singing? What will you be singing? What will they be singing?

Example of typical use:

Events – often planned – that will be going on at a certain time in the future when another event occurs:
You will be sleeping by the time I get home.

Future perfect simple

Positive sentences	Negative sentences	Questions
I will have finished. You will have finished. He/she/it will have finished. We will have finished. You will have finished. They will have finished.	I won't have finished. You won't have finished. He/she/it won't have finished. We won't have finished. You won't have finished. They won't have finished.	Will I have finished? Will you have finished? Will he/she/it have finished? Will we have finished? Will you have finished? Will they have finished? Questions with question word: When will I have finished? When will you have finished? When will he/she/it have finished? When will we have finished? When will you have finished? When will they have finished?
! Be careful with irregular verbs		

Example of typical use:

Future activities that take place before other future activities to show a relation between them. The simple present is used for the other activities:
Joanna will have finished the college course by the time she is 20.

Future perfect progressive

Positive sentences	Negative sentences	Questions
I will have been waiting.	I won't have been waiting.	Will I have been waiting?
You will have been waiting.	You won't have been waiting.	Will you have been waiting?
He/she/it will have been waiting.	He/she/it won't have been waiting.	Will he/she/it have been waiting?
We will have been waiting.	We won't have been waiting.	Will we have been waiting?
You will have been waiting.	You won't have been waiting.	Will you have been waiting?
They will have been waiting.	They won't have been waiting.	Will they have been waiting?

Example of typical use:

Used in the same way as the future perfect simple but placing more emphasis on the activity:
They will have been studying English for eight years before they take the exam.

Conditional I

Positive sentences	Negative sentences	Questions
I would play football.	I wouldn't play football.	Would I play football?
You would play football.	You wouldn't play football.	Would you play football?
He/she/it would play football.	He/she/it wouldn't play football.	Would he/she/it play football?
We would play football.	We wouldn't play football.	Would we play football?
You would play football.	You wouldn't play football.	Would you play football?
They would play football.	They wouldn't play football.	Would they play football?
		Questions with question word:
		Why would I play football?
		Why would you play football?
		Why would he/she/it play football?
		Why would we play football?
		Why would you play football?
		Why would they play football?

Examples of typical use:

1. For suggestions, polite questions and requests:
   Which ring would you take? – Well, I would take that ring.
   Would you like a drink?
   Would you help me, please?
2. In 'if'-clauses Type 2 – future situations that are improbable/unlikely:
   If you studied hard, you would pass the exam.

Conditional II

Positive sentences	Negative sentences	Questions
I would have helped. You would have helped. He/she/it would have helped. We would have helped. You would have helped. They would have helped.	I wouldn't have helped. You wouldn't have helped. He/she/it wouldn't have helped. We wouldn't have helped. You wouldn't have helped. They wouldn't have helped.	Would I have helped? Would you have helped? Would he/she/it have helped? Would we have helped? Would you have helped? Would they have helped? Questions with question word: Why would I have helped? Why would you have helped? Why would he/she/it have helped? Why would we have helped? Why would you have helped? Why would they have helped?
! Be careful with irregular verbs		

Example of typical use:

In 'if'-clauses Type 3 – past situations that are unreal/impossible/hypothetical:
If you had studied hard, you would have passed the exam.

If-clauses

There are three main types of 'if'-clauses (or conditional sentences) in English. They are basically used in the same way as conditional sentences in German. You can put the 'if'-clause at the beginning or at the end of the sentence.

1. Type 1 - Future situations (probable/possible):

a.	'if'-clause: simple present – main clause: 'will'-future If you study hard, you will pass the exam. Wenn du fleißig lernst, wirst du die Prüfung bestehen.
b.	'if'–clause: present perfect – main clause: 'will'- future If you have studied hard, you will pass the exam. Wenn du fleißig gelernt hast, wirst du die Prüfung bestehen.
c.	'if'-clause: simple present – main clause: can + infinitive If you study hard, you can pass the exam. Wenn du fleißig lernst, kannst du die Prüfung bestehen.
d.	'if'-clause: simple present – main clause: might + infinitive If you study hard, you might pass the exam. Wenn du fleißig lernst, wirst du eventuell die Prüfung bestehen.

2. Type 2 – Future situations (improbable/unlikely)

a.	'if'-clause: simple past – main clause: conditional I (would + infinitive) If you studied hard, you would pass the exam. Wenn du fleißig lernen würdest, würdest du die Prüfung bestehen.
b.	'if'-clause: simple past – main clause: could + infinitive If you studied hard, you could pass the exam. Wenn du fleißig lernen würdest, könntest du die Prüfung bestehen.

3. Type 3 – Past situations (unreal/impossible/hypothetical)

a.	'if'-clause: past perfect – main clause: conditional II (would + have + past participle) If you had studied hard, you would have passed the exam. Wenn du fleißig gelernt hättest, hättest du die Prüfung bestanden.
b.	'if'-clause: past perfect – main clause: could + have + past participle If you had studied hard, you could have passed the exam. Wenn du fleißig gelernt hättest, hättest du die Prüfung bestehen können.
c.	'if'-clause: past perfect – main clause: might + have + past participle If you had studied hard, you might have passed the exam. Wenn du fleißig gelernt hättest, hättest du eventuell die Prüfung bestanden.

! Exceptions to the rules:

1. The present tense is used in both clauses in general statements and for repeated activities or habits:
   If plants don't get enough water, they die. – If she has time, she goes to the fitness club.
2. For recommendations and advice use 'were' in the 'if'-clause and conditional I in the main clause:
   If I were you, I would study a bit harder.
3. 'If' can be left out when the order of the verb and subject are reversed:
   Had I studied harder, I would have passed the exam.

! Frequently made mistakes:

1. Be careful with commas. If you start with an 'if'-clause, use a comma. Don't use a comma if you start with the main clause:
   If you study hard, you will pass the exam.
   You will pass the exam if you study hard.
2. Don't use 'will' in the 'if'-clause, except to express willingness:
   They can come to Britain if they'll work.
3. Don't use 'would' in the 'if'-clause except when you are making a polite request:
   I would be grateful if you would hand in your homework on time in future.

The passive

The passive is often used when the action is more important than who or what performed it. The passive is frequently used in scientific and technical writing. The passive can be formed with or without an 'agent'. The 'agent' is the person or thing that causes an action to occur.

Form the passive using a form of 'to be' + past participle **(+ by + agent)**

Bank robbers often steal money.

Money is often stolen **by bank robbers**.

Simple present	Present progressive
I am invited to the party. You are invited to the party. He/she/it is invited to the party. We are invited to the party. You are invited to the party. They are invited to the party.	I am being terrorised by the neighbours. You are being terrorised by the neighbours. He/she/it is being terrorised by the neighbours. We are being terrorised by the neighbours. You are being terrorised by the neighbours. They are being terrorised by the neighbours.
Simple Past	Past progressive
I was invited to the party. You were invited to the party. He/she/it was invited to the party. We were invited to the party. You were invited to the party. They were invited to the party.	I was being terrorised by the neighbours. You were being terrorised by the neighbours. He/she/it was being terrorised by the neighbours. We were being terrorised by the neighbours. You were being terrorised by the neighbours. They were being terrorised by the neighbours.
Present perfect	Modal verbs
I have been invited to the party. You have been invited to the party. He/she/it has been invited to the party. We have been invited to the party. You have been invited to the party. They have been invited to the party.	I can be found in the office. You must be informed. He/she/it mustn't be informed. We needn't be informed. You ought to be informed. They should be informed.
Future	Future perfect
I will be invited to the party. You will be invited to the party. He/she/it will be invited to the party. We will be invited to the party. You will be invited to the party. They will be invited to the party.	I will have been invited to the party. You will have been invited to the party. He/she/it will have been invited to the party. We will have been invited to the party. You will have been invited to the party. They will have been invited to the party.
! Be careful with irregular verbs	

Relative clauses

Relative clauses are used to describe people or things. A relative clause usually begins with a relative pronoun.

Relative pronoun	refers to
who	people (subject or object)
whom	people (object), formal English
which	things
that	people or things (subject or object)
whose	possessions

1. Defining relative clauses:
   A defining relative clause is important for the meaning of the sentence. Without the relative clause the sentence would not make sense. Defining relative clauses are not set off from the rest of the sentence by commas:
   The house that/which we live in is very old.
   This is the woman who(m) I saw yesterday.
   This is the boy whose bike was stolen.

   The pronoun 'that, which, who(m)' can be left out if the pronoun is the object of the relative clause. This type of relative clause is known as 'contact' clause:
   The house we live in is very old.
   This is the woman I saw yesterday.

2. Non-defining relative clauses:
   In non-defining relative clauses the information is additional descriptive information. The sentence is clear even without a relative clause. These relative clauses are separated with commas:
   My grandmother, who will be 85 in December, walks her dog every morning.

Adjectives

Adjectives describe people and things: the tall man – bright lights

1. The comparison of adjectives

Positive form	Comparative form	Superlative form
cold hot funny modern	colder hotter funnier more modern	the coldest the hottest the funniest the most modern
! Remember the irregular forms:	good – better – the best much – more– the most bad – worse – the worst far – further – the furthest	

2. Making comparisons:
Use more/-er than, not as … as and as … as to make comparisons:
The black car is more modern than the red car.
The blue car is newer than the red car.
The red car is not as new as the blue one.
The white car is as new as the blue one.

3. Adjectives used as collective nouns:
Adjectives can be used as collective nouns. In such cases, the + adjective refers to a particular group of people as a whole:
We raised money for the blind.
The very young and the very old are particularly at risk.

4. Participles as adjectives:
The present participle (-ing form) and past participle of verbs can often be used as adjectives:
an interesting book
the finished report

5. Verbs followed by adjectives:
Verbs are usually followed by adverbs, however some verbs are followed by adjectives:

to be	Sally was tired.
to become	Anne became ill.
to feel	Thomas felt happy.
to get	The child got dirty.
to look	Mary looks sad.
to seem	Her new boyfriend seems very nice.

Adverbs

Adverbs are formed by adding -ly/-ily to an adjective.

Adjective	Adverb
safe happy real reasonable	safely happily really reasonably
! Remember the irregular forms:	good – well fast – fast hard – hard

1. Adverbs which describe actions (verbs): He walked quickly.
   She spoke slowly.
2. Adverbs before other adjectives: This is an extremely good essay.
3. Adverbs before other adverbs: He was driving incredibly fast.
4. Adverbs before past participles: Credit cards are frequently accepted.
5. The comparison of adverbs:

Positive form	Comparative form	Superlative form
fluently	more fluently	the most fluently
! Remember the irregular forms:	well – better – the best badly – worse – the worst fast – faster – the fastest	

6. Some useful adverbs: always, usually, often, frequently, sometimes, seldom, rarely, never, recently, soon, lately, in the past, in the future, largely, for the most part, partly, probably, possibly, hardly, definitely, obviously, clearly, basically, consequently, as a result

Question tags

A question tag is added to the end of a sentence turning it into a question. In German you use expressions like '…, nicht wahr?' and '…, oder?' in a similar way.

1. If the statement is positive, the questions tag is negative:
   He likes chocolate, doesn't he?
2. If the statement is negative, the question tag is positive:
   He doesn't like chocolate, does he?
3. The subject of the verb is the same in the statement and in the question tag:
   He likes chocolate, doesn't he?
4. If the statement is in the simple present or simple past tense, the question tag uses 'do/don't' or 'did/didn't':
   He likes chocolate, doesn't he?
   He went to England, didn't he?
5. If the statement uses an auxiliary verb (to be, to have, will, etc.) or a modal (can, must, etc.), use the modal or auxiliary in the same tense in the tag:
   Tom is here, isn't he?
   Roger has bought a new car, hasn't he?
   Jill will be at the party, won't she?
   You can speak English, can't you?

Modal auxiliaries

1. Will/would/can/could/may:

Asking someone to do something: Will/Would/Can/Could you do me a favour?
Asking for permission/giving permission: May I use your phone? – Yes, of course, you may.
Talking about abilities: She can speak English.

2. Must/mustn't/needn't:

Instructing someone to do something or not to do something: You must wear a safety helmet. You mustn't smoke in the office.
Talking about a necessity or duty: I must finish the project by Friday. You needn't pay in advance.

3. May/might/could/must/will:

Expressing a possibility or probability: It may/might/could/will rain. You must be Mr Jones.
Making a suggestion: We could go to that new Spanish restaurant.

4. Should/ought to/shouldn't/ought not to:

Giving advice: You should/ought to use a dictionary. You shouldn't arrive late for the interview.

5. Modal auxiliaries only have a present and/or past tense form. For other tenses substitutes are used:

Modal auxiliary	Substitutes	Examples
can/could	be able to	He won't be able to lift the piano.
may/mustn't	be allowed to not be allowed to	We were allowed to visit the church. We weren't allowed to see the pope.
must/needn't	have to not have to	The Millers will have to sell their house. We didn't have to wait long.

-ing forms

An -ing form can be either a present participle or a gerund.

The present participle

1. The present participle is used in the progressive tenses (present progressive, past progressive, etc.):
   Mary is playing the guitar. – The plane was flying at a height of 10,000 metres.
2. The present participle can be used as an adjective: the winning party – a growing child
3. The present participle can be used to shorten clauses, often after a conjunction, e.g: after, while, before, when
   I was riding my bike to work when I met her. → While riding/Riding my bike to work, I met her.
   I saw a woman who was wearing a silly hat. → I saw a woman wearing a silly hat.
   After we had eaten a burger, we went home. → After eating a burger, we went home.
   Read the text before you answer the questions. → Read the text before answering the questions.
   Although I felt tired, I couldn't sleep. → Although feeling tired, I couldn't sleep.

The gerund

1. The gerund is used after prepositions: You're very good at speaking English.
2. The gerund is often used after certain verbs: like, hate, enjoy, love, mind, prefer
   I don't mind watching TV but I prefer reading and I also enjoy playing computer games.
3. The gerund can be used as a noun: Laughing is good for you. – Studying is very important.
4. Some verbs have the construction verb + preposition + gerund:
   to be afraid of, to look forward to, to feel like, to talk about, to insist on, to decide against, to think about/of, to succeed in, to apologise for
   I'm afraid of flying.
5. When the following expressions are followed by a verb, use the gerund:
   There's no point in waiting any longer.
   It's not worth going to see the new James Bond film.
   A waste of money/time: It's a waste of time talking to you.
   To spend/waste/time/money: He spent all his money playing on the fruit machines.

Reported speech

Reported speech (or indirect speech) is used to report what someone has said without quoting them.

1. Start the reported speech with a reporting verb:

   a. Statements: say (that), tell sb. (that), answer, mention, explain, reply, etc.
      "I'm tired." → She says (that) she's tired.

   b. Questions: ask, want to know
      "Are you hungry?" → She asks me if I'm hungry.
      "Where do you go to school?" → She wants to know where I go to school.

   c. Commands: tell sb. to + infinitive
      "Leave me alone!" → She told me to leave her alone.

2. If the reporting verb is in the present, present perfect or future tense, the tense stays the same:
"Watching TV is bad for your eyes". → Mr Jones says watching TV is bad for our eyes.
→ Mr Jones has said watching TV is bad for our eyes.
→ Mr Jones will say watching TV is bad for our eyes.

3. If the reporting verb is in the past tense, the tense of the reported speech changes:

simple present "I walk the dog every day."	→	simple past She said she walked the dog every day.
present progressive "I'm walking the dog."	→	past progressive She said she was walking the dog.
simple past "I walked the dog last night."	→	past perfect She said she had walked the dog last night.
past progressive "I was walking the dog."	→	past perfect progressive She said she had been walking the dog.
present perfect "I have walked the dog."	→	past perfect She said she had walked the dog.
present perfect progressive "I have been walking the dog."	→	past perfect progressive She said she had been walking the dog.
past perfect "I had walked the dog."	→	past perfect She said she had walked the dog.
past perfect progressive "I had been walking the dog."	→	past perfect progressive She said she had been walking the dog.
will future "I will walk the dog every day."	→	conditional I She said she would walk the dog every day.

4. Questions follow the same tense changes as statements:
"Where did you park the car?" → The policeman asked the man where he had parked the car.

5. Some adverbs of time also change in reported speech, for example:

now	→	then
yesterday	→	the day before/the previous day
here	→	there
last year	→	the year before/the previous year
today	→	that day
tomorrow	→	the next day

6. Statements involving truths and facts do not have to change:
"Cats eat mice". → The teacher said that cats eat mice.

Videotraining: Englische Aussprache

Perfekte englische Aussprache leicht gemacht: Mit dem Lernprogramm zur englischen Lautschrift können Sie alle Laute einüben. Wählen Sie einfach in der Navigation rechts den entsprechenden Reiter (*Vowels* oder *Consonants*) aus und dann klicken Sie auf das gewünschte phonetische Symbol. Sprechen Sie die Wörter laut nach.
Unter www.klett.de geben Sie einfach den Online-Link 808201-1000 ein. Von dort aus können Sie die Webanwendung online starten.

Abkürzungen

etw. = etwas	sb. = somebody	BE = britisches Englisch
jmdm = jemandem	coll. = umgangssprachlich	AE = amerikanisches Englisch
jmdn = jemanden	sg = Singular	fml = formal
sth. = something	pl = Plural	infml = informal

Pronunciation

In this book the following phonetic symbols are used:

Consonants		Vowels		Diphthongs	Additional symbols
[ŋ] morning	[ʃ] she	[ɑ:] father	[i] happy	[aɪ] I, my	['] Primary stress on the following syllable
[r] red	[tʃ] lunch	[ʌ] but	[i:] teacher, she	[aʊ] now, house	[ˌ] Secondary stress on the following syllable
[s] this	[ð] the	[e] pen	[ɒ] got	[eə] there, pair	[‿] Link between two words
[z] is	[θ] thanks	[ə] a sister	[ɔ:] ball	[eɪ] name, they	[x] Pronounced like the German acht
[ʒ] television	[v] video	[ɜ:] girl	[ʊ] book	[ɪə] here, idea	
[dʒ] page	[w] wow, one	[æ] flat	[u] January	[ɔɪ] boy	
		[ɪ] it	[u:] too, two	[əʊ] hello	
				[ʊə] sure	

All other letters are pronounced roughly the way they are written, e.g [b], [j], [l] etc.

The page numbers refer to the first occurrence of the word.

A

to abandon [ə'bændən] verlassen, aufgeben 28

to abolish [ə'bɒlɪʃ] abschaffen 226

abundant [ə'bʌndənt] reichlich 46

abuse [ə'bju:s] Missbrauch 40

abused [ə'bju:zd] missbraucht 48

to accelerate [ək'seləreɪt] beschleunigen 143

to access ['ækses] erreichen 14

access ['ækses] Zugang 46

accessible [ək'sesəbl] zugänglich 75

accommodation [əˌkɒmə'deɪʃn] Unterbringung 142

to accompany [ə'kʌmpənɪ] begleiten 282

accomplishment [ə'kʌmplɪʃmənt] Leistung 148

to account for [ə'kaʊnt fɔ:] ausmachen, (eine Anzahl) stellen 96

to accumulate [ə'kju:mjəleɪt] anhäufen, (sich) ansammeln 28

accusation [ˌækjʊ'zeɪʃn] Anschuldigung 136

to achieve [ə'tʃi:v] erreichen 20

acid rain [ˌæsɪd 'reɪn] saurer Regen 61

to acknowledge [ək'nɒlɪdʒ] anerkennen 137

acquaintance [ə'kweɪntəns] Bekannte(r) 27

to acquire [ə'kwaɪə] erwerben 16

to act on sth. ['ækt‿ɒn ˌsʌmθɪŋ] auf etw. reagieren 146

addiction [ə'dɪkʃn] Sucht 17

addictive [ə'dɪktɪv] süchtig machend 147

additive ['ædɪtɪv] Zusatzstoff 51

to adjust [ə'dʒʌst] anpassen, sich anpassen 288

admiration [ˌædmɪ'reɪʃn] Bewunderung 188

adolescent [ˌædə'lesənt] Heranwachsender 15

to adopt [ə'dɒpt] annehmen 280

to advance [əd'vɑ:ns] fortführen, vorangehen 154

advance [əd'vɑ:ns] Fortschritt, Vorstoß 156

advantage [əd'vɑ:ntɪdʒ] Vorteil, Vorzug 124

adventurous [əd'ventʃərəs] abenteuerlich 53

adverse ['ædvɜ:s] widrig 285

advice [əd'vaɪs] Rat 282

adviser [əd'vaɪzə] Ratgeber(in) 94

advocate ['ædvəkət] Befürworter(in) 240

aerospace ['eərəʊspeɪs] Luft- und Raumfahrt 164

affair [ə'feə] Affäre 28

to affect [ə'fekt] betreffen, beeinflussen, Einfluss nehmen auf 18

affection [ə'fekn] Zuwendung; Zuneigung 28

affiliation [əˌfɪlɪ'eɪʃn] Verbindung, Zugehörigkeit 238

to afford sth. [ə'fɔ:d] sich etw. leisten können 142

affordable [ə'fɔ:dəbl] bezahlbar 136

agenda [ə'dʒendə] Tagesordnung 165

agility [ə'dʒɪlətɪ] Gewandtheit 267

agriculture ['ægrɪkʌltʃə] Landwirtschaft 263

to aid [eɪd] helfen, unterstützen 124

aid [eɪd] Hilfe 136

to aim at ['eɪm‿ət] zielen auf 96

air-freighted ['eəˌfreɪtɪd] per Luftfracht 242

allegedly [ə'ledʒədlɪ] angeblich 204

alongside [əˌlɒŋ'saɪd] neben 200

ambitious [æm'bɪʃəs] ehrgeizig 46

ancient ['eɪnʃənt] antik 48

to announce [ə'naʊns] ankündigen, verkünden 46

annually ['ænjʊəlɪ] jährlich 34

to anticipate [æn'tɪsɪpeɪt] erwarten 96

anxiety [æŋˌzaɪətɪ] Angst 196

to apologise [ə'pɒlədʒaɪz] sich entschuldigen 122

appeal [ə'pi:l] Anziehung(skraft), Anreiz 18

to appeal [ə'pi:l] ansprechen 53

appearance [ə'pɪərəns] Aussehen 139

applicant ['æplɪkənt] Bewerber(in) 113

application [ˌæplɪ'keɪʃn] Anwendung 263

to apply [ə'plaɪ] anwenden 88

to apply to sb. [ə'plaɪ tə ˌsʌmbədɪ] für jdn gelten 96

to appoint [ə'pɔɪnt] ernennen, verpflichten 128

to appreciate [ə'prɪ:ʃɪeɪt] schätzen, zu schätzen wissen 29

appreciation [əˌpri:ʃɪ'eɪʃn] Wertschätzung 64

apprenticeship [ə'prentɪʃɪp] Berufsausbildung, Lehre 144

approach [ə'prəʊtʃ] Ansatz, Haltung, Herangehensweise 46

appropriate [ə'prəʊprɪət] angemessen, passend 12

approval [ə'pru:vl] Billigung, Zustimmung, Beifall 156

to approve [ə'pru:v] genehmigen, billigen 201

approximately [ə'prɒksɪmətlɪ] ungefähr 49

arid ['ærɪd] trocken, dürr 61

to arise [ə'raɪz] anfallen 269

to ascend [ə'send] aufsteigen 114

aspirational [ˌæspɪ'reɪʃənl] erstrebenswert 237

to aspire [ə'spaɪə] anstreben 125

to assault [ə'sɒlt] angreifen 204

to assemble [ə'sembl] zusammenstellen 140

assembly [ə'semblɪ] Versammlung, Rat 127

to assess [ə'ses] beurteilen, bewerten 52

asset ['æset] Vermögen(swerte) 228

association [əˌsəʊʃɪ'eɪʃn] Verbindung 40

assumption [ə'sʌmpʃn] Annahme 188

astonishing [ə'stɒnɪʃɪŋ] erstaunlich 146

at one's disposal [ət wʌnz dɪ'spəʊzl] zur Verfügung 237

attainable [ə'teɪnəbl] erreichbar 107

attempt [ə'tempt] Versuch 50

attitude ['ætɪtju:d] Haltung 15

audience ['ɔ:dɪəns] Publikum 28

authoritarian [ˌɔ:θɒrɪ'teərɪən] autoritär 116

authorities [ɔ:'θɒrətɪz] Behörden 13

average ['ævrɪdʒ] durchschnittlich 282

aware [ə'weə] bewusst 164

awareness [ə'weənəs] Bewusstsein 192

awkward ['ɔ:kwəd] seltsam 242

B

to back [bæk] unterstützen 262

to back up [ˌbæk‿'ʌp] absichern 47

backdrop ['bækdrɒp] Hintergrund 92

ball bearing [ˌbɔ:l'beərɪŋ] Kugellager 171

to ban [bæn] verbieten 12

to banish ['bænɪʃ] verbannen 28

barely ['beəlɪ] kaum 14

barrier ['bærɪə] Hindernis 92

battery farm ['bætərɪ ˌfɑ:m] Legebatterie 43

to battle ['bætl] für/um etw. kämpfen 144

to be at a loose end [bɪ‿ət ə ˌlu:s 'end] nicht wissen, was man mit sich anfangen soll 24

to be exposed to sth. [bɪ‿ɪk'spəʊzd tə] etw. ausgesetzt sein 206

to be held responsible for [bɪ ˌheld rɪ'spɒnsəbl fə] verantwortlich gemacht werden für 190

to be in charge of sth. [bɪ‿ɪn 'tʃɑ:dʒ əv] zuständig sein für etw. 128

to be more likely to do sth. [bɪ ˌmɔ: 'laɪklɪ tə 'du:] es ist wahrscheinlicher, dass man etw. tut 152

to be opposed to sth. [bɪ‿ə'pəʊzd tə ˌsʌmθɪŋ] gegen etw. sein 132

to be rewarded [bɪ rɪˈwɔ:dɪd] belohnt werden 139

to be set [bɪ ˈset] erwartet werden 152

to be split over [ˈsplɪt ˌəʊvə] geteilter Meinung sein über 242

to be struck by sth. [bɪ ˈstrʌk] von etwas beeindruckt sein 73

to be sworn in [bɪ ˌswɔ:n ɪn] vereidigt werden 113

to bear in mind [ˌbeər‿ɪn ˈmaɪnd] beachten 173

behaviour [bɪˈheɪvjə] Verhalten 236

to belong to [bɪˈlɒŋ tu:] gehören zu 29

beneficial [ˌbenəˈfɪʃl] förderlich, nützlich 137

benefit [ˈbenəfɪt] Vorteil, Leistung, Nutzen 34

betrayal [bɪˈtreɪəl] Verrat, Treuebruch 110

beverage [ˈbevrɪdʒ] Getränk 51

beyond [bɪˈɒnd] jenseits, außerhalb 232

biased [ˈbaɪəst] voreingenommen 57

bidder [ˈbɪdə] Bietende(r) 142

bill [bɪl] Rechnung 16

billion [ˈbɪljən] Milliarde 34

binding [ˈbaɪndɪŋ] bindend 46

biodiversity [ˌbaɪəʊdaɪˈvɜ:sətɪ] Artenvielfalt 45

biotechnology [ˌbaɪəʊtekˈnɒlədʒɪ] Biotechnologie 164

to blame sb. [bleɪm] jmdm die Schuld geben für 24

blank [blæŋk] unbeschrieben, leer 200

to blend [blend] mischen 189

to bless [bles] segnen 191

blessing [ˈblesɪŋ] Segen 231

blog [blɒg] Internet-Tagebuch 93

to blush [blʌʃ] rot werden 15

to boast [bəʊst] angeben 15

bold [bəʊld] mutig, entschlossen 100

bone marrow [ˈbəʊn ˌmærəʊ] Knochenmark 159

to boost [bu:st] stärken, erhöhen, in die Höhe treiben 64

to bother [ˈbɒðə] sich die Mühe machen 148

boundary [ˈbaʊndrɪ] Grenze 45

branch [brɑ:ntʃ] Sektor 51

brand [brænd] Marke 236

brand value [ˌbrænd ˈvælju:] Markenwert 225

breakthrough [ˈbreɪkθru:] Durchbruch 196

breed [bri:d] (hier:) Generation 191

to bridge [brɪdʒ] überbrücken 282

broad [brɔ:d] weitgehend 290

broadband [ˈbrɔ:dbænd] Breitband 14

to broadcast [ˈbrɔ:dkɑ:st] übertragen, senden 13

broadcasting [ˈbrɔ:dkɑ:stɪŋ] Rundfunk und Fernsehen 90

brochure [ˈbrəʊʃə] Prospekt, Broschüre 80

to bully [ˈbʊlɪ] mobben 40

burden [ˈbɜ:dn] Last 29

byproduct [ˈbaɪˌprɒdʌkt] Nebenprodukt 225

C

to call for [ˈkɔ:l fɔ:] verlangen 248

calling [ˈkɔ:lɪŋ] Berufung 149

canning [ˈkænɪŋ] Konserven- 171

canvas [ˈkænvəs] Segeltuch 200

capability [ˌkeɪpəˈbɪlətɪ] Möglichkeit, Fähigkeit 47

capable [ˈkeɪpəbl] fähig 131

capital [ˈkæpɪtl] Hauptstadt 67

carbon dioxide [ˌkɑ:bndaɪˈɒksaɪd] Kohlendioxid 44

carriage [ˈkærɪdʒ] Wagen (eines Zuges etc.) 72

cash machine [ˈkæʃ məˌʃi:n] Bankautomat 285

to cast (a vote) [kɑ:st] (hier:) (Stimme) abgeben 113

casual [ˈkæʒjʊəl] Gelegenheits- 290

casualty [ˈkæʒjʊəltɪ] Opfer 93

to cater for [ˈkeɪtə fə] sorgen für 53

cautious [ˈkɔ:ʃəs] vorsichtig 127

CCTV (closed circuit television) [ˌsi:si:ti:ˈvi:] Videoüberwachung 123

censorship [ˈsensəʃɪp] Zensur 92

census [ˈsensəs] Volkszählung 287

to challenge [ˈtʃælɪndʒ] herausfordern 195

challenge [ˈtʃælɪndʒ] Herausforderung 223

channels [ˈtʃænlz] Wege, Kanäle 93

characteristic [ˌkærəktəˈrɪstɪk] Merkmal, Charakteristikum, Eigenschaft 30

charity [ˈtʃærɪtɪ] Wohltätigkeit, Wohltätigkeitsorganisation, -verein 142

to chart [tʃɑ:t] vermessen, skizzieren 178

chit-chat [ˈtʃɪttʃæt] Geplauder 266

citizen [ˈsɪtɪzn] Bürger(in), Staatsangehörige(r) 196

civic [ˈsɪvɪk] bürgerlich 201

civil service [ˌsɪvɪl ˈsɜ:vɪs] öffentlicher Dienst 124

climate change [ˈklaɪmət ˌtʃeɪndʒ] Klimawandel 44

cloak [kləʊk] Umhang 181

to clone [kləʊn] klonen 156

clone [kləʊn] Klon 164

coastline [ˈkəʊstlaɪn] Küstenlinie 46

to coin [kɔɪn] prägen, erfinden 92

to coincide [ˌkəʊɪnˈsaɪd] übereinstimmen 237

coincidence [kəʊˈɪnsɪdəns] Zufall 31

to collaborate [kəˈlæbəreɪt] zusammenarbeiten 221

to collapse [kəˈlæps] einstürzen 64

to combat [ˈkɒmbæt] bekämpfen 237

combustion [kəmˈbʌstʃn] Verbrennung 47

commander-in-chief [kəˌmɑ:ndər‿ɪn ˈtʃi:f] Oberbefehlshaber 112

to commission [kəˈmɪʃn] in Auftrag geben 78

commitment [kəˈmɪtmənt] Bindung, Engagement 53

committed [kə'mɪtɪd] motiviert, entschlossen 175

common ['kɒmən] normal, üblich 280

commute [kə'mju:t] Pendelstrecke 120

compassion [kəm'pæʃn] Mitgefühl 34

compelling [kəm'pelɪŋ] faszinierend 101

to compensate ['kɒmpənseɪt] entschädigen 53

to compete [kəm'pi:t] konkurrieren, mithalten, teilnehmen 221

competitive [kəm'petɪtɪv] konkurrenzfähig 223

to compile [kəm'paɪl] zusammenstellen 52

to compliment sb. ['kɒmplɪmənt] jmdm Komplimente machen 110

to comply [kəm'plaɪ] übereinstimmen 140

to comprise [kəm'praɪz] umfassen 200

compulsory [kəm'pʌlsrɪ] obligatorisch, vorgeschrieben, verpflichtend 94

to compute [kəm'pju:t] rechnen 165

conclusion [kən'klu:ʒn] Schlussfolgerung 72

to conduct [kən'dʌkt] ausführen 156

confidence ['kɒnfɪdəns] Selbstvertrauen, Sicherheit 19

confident ['kɒnfɪdənt] sicher, selbstbewusst 139

confidential [ˌkɒnfɪ'denʃl] vertraulich 140

congestion [kən'dʒestʃn] Verkehrsstau 260

to conquer ['kɒŋkə] besiegen, erobern 124

conscience ['kɒnʃəns] Gewissen 223

consciousness ['kɒnʃəsnəs] Bewusstsein 48

consistent with [kən'sɪstənt wɪð] übereinstimmend mit 240

to console [kən'səʊl] trösten 35

to consolidate [kən'sɒlɪdeɪt] vereinigen 291

constituency [kən'stɪtjʊənsɪ] Wahlbezirk, Wahlkreis 128

to constitute ['kɒnstɪtju:t] darstellen, bilden 28

constitution [ˌkɒnstɪ'tju:ʃn] Verfassung 128

construction [kən'strʌkʃn] Baugewerbe 164

consumption [kən'sʌmpʃn] Verbrauch 20

contemporary [kən'temprərɪ] zeitgenössisch, gegenwärtig 15

content ['kɒntent] Inhalte 281

contentious [kən'tenʃəs] umstritten 142

contest ['kɒntest] Wettbewerb 33

contestant [kən'testənt] Teilnehmer(in) an einem Wettbewerb 180

contract ['kɒntrækt] Auftrag, Vertrag 225

to contribute [kən'trɪbju:t] beitragen 97

convenience [kən'vi:nɪəns] Annehmlichkeit, Bequemlichkeit 172

convention [kən'venʃn] (hier:) Parteitag 113

convergence [kən'vɜ:dʒəns] Zusammenlaufen, Annäherung 165

to convert [kən'vɜ:t] verwandeln, umwandeln 258

to convey [kən'veɪ] vermitteln 78

convulsive [kən'vʌlsɪv] erschütternd 191

core [kɔ:] Kern; Kern-, Haupt- 16

corporate ['kɔ:pərət] Unternehmens- 237

to counter ['kaʊntə] erwidern, dagegen sprechen 57

counterpart ['kaʊntəpɑ:t] Gegenstück, Pendant 36

to cover ['kʌvə] senden 248

to crawl [krɔ:l] krabbeln 114

to credit sb. with sth. ['kredɪt] jmdm etw. zuschreiben 104

criticism ['krɪtɪsɪzm] Kritik 116

crop [krɒp] Feldfrucht, Getreide 288

crowd [kraʊd] (Menschen)menge 13

to crowd [kraʊd] überfüllen 140

crucial ['kru:ʃəl] entscheidend, äußerst wichtig 69

to crush [krʌʃ] unterdrücken 93

curative ['kjʊərətɪv] heilend 157

to cure [kjʊə] heilen 156

curious ['kjʊərɪəs] wissbegierig 53

currency ['kʌrənsɪ] Währung 225

current ['kʌrənt] aktuell, gegenwärtig 45

current affairs [ˌkʌrənt‿ə'feəz] aktuelle Nachrichten, Zeitgeschehen 238

curriculum [kə'rɪkjələm] Lehrplan 94

curse [kɜ:s] Fluch 231

custody ['kʌstədɪ] Gewahrsam 13

cut [kʌt] Senkung, Kürzung 144

to cut ties [kʌt‿'taɪz] Verbindungen lösen 60

cute [kju:t] süß 227

cynical ['sɪnɪkl] zynisch 53

D

damage ['dæmɪdʒ] Schaden 49

data protection ['deɪtə prəˌtekʃn] Datenschutz 43

dawn [dɔ:n] Morgendämmerung, Beginn 262

to debrief ['pækɪdʒ] einen Einsatzbericht abgeben 83

debt [det] Schuld, Schulden 142

debts [dets] Schulden 16

decade ['dekeɪd] Jahrzehnt 96

declaration [ˌdeklə'reɪʃn] Erklärung 60

to decline [dɪ'klaɪn] sinken, zurückgehen, abnehmen 40

decline [dɪ'klaɪn] Rückgang 130

to decrease [dɪ'kri:s] zurückgehen, sinken 19

decreasingly [dɪ'kri:sɪŋlɪ] immer weniger 126

to dedicate ['dedɪkeɪt] widmen 16

deep-seated [ˌdi:p'si:tɪd] tiefsitzend 116

deficit ['defɪsɪt] Defizit 132

defining [dɪ'faɪnɪŋ] entscheidend 114

degeneration [dɪˌdʒenəˈreɪʃn] Abnahme, Degeneration 156

to delay [dɪˈleɪ] hinauszögern 263

deliberate [dɪˈlɪbrət] absichtlich 57

delicate [ˈdelɪkət] empfindlich 188

delinquency [dɪˈlɪŋkwənsɪ] Straffälligkeit 284

delivery times [dɪˈlɪvrɪ ˌtaɪmz] Lieferzeiten 80

to demand [dɪˈmɑːnd] verlangen, fordern 52

demand [dɪˈmɑːnd] Anforderung 77

demographic [ˌdeməˈgræfɪk] demografisch 290

denial [dɪˈnaɪəl] Ablehnung 270

to denounce [dɪˈnaʊns] verurteilen 142

densely [ˈdenslɪ] dicht 67

densely populated [ˌdenslɪ ˈpɒpjəleɪtɪd] dicht bevölkert 113

to deny [dɪˈnaɪ] abstreiten, verweigern, vorenthalten 95

dependency [dɪˈpendənsɪ] Abhängigkeit 174

to deploy [dɪˈplɔɪ] einsetzen 132

to deposit [dɪˈpɒzɪt] ablagern 258

to depreciate [dɪˈpriːʃɪeɪt] abschreiben 121

depression [dɪˈpreʃn] (hier:) Tiefdruckgebiet 67

deprived [dɪˈpraɪvd] heruntergekommen 287

depth [depθ] Tiefe 28

to derive from [dɪˈraɪv frəm] sich ableiten von 196

to derive sth. from [dɪˈraɪv frəm] etw. beziehen aus 163

derogatory [dɪˈrɒgətrɪ] abschätzig, abwertend 213

desertification [dɪˌzɜːtɪfɪˈkeɪʃn] Versteppung 61

desirable [dɪˈzaɪərəbl] wünschenswert, erstrebenswert 209

desire [dɪˈzaɪə] Wunsch, Verlangen 29

desolate [ˈdesələt] verlassen 120

to despise [dɪˈspaɪz] verschmähen 111

despite [dɪˈspaɪt] trotz 146

destination [ˌdestɪˈneɪʃn] (Reise-)ziel 52

destructive [dɪˈstrʌktɪv] zerstörerisch 282

to detain [dɪˈteɪn] in Gewahrsam nehmen 13

deterioration [dɪˌtɪərɪəˈreɪʃn] Verschlechterung 115

to determine [dɪˈtɜːmɪn] bestimmen, feststellen 148

determined [dɪˈtɜːmɪnd] bestimmt, entschlossen 16

to devalue [ˌdiːˈvæljuː] abwerten 37

development [dɪˈveləpmənt] Entwicklung 62

to devise [dɪˈvaɪz] erfinden 69

to diminish [dɪˈmɪnɪʃ] kleiner werden 179

disability [ˌdɪsəˈbɪlətɪ] Behinderung 152

disadvantaged [ˌdɪsədˈvɑːntɪdʒd] benachteiligt 144

to discard [dɪˈskɑːd] wegwerfen, abwerfen 181

discomfort [dɪˈskʌmfət] Unannehmlichkeit 68

discount [ˈdɪskaʊnt] Rabatt, Nachlass 81

to discourage [dɪˈskʌrɪdʒ] abschrecken, abhalten 18

to discriminate against sb. [dɪˈskrɪmɪneɪt‿əˌgenst ˌsʌmbədɪ] jdn diskriminieren 97

discrimination [dɪˌskrɪmɪˈneɪʃn] Diskriminierung 125

to disguise oneself [dɪsˈgaɪz ˌwʌnself] sich verkleiden 208

to dishonor [dɪˈsɒnə] entehren 110

to dismiss sth. [dɪˈsmɪs] etw. als … abtun 56

to disobey [ˌdɪsəˈbeɪ] nicht gehorchen 209

disparity [dɪˈspærətɪ] Ungleichheit 115

to dispel [dɪˈspel] verbannen 40

to disperse [dɪˈspɜːs] verstreuen 286

to displace [dɪˈspleɪs] ersetzen 261

dissent [dɪˈsent] Widerspruch 191

to dissolve [dɪˈzɒlv] auflösen 51

to distinguish [dɪˈstɪŋgwɪʃ] unterscheiden 131

distinguished [dɪˈstɪŋgwɪʃt] angesehen, bedeutend 180

distributed [dɪˈstrɪbjuːtɪd] verteilt 47

disunited [ˌdɪsjuːˈnaɪtɪd] entsolidarisiert, uneinig 126

to ditch [dɪtʃ] aufgeben 152

diverse [daɪˈvɜːs] unterschiedlich, vielfältig, verschieden 53

doable [ˈduːəbl] machbar 46

domestic market [dəˌmestɪk ˈmɑːkɪt] Heimatmarkt 225

to dominate [ˈdɒmɪneɪt] beherrschen 196

dominion [dəˈmɪnjən] Herrschaft, Machtgebiet 125

to donate [dəʊˈneɪt] spenden 142

donation [dəʊˈneɪʃn] Spende 64

doomed [duːmd] verdammt 131

double-edged sword [ˌdʌblˌedʒd ˈsɔːd] zweischneidiges Schwert 155

doubt [daʊt] Zweifel 147

downturn [ˈdaʊntɜːn] Abschwung 232

to draft [drɑːft] entwerfen 192

drenched [drentʃt] durchnässt 72

drill [drɪl] Übung 104

drought [draʊt] Dürre 45

dull [dʌl] langweilig 147

duty [ˈdjuːtɪ] Pflicht 12

dystopia [dɪsˈtəʊpɪə] Dystopie, Antiutopie 196

E

eager [ˈiːgə] eifrig 188

early riser [ˌɜːlɪ ˈraɪzə] Frühaufsteher 139

ease [iːz] Erleichterung, Bequemlichkeit 37

economic cycle [ˌiːkənɒmɪk ˈsaɪkl] Konjunktur 225

edible [ˈedɪbl] essbar 289

eerie [ˈɪərɪ] gespenstisch 114

effect [ɪˈfekt] Auswirkung 44

elaborate [ɪ'læbrət] kompliziert 74

to elaborate [ɪ'læbəreɪt] näher ausführen 230

electricity grid [ˌelɪk'trɪsətɪ ˌgrɪd] Stromnetz 47

to eliminate [ɪ'lɪmɪneɪt] abschaffen, beseitigen 124

elusive [ɪ'lu:sɪv] (hier:) schwer zu erreichen 184

embarrassment [ɪm'bærəsmənt] Beschämung, Peinlichkeit 236

embedded [ɪm'bedɪd] tief verwurzelt; eingelassen 40

embryonic [ˌembrɪ'ɒnɪk] Embryo- 156

to emerge [ɪ'mɜ:dʒ] herauskommen 120

emergence [ɪ'mɜ:dʒəns] Entstehung 196

emerging [ɪ'mɜ:dʒɪŋ] neu 47

to emigrate ['emɪgreɪt] auswandern 60

emission [ɪ'mɪʃn] Emission, Ausstoß 44

to emit [ɪ'mɪt] ausstoßen, emittieren 44

emitter [ɪ'mɪtə] Erzeuger 61

empathic [em'pæθɪk] einfühlsam 37

empathy ['empəθɪ] Empathie, Mitgefühl 36

emphasis ['empfəsɪs] Betonung 97

to emphasise ['emfəsaɪz] betonen 92

to employ a strategy [ɪm'plɔɪ] (hier:) eine Strategie anwenden 21

to empower [ɪm'paʊə] befähigen 194

to enable [ɪ'neɪbl] ermöglichen 194

to encompass sth. [ɪn'kʌmpəs] etw. umfassen 124

encounter [ɪn'kaʊntə] Begegnung 24

to encourage sb. [ɪn'kʌrɪdʒ] jdn ermutigen, animieren 18

encouragement [ɪn'kʌrɪdʒmənt] Ermutigung 238

endangered [ɪn'deɪndʒəd] gefährdet; (hier:) vom Aussterben bedroht 63

to endorse [ɪn'dɔ:s] billigen, unterstützen 204

enemy ['enəmɪ] Feind 49

to engage [ɪn'geɪdʒ] involvieren 195

to engage in sth. [ɪn'geɪdʒ] sich an etw. beteiligen 24

engaged [ɪn'geɪdʒd] verlobt 209

engaging [ɪn'geɪdʒɪŋ] einnehmend, faszinierend 179

to enhance [ɪn'hɑ:ns] verbessern, steigern 79

enhancement [ɪn'hɑ:nsmənt] Verbesserung 164

to enlist [ɪn'lɪst] (hier:) in Anspruch nehmen 236

enquiry [ɪn'kwaɪərɪ] Anfrage 80

to enslave [ɪn'sleɪv] versklaven 196

to ensure (that) [ɪn'ʃɔ:] sicherstellen, garantieren, gewährleisten; dafür sorgen (, dass) 46

to entail [ɪn'teɪl] beinhalten 269

entire [ɪn'taɪə] ganz 97

entirely [ɪn'taɪəlɪ] ganz, vollständig 132

entitlement [ɪn'taɪtlmənt] Anrecht, Anspruch 36

envious ['envɪəs] neidisch 69

epidemic [ˌepɪ'demɪk] Epidemie, Seuche 36

equal ['i:kwəl] gleich 95

to eradicate [ɪ'rædɪkeɪt] beseitigen 40

essential [ɪ'senʃl] notwendig, wesentlich 178

to establish [ɪ'stæblɪʃ] aufbauen 77

to estimate ['estɪmeɪt] schätzen 34

estimate ['estɪmət] Schätzung 44

ethics ['eθɪks] Werte 149

even ['i:vn] gleichmäßig 284

event [ɪ'vent] Ereignis, Veranstaltung 12

to evict [ɪ'vɪkt] jmdn hinauswerfen, (hier:) ausschließen 180

evidence ['evɪdəns] Beweis, Nachweis 12

evident ['evɪdənt] offensichtlich 179

evidently ['evɪdəntlɪ] offensichtlich 131

exaggeration [ɪgˌzædʒə'reɪʃn] Übertreibung 175

to exceed [ɪk'si:d] übertreffen, übersteigen 46

excessive [ɪk'sesɪv] übermäßig 57

excluded [ɪk'sklu:dɪd] ausgegrenzt 191

executive [ɪg'zekjətɪv] Führungskraft 64

executive [ɪg'zekjʊtɪv] leitend(e/r) 148

to exert [ɪg'zɜ:t] ausüben 291

exhaustive [ɪg'zɔ:stɪv] erschöpfend, umfassend 29

exhibition [ˌeksɪ'bɪʃn] Ausstellung 245

to expand [ɪk'spænd] (sich) ausdehnen 229

expansion [ɪk'spænʃn] Expansion, Erweiterung 286

to expel [ɪk'spel] ausschließen 114

to expend in [ɪk'spend] aufwenden für 34

expenditure [ɪk'spendɪtʃə] Auslagen, Ausgaben 136

expense [ɪk'spens] Kosten 194

to exploit [ɪk'splɔɪt] ausbeuten 142

exploit [ˌeksplɔɪ'teɪʃn] Tat 244

exploitation [ˌeksplɔɪ'teɪʃn] Ausbeutung 137

to explore [ɪk'splɔ:] erkunden 195

to expose sth. [ɪk'spəʊz ˌsʌmθɪŋ] etw. enthüllen 56

to expose [ɪk'spəʊz] aussetzen (einer Gefahr, einem Risiko) 88

exposure [ɪk'spəʊʒə] Aussetzen 37

to extend [ɪk'stend] verlängern, ausdehnen 72

extent [ɪk'stent] Ausmaß 44

to extinguish [ɪk'stɪŋgwɪʃ] löschen 13

F

facade [fə'sɑ:d] Fassade 73

face value [ˌfeɪs 'vælju:] Nennwert, eingetragener Wert 29

to facilitate [fə'sɪlɪteɪt] erleichtern 15

facility [fə'sɪlətɪ] Einrichtung 228

to factor in [ˌfæktər‿ɪn] berücksichtigen, einbeziehen 242

failure ['feɪljə] Versagen 232

famine ['fæmɪn] Hungersnot 60

fault [fɒlt, fɔ:lt] Fehler 16

feasible ['fi:zəbl] machbar 125

to feature ['fi:tʃə] (als Besonderheit) aufweisen, groß herausbringen, zeigen 89

fee [fi:] Gebühr 142

to feel guilty [ˌfi:l 'gɪltɪ] sich schuldig fühlen 282

fertility [fə'tɪlətɪ] Fruchtbarkeit 156

fertiliser / fertilizer ['fɜ:tɪlaɪzə] Dünger 61

to file for divorce [ˌfaɪl fə dɪ'vɔ:s] die Scheidung einreichen 158

fish fingers [ˌfɪʃ'fɪŋgəz] Fischstäbchen 172

flattering ['flætərɪŋ] schmeichelhaft 158

flawed [flɔ:d] fehlerhaft 217

fluency ['flu:ənsɪ] Flüssigkeit 96

to forecast ['fɔ:kɑ:st] voraussagen 46

to foreclose [fɔ:'kləʊz] zwangsvollstrecken 120

foremost ['fɔ:məʊst] führend 62

forerunner ['fɔ:ˌrʌnə] Vorreiter(in) 291

foreseeable [fɔ:'si:əbl] absehbar 164

to forge [fɔ:dʒ] schmieden 192

fortnight ['fɔ:tnaɪt] vierzehn Tage 191

fortunate ['fɔ:tʃənət] glücklich 211

fossil fuel [ˌfɒsl 'fjʊəl] fossiler Brennstoff 44

fossil-fuelled [ˌfɒsl'fju:ld] fossil befeuert 46

to found [faʊnd] gründen 60

fraction ['frækʃn] Bruchteil 104

fragile ['frædʒaɪl] zerbrechlich, schwach 207

freedom ['fri:dəm] Freiheit 107

free-range [ˌfri:'reɪndʒ] Freiland- 43

frequently ['fri:kwəntlɪ] häufig 241

fried [fraɪd] frittiert 172

fringe [frɪndʒ] Rand 202

from scratch [frəm 'skrætʃ] ganz von Anfang an 172

to frown [fraʊn] die Stirn runzeln 29

to fulfil [fʊl'fɪl] erfüllen 107

full-time [ˌfʊl'taɪm] Vollzeit 283

to fund [fʌnd] finanzieren 152

fungus ['fʌŋgəs] Pilz 60

G

gain [geɪn] Gewinn, Vorteil 152

to gain [geɪn] gewinnen 194

to gain ground [ˌgeɪn 'graʊnd] an Boden gewinnen 92

to gain momentum [ˌgeɪn mə'mentəm] an Boden gewinnen 120

gate [geɪt] Tor 24

to gather ['gæðə] zusammenkommen, sammeln 64

to gauge [geɪdʒ] nachprüfen 156

GDP (Gross Domestic Product) [ˌdʒi. di:'pi: ˌgrəʊs dəˌmestɪk 'prɒdʌkt] Bruttoinlandsprodukt 133

gender ['dʒendə] Geschlecht 37

generous ['dʒenərəs] großzügig, freigebig 148

genetic [dʒə'netɪk] genetisch, Gen- 156

gentle ['dʒentl] sanft 185

to gentrify ['dʒentrɪfaɪ] verbürgerlichen 120

genuine ['dʒenjʊɪn] echt, aufrichtig 180

genuinely ['dʒenjʊɪnlɪ] echt, aufrichtig, von Grund auf 28

to get out of control [get ˌaʊt‿əv kən'trəʊl] außer Kontrolle geraten 13

to get out of hand [ˌget‿aʊt‿əv 'hænd] außer Kontrolle geraten 196

the gist [ðə 'dʒɪst] Kernaussage, das Wesentliche 172

glacier ['glæsɪə, 'gleɪʃə] Gletscher 44

gloomy ['glu:mɪ] düster 120

to glue [glu:] kleben 280

GM food [ˌdʒi:'em ˌfu:d] gentechnisch verändertes Lebensmittel 43

gorgeous ['gɔ:dʒəs] sehr schön 148

to gossip ['gɒsɪp] tratschen, lästern 15

to govern ['gʌvn] leiten, lenken 132

grant [grɑ:nt] Beihilfe, Unterstützung, Subvention 144

grape [greɪp] Traube 288

to grapple with sth. ['græpl wɪð] sich mit etw. auseinandersetzen 115

gravy ['greɪvɪ] (Braten-)Soße 172

to grieve [gri:v] trauern 180

to grind sb. down [graɪnd‿'daʊn] jmdn zermürben 72

groundbreaking ['graʊndˌbreɪkɪŋ] bahnbrechend 170

to grow [grəʊ] anbauen 222

growth [grəʊθ] Wachstum 132

guardian ['gɑ:dɪən] Erziehungsbeauftragte(r) 150

guess [ges] Vermutung 30

to guess [ges] glauben, schätzen 226

guidance ['gaɪdəns] Anleitung, Beratung, Ratschläge 174

H

habit ['hæbɪt] Gewohnheit 88

habitat ['hæbɪtæt] Lebensraum 45

hallmark ['hɔ:lmɑ:k] Kennzeichen 78

handicapped ['hændɪkæpt] Behinderte(r) 146

to hang on to sth. [ˌhæŋ‿'ɒn tə] etw. behalten 78

to harm [hɑ:m] schädigen, schaden 53

harvest ['hɑ:vɪst] Ernte 60

to harvest ['hɑ:vɪst] ernten 290

hazard ['hæzəd] Gefahr 155

hazardous ['hæzədəs] gefährlich 43

healthcare ['helθkeə] Gesundheitspflege 156

heap [hi:p] Haufen 64

heathen ['hi:ðən] Ungläubige(r) 111

heir [eə] Erbe; Thronfolger 130

hence [hens] daher, deshalb 124

to hesitate ['hezɪteɪt] zögern 104

high-flying [ˌhaɪ'flaɪɪŋ] erfolgreich 152

to highlight ['haɪlaɪt] hervorheben 212

to hijack ['haɪdʒæk] entführen 64

to hinder ['hɪndə] behindern 88

to hinge [hɪndʒ] abhängen 242

to hire [haɪə] einstellen 275

hole [həʊl] Loch 17

honesty ['ɒnəstɪ] Aufrichtigkeit, Ehrlichkeit 148

to hook up [hʊk 'ʌp] (hier:) zusammenfügen 158

horrendous [hə'rendəs] übermäßig, horrend 243

horrified ['hɒrɪfaɪd] entsetzt 64

host [həʊst] Gastgeber(in) 53

humble ['hʌmbl] bescheiden 258

to humiliate [hju:'mɪlɪeɪt] demütigen 29

to hurl [hɜ:l] schleudern 26

hybrid ['haɪbrɪd] Hybrid, Misch- 90

hyphen ['haɪfən] Bindestrich 146

hypocritical [ˌhɪpə'krɪtɪkl] scheinheilig, heuchlerisch 227

I

illiteracy [ɪ'lɪtrəsɪ] Analphabetismus 194

imaginary [ɪ'mædʒɪnərɪ] erfunden 196

immigrant ['ɪmɪgrənt] Einwanderer, Einwanderin 178

immigration [ˌɪmɪ'greɪʃn] Einwanderung 60

impact ['ɪmpækt] Auswirkung 40

to impair [ɪm'peə] beeinträchtigen 165

impediment [ɪm'pedɪmənt] Hindernis 115

to implement ['ɪmplɪment] einführen, umsetzen 132

to impose sth. [ɪm'pəʊz] jmdm etw. aufzwingen, auferlegen 93

impressive [ɪm'presɪv] beeindruckend 227

to improve [ɪm'pru:v] besser werden, sich verbessern 19

improvement [ɪm'pru:vmənt] Verbesserung 46

in advance [ɪn əd'vɑˌɛns] im Voraus 12

in demand [ˌɪn dɪ'mɑ:nd] gesucht/gefragt 152

inability [ˌɪnə'bɪlətɪ] Unfähigkeit, Unvermögen 174

inaccurate [ɪn'ækjərət] ungenau, falsch 291

inadequates [ɪ'nædɪkwəts] sozial Benachteiligte 14

inappropriate [ˌɪnə'prəʊprɪət] unpassend, unangemessen 248

inauguration [ɪˌnɔ:gjə'reɪʃn] Amtseinführung 113

incentive [ɪn'sentɪv] Anreiz 47

inclined [ɪn'klaɪnd] geneigt 230

inconsiderate [ˌɪnkən'sɪdərət] rücksichtslos 260

inconvenience [ˌɪnkən'vi:nɪəns] Unannehmlichkeit(en) 34

inconvenient [ˌɪnkən'vi:nɪənt] ungünstig 56

to increase [ɪn'kri:s] (an)steigen, steigern, erhöhen 15

increase ['ɪnkri:s] Zunahme, Anstieg 144

increasingly [ɪn'kri:sɪŋlɪ] zunehmend 148

independence [ˌɪndɪ'pendəns] Unabhängigkeit 60

to indicate ['ɪndɪkeɪt] zeigen 286

indigenous [ɪn'dɪdʒɪnəs] einheimisch 53

indigenous people [ɪnˌdɪdʒɪnəs 'pi:plz] Einheimische 124

indignation [ˌɪndɪg'neɪʃn] Empörung 191

indistinguishable [ˌɪndɪ'stɪŋgwɪʃəbl] nicht unterscheidbar 154

to indulge in sth. [ɪn'dʌldʒ ɪn] sich etw. hingeben 178

inevitable [ɪ'nevɪtəbl] unvermeidlich 41

infant mortality [ˌɪnfənt mɔ:'tælətɪ] Säuglingssterblichkeit 115

inferior [ɪn'fɪərɪə] minderwertig 202

infrequently [ɪn'fri:kwəntlɪ] selten, unregelmäßig 146

ingredient [ɪn'gri:dɪənt] Zutat 51

inhospitable [ˌɪnhɒs'pɪtəbl] ungastlich 69

initial [ɪ'nɪʃl] erste(r,s) 64

injection [ɪn'dʒekʃn] Spritze, Injektion 157

to injure ['ɪndʒə] verletzen 64

injustice [ɪn'dʒʌstɪs] Ungerechtigkeit 137

inn [ɪn] Gasthaus 110

innocent ['ɪnəsnt] harmlos 76

innovation [ˌɪnəʊ'veɪʃn] Neuerung 170

inspirational [ˌɪnspɪ'reɪʃənl] inspirierend 101

instant ['ɪnstənt] sofort 51

instantly ['ɪnstəntlɪ] sofort, augenblicklich 244

insurance [ɪn'ʃɔ:rəns] Versicherung 195

to integrate ['ɪntɪgreɪt] integrieren 280

intended [ɪn'tendɪd] (hier:) bestimmt 80

to intensify [ɪn'tensɪfaɪ] verstärken 196

interconnected [ˌɪntəkə'nektɪd] vernetzt 47

interest ['ɪntrəst] Zinsen 285

interface ['ɪntəfeɪs] Schnittstelle 179

to interfere with [ˌɪntə'fɪə] sich einmischen; (hier:) verhindern 63

to intervene [ˌɪntə'vi:n] sich einschalten, einschreiten 12

intimacy ['ɪntɪməsɪ] Intimität, Nähe 28

to intimidate [ɪn'tɪmɪdeɪt] einschüchtern 213

intriguing [ɪn'tri:gɪŋ] faszinierend, fesselnd 259

intruder [ɪn'tru:də] Eindringling 165

invaluable [ɪn'væljʊəbl] außerordentlich wertvoll, unschätzbar 269

invention [ɪn'venʃn] Erfindung 124

to investigate [ɪn'vestɪgeɪt] erforschen, untersuchen, recherchieren 274

invincible [ɪn'vɪnsəbl] unbesiegbar 191

invoice ['ɪnvɔɪs] Rechnung 81

irreversible [ˌɪrɪ'vɜ:səbl] unumkehrbar 114

issue ['ɪʃuˌɛ] Thema, Frage, Problem 44

to issue ['ɪʃu:] ausgeben 268

itinerary [aɪ'tɪnərərɪ] Reiseroute, Reiseplan 69

J

janitor ['dʒænɪtə] Hausmeister 64

to join forces [ˌdʒɔɪn 'fɔ:sɪz] zusammenarbeiten, sich zusammenschließen 222

judiciary [dʒu:'dɪʃərɪ] Gerichtsbarkeit 128

juncture ['dʒʌŋktʃə] Punkt 84

justice ['dʒʌstɪs] Gerechtigkeit 227

justifiable ['dʒʌstɪfaɪəbl] gerechtfertigt 53

juvenile ['dʒu:vənaɪl] Jugendliche(r); Jugend- 24

K

to keep track of sth. [ˌki:p 'træk‿əv] über etw. Aufzeichnungen machen 210

key [ki:] wesentlich 282

key [ki:] Haupt-, Schlüssel- 91

to kid [kɪd] Spaß machen 72

kidney ['kɪdnɪ] Niere 14

L

to label ['leɪbl] beschriften, nennen 26

laboratory [lə'bɒrətrɪ] Labor 164

labour ['leɪbə] Arbeitskräfte 222

to lack sth. ['læk ˌsʌmθɪŋ] etw. vermissen lassen 146

lack of sth. ['læk‿əv] fehlend, Mangel an 36

large-scale [ˌlɑ:dʒ'skeɪl] großflächig, in großem Maßstab 222

the latter [ðə 'lætə] Letztere(r,s) 104

to launch [lɔ:ntʃ] auf den Markt bringen 240

launch [lɔ:ntʃ] Markteinführung 264

law-abiding ['lɔ:əˌbaɪdɪŋ] gesetzestreu 285

layer ['leɪə] Schicht 263

to leap [li:p] springen 101

to lessen ['lesn] verringern 125

letter of application [ˌletər‿əv æplɪ'keɪʃn] Bewerbungsschreiben 140

license plate ['laɪsəns ˌpleɪt] Autokennzeichen, Nummernschild 110

licensees [ˌlaɪsən'si:z] Lizenznehmer 243

likelihood ['laɪklɪhʊd] Wahrscheinlichkeit 132

limitless ['lɪmɪtləs] grenzenlos 189

lingua franca (Latin) [ˌlɪŋgwə 'fræŋkə] internationale Verkehrssprache 92

literacy ['lɪtrəsɪ] Lese -und Schreibfähigkeit 78

literate ['lɪtrət] lese- und schreibkundig 78

littered ['lɪtəd] übersät 291

livestock ['laɪvstɒk] Vieh 289

loads [ləʊdz] Mengen von 14

loan [ləʊn] Darlehen, Kredit 143

longing ['lɒŋɪŋ] Sehnsucht 124

to loom [lu:m] sich abzeichnen 179

to lose out on s.th. [ˌlu:z‿'aʊt ɒn ˌsʌmθɪŋ] ins Hintertreffen geraten 288

loss [lɒs] Verlust, Einbuße 125

lot [lɒt] Grundstück 63

M

magnitude ['mægnɪtju:d] Ausmaß, Größe 64

to maintain [meɪn'teɪn] aufrechterhalten, beibehalten; behaupten 77

majority [mə'dʒɒrətɪ] Mehrzahl, Mehrheit 80

to make a living [ˌmeɪk‿ə 'lɪvɪŋ] seinen Lebensunterhalt verdienen 222

to make amends [ˌmeɪk‿ə'mendz] etw. wiedergutmachen 82

to make choices [meɪk 'tʃɔɪsɪz] Entscheidungen treffen 179

to make sth. worth one's while [meɪk ˌsʌmθɪŋ ˌwɜ:θ wʌnz 'waɪl] jmdn für etw. belohnen 34

malnourished [ˌmæl'nʌrɪʃt] unterernährt 136

manipulation [məˌnɪpjə'leɪʃn] Manipulation, Beeinflussung 98

to manoeuvre [mə'nu:və] manövrieren 78

manufacturer [ˌmanjə'fæktʃərə] Hersteller 172

to marginalize ['mɑ:dʒɪnəlaɪz] an den Rand drängen 111

to mask [mɑ:sk] verbergen 202

mass transit [ˌmæs 'trænzɪt] öffentliche Verkehrsmittel, Massenverkehr 62

to match [mætʃ] übereinstimmen 41

mate [meɪt] Kumpel 28

to mature [mə'tʃʊə] reifen 237

maturity [mə'tjʊərətɪ] Reife 19

mayhem ['meɪhem] Chaos 24

mayor [meə] Bürgermeister(in) 12

means of communication [ˌmi:nz‿əv kəˌmju:nɪ'keɪʃn] Kommunikationsmittel 74

measurable ['meʒərəbl] messbar 193

mediocre [ˌmi:dɪ'əʊkə] mittelmäßig 69

medium ['mi:dɪəm] Medium 90

to meet [mi:t] erreichen 46

memorial [mə'mɔ:rɪəl] Denkmal 65

merchant ['mɜ:tʃənt] Händler, Kaufmann, Handelsmann 173

mere [mɪə] bloß 200

merely ['mɪəlɪ] lediglich 193

might [maɪt] Macht 35

millennium [mɪ'lenɪəm] Jahrtausend 164

mind-set ['maɪndset] Einstellung 149

minimally invasive surgery [ˌmɪnɪməlɪ ɪnˌveɪzɪv 'sɜ:dʒərɪ] minimalinvasive Operationstechnik 155

to miss out on sth. [ˌmɪs‿'aʊt‿ɒn] etw. verpassen 78

model ['mɒdl] Vorbild 176

monitoring ['mɒnɪtərɪŋ] Kontrolle, Überwachung 12

monopoly [mə'nɒpəlɪ] Monopol 124

mother tongue [ˌmʌðə 'tʌŋ] Muttersprache 209

mother-in-law ['mʌðərɪnˌlɔ:] Schwiegermutter 26

motive ['məʊtɪv] Antrieb 124

mountain range ['maʊntɪn ˌreɪndʒ] Bergkette 67

mystery ['mɪstərɪ] Rätsel 158

N

nanotechnology [ˌnænəʊtek'nɒlədʒɪ] Nanotechnologie 164

narcissism ['nɑ:sɪsɪzm] Selbstverliebtheit 36

native ['neɪtɪv] eingeboren, einheimisch 90

native ['neɪtɪv] Ureinwohner(in) 178

native speaker [ˌneɪtɪv 'spi:kə] Muttersprachler(in) 90

natural resource [ˌnætʃərl rɪ'zɔ:s] Bodenschatz 46

necessity [nə'sesətɪ] Notwendigkeit 46

need [ni:d] Bedürfnis 15

to negate [nɪ'geɪt] zunichtemachen 115

neglect [nɪ'glekt] Nichtbeachtung 232

to negotiate [nɪ'gəʊʃieɪt] verhandeln 272

negotiation [nɪˌgəʊʃɪ'eɪʃn] Verhandlung 90

notion ['nəʊʃn] Konzept, Idee 126

to nourish ['nʌrɪʃ] ernähren 291

nuclear ['nju:klɪə] nuklear, Atom- 155

to nurture sth. ['nɜ:tʃə ˌsʌmθɪŋ] etw. fördern 148

nutrition [nju:'trɪʃn] Ernährung 194

O

obesity [ə'bi:sɪtɪ] Fettleibigkeit 63

objective [əb'dʒektɪv] Ziel, Absicht 140

obligation [ˌɒblɪ'geɪʃn] Verpflichtung 269

obsessed [əb'sest] besessen 76

obsession [əb'seʃn] Obsession, Besessenheit 17

obvious ['ɒbvɪəs] offensichtlich 236

obviously ['ɒbvɪəslɪ] offensichtlich 227

occasionally [ə'keɪʒənlɪ] gelegentlich 53

offender [ə'fendə] Straftäter(in) 204

offer ['ɒfə] Angebot 80

official language [əˌfɪʃl 'læŋgwɪdʒ] Amtssprache 90

to offset [ˌɒf'set] kompensieren, ausgleichen 243

offshore [ˌɒf'ʃɔ:] vor der Küste 47

ongoing [ˌɒn'gəʊɪŋ] in Gang befindlich, laufend 28

open source [ˌəʊpn'sɔ:s] offener Quellcode (bei Software) 104

opponent [ə'pəʊnənt] Gegner(in) 133

oppressive [ə'presɪv] unterdrückend 116

to opt out [ɒpt 'aʊt] aussteigen 24

order ['ɔ:də] Bestellung, Auftrag 80

ordinarily [ˌɔ:dən'erılı] für gewöhnlich, normalerweise 146

otherwise ['ʌðəwaɪz] ansonsten 195

outcome ['aʊtkʌm] Ergebnis 96

outstanding [aʊt'stændɪŋ] herausragend 52

to outstrip [ˌaʊt'strɪp] übersteigen 47

to outweigh sth. [ˌaʊt'weɪ] schwerer wiegen als etw. 173

overpaid [ˌəʊvə'peɪd] überbezahlt 146

overseas [ˌəʊvə'si:z] ausländisch; im Ausland 132

overwhelming [ˌəʊvə'welmɪŋ] überwältigend 29

P

pace [peɪs] Geschwindigkeit, Gangart 179

(cardiac) pacemaker [ˌkɑ:dɪæk 'peɪsˌmeɪkə] Herzschrittmacher 171

painstakingly ['peɪnzˌteɪkɪŋlɪ] gewissenhaft, sorgfältig 78

partially ['pɑ:ʃəlɪ] teilweise 152

to participate [pɑ:'tɪsɪpeɪt] teilnehmen 47

to partition [pɑ:'tɪʃn] aufteilen 125

to partner with ['pɑ:tnə wɪð] sich mit jmdm zusammenschließen 290

passionate ['pæʃənət] leidenschaftlich 17

patriotism ['pætrɪətɪzm] Vaterlandsliebe 173

pattern ['pætn] Muster 96

to pave the way [ˌpeɪv ðə 'weɪ] den Weg ebnen 172

peak [pi:k] Höhepunkt 190

peer [pɪə] Gleichaltrige(r) 40

peer pressure ['pɪə ˌpreʃə] Gruppenzwang 19

to perceive [pə'si:v] wahrnehmen 237

perception [pə'sepʃn] Wahrnehmung 216

performance [pə'fɔ:məns] Leistung 284

peril ['perəl] Risiko 184

periodical [ˌpɪərɪ'ɒdɪkl] Zeitschrift 90

perishable ['perɪʃəbl] (leicht) verderblich 173

to permit [pə'mɪt] erlauben 133

persecution [ˌpɜ:sɪ'kju:ʃn] Verfolgung 60

pertinent ['pɜ:tɪnənt] relevant 243

pesticide ['pestɪsaɪd] Pestizid, Schädlingsbekämpfungsmittel 61

phenomenon [fə'nɒmɪnən] Phänomen, Erscheinung 12

pillow ['pɪləʊ] Kopfkissen 110

placement ['pleɪsmənt] Praktikum 283

policy ['pɒləsɪ] Strategie, Richtlinie 96

poll [pəʊl] Umfrage 180

polluting [pə'lu:tɪŋ] umweltverschmutzend 53

population [ˌpɒpjə'leɪʃn] Bevölkerung 67

population density [ˌpɒpjəleɪʃn 'densɪtɪ] Bevölkerungsdichte 67

portfolio [pɔ:t'fəʊlɪəʊ] Mappe 140

to portray [pɔ:'treɪ] darstellen 196

to pose [pəʊz] darstellen 242

post [pəʊst] Ziel(markierung) 129

poultry ['pəʊltrɪ] Geflügel 243

power plant ['paʊə ˌplɑ:nt] Kraftwerk 155

praise [preɪz] Lob 148

to praise [preɪz] loben; anpreisen 148

pre-booking [ˌpriːˈbʊkɪŋ] Vormerkung 72

precious [ˈpreʃəs] wertvoll 158

predecessor [ˈpriːdɪˌsesə] Vorgänger(in) 191

to predict [prɪˈdɪkt] vorhersagen 62

predictable [prɪˈdɪktəbl] vorhersehbar 46

prediction [prɪˈdɪkʃn] Vorhersage 164

predominance [prɪˈdɒmɪnəns] Vorherrschaft 93

pre-industrial [ˌpriːɪnˈdʌstrɪəl] vorindustriell 44

prejudice [ˈpredʒʊdɪs] Vorurteil 32

premonition [ˌpreməˈnɪʃn] Vorahnung 114

pre-requisite [ˌpriːˈrekwɪzɪt] Voraussetzung 143

to preserve [prɪˈzɜːv] bewahren 62

to preside over sth. [prɪˈzaɪd ˌəʊvə] über etw. walten 115

presidency [ˈprezɪdənsɪ] Präsidentschaft 113

pressure [ˈpreʃə] Druck 19

to pressure sb. [ˈpreʃə] jmdn unter Druck setzen, Druck ausüben 116

prevalent [ˈprevələnt] vorherrschend 14

to prevent [prɪˈvent] verhindern, vermeiden 232

to prevent sth. from happening / sb. from doing sth. [prɪˈvent] verhindern 47

preventable [prɪˈventəbl] vermeidbar 228

previous [ˈpriːvɪəs] vorherig 65

pricy [ˈpraɪsɪ] teuer 72

primarily [praɪˈmerɪlɪ] hauptsächlich, vornehmlich 221

primary [ˈpraɪmərɪ] Vorwahl 113

privacy [ˈpraɪvəsɪ] Privatsphäre 80

privilege [ˈprɪvɪlɪdʒ] Privileg 142

to proceed [prəˈsiːd] fortfahren 80

to process [ˈprəʊses] verarbeiten 197

production costs [prəˈdʌkʃn ˌkɒsts] Herstellungskosten 225

production facilities [prəˈdʌkʃn fəˌsɪlɪtɪz] Produktionsanlagen 225

profoundly [prəˈfaʊndlɪ] stark 65

progress [ˈprəʊgres] Fortschritt 80

to prohibit [prəʊˈhɪbɪt] verbieten 12

prohibition [ˌprəʊhɪˈbɪʃn] Untersagung, Verbot 269

projection [prəˈdʒekʃn] Projektion, Hochrechnung, Fortschreibung 286

to promote [prəˈməʊt] fördern, unterstützen 136

to prompt [prɒmpt] hervorrufen 262

property [ˈprɒpətɪ] Grundbesitz, Eigentum; Eigenschaft 63

proponent [prəˈpəʊnənt] Befürworter(in) 133

proposal [prəˈpəʊzl] Vorschlag 240

to propose [prəˈpəʊz] vorschlagen 48

to propose to sb. [prəˈpəʊz tə ˌsʌmbədɪ] jmdm einen Heiratsantrag machen 120

prospect [ˈprɒspekt] Aussicht 96

prosperity [prɒsˈperətɪ] Wohlstand 192

prosperous [ˈprɒspərəs] wohlhabend, florierend 232

to provide (for) [prəˈvaɪd] geben, bieten; sorgen für, versorgen 129

public order [ˌpʌblɪk ˈɔːdə] öffentliche Ordnung 12

punctuation [ˌpʌŋktʃʊˈeɪʃn] Interpunktion 78

punishment [ˈpʌnɪʃmənt] Strafe, Bestrafung 212

to purchase [ˈpɜːtʃəs] erwerben 132

purpose [ˈpɜːpəs] Zweck, Absicht 50

to pursue sth. [pəˈsjuː] etw. verfolgen 143

to pursue sb. [pəˈsjuː] jmdn bedrängen/jagen 208

pursuit [pəˈsjuːt] Streben 189

to put at risk [ˌpʊt‿ət ˈrɪsk] gefährden 12

Q

quotation [kwəʊˈteɪʃn] Angebot, Kostenvoranschlag 80

R

radical [ˈrædɪkl] radikal 109

to rage [reɪdʒ] toben 15

to raise money [ˌreɪz ˈmʌnɪ] Geld beschaffen 284

ramification [ˌræmɪfɪˈkeɪʃn] Auswirkung 130

random [ˈrændəm] per Zufall, willkürlich 95

range [reɪndʒ] Reichweite 260

to ratify a treaty [ˌrætɪfaɪ‿ə ˈtriːtɪ] einen Vertrag ratifizieren, anerkennen 112

ready-made [ˌredɪˈmeɪd] Fertig- 172

to reap [riːp] ernten 290

to rear [rɪə] großziehen 157

to recede [rɪˈsiːd] sich entfernen 111

recent [ˈriːsənt] kürzlich, letzte/r/s 12

recession [rɪˈseʃn] Konjunkturabschwung, Rezession 132

recipe [ˈresɪpɪ] Rezept 149

to reckon [ˈrekən] vermuten 14

recognition [ˌrekəgˈnɪʃn] Erkenntnis; Anerkennung; Erkennung 141

to recommend [ˌrekəˈmend] empfehlen 271

recommendation [ˌrekəmenˈdeɪʃn] Empfehlung 140

to recount [rɪˈkaʊnt] erzählen 213

to recover [rɪˈkʌvə] sich erholen 19

to redefine [ˌriːdɪˈfaɪn] neu definieren 190

redistribution [riːdɪstrɪbjuːʃən] Umverteilung 184

reference [ˈrefrəns] Referenz, Bezug 140

referendum [ˌrefəˈrendəm] Bürgerentscheid 126

refuge [ˈrefjuːdʒ] Zufluchtsort 120

refugee [ref.jʊˈdʒiː] Flüchtling 189

to regard [rɪˈgɑːd] betrachten 133

regardless of [rɪ'gɑːdləs‿əv] ungeachtet, unabhängig von 126

regenerative [rɪ'dʒenərətɪv] regenerativ 157

regime change [reɪ'ʒiːm ˌtʃeɪndʒ] Regimewechsel 116

to reinforce [ˌriːɪn'fɔːs] verstärken 131

to reject [rɪ'dʒekt] ablehnen 140

relapse ['riːlæps] Rückfall 159

to relate to sth. [rɪ'leɪt tə] sich mit etw. identifizieren 206

to release [rɪ'liːs] entlassen, veröffentlichen 36

relentless [rɪ'lentləs] gnadenlos, (hier:) unablässig 62

reliability [rɪˌlaɪə'bɪlətɪ] Glaubwürdigkeit, Vertrauenswürdigkeit 238

reliable [rɪ'laɪəbl] zuverlässig 110

reliance [rɪ'laɪəns] Verlass 175

relief [rɪ'liːf] Erleichterung 227

reluctant [rɪ'lʌktənt] widerwillig, widerstrebend 205

reluctantly [rɪ'lʌktəntlɪ] zögerlich 60

to rely on [rɪ'laɪ‿ɒn] sich verlassen auf 133

to remain [rɪ'meɪn] bleiben 80

remark [rɪ'mɑːk] Bemerkung, Äußerung 192

remarkably [rɪ'mɑːkəblɪ] bemerkenswert 191

remote working [rɪˌməʊt 'wɜːkɪŋ] Telearbeit 152

to remove [rɪ'muːv] entfernen 248

renewable [rɪ'njuːəbl] erneuerbar 196

renewable energy [rɪˌnjuːəbl‿'enədʒɪ] erneuerbare Energie 43

renewed [rɪ'njuːd] erneut 227

rent [rent] Miete 16

to replace [rɪ'pleɪs] ersetzen 94

reputation [ˌrepjə'teɪʃn] Ruf 172

to require [rɪ'kwaɪə] benötigen 46

requirement [rɪ'kwaɪəmənt] Anforderung 96

research [rɪ'sɜːtʃ] Forschung 96

researcher [rɪ'sɜːtʃə] Forscher(in) 29

to resemble [rɪ'zembl] ähneln 258

reserve [rɪ'zɜːv] Scheu, Förmlichkeit 266

to reshape [ˌriː'ʃeɪp] umformen, wieder verformen 136

to reside [rɪ'zaɪd] seinen Sitz haben 200

resident ['rezɪdənt] Einwohner(in) 210

residential neighborhood [ˌrezɪ'denʃl] Wohngebiet 63

residual [rɪ'zɪdjʊəl] restlich 130

resistance [rɪ'zɪstəns] Widerstand 196

to resolve [rɪ'zɒlv] lösen 15

resource [rɪ'zɔːs; 'riːsɔːs] Vorrat, Rohstoff 61

respectively [rɪ'spektɪvlɪ] beziehungsweise 129

to respond to [rɪ'spɒnd] (hier:) reagieren auf 64

responsibility [rɪˌspɒnsə'bɪlətɪ] Verantwortung 116

to restore [rɪ'stɔː] wiederherstellen 157

to restrict [rɪ'strɪkt] begrenzen 18

résumé [ˌrezjʊ'meɪ] Lebenslauf 140

to retain [rɪ'teɪn] behalten 201

retirement [rɪ'taɪəmənt] Ruhestand 46

to retreat [rɪ'triːt] zurückgehen 44

to reveal [rɪ'viːl] bekannt geben, enthüllen, aufdecken, aufzeigen 29

to reverberate [rɪ'vɜːbəreɪt] nachhallen 114

to reverse [rɪ'vɜːs] umkehren 130

to revise [rɪ'vaɪz] wiederholen, noch einmal durchsehen 14

to revitalize [ˌriː'vaɪtəlaɪz] wiederbeleben 120

to reward [rɪ'wɔːd] belohnen 53

reward [rɪ'wɔːd] Belohnung 148

ridiculous [rɪ'dɪkjələs] lächerlich 77

rigorous ['rɪgərəs] peinlich genau, gründlich 157

to ring out [rɪŋ 'aʊt] schallen 114

riot [raɪət] Aufruhr 93

rise [raɪz] Anstieg, Zunahme 96

risk [rɪsk] Risiko 280

rival ['raɪvl] Konkurrent(in) 201

robotic [rəʊ'bɒtɪk] Roboter- 155

role models ['rəʊl ˌmɒdlz] Rollenvorbilder 144

root [ruːt] Wurzel 232

roughly ['rʌflɪ] ungefähr 96

row [raʊ] Auseinandersetzung 17

rubbish ['rʌbɪʃ] Müll 13

rudely ['ruːdlɪ] unhöflich 72

to rule [ruːl] herrschen, regieren 178

to rule out [ˌruːl‿'aʊt] ausschließen 268

rundown [ˌrʌn'daʊn] heruntergekommen 120

runoff ['rʌnɒf] Sickerwasser 61

rural ['rʊərəl] ländlich 62

S

sacrifice ['sækrɪfaɪs] Opfer 65

to sample ['sɑːmpl] ausprobieren 24

sample ['sæmpl] Beispiel 140

satisfaction [ˌsætɪs'fækʃn] Zufriedenheit 147

scale [skeɪl] Ausmaß, Umfang, Maß, Maßstab 46

scarce [skeəs] knapp 45

scarcely ['skeəslɪ] kaum 92

sceptic ['skeptɪk] Skeptiker(in) 56

scope [skəʊp] Ausmaß, Umfang 177

to scramble for sth. ['skræmbl ˌfɔː] um etw. kämpfen 124

screen [skriːn] Bildschirm 14

scrutiny ['skruːtɪnɪ] Kontrolle, Prüfung 130

secretive ['siːkrətɪv] geheimnisvoll 76

to secure [sɪ'kjʊə] absichern, unter Vetrag nehmen 101

sedentary ['sedəntrɪ] sitzend 176

to seek [siːk, sɔːt, sɔːt] versuchen 53

segregation [ˌsegrɪ'geɪʃn] Rassentrennung 109

selective [sə'lektɪv] wählerisch 53

self-absorbed [ˌselfəb'zɔːbd] mit sich selbst beschäftigt 36

self-esteem [ˌselfɪ'stiːm] Selbstwertgefühl 194

self-evident [ˌself'evɪdənt] selbstverständlich 110

selfish ['selfɪʃ] egoistisch 77

self-respect [ˌself rɪ'spekt] Selbstrespekt 29

self-worth [ˌself'wɜːθ] Selbstwert 29

sensible ['sensɪbl] vernünftig, sinnvoll 53

sentiment ['sentɪmənt] Ansicht 213

separation [ˌsepər'eɪʃn] Trennung 238

to set out [set 'aut] (hier:) darlegen 243

settler ['setlə] Siedler(in) 108

shameless ['ʃeɪmləs] schamlos 20

to shape [ʃeɪp] formen 179

share [ʃeə] Anteil 181

shares [ʃeəz] Aktien 225

sharp [ʃɑːp] steil, stark, scharf 286

to shatter ['ʃætə] zerschmettern 126

shift [ʃɪft] Veränderung 40

to shift [ʃɪft] sich verschieben, wechseln 45

shortcut ['ʃɔːtkʌt] Kurzform 88

to showcase ['ʃəʊkeɪs] demonstrieren 140

sick leave ['sɪk ˌliːv] Fehlzeit durch Krankheit, Krankenstand 85

side effect ['saɪd‿ɪˌfekt] Nebeneffekt 155

significance [sɪg'nɪfɪkəns] Bedeutung 40

sincere [sɪn'sɪə] aufrichtig 148

single-handedly [ˌsɪŋgl'hændɪdlɪ] im Alleingang 34

to skip sth. [skɪp] ausfallen lassen 152

to slaughter ['slɔːtə] schlachten 56

slave [sleɪv] Sklave/Sklavin 219

slope [sləʊp] Hang 61

small-scale [ˌsmɔːl'skeɪl] in kleinem Umfang 53

smooth [smuːð] fließend 202

to soar [sɔː] hochschnellen 192

social networking site [ˌsəʊʃl 'netwɜːkɪŋ ˌsaɪt] Internetseite eines sozialen Netzwerks 12

social worker ['səʊʃl ˌwɜːkə] Sozialarbeiter(in) 13

sociogram ['səʊsɪəʊgræm] Soziogramm 26

solar energy [ˌsəʊlər‿'enədʒɪ] Solarenergie 197

solar panel [ˌsəʊlə 'pænl] Sonnenkollektor 155

sole [səʊl] einzig, ausschließlich 92

solicitor [sə'lɪsɪtə] Anwalt/Anwältin 152

sophisticated [sə'fɪstɪkeɪtɪd] hoch entwickelt 162

sore [sɔː] Wunde 115

source [sɔːs] Quelle 282

to spark [spɑːk] entzünden 116

to speculate ['spekjəleɪt] spekulieren 121

spinal cord [ˌspaɪnl 'kɔːd] Rückenmark 156

spirit ['spɪrɪt] Geist 191

to spoil (a child) [spɔɪl] verwöhnen 49

to spoil [spɔɪl] verderben 173

to spot [spɒt] entdecken 204

to spread [spred] verbreiten, ausbreiten 93

staff [stɑːf] Angestellte(r), Personal 245

stain [steɪn] Fleck 209

state [steɪt] Zustand 94

stereotype ['sterɪətaɪp] Stereotyp, Klischee 32

to stigmatise ['stɪgmətaɪz] brandmarken 40

storage ['stɔːrɪdʒ] Speicherung 171

straightforward [ˌstreɪt'fɔːwəd] geradlinig, unkompliziert, einfach 14

strain [streɪn] Belastung 126

strategic [strə'tiːdʒɪk] strategisch 94

to strengthen ['streŋkθn] verstärken 117

strife [straɪf] Streit 35

strike [straɪk] Schlag 64

to strike [straɪk] treffen 64

striking ['straɪkɪŋ] verblüffend 200

to strive [straɪv] streben nach 233

stroke [strəʊk] Schlaganfall 174

to struggle ['strʌgl] kämpfen, sich abmühen 97

stunned [stʌnd] betäubt 64

to stunt [stʌnt] hemmen 47

subliminal [sʌb'lɪmɪnəl] unterschwellig 204

to submit [səb'mɪt] vorlegen, abschicken 122

subsequent ['sʌbsəkwənt] anschließend, nachträglich 190

subsidised ['sʌbsɪdaɪzd] subventioniert 56

substantial [səb'stænʃl] beträchtlich 114

substitute ['sʌbstɪtjuːt] Ersatz 75

subtle ['sʌtl] dezent 237

to succeed [sək'siːd] erfolgreich sein 95

to suffer ['sʌfə] leiden, erleiden 29

sufficient(ly) [sə'fɪʃənt, sə'fɪʃəntlɪ] ausreichend 97

suitability [ˌsuːtə'bɪlətɪ] Eignung 142

superstition [ˌsuːpə'stɪʃn] Aberglaube 202

supervision [ˌsuːpə'vɪʒn] Beaufsichtigung 152

supervisor ['suːpəvaɪzə] Leiter(in), Kontrolleur(in) 148

supplies [sə'plaɪz] Vorräte 262

supply [sə'plaɪ] Vorrat, Angebot 45

to supply [sə'plaɪ] liefern, zur Verfügung stellen 223

supposedly [sə'pəʊzɪdlɪ] angeblich 130

surface ['sɜːfɪs] Oberfläche 162

surgery ['sɜːdʒərɪ] Operation 155

to surmise [sə'maɪz] mutmaßen 37

to surpass [sə'pɑːs] (hier:) überholen 291

surveillance [sə'veɪləns] Überwachung 165

survey ['sɜːveɪ] Umfrage 40

to survive [sə'vaɪv] überleben 222

suspicion [sə'spɪʃn] Misstrauen, Verdacht 147

sustainability [səˌsteɪnə'bɪlətɪ] Nachhaltigkeit 237

sustainable [sə'steɪnəbl] nachhaltig 192

to swap [swɒp] tauschen 14

sweatshop ['swetʃɒp] Ausbeutungsbetrieb 219

to sweep [swi:p] rauschen, fegen 288

swiftly ['swɪftlɪ] schnell 72

sympathetic [ˌsɪmpə'θetɪk] mitfühlend 148

T

to tackle ['tækl] etw. angehen, in Angriff nehmen, bewältigen, bekämpfen 18

to take off [ˌteɪk‿'ɒf] abheben 136

to take pride in [ˌteɪk 'praɪd‿ɪn] auf etw. stolz sein 88

to take sth. for granted [ˌteɪk fə 'grɑ:ntɪd] etw. als selbstverständlich/gegeben hinnehmen 46

to take the initiative [ˌteɪk ðɪ‿ɪ'nɪʃətɪv] die Initiative ergreifen 117

target ['tɑ:gɪt] Ziel 46

to target sb. ['tɑ:gɪt] jmdn als Zielgruppe haben, auf jmdn abzielen 96

to target ['tɑ:gɪt] zielen auf, ins Visier nehmen, anpeilen 173

taste [teɪst] Geschmack 282

tax bill ['tæks ˌbɪl] Steuerabrechnung 62

to tease someone [ti:z] jmdn hänseln 15

temperate ['tempərət] gemäßigt 67

temporary ['temprərɪ] vorübergehend, zeitweilig 144

tense [tens] angespannt 272

tension ['tenʃn] Spannung 131

tentative ['tentətɪv] vorsichtig 191

to terminate ['tɜ:mɪneɪt] beenden 136

terrifying ['terəfaɪɪŋ] furchterregend 196

testimony ['testɪmənɪ] Zeugnis, Beweis 156

theft [θeft] Diebstahl 280

therapeutic [ˌθerə'pju:tɪk] therapeutisch 165

therapy ['θerəpɪ] Behandlung 156

think tank ['θɪŋk ˌtæŋk] Expertenkommission, „Denkfabrik“ 262

threadbare ['θredbeə] schäbig 24

tidal ['taɪdl] Gezeiten- 47

tie [taɪ] Bindung 97

tight [taɪt] knapp 193

tissue ['tɪʃu:] Stoff, Material 156

tongue-in-cheek [ˌtʌŋɪn'tʃi:k] ironisch 122

totalitarian [təˌtælɪ'teərɪən] totalitär 93

tough [tʌf] (hier:) hart, schwer 65

to track [træk] verfolgen 28

track record ['træk 'rekɔ:d] Erfolgsgeschichte 83

to trade in [ˌtreɪd‿'ɪn] eintauschen 288

trait [treɪt] Charakterzug, Eigenschaft 140

tranquil ['træŋkwɪl] ruhig, friedlich 73

to transform [træns'fɔ:m] verwandeln 178

transition [træn'zɪʃn] Übergang 263

to trap sth. [træp] etw. auffangen 44

to trash [træʃ] verwüsten 24

to treat [tri:t] behandeln 108

treatment ['tri:tmənt] Behandlung 109

trial [traɪəl] Versuch 156

to triple ['trɪpl] verdreifachen 145

to trust sb. [trʌst] jmdm vertrauen 28

tuition [tjʊ'ɪʃn] Unterricht, Unterweisung 145

to turn over [ˌtɜ:n‿'əʊvə] umsetzen 225

turnover ['tɜ:nˌəʊvə] Umsatz 225

twice [twaɪs] zweimal 14

U

ultimately ['ʌltɪmətlɪ] schließlich 64

unanimously [ju:'nænɪməslɪ] einhellig, einstimmig 93

unashamed [ˌʌnə'ʃeɪmd] schamlos 291

uncanny [ʌn'kænɪ] unheimlich 114

unchallenged [ʌn'tʃælɪndʒd] unbestritten 92

unchecked [ʌn'tʃekt] ungehindert, unkontrolliert 62

to undermine sth. [ˌʌndə'maɪn ˌsʌmθɪŋ] etw. untergraben 133

to underwrite [ˌʌndə'raɪt] Risiko übernehmen, versichern 47

undoubtedly [ʌn'daʊtɪdlɪ] zweifellos 126

unfortunate [ʌn'fɔ:tʃənət] bedauernswert 31

unharmed [ʌn'hɑ:md] unbeschädigt 51

unimaginably [ˌʌnɪ'mædʒɪnəblɪ] unvorstellbar 52

unintelligible [ˌʌnɪn'telɪdʒəbl] unverständlich 69

union ['ju:nɪən] Gewerkschaft 248

unique [ju:'ni:k] einzig, einmalig, einzigartig 53

unjust [ʌn'dʒʌst] ungerecht 109

to unleash [ʌn'li:ʃ] freisetzen 136

unparalleled [ʌn'pærəleld] beispiellos 92

unprecedented [ʌn'presɪdəntɪd] beispiellos, nie dagewesen 45

unpredictable [ˌʌnprɪ'dɪktəbl] unvorhersehbar, unberechenbar 272

unrecognizable [ʌn'rekəgnaɪzəbl] unerkennbar 40

unruly [ʌn'ru:lɪ] wild, ungebändigt 73

uprising ['ʌpˌraɪzɪŋ] Aufstand 190

urban ['ɜ:bən] städtisch, urban 67

urge [ɜ:dʒ] Drang, Trieb 124

to urge [ɜ:dʒ] drängen, ermahnen 149

urgency ['ɜ:dʒənsɪ] Dringlichkeit 35

urgent ['ɜ:dʒənt] dringend 232

V

vacancy ['veɪkənsɪ] Stellenangebot, Leere, Lücke 144

vacant ['veɪkənt] leer stehend, frei 63

valuable ['væljʊəbl] wertvoll 194

value ['vælju:] Wert 93

valued ['vælju:d] (wert)geschätzt 152

varying ['veərɪɪŋ] wechselnd 127

vehicular language [vɪˌhɪkjələ 'læŋgwɪdʒ] Verkehrssprache 92

venture ['ventʃə] Unternehmen, Unterfangen 101

venue ['venju:] Veranstaltungsort 195

to verify ['verɪfaɪ] belegen 140

to veto a law [ˌvi:təʊ‿ə 'lɔ:] ein Gesetz ablehnen 112

vice versa [ˌvaɪs'vɜ:sə] umgekehrt 50

violation [ˌvaɪə'leɪʃn] Verletzung, Nichteinhaltung 136

virtue [vɜ:tju:] Tugend 189

vocational [vəʊ'keɪʃənl] beruflich, Berufs- 274

to voice [vɔɪs] äußern, zum Ausdruck bringen 93

volunteer [ˌvɒlən'tɪə] Freiwillige(r) 64

to vow [vaʊ] schwören 64

vulnerable ['vʌlnərəbl] angreifbar, verwundbar 144

W

weapon ['wepən] Waffe 20

weight [weɪt] Gewicht 194

whereas [weə'ræz] während, wohingegen 147

to withdraw [wɪð'drɔ:] sich zurückziehen 109

withdrawal [wɪð'drɔ:əl] Ausstieg 133

to witness ['wɪtnəs] mitansehen, beobachten 64

working knowledge [ˌwɜ:kɪŋ 'nɒlɪdʒ] praktische Kenntnisse 90

worthwhile [ˌwɜ:θ'waɪl] lohnend 53

Y

yearning ['jɜ:nɪŋ] Verlangen 29

to yield [ji:ld‿'ɪntrəst] hervorbringen 287

Z

zest [zest] Eifer, Ziel 175

Bildquellennachweis

4.1; 4.4 Thinkstock (iStockphoto), München; **4.2** shutterstock (Patrizia Tilly), New York, NY; **4.3** Fotolia.com (Alexander), New York; **5.1** iStockphoto (Anna Bryukhanova), Calgary, Alberta; **5.2** iStockphoto (The Power of Forever Photography), Calgary, Alberta; **5.3** iStockphoto (LifesizeImages), Calgary, Alberta; **5.4** Getty Images (Dan Kitwood), München; **6.1** shutterstock (mihaicalin), New York, NY; **6.2** iStockphoto (Vladislav Ociacia), Calgary, Alberta; **6.3** iStockphoto (David Jones), Calgary, Alberta; **6.4** Picture-Alliance (abacausa), Frankfurt; **7** www.CartoonStock.com (Jonny Hawkins), Bath; **7.1** Perez, Armando, McLean; **7.2** Corbis (Pawel Kopczynski/Reuters), Düsseldorf; **7.3** shutterstock (RF/Losevsky Pavel), New York, NY; **8.1; 8.2; 8.3; 8.4; 8.6; 8.7; 8.8** BBC Information and archives, London; **8.5** Video(s) supplied by BBC Motion Gallery, London; **9.2** Thinkstock (iStockphoto), München; **10.1** Fotolia.com (diego cervo), New York; **10.2** iStockphoto (craftvision), Calgary, Alberta; **10.3** iStockphoto (Karen Mower), Calgary, Alberta; **10.4** Thinkstock (iStockphoto), München; **10.5** shutterstock (My Portfolio), New York, NY; **10.6** Fotolia.com (Monkey Business), New York; **11** www.CartoonStock.com (Jonny Hawkins), Bath; **14.2** BigStockPhoto.com (monkeybusinessimages), Davis, CA; **16** www.willyrussell.com, Whiston, Merseyside; **18.2** iStockphoto (Piotr Marcinski), Calgary, Alberta; **20** dreamstime.com (Wanderlust), Brentwood, TN; **24.2** iStockphoto (Luca Cepparo), Calgary, Alberta; **25** Cagle Cartoons (Dave Granlund), Santa Barbara, CA; **26.1** Thinkstock (Monkey Business), München; **26.2** iStockphoto (Chris Gramly), Calgary, Alberta; **26.3** shutterstock (Patrizia Tilly), New York, NY; **27.1** Fotolia.com (Thomas Pajot), New York; **27.2** Thinkstock (Monkey Business), München; **27.3** iStockphoto (Logorilla), Calgary, Alberta; **28** www.CartoonStock.com (Delgado, Roy), Bath; **30** iStockphoto (GYI NSEA), Calgary, Alberta; **32.1** shutterstock (Robert Adrian Hillman), New York, NY; **33** www.CartoonStock.com (Bacall, Aaron), Bath; **35.1** www.bilderbox.com (www.BilderBox.com), Thening; **35.2** Ullstein Bild GmbH (Wolter), Berlin; **35.3** Alamy Images (Jeremy Hoare), Abingdon, Oxon; **35.4** FEMA (PD/Greg Henshall), Washington, D.C.; **36.2** iStockphoto (Joan Vicent Cantó Roig), Calgary, Alberta; **39** nach: Statistisches Bundesamt, Wiesbaden 2011; **40.2** Alamy Images (Peter Marshall), Abingdon, Oxon; **41** nach: Journal of Adolscent Health, 2006 (http://www.sprc.org/sites/sprc.org/files/library/SPRC_LGBT_Youth.pdf); **42.1** Fotolia.com (Alexander), New York; **42.2** iStockphoto (narvikk), Calgary, Alberta; **42.3** shutterstock (MarcelClemens), New York, NY; **43.1** iStockphoto (eskaylim), Calgary, Alberta; **43.2** iStockphoto (Lucía Cóppola), Calgary, Alberta; **43.3** iStockphoto (Maridav), Calgary, Alberta; **43.4** iStockphoto (Bart Coenders), Calgary, Alberta; **43.5** iStockphoto (Jani Bryson), Calgary, Alberta; **45** iStockphoto (Andy Green), Calgary, Alberta; **46.1** Federal Coordinator, Alaska Natural Gas Transportation Projects, 2012; **46.2** Copyright Guardian News & Media Ltd 2011, London; **48** Corbis (Lynn Goldsmith), Düsseldorf; **50** Avenue Images GmbH (Stockbyte), Hamburg; **51** MEV Verlag GmbH, Augsburg; **52.1** Copyright Guardian News & Media Ltd 2011, London; **52.2** ifotoStock (Frank Sánchez), Madrid; **53** Madden, Chris, ..; **56.1** Telegraph Media Group Limited, London; **56.2** Fotolia.com (Eky Chan), New York; **58.1** Fotolia.com (Birgit Urban), New York; **58.2** iStockphoto (Richard Semik), Calgary, Alberta; **58.3** shutterstock (Jiri Moucka), New York, NY; **58.4** shutterstock (Palette7), New York, NY; **58.5** Fotolia.com (chasingmoments), New York; **58.6** iStockphoto (S. Greg Panosian), Calgary, Alberta; **59.1** Thinkstock (iStockphoto), München; **59.2** shutterstock (Brendan Howard), New York, NY; **59.3** Thinkstock (Ron Chapple Studios), München; **59.4** iStockphoto (Mark Stay), Calgary, Alberta; **59.5** shutterstock (Timo Kohlbacher), New York, NY; **59.6** Fotolia.com (sumikophoto), New York; **60** akg-images, Berlin; **62** www.CartoonStock.com (Andrew Toos), Bath; **64.2** iStockphoto (Charles Daniel Howell), Calgary, Alberta; **66.1** www.CartoonStock.com (Robert Thompson), Bath; **66.2** Pauline Ashworth, Stuttgart; **67** iStockphoto (Bob Duffy), Calgary, Alberta; **68.1** Getty Images (Ulf Andersen), München; **68.2** iStockphoto (Ismail Akin Bostanci), Calgary, Alberta; **72** Fotolia.com (oscity), New York; **73** shutterstock (QQ7), New York, NY; **74.1** The Cartoonist Group (Dan Piraro), Seattle; **74.2** iStockphoto (Anna Bryukhanova), Calgary, Alberta; **74.3** iStockphoto (Daniel Laflor), Calgary, Alberta; **75.1** iStockphoto (Sanne Berg), Calgary, Alberta; **75.2** [Lichtenstein, Roy: Oh, Jeff... I love you, too... but...] © VG Bild-Kunst, Bonn 2012. ddp images GmbH (AP Photo/Courtesy the Estate of Roy Lichtenstein via The Art Institute of Chicago), Hamburg; **75.3** iStockphoto (HultonArchive), Calgary, Alberta; **76.2** iStockphoto (Jacob Wackerhausen), Calgary, Alberta; **77** www.CartoonStock.com (Love, Jason), Bath; **78.2** iStockphoto (Aldo Murillo), Calgary, Alberta; **79** www.CartoonStock.com (McPherson, John), Bath; **80.1** iStockphoto (Blend_Images), Calgary, Alberta; **80.2** iStockphoto (Lise Gagne), Calgary, Alberta; **81** www.CartoonStock.com (Fran), Bath; **82** iStockphoto (Daniel Laflor), Calgary, Alberta; **86** Reuters, Frankfurt; **88.2** iStockphoto (TommL), Calgary, Alberta; **89** www.CartoonStock.com (Bucella, Marty), Bath; **92.2** Agency: Ogilvy & Mather Budapest. Creative: Dalbir Singh.; **94.2** iStockphoto (The Power of Forever Photography), Calgary, Alberta; **96.2** Mauritius Images (Alamy), Mittenwald; **97** John C Fewings, Peterborough, On; **98** www.CartoonStock.com (Goddard, Clive), Bath; **99** shutterstock (c.), New York, NY; **101** Classical Comics Ltd, Litchborough,Towcester; **103** Mit freundlicher Genehmigung der Berliner Stadtreinigung und der Heymann Brandt de Gelmini Werbeagentur AG; **106.1** Getty Images (Digital Vision), München; **106.2** Getty Images (AFP/Paul J. Richards), München; **106.3** iStockphoto (LifesizeImages), Calgary, Alberta; **107** Ullstein Bild GmbH (AP), Berlin; **107.1** iStockphoto (Juanmonino), Calgary, Alberta; **107.2** Alamy Images (Jeff Greenberg), Abingdon, Oxon; **108.1** Corbis (Brian A. Vikander), Düsseldorf; **108.2** Alamy Images (PhotoStock-Israel), Abingdon, Oxon; **109.1** Corbis (Leif Skoogfors), Düsseldorf; **109.2** Getty Images (Craig Allen), München; **110** The Guardian, London; **110** The Mirror, London; **110** Wikimedia Deutschland (PD), Berlin; **112.1** JupiterImages photos.com (photos.com), Tucson, AZ; **112.2** Wikimedia Deutschland (PD), Berlin; **112.3** Corbis (Wally McNamee), Düsseldorf; **113** Corbis (SABA/Freeland), Düsseldorf; **114.1** Picture-Alliance (dpa), Frankfurt; **114.2** Süddeutsche Zeitung Photo, München; **116.1** Süddeutsche Zeitung Photo (AP), München; **116.2** Das Fotoarchiv (Markus Matzel), Essen; **117.1** Corbis (Sygma/Stone), Düsseldorf; **117.2** Fotosearch Stock Photography (Design Pics), Waukesha, WI; **117.3** Corbis (Anthony Dobson/US Navy/Hanout/CNP), Düsseldorf; **120.2** Picture-Alliance (dpa/EPA/JUSTIN LANE), Frankfurt; **122.1** Ullstein Bild GmbH (Liverani), Berlin; **122.2** iStockphoto (Duncan Walker), Calgary, Alberta; **122.3** Corbis (Ashley Cooper), Düsseldorf; **123.1** Topham Picturepoint, Edenbridge Kent; **123.2** shutterstock (Pres Panayotov), New York, NY; **125** Schrank, Peter, Aldeburgh; **126.2** Getty Images (Dan Kitwood), München; **128.1** Corbis (Bettmann), Düsseldorf; **128.2** Ullstein Bild GmbH (Reuters), Berlin; **128.3** Getty Images (Tim Graham), München; **129** Klett-Archiv (nach: The Huddersfield Daily Examiner), Stuttgart; **130.2** Getty Images (Chris Jackson), München; **130.3** Getty Images (BEN STANSALL/AFP), München; **132.2** iStockphoto (pagadesign), Calgary, Alberta;

Textquellennachweis

12/13 © DW Deutsche Welle, 2011; **14/15** Teenagers and technology: 'I'd rather give up my kidney than my phone', Jon Henley, 16 July © Guardian News & Media Ltd. 2010; **16/17** From: Willy Russell, The Wrong Boy, p. 80–82 © Black Swan edition 2001; **18/19** What teenagers think about binge drinking, Poppy Robertson © Guardian News & Media Ltd. 2010; **20/21** The Fear Text: Allen, Lily/Kurstin, Gregory Allen © EMI April Music Inc./Kurstin Music/Universal Music Publishing Ltd./ EMI Music Publishing Germany GmbH & Co. KG, Hamburg/ Universal Music Publ. GmbH, Berlin; **24** What's wrong with today's youth?, Idle hands, idle minds, Cristina Odone, The Observer, 6 January 2002 © Guardian News & Media Ltd. 2002; **28/29** From: Friends ain't friends... How social media has changed the way young people form friendships. By Philip Jenkinson © Copyright Young Life Australia.; **30/31** From: Klett English editions, ISBN 579822 © Original: Puffin Books, 2007; **32/33** From: Das bisherige Rollenmodell bleibt etabliert, Armin Lehmann © Der Tagesspiegel; **34** © Network for Good; **35** © Kenneth R. Thompson; **36/37** Source: www.psychologytoday.com / BLOGS What The Wild Things Are © 2010, Samantha Smithstein, Psy. D; **40/41** Homophobia is declining in schools, study claims, Tracy McVeigh, The Observer, 3 March © Guardian News & Media Ltd 2012; **44/45** Source: National Environment Research Council Brochure, June 2007, www.nerc.ac.uk/publications; **46/47** Juliet Davenport, Britain could be running on 100% renewable energy by 2050, 14 December 2010 © Guardian News & Media Ltd. 2010; **48/49** From: T.C. Boyle, A Friend of the Earth © Penguin, 2000; **50/51** © 2007 BBC Focus, Bristol Magazines Ltd.; **52/53** What it means to travel green, John Vidal, 20 February © Guardian News & Media Ltd 2010; **56/57** From: New film exposes unsavoury side of US food industry by Leonard Doyle, 14 Jun 2009 © Telegraph Media Group Ltd.; **62/63** What Urban sprawl costs you, Used with permission of the Orlando Sentinel © 2006; **64/65** © 2009 Advameg, Inc.; **68/69** Extract from THE KINGDOM BY THE SEA by Paul Theroux. Copyright © 1983, Paul Theroux, used by permission of The Wylie Agency (UK) Limited; **72/73** Adapted from: www.helium.com © 2002-2010 Helium, Inc. All rights reserved. **76/77** From: 'FAMILY MATTERS: Time spent chatting online is time lost with family' Posted: February 25, 2010 by Jim May, Midland Reporter-Telegram. Source: MyWestTexas.com © Copyright 2011, Mywesttexas.com; **78/79** A fifth of children have never received a letter', Rachel Williams, 21 May 2010 © The Guardian News & Media Ltd., 2010; **82-85** From: Martin Lukes, Who Moved My BlackBerry? © Penguin Books Ltd., 2006; **88/89** From: The University of Alabama Computers and Applied Technology Program (2009). Technology education: A series of case studies. Available at http://www.bamaed.ua.edu/edtechcases.; **91** From: English Next. Why global English may need the end of 'English as a Foreign Language' by David Graddol © copyright British Council; **91** Source: "European Union, Eurobarometer" http://ec.europa.eu/public_opinion/archives/ebs/ebs_243_sum_en.pdf. The European Union does not endorse changes, if any, made to the original data and, in general terms to the original survey, and such changes are the sole responsibility of the author and not the EU; **91** Quelle: Job Trends Deutschland 2011 © 2011 by Staufenbiel Institut GmbH; **92/93** Source: Lingua Franca: Chimera or Reality? Studies on translation and multilingualism 1/2011 © European Commission, 2011; **94/95** © Independent News and Media Ltd. 2007; **96/97** Joe Friesen, "Canada to raise language bar", 19 June 2012 © Guardian News & Media Ltd 2012; **100/101** Alison Flood "Schools test 'interactive graphic novel' version of Macbeth" 1 March 2010 © Guardian News & Media Ltd. 2010; **104** By Ruth Walker. Reprinted with permission from the June 30, 2010 issue of The Christian Science Monitor. © 2010 The Christian Science Monitor (www.CSMonitor.com); **110/111** Copyright © 2006 by Greil Marcus. Delivered as a commencement address at the University of California at Berkeley, May 19, 2006. Published by Salon.com on 4 July 2006. Veröffentlicht mit Genehmigung der Paul & Peter Fritz AG in Zürich.; **114/115** 40 years after King's death …, Ed Pilkington, 03 April 2008 © Guardian News & Media Ltd.2008; **120/121** Lara Farrar, Is America's suburban dream collapsing... From CNN.com, 6/16/ © 2008, Cable News Network, Inc.. All rights reserved. Used by permission and protected by the Copyright Laws of the United States. The printing, copying, redistribution, or retransmission of this Content without express written permission is prohibited.; **126/127** © Guardian News & Media Ltd 2011; **130/131** Stuart Jeffries, "How the royals became cool", 11 April 2012 © Guardian News & Media Ltd. 2012; **132/133** © Independent News and Media Ltd. 2012; **136/137** Praful Bidwai, "Why India needs aid", 7 Febr 2012 © Guardian News & Media Ltd.; **140/141** By Mary Nestor-Harper. From: eHow.com © 2011, Demand Media, Inc.; **142/143** Career-boosting internships for sale', Rachel Williams, 24 May 2011 © Guardian News & Media Ltd. 2011 144/145 © BBC News at bbc.co.uk/news; **146/147** From: THEN WE CAME TO THE END by Joshua Ferris. Copyright © 2007 by Joshua Ferris. By permission of Little, Brown and Company. All rights reserved.; **148/149** By Marily Gardner. Adapted with permission from the January 28, 2008 issue of The Christian Science Monitor. © 2008 The Christian Science Monitor (www.CSMonitor.com)".; **152** © Independent News and Media Ltd. 2005 156/157 © Telegraph Media Group Ltd. 2011; **158/159** From "My Sister's Keeper" by Jodi Picoult © Hodder & Stoughton, London 2004, pp. 7–8/9–10 160/161 © SPIEGEL ONLINE 2008; **162/163** © BBC News at bbc.co.uk/news; **164/165** From: Richard Watson 'Future files: A brief history of the next 50 years', p. 40 © Nicholas Brealey Publishing, 2009; **168/169** © ZEIT ONLINE GmbH; **172/173** The rise and rise of convenience food', Tim Dowling, 19 May 2006 © The Guardian News & Media Ltd., 2006; **174/175** Jerome Monahan and Joe Clancy, Lifelong learning is the secret to happiness in old age, 17 May 2011 © Guardian News & Media, 2011; **175** © SPIEGEL ONLINE 2010; **176/177** From: www.life123.com © Text: LuAnn Schindler; **178/179** From: Sunday Times © Times Newspapers Ltd.; **180/181** From: Dead Famous by Ben Elton © Bantam Press (a division of Random House) 2001; **184/185** Anna Coote, "A shorter working week would benefit society", 30 July 2010 © Guardian News & Media Ltd. 2010; **188/189** Michael White, Why national dream is a foreign concept 5 February 2011 © Guardian News & Media Ltd. 2011; **190/191** John Harris, Global protests: is 2011 a year that will change the world? 15 November 2011 © Guardian News & Media Ltd. 2011; **192/193** From: Remarks to Non-Governmental Organizations. Source: UN News Center Website, 19.10.2012; **194/195** From: Society Guardian.co.uk © Guardian News and Media Limited 2011; **197** Quelle: Rainer Hermann, Hightech für die Umwelt: Die Stadt der Zukunft. Deutschland Online, 2007.; **200/201** © BBC 202 Jacky Kay, In my country. From: Other Lovers © Bloodaxe Books Ltd., 1993; **202** "Legal Alien" is reprinted with permission from the publisher of "Chants" by Pat Mora (© 1994 Arte Público Press-University of Houston); **203** Windrush Child by John Agard. From: Half-Caste and other Poems by John Agard © Hodder Children's Books, 2005; **204/205** Marguerite Rigoglioso, Racial Stereotypes Can Be Unconscious but Reversible © Stanford Graduate School of Business Board of Trustees, Leland Stanford Junior University Stanford, Calif.; **206/207** Transcript from American Public Media's Speaking of Faith (now on Being) © 2008 American Public Media. Used with permission. All rights reserved.; **208/209** From: Chris Cleave, Little Bee, pp. 1-3 © Simon & Schuster UK, 2010; **210/211** © Armando Perez, Virginia, USA; **212/213** Stephen Brook, "It's Australia Day. Don't let the 'we grew here, you flew here' crew spoil it", 26 Jan 2011 © Guardian News & Media Ltd. 2011; **216/217** From: Welcome to Everytown by Julian Baggini © granta Books, 2007; **219** Globalization Blues © words and music: Ray Korona; **220/221** From: Thomas L. Friedman, A World is flat: A brief history of the twenty-first century © 2005 Farrar, Straus and Giroux, Penguin, 2006; **222/223** © Fairtrade International; **224/225** Quelle: www.boerse-online.de © 1996 - 2012 BÖRSE ONLINE; **226/227** From Jennifer Government by Max Barry, copyright © 2003 by Max Barry. Used by permission of Doubleday, a division of Random House, Inc.; **228/229** © Global Water Challenge; **232/233** © Kofi Annan Foundation; **236/237** Sylvia Rowley, Can brands make consumers see sustainable behaviour as desirable?, 5 October 2011 © Guardian News & Media Ltd. 2011; **238** New media fail to click on the reliability scale by Ari Sharp. From: The Sydney Morning Herald, March 16, 2010 © Text: Ari Sharp; **239** Quelle: WinFuture.de, Berlin; **240/241** Used with permission of Network World Copyright © 2012. All rights reserved; **242/243** Organic movement split over air-freighted food, Martin Hickman, 29 May 2007 © Independent News & Media Ltd. 2007; **244/245** From: Steve Martin, An object of beauty, pp. 5 - 8 © Orion Publishing Group, 2010; **248** © Independent News & Media Ltd. 2007; **258/259** © BBC; **260/261** © BBC; **262/263** Dawn of the age of robots, Dominic Rushe, 30 December 2010 © Guardian News & Media Ltd. 2010; **264/265** Mark King, "A working life: The app developer", 5 March 2011 © Guardian News & Media Ltd. 2011; **266/267** Copyright © The Economist Newspaper Limited 2009. All rights reserved; **268/269** Olivia Perrott and Nick Atkins, "Top tips for web startups", 21 Aug 2012 © Guardian News & Media Ltd.; **270/271** Gozde Zorlu, "New holistic approach to treat child obesity", 1 Aug 2012 © Guardian News & Media Ltd. 2012; **272/273** Guardian Professional "Just another day in court as a social worker", 13 Jan 2012 © Guardian News & Media Ltd. 2012; **274/275** Jessica Shepherd, "Has England finally found the formula for vocational education?" 31 May 2012 © Guardian News & Media Ltd. 2012; **280/281** © Daily Mail, London 2011; **284/285** © EndPlay, Inc.; **286/287** Mark Tran, Ethnic minorities to make up 20% of UK population by 2051, 13 July 2010 © Guardian News & Media Ltd. 2010; **288/289** © The Times, 2007; **290/291** From: Naomi Alderman, Get down on the FarmVille, 13 May 2011 © Guardian News & Media Ltd. 2011